Redemptive Transformation in Practical Theology

James E. Loder Jr.
1931-2001

Redemptive Transformation in Practical Theology

ESSAYS IN HONOR OF

James E. Loder Jr.

Edited by

Dana R. Wright and John D. Kuentzel

William B. Eerdmans Publishing Company
Grand Rapids, Michigan / Cambridge, U.K.

Wm. B. Eerdmans Publishing Co.
255 Jefferson Ave. S.E., Grand Rapids, Michigan 49503 /
P.O. Box 163, Cambridge CB3 9PU U.K.

Printed in the United States of America

09 08 07 06 05 04   7 6 5 4 3 2 1

Library of Congress Cataloging-in-Publication Data

Redemptive transformation in practical theology: essays in honor of
James E. Loder, Jr. / edited by Dana R. Wright and John D. Kuentzel.
p. cm.
Includes bibliographical references.
ISBN 0-8028-2689-X (alk. paper)
1. Theology, Practical. 2. Loder, James E. (James Edwin), 1931-2001
3. Loder, James E. (James Edwin), 1931 — Bibliography
I. Loder, James E. (James Edwin), 1931-2001 II. Wright, Dana R.
III. Kuentzel, John D.

BV3.R33 2004
230 — dc22

2004047244

www.eerdmans.com

Contents

III. Redemptive Transformation *beyond* Practical Theology

Foreword

By any measure, Jim Loder was a remarkable human being and scholar. I was privileged to be his colleague in the School of Christian Education at Princeton Theological Seminary during the last years of his life. Perhaps more than any individual I have known, Jim was able to integrate in his person, teaching, and writing elements that typically do not hang together in the contemporary academy: personal piety and intellectual rigor, spiritual practice and an open search for truth.

Jim came to Princeton Seminary as a brilliant young scholar, deeply committed to the sort of intellectual rigor he learned while studying in the graduate school of Harvard University. During his early years of teaching, students both loved and feared his formidable intellect. Yet his approach to the academic life was to change dramatically through a near encounter with death when Jim was trapped under a car after he and his family, on vacation, stopped to help two women experiencing car trouble on the New York thruway. He would later describe this life-changing event in *The Transforming Moment* as the singular event that gave birth to an entirely new personal spirituality that regrounded and reoriented his whole understanding of the life of the mind.

In Jim's writings, lectures, and personal conversations, he often described this transforming moment in terms of a new appreciation of the presence and power of the Holy Spirit. Those of us who knew him well were keenly aware of the sense of joy and vitality that he brought to his work. Every morning when he entered the suite of offices of the School of Christian Education, he would pause, lift up his hand, and smile at the staff, saying, "Blessings." His daily life and relationships were filled with many such small acts of sanctification, which communicated the spirit of a life walking in the presence of God's Spirit. Yet at no point did this deep and overflowing personal piety interrupt his commitment to intellectual rigor. If anything, Jim's new appreciation of the presence and power of the Holy Spirit set him on an ambitious intellectual project that brought together the life of the mind and the love of God.

In his writings, Jim often spoke of this spiritual intelligence in terms of convictional knowing. He found Michael Polanyi to be a helpful dialogue partner in articulating the tacit and personal dimensions of all scientific and scholarly activity. It was no longer necessary to fall into the modernist trap of bifurcating the individual's convictional and tacit knowing from the scientist's or scholar's rigorous inquiry. Much of Jim's scholarly work after his fundamental reorientation to life in the Spirit was to develop a theological and interdisciplinary account of this insight. An important part of this new intellectual project was to articulate the parameters of a four-dimensional universe — a universe in which God's Spirit is active and present in manifold ways — in relation to developmental psychology *(The Logic of the Spirit)*, physics *(The Knight's Move)*, and other areas of life. No one who ever heard Jim Loder lecture or who read one of his books could accuse him of allowing his piety to cut the nerve of his intellectual rigor. His capacity to hold these together in his person and to articulate how they ought to be held together in contemporary theology and science is one of his most important and lasting intellectual contributions.

Jim also held together and integrated other elements that often are sundered in the contemporary academy, including much theological education: spiritual practice and open, intellectual questioning. Those of us who were his closest colleagues knew firsthand the seriousness and intensity with which he approached his teaching, committee work, and counseling relationships. These were not merely mundane institutional activities. For Jim, they were forms of spiritual practice.

This was especially evident in the way he approached teaching and counseling. Jim's courses were always among the most demanding in the academic curriculum of Princeton Theological Seminary. His assigned readings were difficult and lengthy; his lectures were challenging and often difficult to understand. Yet year after year, his courses typically had the largest student enrollment of any elective course in the curriculum. He had to limit enrollment in his upper-level seminars in order to keep them small enough to allow discussion. I have heard more than one colleague wonder how it was possible for such an academically demanding teacher to generate such student enthusiasm.

The secret I have come to believe was the unique way that Jim challenged his students to strive for depth and personal authenticity in their engagement of his course. He was not satisfied with merely presenting a body of knowledge. He strove to evoke a deeply personal engagement with course content in relation to students' questions and life-issues. Teaching was nothing less than a form of spiritual practice. Jim's mentor in this regard was Søren Kierkegaard, the master of paradox and personal engagement in the quest for truth. Like Kierkegaard, Jim offered students a spiritual and theological grounding for open questioning that was quite different from that found in the Enlightenment's commitment to autonomous reason or in modernity's cynical distrust of all authority. Rather, an authentic and open search for truth was grounded spirituality — in a love for God and the quest for a truthful life before God. An entire generation of students at Princeton was privileged to learn at Jim Loder's feet what it means to teach as a spiritual practice. The church is much the better for it!

A second form of spiritual practice which Jim offered many students was his counseling. He was deeply steeped in the wisdom of contemporary psychotherapy and trained at one point at the Menninger Clinic. Yet, Jim did not view his many counseling relationships with students as simply a form of psychotherapy. Rather, his counseling was a kind of spiritual practice in which he attempted to evoke in one-on-one relationships the same sort of search for authenticity before God embodied in his teaching. He offered healing and care, to be sure. But he also sought to invite his student counselees to probe the ways their lives were moving down false paths, driven by an achievement orientation or by an inordinate fear of affirming the unique life and vocation that God had given to them. His larger goal was always to open them up to a life of authenticity before God.

One of the many losses that resulted from his untimely death was that Jim did not have the opportunity to write up in book form his approach to spiritual counseling. My sense is that his counseling was something quite unique among contemporary approaches to spiritual formation and direction, for it took so seriously the insights of depth psychology without being reduced to another form of psychotherapy. In his approach to spiritual counseling, Jim embodied his intellectual commitment to the Chalcedonian pattern of interdisciplinary work — a pattern in which the insights of the human and natural sciences are negated and then reappropriated in an explicitly theological framework. He learned from psychotherapy while placing its insights in a fundamentally different pattern of spiritual practice.

Jim's practice of spiritual counseling is only one of many areas that must be brought forward by his students and colleagues because of his sudden death. In personal conversation with him not long before he died, I found him to be positively glowing with excitement about the intellectual projects he was beginning to pursue on his sabbatical. These were never brought to fruition, and more than a few of us were left with the profound sense that he died too soon. He had so much more to offer. Ironically, however, my guess is that leaving things incomplete and open-ended would have suited Jim just fine. It remains for his students, former colleagues, and new readers to harvest in the years ahead the fields he planted. Thus, this volume of splendid essays becomes far more than a fitting tribute to this remarkable scholar and human being. It becomes the first step toward building on the intellectual legacy that Jim Loder has left us, a task that is likely to continue for generations to come.

RICHARD R. OSMER
Princeton Theological Seminary
Easter, 2004

Acknowledgments

The contributors to this *Festschrift* were by no means only those former students of Dr. Loder's who wrote the essays and/or coedited this volume. We wish to acknowledge Daisy and Ajit Prasadam for their loving support and willingness to help with so many of the editing details during a hectic time in their own lives. We also thank those tireless staff persons in the Christian education office of Princeton Theological Seminary, past and present — Kay Vogen, Margo Dudak, and Pat Heran, along with many student helpers whom they called on to help us in "crunch time," never losing their cheerfulness in the process. Along with them, we appreciate the help of Speer and Reigner Library staff persons, especially Sarita Ravinder, Donna Quick, David Stewart, and Kate Skrebutenas, all of whom can track down anything you want to find in print or out of print. Further, special notes of thanks to Richard Osmer for writing the foreword, and to Kim Loder Engelmann for her encouragement of this project, especially through the excruciating times following her father's death. We also thank Eerdmans Publishing Company, especially Jennifer Hoffman, for their expert help and advice. And finally, we salute our families, who kept us ever mindful of, and accountable to, the things in life that really matter beyond academics.

Dana would like to tip his hat to Dean Armstrong and the Faculty Grant Committee of Princeton Theological Seminary for their research grant in 2001-2002, and to the folks who gave of their time to be interviewed regarding their knowledge of Dr. Loder and his work — D. Campbell Wyckoff, Frank Rogers, Elizabeth Frykberg, Kim Loder Engelmann, Ray Anderson, Freda Gardner, Joe Williamson, and Randy Nichols. Dana would also single out his doctoral seminar students at Princeton — Michael Langford, Theresa Latini, Andrew Root, Ajit Prasadam, Sandra Kunz, and Troy Morgan — who spent the 2002-2003 school year working through virtually the whole of Loder's corpus. Out of that immersion they wrote excellent papers that they delivered in rough-draft form under conference-like conditions. Their love for Christ and their fun-loving attitudes were balm for my soul during what proved to be for me, for several reasons, a most difficult year. Also participating regularly in that seminar were Alwin Maben, J. Wesley Brown, and Matthew Frawley, all of whom contributed to our "learning Loder" that year.

Finally, let us say on behalf of all the contributors a special thanks to Princeton Theological Seminary's president emeritus Thomas Gillespie, who, when Dana approached him in the spring of 2001 with an idea to put together a *Festschrift* for Dr. Loder, enthusiastically embraced the idea and put the resources of the seminary behind it to make it possible. We hope his eager willingness to make this book happen pays rich dividends for the Kingdom, not only by honoring the memory of Dr. Loder, but also by making a worthwhile contribution to the current worldwide renaissance taking place in practical theology.

Dana R. Wright
John D. Kuentzel

INTRODUCTION

Are You There? Comedic Interrogation in the Life and Witness of James E. Loder Jr.

Dana R. Wright, with John D. Kuentzel

A Raconteur of Close Encounters

I'll always remember May 3, 1988, in Seattle, my first live encounter with James Edwin Loder Jr., that I knew I was in the presence of someone special. We had just heard, many of us for the first time, Dr. Loder gossip[1] one of his famous case studies, a counseling story "in the Spirit" designed to confront us with the Reality about which he had just spoken in more academic terms. In this story, a woman in despair, contemplating suicide in her room late one evening, had literally been knocked to the floor by an overpowering Presence who convinced her that her shattered life was but the seedbed of a rebirth to new possibilities. In the afterglow of this extraordinary awareness, she found herself hopeful, joyous, and oriented to the Good for the first time in her life.

Through this dramatic account of redemptive transformation, Loder staged an event for us that morning that I later learned typified his pedagogical complicity with the Spirit of God. He situated us in the theater of *Spiritus Creator* made up to look suspiciously like a classroom, warned us that the Spirit

1. By "gossip" I obviously don't mean that Loder irresponsibly breached ethical boundaries in his counseling. Rather, I am using "gossip" metaphorically according to the original meaning of the word (god + sip, in which "sip" meant "akin" or "related") as "one who has contracted a spiritual affinity with another by acting as a sponsor at baptism" (see James Fowler, *Becoming Adult, Becoming Christian* [San Francisco: Harper & Row, 1984], p. 17). In telling these stories of transformation, Loder vicariously testified on behalf of those profoundly changed by their "baptism in the Spirit," that new life was indeed an ever-present possibility for all of us.

John Kuentzel read and commented on this introductory essay at many points. Especially valuable were his comments on the summaries of the essays in this volume at the end of the introduction. Those summaries were composed with notes from John's close reading of these essays situated close at hand. — Dana R. Wright

hovered there, and then rolled back the curtain just far enough for us to behold the Glory ourselves. In so doing, this passionate *raconteur* of divine-human encounters transformed a critical lecture into an opportunity for liturgy. Indeed, Loder, I soon found out, had a way of effectively rendering almost every interchange with him — academic, pastoral, or personal — into witness and worship. I still remember how, during the telling of the story that morning, a stillness enveloped the classroom. In the interlude some cheeks moistened. Others nodded in recognition. A tentative "Amen" filtered in from the back of the room. Others no doubt felt some awkwardness. "What is he talking about?" "Has he completely abandoned academic protocol for 'anecdotes' or, worse still, lapsed into mysticism?" After all, had we not gathered together at the First Presbyterian Church on Seattle's Capitol Hill for instruction *about* "The Creator Spirit in Faith Formation"? And had not Loder confronted us with the existential state of our own faith condition? We waited.

One thing was sure. Loder felt no embarrassment about our confrontation with the *mysterium tremendum et fascinans* in a continuing education event. He apparently had no problem with the Holy Spirit's comedic disregard for academic territorial protocol in her pursuit to redeem all of us from our insipid religiosity, our intellectual sophistries, our presumptuous certitudes, or our defensive posturing — not to mention our less socially acceptable sins that also need redemption. He had no trouble at all putting our intellectual pursuits in the context of the Spirit's transformational initiative. In fact, he appeared to be exposing us through his storytelling to the outer boundaries of our own experience where the Holy Spirit likes to "work the house" to confront every distortion of the human spirit destined toward death with what Ralph Wood called "the comedy of redemption."[2] My suspicions were confirmed when he delivered the evangelical punch line. "You have only two options," Loder offered in his best Kierkegaardian impersonation, "the absurdity of unbelief or the absurdity of the God-man. You cannot play it cool. Now let's think about *that!*"

As we sat there, somewhat stunned by the boldness of the professor-turned-evangelist, we also became aware that this remarkable servant of Christ possessed an uncanny ability to connect the highest levels of intellectual pursuit to the experience of salvation without destroying the integrity of either. For Loder, the Holy Spirit's action always put persons and/or communities *into* the world, *into* the body, *into* the life of the mind, and living faith *always* led to the pursuit of understanding. Genuine experiences of the Spirit were always "reality restoring" events for Loder that uncovered the hidden orders of meaning and

2. Ralph *Wood, The Comedy of Redemption* (Notre Dame: University of Notre Dame Press, 1988).

purpose that make life truly intelligible — as if one could know life itself again for the first time (Loder called knowing the ordinary through the Spirit "mundane ecstasy").[3] For us that day, the full convictional potential of the academic moment, and the academic potential of the convictional moment, interpenetrated, and the magic of it all lingered for some time. Then Loder himself broke the spell with what first seemed to me to be a return to "mere" academics. He simply asked us, "Are you there?" He might have said, "Do you understand the lecture?" "Are we ready to move to the next topic?" "Any questions?"

No doubt that is all he meant. But by the time he started to lecture again, the deeper meaning of those three little words had taken up permanent residence in my soul. *"Are you there?"* "Dana, are *you* there?" I felt both compelled to respond to the Spirit's interrogation but at the same time fearful and unsure of what it all might mean for me, my family, or my ministry, to allow the Spirit to inhabit every dimension of our lives. *"Are you there?"* "Yes!" I wanted to say with conviction. "Are *you* there?" "No!" I knew was closer to the truth. Like Jesus holding his followers in the palm of his hand and placing their existence "under question" one by one — "Peter, do you love me?"; "Thomas, do you believe me?"; "Jairus, are you still afraid?" — Loder, disguised as Christ's comedic understudy, called me to "wise up" to what was really going on around me. "Do you see what all this means?" "Do you have the courage to go there?" *"Are you there?" "Yes . . . !" "No . . . !"* "I don't know . . . !" And then, right on cue, came a second punch line. "Be very careful!" Loder warned (or promised!), "Once you wise up to this Reality you can't wise down!" Indeed!

Wising Up in Practical Theology: A Loderian Interrogative

As I reflect once again on this powerful first encounter with this comedic understudy of Jesus Christ, this gossip of the Spirit, and especially now in light of the passing away of our *Doktorvater,* friend, and colleague, the "Loderian interrogative" lingers still. Indeed, for me "Are you there?" has become a kind of subtext underlying my involvement coediting this collection of essays in his honor, calling all of us (writers and readers) to "wise up" to the reality that confronts us in Jesus Christ and that compels us to bear urgent, yet buoyant witness to him in an increasingly dangerous and spiritless age.[4] "Are you there?"

3. Loder, *The Transforming Moment,* 2nd ed. (Colorado Springs: Helmers & Howard, 1989), pp. 107-111.

4. These essays began to take shape in the shadow of 9/11 and the events leading up to, and including, the second war in Iraq. Has there ever been a time more in need of the Holy Spirit's presence?

addresses pastors and practical theologians, Christian educators and their disciples, evangelists, laypersons, and psychologists, and especially persons around the world who took Loder's courses, who read his books, who heard him lecture, and who are reading (or editing and writing) this volume. "Do you know how big the Spirit's Presence is?" "How adequate the Spirit's power?" "How fearsome and glorious it is when God shows up?"

Loder loved to tell another story of a young seminarian who boldly entreated him after a lecture to pray that he might receive the Holy Spirit. As he placed his hands on the young man's shoulder and began to call upon the Spirit, the student awakened to the dangerous thing he was asking God to do and, shell-shocked, abruptly pulled away shouting, "Wait! Hold it! I'm not ready for this! Stop!"[5] Like the young monk Martin Luther, rendered catatonic at the prospect of serving his first communion before the terrible mystery that confronted him, the very thought of nearing the Holy Place traumatized this student as well. And well it should! Can any of us really face up to the prospect of being confronted by the Holy Spirit of Christ calling for the redemptive transformation of all things, including the hubris that infects the heart of so many of us, and that inevitably seeps into the fabric of our academic or pastoral work — our prized theories and/or our pet projects? "Wait! Hold it! Stop! I'm not ready for this. I have tenure and a reputation to protect." "No, not now. I have my ministry just where I want it."

Loder communicated this evangelical "Are you there?" through compelling classroom lectures, rigorous publications, prayerful counseling sessions, faculty gatherings, and ordinary conversations. He communicated with passion and (especially in his later years) infectious playfulness and humor born of conviction.[6] He demonstrated to so many of us the Spirit's kindness and patience, and what Loder called the "non-possessive delight in the particularity of the other" that lies at the center of the Spirit's intimate and generative movement human-ward. Indeed, he had great faith in the power and constancy and timing of the divine Pedagogue to inspire his students and colleagues to find their own responses to the Spirit's promptings.

Yet in the midst of this buoyant confidence and joy in *Spiritus Creator* to inspire all of us, one could also detect in Loder's "Are you there?" a measure of frustration, like a kind doctor might feel when her patient fails to respond to a

5. This event was retold in Loder's ED 105 lectures. See the notes of those lectures on file in Speer Library, Princeton Theological Seminary, lecture V, p. 82 (2001 version).

6. Loder likened good practical theological process to scientific discovery and argued that, in good science, humor is a crucial indication that something important is taking place. See Loder, "The Place of Science in Practical Theology: The Human Factor," *International Journal of Practical Theology* 4, 1 (2000), see esp. pp. 25 and 26.

warning to quit smoking, or responds to the warning by taking up chewing tobacco. I think Loder grieved over the kinds of issues and priorities that often captured the primary attention of both church and academy to the neglect or even exclusion of what he believed fundamentally mattered. He grieved especially over the church's ignorance of Jesus Christ — that is, her lack of passionate concern to testify to the rightful place of Christ and his Passion at the center of reality, and her failure to underscore the power of the living Christ to reveal himself to us and through us to the world. Thus, while many practical theologians turned to the works of Aristotle, Heidegger, Gadamer, Habermas, et al. for clues to a rigorous interdisciplinary methodology, Loder wanted to construct even the methodological question christologically, and so confront every unredeemed form of dialogical praxis, communicative action, or hermeneutical structure with the news of humanity's ultimate destination in the trinitarian reconciliation of all things in Christ.[7]

Ecumenical-minded theologians wanted to talk about the apologetics of civility and the rules of inter-denominational and inter-religious dialogue, an urgent task for all responsible thinkers. But Loder's theological instincts gave priority to what Paul Lehmann called "the God-man structure of reality" revealed in the incarnation, to the politics of the Spirit's testimony to the scandal of God-in-the-flesh, and to the apologetics of Christ crucified crucifying the world, placing every effort by human beings to understand our connection to the mystery that determines us (including his own effort) under the judgment of the gospel.

Pastors wanted to inquire about the latest strategies and techniques for enhancing ministerial effectiveness, like small group discipleship or church growth principles, important concerns to be sure. But Loder sought first to inspire pastors to awaken to their vocation as provocateurs of the New Humanity who inspire their congregations to center their existence and ministries in "the logic of the Spirit" in the confidence that the Spirit always brings new life out of disorder and death.

Laypersons wanted to speak with Loder about their faith experiences and about their frustrations and failures trying to adjust themselves in measured terms to the demands of a therapeutic society. Loder responded by awakening in them their deeper longing for a relationship with a personal Presence beyond all human measure, who calls them to know this Presence with such fiduciary

7. See Loder, "Normativity and Context in Practical Theology: 'The Interdisicplinary Issue,'" in *Practical Theology: International Perspectives,* ed. F. Schweitzer and J. van der Ven, Erfahrung und Theologie: Schriften zur Praktischen Theologie (Frankfurt am Main: Peter Lang, 1999), pp. 359-381.

passion that they come to measure their own lives and the world itself according to the nature of that relationship.

Special interest groups and advocates of liberation sought to press their agendas and to conscript practical theology into the service of this or that preferred ideology. But Loder upheld the freedom and power of *Spiritus Creator* and testified to the need to purify all human interests by the holy Presence of Christ, so that all contingent reality might find its "Amen" in the ontological Source of human freedom generating sacrificial love.

And while legions of the churched squandered their confessional heritage through neglect or abdication, and either sought to identify with the cultural despisers of passionate faithfulness, or to fight for a seat at the table of the cultural respectability, or to run after the latest version of spirituality *du jour* in order to feel connected to something beyond themselves, Loder mined the deeper veins of catholic Christianity and appropriated the insights of postmodern science in order to bring every thought captive to the obedience of the One who holds all things in heaven and earth together and apart according to his own nature.

Of course, Loder recognized the radical limitations of every human attempt (including his own) to fully grasp the Mystery of holiness *pro nobis.* He knew that even the most perspicuous of us see only "through a glass darkly," and that every practical theological proposal is finally only "a broken statement about human brokenness" (Luther). Indeed, as he loved to acknowledge freely and often: in relation to God we are always in the wrong (Kierkegaard)! Moreover, Loder also knew that his theological science no doubt appeared to many practical theologians and religious educators to be inelegantly out of step with pluralism, multiculturalism, and the apologetic demands of our globalized world, if not downright christologically imperialistic. Nevertheless, he sought to be obedient to the scandal of the cross, and to let his own work be justified finally in relation to this scandalous Datum that he considered to be revealed to the church in the Spirit. Indeed, like Paul of old, Loder seemed compelled, even captured, by the love of the living Christ, and he sought to answer Christ's interrogation of him first of all: "Jim, are *you* there?" Perhaps in time, as the apologetic concerns of practical theology and religious or Christian education struggle for clarification, as the impotence of many current public theological proposals to inspire prophetic critique in the face of the principalities and powers is revealed, and as the scandal of Christ becomes more compelling to us all, some of those who initially regarded Loder's work to be fideistic, eccentric, or imperialistic will take a second look. And perhaps then they will resonate to the practical theological vision of this Kierkegaardian comedian and glimpse a little more fully what he was up to when he, with a wry smile on his face, a palpable joy in his heart, a little tinge of frustration in his voice, and his own sense of fragility and contingency center stage, echoed the Spirit's interrogation of himself and all of us: "Are you there?"

Practical Theology according to the God-Man Structure of Reality

Of course, the "there" for Loder was always "life in the Spirit," which for him was nothing less than our existential participation Spirit-to-spirit in the "God-man structure of reality" transforming every dimension of created life according to Christ's nature. Like his primary interlocutor Kierkegaard, Loder was a conceptual genius who learned convictional, intellectual, imaginative, and vocational obedience from the things that he suffered at the hands of *Spiritus Creator.* Through "suffering divine things" (Reinhard Hütter), Loder was inspired to create interdisciplinary theoretical lenses capable of disclosing the hidden orders of intelligibility underlying, infusing, and potentially transforming every dimension of the social construction of reality (bodily, psychic, social, and cultural) through the power of the Holy Spirit.

From a convictional standpoint, and with perhaps unmatched interdisciplinary breadth (Loder's work reveals a profound understanding of disciplines ranging from what he called the "little infinity" of quantum reality to the "big infinity" of cosmology and astro-physics), and astounding anthropological depth (he was especially fluent with all of the disciplines that inform the knowledge of the human, including the neuro-biological), Loder sought to indwell the inner nature of divine-human interaction and to articulate from there what he felt compelled to identify as "the core generative problematic" of practical theology. By this core problematic he meant the deepest discernment possible of *why* practical theology is a problem at all for human beings.[8] This theological "Why?" at the heart of practical theology is the problematic that inevitably *must* emerge from a long-term, passionate, and patient critical attentiveness to this subject, one that compels the human knower who "allow[s] the gap that stretches from experience to idea to be bridged by an intuitive surmise evoked by deepening coherences that gradually emerge from the interaction between the knower and the known and eventually lay bare the internal structure of the reality being investigated."[9] This indwelling and explicating exercise

8. Loder, "Normativity and Context in Practical Theology," p. 359 n.1. See also "The Place of Science in Practical Theology: The Human Factor," pp. 22-24.

9. Loder, "The Place of Science in Practical Theology: The Human Factor," p. 29.

of "fiduciary passion" was for Loder the central task of any true science, including practical theological science.

What set practical theology apart for Loder was the immensity of its subject matter. He took the God-man to be the tacit relational Reality underlying every differentiation and hierarchy created by human science to bring order and give meaning to human existence, so that every transformational experience (bodily, psychological, social, or cultural, Christian or not) was but a proximate form of the definitive transformation of all things accomplished in and through Christ. Over a span of forty years, Loder worked out the "grammar" of transformation that revealed at the center of existence a bipolar, differentiated, relational unity shaped by, and conformed to, the dimensions discerned at Chalcedon. He thus created conceptual lenses that allowed him to indwell the human condition *coram Deo* with disclosive power to reveal what the Spirit was doing to make and keep human life human (Paul Lehmann) according to Christ's nature. He argued that practical theologians who allowed their minds to be conformed to this christological relationality could not simply assume that theology and the human sciences can be integrated, using whatever conceptual resources seem workable. Rather, they would be compelled by the nature of the reality being investigated and by their own redemptive experience of that reality to first question the very possibility of such integration from the human side, given the ontological incommensurability between divine and human orders revealed in Christ.

Only when practical theologians are humbled to take this incommensurability seriously as revealing the nature of reality itself can they begin to think *theologically* about practical theology's constructive and operational commitments. In one of his last published articles, Loder articulated this "core generative problematic" for practical theology as follows:

> The *core generative problematic* [for practical theology] *is that such issues* (like practices, programs, organizations, spiritual life, *etc.) require that two ontologically distinct realities, the divine and the human, be brought together in a unified form of action that preserves the integrity of both and yet gives rise to coherent behavior.* This paradoxical problematic implies that God's action and human action, although ontologically distinct, are not ultimately dichotomous.[10]

Of course, "ontologically distinct realities" are "not ultimately dichotomous"

10. Loder, "The Place of Science in Practical Theology: The Human Factor," p. 23 (emphasis in the original). Loder is not thinking here in terms of *analogia entis* but in terms of *analogia fidei* and *analogia spiritus*.

only because God has acted, and continues to act, in Jesus Christ through the Holy Spirit to make it so. As Barth taught, God refuses to be God without humanity, and this datum alone supplies our confidence for salvation. Loder argued that Christ alone supplies our confidence for interdisciplinary method as well. Thus, out of this "core generative problematic" Loder sought to construct a critical, confessional, practical theological science of redemptive transformation[11] that places divine and human action in their proper relation according to the nature of Christ. He sought to retain for all practical theological concerns Barth's notion of preaching as an "impossible possibility." Indeed, his work as a whole may at some level be considered neo-Barthian practical theology, in that he sought to develop a conceptual framework that took full account of Barth's concern to preserve the scandalous mystery at the heart of all divine-human intercourse, even while he sought also to go "beyond Barth" to appropriate a fuller contribution from the human sciences in relation to divine science (revealed theology).

This effort to take both the human sciences and the Christian scandal of particularity seriously for constructive practical theology certainly makes his work appear fideistic or naive to some, unworkable to others, unintelligible to still others, and unforgivable to a few. But for those like myself and the writers of this collection, Loder's *oeuvres* provide an incredibly generative resource by which the relevance of the gospel to a scientific culture can be both celebrated and critically examined, taking seriously the full force of the gospel's prophetic judgment on the social construction of reality. Loder himself remained convinced that the Chalcedonian framework liberated practical theologians to take the natural and human sciences more seriously than do the natural and human scientists themselves. Such critical confessional vision (1) presses science and theology to "see things whole" by calling theorists to take the "tacit" domain of "personal knowing" (Polanyi) more seriously, and (2) presses science and theology to "see things broken" by calling theorists to take the creaturely limitations and the contingent nature of all human knowing (Calvin) equally seriously. Loder called this complex "seeing things whole" and "seeing things broken" good science because it takes seriously (1) the nature of the knower, the (2) na-

11. The title and theme of this book, *Redemptive Transformation in Practical Theology,* is Loder's own. He selected the writers of the essays collected here (with one exception), and had planned to respond to them in a final chapter. Loder was concerned that the theme of "transformation" itself had become rather domesticated in its current usage, and he wanted to distinguish human transformations of all types from the divine transformation of human transformation that is the work of the Holy Spirit. This work of the Holy Spirit that "transforms transformation" is what Loder meant by the phrase "redemptive transformation."

ture of the reality being known, and (3) the relationality that unites them to be constitutive of the event of knowing anything at all.

Loder's work included but transcended the contemporary concern for public theology, a concern that often lets culture provide the fiduciary framework within which theology is called to make a contribution. Instead, Loder sought to generate a conceptual revolution by giving Christ preeminence, so that Christ provides the fiduciary framework within which scientific culture itself becomes more self-aware of the implications of its tacit participation in the Chalcedonian reality at the heart of all things. In the preface to *The Knight's Move,* which he coauthored with physicist Jim Neidhardt, this concern to foster generative insights into the theology-science dialogue according to the God-man structure of reality as the tacit ground of every constructive scientific insight and dialogue comes into view:

> This book is addressed to a wide spectrum of persons with the intention that interrelationships which pertain between theology and science may be brought out of any disciplinary ghetto and put into open dialogue. It is hoped that theologians who discuss theology and science largely within their own discipline may find here fresh avenues for interdisciplinary dialogue with scientists. Scientists who are concerned with the meaning and purpose of their emerging views of the universe may find here ways and reasons to examine such concerns with theologians from within the history and practice of theological reflection. Those . . . who find their lives and their values increasingly defined by the advancing power of a scientific and technological culture and who wonder about its purpose and meaning should also find here foundations for a deeper reflection and perhaps even a basis for renewed personal resolve to deepen that dialogue. Those caught up in the spiritual and theological confusion of our time and who wonder how science may inform their quest for some correlation or convergence among God, persons, and the physical universe may find here lines of thought that will inform spiritual discernment in directions that are also compatible with the nature of the created order. There are others . . . who are already engaged in the theology/science dialogue as a vocation [for whom] . . . we hope this book supplies some further stimulation and substance which can forward the direction in which . . . [they] have already begun to move. Finally, some may find the book challenging in its efforts to put familiar figures (Kierkegaard, Bohr, Piaget, Einstein, and others) into the theology/science dialogue in unanticipated ways.[12]

12. Loder and Niedhardt, *The Knight's Move: The Relational Logic of the Spirit in Theology and Science* (Colorado Springs: Helmers & Howard, 1992), pp. xiii-xiv.

From this extended quote it is obvious that Loder's concern for practical theology reached beyond the boundaries normally associated with this field of inquiry. Loder believed that practical theology, when understood relationally and constructively in the light of Christ, was a true science in every sense of the word, and no less rigorous in principle for its being imagined according to the contours defined by Chalcedon than it would be if imagined through the contours of any other fiduciary or convictional stance, say feminist or Marxist or capitalist. While the fully Chalcedonian dimensions of his practical theological science do not become explicit in his own work until the 1980s through his collaboration with Neidhardt, these dimensions were implicit and powerfully at work from the very beginning, due mainly to his redemptive experiences of Christ in 1957 and 1970, and to his lifelong reading of Kierkegaard (see below). His life is an example of the persistence of passionate faith to seek profound understanding of all things in relation to the God-man. Loder understood that his own intellectual vocation had been immersed in the core problematic "Why?" of practical theology from the beginning. In a 2001 interview he confessed:

> I had a restlessness about [theoretical coherence and completeness in practical theology]. . . . I just wanted to see [practical theology] have structure. You see, practical theology has really been for me a genuine interest. It's not like I had an interest in something else and tried to work it into practical theology. It is really to try to see as clearly and substantially and systematically as I could the way in which theology came into [human] action, and the way in which action shaped theological thinking. That area of search was always for me of genuine interest and passion. And I think this is really because of Kierkegaard. That is what Kierkegaard was after. To see how the theological construction of . . . the God-Man, the Chalcedonian understanding, was actually in some ways inherently bound to the way in which we are made and therefore capable of reversing it, like in a conversion. So I think my being driven so much by Kierkegaardian understanding was leading me into practical theology. And the gracious thing was that when I came [to Princeton Seminary in] Christian education . . . the whole arena of the foundational disciplines was wide open so that I could move right into it in a way that I could just create in that area anything at all I felt was relevant. . . . I wanted [Christian education and practical theology] bigger. I wanted it more like what [Seward] Hiltner envisioned but really didn't work out very well. The drive toward practical theology was in my soul.[13]

13. Interview with Dana Wright, April 20, 2001.

One conviction that binds the writers of these present essays in Loder's honor is that his practical theological vision has not received the level of scrutiny that it so richly deserves. The full measure of his insights into the human condition *coram Deo* in light of the Christ event and the work of the Holy Spirit integrated theologically with the wisdom of human science has not yet been adequately comprehended or appreciated, nor has his work *as a whole* really been seriously studied or examined at any comprehensive level by seasoned practical theologians. If this present work helps make Loder's generative vision more accessible to the guild, or more available to pastors and to leaders, for both affirmation and critique, we will be grateful on behalf of Loder's overriding concern to contribute to the redemptive transformation of persons, churches, and cultures in a perilous age.

Because Loder argued for, and demonstrated in all of his work, that the nature of the knower inevitably determines the substance and meaning of what is known, his own experiences of redemptive transformation become crucial generative sources for discerning the significance of his practical theological science. Thus, we need to appreciate Loder's own faith journey of intensification seeking deeper understanding in order to grasp the meaning of his work.[14] I therefore will sketch out a biography of this Christian thinker, educator/teacher, counselor, practical theologian, and disciple, whose experience of redemptive transformation, like Luther and Kierkegaard before him, "fired him into the world with a velocity not his own" (Luther).

A Biographical and Bibliographical Sketch

James Edwin Loder Jr. was born in Lincoln, Nebraska, on December 5, 1931, the oldest child and only son of Edwin and Frances Loder. He spent most of his childhood in Lincoln until the family moved to Kansas City, Missouri, where young Jim attended high school. Upon graduation Loder matriculated at Carleton College in Northfield, Minnesota, majoring in philosophy (he entered as a physics major but his professors soon acknowledged that he asked too many "Why?" questions for a physicist, and suggested he take up *meta*physics, which he did!). Loder graduated from Carleton in 1953 and entered Princeton Theological Seminary in 1954, completing his B.D. degree there in 1957.

14. A more complete biographical account of Loder's life and work can be found in Dana R. Wright, "James E. Loder, Jr.," a research entry to a database website project entitled "Christian Educators of the 21st Century," Kevin Lawson, gen. ed. (La Mirada, CA: Talbot School of Theology, 2003). Go to www.talbot.edu/ceacademic.

While at Princeton, two significant events shaped his emerging sense of himself and his vocation. In his senior year he and several other students resisted the approach D. Campbell Wyckoff had taken in his Christian education course because to them it lacked the philosophical depth and theoretical breadth they craved. So Wyckoff in his wisdom gave them permission to redesign the course in a way that satisfied both their intellectual curiosity and the course requirements.[15] This event launched Loder on his life-long critique of the conceptual coordinates of Christian education in particular and practical theology in general.

However, the impetus underlying and sustaining this vocational awakening arose out of another, even more significant event in Loder's life. During his junior year of seminary, his father was stricken with brain cancer and died. At home, and in despair over his father's untimely death, Loder himself became seriously ill and was confined to bed. From there he searched in vain for consolation and comfort in the midst of this meaningless tragedy. Finally, in desperation, he called out for God to "Do something!" As Loder recalled it, God did indeed "Do something," something quite unexpected for a budding philosopher. As he cried out, the young seminarian was met from the "other side" by a warming Presence that enveloped his body (he likened it to being immersed in "liquid heat"), and awakened his spirit in joy and assurance that all was well. Arising from his bed he (quite uncharacteristically) broke out in song — "Blessed Assurance, Jesus Is Mine" — and then (more characteristically) he picked up one of his seminary texts — Emil Brunner's *The Scandal of Christianity* — and literally "recognized" its truthfulness as a testimony to the power of God he had just experienced. Through this event of transformation Loder insisted that his despair had been "scandalized" by the Presence of Christ, that gracious new life had been bestowed upon him "from above," and that the deeper dimensions of life's final meaning had been revealed to him. Thus, knowing convictionally that what he had experienced of Christ could not be reduced to psychological or social dimensions alone, he returned to Princeton to seek faith's understanding of his proleptic experience.[16]

15. Both Loder and Wyckoff confirmed this episode in separate interviews with Dana Wright.

16. Loder argued that good science requires "fiduciary passion" that depends upon what Polanyi called *prolepsis*, "an anticipatory glimpse, a proleptic conception . . . and implicit apprehension that is imprinted upon the informed mind because the internal structure of the phenomenon bears a kinship to our knowing and what we can know as we allow ourselves to indwell the phenomenon." Perhaps Loder's experience can be understood as a *prolepsis*, anticipating all that was to come. See Loder, "The Place of Science in Practical Theology: The Human Factor," pp. 28-29.

When he told his story to Hans Hofmann, a Swiss theologian who had studied with Brunner and who knew of the Reality of which Loder spoke, Hofmann put the young prodigy on to Kierkegaard as one who might offer him a way to make sense of this liberating experience theologically and psychologically. Loder responded enthusiastically to Kierkegaard's work (he called it "language for my head") and to Hofmann's tutelage. After graduation, Loder accompanied Hofmann to Harvard, where the elder scholar had been chosen by the federal government to conduct interdisciplinary research on the relation of religion to mental health. Hofmann chose Loder as one of his four research students. Over the next half decade Loder earned his Th.M. from the Divinity School at Harvard (1958) and his Ph.D. in the History and Philosophy of Religion from Harvard's Graduate School of Arts and Sciences (1962). He finished his dissertation on the power of criterional imagination in Freud and Kierkegaard to restore mental health while he was a Danforth scholar at the Menninger Foundation in Topeka, Kansas.[17] During these five critical years Loder engaged some of the greatest minds of the day in theology and the human sciences — Talcott Parsons, David McClelland, Paul Tillich, James Luther Adams, Seward Hiltner, Paul Pruyser, etc., along with able young scholars like Robert Bellah, Donald Miller, and Harvey Cox — all of whom Loder interpreted in relation to the ever-present Kierkegaard, in order to forge the conceptual contours of his scientific understanding of transformative religious experiences.

In 1962 Loder, who was now married to his beloved Arlene, was called back to Princeton Theological Seminary as an instructor in Christian education, with a charge to focus on teaching the foundational disciplines that shape Christian education as a sub-field of practical theology. Loder proved to be not only a keen scholar but also a compelling and original teacher who made the often staid subject of Christian education come alive for the many students who flocked to his classes.[18] He also counseled many of his students, providing the seminary with a rich counseling resource it lacked in those days.[19] By the late

17. Loder's dissertation integrated the insights of Freud and Kierkegaard concerning "reality restoring" therapeutic experience and the therapeutic power of imagination in religious experience. This dissertation, "The Nature of Religious Consciousness in the Writings of Sigmund Freud and Søren Kierkegaard: A Theoretical Study of the Correlation of Religious and Psychiatric Concepts" (Harvard University, 1962), was later written up and published as *Religious Pathology and Christian Faith* (Philadelphia: Westminster Press, 1966).

18. Both D. Campbell Wyckoff and J. Randall Nichols confirmed in private interviews Loder's profound effect on Christian education at Princeton. One student likened his teaching to that portrayal of Mr. Keating by Robin Williams in the film version of *Dead Poets Society.*

19. The stories that illuminate Loder's insights into the work of the Spirit, that are found throughout his writings and that were spoken about in his classes, came largely from Loder's almost forty-year counseling ministry at the seminary.

1960s Loder began to attract a high caliber of doctoral students to help him revitalize the academic integrity of a field desperately lacking theoretical and interdisciplinary substance. He offered these students an interdisciplinary and constructive approach to practical theology he had learned at Harvard. By the end of the decade, Loder was ascending to the upper regions of academic service, helping to redefine his discipline from the ground up. His academic future seemed to know no limits. He and Arlene were raising two adorable daughters, Kim and Tami, and Loder himself traveled the world as a bona fide expert in Christian education. And then . . .

In the late summer of 1970, as the Loder family headed toward Toronto on the New York thruway to enjoy the fruits of their labor, they stopped their camper by the side of the road to give aid to two women. While Loder secured a jack to change a tire on the women's ancient sedan, a truck driver fell asleep and crashed his vehicle into the car, flipping it over and dragging the helpless Loder underneath it for some distance over gravel. This horrific experience, which is recorded in detail in his book *The Transforming Moment,* and which was renarrated for all of his students from the early 1970s on, threw Loder again into an existential conflict so powerful that it ultimately forced him to radically reconsider the very core of his self-understanding and the very meaning of his life's vocation. As Loder recalled, "This episode . . . raised countless new questions [for me], disturbed several personal relationships, and forced me to reenvision the spiritual center of my vocation — not an easy matter when one is already teaching in a theological seminary. It undoubtedly presented me with the reality to which I have had to be true and from which I have departed only with a keen sense of having violated my own soul."[20] This experience also compelled him to reassess the meaning and substance of his academic work from the same convictional standpoint. In the 2001 interview Loder responded to the question "What changed in your academic work after the accident?" in the following way:

> That's a good question, because before 1970 I was doing all of my teaching within a basic psychoanalytic model, that conflict learning is basic to psychoanalysis. So I was upgrading psychoanalysis a little bit. But that was the basic shape of my understanding. After 1970 I realized it was the Spirit of God who creates the problem and guides us into truth. And the whole convictional picture in four dimensions began to become a way for me to talk about what I know had happened, and what could happen. And so, it

20. Loder, *The Transforming Moment,* 2nd ed. (Colorado Springs: Helmers & Howard, 1989), p. 13.

> was still conflictual, but now it had shifted into a much bigger perspective. And the dynamics involved were not just limited to the human spirit but also to the divine redemption in action.[21]

As was mentioned earlier, this realization of new life and vocation did not come easy. Indeed, some two years after the accident, fighting his own internal struggles and facing considerable skepticism from some of his colleagues who regarded his "turn to the Spirit" an egregious lapse into uncritical mysticism unfit for Reformed theological consumption, Loder nonetheless concluded that his life and academic ministry only made sense "in the Spirit." That is "in the Spirit" also had to make intellectual sense to himself as well, and the dynamics involved needed to be brought to articulation in a way that held integrity with both the human sciences and with the best insights of the church, especially the Reformed tradition.

In time Loder came to recognize from a convictional standpoint that the pattern of the creative human spirit he had been investigating since his days at Harvard bore an analogical relationship to the Christomorphic pattern of the Holy Spirit that he had experienced at the death of his father and later through the accident that nearly took his own life. Loder now sought to overcome the theological reductionism he was convinced permeated his Harvard work and to understand and explicate theologically the redemptive dynamism of *Spiritus Creator* in relation to the creative action of the human spirit. He pored over the catholic Christian tradition for its teachings on the work of the Holy Spirit in relation to the human spirit, and found particular help from Regin Prenter's study of Luther's doctrine of the Spirit, *Spiritus Creator,* and from George Hendry's Reformed study *The Holy Spirit in Christian Theology.*[22] Loder discerned in this intense study of the church's confession of the Holy Spirit that our human participation in the work of the Spirit is actualized through the conviction-generating power of the Spirit, and not from the autonomous transformational capacities of the human spirit alone. Christian experience consists of the divine transformation of human transformation by the Holy Spirit, generating the convictional courage to live in the world in the power of the Spirit.

After several years of wrestling with these convictional and vocational matters Loder successfully articulated the theological meaning of the relational dynamics of convictional experience in scientific terms in a groundbreaking

21. Interview with Dana Wright, April 13, 2001.

22. George Hendry, *The Holy Spirit in Christian Theology* (Philadelphia: Westminster, 1961), chapter 5, "The Holy Spirit and the Human Spirit"; and Regin Prenter, *Spiritus Creator* (Philadelphia: Muhlenberg, 1953), especially the introduction and chaps. 1 and 3.

book entitled *The Transforming Moment.*[23] This carefully crafted book laid out Loder's theological reconstruction of his earlier emphasis on the transformational dynamics of therapeutic creativity and gave conceptual clarity to how Reformed theologians might understand the Holy Spirit's recreative interaction with the human spirit in convictional experiences that transform transformation by redeeming the human knower ontologically. Loder wanted to forge "a new understanding of knowing commensurate with the nature of convictional experience" (21). He argued that convictional experiences of the Presence of Christ initiated in and through the Holy Spirit constitute "four-dimensional knowing events" generated out of "a patterned process by which the Holy Spirit transforms all transformations of the human spirit . . ." (93). Convictional experiences place persons "inside" their convictions and "outside" the social construction of reality at the same time, so to speak. In relation to "inside" their convictions, Loder wrote of the Eucharist:

> The four-dimensional transformation of the Eucharist requires that one be inside what is believed in order to "see" whatever is out there, in here, and everywhere in terms of Christ's intention for all creation, from the commonest bread crumbs to the Kingdom of God. Everyday Christian experience badly needs what the transforming moment does to place people inside their convictions, just as the transforming moment needs everyday Christian experience as its substantive content. (119)

Convictional experiences also open up for the believer the theological meaning and christomorphic dimensions of normal human development redemptively transformed. Loder advocated a "figure-ground reversal" for human development that (1) made the dynamic creativity of the human spirit itself conceptually and existentially prior to the "products" created by the spirit, like ego or the stages of development, or social roles; and that (2) allowed *homo religiosus* to be understood as the normative expression of being human, whose "very nature was constructed around intrinsically and inextricably religious matters [so that] his personal identity as a member of his society was taken over and shaped by the question of his existential identity as a human being before God" (140). Citing Luther's experience of convictional transformation, Loder meant that

> the final stage in the ordinary course of human development, namely confronting one's own death and the ultimate meaning of life in light of that

23. Loder, *The Transforming Moment* (San Francisco: Harper & Row, 1981). Page references to this work are given parenthetically in the text.

> death, is inextricably tied to the ongoing sense of void at every stage in one's life. Thus, the final crisis in normal people is the lifelong crisis for the religious personality, and the scale of normal development cannot contain, much less explain, a person who brings his or her solution to life's final stage into every intervening stage. In effect, this is to reverse development from a standpoint implicitly outside it. (140)

Convictional experiences therefore testify to the Holy Spirit's initiative to place believers in a sufficiently bounded existential conflict in which the resources generated by the autonomous human spirit, formerly under the aegis of ego and culture, become depleted and call out for a theological resolution not grounded in the social construction of reality or the powers of the human spirit. In essence, through the Spirit, Christ becomes "the ground of the self without absorbing the self, the living center of the personality displacing but not destroying the ego" (144). "*Spiritus Creator* acts from outside the stage sequence frame of human development" while at the same time the Spirit "follows the pattern of transformational logic that is so deeply ingrained in the dynamics of human development" (145). From this convictional standpoint Loder argued that normal human development under the "triumph of negation" ("negation incorporated") is redemptively transformed by and through the Spirit of Christ, freeing human beings and communities to take up the way of love.

Loder's Theological Challenge to Practical Theology

The Transforming Moment appeared virtually simultaneously with two other important treatises in practical theology that gained considerably more attention over the years — James Fowler's *Stages of Faith* and Thomas Groome's *Christian Religious Education.*[24] In relation to the first book, Loder's *Transforming Moment* posed a considerable challenge to the near normative status that Fowler's work enjoyed at that time. Fowler and Loder in fact participated in a debate sponsored by the Religious Education Association in Lansing, Michigan, in 1982, in which each one had a chance to affirm and critique the other's work.[25] Loder applauded Fowler's research model but argued that

24. James Fowler, *Stages of Faith* (San Francisco: Harper & Row, 1981); Thomas Groome, *Christian Religious Education* (San Francisco: Harper & Row, 1981).

25. The substance of the debate is written up in James E. Loder and James W. Fowler, "Conversations on Fowler's *Stages of Faith* and Loder's *The Transforming Moment*," *Religious Education* 77, 2 (1982): 133-148.

Fowler's focus on the constructive powers of human ego to form increasingly complex structures of faith through the life span failed to adequately account for the spiritual nature of human beings or for the redemptive work of the Holy Spirit revealed in Scripture and tradition. Fowler affirmed the profundity of Loder's vision but criticized Loder for his lack of empirical research and for overstating his emphasis on "crisis" experiences. Fowler's work has attracted much more critical attention in the intervening years since this milestone debate. Perhaps part of the reason for this is that Loder's fuller articulation of his alternative understanding of human development came some seventeen years later with the release of *The Logic of the Spirit: Human Development in Theological Perspective,* in 1998, long after Fowler's work had received its closest scrutiny.[26]

Nonetheless, *Logic of the Spirit* offers a compelling alternative to Fowler's developmental paradigm of the whole human life span and its struggle to make meaning and to find hope in this kind of world in the context of the Holy Spirit's transformational initiative. Loder argued that the "logic of transformation" intrinsic to the human spirit's native capacities to create and compose the world unfolds through the life history of persons under the power of negation. Our profound longing to understand *what* human life means and *why* human beings exist gets buried under the repressive powers of "normal" human development. But the "secret secretes" as we navigate the epigenetic timetable where human identity and significance come up for renegotiation. Time after time the Holy Spirit exposes human beings to the outer limits of creaturehood in order to recognize the Living Ground of human existence beyond the social construction of reality and to live in relation to that Ground. Using insights from the human sciences (Freud, Erikson, Piaget, Kohlberg, and Fowler) and theological insights from the patristics, Kierkegaard, Luther, Barth, Pannenberg, and others, Loder constructed a practical theology of human developmental experience that reconsidered the question of "normal" human development in christological and trinitarian dimensions. Loder wrote: "the larger aim of my inquiry is to demonstrate the overall context that a Christian theology of the Spirit provides for the study of human nature, and especially for issues of purpose and meaning implicit in and often insufficiently articulated through the facts and theories of human development" (xiii). Centered on the power of the human spirit, Loder argued:

26. Loder, *The Logic of the Spirit: Human Development in Theological Perspective* (San Francisco: Jossey-Bass Publishers, 1998). Page references to this work are given parenthetically in the text.

> What is at stake in this study is the integrity, the hidden wisdom, and the frequent genius of the human spirit alongside its groundlessness, contaminations, and frequent perversities. To understand the human spirit is to gain entree to the central driving force in human development that separates humanity from the rest of nature . . . it is vitally important to study human uniqueness; otherwise the act of studying itself, a uniquely human enterprise, would not make sense. This quest for human uniqueness leads us into a study of the human spirit. (4)

The self-transcending human spirit generates and inspires human intelligence, adaptation, and the symbolic "worlds" necessary for human survival. The human spirit orders experience, participates in the inevitable disordering of that experience, and reconstructs new order out of the disorder, and in some sense discerns hidden orders of meaning in the process. Yet the human spirit remains "a loose cannon of creativity" that is finally "unintelligible even to itself" until it finds its proper grounding beyond itself in the "self-knowledge of God." Thus, "the human spirit makes all acts of human intelligence self-transcendent and self-relational," but "when God acts, Spirit-to-spirit, then human intelligence is transformed into a 'faith seeking understanding' of God's self-revelation — that is, the disclosure of God's mind in the Face of God in Jesus Christ" (12). In *The Logic of the Spirit* Loder took the *analogia spiritus* he developed in *The Transforming Moment* and the Chalcedonian framework he developed in another study, *The Knight's Move* (see below), to re-envision human development according to the New Creation in Christ, the ontological center of "life in the Spirit." He carefully delineated how the Holy Spirit (1) *affirms* the human spirit's ability to reconstruct itself through the life span, (2) *crucifies* the human spirit's futile efforts to order and reorder ultimate meaning and purpose according to its constructive capacities alone by revealing to the spirit its destiny in death, so as to (3) *liberate (resurrect)* the human spirit to live kinetically in relation to the transformational dynamism of the divine life acting to redeem all of creation christologically. This work of the Spirit is nothing less than the restoration of the *imago Dei* in human experience — human beings fully alive and flourishing — which is the glory of God.

That it took Loder seventeen years to develop and articulate what might be considered his full response to Fowler's *Stages of Faith* is understandable given (1) Loder's (and Fowler's) general disinterest in professional or academic gamesmanship, and (2) Loder's overriding concern to work out a comprehensive theo-anthropological framework for his *analogia spiritus* grounded in the reality of Chalcedon. Though Chalcedon is implicit in all of Loder's early work on Kierkegaard (1957-70) and in his working out the *analogia spiritus* developed in *The Transforming Moment* (1970-81), much of his effort after 1982 until the release of his next book, *The Knight's Move: The Relational Logic of the Spirit in Theology and Science* (see footnote 12), was devoted to spelling out the Chalcedonian dimensions of the Spirit's transformational initiative humanward. In dialogue with theologians like Kierkegaard, T. F. Torrance, and Pannenberg, and drawing insights from the human and natural sciences (in particular through his six-year collaboration with physicist Jim Neidhardt, the coauthor of *The Knight's Move*), Loder's "turn to Chalcedon" resulted in his constructing a comprehensive christological conceptual framework through which he further refined his *analogia spiritus* as a generic epistemological lens with extraordinary generative power to connect scientific culture to its tacit grounding in the reality of Christ. Loder and Neidhardt drew upon the work of the "hard" sciences represented by the likes of James Clerk Maxwell, Michael Polanyi, Albert Einstein, Niels Bohr, Werner Heisenberg, and Illya Prigogine; from the "soft" sciences represented by Sigmund Freud and Jean Piaget; and from theological sciences represented by Torrance, Barth, Pannenberg, the early church fathers, and the ubiquitous Kierkegaard, to make their case that Christianity possessed the conceptual resources to revolutionize postmodern ecclesial and cultural meaning-constructive capacities.

The Knight's Move bore testimony to Loder's conviction that the two-fold crisis of late modernity or postmodernity — the crisis of science (discerning the nature and limits of human knowing) and the crisis of spirit (reaffirming the importance of human participation in scientific knowing) — was profoundly addressed in the reality of Jesus Christ. This work recapitulated the staggering breadth of Loder's theoretical vision beyond the usual concerns of Christian education and practical theology and supported his conviction that the Reformed and catholic Christian tradition offered postmodern culture extraordinary generative conceptual resources for imagining a more humane personal, social, and cultural order.

After *The Logic of the Spirit* came out in 1998, Loder wrote two published articles and a final (yet unpublished) book, which, taken together, outline his vision for a critical, confessional, practical theological science that builds upon all of this previous work. In his 1999 essay "Normativity and Context in Practical Theology: The 'Interdisciplinary Issue,'" Loder argued that the methodological dimension of practical theology, the integrative key to all other dimensions (historical, contextual, ecclesial, and operational), must always fundamentally address the "core generative problematic" of the discipline, or "*why* practical theology itself is a problem."[27] Since practical theology inquires

27. Loder, "Normativity and Context in Practical Theology," pp. 359-382.

about the nature of the relation of divine to human action, the core generative problematic requires a *theological* answer commensurate with the nature of this relation *as an ongoing problem* in order to have integrity. This theological answer, for Loder, was the actuality of the *hypostatic union* revealed through the Holy Spirit to the church. Loder argued that "the relationality that pertains between theology and the human sciences only becomes what it is through the transforming action of Christ's Spirit in and through the human spirit," so that "the Christomorphic relationality at stake in interdisciplinary studies calls forth *a transformational dynamic* which is repeatedly awakening us to contradictions between theology and the human sciences, intensifying oppositions until there is a new insight, finally bringing about a reappropriation of the original situation as parabolic of the relationality in Christ."[28] Loder outlined the difference it makes to the other dimensions of practical theology to envision this christological actuality at the generative center of the discipline.

Then, in 2000, Loder wrote another important essay entitled "The Place of Science in Practical Theology: The Human Factor."[29] In this article he again defined the core generative problematic for practical theology: *The core generative problematic is that [all issues related to practical theology] require that two ontologically distinct realities, the divine and the human, be brought together in a unified form of action that preserves the integrity of both and yet gives rise to coherent behavior.*"[30] He then proceeded to demonstrate from an extended discussion of the nature of true science, why the practical theologian herself must be self-involved in this theological problematic if she is to allow "deepening coherences [to] gradually emerge from the interaction between [herself] and the known and eventually lay bare the internal structure of the reality being investigated." When this self-involved knowing becomes the passion of faith (faith seeking understanding), the insight that emerges is indeed startling and definitive:

> God is irreducibly Subject; the presumed object of the inquiry turns out to be its origin and its destiny making the investigator the object of grace and the inquiry of faith a response to God's initiative. Indwelling the inner life of God is to come to the remarkable realization that such an indwelling is derivative, a human mirror of the indwelling presence of God's Spirit in the investigator.[31]

28. Loder, "Normativity and Context in Practical Theology," pp. 366-367 (emphasis in the original).

29. Loder, "The Place of Science in Practical Theology: The Human Factor," pp. 22-41.

30. Loder, "The Place of Science in Practical Theology: The Human Factor," p. 23 (emphasis in the original).

31. Loder, "The Place of Science in Practical Theology: The Human Factor," p. 29.

Through this christological transformation of the knower, the practical theologian learns to know every domain of human experience according to Christ's knowing of her, so that "by the universal replication of this Christomorphic pattern . . . we address the core of practical theology where theology and science converge in the person of Jesus Christ to shape the interplay and coherence of Divine and human action."[32]

As Loder neared his retirement, his desire to continue honing his neo-Chalcedonian theory of practical theology witnessed to in the gospel continued unabated right up until his untimely death in November 2001. Days before he died, he essentially finished his only book on Christian education, *Educational Ministry in the Logic of the Spirit,* developed over decades from his ever-popular course at Princeton, ED 105. As we noted, this book has yet to be published. Yet one may consider it to be Loder's alternative vision for practical theology to Thomas Groomes' influential *shared praxis* approach.

Groomes' own influential book, *Christian Religious Education,* has almost nothing explicitly theological to say about the transformative action of the Holy Spirit transforming the knower. Loder's work on Christian education, on the other hand, is crucial for understanding the christological, pneumatological, and anthropological dimensions of divine-human relationality that constitute "life in the Spirit" and that generate insights into the nature of the Spirit's transforming initiative in every dimension of human action.[33] Using a modified version of Talcott Parson's theory of human action (bodily, psychic, social, and cultural dimensions in isometric relations) under the powers of socialization ("tension-reduction, pattern maintenance" movement) and transformation (the dynamics governing the emergence of hidden orders of intelligibility generating paradigmatic reconstructions of human life), Loder argued that the pedagogical work of the Holy Spirit was to negate the negation riven into every dimension of human action at crucial stages through dominant socialization dynamics (bodily development/deteriorization, the creation of ego, semiotic function, the development of role structures, the formation of identity, the creation and maintenance of cultural capital), and to release the transformative capacities of the human spirit (personal and corporate) from

32. Loder, "The Place of Science in Practical Theology: The Human Factor," p. 39.

33. The importance of this book for understanding Loder's whole project cannot be overestimated. Since it has not yet been published, we have included in the *Festschrift* a summary of its content and uniqueness, written by Russell Haitch (chapter 11). Publication of this book would help dispel certain myths that surround Loder's work — for example, that he was interested only in "crisis" experiences and individual transformations or conversion experiences, and that his main contribution is to the function of the imagination in learning and teaching.

their bondage to socialization to become the dominant dynamic for constructing human order "in the Spirit." Under the impact of the Spirit, organic life-unto-death becomes the bearer of divine life and love even in the face of death. Defensive ego boundaries soften under the Spirit's work to make room for the otherness of the other. In the Spirit, role structures become reversible so that intimacy becomes possible across sexual, cultural, racial, and class boundaries. And in terms of culture, images, narratives, values or artifacts are rendered transparent in the service of living in and through the power of the divine Presence. This Loderian vision placed an enormously important challenge in front of religious educators and practical theologians to take more seriously both the work of the Holy Spirit and the dynamics of the human spirit (and their interaction at every level of human action) for theory construction and practice.

Beyond this book on Christian education Loder had hoped to finish a major work on the practical theological implications of Kierkegaard for seminary students, and to write a commentary on the Gospel of John to show the hermeneutical significance of the transformational pattern for biblical studies.[34]

While Loder's total academic output was rather small by some standards, the depth and breadth of his fecund output cannot be understood in any sense to be small. We who have collaborated to create this *Festschrift* in his honor believe that the generative power of his vision offers a uniquely valuable source of insight at the meta-theoretical level for Christian educators, practical theologians, and those concerned about cultural transformation. Loder has not gone unnoticed or unread, but his entire corpus needs a comprehensive critique by the practical theologians and religious educators, and by those involved in the reconstruction of public life in postmodern culture. We hope this *Festschrift* generates other, careful readers of Loder's work, even while we disavow with Loder the establishment of anything like a "Loderian school" of practical theology. Quite simply, however, we do believe that Loder was "fired on the world with a velocity not his own" and that the greatest tribute we could give to him is to allow this same "alien velocity" to inspire in us and in the readers of these essays a deeper probing into the redemptive transformation that Loder believed to be at the heart of all things human and divine.

* * *

34. Loder had in part been inspired to think about this project in light of a treatise he had read by New Testament scholar Paul Anderson on John 6, in which Anderson used both Loder and Fowler to talk about the meaning of Johannine authorship. See Anderson, *The Christology of the Fourth Gospel* (Tübingen: Paul Siebeck, 1996), especially chaps. 7 and 8.

A Short Review of the Essays

We have ordered the essays contained in this *Festschrift* around three themes, which seem to have emerged quite felicitously as various authors submitted their work for review. These themes, which inevitably show Loder's influence even when he is not directly quoted and even (or especially) when some level of disagreement with him emerges, therefore give (explicit or implicit) testimony to the breadth and depth of Loder's generative mentoring of us all. These themes are:

(1) Redemptive Transformation *within* Ecclesial Praxis
(2) Redemptive Transformation *of* Practical Theology
(3) Redemptive Transformation *beyond* Practical Theology

The six essays comprising Part I, "Redemptive Transformation *within* Ecclesial Praxis," take up six core practices of the church — baptism, communion, preaching, biblical interpretation, leadership, and youth ministry — and explore their meanings as embodied actions of redemptive transformation. All of these essays powerfully challenge the domesticating forces at work in congregations today and call them to recover what Loder called human participation in "the logic of the Spirit" at the center of redemptive transformation. Loder believed that "life in the Spirit" was fully "embodied" life, and "reality-restoring," and therefore connecting practical theological vision (the Mind of Christ) to redemptive ecclesial praxis (the Body of Christ) was crucial to actualizing the church's experience of the Spirit's redemptive work in and through her life together in witness to the world. These essays should give congregational leaders significant insight into the work of the Spirit generating core Christian practices.

A theology of baptism and its relevance to the transformation of human life is the focus of the initial essay by **Russell Haitch**. Haitch orients his discussion to one of the most important generative concepts Loder developed to uncover the hidden dimensions of human reality — the concept of "double negation" which lies at the heart of divine-human redemptive interaction. Haitch first examines the developmental origins of negation that emerge at birth and in infancy, when the baby's primal assurance, incarnate in the mother's face, goes away. The child negates the negative environment by forming an ego, but with ego formation comes an inevitable repression of the power to give and receive love. Thus, "normal" human development is, theologically considered, "negation incorporated." This negation of the human spirit must itself be negated and transformed by the Holy Spirit to release the creative potential of humanity's groundedness in *Spiritus Creator*. Here Haitch clarifies that Loder does not envision the elimination of ego in the redemptive double negation, but its reconstitution in a dynamic, dialectical relationality. Transformed, the ego defenses serve a higher purpose than adaptation, becoming energies of life in the Spirit. Moreover, the negation of negation ramifies through every realm of human action (psychological, social, cultural, organic) wherever the relationality of the human spirit and Holy Spirit is active. Haitch then describes how Loder's understanding of double negation fits into a theology of baptism. The meaning of baptism is found in Christ's crucifixion, whose pattern of double negation is heard in the Orthodox hymn, "Christ has risen from the dead, trampling down death by death." Because "life" is in God, and "death" is separation from God, the death of Christ destroys death. Because his voluntary death is the final expression of his life, a life that consists completely in the love of God, "there is no 'death' in His death." Christ "fill[s death] with Himself" and renders it a "Passover into fuller life" (Schmemann). Haitch then offers practical theological guidelines, suggesting how understanding baptism in this way can help the church to teach on death and dying, as well as to address contentious issues, such as infant baptism versus believer's baptism, and the relation of water baptism to Spirit baptism.

A deep pastoral concern for persons shattered by experiences of horrendous evil runs throughout **Marilyn McCord Adams**'s passionate and raw essay provocatively titled "Biting and Chomping Our Salvation: Holy Eucharist, Radically Understood." Adams argues that even in a world like this one, in which "horror-participation" is a constitutive element of human vulnerability to dissolution and meaninglessness, nonetheless the Gospel affirms that our "enmatteredness" really *matters* to God. God, Adams insists, relentlessly "mixes it up" with the vulnerability intrinsic to our material reality (a core implication of the meaning of the Incarnation) in order to fill material reality with God's Presence so as to render human life in this kind of world blessed rather than accursed. The church enacts God's accommodation to human "enmatteredness" in the Eucharist, in the celebration of which God-with-us and God-for-us "shar[es] with us the costs of God's remarkable project" to defeat human "horror-participation" in order to render human life worthwhile. Against the tendency to "spiritualize" this Christian practice, which Adams believes permeates Protestant understandings (perhaps even Loder's work), Adams argues that Christ is present in the bread *impanationally* — meaning that "if the Divine Word assumes the eucharistic bread the way he assumes human nature, it follows that Christ's Body has two natures — human nature and bread nature." Christ's post-resurrection body, no longer vulnerable to horrors, is "causally interactive" with its environment according to its "bread nature," so that it can be touched and handled, seen and tasted. In light of Christ impanationally present, we bring to the Eucharist the kinds of raw hostility and agony that we bring to food under the assault of mastication, a process of destruction essential for allowing the food to become nurturant for us. We bring to the Eucharist our "masticated" lives and our "bitten and chomped" relations with others, especially those with whom we regularly eat. And there we literally "feed" on Christ's flesh, chomping and biting and tearing and shredding God's body and "getting even . . . for the way God has allowed horrors to shred the fabric of our lives." In doing so we overcome our tendency to defer to God's will and thereby "to hide from the terrifying truth that God is radically vulnerable to horrors, and so are we." Drawing on the psychological notion of "regression in the service of ego advancement," Adams argues that this raw approach to the Eucharist may better serve persons in congregations who live in this kind of world. The Eucharist enacts our inauguration into *ante-mortem* experience of the New Order promised in Christ.

Facing the full force of human resistance to being truly open to the otherness of the other, and upholding a strong Reformed conviction that Gospel preaching can liberate persons and communities to love, **John S. McClure** engages in an interdisciplinary analysis entitled "The Way of Love: Loder, Levinas, and Ethical Transformation through Preaching." McClure, working at the intersection of hermeneutics, homiletics, and ethics, argues that the view of preaching as an imaginative ethical and theological re-scripting through, and dialectic of, testimony and countertestimony — advocated in the works of Ricoeur and made accessible through the improvisations of Walter Brueggemann — is important but finally inadequate for inspiring ethical renewal. Rather, ethical preaching must move beyond aesthetic modes of re-scripting reality by taking more seriously the Spirit's redemptive work to transform the defensive patterns of ego that destroy and distort moral agency in the first place. The Spirit creates *ex nihilo,* according to McClure, to de-center and extradite ego from its defensive posture and liberate the human spirit to flourish as the "way of love." To develop this understanding, McClure creates the concept of "erasure testimony." He combines (1) Loder's concepts of the "logic of transformation" and the "negation of negation" in relation to the "Face," and (2) the tension in Levinas's work between "totality" ("making same") and "infinity" ("acknowledging the other"), and the relation of "the said" to "the saying," and asserts that "erasure testimony" "can occur only as the ego's efforts to 'make same' are radically displaced and reoriented by and toward the glory of the Infinite" as encountered in the other. For McClure, "the event of proclamation" must become "a second, passive and non-binary form of erasure-testimony" beyond countertestimony, a "deeply passive 'act' of *proxemics* — of 'exposure' to the other, of 'extraditing' oneself 'to the neighbor'" (Levinas). He continues, "In

Loder's terms permutational ethical transformation issues from a transformational negation, in this case mediated by what Levinas calls the 'glory of infinity' revealed in the face of the human other." Finally, McClure turns to Rebecca Chopp, who draws out a distinction between testimony in "words" and testimony in "life" to argue that Jesus Christ, the Word, as "perfectly open sign" is the living reality out of which preaching is empowered to resist "making same" and to fulfill humanity's "infinite ethical obligation" to love the human other.

In the fourth essay **Daniel S. Schipani** emphasizes the relevance of Loder's "transformational logic" to the Christian practice of biblical interpretation toward discipleship, arguing that biblical interpretation best participates in prophetic transformation when the interpreting community or person is taught to enter the text from the "margins." His essay, "Transforming Encounter in the Borderlands: A Study of Matthew 15:21-28," makes an affirmative and critical evaluation concerning Loder's "transformational logic" and its relevance for providing "a key to [interpreting] biblical narrative" from the margins. After summarizing what Loder means by "transformational logic," Schipani outlines a liberation hermeneutic structured around the three movements of *"seeing"* (assessing the structural meaning of a text in all of its strangeness and surprise), *"judging"* (discerning the significance of a text in all of its power to overturn or heal) and *"acting"* (responding to the call of the text to transformed living). In the *"seeing"* section, he interprets a notoriously difficult passage, Matthew 15:21-28, depicting Jesus' encounter with the Canaanite woman. First, he establishes the Matthean text. He then arrives at a surprising conclusion — that Jesus, not the foreign woman, is the primary object of the conflict narrated in the pericope. In being confronted with the woman's need, Jesus is exposed as one who initially accepts the underlying injustice and inhumanity of Jewish exclusivism into which he was socialized (Jesus is "fully human"). For Schipani, the text asks, Will Jesus "accommodate to tradition (of exclusion) while disobeying the will of God?" In the *"judging"* stage, Schipani notes how the text portrays Jesus in confict with his Jewish identity and the woman as the unlikely "mediator" of the negation of the negation voiced by Jesus against the woman (indicating Jesus being "tempted in all things as we are"). However, Jesus nonetheless resists the reality principle enshrined in Israel's exculsivism (he was "tempted in all things as we are, apart from sin"), and comes to accept the Gentile woman as true subject. Schipani suggests that the pericope celebrates the woman's role in "mediating" this understanding to Jesus, even as its place in the canon affirms Jesus as the Mediator! In the final act of interpretation, *"acting,"* Schipani uses Loder's five-step transformational grammar in the service of education-to-discipleship, showing how this text prompts us to develop guidelines for faith and ministry that appreciate the hermeneutical significance of marginalized experience, the transformational potential of conflict, and the power made perfect in weakness.

In the fifth essay in this section, **Robert K. Martin** addresses the important subject of transformation in relation to shared congregational leadership, the exercise of power, and reconciliation. Entitled "Leadership and Serendipitous Discipleship: A Case Study of Congregational Transformation," Martin draws upon Loder's understandings of "transformational logic" and "fourfold knowing events" to discern the work of the Spirit in the life-experience of an ordinary congregation facing potential dissolution and loss of identity through a crisis of leadership. Placing his analysis in the context of the domination of effectiveness-production models of church leadership that exist today, and more broadly in the technological rationality of modernity, he argues that such "enterprise culture" moves against genuine transformation understood theologically. Martin asks what transformed congregational leadership might look like under the power of the Spirit of God, and proposes a model of "serendipitous leadership" emerging out of conflicts that confront congregations and their leaders with personal and corporate non-being. Martin "gossips" a story in Loderian fashion of how leadership reorganized itself redemptively when the Auburn United Methodist Church of Auburn, Nebraska, and its pastor both passed through the crucible of uncertainty, self-doubt, potential alienation of affection, and the loss of trust. Out of this crisis, the transformational potential of the human spirit was released into the personal and corporate life of the congregation through a fourfold knowing event that bore the marks of the Holy Spirit's dynamic integrity. Of the impact of the Spirit on this ordinary congregation, especially in relation to a Christmas Eve worship service in which "a spontaneous eruption of love between pastor and congregation" was felt with convictional force, Martin notes: "Subsequently, as the conflict was resolved, greater energy was available to invest in their common life and ministry . . . as the tacit insight, which was the basis of the revolution, has become more explicit and to the extent that they have chosen for it, the relationality of their common life has come to reflect to a greater degree the 'communion-creating activity of the Holy Spirit.'" Martin helpfully concludes his essay by outlining several guidelines for aiding church leaders to "prepare the way for the Lord": (1) to resist the twin temptations of over-control through coercion and over-preoccupation with transformation itself, (2) to develop a sacramental understanding of leadership, and (3) to develop sensitivity to the work and shape of the Spirit's presence in the community of faith and to the cruciform nature of human response to the Spirit's ministry among us.

The final essay of Part I, "Youth, Passion, and Intimacy in the Context of

Koinonia: James E. Loder's Contributions to a Practical Theology of *Imitatio Christi* for Youth Ministry," takes up aspects of a vision for grounding youth ministry theologically in the Passion of Christ. This thesis was originally articulated by **Kenda Creasy Dean** (for her book *Practicing Passion*), but here **Dana R. Wright** puts elements of this vision in conversation with an interpretation of Loder's transformational understanding of adolescent development in order to propose a passionate practical theology of youth ministry as *imitatio Christi.* Dean argued that the passionate nature of adolescence itself demands a theological approach to youth ministry centered on the Passion of Christ, and highlights the Christian passion's power for overcoming and transforming the ego and socialization. Wright decodes Dean's debt to Loder and proposes that the adolescent demand for a cause or relationship "to die for" finds its true generative ground in the living Christ who authorizes Spirit-to-spirit intimacy with young people. Christ transforms adolescent fidelity based on the meaning-making capacities of the ego into convictional fidelity, a theological identity born of the Spirit. This interpretation of Loder's generative influence on both Dean and Wright seeks to illuminate various dimensions of this fiduciary identity created through convictional experience. In the convicting power of the Spirit, adolescents confront the full force of nothingness that infuses and envelops the inner and outer landscapes they inhabit, only to be "astonished by being" when and as Christ reveals himself there to be "the self-confirming presence of the loving Other" who releases them from the fear of abandonment and/or the fear of absorption that threatens them existentially.

Wright then explores Loder's critique of Erik Erikson's interpretation of Martin Luther as an exemplar of adolescence transformed by convictional experience. He discusses the nature of Spirit-to-spirit intimacy that results from convictional experiences, unpacks the relational structure of Christian identity (dialectical intimacy — I yet not I but Christ), and points to the relational context of this identity (the *koinonia*). Finally, Loder's insights on these inner dynamics of convictional experience are connected to Dean's concept of *mimesis* and to Sarah Coakley's concept of "deepening practices," to illuminate how the Spirit transforms socialized practices into the corporate form of fiduciary conviction, the *imitatio Christi* — which communities of faith experience when the relationality between divine and human action becomes a positive third term. Young people, note Dean and Wright, would "die for" a place in this kind of community. Loder's work suggests that youth ministry, in order to have integrity with, and to give meaning to, young people, must be conceived theologically in something like these passionate, convictional, and relational terms.

Part II, "Redemptive Transformation *of* Practical Theology," consists of five essays that focus more broadly on the meaning and shape of practical theology to discern and to give order to the relation of divine action to human action revealed in Christ. Here we come to the very center of Loder's concern to develop a critical confessional practical theology of redemptive transformation that challenges all of us to think theologically about the relation of divine and human action for guiding the church's practice in the world.

The initial essay by **Susanne Johnson** takes up the cause of re-conceiving congregational self-identity itself as a complex, constitutive, transformative praxis that understands and orders its life around God's praxis of "remembering the poor." Her essay, simply entitled "Remembering the Poor: Transforming Christian Practice," is a passionate apologetic for radically reenvisioning the church's understanding of, and relationship to, exercise of power in the cause of God's justice. Disavowing the traditional way congregations think about their responsibility to the poor, and basing her argument on an extended critique of the ethical vision of Craig Dykstra's *Vision and Character*, Johnson asserts that what is required today is a radical reordering of power and vision "poor-ward," a taking sides with the poor so that the community of faith actually envisions the social construction of reality from the side of the poor, at a time when predatory globalization makes this kind of radical discipleship more difficult than ever.

After laying out in broad strokes the nature of the church as an ecology of interlocking practices, and assessing the power of globalized capitalism to promote conditions that favor the rich over the poor, Johnson then brings the church's conventional ministry paradigm — what she calls the "service paradigm" — under scrutiny. She argues that this "service" model is wholly inadequate for several reasons, including: (1) it does not rely on the indispensable task of discerning the nature of the sociocultural context in which poverty takes place (including our own culpability in the structures that systematically oppress people); (2) it does not understand that ministry cannot simply be "to" the poor (as if it were an adjunct exercise dependent upon some native altruistic impulse), but must be conceived "with" the poor and on the side of the poor against the powers that perpetuate systemic poverty and oppression; and (3) its one-sided view of the nature of power (i.e., that power must be repudiated) ignores the positive value power has under the impact of the Spirit of Christ. Johnson writes: "Remembering the poor can be defined as a practice through which the church brings itself into a mutually transforming presence with actual persons and groups living in poverty and engages with them in strategies that challenge and change asymmetrical, unjust power structures . . . , creating conditions for diverse persons and groups to flourish more equitably through their common life together." Without reordering the life-stance of a community of faith around the practice of remembering the poor, Christian congregations offer little hope to embody the communion-creating power of the Spirit in this kind of world. Education in the congregation is propaedeutic to enabling this kind of radical remembering.

In the second essay, **Dana R. Wright** develops a biblical interpretation of the theological significance of Loder's overall project as neo-Chalcedonian practical theological science. Wright's essay, "Paradigmatic Madness and Redemptive Creativity in Practical Theology: A Biblical Interpretation of the Theological Significance of James E. Loder's Neo-Chalcedonian Science for the Postmodern Context," makes an informed intuitive connection between a *theological* reading of the function of the epistle to the Ephesians for the early church in relation to the *Pax Romana* and what Wright imagines to be the *biblical* significance of Loder's critical confessional science for the postmodern church in relation to the *Pax Americana.*

Wright argues that the author of Ephesians, under pressure from the dying-off of the apostles and the threat of the Empire, improvised a new interpretation of the meaning and purpose of Christian congregations situated in the *Pax Romana.* Ephesians envisions congregations "adapting" to life in Rome by assimilating Roman moral and institutional structures to give order to Christian life, but radically reordering these structures according to the generative and determinative blessedness of the presence of Christ in the church and the world. Ephesians uses the metaphor *plērōma* (fullness) to inspire Christian congregations in Rome to engage in what Wright calls "*pleromic* improvisation" ("filling up the fullness of Christ"), by affirming ordinary practices of everyday life (like conversation, honesty, and forgiveness), and ordinary social role relations (like marriage, parent-child and master-slave relations), but turning these practices and relations "odd" under the redemptive impact of Christ's powerful presence.

In the context of everyday existence this call to redemptive creativity in view of the *plērōma* is nothing short of the re-discovery of Christ in the context of the *Pax Romana,* as transformed relations become like "holograms" of Christ's eschatological redemption of all things. Wright then argues that the work of James Loder can be interpreted "biblically" as an Ephesians-like vision of redemptive creativity for a scientific context, one that orients Christian life in the *Pax Americana* to the God-man structure of reality. Wright traces Loder's early efforts to get "inside" the dynamic structure of "reality-restoring" imagination (the hypnagogic paradigm) in religious experience (using Freud and Kierkegaard), and he shows how this paradigm illuminated Loder's creative 1969 interpretation of generation-gap conflicts plaguing American society, based on his reading of Eph. 6:1-4. Wright then argues that this early paradigm was trapped within a psychoanalytic framework that eclipsed the full christological immensity and christomorphic relational structure of the Holy Spirit's initiative in restoring human beings to reality (convictional experiences). Only after an accident that threatened his life did Loder discern the analogy between the dynamics of the human spirit and the redemptive creativity of the Holy Spirit (his *analogia spiritus*) and go on to reconceive his later theological exposition of the Christological grounds of human participation in the redemptive creativity of the Spirit. Wright argues that Loder's Ephesians-like effort to inspire a comprehensive understanding of "life in the Spirit" in the context of Empire deserves to be studied thoroughly and carefully by practical theologians, religious educators, and cultural theorists.

In the third essay, entitled "George Lindbeck and Thomas F. Torrance on Christian Language and the Knowledge of God," **Thomas J. Hastings** looks for a way to get "beyond the fractured Protestant epistemologies of 'objectivism,' 'subjectivism,' and 'volitionalism'" that plague faith communities, in a way that has theological integrity with the nature of Jesus Christ. Hastings's analysis highlights the insights of one of the most influential theologians in Loder's career, Thomas F. Torrance. Hastings, using Torrance, seeks to clarify what is at stake theologically in the language games we use in Christian education by placing Torrance's view of language into relationship with the influential postliberal theologian George Lindbeck, generally criticizing Lindbeck by means of Torrance. The issue behind this discussion is the confusion that exists concerning the Christological grounding of Christian language for the teaching ministry of the church.

After introducing both Lindbeck and Torrance in broad outline, Hastings analyzes the former's classical work *The Nature of Doctrine* in some detail. He then argues via the latter that Lindbeck's philosophical and cultural assumptions cannot do adequate justice to the true nature of doctrine grounded in Jesus Christ. Lindbeck's theory suffers from what Hastings calls a "fatal deistic disjunction" between God and the world that ignores both the Christological reality which holds heaven and earth together and apart according to the nature of Jesus Christ and the "pathic self-investment" demanded of one who seeks to know (or be known) by this reality. From Torrance, Hastings argues for an epistemology that has integrity with the nature of reality as it has been revealed in Christ. For Hastings, Torrance's claim that both theology and the natural sciences operate within "the same 'field limitations' of the unitary rationality of the universe, its contingent intelligibility, and contingent freedom" provides the theoretical key to a unified epistemology. Only a theologically discerned epistemology grounded in the Chalcedonian reality underlying all contingent realities, what Torrance calls *a posteriori objective realism*, provides an adequate framework for speaking intelligently of God and humanity. Such an epistemology is resonant both with Einsteinian scientific discoveries of the "singular constant of the speed of light" of postmodern physics and with the "epistemological singularity of Jesus Christ . . . 'God in his own Being and Act come among us.'"

The fourth essay in this section, by **Margaret A. Krych**, inquires about the relevance of Loder's work for Krych's own Lutheran tradition. Asking about the place of "Transformational Narrative in a Non-Transformational Tradition," Krych looks at the subject of transformational narrative from the standpoint of a *theologia crucis,* and asks the difficult question, "How does one express transformational logic in a tradition that shies away from terms like 'transformation' because it bears a cruciform understanding of sanctification?" After outlining Loder's basic structure of transformation, noting both continuity and discontinuity intrinsic to transformation and the need for transformation to be transformed in the service of Christ, she deftly and appreciatively "exegetes" crucial passages in Loder's *The Transforming Moment* and *The Logic of the Spirit* to find there profound understandings of Christ-mediated transformational narrative to which she resonates as a Lutheran theologian and educator. In particular she notes Loder's concentration on Luther's *Anfechtungen* (the struggles) as constitutive of Christian life confronted by, and dependent upon, the Holy Spirit. Yet she also detects in Loder's analysis and constructive proposal the Calvinist "upward movement" that, from a traditional Lutheran perspective, overemphasizes "positive growth in grace" (sanctification) by subordinating justification to sanctification and distorting the *simul iustus et peccator* nature of Christian experience. That is, in Krych's judgment, Lutheran theology corrects Loder's Reformed commitments to the "more and more" of sanctification by accepting the full implications of Luther's *simul iustus et peccator* for theological anthropology and transformation. Krych wants to take the full force of justification in theological anthropology that insists that God's justifying movement human-ward is never "left behind" to get to the more positive movement of growth in sanctification.

In the end Krych would allow Lutherans to accept the transformational paradigm of Loder's work provisionally. Transformation is acceptable if (1) Lutherans retain the agonistic nature of Christian life reflecting Luther's commitment to the bondage of the will even in mature Christians; if they (2) place full emphasis on the mercy of Christ as mediating reality of transformation; if they (3) conceive sanctification "cyclically" as a profound recapitulation of our dependency on the benefits of Christ, not on positive change; and if they (4) confirm over and over again that human life must ever be justified by God's mercy and forgiveness mediated through core Christian practices, especially preaching and the sacraments, every day. In short, Krych would emend Loder's christomorphic relational emphasis by reshaping redemptive transformation along the lines of Luther's *theologia crucis* with its "cruciform" relationality as the proper structure of divine-human interaction.

Russell Haitch concludes Part II (at the editors' request) with an important summary of the context and content of Loder's only book on Christian education, the yet-to-be-published *Educational Ministry in the Logic of the Spirit.* Haitch's essay, entitled "A Summary of Teaching in the Spirit: James Loder's Theory of Christian Education," outlines key features of Loder's complex transformational theory of Christian education in a way that bears witness to Loder's very unique understanding of the pedagogical work of the Holy Spirit in congregational contexts. Haitch locates Loder's theory historically as a response to the charge Edward Farley made in 1965 to religious educators that the Holy Spirit functioned as a kind of X-factor in Christian or religious education. In essence, Loder took Farley's criticism to heart and set out to construct a theory that took the Spirit as the fundamental reality.

Organizing his chapter around three Loderian themes of "transformation," "four-dimensionality," and "christocentrism," Haitch notes how Loder shaped his theory of education to address the immensely powerful forces of socialization that (1) distort the transformational potential of the human spirit (e.g., as in authoritarian cultures that distort power or achievement cultures that distort love), (2) repress the four-dimensional life revealed in Christ to two dimensions under the *aegis* of the ego (e.g., raising functional concerns above existential concerns), and (3) reduce Christ to the dimensions of socialized existence by placing the church in the service of culture. Haitch discusses Loder's understanding of the relation of transformation (creativity) to socialization (order) using the relational nature of the human spirit as the clue to transformation's priority in the relation. But he notes that for Loder, the human spirit itself is ungrounded and needs to participate in a christomorphic pattern of relationality to find and express its true nature. This pattern, which is described as a bipolar, asymmetrical relational unity, is in human beings and structures (like the self, itself) a proximate form of the ultimate bipolar, asymmetrical relational unity in the God-Man. Christian "life in the Spirit" requires that the ultimate pattern of relationality revealed in Christ become the underlying reality of human praxis, such as Christian education and Christian worship. But Loder argued that the pattern itself is not enough. The transformation of praxis occurs when the full power of the absence of being (the Void) confronts our social constructions of reality (and the ego-centered structure that created it) and reveals their groundlessness. Haitch argues, "if we come to the conviction that these patterns [of christomorphic relationality] are not just abstractions, but actualities, then one's approach moves from being christomorphic to christocentric." Haitch points to convergences between Loder's work and the proposal of Thomas Groome for critical consciousness-raising. But he describes how Loder's work tries to go deeper by relating the generative power of consciousness, the human spirit, with the generative source of transformation, the Holy Spirit. Haitch concludes by offering several implications of Loder's work for practical theology and educational practice: the priority of theory, the priority of spirit in education theory, and the priorty of the Holy Spirit in the life of the church.

Part III addresses "Redemptive Transformation *beyond* Practical Theology." The three essays located here, taken together, demonstrate the breadth of Loder's own scholarship by putting his work in dialogue with philosophy and mystical theology, and show how attuned he was to the times in which he lived. Loder's relevance beyond the boundaries of his own discipline are apparent here in these essays. They focus on three fundamental themes in Loder's corpus — the themes of relationality, the proximity of non-being to all things human, and the nature of authentic spirituality — all of which have emerged as crucial for understanding our postmodern context.

In the first essay, **F. LeRon Shults** surveys the theme of relationality in Western philosophy as a kind of "propaedeutic to reading Loder" (and no doubt to reading our times in general). He argues that this theme "pervaded" Loder's writings "as well as his pedagogical and therapeutic practice," so that Loder's placing "the logic of relationality . . . at the heart of practical theology, both methodologically and materially" places his work at the cutting edge of the highest levels of the current postmodern conversation. Shults first asks why the philosophical turn to relationality is so important, not only to practical theology but to every human endeavor. He then moves on to identify several key "pivotal points" in philosophy's development from essentialist and substantivist thinking to relational thinking, breaking up this history into two broad sections, "Aristotle to Kant" and "Hegel to Levinas."

In the first section Shults summarizes the thought of Aristotle, the neo-Platonist Plotinus, and Porphyry's distinction between substance and accidents, and he then moves quickly through nominalism (Ockham) to Descartes, Locke, Hume, and finally Kant. He raises two important issues in Kant that laid the foundation for a turn to relationality: (1) Kant's decision to make "substance" and "accidents" sub-categories of "relation," and (2) Kant's "unleashing of relationality" from "quantity." In the second period of review, Shults discusses the contributions of Hegel to relationality (his notions of self-relatedness, process, and the ultimate relational reality of finitude and infinitude), the insights of Kierkegaard (infinite qualitative distinction between God and humanity, the self as intrinsically relational), and Charles Sanders Peirce (synechism). Then he traces the relationality theme in two streams of twentieth-century philosophy, the analytic (the relation of logic and language) and the phenomenological (especially Husserl's emphasis on categorical intensionality), in existentialism (Sartre and Heidegger), process thought (Whitehead), Buber, object relations, and Emmanuel Levinas's concern with the ethical relation to the otherness of the other. Shults concludes this whirlwind tour by arguing that practical theology is also in fact partially responsible for the "turn to relationality" in philosophy. In doing so he implies that Loder's consistent emphasis on the constitutive relationality at the heart of reality gives his work a kind of prophetic position in the current discussion.

John D. Kuentzel continues this dialogue between practical theology and philosophy by exploring the theme of negation central to Loder's soteriology. Kuentzel argues that Loder's concept of negation appears to have been shaped in fundamental ways by his reading of Martin Heidegger. His essay, "The Heidegger in Loder (Or, How the Nothing Became the Void): Provoking Wonder in Education," begins by "exegeting" Heidegger's inaugural lecture "What Is Metaphysics?" (a work Loder assigned to his students) to show its probable impact on Loder's construction of ontology. Heidegger's concern in "Metaphysics" is to "discern what is metaphysically essential to every mode of human knowing." He focuses on being itself (the whole), the knower's being questioned by being, and the nothing, themes that Kuentzel finds resonate to Loder's theological anthropology and to his scientific understanding of self-involved knowing. Kuentzel takes us on a journey through Heidegger's development of the theme of the void, which is "not beyond human experience." Phenomenologically, the void is not a "thing" to be comprehended (an idea) but is apprehended in a "mood" in which one finds oneself. Thus, while experiences of boredom or joy reveal the wholeness of being, the most profound experience of one's situatedness in being is anxiety, a sense of indeterminedness (the German *unheimlich* means "not-being-at-homeness" that is literally indescribable). Yet for Heidegger, the nothing as a "repelling gesture" is the dynamic source of transformation because it allows us to ask the most basic question of all, "Why is there being and not nothing?"

Kuentzel then goes on to critique Heidegger in light of Loder, arguing that Loder's theological position offers what Heidegger's philosophy cannot deliver — an encounter with the Holy on the other side of one's apprehension of the totality of life and death. Loder contends that awakening to being, including the experience of void, points one to the ground of one's existence beyond void. In four-dimensional transformation, the convicted person or community experiences the negation of Heidegger's negation, placing even the void in the service of redemptive transformation. Kuentzel concludes his discussion by comparing notions of "wonder" in Heidegger and Loder, who both understand confrontation with the nothing as essential to the generative dynamic structure through which wonder is experienced. He offers some guidelines for generating wonder-full learning experiences in secular and religious education settings.

Eolene Boyd-MacMillan writes the concluding essay in this section, entitled "Loder and Mystical Spirituality: Particularity, Universality, and Intelligence." She provocatively interprets Loder as a "Protestant mystical theologian" whose work, in accord with specific depictions of mystical theology, (1) centers on "transformative encounters with God," (2) addresses problems of humanity at the extremities of human experience, and (3) reconceptualizes and transforms the nature of intelligence as an expression of love and reason.

First, Boyd-MacMillan argues that Loder's transformational theology is grounded in the Chalcedonian reality that is the generative source and goal of transformation. So central is the logic of transformation to human experience that it undergirds the Christian life of turning points, stillness, and movement, supported by neural correlates in the intensification process, and it accords with the dynamic structure of classic Christian views on spirituality.

Second, she argues that the validity of Loder's mystical theology shows itself in its ability to address major issues in mystical theology, for example the relationship between universality and particularity. By creating a conversation between Loder's transformational theology and James Hillman's theory of ego-relativization, Boyd-MacMillan argues that Loder's theory relates these polarities in a way valuable for spirituality discourse in general as well as for discussions about Christian transformation in particular. Loder's relational approach discerns through faith the actual and eternal union of particularity and universality in Jesus Christ and, ultimately, in the Trinity. This primal unity is tacitly present to infants, though in the course of human development they repress this knowledge and ever seek alternative ways to relate these polarities again, failing to do so unless and until Christ reveals himself to them in convictional experiences.

Third, Boyd-MacMillan shows that Loder's work bears affinity with the mystical tradition generally that "love is the central movement of intelligence." Highlighting the role of imagination in all knowing, she shows how Loder's analysis of convictional knowing, which is radically self-involved knowing, reveals the knower's contingent relation with God, who may be recognized as "the condition for the possibility of knowing anything at all." Intelligence itself can bear the mark of Christ's nature, so that all knowing "in the Spirit" can serve reconciliation, love, and the human quest for meaning and purpose.

Boyd-MacMillan asserts that this integration of knowing and love is a powerful prophetic critique of our dehumanizing rationalities and our loveless intellection.

* * *

A Concluding Ironic Interlude

Dr. Loder himself had wanted to respond to these essays in a final chapter of the *Festschrift*. He looked forward to the publication of this collection, and he was very appreciative that such a collaboration was "in the works." His involvement was cut short by his death. Perhaps from his own transformational standpoint, however, the fact that he did not get a chance to respond directly has considerable meaning for us. We recall his story of going to the Royal Library in Denmark in Copenhagen to read the account of Kierkegaard's awakening to faith, only to find the passage cut out of the manuscript by a razor.[35] His initial disappointment evaporated, however, when he realized the "Kierkegaardian irony" underlying this experience, an irony central to Kierkegaard's own teaching. Kierkegaard's *modus operandi* was "to provoke and to explore the inner contradictions in his readers, but then to vanish so his reader might find her or his own unique stance before the Truth."[36] Loder then wrote of his ironic interlude with Kierkegaard, "It was almost as if he had cut it out himself to make sure that the experience, important and decisive as it might be in its own right, became transparent to the reality that embodied it . . . [so that] the reader's experience of it could then be as unique to him or her as this account was for Kierkegaard himself."[37]

Loder, like his mentor Kierkegaard, has vanished. And now, in the midst of the contradictions of life that shape all of us, his former students have had to find "their own unique stance before the Truth." Each of us has tried to articulate aspects of that stance through these chapters written in honor of our beloved mentor. And, ironically, it is almost as if he himself decided not to comment on the essays contained in his *Festschrift,* in order to make sure that our own experiences of writing became as unique for us as Loder's experiences of writing were for him — that is, a way for all of us (and our readers) to engage

35. Loder, *The Transforming Moment,* p. 2.
36. Loder, *The Transforming Moment,* p. 2.
37. Loder, *The Transforming Moment,* p. 2.

transparently in the generative Source of redemptive transformation that we hope inspires us.

Still, we miss him. We wish we could run these essays by him at least once, just to get his encouragement one more time. Nonetheless, we rejoice in the privilege of so honoring him with this work of love. If these essays sound forth even faint echoes of the Truth that has come to us in Jesus Christ, to whom our mentor bore such passionate testimony, we will be grateful. And we will laugh with Jim Loder at the irony of it all!

I. Redemptive Transformation *within* Ecclesial Practice

1. "Trampling Down Death by Death": Double Negation in Developmental Theory and Baptismal Theology

Russell Haitch

The aim of this essay is threefold: to explain the concept of "double negation," which is central to James Loder's developmental theory; to show how this concept fits into a theology of baptism; and to suggest how the developmental and theological insights thus gained may be used in teaching on baptism and the topic of death and dying.

James Loder's Developmental Theory

Looking for Divine Order

I recall the conversation I had with Professor Loder a few weeks after September 11, 2001, and shortly before his death.

We had all seen the planes going in and the towers coming down; repeatedly and in slow motion had watched the awful televised images. But faith comes through hearing, and in the background of those images, so often it seemed, was the voice of someone crying out: "O God!" or, "Oh my God!"

"'*Oh my God!*' — what's going on there?," Jim asked. "Is this just a cry of desperation?" "No," he said, "I think it is more than that. I think it is a kind of primitive prayer. It is saying that in the midst of this horror there is still a higher order. It is calling out for this divine order to reassert itself." This was what he heard in that voice; in hearing him I heard it too, and what we heard that day became emblematic for me of how his mind worked. Whether as therapist or theologian, James Loder sought always to listen beneath the surface.

It is sometimes thought that he focused too much on the moment of crisis, extreme example, or sudden conversion. He valued these events because he felt that they had been devalued by his church and academic peers. Moreover, he had witnessed sudden gracious power in his own life and in the lives of those he counseled, and he could not but speak of what he had seen and heard. At the same time, he was careful to say the point was not to be always living at the extremities, but rather to see how the experience of extremity could reveal what matters most when living in the middle. Sometimes his critics disbelieved this caveat, and sometimes his students remembered mainly the stories he told of remarkable spiritual events. However, he himself was concerned with both the transforming moment and the underlying structure of reality it revealed; with both the epiphany of Christ and the christomorphic patterns displayed (if half hidden) across the universe. Charismatic and structuralist concerns coalesced in his mind. As in the case of the World Trade Center Towers, he was always looking and listening for divine order.

He has, I think, left to the field of practical theology a cache of highly generative concepts regarding this order. What lies ahead is the work of continuing to connect these concepts to empirical research on the one hand and the life of church communities on the other. This essay will focus on one of these concepts, which Loder calls "double negation," or sometimes "the negation of negation." While this concept has not been ignored by his readers, it has probably not received the full attention it deserves. Loder is best known for his model of transformation, and in one place he calls this concept of double negation "the key to transformation."[1] This view he reiterates in *The Transforming Moment,* saying double negation is "essential to transformation."[2] And in telling how certain images mediate transformation, he notes, "the centrality of double negation . . . cannot be overemphasized."[3] As the Chalcedonian pattern is central to his christology, the pattern of double negation may be central to his pneumatology, especially understanding of how the human spirit and Holy Spirit work in the world.

Double Negation in Developmental Transformation

What then do these concepts mean — "negation" and "double negation"? Negation figures importantly in Hegel's philosophy, and the background to Loder's understanding may be Kierkegaard's critique of Hegel.[4] The other im-

1. "Negation and Transformation: A Study in Theology and Human Development," in *Toward Moral and Religious Maturity,* ed. Christiane Brusselmans et al. (Morristown, NJ: Silver Burdett Co., 1980), p. 166.

2. *The Transforming Moment,* 2nd ed. (Colorado Springs: Helmers & Howard, 1989), p. 103.

3. *The Transforming Moment,* pp. 105-106.

4. I wish to thank Donald Miller, a fellow student with Loder at Harvard, for suggesting

portant intellectual influences, Heidegger and Lévi-Strauss, also come into play. However, when illustrating "negation" to others, Loder referred most often to the developmental theory of René Spitz, bringing to it what he himself knew of the maternal bond and what he heard in the voice of the small child who first learns to say "No."

In the first year and a half of life, according to Spitz and Loder, the child goes through a remarkable sequence of changes. Initially the primary connection to the world is the child's *mouth,* through which she receives maternal nourishment. Then with the development of physical eyesight, attention focuses upon the mother's *face,* for this face composes the child's world. What matters most here is the loving presence of the other, a presence that can still be experienced if the child is physically blind or the primary caregiver is not the biological mother. (Loder notes how in both the Hebrew *pānîm* and Greek *prosōpon,* "face" and "presence" are the same word.)

In time, however, the child not only senses this loving presence, but also becomes more acutely aware of its absence: the child knows when the mother is leaving the room. Now *anxiety over absence* becomes the central feature and gripping conflict of the infant's life. The mother returns and the world is right again; but then the mother departs and the world falls apart. To exist so precariously is unendurable; instinctively the small child scans for a solution. . . . If I wail — if I cry out with full lung capacity, this gets the desired result. But then comes the day or the long night when the mother is simply not there; and eventually, painfully comes also the insight: I can learn to say *"No."*

What is going on here — why does the child learn to say "No" with such vigor and predictable repetition? Psychologically, such an act in later life could be called a "reaction formation," doing the opposite of what one wants to do, but with all the energy that would have been invested in the original deed. The child would like with all her heart to be able to say "Yes" to the mother's face, to say yes and to exist fully in this loving presence. But the anxiety of absence grows too intense; the child cannot let her identity be so wrapped up in the mother, in another. Thus the child learns to say in effect, "no — not you, but me." This move is formative for the creation of the ego; all the little "no's" the small child spouts help establish a separate identity. The parent's absence was already a form of "no"-saying; and then too even when the parents are there physically, their "gesture, word, and affect"[5] may negate those of the child. In response, the child "incorporates negation and inflicts it upon the environment

---

this connection to Kierkegaard. For an extensive discussion of Heidegger's impact on Loder's understanding of negation, see John Kuentzel's essay in this volume, chapter 13.

5. "Negation and Transformation," p. 172.

so as to carve out and defend an emerging autonomy against the incursions of [parental] negation."[6] The child is developing an ego.

The ego is the most remarkable creation of the human spirit, the seminal act of human transformation.[7] However, it is built on negation — on a repression of the longing to receive and give love. Hence this negation of the human spirit must in turn be negated, and the transformation it produces must in turn be transformed by the Holy Spirit. While the process of this *double negation* takes a lifetime, its correct "formula" can be found in Galatians 2:20, where Paul says: "I am crucified with Christ: nevertheless I live, yet not I, but Christ liveth in me: and the life which I now live in the flesh I live by faith in the Son of God, who loved me, and gave himself for me." Whereas the ego says, "not you, but me (or I)," the Christian here declares "I, yet not I, but Christ." Here Christ becomes the loving presence of the other, to whom one can say "yes" and not be afraid. In him is revealed the face of God that will never leave or forsake, but abide always.

This is the essential pattern of double negation, but more must be added to avoid misconstrual. Paul's ego here has been de-centered, or re-centered around Christ, but his sense of self is not swallowed up. After the negation of the "I," he still goes on to say, "the life *I* live in the flesh." In other words, he has an intimate dialectical identity, whereby the statement "I, not I, but Christ" is also in some sense reversible. There are times (e.g., 1 Cor. 7:12) where he says, "I, not the Lord. . . ." As a general point, therefore, when Loder uses the term "double negation," he does not mean it simply in a mathematical sense whereby two negatives cancel each other out and become a positive. Rather double negation refers to a relationality, whereby whatever is good or redeemable within the first negation becomes saved, purified, and perfected through the mediation that negates it.[8] At least this is the case where Christ mediates and God's Spirit governs the second negation.[9]

6. "Negation and Transformation," p. 172.

7. This transformation is prototypical of the five-step pattern or "grammar" that Loder finds in all transformations of later life. (1) *Conflict* ("I want this loving presence, but fear its absence") is followed by a period of (2) *scanning* (evinced in various sounds of distress), yielding (3) *insight* (I can "reject" — say "no" — before I am rejected); from the insight comes (4) *release* of the energy that had been bound up in the conflict (I can say "no" repeatedly), and then there is a period of (5) *verification* in which the insight is tested to see whether it coheres internally and corresponds externally to how other people think and act (it is deemed good to have an independent sense of oneself).

8. See *The Transforming Moment*, p. 223; cf. "The Place of Science in Practical Theology: The Human Factor," *International Journal of Practical Theology* 4, 1 (2000): 23n.1.

9. Loder refers to the formula from Lévi-Strauss's *Structural Anthropology:* $f_x A : f_y B :: f_x B : f_{A-1} Y$. Here B is the mediator by which an initial negative condition ($f_x A$) is negated, and a new transformed condition ($f_{A-1} Y$) is established. (See *The Transforming Moment*, p. 159; cf. "Negation and Transformation," p. 191.) Double negations are transformational in that there is a me-

As the Holy Spirit negates and reconstitutes the negation-based ego of the human spirit, so likewise are the "ego defenses" transformed when the self is centered in Christ.[10] For example, "repression" — as an inhibition (negation) of activity or consciousness — becomes negated, and this capacity of the ego is reconstituted as patience and self-control. "Projection" — as a hiding (negating) of one's own feelings by placing them onto another — becomes negated, and this capacity is reconstituted as empathy. "Denial" — as an effort to deny (negate) the reality of a situation — becomes negated and reconstituted as part of the capacity to forgive and forget. "Fantasy formation" — as the negation of quotidian reality — becomes negated and resurrected in the capacity to embrace divine dreams and visions. "Reaction formation" — as the negation of an instinctive urge — becomes negated and redeemed in the ability to return good for evil. All of these double negations are transformational. As Loder uses the term, "transformation" is not simply a synonym for change but rather has a precise meaning: within a given frame of reference or experience, a new and hidden order emerges that has power to redefine the original frame and reorder its elements.[11]

Double Negation across the Spectrum of Human Action and Divine-Human Interaction

Thus Loder uses "negation" to refer to many sorts of nullifications — such as "denial, reduction, minimizing, ignoring, perverting, and the like"; all of these are forms of no-saying that point ultimately to "nothingness and non-being."[12] He finds the dynamics of negation and double negation at work across the whole spectrum of human action; he explains how by drawing on Talcott Parsons' depiction of this spectrum in terms of four overlapping spheres — organism, psyche, society and culture. In the sphere of the *psyche,* as just outlined, the ego with its seminal act of negation strives to ensure survival. Yet paradoxically, the ego grows to stifle and deaden the capacity to receive and give the love one needs truly to live. (In fact, says Loder, the ego "incorporates" death.[13]) New life is given through double negation, in the faith that says, "I, not I, but Christ."

---

diator and to the degree that the new condition establishes a gain over the original state. The human spirit can accomplish double negations, as has been shown, but cannot of itself negate the power of death or ultimate nothingness.

10. *The Logic of the Spirit: Human Development in Theological Perspective* (San Francisco: Jossey-Bass Publishers, 1998), p. 197.

11. *The Transforming Moment,* p. 229.

12. "The Place of Science in Practical Theology: The Human Factor," p. 23.

13. *The Logic of the Spirit,* p. 116.

A parallel dynamic transpires at the level of *society.* Role structures are the social equivalent of ego defenses. They are meant to facilitate social interaction and thus to assure survival of the group. Yet when social roles predominate they deaden the longed-for intimacy that is the lifeblood of social relations. This negation also needs to be negated. Transformation occurs when the social group, as the Body of Christ, can come to say, "we, not we, but the *koinonia* of Christ." Once again a dialectical identity is given, in which both the unity of the group and the particularity of its members are deepened simultaneously.

At the level of *culture,* parallel dynamics occur in respect to language, the matrix of culture. Loder proposes, with reference to Paul Ricoeur, that "root metaphors" or "master images" are structures deeper than language. Equivalent to role structures in society and ego defenses in the psyche, these master images shape how language is used. Yet language also negates reality, not only when words are used intentionally to deceive, but because — as the long tradition of the hermeneutic of suspicion points out — even with the best of intentions, language may conceal as much as it reveals. And yet again, through God's Spirit this negation can be negated; by a kind of double negation, the Bible can become the life-giving Word of God.

Even at the level of *organism,* there is an inherent negation in the struggle to survive. As the body grows, it deteriorates; from the start of life it moves inexorably toward death, so negation is present from birth or before. Even in the idea of reincarnation the seeds of death are present at birth. Yet the hope of receiving a resurrection body can negate this organic negation. While some of the foregoing is an extrapolation of what Loder has written, I think it is consistent with his comprehensive application of the concept. He finds the dynamics of negation across the panoply of human action, and those of double negation in each divine and human interaction.

We can review the matter not only horizontally, across the whole range of human action, but also vertically, so to speak. Whether viewing reality "top down" or "bottom up," from biblical theology to quantum physics, the theme of double negation is equally in evidence. In the biblical account of original sin, Loder sees an analogy to the developmental negation just outlined. Drawing on Kierkegaard's analysis of anxiety,[14] he notes how Adam and Eve enact a primordial negation. From face-to-Face interaction with God, they move to a posture of anxiety over God's command. The resolution to this anxiety is the negation, the no-saying, to a relationship of obedience with God. From this negation flow the consequences — their repressive hiding of nakedness, their loss of intimacy with God, their striving to earn life through labor. This negation stands in need

14. *The Logic of the Spirit,* pp. 122-124.

of being negated through the free gift of life in Christ: to be hidden in him is to be found clothed in obedience and seated close to God in the heavenlies.

Moving from the heavenlies to the physical universe and from theology to science, negation is seen in the way that chaos dissipates systemized forms of energy, according to principles of thermodynamics. But the chaos theory of Prigogine and others proposes a kind of double negation. From the chaos, due to the interrelation of all things, "strange attractors" draw forth new kinds of order. Here science gives theological pointers: in addition to being the door or bread of life, Jesus Christ can be seen as "the ultimate 'strange attractor.'"[15] For Loder, the physical universe gives more than metaphors for the spiritual realm; rather there is an analogous order between the two. Creation prefigures the new creation.

To conclude this whistle-stop review of negation and double negation in Loder's work, we might return to the first year of human development, and to the act of birth itself. In the so-called "birth trauma," even in the normal course of events the child moving through the birth canal comes close to suffocation after the mother's umbilical cord is squeezed shut and before the infant first takes oxygen through the mouth and nose. This proximity to death Loder calls "the primal existential negation."[16] And even aside from the trauma of the birth event, Loder believes that negation is intrinsic to birth, since birth always entails a loss of original unity with the mother. He notes how Spitz's research points to "a generalized sense of loss that was laid down across the whole of the child's brain and recorded in the hypothalamus." Thus he concludes, "negation is a major theme in development, yet most major theorists ignore it."[17]

From this developmental perspective, negation is present at the start of life, a fact that lends credence to Sartre's dictum that "nothingness haunts being." But if the act of birth is itself an instance of negation, then the appearance of the mother's face — the loving presence that sets things right again — becomes a double negation, or "transformation of the existential negation of birth."[18] Thus modifying my previous description, the child learning to say "no" would represent a negation of this double negation, and then the subsequent presence of the divine Face would be the ultimate double negation of the child's negation of the mother's double negation.

15. "The Place of Science in Practical Theology: The Human Factor," p. 39.

16. "Negation and Transformation," pp. 170-173; *The Transforming Moment*, p. 162.

17. *The Logic of the Spirit*, p. 83.

18. "Negation and Transformation," p. 173.

Ramifications and Criticisms

This may be a good place to pause and suggest some reasons why these concepts are not so much double-talk. Three come to mind. First, in every developmental discussion, Loder was eager to point out that a relationship with God is not only something supernatural, but also in another sense quite natural. The entire life span points to our existential need and capacity for this relationship. We are, he often said, "high-wired" for it.[19] In the movement from womb to world, and in the drama of first-year development, the stage is set for later religious life. The birth trauma that signals physical death and the no-saying that recapitulates spiritual death both point the way to the new birth that comes through dying in and with Christ. Like the physical universe, the "psychic universe" reflects divine order. Notably, it is more than metaphor — but also less than determinant cause. Even given the great importance Loder attaches to maternal relations and the first year of life, he is clearly not a psychologist who views all religious issues as reprisals of parental issues, or all religious experiences as re-creations of infantile states.[20]

19. Loder's anthropology is consistent with that of some Orthodox Christian theorists, even though he interacts more with Protestant and Catholic positions. For example, Christos Yannaras writes: "What every human being seeks, from the moment of separation from the womb, is the immediacy and fullness of a relationship — *coessentia*. Not to be, at first, as a biological self and then to have relationships, but rather to draw existence from relationship — to exist as an event of relationship" ("Psychoanalysis and Orthodox Anthropology," in *Personhood: Orthodox Christianity and the Connection Between Body, Mind, and Soul,* ed. John Chirban [Westport, CT: Bergen & Garvey, 1996], p. 84).

20. The editors of this book asked me to address a potential criticism of Loder's developmental theory — viz., that it overemphasizes early childhood events. They referred me to Jerome Kagan, who, in his essay "The Allure of Infant Determinism," argues against the idea that "a mother's care of her infant in the first two years sets the child's future in a significant way" (*Three Seductive Ideas* [Cambridge: Harvard University Press, 1998], p. 147). Kagan says the facts point rather toward a congeries of environmental influences, of which maternal care is only one; further, one must note the child's "developmental malleability" (89, 105) in adapting to circumstances. Kagan criticizes those who overemphasize maternal nurture and so overlook socioeconomic problems: "it is considerably more expensive to improve the quality of housing, education, and health of the approximately one million children living in poverty in America today than to urge their mothers to kiss, talk to, and play with them more consistently" (91). But "the social class of a child's family is a better predictor of an adult's vocation and personal traits than the child's psychological profile at age two" (149).

Without evaluating the merits and faults of Kagan's essay, let me say why I think the developmental theory it attacks is not the developmental theory Loder espouses. First, Loder, like Kagan, opposes determinism. He too finds developmental malleability, though he attributes it to the human spirit rather than evolutionary forces of adaptation (Kagan's option, which may be another kind of determinism); for Loder, the ultimate defeat of determinism is the Holy

A second observation concerns the way that ontogenetic development impacts all intellectual enterprises, from science to practical theology. The no-saying of the infant fuels the development of autonomy, and autonomy in turn inclines a person to view the world "objectively." This objectivity represses (thus negates) subjective states — such as the relational experience of the loving face, or the anxiety over its absence, or the longing for a face that will never go away. The achievement of this objectivity has been a benchmark of critical inquiry, because it entails the ability to negate subjective, egocentric distortions of the mentation process. But because it also closes us off from the more basic subjective resources of our understanding, some kind of postcritical method is needed. This would be a method that negates this negation in order to reclaim personal involvement in knowledge — by honoring the relationality between subject and object, the role of the body in knowing, and the importance of passion, hunches and intuition.[21] Loder finds this method precisely in the epistemology of Michael Polanyi, and abundant examples of its implementation in the discoveries of Einstein and other imaginative scientists.

A third point relates most directly to the next concern of this essay,

---

Spirit's power to give liberty to God's children. Second, Loder, like Kagan, would oppose blaming poor mothers for, say, their child's illiteracy. To Kagan's social critique, Loder adds the psychological and theological critiques outlined in this essay: even children of wealth who grow up to acquire socially desirable "vocations and personal traits" are equally subject to the negating, death-based patterns of psychic, social, cultural and organic interaction. Thus a third point, Loder's theory never proposes that any human mother could negate these negative patterns for her child. He does not suggest, for example, that the mother could prevent the infant's separation anxiety by never leaving the room. The departure of the mother's face, like the severing of the umbilical cord, is eventually inevitable. The infant truly longs for the face of God, which negates fear, loneliness, and death. The mother's presence both quickens and partly satisfies this infant longing; but it can and should satisfy it only partly and only temporarily. The mother's face is not the face of God, and if one tried to make it that, it would become an idol.

In sum, Loder attributes more importance to maternal influence than does Kagan, but he is not a determinist or blamer of mothers, nor does he suggest that their early nurture can surmount all socioeconomic, let alone existential, obstacles to happiness.

21. Loder distinguished "relationality" from "relationship." He saw relationality as being more kinetic, less static. Further, the *relationship* between two or more things for him connotes an emphasis on their distinctness, and sometimes their polarity. Yet in a dynamic relationship there are not just the distinct things, for the relationship between them takes on a life of its own, and this reality is signified by the term *relationality.* In other words, two or more things comprise a relationship; but where it is understood that the relationship *comprises them,* then relationality comes into play. As an example Loder cited often, the marriage relationship needs to be viewed as relationality. Relationality is evident elsewhere as well, from quantum field theory to divine–human encounters. See the essay by F. L. Shults in this volume, chapter 12.

Christian baptism. Just as death and birth are intertwined in earliest human development, so in the Christian tradition death and new birth are dyadic: the baptismal font has been called both the womb and tomb of the church. In both cases, the pattern of transformation follows the dynamics of double negation.

In all of the above, Loder's basic argument about the relationship between human development and spiritual transformation is this: transformations of the human spirit occur at every stage of human development, but these transformations need in turn to be transformed by the Holy Spirit. Not only in the formation of the ego, but in each successive stage of life, the human spirit evinces remarkable creativity. Its efforts are to be admired, not devalued, for they witness to the *imago dei.*

At the same time, they are ultimately deficient. For while the human spirit can negate and create many things, it cannot negate death and nothingness. This fact is something of a premise or direct apprehension. In times of death or moments of intense loneliness, one apprehends the void or nothingness that underlies all we think or say or do. At death we break up. Even the sanguine psyche that says we merge molecularly with the universe must face the fact that gradually the universe is also running down. The logical mind may dismiss the spectre of nothingness as something we can do nothing about, but the psychologist can observe that people do in fact do much about it — they labor hard to repress it. To the mystic who says the nothingness is really something, the vacancy a plenitude, Loder might respond that this turning the problem into a solution also represents repression: the intense striving to survive testifies to a human intuition that death is not meant to be.

If the ultimate negation is what Loder calls this void, of which human death is the definitive face, then the ultimate desire of the human soul is somehow to negate this negation. Indeed people can negate the proximate forms of this negation — that is exactly what human transformations do all the time — but these are only proximate and temporary solutions; for still the void lies beneath all earthly endeavors. That is why human transformations must be in turn transformed by God; or to put it more precisely if strangely, why human double negations must be doubly negated by God. The human spirit is remarkable but inadequate; but though inadequate, redeemable. Thus a higher order transformation cannot be done without the participation of the human spirit; yet neither can it be done by the human spirit alone.

Objections may be raised to this basic position. To say that it sounds too morbid is saying too little, for that response may be simply a form of denial. The comment that it is too individualistic may be true but beside the point. For once the situation is framed in terms of a dichotomy of being and non-being, it must be conceded that a human community or collective does not stand against the void in a position qualitatively different from that of the individual. Perhaps the most valid objection from the Christian standpoint would be to say that because of the Incarnation and Pentecost, the void has been definitively nullified, death has been swallowed up — and this condition of grace is already universal, because Christ has been made progenitor of a new humanity and God's Spirit has been poured out on all flesh. To focus on the Incarnation and Pentecost this way may be a valuable corrective to certain streams of Protestant theology; but to focus on them exclusively overlooks the fact that this condition of abundant grace is costly. It involves God's intimate, agonizing interaction with the world and against the spiritual forces of wickedness. Likewise the instantiation of this condition in particular human beings involves their involvement, their active consent and participation in God's activity. It means confronting and not avoiding the void. Recognition of that fact brings us directly to the Christian events of Death and Resurrection, and to the topic of baptism.[22]

How Loder's Theory Illumines a Theology of Baptism

The Important Obvious Question about Baptism

Scripture calls baptism union with Christ in his death. This meaning is clearest in Romans 6:3-5 and Colossians 2:12. Jesus speaks of his impending death as a

22. This review has touched on, without naming as such, Loder's typology of negation. He sees four basic types: "methodological" or "calculative" negation, which refers mainly to the cognitive or intellectual process by which "subjective or egocentric distortions" are negated for the sake of "presumably objective . . . truths"; "functional" negation, which refers to negation involving psychological functions; "existential" negation, which refers to the negation of one's own being; and "transformational" negation, which refers to "the negation of negation via a mediator such that new integration emerges, establishing a gain over the original negated state" (see "Negation and Transformation," pp. 167-169; *The Transforming Moment,* p. 226).

I have not stressed this typology as much as Loder does, because the distinctions between the four types become blurry, the more I read his descriptions. For example: the capacity for *methodological* negations is built on the *functional* negations that give rise to abstract thinking and the "reality principle"; and *functional* negations are based on the formation of the ego, which occurs in response to *existential* negation; meanwhile *existential* negation is a component of both *methodological* and *functional* negation, since these negations take place against the backdrop of nothingness and cosmic loneliness; and given this pervasive backdrop, every negation can be portrayed as negating some prior negation — hence all three of these types are potentially *transformational* negation, even if the "gain" is temporary and limited (in cases where Christ is not the mediator).

kind of baptism in Mark 10:35-40 and Luke 12:50.[23] Also implicit in baptism is the idea of new birth, as seen in Titus 3:5 and arguably in John 3:5.[24]

Churches have held different views on baptism, and sometimes attacked each other from those vantage points. The issues of contention are many. When verses such as Romans 6:3 or Galatians 3:27 speak of being baptized, does this mean water baptism or Spirit baptism; or if both, how are the two related? Acts clearly speaks of a water ritual; is this event identical to mystical union with Christ, or are the two different? If different, should it be said that water baptism "causes" union with Christ, that it "expresses" this union, that it "symbolizes" or "represents" or "re-presents" it? In debates of these and other questions, such as whether baptism removes sin, the typical desire may be to pin down what baptism *does*. But if like Loder one is looking for divine order, then it is equally important to ask what baptism *is*, in its underlying order, its structure or "grammar."

As a baseline, Christian baptism here refers to the action of being plunged (from *baptizō*, to be plunged) into the death of Christ: "as many as were baptized into Christ Jesus were baptized into his death" (Rom. 6:3). But if "baptism" is "death," then the obvious question a child might ask is how this could be a good thing. Perhaps the Christian education most adults have received does not equip them to answer this question very well. For example, if the death of Christ is seen exclusively in terms of his bearing sins for the sake of others' forgiveness, then the logical entry point for Christians would seem to be resurrection — receiving new life as a consequence of Christ's sin-bearing. But there remains the task of explaining why Jesus tells James and John they must be baptized with his baptism, why Paul says baptism is primarily a baptism *into death*, and why for that matter Paul also says, "may I never boast except in the cross [not resurrection] of our Lord Jesus Christ" (Gal. 6:14). As a diagnosis, I would say the educational problem starts with an inadequate definition of death, hence an incomplete view of Christ's death, and thus a confusion about why it is good for a person to be united with Christ in this death. Baptism in churches manifests this confusion, but also offers occasion to teach toward clarification, which is where Loder's elucidation of double negation comes into play.

23. Rom. 6:3: "Or don't you know that all of us who were baptized into Christ Jesus were baptized into his death?"; Luke 12:50: "But I have a baptism to undergo, and how distressed I am until it is completed!"; Mark 10:39: "Jesus said to them, 'You will drink the cup I drink and be baptized with the baptism I am baptized with.'"

24. Titus 3:5: "He saved us through the washing of rebirth and renewal by the Holy Spirit"; John 3:5: "Jesus answered, 'I tell you the truth, no one can enter the kingdom of God unless he is born of water and the Spirit.'"

Double Negation: How the Death of Jesus Destroys Death

What Paul seems to be saying about baptism in Romans 6 is interesting. He says not only that baptism is into Christ's death, but also that baptism and Christ's death have the same "likeness" *(homoiōma)* — baptism is "a death like his" (Rom. 6:5). On the surface, it would seem that baptism is no death at all, let alone one like crucifixion. Even by triple immersion, there are no recorded cases of persons drowning. To make sense of Paul's statement, one must first assume that "death" means more than a flatline on the heart monitor. Intuition tells us this assumption is right. Physical death is severe, perhaps in our era the most severe event imaginable. But we also sense that death is more than expiration, because we know that life is more than physical breathing. A person will say, "I don't want merely to exist — I want truly to live." When the fourth Gospel says of Jesus, "in him was life" (John 1:4), this "life" refers to a relationality with God, and thence with people and the world. This relationality is one of love, joy, peace, goodness — all these betoken life.

Therefore, death as the negation of this life means that one is cut off or separated from this life. Since physical death is seen to precipitate such separation, it is greatly feared. Yet the appearance is somewhat deceiving, for Scripture claims that physical death is not the cause of this separation, but rather its consequence. Physical death came into the world because of prior spiritual death, because of separation from God and thus from true life. Alexander Schmemann says that in the Christian vision, biological or physical death is not the whole of death or even its ultimate essence. Rather "death is above all a *spiritual reality*."[25] Death as a spiritual reality is something of which one can partake while walking to work; or by the same token, from which one can be free while lying in the grave. For "death" really means separation from life — "from God Who is the only Giver of life."[26]

The first step, then, is to see how "death" is the negation of life — of life as love and light in the presence of God. The second step is to see how Jesus' death negates this negation. From the start, his earthly existence is the apotheosis of life: it consists purely in the love of God and therefore love for the world; in obedience to God and therefore in the desire to save people and destroy that which enslaves them. Nor in this respect did his death differ from his life. His desire to "drink this cup" and be plunged into the baptism of crucifixion was an extension of his life, the final expression of its love and obedience. But — here

25. Alexander Schmemann, *Of Water and the Spirit* (Crestwood, NY: St. Vladimir's Seminary Press, 1974), p. 62.

26. Schmemann, *Of Water and the Spirit,* p. 63.

is the crucial juncture — if death is actually the absence of this love and obedience, then this death, *his* death, is "deathless." As Schmemann says: "because His death is nothing but love, nothing but the desire to destroy the solitude, the separation from life, the darkness and despair of death, nothing but love for those who are dead — *there is no 'death' in His death.*"[27]

From this perspective, the resurrection is not bizarre, but the expected outcome of Christ's life. If spiritual life and death have conceptual priority and exercise marginal control in relation to physical life and death, then it is not impossible for Jesus to rise physically from the dead; rather, as Peter preaches in Acts, "it was impossible for him to be held in death's power" (Acts 2:24). Thus Jesus not only overcomes death; he destroys its power. The Easter liturgy of the Orthodox Church says, "Christ has risen from the dead, trampling down death by death, and upon those in the tombs bestowing life." This trampling down of death by death is the quintessential act of double negation. This is the declaration made in baptism.

There remains another obvious question a child might ask: if Christ has destroyed death, then why do people still die physically? Schmemann writes:

> [Christ] does not "abolish" or "destroy" the physical death because He does not "abolish" this world of which physical death is not only a "part" but the principle of life and even growth. But He does infinitely more. By removing the sting of sin from death, by abolishing death as a spiritual reality, by filling it with Himself, with His love and life, He makes death — which was the very reality of separation and corruption — into a shining and joyful "passage" — passover — into fuller life, fuller communion, fuller love. "For to me to live is Christ," says St. Paul, "and to die is gain" (Phil. 1:21).[28]

It was said before that in double negation, the elements of the first negation are not merely cancelled out, but transformed, so that what is good becomes retained and reordered around the mediator of the second negation. Here this structure may be said to pertain even with respect to the ultimate negation, death. Death has finality; it separates and blots out. Scripture notes how that can be a good thing: "reckon yourselves to be dead indeed to sin . . ." (Rom. 6:11). Somewhat similarly, a good aspect of physical death may be that it can separate people from sickness or suffering. However, because physical death also separates us from people we care about, even love dearly, Schmemann's assurance that death has been transformed "into a shining and joyful passage" may need to be tempered with the acknowledgement that aspects of death still

27. Schmemann, *Of Water and the Spirit,* p. 64.

28. Schmemann, *Of Water and the Spirit,* p. 64.

await fuller negation and transformation. As Paul says, "the last enemy to be destroyed is death" (1 Cor. 15:26).

How Baptism Is Connected to the Double Negation of Christ's Death

Now the work of the teacher is to relate yet also distinguish the spiritual, emotional and physical aspects of death, for human beings who are simultaneously spirit, soul and body. Baptism offers an ideal setting for such teaching. It does so by first raising a question about itself. If the first step is to say what "death" means, and the second to see how Christ's death tramples down death, then the third step is to answer how baptism is related to Christ's death and its victorious double negation. The question becomes more acute when we recall that Paul describes baptism as being "a death like his" (Rom. 6:5). How can this be?

Since the patristic period, preachers have remarked how baptism is a death like Christ's because going under the water is like his going into the tomb. This similitude has imaginative and heuristic power. At the same time, it is inexact. The death of Christ includes the crucifixion as well as his going into the grave, and in terms of physical resemblance crucifixion was nothing like water. There may be another reason why Paul implies that baptism has the likeness of Christ's death. One thing especially distinctive about Christ's death — which is similar to Paul's baptism — was its voluntary nature. Knowing what was to befall him, Christ chose to die. Paul implies that baptism is likewise a voluntary death; as he goes on to say in Romans 6, it is a death to sin. For all the obvious differences between Christ's crucifixion and Paul's baptism, the point of likeness is that both entail faithful obedience. The obedience that comes through faith (Rom. 1:5) is a central theme Paul establishes at the letter's outset.

Hence, as Jesus negates any negation of God's will in order to say "yes" to God ("not my will but thine be done"), so too does the believer who says "yes" to God in baptism. Theologically, one dies to sin, to self-destruction. Psychologically, it is saying "no" to one's no-saying ego. This double negation evinces the dialectical identity of "I, not I, but Christ." It sets in motion the transformation of the ego's capacities.

We can strengthen the connection between the double negation of Christ's death and the double negation of baptism by reexamining the developmental sequence. While it is risky to look at the biblical Jesus through the lens of psychology, the Bible itself prompts some degree of reflection. When Jesus says at Gethsemane, "my soul *(psychē)* is overwhelmed with sorrow" (Matt. 26:38), it seems apparent he is experiencing anxiety, especially when he falls "with his face to the ground" and prays, "if it is possible, may this cup be taken from me" (v. 39). Does the ego psychology of Spitz and Loder offer any insight into such anxiety? Just as before birth Jesus lived in his mother's womb, we may assume that as an infant he experienced the world first through his mouth, then in relation to her face. According to the previously-outlined pattern, next would come the anxiety of separation, leading to a negation of the loving face and the formation of the ego. However, it could be surmised that Jesus did not in fact develop this way, that anxiety at separation from his mother would right away have been negated by his awareness of God's loving presence. For in his adolescence, a time when infantile issues are revisited, it is Jesus' parents who experience anxiety when separated from him after the Passover; he meanwhile says, "Did you not know that I must be about my Father's business?" (Luke 2:49). Whereas ordinarily the ego's stance says, "not you, but me," already Jesus, developing in wisdom and stature, seems to have arrived at a dialectical identity that will declare in effect: "I, not I, but the Father" is speaking to you; or "I, not I, but the Father" is doing the miracles you see.

His agony in the garden, therefore, may be seen as an anxiety over separation from God. Clearly too, on the organic level, he would recoil from the violent pain of crucifixion; but the prospect of God-forsakenness may be yet more dreadful. As Loder and others have noted, the twin fears of absorption and of abandonment (which point to opposite ends of the life span) are the twin enemies of human intimacy; and it may be added, of obedient intimacy with God as well. But the step of obedience — that is, of obedience *to* God — actually undoes the anxiety. Jesus, who comes to be "tempted in every way, just as we are" (Heb. 4:15), undergoes this anxiety in order to undo it. In obedience, he undergoes baptism, first in the Jordan, then at Calvary. His baptism in the Jordan, as a step of solidarity with sinners, is also a step of obedience to the Torah as interpreted by Rabbi John, and a first step toward the Cross that completes this baptismal obedience.

Likewise, baptism becomes the prototypical act of Christian obedience, the first step that sets the pattern for subsequent steps. It is the specific command Christ couples with teaching (Matt. 28:19-20), and typically the first command issued in response to Gospel preaching: repent and be baptized (Acts 2:38). In this baptism, believers may well have undergone anxiety, not only fear at the prospect of physical persecution or death, but also existential and psychological anxiety over ego absorption and abandonment. If I am united with Christ, becoming reborn ("planted together," Rom. 6:5) with him, I will be absorbed into Christ, and nothing will be left of me; fear of absorption hearkens back to physical birth and the instinct to avoid being absorbed or drawn back into the womb. Then too if I am united with Christ, dying to my "old self" (Rom. 6:6), I will be abandoned by my family or society; fear of abandonment anticipates physical death and the instinct to avoid being cut off from the world.

Baptism intends to negate these anxious voices that would say "no" to God. In obedient union with Christ, absorption and abandonment are taken into the relationship and undone. The self can say, yes, I am "absorbed" into Christ — "for you died and your life is hidden with Christ in God" (Col. 3:3) — but not in such a way that I lose myself. Rather, I truly find myself, for he, Jesus, knows better than I do what it means for me to be me. In giving my life to Christ, I am abandoned by the world and lost to it; but through Christ the world is given back to me as an object of non-possessive love. In this pattern of double negation, birth and death are sanctified, so that one's relationship to God, to oneself and to the world is set right.

How These Ideas Apply to Baptismal Teaching

Spirit Baptism versus Water Baptism

Understanding baptism in terms of double negation may help Christian teachers educe certain guidelines for taking a balanced approach to the great baptismal debates. What follows is an attempt to address three contentious issues: Spirit baptism versus water baptism; infant versus believer's baptism; and death-and-resurrection versus other baptismal meanings, such as new birth or washing from sin. In each case the discussion does not hinge solely on these concepts of negation and double negation, but includes scriptural and theological concepts; what I hope to show is consistency between the former and latter.

Perhaps the central baptismal question of the last century was that of Spirit baptism versus water baptism. Pentecostals have pressed this issue, by teaching a clear distinction between the two, and among Reformed theologians Karl Barth also was adamant that Spirit baptism be distinguished from water baptism. The developmental pattern of double negation suggests how physical and spiritual realities are indeed distinct, but at the same time related. The mother's face is an organic fact, but as the loving presence that composes the child's world, it deeply influences the infant's spirit. (Here I am construing the human spirit as comprising the human capacity for relationality.)[29] Likewise

29. I believe the human spirit is distinct from the Holy Spirit and the human spirit in communion with the Holy Spirit is distinct from the human spirit without that communion. Common to all, though, is the focus on relationality. The Holy Spirit, as Loder sometimes noted, has been helpfully if crassly called the "go-between God." Whereas Scripture says "God *is*

the infant's no-saying is a physical action of spiritual consequence: negating the face resolves anxiety by repressing exocentricity and openness to relationality, for the sake of egocentricity and psychic survival. Yet the movement is not only from physical to spiritual, but even more the reverse; the infant's spirit, struggling to make a place in the world, initiates the physical actions of rejecting continual intimacy with caregivers. But the point is that the negation is both physical and spiritual, and so it is fitting for the negation of this negation — the transformation of the ego — to be both physical and spiritual. Further, if baptism mediates this double negation, then it makes sense that baptism should be both spiritual and physical, both Spirit baptism and water baptism. However, more needs to be said about the nature of the relation between the two.

It has been duly noted that in double negation the second, transformative negation does not merely cancel out the first negation, but reconstellates its elements into a new order; and the nature of this order depends on the nature of the person or thing that mediates the double negation. Here it may be said that Christ is the mediator who brings together transcendent and immanent dimensions according to his divine-human hypostasis. Baptism is reflective of this order. It is transcendent and spiritual, a union with Christ that takes place by faith; but it is also immanent and physical, in that it takes place in water.

Not only water, but other elements of physical creation are involved in baptism. As something of an original discovery, at least one I've not found elsewhere, it could be said that in Scripture all four basic elements of the ancient world — water, earth, air, and fire — are referred to in baptism. The waters of Jordan, the earth of the borrowed tomb, the wind and tongues as of flame at Pentecost are all involved in baptism. This observation about physical elements does not denigrate Pentecostal emphases on Holy Spirit baptism and receiving spiritual power for ministry; rather it heightens awareness of the Holy Spirit's power to transform all created elements, restoring them to their rightful place as a means of communion with God. In baptism, simultaneously one is plunged more deeply into creation and into the inner life of God.

Hence one may say that in the structural order of baptism, Spirit baptism and water baptism are neither one and the same, nor completely separate. They are conceptually distinct, and empirically one may precede the other in time, as the Acts narratives show (see especially 8:14-17 and 10:44-48). But as these nar-

Spirit," it is more commonly said that humans *have* a spirit; and yet it could also be said that humans are spirit, especially, if like Kierkegaard (and Loder) one views the self in terms of relationality: "the self is a relation that relates itself to itself." Thus the human spirit could be seen as existing in the capacity for relationality within the person (i.e. between body and soul), among persons, between people and the universe, and between people and God.

ratives also indicate, each calls for and completes the other. When the people of Samaria receive water baptism, Peter and John are sent so that they may receive also the Holy Spirit. When Cornelius and other gentiles receive Spirit baptism, Peter straightway calls for them to be baptized in water. Regardless of chronological order, in the divine order water baptism and Spirit baptism are distinct yet unified events, as exemplified in Jesus' baptism at Jordan. In this way baptism is both transcendent and concrete.

Working from baptism back to human development, specifically to death and dying, one can see it is fitting for baptism, as the eventful negation of death's power, to be both concrete and transcendent. For that is how death is experienced, for the dying person and those who love him or her. There is the specific diagnosis of the doctor, the exact time of death; or afterwards, in going through personal effects, there are the shoes and dresses she wore, the letters he wrote, the detailed financial records that must be sorted through. Death is experienced not only as an abstract void, but in its sorrowful particulars. Thus in teaching beforehand about the negation of death's power, one does well to note the concreteness of the crucifixion and the particularity of a person's union with Christ. It is also good to recall that the essential defeat of death occurs not only in the resurrection but already in this death-destroying crucifixion and this personal union with Christ; for when someone has died, it is seen only that the person has died, not yet that he or she will be resurrected.[30]

30. Here I am offering an interpretation of Loder's theory that differs somewhat from that of James Fowler, and perhaps Loder himself. Fowler describes Loder's theory thus: "with the death of Christ our sin, which he takes on, is negated. And then in his resurrection the negation is negated and we are restored to freedom to choose alignment with the Author of our transformation" ("Conversations on Fowler's *Stages of Faith* and Loder's *The Transforming Moment*," *Religious Education* 77, 2 [1982]: 142).

As to differences, Fowler focuses on sin rather than death and sees the double negation occurring in the resurrection rather than the crucifixion. These differences may be more of emphasis than contradiction, since this concept of negation is polyvalent. Still, I would quibble. Explaining Loder's book (see *The Transforming Moment,* p. 161), Fowler says that Christ negates sin by taking it into himself. Sin is already a negation, which means this negation of sin would be a double negation. The point is not mere technicality, for as I have just quoted, Fowler goes on to say, "in his resurrection the [double] negation [of sin] is negated and we are restored to freedom." But what does it mean that "sin" is being restored in some form, integrated into the new transformed state? Perhaps one could explain that "freedom" is the element of sin that now becomes used rightly instead of sinfully, but Fowler does not say this, nor does Loder so far as I know. Loder *does* say: "In Christ, death dies; by his becoming sin, all sin is canceled" (161). I have tried to show that death dies even *in* Christ's death, before the resurrection that confirms and fructifies the victory. Regarding sin, one could say that sin is cancelled even *in* Christ's act of becoming sin, for that act is one of sinless obedience. Thus in both cases the double negation occurs already in the crucifixion. An alternative construal would be to say that in the crucifixion

The grammar of double negation means the hope of future resurrection can be supported by a spiritual rationale. If for a person the power of death has been destroyed, then it is impossible for her or him to be held forever in this power (cf. Acts 2:24). Further, if personhood is understood to be, like baptism, a union of spiritual and physical, then it makes sense for there to be an eventual bodily resurrection, even if one cannot begin to say scientifically how such a thing could occur.

Accordingly, a lesson plan based on Scripture that teaches about death could go something like this. In the beginning, God creates the *'ādām* ([hu]man) out of dust *('ădāmāh)* of the earth. This means the man and woman are fully physical, but matter does not fully account for who they are: God also breathes spirit into this dust and *Adam* becomes a living soul (Gen. 2:7). Implicit at the start, then, are the dimensions of spirit, soul and body: the bodily connection to the universe; the spiritual capacity for relationality with God (and through God with one another and all creation); and between them, perhaps as conjunction of spirit and matter, the psyche that mediates transcendent and immanent dimensions through its reason, will and emotions.

Given that the man and woman are created as "doxological, eucharistic beings"[31] (cf. Rom. 1:21), given that they are made for mutual love and creative interaction with the world, their primordial sin is something of a surd.[32] But

---

the negations of sin and death *are intensified;* then in the resurrection these negations are negated. I have not chosen this latter line of reasoning, because I think the former aligns better with scriptural teachings on Christ's death and baptism. As Fowler's summary shows, Loder may conflate the two lines of reasoning, and the result is a bit confusing.

31. Thomas Hopko has used this phrase, though I think he is actually quoting someone else.

32. I am less inclined than Kierkegaard or Loder to see primordial sin as resulting from anxiety. Kierkegaard speculates that dizzying freedom over the possibility of disobedience precipitates the self-alienating act. If I understand Kierkegaard correctly (and I'm not sure I do) this conceptual scenario turns freedom into a kind of causality, whereas freedom is better seen as a condition of specific relationships; and in the God-human relationality, freedom is peaceful, not anxious (Rom. 8:6-7). In other words, I see no reason why human freedom before the fall should be any more anxiety-laden than the "glorious liberty" (Rom. 8:21) of God's reconciled children. Loder builds on Kierkegaard's concept of anxiety, and, as I mentioned earlier, he says the sequence of primordial sin is parallel to the formation of the ego in the first eighteen months of life (*The Logic of the Spirit,* p. 123). I think this comparison has heuristic value, for it demonstrates that spiritual struggles are not divorced from psychic ones; but in looking for parallels one should also recognize dissimilarities. The face of the mother is not a direct equivalent to the face of God. If given God's steadfast loving presence, even the extreme anxiety of the Second Adam can be resolved in the direction of obedience, then one is hard-pressed to say why the first Adam should have chosen disobedience. A different line of thinking is suggested by scriptural descriptions of the serpent and Satan: essentially the primordial couple, for all their im-

even if we cannot explain the emergence of sin, we can understand how it leads to death. God says that when they eat from the tree of the knowledge of good and evil, they will surely die (Gen. 2:17). They do eat; in disobedience they obtain knowledge of evil by doing it, and having done it, lose the power of choosing otherwise. Satan tempts them by saying they can become like God by disobeying God (Gen. 3:5). This desire to be like God *apart from God,* and to enjoy creation's benefits apart from God, is the primordial sin that leads to death. Death ensues, because life is in God. Separated from God, they die spiritually, and then also physically — since spirit, soul and body are interrelated. In their psychic life, they fall into idolatry (a kind of death), because their relationship to themselves and the world is not grounded in God. They are still doxological, eucharistic beings, but they begin worshipping created things rather than the Creator (Rom. 1:25).

When death is understood this way, then it can be better grasped how Christ's voluntary death is the double negation that defeats the power of death; and how baptismal union with Christ in his death liberates people for new life (though teachings may vary on the precise relationship between this union and the water ritual). The physical fact and psychic pain of death are to be recognized and not brushed aside; but they do not have the last word when it is seen that spiritual realities have conceptual priority. The pain of separation from a loved one, which points back to the infant's trauma at the loss of the face, is assuaged by the continual presence of Christ, a presence that is both spiritual and physical. In some churches, this life-giving presence may be experienced most intensely through Spirit baptism and physical manifestations of spiritual gifts; in others, it may be through the Eucharist. I recall how after my mother's death, a member of her congregation consoled me with words about their friendship, adding " — and of course your mother is still with us each time we celebrate the Eucharist, if we rightly discern the Body."

The basic points here are that spiritual and physical death are distinct but related, such that the negation of the one also negates the power of the other; second, that Christ is the mediator of the double negation that destroys death, both spiritually and physically; and third, that baptism as the event that instantiates this reality is likewise both spiritual and physical, both Spirit baptism and water baptism: thus the two are distinct but connected.

---

portance, are thrust into the midst of a cosmic battle they did not initiate. Though they, like we, are responsible for how they deal with it, nevertheless they are drawn toward their suicidal choice by the one who was "a liar and a murderer from the beginning" (John 8:44). This "explanation" does not explain why they chose as they did, but at least it acknowledges that larger forces than flesh and blood are involved (cf. Eph. 6:10-12).

Infant Baptism versus Believer's Baptism

Another contentious baptismal issue has been the question of infants versus believers. It was noted that the Romans passage seems to speak of both vicarious death and co-death — saying that baptismal union with Christ is both "into his death" (6:3) and "a death like his" (6:5). Given the latter claim, the pattern of double negation further reinforces the need for baptism to involve human decision. If primordial death comes through a human choice to disobey, if Christ's defeat of death comes through his voluntary death, then it makes perfect sense for humanity's union with Christ in "a death like his" to be likewise a voluntary choice. This much, it seems to me, is apodictic.

Then comes the question of whether humanity is to be seen in the singular or plural, as unique persons or corporate body. One may say the believer should freely request baptism of the church; or that the church should freely request baptism for the infant. Perhaps the question of infants versus believers is ultimately a question of whether to focus on the members of the Body or the Body of the members. Given the abundant biblical examples of believers being baptized, and the fact that human volition is clearest when it involves a particular person, believer's baptism may be theologically the safer course. On the other hand, there is the long-standing tradition of infant baptism; it is supported both by Schmemann, even though he stresses the voluntary nature of Christ's death, and by Loder, even though he stresses the importance of the individual self. Schmemann says that faith is needed for baptism, but any merely human faith would be lacking. The only adequate faith is that of Jesus Christ, which is instilled into his body, the Church. Thus the Church requests baptism, and within the Church the infant represents all the people, while the people for their part undertake to participate in vows addressed to the infant. In conversation, Loder's line of reasoning was more like Luther's: because baptism is so closely affiliated with salvation (whether as enactment or re-presentation of salvation), it must be seen as something that God does, and God's sovereign action is clearest in the case of infants. At some point, however, a space must be made for a person's consent — which confirmation may try to do — and then arises a predicament Kierkegaard noted well. If infant baptism makes people Christians, then one must transform an initial being-Christian into a future possibility, so that one can become a Christian by choice.[33] In other words, baptism must first be undone, at least conceptually, in order to be personally ap-

33. Søren Kierkegaard, *Concluding Unscientific Postscript to Philosophical Fragments,* Hong and Hong edition (Princeton: Princeton University Press, 1992), p. 365.

propriated. Perhaps it may mollify this perplexity to think that personal choice does not have to undo in order to ratify what was first chosen for one.

I won't try to resolve a problem that has roiled since ancient times; but in regard to the structure of double negation and the developmental issues at hand, two bits of advice may be given to the Christian educator regarding infant versus believer's baptism. The first is to reinforce that baptism is a good setting to teach about death, whether this teaching takes place in the sanctuary or study. Unfortunately where the practice is one of infant baptism, the teacher may be less apt to stress this scriptural connection between baptism and Christ's death. If for many parents the idea of their newborn infant being reborn seems odd enough, the thought of their baby becoming crucified with Christ may be downright abhorrent; perhaps especially so in churches where teaching has emphasized the connection between crucifixion and sin, or neglected the connection between crucifixion and victory over the powers of death. These situations call for careful teaching, and baptismal teaching can take place even when a baptism is not about to happen. In any event and at all costs, it is important to preserve the scriptural connection between baptism and Christ's death.

Another word of advice concerns baptism and the human family. While families may well be the reason infant baptism was first instituted, the teacher should convey that the context of baptism is much larger than family dynamics. If it is within the context of those dynamics that the ego is formed, then it must be seen that the context of the ego's negation and transformation is created by the Spirit of Christ, within the Church that is his presence and power in the world. In other words, baptism should not be seen as something the family does, or that one does simply because one belongs to a family — a misperception that can occur even with adolescent believer's baptism. This position is not anti-family; it simply recognizes that the negative dynamics of the family must be negated, in order to be christocentrically reconstellated ("If anyone comes to me and does not hate his father and mother, his wife and children, his brothers and sisters . . ." — Luke 14:26).

The Central Pattern of Baptism

A third important question has been: what is the most basic depiction of baptism? I have focused on the scriptural meaning of baptism as union with Christ in his death and into a death like his. But other scriptural images may come to mind: for example, baptism can be seen as new birth; washing from sin; receiving the true circumcision of the heart; or putting on new apparel (white robe, wedding clothes, spiritual armor). This study suggests that, both theologically and developmentally, the pattern of death and resurrection is the most basic of all.

For the existential fault line runs deep. Approaching it from the standpoint of human sin may prompt back-and-forth arguments about the extent of this depravity, since most human actions are ambiguous enough to be judged either as hopelessly defective or as showing some glint of the *imago dei.* The message about death is less ambiguous. People who doubt they are sinners still know they will die; empirical evidence of death's universality abounds. In Scripture, death is described as a ruling power: ". . . Death reigned from the time of Adam to the time of Moses, even over those who did not sin by breaking a command . . ." (Rom. 5:14). Other passages reinforce that death affects soul and spirit as well as body. Of the spirit aspect, Ephesians states: "You were dead through your trespasses and sins in which you once lived, following . . . the spirit that is now at work among those who are disobedient" (Eph. 2:1-2). Of the soul or psyche aspect, Hebrews says: "Since the children have flesh and blood, he too shared in their humanity so that by his death he might destroy him who holds the power of death — that is, the devil — and free those who all their lives were held in slavery by their fear of death" (Heb. 2:14-15).

This last quotation relates most directly to the developmental features just considered. Death is a lifelong fear, incipiently present even in the birth trauma. Loder argues that death catalyzes the formation of the ego, and all subsequent ego competencies are extensions of the process by which death gets incorporated into the ego.[34] Therefore the defeat of death, the negation of this negation, needs to precede all attempts to renew ourselves or grow in Christian character. Conviction of sin and disciplines of mortification surely can play a part in this process, but the essential starting point is union with Christ in his

34. To review, ego formation is based on death because it is based on separation from the presence of the parents or caregivers who represent the face of God. The infant spirit attempts to overcome the anxiety of separation, but the attempt issues in an independence that solidifies the separation, leading to an enduring sense of "cosmic loneliness" (a phrase Loder uses often). Since death and separation from God are the same, the infant attempt to overcome death in the drama of the parental face may even be analogous to the primordial sin, in that it tries to do what God does (overcome death) apart from God. However, the spontaneous infant actions are not all sinful, but show glimmers of the *imago dei.* For the initial response to the parental face can be seen as infantile longing for the face of God to transform the separation (negation) that occurs in birth; and the rejection of the parental face can be viewed as infantile recognition that the parent does not in fact provide God's steadfast presence.

Still, the basic posture of the ego is separation, hence death. Untransformed ego competencies "incorporate" death because they are self-centered, rather than being grounded in the self's relationality with the One who overcomes death and cosmic loneliness; thus the ego can grow simultaneously stronger and lonelier.

death-trampling death. The beauty of baptism here is not that it is quick and clean, but gracious and Christ-centered. Without such a context, will not mortification or ascesis too easily become a "superego" activity ridden with self-centered guilt and anxiety? One recalls Luther's journey, and his eventual refrain against Satan's attack on his conscience: "I have been baptized!"

From these theological and developmental perspectives, baptism as death (leading to resurrection) serves as the central image for all other baptismal images. I agree with Barth that the idea of baptism as washing from sin points to the "total cleansing and renewal in Christ's death."[35] So too the new birth, the new heart, the new clothing are all made possible by the defeat of death that comes from being united with Christ in his death.

Final Words

One final bit of teaching advice would be to heed a principle partly neglected in this essay: in almost any classroom or audience will be those for whom the fact of death, fear of death, or sorrow of death has recently become an acute reality. While I was writing this essay, a close friend called to tell me her grandmother had just died. She was nearly one hundred years old. She had lived a full, joyful life, yet her death brought an unspeakable sadness. The point is not that teachers should avoid talk of death for fear of saying the wrong thing — the subject may be too taboo already, and further repression only deepens the negation. But one does well to recognize a certain pastoral or counseling dimension to teaching. Continually the Christian message offers hope: *Christ has risen from the death, trampling down death by death.*

There was a passage in Loder's *Logic of the Spirit* that bothered me, but has made more sense with time. Near the start, in speaking about the human spirit, he wrote in his manuscript: "Even when the spirit itself chooses death in suicide, it is in hope of a better life." Reading it, I suggested an alteration: "Even when the spirit itself chooses death, whether in suicide or baptism, it is in hope of a better life."[36] He thanked me, readily accepting the change, though I think for better reasons than mine. I had instinctively recoiled from his stark reference to suicidal death in the first paragraphs of a book on human development. But he had been focusing steadily on the human spirit's thirst to "transcend and transform death."[37] Even with suicide, he asked,

35. Karl Barth, *Church Dogmatics* (Edinburgh: T. & T. Clark, 1956-75), IV/4, p. 140.
36. *Logic of the Spirit,* p. 4.
37. *Logic of the Spirit,* p. 4.

"what's going on here?" and found evidence of hidden hopefulness — hidden order. (The suicidal person may hope that even death will be better than the current life of despair, and may leave a written note in the hope that someone will find it, read it, and finally understand in some way.) But he also readily recognized that baptism spoke a better word, for it referred the reader directly to what God does to negate and transform death, thus bestowing life, indeed, even righteousness, peace, and joy.

In the order of things, there is everywhere the presence of negation, stretching from one end of the life span and the universe to the other. Human efforts to overcome negation are ingenious and often tragic. Yet even in the worst tragedy, we may hear a human voice crying out in primitive prayer for divine order to appear. The Christian message is that God hears this cry and has responded. Though death has been the fact of life, it does not in fact have the final word, because *Christ has risen from the dead, trampling down death by death, and upon those in the tombs bestowing life.*

2. Biting and Chomping Our Salvation: Holy Eucharist, Radically Understood

Marilyn McCord Adams

In the mid-eleventh century, a eucharistic controversy erupted between Lanfranc (later the first Norman archbishop of Canterbury) and Berengar (deacon of the Church of St. Maurice of Angers). Berengar held that in the sacrament Christ was present to the believer *spirit-to-spirit*. Lanfranc contended for transubstantiation, insisting that the body of Christ comes to be literally located where the bread used and still seems to be. Berengar lost the debate and throughout the rest of his career was made repeatedly to swear formulae such as this:

> "I, Berengar, acknowledge . . . that the bread and wine which are placed on the altar are after consecration not only a Sacrament but also the real body and blood of our Lord Jesus Christ, and that with the senses *(sensualiter)*, not only by way of Sacrament but in reality, these are held and broken by the hands of priests and are crushed by the teeth of the faithful."

Although the species of bread and wine remain, so that the faithful "may not shrink through perceiving what is raw and bloody," it is the same body that Mary bore that is bitten into, torn, and chewed.[1]

1. S. Gregorius VII, 1073-1085, Proceedings of his Sixth Council at Rome in 1079, "De ss. Eucharistia: Ius iurandum a Berengario praestitum," in *Enchiridion Symbolorum: Definitionum et Declarationum de Rebus Fidei et Morum*, ed. by Heinrich Denzinger (Freiburg im Breisgau: B. Herder, 1911). Berengar's position was condemned by Leo IX at Rome in 1050, by Victor II at the synod of Florence in 1055, by Nicholas II at Rome in 1059, and by Gregory VII at Rome in 1078 and again in 1079.

I am happy to acknowledge that research for this paper has been supported by a Henry Luce III fellowship in theology.

* * *

One Sunday, when I had preached on the unconditional love of God, as usual, Tony challenged me at the church door. "Do you do pastoral counseling?" The chaos of his life seemed bottomless. His mother was a prostitute and lay dying of AIDS. Two weeks before, police had impounded Tony's car when his father "borrowed" it to haul illegal aliens across the border. As a teenager, Tony had run for refuge to a large charismatic church, whose programs had ordered his life. Tony had a dramatic conversion experience, felt engulfed by white-hot lava-love of the Holy Spirit, even heard a call to Christian ministry. But he was "cast into outer darkness," condemned as a "son of the devil," when they learned he was gay. Tony had taken his own tour through drugs and alcohol, crashing to a halt at skid-row's "rock bottom." At last he was in AA, looking to start a new job in a couple of weeks. The trouble was, he was depressed and couldn't seem to snap out of it.

My mind raced and reeled. My *sotto voce* prayer was desperate. The cross flashed before my mind. Depression is inverted anger. Christ himself seemed to be saying, "Tell him to take his rage, and throw it at me!" Screwing up my courage, I suggested: "Buy a cheap crucifix, bang it on the floor for all you're worth. Yell and tell God exactly what you think of the life he has given you. Do it until you run out of steam!"

Two weeks later, I asked, "Say, Tony, did you get hold of that crucifix?" "No, but I feel better now," he replied. "You know what I did? The very next time I went up for communion, I bit hard into the wafer, and told Jesus, 'Take that, and that, and that!'"[2]

"Corporeal" Presence, Controverted

From the ninth through the fifteenth centuries, it was the dominant position in Western Christendom that when — in the course of the eucharistic prayer — the officiating clergy says the words of institution, the body and blood of Christ come to be literally located where the bread and wine used and still seem to be. Yet, this medieval majority report was energetically challenged in the sixteenth century by Reformed and reforming theologians — including Zwingli, Bullinger, and Calvin — on multiple grounds.

First, they contended, it was *unsupported by Scripture.* Zwingli among others ridiculed Aquinas's and others' literal reading of "This is my body" as rhetorically naive. The Bible is full of figures of speech! Moreover, everyone

2. A suitably disguised true story from my ministry.

agrees that sacraments are signs; how could Aquinas so blatantly fail to observe the distinction between the thing signified and the sign?[3]

Second, they insisted, transubstantiation and other school theological theories *fly in the face of reason and experience* — of philosophy, physics, and common sense. For the senses testify to the continued presence of bread and wine; moreover, such perceptions survive all the usual tests to rule out sensory illusions. Doesn't everyone know, don't philosophy and science agree that it is impossible either for two bodies (e.g., the bread and the body of Christ) to be in the same place at once, or for a single body to be in two places at once (e.g., the body of Christ in heaven at the right hand of God and on each altar where the Eucharist is being celebrated)?[4]

Third, they charged, belief in corporeal eucharistic presence is *pragmatically pernicious.* Combined with the (anti-Donatist) *ex opere operato* provisions of medieval sacramental theology, it turns the Eucharist into a magic trick in which the priest mumbles the secret formula — *'hocus pocus'* was their mocking contraction of *'hoc est corpus meum'* — to summon the presence of a thing whose occult powers work effects for good or ill apart from faith and beyond our knowledge.[5] Besides superstition, such conviction fosters the putative idolatry of eucharistic veneration and the popish pomps of Corpus Christi processions.[6] Enlightenment Anglicans deplored bad consequences of a different sort, pointing to their own history of religious bloodshed, partly provoked by zealous interest in the manner of Christ's real presence in the eucharistic rite.

Nineteenth- and twentieth-century *psychology* add a fourth category of objections. Freud disparages ritualistic behavior as neurotic at best, pathological at worst. Piaget counts concrete operations and material manipulations more elementary than formal operations that are analogically based upon it. Surely this suggests that Calvin was right to shift the attention of mature Chris-

3. Zwingli, "On the Lord's Supper," in *Zwingli and Bullinger,* ed. by G. W. Bromiley (Philadelphia: Westminster, 1953), pp. 188-193; cf. "An Exposition of the Faith," p. 265. John Calvin, *The Institutes of the Christian Religion,* Library of Christian Classics, vols. XX-XXI, trans. Ford Lewis Battles (Philadelphia: Westminster, 1960), IV.17.1-2.1359-1363; 21-23, 25.1385-1390, 1391-92. *Short Treatise on the Holy Supper of Our Lord Jesus Christ,* in *John Calvin: Selections from His Writings,* ed. John Dillenberger (Missoula: Scholars Press/AAR, 1975), 15-16.515-516; 39.528.

4. Ulrich Zwingli, "An Exposition of the Faith," in Bromiley, ed., *Zwingli and Bullinger,* pp. 255-258, 261. Cf. Zwingli, "On the Lord's Supper," p. 186. Calvin, *The Institutes* IV.17.13-18.1379-1381; 26-27.1393-1395. *Short Treatise on the Holy Supper of Our Lord Jesus Christ,* 41-42.529-530.

5. Calvin, *The Institutes* IV.14.4.1279-1280; IV.14.14.1289. *Short Treatise on the Holy Supper of Our Lord Jesus Christ,* 48-52.534-536.

6. Calvin, *Institutes* IV.14.14-15.1289-1291; 17.36-37.1412-1413; 17.39.1416-1417. *Short Treatise on the Supper of Our Lord Jesus Christ,* 43.512-513. Calvin's point of view was enjoined by the Anglican Thirty-nine Articles of Religion, #28.

tians off the material props and onto worthy reception of the gift of Christ's person. James Fowler, too, seems to shove eucharistic devotion into the developmental basement — from the magical numinous of stage one (that takes consecrated hosts home like magic charms) or the literal of stage two that identifies symbol with thing signified (what Zwingli deplored) and leaves meanings imbedded in the narrative form of the rite.[7]

In a way, our friend and mentor James Loder holds a high doctrine of the Eucharist, promoting it — as he does in *The Transforming Moment* — as a paradigm of transformational dynamics.[8] His attention is riveted on psychospiritual process and rarely rests on metaphysical questions. Standing firmly in the Reformed tradition, he takes for granted that Eucharist is meant to be an occasion of personal communion, one in which believer and God meet *spirit-to-Spirit.* His psychological theories make him content to regard the eucharistic drama as a *symbol* of transformation — indeed as the paradigm and pattern of Christian transformation.[9] Reading the rite through the lens of the Emmaus pericope (Luke 24:13-35), Loder stresses how the worthy recipient opens him/herself to a figure-ground shift of cosmic proportions:[10] taking the bread and wine into her/himself looks like an effort to *contain* Christ as an object in *our* world, but instead the believer is *in*corporated into Christ's body and so thrust into and encompassed by *God's* world. Once again, Loder's focus is on the logic of the *Spirit/spirit;* bodily eating functions as a metaphor of the ego's cosmos-sustaining efforts.[11] Alternatively, consuming the bread and wine is a kinship metaphor that symbolizes cutting off the priority of other blood lines.[12] Even when Loder emphasizes that the human spirit is transformed as an *embodied* being for *mundane* ecstacy, he identifies the agent of this change as Christ's Spirit or as the Holy Spirit (the third person of the Trinity).[13] Loder seems

7. James W. Fowler, *Stages of Faith: The Psychology of Human Development and the Quest for Meaning* (San Francisco: Harper & Row, 1981), chaps. 16-17, pp. 122-150.

8. Cf. *The Logic of the Spirit* (San Francisco: Jossey-Bass, 1998), chap. 2, p. 40, where Loder speaks of "the gracious spiritual presence of Christ at the Eucharistic table" or of the Creator Spirit's "making Christ's Person present in that sacred and transforming event."

9. *The Transforming Moment,* 2nd ed. (Colorado Springs: Helmers & Howard, 1989), chap. 2, p. 50, n. 8; pp. 53-55.

10. Echoes of the Reformers can be heard in Loder's comment that participation without readiness for transformation makes the celebration degenerate along a spectrum from "dull ritualism to cannibalism and Dionysian revelry," into "idolatry or sheer folly" (*The Transforming Moment,* chap. 4, p. 118).

11. *The Transforming Moment,* chap. 4, pp. 103-107, 117-119; chap. 5, p. 126.

12. *The Transforming Moment,* chap. 4, p. 120.

13. *The Transforming Moment,* chap. 4, pp. 107-111, 114-117, 119, 120-121, and 121 n. 13; chap. 5, pp. 153-154.

never to have asked whether wholesome human development requires regular encounters with a literally located and literally embodied God!

The cloud of witnesses testifying against corporeal eucharistic presence of Christ's body and blood is ancient and honorable, recent and venerable. All the same, I beg to differ. Despite the impressive range of the above arguments and the cumulative case mounted by them, I find them far from decisive. Rather, eucharistic controversies — with so many conflicting positions claiming to base themselves on the Bible — combine with higher critical methods of biblical interpretation, to yield the verdict that sacramental theology is *underdetermined* by Scripture. Deep disagreements among theological professionals have always undermined the notion that the Bible is self-interpreting. If I disagree with Aquinas and Luther that literal location is demanded by relevant biblical passages, I would contend against Zwingli that it is not excluded either. So far as I know, no one has claimed that any positive position about eucharistic presence can be proved by reason and/or experience in such a way as to convince all rational persons. But Zwingli's and Calvin's philosophical and scientific objections to literal location are shown up as philosophically narrow-minded and unduly polemical, when they simply ignore the variety of alternative philosophies of body developed by school theology to show how it is far from unintelligible that one body could be in two places or two bodies in one place at the same time. Moreover, the alleged dichotomy between attention to material things and focus on the personal is false, insofar as human beings are and are typically present to one another as *embodied* person to *embodied* person. The fact that I can recognize you as a person without developing any position on the philosophical mind-body problem, or that I can encounter Christ personally in the Eucharist without endorsing any particular view about how we make the connection, neither makes it perverse for a philosopher to probe for such a theory nor excises the task of explaining eucharistic presence (or the lack thereof) from a theologian's job! Likewise, the fact that embodied personal presence — ours or Christ's — makes it possible for us to be objectively present to people who nevertheless do not notice or treat us as persons, does not, by itself, make embodied personal presence a bad idea.

For my part, I want to commend a strong doctrine of literal location — one that would underwrite the above-summarized declaration that Berengar was made to swear — as pragmatically fruitful and systematically coherent. In particular, I want to defend a recurrent minority report in Christian history sometimes referred to as "impanation."[14] According to this theory, just as the

14. Cf. Darwell Stone, *A History of the Doctrine of the Holy Eucharist,* 2 vols. (London, New York, Bombay, and Calcutta: Longmans, Green, & Co, 1909), who traces views of

divine Word becomes in-carnate (en-fleshed) when it assumes a particular human nature into hypostatic union with itself; so the divine Word becomes impanate (em-breaded) when — at the moment of consecration — it hypostatically assumes the eucharistic bread nature on the altar. My contention is that impanation is more helpful than competing accounts of eucharistic presence in suggesting how human participants in the very worst evils might make *ante-mortem* progress towards being reconciled to the Goodness of God!

The Place of the Material

Sacramental theology has to do with individual and corporate appropriation of divine benefits in this life between birth and the grave, and so presupposes an understanding of God's character and purposes. Sacraments are *material* signs. My contention is that the material is sufficiently entrenched in God's creative aims generally, and in what it is to be human in particular, as to make divine provision of sacraments a skillful means and natural step in forwarding God's plans. Because — in my judgment — this conclusion takes its urgency from soteriology, I begin my explanation with the evils from which we need to be saved and project backwards to God's positive aims in creation.[15]

The "Negative" Argument from Horrendous Evil

Soteriology deals with twin problems: that the human condition generally, and divine-human relations in particular are non-optimal. Centuries of Christian tradition have traced the root of these non-optimality problems to a primordial misuse of created freedom, and marshalled multiple conceptualities — of sin

---

eucharistic presence from the New Testament to the early twentieth century. The theory only sometimes *called* impanation — with its putative parallel between the incarnation and eucharistic presence — is strongly suggested by Theodoret (Stone I.3.i.99-102); Gelasius (I.3.i.101-102); Leontius of Byzantium (I.4.i.135); Ephraim of Antioch (I.4.i.135-136); John of Paris (ca. 1300) (I.8.i.361-362); and the Anglican divine Lancelot Andrewes (1555-1626) (II.xiii.ii. 258, 265). It also seems to have been advanced by Rupert of Deutz (+1135) (cf. John H. Van Engen, *Rupert of Deutz* [Berkeley, Los Angeles, and London: University of California Press, 1983], chap. 4, pp. 140-141), and was attributed to Luther by the 1552 session of the Council of Trent (Stone II.9.x.88) and the 1672 Council of Jerusalem/Bethlehem (II.4.vi.181-182).

15. Obviously, space limitations will not allow me a full defense of my soteriological position. Here I summarize the argument of my book *Horrendous Evils and the Goodness of God* (Ithaca and London: Cornell University Press, 1999) and my not-yet-published Gifford lectures to be entitled *The Coherence of Christology.*

and satisfaction, of freedom and bondage, of guilt and justification, of purity and defilement, of honor and shame — to interpret what these non-optimalities mean. My own view is that these difficulties are fundamentally structural and systemic, at bottom not a function of what we *do*, but of what God is and of what we and the other things in our environment *are*. I arrive at this conclusion by focusing the human predicament through the lens of horrendous evil, and so by grappling with the contentions that the human condition is non-optimal because we are radically vulnerable to horrors, while divine-human relations can seem bad because God has "set us up" for horrors by creating us in a world such as this!

Defining the Category I define horrendous evils as evils the participation in the doing (or suffering) of which constitutes *prima facie* reason to doubt whether the participant's life could (given their inclusion in it) be a great good to him/her on the whole. Examples include the rape of a woman and axing off of her arms, psycho-physical torture whose ultimate goal is the disintegration of personality, schizophrenia, severe depression, personality-destroying diseases such as Alzheimer's, cannibalizing one's own off-spring, child-abuse of the sort described by Ivan Karamazov, parental incest, participation in the Nazi death camps, the explosion of nuclear bombs over populated areas, being the accidental and/or unwitting agent in the disfigurement or death of those one loves best. Participation in horrors furnishes *reason* to doubt whether the participant's life can be worth living, because it engulfs the positive value of his/her life and penetrates into his/her meaning-making structures seemingly to defeat and degrade his/her value as a person. This criterion is objective but relative to individuals. Personal strengths vary: what crushes some may be bearable by others. Curmudgeons and people who know how to make the worst of a good situation may mistakenly estimate their predicament as horrendous. But without being infallible, the participant is an expert on how ruinous a given episode or condition is for her/him.[16]

16. Loder would recognize horrors as one face of the void or nothingness, a comprehensive existentialist category that encompasses loneliness, meaninglessness, and death. (Cf. *The Transforming Moment*, ch. 3, pp. 84-85.) I at least flirt with the idea that horror participation is a fate worse than death, a condition that makes it *prima facie* plausible to suppose that it would have been better for the participant never to have been born, whereas Loder's Carnegie-Lake parable suggests that every human career — no matter what its personal connections or achievements — is *prima facie* meaningless because it will be (in the medium if not the short run) completely forgotten. I want to say that horrors make matters worse, because they seem *prima facie* to rob participants' lives of any temporary positive meaning.

Horrendous Facts of Life Given this definition, a number of things become obvious. First, human history is riddled with horrendous evil. Moreover, it is comparatively easy for human beings to cause (be salient members in causal chains leading to) horrendous evils. A few seconds of lapsed attention behind the wheel can turn someone into a paraplegic; careless exposure to measles during pregnancy can produce mental retardation and/or deprive the fetus of hearing or sight. Clearly, an individual's capacity to produce suffering (horrendous and otherwise) unavoidably exceeds (both quantitatively and qualitatively) his/her ability to experience it. Hitler, Stalin, and Pol Pot lacked the psychic capacity to suffer, within the framework of their own individual lives, all of the terrors they perpetrated on so many thousands of others. Again, what could seventeen-year-old male soldiers experience anything like horrific enough to a mother's torment as she watches them bounce her baby on the sharp tips of bayonettes? Because — where suffering is concerned — capacity to conceive follows capacity to experience, our ability to cause horrors unavoidably exceeds our powers of conception, so that — in an important sense — we know not what we do. Finally, virtually every human being is complicit in actual horrors merely by living in his/her nation or society.

Structural Misfits Notice that human radical vulnerability to horrors cannot have its *origin* in misused created freedom, because — on traditional Adam's-fall approaches — even in Eden humans were radically vulnerable to horrors. For the framework within which the primal ancestors made their choices was such that obedient choices meant persistence of the *status quo,* while disobedient choices would result in the horrendous disarray such as humans have experienced ever since. Even if Adam's and Eve's choices are supposed to be somehow self-determined, the fact that the consequences amplify far beyond their capacity to conceive and hence to intend — viz., to horrors of which they had no prior experience and of which they could therefore have no adequate conception — is not something for which humans are responsible. Rather it is a function of the interaction with human agency and the wider framework within which it is set, and *God* is responsible for creating them in such a framework.

In fact, ready examples show that playing a salient role in horror perpetration is not neatly correlated with an individual's moral guilt or innocence. In a world such as this, not only do bad things happen to good people; morally innocent people sometimes perpetrate horrors on others, sometimes even those they love the most (e.g., the devoted parent who non-negligently backs out of the driveway and runs over the beloved toddler who has suddenly but not visibly moved into the car's path). Neither could God confer dignity on human nature by leaving it "up to" humans whether the world's potential for horrors is actualized or not. Crushing responsibility does not honor the agents on whom it is imposed. Even if different choices may avert this disaster or that, we do not have enough wisdom, enough individual and/or collective control over ourselves and our environment, reliably to steer clear of any and all horrors. Nor could retributive justice set things right: horror for horror multiplies the *prima facie* personal ruin; it neither defeats horrors nor brings them to an end.

My own hypothesis is that human radical vulnerability to horrors is rooted in *the character of human nature* as personalized material or enmattered spirit. Tying personality to the developmental structure of animal life — one that begins in groping immaturity and dependence, stumble-bumbles by trial and error towards higher functioning, only to peak and slide towards diminishment — makes our meaning-making capacities easy to twist, even ready to break, when inept caretakers and hostile surroundings force us to cope with problems off the syllabus and out of pedagogical order. By building into animal nature both an instinct for life and the seeds of death, biology makes human persons naturally degradable. Real and apparent scarcity amplifies the desperation of human struggles to survive.

Global Goodness vs. Goodness-to Created Persons The Bible and hence traditional theology and philosophy represent God as invested in cosmic projects, and advertize divine goodness at producing excellences in the cosmos over-all. But they also represent God as disposed to be good-to created persons. While denying that created persons have any rights against their Creator, my hypothesis is that God's positive projects in creation involve God's putting a high value on created persons. Divine love for created persons would mean that God does not have merely global goals (e.g., to produce the best of all possible worlds, a cosmos displaying maximum variety with maximum unity, or a world with as favorable a balance of moral good over moral evil as God could get) but aims to be good-to individual created persons God makes. Put otherwise, the global goals of divine love would be utopic, integrating any cosmic excellence at which God aimed with well-being and positive meaning for any created persons involved. My contention is that *God cannot be good to an individual created person unless God guarantees to him/her a life that is a great good to him/her on the whole, and unless God makes good on any horror participation by that individual, not merely within the context of the cosmos as the whole, but within the framework of that individual horror participant's own life.*

Balancing Off vs. Defeat For God to *make good on* horror participation is for God to overcome it with some great enough good. But the notion of "overcoming" is ambiguous, because there are different kinds of relations that value-parts can bear to value-wholes. There is the quasi-arithmetical notion of *balancing off*, in which one merely adds to a negatively (positively) valued part a positively (negatively) valued part of greater value. For example, one might balance off a painful hour in the dentist's chair with a stunning concert in the evening. By contrast, *defeat* involves a relation of organic unity between the negatively (positively) valued part and the whole, with the result that a significantly smaller negatively (positively) valued part can actually increase (decrease) the value of the whole of which it is a part. For instance, a square centimeter of ugly bilious green may be just right to depict the light on Rouen cathedral in early morning, while replacing it with a square centimeter of gorgeous blue would spoil the design. Mere balancing-off of horrors does not confer any positive meaning on them, and so would leave open the question, why a good God would not — since horror participation contributes nothing of positive significance — omit the horrendous segments altogether (e.g., deleting apocalyptic terrors of this present world and proceeding immediately to the bliss that is to come). But meaning-making is distinctive of personal functioning, while horrors make it *prima facie* impossible for human horror participants to make any positive sense of their lives. My conclusion is that a God who loved individual created persons would not merely balance off but defeat any horror participation within the context of the individual person's life.

How Valuable a Defeater? Horrors are so bad that no package of merely created goods will balance off much less defeat them. Aharon Appelfeld's novels vividly depict the psychic wasteland of holocaust survivors surrounded by new families, professional success, and personal luxury.[17] But God is the incommensurate good, while intimate relationship with God that is on the whole and in the end beatific is incommensurately good-for creatures. My conclusion is that the only currency valuable enough to make good on horrors is God, and the horror participant's overall-beatific intimacy with God.[18]

Three Stages of Defeat (1) First Stage: To defeat horror participation within the individual created person's life, God must weave it into the fabric of that individual's intimate and (overall and in the end) beatific personal relation with God. My claim is that establishing such a relation of organic unity between the

17. See Aharon Appelfeld, *The Immoral Bartfuss* (New York: Harper & Row, 1989); and Appelfeld, *For Every Sin* (New York: Weidenfeld and Nicholson, 1989).

18. This is a version of Loder's point that only the holy can swallow up the void (cf. *The Transforming Moment,* chap. 3, pp. 80-91).

individual's horror participation and a relationship incommensurately good-for the individual, would constitute the ingredients for defeating the presumption that horror participation has ruined the individual's life.

(2) Second Stage: Nevertheless, horror defeat within the context of the individual horror participant's life requires that the created individual recognize and appropriate some dimensions of positive meaning conferred by their integration into his/her relationship with God. By definition, horror participation stumps — in the event, the trauma of horror often breaks the human participant's capacities for meaning-making. Moreover, for many, no *ante-mortem* remedy is forthcoming. Many horror participants die bitter and bewildered. To defeat horror participation within the individual created person's life, God must heal, enable, and instruct our meaning-making capacities, so that we can collaborate with God to actually make some positive sense of our lives. Among other things, horror participants will need to appreciate how God can be trusted to be *for us,* given that God has set us up for horrors by creating us as personal animals in a material world such as this. For some, probably for all of us, this must (continue to) happen after we die.

(3) Third Stage: For God to put our non-optimality problems to rest, God must "change the system," by re-creating our relation to our material world, so that we are no longer radically vulnerable to horrors. The *bodily* resurrection of Christ is a representative down-payment on this. Theologians who treat the material world as a temporary and passing thing, might represent divine rescue of the elect in terms of a final liberation of spirit from matter. My own reasoning runs in the opposite direction. By contrast with angels, we humans are *by nature* personalized *material, enmattered* spirits. The misfit between these dimensions and between human nature and our material environment brings with it the curse of radical vulnerability to *prima facie* personal ruin. For God to deliver us from horrors by ripping human personality out of its material context, would signal a lack of divine follow-through, a failure on God's part to make good on what it is to be *human* being. *Divine victory should resolve the plot by harmonizing our personal with our material dimension, by making our hybrid nature and material environment a blessing rather than a curse.* Doesn't the Bible often promise a land of milk and honey, look forward to heavenly banqueting with abundant wine and bread from finest flour?

Sacraments are meant to inaugurate us into *ante-mortem* participation in this new world order. If our human nature as personalized material or enmattered spirits bears the *ante-mortem* curse of *prima facie* personal ruin, then — even *ante-mortem* — the material should be a medium of divine blessing. Why then should we be surprised if our Lord prescribes not only Spirit but *water* baptism? Is it any wonder if in the meantime he does not promise daily, weekly, or quarterly out-of-the-body experiences, but commands us to break bread to show forth his death, and feeds us with his body and blood!

The "Positive" Approach from Creation

In view of the problems horrendous evils cause, we can scarcely help asking, what could God have been thinking to create us in a world such as this? My estimate of the prices paid to personify the material in a world such as this drives me to the hypothesis that God must love material creation, and that "mixing it up" with matter must number among God's primary objectives in giving being to things other than Godself. Such interests could explain divine production of human beings in this world, twice over. First, because — like any good parent with its offspring — God would want as far as possible for creatures to be God-like and yet still possess their own integrity. In biblical language, God wants the whole world to be filled with, to be a reflection of divine glory. Thus, God makes chemicals and stuffs dynamic, plants and animals vital, human beings personal. Human nature can be seen as the crown of divine efforts to make material creation — while yet material — more and more like God. Second, love seeks union with its object (in this case, God with material creation). In liturgical language, God is out to marry heaven to earth and earth to heaven. Human nature stands at the frontier of material creation, the point at which God makes matter personal, and so the point at which God can enter into loving intimacy and consciously acknowledged collaboration with it.

Divine desire to "mix it up" with matter would find its culmination in the incarnation, where God becomes part of material creation, by joining God's very self to human being in personal union — in biblical language, so that the dwelling of God is with humankind. God incarnate in this very material world, God-with-us sharing with us the costs of God's remarkable project, seems a promising vehicle for the first stage of horror defeat — the means to weave individual human horror participation up into the individual's own (overall and in the end) beatific relation with God.

That same positive orientation to matter would underwrite divine provision of sacraments as material means of grace for us embodied persons, in the midst of our *ante-mortem* struggles to discern whether our lives can be worth living, whether God is for us or against us or just plain doesn't care. My question is, what's to stop divine hankering for material connection from going all the way, from maintaining not merely spiritual but some form of *corporeal* presence with us even after the ascension? Why wouldn't God — to use Luther's words — continue the incarnation, not only by becoming literally located where the eucharistic elements still appear to be, but by assuming the bread and wine into hypostatic union, so that they are literally the body and blood of Christ?

Dinner-Table Dynamics, Pragmatic Function

Distancing himself from Roman interpretations of the sacrifice of the mass, Calvin preferred to speak instead of "the Lord's Supper," "the Holy Banquet."[19] The Lord's table is a groaning board, heavy laden with the Heavenly Father's provisions, where adoptive sons and daughters gather to eat, drink, and be satisfied, to commune with one another and with God.[20] Yet, angels do not gather around family dinner tables; lacking bodies, they do not biologically reproduce or come in families; pure spirits that they are, angels have no need to eat. Family dinner tables would be an irrelevant setting for God's spiritually forming and informing them. By contrast, dinner tables figure deeply in the psycho-spiritual formation of human beings, because dinner tables are places where we meet *embodied* persons to *embodied* persons, to eat and drink, to bite and chew our way into who we are.

Table fellowship is a risky business. For eating betrays our vulnerability. By opening our mouths, taking something from outside in, we prove that we are *not self-contained.* To be sure, our human bodies have a natural shape, boundaries giving definition. Paradoxically, these cannot be sustained unless they are regularly compromised — food, water, oxygen enter to become part of us; carbon dioxide, useless leftovers expelled, in and out according to natural rhythms, necessary for life. The body's doors couldn't serve if they didn't open on passages that reach deep within us. Yet, precisely because they do, they put us at risk, allow the wrong things to penetrate too deeply, lock them inside for too long. Little wonder if the distinction between clean and unclean foods becomes sacred. What happens around the table is literally a matter of life and death!

At dinner tables, families bond, weave lives together. Where food is scarce, sharing means our lives are so tied together that I do not stand to gain by refusing you, while you win no advantage by withholding from me. If you give me the food that would sustain your life, by eating it I ingest part of your life, take

19. Calvin, *Short Treatise on the Holy Supper of Our Lord Jesus Christ,* 507-541. Cf. B. A. Gerrish, *Grace and Gratitude: The Eucharistic Theology of John Calvin* (Minneapolis: Fortress Press, 1993), 1.13.

20. Calvin, *Short Treatise on the Holy Supper of Our Lord Jesus Christ,* 3.508-509.

part of you into myself, and vice versa. In a suspicious world, reciprocity is important. If I receive food from your hand, I not only consume something that you could have eaten. I take into myself something you have touched, prepared. I trust you not to be offering me poison. If I give, I reassure you by sipping first. Willingness to offer and to receive food from one another is a sign of covenant, a decision not to regard each other as enemies or strangers.

Family tables are meant to nurture, from cradle to grave, from infancy to Alzheimers, to be centers of feeding and being fed. Our presence is required not only in periods of eager anticipation, vigorous work, and joyful accomplishments, but also in the midst of angry quarrels and hard-won resolutions, through seasons of grief and depression, frustration and diminishment. They are meant to be places where we grow up, from milk to pablum to solid food that has to be bitten, chomped, and chewed. Daily bread, broken and shared, is a tie that binds — for better, for worse, for richer, for poorer, in sickness and in health, for all seasons. Daily bread, broken and shared, makes us members of one another.

Yet, all too often and notoriously, dinner tables are scenes of mutual abuse and trust betrayed — places where boundaries are violated, where families "eat at each other," "bite each other's heads off," gnaw away at self-confidence, throw up bones of contention, devour one another's sense of self-worth. Dinner tables can be set with venom and poison, children force-fed, their manners ritually mocked and insulted, while providers are heartily hated and scorned. How easily dinner tables become altars on which we make holocaust of others lest in flames of fury we destroy ourselves.

Other family tables freeze solid, iced by etiquette that folds indigestible truths in starched napkins and silently passes them under the table to the dog — tables where mile-thick defenses guarantee disconnection, where dead and estranged families abort further conversation by appeal to their one mediator, the common TV.

So too, Christ invites us, each and all to his table, sets the appointment to meet us, embodied person to embodied persons, appearing under forms of bread and wine. Because we are horror participants, Christ sets a specific agenda: all conflicts out on the table, immediately! For we come, first and foremost, to show forth the Lord's death: "This is my body!" "This is my blood!" "Do this for the remembrance of me!" Christ crucified is "in our face," Christ crucified is "in *God's* face," re-presenting, reminding God how in establishing material creation, God "set us up," how in creating human being God has put us in the position of being radically vulnerable to horrors.

God in Christ crucified insists on swapping lunches, demands we bring our cups of spiced and foaming wine, our liquefying rage, the wormwood of our bitterness, the festering inflammations of horror-torn creation. God in Christ crucified stretches out loving arms, drains the dregs of our poisons, sucks dry the pus out of our wounded world. God in Christ crucified offers us his flesh to chomp and bite and tear with our teeth, invites us to get even, horror for horror, urges us to fragment God's own body in return for the way God has allowed horrors to shred the fabric of our lives. God in Christ crucified invites us to come with anger and tears, with shame and humiliation poured out to the point of exhaustion. "I hunger and thirst for it all. For heaven's sake, don't keep swallowing it or try to force it down someone else's throat!"

God in Christ crucified refuses to leave the table; Emmanuel still plights his troth — for better, for worse, for richer, for poorer, for horrors descending down into the grave. "For heaven's sake, don't hold back! I can take it all in, and still rise on the third day!" Not always but in some cases, not right away but eventually, not all at once but from time to time and fleetingly, as we catch our breaths between bouts of thrashing and sobbing, the Easter recognition begins to dawn. This family will not break. This quarrel is between lovers. Love bade us welcome. Willy nilly, recognized or not, Love has held on to us, all the while comforting us with its touch. From time to time, eventually, the storm may break, the air clear, the bread and wine bear the passion of lovers' kiss, of pleasurable embrace, of taking in one another's life.

The Superiority of Impanation, *Ego Berengarius* Revived!

So far, I have been trying to suggest how the doctrine of impanation is *congruent* with divine determination to "mix it up" with matter, the horrendous predicament in which we find ourselves, and the dinner-table image of the eucharistic rite. What makes theology systematic, however, is its balancing and adjusting of a wide range of *prima facie* desiderata into a consistent, coherent whole. Opponents of *Ego Berengarius* surely reckon that whatever positive orientation God might have to the material is trumped by the repulsive cannibalistic connotations of the impanationist view.[21] Likewise, Calvin could not countenance my analysis of the roots of our twin non-optimality problems, any more than he could recognize Tony's angry biting and chomping as a case of worthy reception. For Calvin, railing at God is blasphemy, accusing God a sure sign of impiety at heart. Without either reneging on or further defending my own soteriological position and its pragmatic implications, I do want to com-

21. Zwingli, "On the Lord's Supper," 190-197; cf. "An Exposition of the Faith," 254-255, 258, 261. Calvin, *Institutes* IV.17.12.1372-1373.

ment further on why impanation fits them better than competing accounts of eucharistic presence do.

Spiritual Eating, Flesh-and-Blood Food

In *Grace and Gratitude*,[22] Brian Gerrish argues that — despite Platonizing philosophical tendencies — Calvin does not think Christ meets us in the Supper merely Spirit-to-spirit, but rather *embodied* person to *embodied* person. For while Calvin repeatedly affirms that Jesus Christ is the gift and *spiritual* food in the sacrament, he also speaks of Christ's feeding us in the supper with his body and blood.[23] The *food* is not merely spiritual. But because Christ's body and blood have ascended into heaven to the right hand of God, the *eating* must be spiritual: it is not possible literally to bite and chomp a body that is not located in the same place where the consumer's mouth and teeth are! For Gerrish's Calvin, the real presence of Christ's body and blood and so of the embodied Christ to the faithful participant is not *spatial*, but *mysterious* and *spiritual*, because effected in some mysterious way by the Holy Spirit of God.[24] Likewise, the nourishment effected by this spiritual eating of the flesh of Christ is *spiritual* — a quickening, not just of the mind's cognitive faculties, but of the whole soul.[25]

This view has the merit of emphasizing how the holy banquet is an occasion of *personal* encounter between the faithful and Christ. The pragmatic thrust of Calvin's critique of scholastic views is to steer our attention away from the physical onto the personal dimensions of the rite (hence his antipathy to liturgical ornamentation).[26] Calvin's account makes the literal eating and drinking of the elements *a metaphor* or *analogy* for the soul's feeding on the flesh and blood of Christ.[27]

Nevertheless, however much this account may seem to anticipate Piaget, I think it misunderstands dinner table dynamics. It is true that my grasping of the cup is a metaphor, and *only* a metaphor, of my grasping the idea of a cup. This is because my grasping of the cup in no way constitutes my grasping of the

22. Gerrish, *Grace and Gratitude.*

23. Calvin, *Short Treatise on the Holy Supper of Our Lord Jesus Christ*, 3-4.509; 5.510; 11.512-513.

24. Calvin, *Institutes* IV.17.1-5.1359-1365; 8-10.1368-1371; 32-33.1403-1408. Cf. Gerrish, 1.7-9; 5.137-138.

25. Calvin, *Institutes* IV.17.5.1364-1365; 8-9.1368-1369; 11.1372.

26. Calvin, *Institutes* IV.15.19.1319-1320.

27. Calvin, *Short Treatise on the Holy Supper of Our Lord Jesus Christ*, 17.516. Cf. Gerrish, *Grace and Gratitude*, 1.11-12.

idea. They are two entirely distinct actions. But at the dinner table, opening my mouth in your presence is not just an outward and visible sign of inward and spiritual vulnerability. It *is* a personal risk of vulnerability in relation to you. Eating what you prepare *is* an act of trust, sharing food *is* an act of social bonding. When I as an embodied person do these things, the one act *constitutes* the other.

Put otherwise, willy nilly, human family dinner tables make the material the medium of the psycho-spiritual in such a way that they are humanly impossible to disentangle. Attempts to deprive bodily feeding of personal significance, or to pursue social bonding and personal nurture *only* outside the context of eating, are themselves psycho-spiritual moves, normally fraught with momentous psycho-spiritual consequences. I have no wish to deny that God provides divine-to-human personal nurture outside the context of physical eating (as when the Word is preached or Scripture is read), or that God sometimes meets human persons spirit-to-Spirit (as in mystical contemplation). What I don't see is why God would invite us to *dinner* and then try to split table *fellowship* from the act of eating itself.

Calvin's position is also philosophically underdeveloped by his own admission. We can see how God can be present to the faithful spirit-to-Spirit, because God is Spirit and God is omnipresent, literally and/or at least in divine power to produce effects. We know from experience how encounters of embodied person to embodied person build up trust and confidence. From some philosophical points of view (e.g., Aquinas's), we can understand how God might use the locally present bread and wine as instrumental causes to produce spiritual benefits in the soul. But how does the Spirit make it possible for us to meet or be united *embodied* person to *embodied* person when Christ's body is not located within the range of any of our sensory faculties?[28]

Location without Extension

In thirteenth- and fourteenth-century eucharistic theology, both *transubstantiation* — the view that the whole substance of the bread (wine) is converted into the substance of the body (blood) of Christ, the bread (wine) accidents remaining — and *consubstantiation* — the view that the bread and wine remain as before but the body and blood of Christ come to be present *with* them where they are — continued to command attention. These positions shared the philosophically innovative thesis that bodies (like angels and souls) can be literally lo-

28. Cf. Gerrish, *Grace and Gratitude*, 6.177.

cated in a place without being extended in it. For a thing to be extended in a place (in their terminology, to be in place *circumscriptively*) is for the whole thing to exist in the whole of the place and part of the thing to exist in part of the place — different parts in different places, so that some parts of the thing are at a distance from others of its parts. Taking their cue from Augustine, scholastic philosophers reasoned that angels and intellectual souls cannot be extended in a place because they are simple and so lack parts that could be positioned at a distance from one another. But a human being's intellectual soul is located in his/her body throughout his/her *ante mortem* career. Hence, the intellectual soul must be whole in the whole body, and whole in each part of the body (which Scotus and Ockham call being *definitively* in place). By contrast, material things do have parts, and their natural way of existing is to be extended in place, with some parts at a distance from others.

Confronted with the problem of eucharistic presence, however, Aquinas, Scotus, and Ockham all reasoned that just because material things have parts and so can be and normally are in a place by being extended in it, it doesn't follow that it is metaphysically impossible for material things to be located in a place without being extended in it. Why would it be impossible for divine power to make a material thing to exist in place definitively, so that the whole thing was in the whole of the place, and the whole thing was in each part of the place as well? Instead of making each part of a thing exist in a different part of place, God could make all the parts of the thing exist in each and all parts of the place at once. Normally, there is no reason for God to exercise this power, perhaps even considerable reason against it. But in the Eucharist, this isn't so. God brings it about that the body (blood) of Christ, which is literally located and extended (exists circumscriptively in place) in heaven, also exists definitively in the place where the bread and wine accidents are still extended. Theoretically, Aquinas and Scotus observe, this allows the body (blood) of Christ to be literally located in heaven and on multiple altars at once without violating the intuition that two things can't be *extended* in the same place at once, and a single thing can't be *extended* in two places at once.[29]

In my judgment, these scholastic positions win a pragmatic advantage over Gerrish's Calvin, insofar as they allow the body and blood of Christ concrete locations in our world. God is Spirit, but we are personalized material. God is everywhere, but we are somewhere in particular, and it is difficult for us

29. In fact, neither Scotus nor Ockham holds these commonsense theses to be metaphysically necessary. For a thorough discussion of the metaphysical merits and demerits of these positions as well as a fuller exposition of them, see my article "Aristotle and the Sacrament of the Altar: A Crisis in Medieval Theology," *Canadian Journal of Philosophy*, Supplementary volume 17 (1991): 195-249.

to notice and pay attention to what is not anywhere in particular. Like the incarnation, literal location where the bread and wine seem to be, is a concession to our condition: in the Eucharist, the body and blood of Christ come to meet us literally where we are. That is why eucharistic veneration is not idolatry. We do not bow ourselves to bread and wine or their accidents (any more than we curtsey to the king's clothes). Rather we bend the knee to the really present, because literally located, body and blood of Christ, which are themselves hypostatically united to the divine Word who is worthy of all worship.

Adherents of literal-location-without-extension counted it a further advantage that the body and blood of Christ could be thus present without being causally interactive with that environment. What is not extended in a place cannot be literally chewed and torn there. Neither can it be seen with the bodily eye or touched with the bodily hand or mouth. There is no need to wonder about whether the body and blood of Christ are digested or excreted by the normal biological routes. These conclusions were all the more important to them, because they believed Christ's post-resurrection body to be impassible. Thus, their theologically buttressed philosophical account allowed them to distance themselves from the more vivid language of the *Ego Berengarius* formula.[30]

Ubiquity

If Luther often disparaged, he also entered the speculative fray in his zeal to preserve the corporeal presence of the body and blood of Christ in the Eucharist.[31] He was singularly unimpressed with Zwingli's (and then Calvin's) insistence that the body and blood of Christ could not be literally located on the altar because they had ascended to the right hand of God. First, Luther denies that "the right hand of God" refers to a place (as if Christ were imprisoned in heaven like a bird in its nest); on the contrary, Luther contends, it refers to the hypostatic union of divine and human natures.[32] Second, Luther rejects their philosophical assumption that a single body cannot be in more than one place at a time. Reviewing scholastic options, Luther denies that the body and blood of Christ are extended (circumscriptively) in place the way the bread and wine are, or that they are

30. E.g., Aquinas, *Summa Theologica* III, q.77, aa.3-7, exp. a.7, obj.3 & ad 3um; q.81, aa.3-4.

31. Marc Lienhard puts Luther's reflections on the Eucharist in the context of his wider Christology, in *Luther: Witness to Jesus Christ,* trans. Edwin H. Robertson (Minneapolis: Augsburg, 1982), esp. chaps. 4-5, pp. 195-267.

32. Martin Luther, *Against the Heavenly Prophets in the Matter of Images and Sacraments* (1525), *Luther Works* (= LW) 40.216, 220-221. *That These Words of Christ, "This is my body," Stand Firm against the Fanatics* (1527), LW 37.55-70.

whole in the whole and whole in the parts of that place (definitively in that place) the way angels are. Instead, he maintains that the body and blood of Christ are in place repletively *(repletive)* in such a way as to fill all things.[33]

By way of explanation, Luther applies the ancient and honorable doctrine of *communicatio idiomatum* in a distinctive and philosophically questionable way. In patristic and medieval sources, the understanding is that because one person subsists in two natures, predicates from both natures apply to that person; and in consequence, one can make true statements of the form "*S* is *P*" where "*S*" is a description taken from one of the natures and "*P*" is a descriptive predicate from the other. For example, "The babe in the manger sustains the world," or "The divine Word was born of Mary, suffered, died, and rose again" are both thought to come out true by virtue of the hypostatic union of the divine Word to the human nature. This works because *the person* falls under both descriptions, both of which in turn can refer to it. Luther, however, conflates this construal of *communicatio idiomatum* according to which properties from both natures belong to *the person,* with an alternative doctrine according to which properties from one nature can be truly predicated of the other *nature.* Thus, Luther reasons that because the divine essence is everywhere, *the human nature* is also everywhere, with the result that Christ's body and blood are too. This implies that the embodied Christ is *physically* as near to us as he was to Mary, Simeon, and the shepherds,[34] and that Christ is not only eaten spiritually by faith in the heart but physically with the mouth.[35] Yet, even in the mouth, Christ's body is spiritual food that changes us into itself rather than corporeal food that gets changed into the consumer's body.[36]

To the objection that "everywhere" is overkill, indeed that it defeats one pragmatic purpose that real corporeal presence was supposed to serve — viz., of providing a particular concrete focus — Luther replies that we are not to seek God everywhere because that might lead to idolatry, but rather where God invites us to seek him — viz., where the Word is present and especially at the Lord's table.[37]

33. Luther, *Confession Concerning Christ's Supper* (1528), LW 37.223; cf. 215-335.

34. Luther, *That These Words of Christ, "This is my body," Stand Firm against the Fanatics* (1527), LW 37.95-96.

35. Luther, *That These Words of Christ, "This is my body," Stand Firm against the Fanatics* (1527), LW 37.87-88.

36. Luther, *That These Words of Christ, "This is my body," Stand Firm against the Fanatics* (1527), LW 37.94, 100.

37. Luther, *That These Words of Christ, "This is my body," Stand Firm against the Fanatics* (1527), LW 37.69; *The Sacrament of the Body and Blood of Christ against the Fanatics,* LW 36.342-345.

Already Zwingli charged that this second version of the *communicatio idiomatum* seems both philosophically incoherent and un-Chalcedonian insofar as it confuses the divine and human natures. In advancing it, Luther seems genuinely to have been puzzled how — if the divine Word really is hypostatically united to the human nature — the divine Word could be anywhere without that human nature. Philosophically, this is worth pondering, but the claim goes to the heart of the Chalcedonian definition: that the person x can be F according to its divine nature and not-F according to its human nature. Although in many places Luther denies that he is thereby confusing the natures, he can also be found to assert that because of such mutual participation the two natures should be called *one nature!*[38]

Impanation

If corporeal eucharistic presence is desirable so that we can meet *Christ* embodied person to embodied person, then it seems better if it is *Christ's* body — rather than mere bread or mere wine or their accidents — that we meet. Impanation gives us this pragmatic desideratum without turning eucharistic reception into the biting and tearing of raw meat. If the divine Word assumes the eucharistic bread the way that he assumes the human nature, it follows that Christ's one body has two natures — human nature and bread nature.[39] If we like, we can take a page from the scholastics and hold that Christ's body is present on the altar without being extended *according to its human nature,* but present and extended *according to its bread nature.* Alternatively, we could hold that Christ's body is not present on the altar according to its human nature at all, but only according to its bread nature. Either way, Christ's post-resurrection body could be impassible or at least no longer vulnerable to horrors *according to its human nature.* But Christ's post-resurrection body would be causally interactive and so capable of being literally touched and handled, tasted and seen, *according to its bread nature.* This makes it metaphysically possible for us to in-

38. Luther, *Confession Concerning Christ's Supper* (1528), LW 37.296.

39. Note that Luther's sometime endorsement of the ubiquity of the body and blood of Christ is *not* tantamount to an acceptance of impanation. Ubiquity implies that the body and blood of Christ are located in the same place as the bread and wine on the altar (just as Christ is located in the same place as everything else in the physical universe). By itself, ubiquity implies no metaphysical connection between Christ's body and the bread other than co-location — which makes the position sound like what Scotus and Ockham meant by consubstantiation, or more recently preferred Lutheran language to the effect that Christ's body is "in, with, and under" the eucharistic bread.

teract with the Christ as with other embodied persons: to reach out for comfort, to ingest for nurture, to strike out in anger and confusion, to grasp and hold with desire, to gaze and gasp with amazement and awe. Just as the divine Word could (but — according to medieval doctrine — never in fact will) lay down the human nature it assumed, so the divine Word could lay down assumed bread natures at any time — once the bread enters the mouth, once it starts to be digested, only after it has ceased to be bread anymore, etc. My own estimate of what it takes to defeat horrors, drives me to reverse medieval reluctance: for the body of Christ to pass through the digestive process *according to its bread nature,* would represent a continuation of divine solidarity that descends to the depths of human degradation to be God-with-us! Thus, impanation underwrites *Ego Berengarius*'s assertion that the body of Christ is held and broken by the hands of priests and crushed by the teeth of the faithful. Because it is *one* body that has two natures, impanation also implies that the very body that Mary bore is present on the altar: Mary bore it according to its human nature, while it is touched and seen, bitten and chomped according to its bread nature. *Ego Berengarius,* revived!

Literal Eating: Regression or Advance?

Holy Eucharist, the Lord's Supper, the Holy Banquet is a ritual — among the dominical sacraments, the oft repeatable ritual. Against degenerate medieval custom, Calvin advocated frequent communion.[40] High-church Anglicans imitate monastic practice by pressing for daily observance. Objections that such eucharistic piety is psychologically abnormal or sub-standard come from many angles and bear down with different weights.

Calvin's "family dinner table" rubric undercuts any suggestion that "daily mass" piety manifests a compulsive disorder, a kind of repetition compulsion that creates a ritual to staunch a need whose primary object is inaccessible and then keeps repeating it because the substitute doesn't really satisfy. Daily dinner is not neurotic; at the animal level, it is a highly appropriate solution to a real biological need. Psycho-socially, it is not "vain repetition" either: oft repeated rituals contribute to social definition and stability, and teach individuals their appropriate roles.[41] This social function is best served if the whole family unit

40. Calvin, *Short Treatise on the Holy Supper of Our Lord Jesus Christ,* 29-32.522-525.

41. Cf. Hans-Gunther Heimbrock, "Religious Development and the Ritual Dimension," in *Stages of Faith and Religious Development: Implications for Church, Education, and Society,* ed. James W. Fowler, Karl Ernst Nipkow, and Friedrich Schweitzer (New York: Crossroad, 1991), part 4, chap. 11, pp. 192-205.

is regularly present for the occasion. But — *pace* Reformed critiques — this fact would not automatically make it psycho-socially perverse for priests to celebrate sometimes without congregations. Even if all of the children are out, there is nothing psycho-socially deficient about mom and dad proceeding to have a quiet dinner together.

All the same, ingesting another's life to satisfy hunger, biting and chomping in frustration and rage, seem to be infantile-to-toddler regressive behaviors. Insofar as the theory of impanation makes this literally possible, doesn't it erode the impetus to psycho-spiritual maturity?

My first thought is to appeal to the psychoanalytic trope and to maintain that this is a case of regression in service of advancement. Individual horror participation is no routine obstacle or medium-sized set-back. It constitutes major trauma that stalemates and/or does significant injury to the participants' abilities to make sense of their worlds. Individual horror participation is precisely the kind of case where regression is to be expected, entered into the better to be reversed.

My second thought is that *what counts as regressive depends on the persons involved in the relationship and their relative personal capacities.* Certainly, it is regressive for an adult son to demand to suck his mother's breast or to throw biting and kicking tantrums. This is because adult children are or should be near-enough peers of their parents, while such behaviors are "normal" in relation to the parent only at certain stages in which the offspring's agent capacities are vastly inferior to and dependent for their further development upon the parent's. Some psychoanalytic theories would concede, however, that in relation to spouse or lover, adult male fascination with breasts and attempts to reenter the womb through sexual intercourse constitute a healthy defense and so are not indicators of neurosis or pathology. But "acting out" such desires on dependent children would be abusive because a violation of what the offspring need from the parent in order to grow up into healthy functioning adults.

Medieval estimates of the "size-gap" between God and creatures muddy the waters of what would or would not be regressive in relation to God. Anselm says that by comparison with God the rest of what there is, is "almost nothing." Scotus argues that creatures are finite, but God is infinite being. Julian of Norwich sees that the whole created universe is no more than a hazelnut in God's hand. Cashing these comments psychologically, I take them to imply that there is almost no comparison between the cognitive and affective relationship capacities of the divine Persons and those of human persons at whatever developmental stage. This is perhaps the metaphysical ground underlying the phenomenology that prompts Benedict J. Groeschel to suggest that the most advanced stages of movement into knowledge and love of who God is, may well reverse ego development.[42]

For Julian of Norwich,[43] the "size-gap" is explicitly her reason for insisting that in relation to God we have to do a developmental double-take. On the one hand, to God we are dear lovely children, who — so far as comparative agent-competency is concerned — will never rise above infancy or at most the toddler stage. On the other hand, Julian's book is arguably addressed to spiritually mature adults who get depressed because they don't feel they are getting anywhere spiritually.[44] It is this human agency — agency as mature as it gets this side of heaven — that Julian claims has the standing of infants or toddlers in relation to divine agent competency. This means that one does not have to regress on Fowler's developmental scale to approach Mother Jesus as an infant to its mother's breast, to feed from her substance. Nor will it be necessarily regressive to bite and chomp our salvation with raging tantrums. *Whether that is so will depend on the relation between the frustrating situation and our developmental capacities to cope with them.* Horrors are, by definition, evils beyond our capacity reliably to prevent or to make good on; they stump and often wreck our meaning-making capacities. And while we adults can come up with partial reasons why God does not prevent horrors, our comprehension of the method in divine madness, or of how it fits with divine love for us, is much less than a two-year-old's grasp of why its parents have made it go through excruciating and terrifying heart-valve surgery. Biting and chomping Mother Jesus for all we're worth, and later calming to experience how she has been lovingly holding us all the while, can be cathartic and trust-restoring for some horror participants. That is why I count it pragmatically fruitful instead of pathologically regressive.

Julian also manages divine-human incommensuration by mounting multiple analogies from horizontal human-to-human relationships, since each captures as well as distorts something about who we are and how we stand in relation to God. To us Jesus is not only birth-mother and nanny, but also courtier, knight in shining armor and would-be lover, trying to woo his lady by un-

42. See Benedict J. Groeschel, *Spiritual Passages: The Psychology of Spiritual Development* (New York: Crossroad, 1984), esp. pp. 118, 185-186.

43. See *A Book of Showings to the Anchoress Julian of Norwich*, Studies and Texts #35, ed. Edmund Colledge, OSA, and James Walsh, SJ (Toronto: Pontifical Institute of Medieval Studies, 1978). For more of my developmental readings of Julian, see my article "Julian of Norwich on the Tender Loving Care of Mother Jesus," in *Our Knowledge of God*, ed. K. J. Clark (Dordrecht and Boston: Kluwer Academic Publishers, 1992), pp. 203-19.

44. So Julia Gatta suggests in her *Three Spiritual Directors for Our Time: Julian of Norwich, The Cloud of Unknowing, Walter Hilton* (Cambridge, MA: Cowley Publications, 1986).

dertaking (on the cross) the most difficult of valiant deeds. Other mystical writers — arguably, so far as we can tell, among the most spiritually advanced of human beings — favor "Mother" and "Lover" to analogize their relationship with God.[45] Why, then, should we count it regressive if the beloved who consents literally reaches out to meet his touch, to receive his kiss, to take in his life? Even Calvin can speak of the Holy Banquet as a means to personal union. Impanation makes the scene of consecration an exchange of marriage vows, of holy kiss and nuptial consummation.[46]

Moments of Truth

Even in the Middle Ages, *Ego Berengarius* was a minority report. However often Berengar was made to swear such things, philosophical theories of eucharistic presence — including that of his opponent Lanfranc — did not allow the body of Christ to be on the altar in such a way as to be bitten and chewed. Aquinas also repeats the patristic explanation that the bread and wine appearances are left to keep us from being scandalized at the prospect of cannibalizing another human being.[47] In opposing corporeal presence, the Reformed tradition turns *Ego Berengarius* to good rhetorical advantage, counting on our civilized revulsion to human sacrifice. Yet, all can agree that cross and table bring us who approach them to judgment. My question is, why are we so squeamish? Is it because *Ego Berengarius* makes the Lord's Supper an occasion of more truth than we would like to face?

There is a strand of Christian piety that wants to protect God from contamination. For Anselm in *Cur Deus Homo*, this sets up a *prima facie* presumption against incarnation — why would God sully divinity by stooping so low? — as well as a *prima facie* presumption in favor of making Christ's human nature as Godlike as possible while still preserving the characteristics (e.g., passibility and mortality) required for Christ's soteriological job. It shows up again in medieval eucharistic theology's worries about whether the really present body and blood of Christ would be vulnerable to digestion and decay. Scripture (1 Cor 11:26) explicitly commands us to observe the rite to show forth

45. See Nelson Pike, *Mystic Union: An Essay in the Phenomenology of Mysticism* (Ithaca and London: Cornell University Press, 1992).

46. Eugene Rogers, in *Sexuality and the Christian Body* (Oxford: Blackwell, 1999), goes further to characterize holy Eucharist as a death-bed marriage. He wants to argue that marriage is an ascetical discipline. The Lord's death, which the eucharistic rite shows forth, stands against casual and sentimental takes on the "happily ever after" theme.

47. Aquinas, *Summa Theologica* III, 1.75, a.5, c.

the Lord's death. But Reformed crosses are empty; catholic crucifixes are typically of ivory, brass, or silver. These several maneuvers enable us to hide from the terrifying truth that God is radically vulnerable to horrors, and so are we.

There is another strong trend in New Testament piety that builds a hedge around irreverence by encouraging us to use court flattery, to be deferential, even sycophantic with God. Energetic sensitivity to blasphemy is not always but often a reaction formation that protests too much and gives itself away with the implicit accusation that God will be furiously angry if we don't mind our prayer book etiquette. But, once again, our Lord gathers us around a *dinner* table, not only presides as host but serves himself as food. And — as Loder often quipped — *eating is a hostile act: we destroy what we eat!* Like the dialogue section of Job and the sassy psalms, *Ego Berengarius* confronts us with our violent, vindictive, and destructive emotions — with the horrifying reality that we can be angry and confused enough to tear ourselves and one another to pieces, even to kill God!

These facts are brutal and revolting. But we have to confront them to appreciate how God in Christ crucified sets us free. And so we come to another pragmatic fruit of the doctrine of impanation with *Ego Berengarius* as its corollary: by taking this theory into our practice, we "set ourselves up" to undo our denial!

3. The Way of Love: Loder, Levinas, and Ethical Transformation through Preaching

John S. McClure

In *The Transforming Moment: Understanding Convictional Experiences,* James E. Loder established the "logic" or "grammar" of transformational knowing as one of the central features of his practical theology.[1] In short, this five-part, flexible logic involves (1) a "conflict" or double-bind, (2) an "interlude for scanning," (3) a "constructive act of imagination" or "insight," (4) a "release of energy," and (5) an "interpretation" that integrates the image/insight into life and community (*Transforming Moment,* 31-38). Loder asserted that this logic is at work deeply and pervasively within the human spirit. If placed within a "four-dimensional" context that includes not only the "self" and the "world," but also the "void" and the "Holy," this logic of transformation can itself be transformed. This constitutes a "transformation of transformation" in which the void is filled by God's Spirit and the self is dramatically displaced and re-centered in relation to the Holy, and, by extension, to itself and the world. This, he contends, is nothing short of the grammar of the *Spiritus Creator* at work in the world transforming all things in and through Jesus Christ (114-116).

At the end of *The Transforming Moment,* Loder asks "*why* this [transformation of transformation] is to take place." "The answer," he says, is "for love's sake" (179). He goes on to articulate what is fundamentally a hypothesis about the original ontological position of the self in relation to the other:

> deeper than consciousness, is the longing to give love, and the willingness to give it sacrificially. . . . [Sacrificial love] is a matter of drawing the other

1. *The Transforming Moment: Understanding Convictional Experiences* (San Francisco: Harper & Row, 1981), pp. 17, 31-45, 52-60, 114-123, 128-152, 157-159. Page references will be given parenthetically in the text. This logic is not strictly linear in nature. It can be entered at any point and tends to complete itself.

> one into the Presence of God. . . . To re-present the Presence of God is after all the point of witnessing (*martureo,* "to witness"). . . . This hypothesis regarding the primal need to give love is only the summary of a position, but its thrust should be clear. The way of love is deeply and enduringly rooted in our nature, but it must inevitably live in an ego-oriented social order that either denies those roots or else subordinates them to incidental expressions in and around the supposed "real business of life"; namely, ego survival and satisfaction. (182, 184)

Although *The Transforming Moment* is subsumed with questions regarding the *what* of transformation (convictional experiences) and the *how* of transformation (its logic or "grammar"), Loder could have started with the *why* of transformation, the "way of love,"[2] and worked toward the *what* and *how,* and arrived at similar places.[3] Loder himself was in favor of this kind of reversibility in practical theological method. We might begin, then, with the hypothesis that "deeper than consciousness is a primal longing to give love and to give it sacrificially." From that vantage point, we can observe that the *how* of the grammar of transformation and the *what* of convictional experiences are actually de-centerings of certain defensive ego-mechanisms that are destroying our ability to give love. These de-centerings open up a space in which this original, ontological longing to "give love" can flourish.[4]

Loder, in *The Transforming Moment,* assumed an existentialist-developmentalist framework for his exploration of transformation in relation to practical theology. This logic of transformation, however, has many potential applications. Daniel Schipani, for instance, places transformation within the historical process of education for liberation in *Conscientization and Creativ-*

2. According to Loder, "It would be fruitful and interesting to pursue the ethics of love as a duty to love the other one as the self has been loved, namely, with a four-dimensional transforming affirmation of human particularity" (*Transforming Moment,* p. 186). By "duty," Loder does not mean "conscience," but the kind of duty suggested by Kierkegaard when speaking of "works of love." He goes on to say that "to continue to love as one has been loved is the only way to abide in the transformation effected by (God's) Spirit."

3. This question of "why" is precisely where Loder starts his book *The Logic of the Spirit,* with what he calls a "theology of human existence." See James E. Loder, *The Logic of the Spirit: Human Development in Theological Perspective* (San Francisco: Jossey-Bass Publishers, 1998).

4. Clearly much of Loder's interest in such de-centerings derives from his keen interest in Kierkegaard. Much of Kierkegaard's concern to move from the esthetic and ethical forms of existence to the religious, and in particular to "religiousness B" is at the heart of Loder's work. One might say that, for Kierkegaard, only the negation (despair) and negation of negation by the paradox of faith at the heart of religiousness B can deal with the guilt of infinite responsibility so that love becomes a possibility. See *Either/Or 1: Kierkegaard's Writings,* Volume 3, ed. Edna Hong (Princeton: Princeton University Press, 1988).

ity.[5] Here, I want to take Loder's transformational logic to its intersections with ethics and with homiletics, to demonstrate its power and usefulness within yet another framework. I hope to show that this logic in its four-dimensional capacity can help homileticians as practical theologians make better sense of another "transforming moment," the moment when preaching begins to move both preacher and hearers onto the holy ground of love.

In particular, I will show how the writings of Walter Brueggemann and Rebecca Chopp, relying on the work of the Jewish philosopher of testimony, Emmanuel Levinas, have led ethical reflection on preaching to the point where this move toward love comes into view. I will demonstrate how the idea of "negation" within Loder's four-dimensional transformation can help to illumine, within a distinctively Christian perspective, the "extradition" of the ego toward the "other" in Levinas's writings on testimony, in a way that can strengthen the Christian act of preaching to empower love. It should be understood that "negation" within the logic of transformation is not the annihilation of the ego, but the negation of certain malignant survival tactics of the ego.[6] Both Loder and Levinas encourage a final move toward the other, what Loder calls the "way of love," or what Levinas calls "welcome."[7] I will argue that this move involves a

5. Schipani, *Conscientization and Creativity* (Lanham, MD: University Press of America, 1984).

6. These potentially love-constricting survival tactics are particular to each human subject and should not be generalized along lines defined by gender, class, race, or culture. For instance, negation should not be confused with an abusive annihilation of the self motivated by fear, avoidance of self (Plaskow's "hiding"), or loss of self (the self that goes nowhere, rather than toward neighbor). See Judith Plaskow, *Sex, Sin and Grace: Women's Experience and the Theologies of Reinhold Niebuhr and Paul Tillich* (New York: University Press of America, 1980). For an excellent reassessment of the kenosis of Christ see Mary M. Solberg, *Compelling Knowledge: A Feminist Proposal for an Epistemology of the Cross* (Albany, New York: SUNY Press, 1997). See also Sally B. Purvis, *The Power of the Cross: Foundations for a Christian Feminist Ethic of Community* (Nashville: Abingdon Press, 1993), and Sally H. Brown, *Preaching Ethics Reconsidered: The Social Construction of Christian Moral Reasoning and the Reimagining of Power in Preaching According to the Cross* (Ph.D. dissertation, Princeton Theological Seminary, April, 2001), pp. 200-224.

7. According to Levinas, "to possess the idea of infinity is to have already welcomed the other" (*Totality and Infinity: An Essay on Exteriority,* trans. Alphonso Lingis [Pittsburgh: Duquesne University Press, 1969], p. 93). Welcome is a pervasive theme in *Totality and Infinity* and, as Derrida so aptly comments, "operates, everywhere . . . in order to speak of the first gesture in the direction of the Other." See *Adieu: To Emmanuel Levinas,* trans. Pascale-Anne Brault and Michael Naas (Stanford: Stanford University Press, 1999), p. 25. Levinas reserves the word "love" primarily for his treatment of *erōs.* According to Levinas, *erōs* is originary of welcome. It is, however, ultimately subsumed by the concern for justice introduced by the "entry of the third party," i.e., once the intimacy of the welcome of the single face is interrupted by the welcome of an infinity of others. Levinas's idea of welcome, I would contend, bears significant resemblances

transformation of the esthetic and ethical transformations that exist in the dynamic relationship between core-testimony and countertestimony in preaching. When this final transformation occurs, testimony bears witness to its own "erasure" or "crossing-through"[8] and preachers can move beyond a theological and ethical re-scripting of reality, and onto the far-ground of love.

Preaching as Rhetorical-Esthetic Re-scripting

Recently, several theologians, biblical scholars and homileticians have been influenced by Emmanuel Levinas's ethical phenomenology of testimony, as attenuated by Paul Ricoeur.[9] These scholars have begun to appeal broadly for an ethical homiletic in which something like Loder's logic of transformation is at work. At the center of this interest in preaching as testimony is the work of Walter Brueggemann. In Brueggemann's writings about preaching, the logic of transformation resembles, to a great extent, a combination of what Loder calls "esthetic knowing" and "therapeutic knowing." According to Loder,

> esthetic knowing waits on and celebrates the imaginative turning point in the transformational knowing event. It is not information or idea, but the intuition or image and its symbolic expression that the artist (of whatever sort) cares for and wants to make known.[10]

Esthetic knowing yields a transformational logic that is rooted in imagination and bonded to the *constructive act of imagination* and *release of energy* that characterize steps 3 and 4 of Loder's transformational logic.

---

to the Christian articulation of *agapē*. For more on the "third party" see Emmanuel Levinas, *Otherwise than Being or Beyond Essence*, trans. Alphonso Lingis (The Hague: Martinus Nijhoff Publishers, 1981), pp. 157-162.

8. The idea of *sous rature*, in which a term goes "under erasure," is actually Jacques Derrida's terminology, and is fundamental to his idea of deconstruction. Derrida often *crosses through* words while leaving them legible in order to show that words are inadequate, indeed their meaning is undecidable (filled with traces of other signs), and yet they are necessary as markers, as traces of what they fail to signify. As I will show later, this term is useful because of its unity of a negation (the crossing through/out/over of a sign) and a negation of that negation (the trace of an "other" sign).

9. The primary essay by Ricoeur on Levinas, shared by both Rebecca Chopp and Walter Brueggemann, is "The Hermeneutics of Testimony," in *Essays on Biblical Interpretation*, ed. Lewis S. Mudge (Philadelphia: Fortress Press, 1980), pp. 119-54. See also Thomas G. Long, *The Witness of Preaching* (Louisville: Westminster John Knox Press, 1989); John S. McClure, *Otherwise Preaching: A Postmodern Ethic for Homiletics* (St. Louis: Chalice Press, 2001).

10. *Transforming Moment*, p. 44.

In *Cadences of Home: Preaching among Exiles,*[11] Brueggemann contends that

> the Bible should be understood as a set of models (paradigms) of reality made up of images situated in and contextualized by narratives. . . . I think it a major gain to see that the Bible in its several models is an artistic, rhetorical proposal of reality that seeks to persuade (convert) to an alternative sense of God, world, neighbor, and self. (12)
>
> Human transformation [happens] through the playful entertainment of another scripting of reality that may subvert the old given text and its interpretation and lead to an embrace of an alternative text and its re-description of reality. (29)
>
> The work of preaching is an act of imagination, that is, an offer of an image through which perception, experience, and finally faith can be re-organized in alternative ways. (32)
>
> I would paraphrase Ricoeur to say that "the image gives rise to a new world of possibility." (33)

In *Texts Under Negotiation,* as well as *Cadences of Home,* Brueggemann argues for the therapeutic "analogue of psychotherapy" for his biblical-homiletical model.[12] Transformation is a matter of "conversion" or "switching worlds" (*Cadences of Home,* 35). The preacher offers a biblical *"counter-script"* that "invites to a *counter-context* that over time may authorize and empower *counter-life*" (36). Preachers invite their hearers into a new "evangelical infrastructure" that "mediates and valorizes a viable world outside that given, privileged advantage of certitude and domination" (36). In a similar way, Loder acknowledges that one of "the most important aspects of esthetic knowing [is] its power to break the numbing spell of 'everydayness,' . . . to break with the tyranny of the obvious and compose some aspect of the world in its (the spirit's) own terms."[13]

11. Walter Brueggemann, *Cadences of Home: Preaching among Exiles* (Louisville: Westminster John Knox Press, 1997). Page references are given parenthetically in the text.

12. *Cadences of Home,* p. 35. See also *Texts Under Negotiation: The Bible and Postmodern Imagination* (Minneapolis: Fortress Press, 1993), p. 21.

13. *Transforming Moment,* pp. 51-52.

Testimony and the Logic of Ethical Transformation

In *Theology of the Old Testament: Testimony, Dispute, Advocacy,* Brueggemann places this esthetic idea of preaching as imaginative re-scripting within the larger context of Israel's practice of testimony. It is here that the work of Emmanuel Levinas, as reshaped by Paul Ricoeur, has "much informed" Brueggemann's thought. For Brueggemann, testimony yields a forensic-fiduciary form of knowledge. The "proper setting for testimony is a court of law in which various and diverse witnesses are called to 'tell what happened,' to give their version of what is true."[14] He goes on to note three qualities of this testimony.

> First, the witness is able to choose the construal to be uttered. . . . Second, when the witness utters testimony, the testimony is a public presentation that shapes, enjoins, or constitutes reality. . . . Third, when the court makes a decision and agrees to accept some version of reality based on some testimony, the testimony is accepted as true — that is, it becomes true. In the decision, by the process of the verdict, the testimony is turned into reality . . . we may say that testimony *becomes revelation.* (121; italics added)

In some respects, this way of knowing resembles Aristotelian *phronēsis* or practical, rhetorical reasoning. The context for speech is *enthymematic.* In other words, the preacher and Sunday morning hearers start from some sort of "tacit consensus" (accumulated body of verdicts) that is conceded in advance in order that the search for knowledge not degenerate into what philosopher of rhetoric P. Christopher Smith calls "an interminable digging for grounds, for the grounds, for the grounds, *ad infinitum,* in which the bottom would drop out."[15] This non-foundational, forensic-fiduciary and rhetorical form of epistemology cannot proceed unless there is some measure of community (the court) to begin with, in which participants have "always already tacitly agreed to agree about some things,"[16] and in which certain things are credited to be true. According to Smith, rather than working from a *logos apophantikon* or "declarative statement of necessary fact," this type of testimonial speech works "from *endoxa* or received opinions" and then reasons "to *doxa* or new opinions."[17]

14. *Theology of the Old Testament: Testimony, Dispute, Advocacy* (Minneapolis: Augsburg Fortress Press, 1997), p. 120. Page references will be given parenthetically in the text.

15. P. Christopher Smith, *The Hermeneutics of Original Argument: Demonstration, Dialectic, Rhetoric* (Evanston, IL: Northwestern University Press), p. 53.

16. Smith, *The Hermeneutics of Original Argument,* p. 53.

17. Smith, *The Hermeneutics of Original Argument,* p. 25.

In a similar way, Brueggemann argues that "core testimony" can never be allowed to become a "final testimony" (*Theology of the Old Testament,* 318). The "verdict" that "becomes revelation" is always subject to further "cross-examination." At this point, we can see the logic of esthetic transformation begin to work backward, or forward, in Loder's model, from the constructive act of imagination in the logic of transformation toward ever-new "conflicts" and processes of "scanning." According to Brueggemann, "Israel's faith is a probing, questioning, insisting, disjunctive faith" (318). Its testimony is always met and reopened by "countertestimony," by new "cross-examinations." Midrash arises and begins to "expose what is hidden" (325). Psychoanalysis discovers "incongruity between what is said and what is hidden and signaled." Holocaust inserts an "unanswerable disruption" into the courtroom (327). Deconstruction requires "that all false starts on the part of YHVH be problematized, critiqued, and subverted" (331).[18]

This rhythm between "core testimony" and "countertestimony" directly parallels Loder's "esthetic transformation" and the dynamic interaction between image/release/interpretation (e.g., core testimony) and conflict/scanning (e.g., countertestimony). One can begin to hear Loder wondering, however, if there might not be another form of transformation in, under, and around this dialectic of scripting and re-scripting, one initiated by the Holy Spirit, that seeks to transform all of these transformations of the human spirit wrought within the rhythms of core testimony and countertestimony. Loder would affirm, with Brueggemann, that creative redescription of reality lies at the heart of the human spirit's constitutive meaning-making capacities as outlined in the developmental literature. He criticized these meaning-making capacities, however, as, in the last analysis, inadequate from a *theological* point of view. A transformation of these redescriptive, re-scripting transformations is required if they are to become a part of the Spirit's transformation of all things.

18. Brueggemann moves on to articulate two other forms of testimony: "unsolicited testimony" and "embodied testimony." Both of these are, in my opinion, supplements to the primary rhythms of esthetic transformation found in core testimony and countertestimony. Unsolicited testimony plays primarily a further interpretative and integrative role (similar to #5 in Loder's transformational logic), so that testimonies are found to be in the largest possible nexus of congruity. Embodied testimony investigates various "mediators" of testimonial re-scriptings of reality: the Torah, kings, prophets, cultic leaders, and sages (a shoring up of #3 in Loder's transformational logic). See especially Loder's use of Lévi-Strauss's formula for the mythic mind in which the qualities of mediation within transformational logic have a lot to do with whether or not a significant "gain" is established "over the original negated state or condition." He goes on to assert that: "Double negation, as accomplished by a mediator, establishes a new state of being that includes the first negation as an essential element of the gain." *The Transforming Moment,* pp. 163, 186 n. 1.

We must ask, however, why, *from an ethical perspective,* this "transformation of transformation" by God's Spirit is necessary. Why is it *ethically* inadequate to ride the dialectic of core testimony–countertestimony further and further into the evangelical infrastructure of biblical re-scripting? In other words, why is constantly revised esthetic "world-switching" not enough for the development of a theological ethic for preaching?

Testimony and Co-optation of the Other

Jacques Derrida, in *Religion,* argues that there is something in the forensic-fiduciary nature of testimonial epistemology that ultimately works to keep both the self and the community from "the other." According to Derrida, the core testimony–countertestimony transformational spiral mirrors the way in which the other is subtly co-opted by hegemonic speech.

> There is no opposition fundamentally between "social bond" and "social unraveling." A certain interruptive unraveling is the condition of the "social bond," the very respiration of all "community." This is not even the knot of a reciprocal condition, but rather the possibility that every knot can come undone, be cut or interrupted. This is where the *socius* or the relation to the other would disclose itself to be the secret of testimonial experience — and hence of a certain faith.[19]

Derrida goes on to argue that without a final deconstruction a dangerous binary continues to exist. This binary exists between what Levinas calls the "same"[20] (social bond, core testimony, revelation-as-verdict) and the "other" (social unraveling, countertestimony, conflict).

According to Derrida, this binary can "auto-immunely"[21] self-create the community of faith and what it believes is true. By auto-immune, Derrida seems to mean that the truth and value of testimonial faith is decided within the court or "community" created by an *automatic* "respiration" between "social bond" ("the same," core testimony) and "social unraveling" ("the other," countertestimony). This makes testimony itself increasingly *immune* from any real encounter with the other beyond what is "imagined" or "scripted" as testimony-countertestimony.

19. Jacques Derrida and Gianni Vattimo, eds., *Religion* (Stanford, California: Stanford University Press, 1996), p. 64.

20. For more on the "same" and "other" see Levinas, *Totality and Infinity,* especially pp. 33 and 113. According to Levinas, ethics is the calling into question of "the same."

21. *Religion,* p. 66.

Beyond the epistemological issues raised by this "auto-immune" binary logic lies the ethical issue of the co-optation of the "other" within *speech*. Another way to say this is that to stand *against* or *in contradistinction to* hegemonic discourse *within* that discourse, or within its logic of self-perpetuation, is merely to prop up that discourse as its "other." In short, the "same" (core testimony) requires the "other" (countertestimony) in order to be the same, thus co-opting the other in service to its own purposes. This has the effect, paradoxically, of keeping those within the circle of testimonial faith (safe) from (real) other(s) and otherness.[22]

To return to Loder's categories, this binary logic, although mirroring the transformational "logic of the Spirit" formally, must be opened up or transformed *so that giving oneself to the other (the "way of love") is truly possible.* For Loder, this opening occurs through convictional knowing, "the patterned process by which the Holy Spirit transforms all transformations of the human spirit."[23] This, it seems to me, points the preacher toward yet another form of testimony beyond countertestimony, what I, for lack of a better term, and with deference to Derrida and to Levinas, will call "erasure-testimony."[24]

This could, of course, simply be deconstructive one-up-man-ship. After all, hasn't Brueggeman already included this final deconstruction in his view of countertestimony? Looking carefully at the work of Levinas, from which this idea is in part taken, we will have to say "no." In order to better understand this "erasure testimony" and its correlation and contrasts with Loder's "transformation of transformation" it is important to revisit the work of Levinas — especially as it pertains to what he calls "proximity," or "the one-for-the-other."[25]

22. Beyond this, according to Derrida, the *fiduciary* aspects of this process, through which countertestimony is "credited" as true, becomes, in fact, an important aspect of the logic at the heart of Western-capitalist societies. According to Derrida, in the techno-capitalist society bequeathed to us by this kind of reasoning, the hegemony + supplement (One + n) dialectic "makes violence of itself, does violence to itself, and *keeps itself from the other*" (italics added). According to the aesthetic philosopher Jean-Luc Nancy, this kind of testimonial scripting and rescripting operates freely in Western society. In its more extreme forms it becomes what a late-Marxist would call the "spectacular market society" or "society of the spectacle" (for us, worship and preaching as spectacle). In this situation, alienation has reached so serious a level that people are contented by "an imaginary appropriation of real appropriation." In other words, a testimonial imagining and reimagining of love (fetishism, sentiment, or even "solidarity") substitutes for love itself. See *Being Singular Plural* (Stanford: Stanford University Press, 2000), p. 49.

23. *Transforming Moment,* p. 92.

24. See footnote 8 for a definition of erasure.

25. See especially chap. III of *Otherwise than Being.* In short, proximity is "the signification of the sensible" which "does not belong to the movement of cognition" (63).

Emmanuel Levinas and Testimonial Erasure

Emmanuel Levinas, a Lithuanian Jew who lived and wrote in France, was consumed by a sense of the priority of the human other as a site for the revelation of the Holy Other, though he never ventured to articulate a theology. Exegetically, Levinas saw in the sixth commandment, "Thou shalt not kill," the proto-theological status of ethical obligation to the human other. For Levinas, "Thou shalt not kill" is the ultimate command against "making same" that which is "other," or making a "totality" out of that which is "infinite."[26] In some ways, this business of taking what is other and "making same" is similar to the work of what Loder calls the "enemies" of love. For Loder, the enemies to giving love are "fear of absorption" and "fear of abandonment." Both of these fears lead to the ego's postulation of defense mechanisms that can result in either the devouring or objectivizing (killing) of others.[27]

These ideas, "totality" and "infinity": the "same" and the "other," are the two overarching ideas that organize Levinas's ethical thought. For Levinas, totality stands for any comprehensive system or structure, including ideologies, theories, explanations, systems of justice, political or legal systems, and philosophies. These totalities are required in order to organize and order human life. Like Loder's ego defenses, they function for survival, but they are ultimately false, because they tend to "make same" that which is infinitely and mysteriously "other."

According to Levinas, the falseness of totality is exposed in face-to-face encounter during which the "glory" of infinite otherness interrupts our attempts to cling to sameness. This rupture of sameness both interrupts my conceptual schemes and introduces a profound ethical obligation into my experience. *In* the eyes of the other, my sameness is ruptured. *Through* the eyes of the other, I become aware of the other's others, and their other's others, and so on.[28] A veritable infinity of obligation confronts me. Levinas calls this the "entry of the third party,"[29] the entry of another other, infinite responsibility. Once this rupture has occurred, I cannot help but realize that, at bottom, all of my totalizing systems (of distributive justice, for example) are partial, and in many

26. See *Totality and Infinity,* pp. 198, 232-237.

27. *Transforming Moment,* pp. 179-182.

28. Paraphrased from O. E. Ajzenstat, "Beyond Totality: The Shoah and the Biblical Ethics of Emmanuel Levinas," in *Strange Fire: Reading the Bible after the Holocaust,* ed. Tod Linafelt (Sheffield: Sheffield Academic Press, 2000), p. 109. Much of the language and shape of this summary is taken from Ajzenstat's excellent essay. See Levinas, *Otherwise than Being,* p. 157.

29. For a summary of Levinas's ideas on the "entry of the third party" see *Otherwise than Being,* pp. 157-162.

respects unjust. In other words, all forms of totalizing ethics are ultimately interrupted and broken across the ethics of infinity.

Although James Loder operates more from developmental premises, for him also, it is primarily the "entry of the third," that is, "the face," that is given proto-theological status. For Loder, the parental face at the crib becomes the organizing center for the child's personality. "In the face-to-face interaction (whether actualized or remaining an innate potential), the child seeks *a cosmic-ordering, self-confirming impact from the presence of a loving other*." He goes on to say that "the primal experience of the face as actual presence and in its significance as symbolic expression provides a prototype for the convicting presence of God."[30] At the end of *The Transforming Moment,* when speaking about ethics or the "way of love," Loder turns this around. He focuses on the child's response to the mother's face as "a unique gift to the mother . . . the gift of sacrificial love, because it calls forth from the mother the repressed longing in her for the face that will not go away."[31]

The developmentalist Loder finds a crisis of abandonment and a longing for a stable face that will not go away at the center of this primal experience of human proximity. The ethicist Levinas discovers something else. For Levinas, in this primal proximity to the other, the crisis is not one of abandonment, but of *infinite obligation,* of response-ability, and ultimately, therefore, of justice *(tsādaq).* For Levinas, the gift offered in the sacrificial love represented in the face of the other is not that it calls forth a repressed longing for a face that will not go away, but that it calls forth an awareness of what he calls "the glory of the Infinite" that has been obscured by the rush toward totality. It is the real openness to the other and to all others that the totality of strategies for closure and system imposed by human consciousness and a survival-bent ego represses, or in fact destroys. One might go so far as to say that, for Levinas, the face that will not go away is made up of an infinity of human faces that prototypically represent God who is not an eternal presence, but is always and in every way "Otherwise than Being."[32]

30. *The Transforming Moment,* p. 167.

31. *The Transforming Moment,* p. 182. Loder's use of the mother's face as primary parallels Levinas's idea of the "feminine." According to Levinas, "before every inhabitant, the welcoming one par excellence, welcoming in itself — the feminine being." *Totality and Infinity,* p. 89. This welcome, however, is both subsumed and exceeded by the entry of the "third." For a summary of several important feminist critiques of this idea in Levinas's work, see Stella Sandford, "Levinas, Feminism and the Feminine," in *The Cambridge Companion to Levinas* (London: Cambridge University Press, 2002).

32. According to Levinas: "If transcendence has meaning, it can only signify the fact that the *event of being,* the *esse,* the *essence,* passes over to what is other than being. . . . Transcendence is passing over to being's other, otherwise than being." *Otherwise than Being,* p. 3.

At this point, the parallels with Loder's existentialist "four-dimensional transformation" begin to become striking. For Loder the crisis of abandonment opens an abyss-as-*absolute existential separation* (the void) that is transformed by being filled to overflowing by the Holy Spirit. For Levinas a crisis of justice opens up an abyss-as-*infinite ethical obligation* that is filled with "traces" of the glory of the Infinite.[33] Encountering this Spirit (for Loder) or this trace of the glory of the Infinite (for Levinas), is a matter of erasure, or what Loder calls "double negation" for the ego and all of its transformations, whether esthetic, therapeutic, or otherwise.[34] For Levinas, this glory makes it possible for the ego to move into full proximity to the other. In his own terms, the ego is "extradited," moving behind the "said" (core testimony and counter-testimony) and onto the ground of "saying," the realm of "exposure" and "proximity" to the other.

This proxemic "saying" *is communication,* but by this Levinas does not mean the "will or intention to make this thought pass into another ego."[35] This "saying" is, as Levinas puts it, "a signifyingness dealt the other prior to all objectivication. It does not consist in giving signs." Levinas calls this "exposure to another . . . the risky uncovering of oneself, in sincerity, the breaking up of inwardness and abandon of all shelter, exposure to traumas, vulnerability."[36] This kind of "erasure-testimony" can occur only as the ego's efforts to "make same" are radically displaced and re-oriented by and toward the glory of the Infinite. The four-dimensional transformation at the heart of this is that the subject of "saying" discovers that he or she is not simply a giver of signs (re-scripter of reality), but indeed "becomes a sign, turns into an allegiance."[37] For Levinas, this is the deepest meaning of the word testimony or witness *(martureō).* The glory of the Infinite brings about an erasure of the "said," and the witness becomes an "allegiance" or indeed a "substitution" for another, grasped fully by the glory of the "Otherwise-than-Being."[38]

This transition from signification to allegiance is directly parallel to the

33. According to Levinas, the trace is "the signification of the Infinite in responsibility." *Otherwise than Being,* 161-162.

34. *The Transforming Moment,* p. 163.

35. *Otherwise than Being,* p. 48. This spirit-to-spirit communication (love) is precisely where the trace of what Loder calls "Spirit-to-spirit" communication comes onto the scene, though this trace is beyond representation. See James E. Loder, *The Logic of the Spirit: Human Development in Theological Perspective,* p. 11.

36. *Otherwise than Being,* p. 48.

37. *Otherwise than Being,* p. 49.

38. *Otherwise than Being,* p. 11. This sense of being grasped is, for Levinas, an "ordination" in which "I am ordered toward the face of the other." The "trace" or "glory" of that which "orders" me "lights up in the face of a neighbor" (11-12). Subsequent page references are given parenthetically in the text.

movement of the self, in Loder's thought, beyond the "self as conscience" to the "self as spirit." This he relates to Kierkegaard's idea that the self must become "transparently grounded in the Power that posits it."[39] In the glossary to the second edition of *The Transforming Moment,* Loder offers this definition of "transparency":

> In Kierkegaardian literature, [transparency is] a direct knowledge of God without intervening persons, images, or symbols. Although Kierkegaard was not a mystic, his understanding was that if the self was to be free of despair it had to be transparently grounded in the Spiritual Presence of Christ. Although sometimes equated with love, this transparency must also be understood as basic to the whole range of Christian experience, including faith and hope. [referring to *Sickness Unto Death*][40]

We can begin to see that, at the far ground of testimony, the esthetic transformations wrought by the "self as conscience" and perhaps even human imagination itself are transformed, as the "said" (core testimony and countertestimony in court) is erased in its "saying" (proximity to the glory of the Infinite in the face of the other). Within this aspect of proclamation, the preacher releases his/her thematizing and imagining control, uncovers oneself and becomes "exposed" to the other. This is possible because the preacher is now (transparently) oriented by and toward a glory that exists beyond or behind our ability to represent or "script" reality. Glory, Levinas says, is "prior to the *logos*" and "breaks up themes." According to Levinas, glory gives itself only in the "extraditing of the subject that rests on itself" (144). This "torn up" subject, the subject torn loose from totalizing efforts (Levinas) or from malignant survival tactics born of abandonment fears (Loder), emerges into the prior reality of the "one-for-the-other" (144). This subject then becomes a "*witness* of the infinite" as the "I" presents itself to the other: "Here I am" *(me voici)* (144-145).

> The ego stripped . . . of its scornful and imperialist subjectivity, is reduced to the "here I am," in a transparency without opaqueness, without heavy zones propitious for evasion. "Here I am" as a witness of the Infinite, but a witness that does not thematize what it bears witness of, and whose truth is not the truth of representation, is not evidence. (146-147)

The preacher as a "witness of the Infinite," "reduced to the 'here I am'" in preaching, testifies to an erasure or "negation of negation." This erasure is the

39. *Transforming Moment,* pp. 77-78.

40. *Transforming Moment,* 2nd ed. (Colorado Springs: Helmers and Howard, 1989), p. 229.

negation of the co-optation of the other that is at work subtly within the esthetic core testimony–countertestimony relationship. Erasure-testimony, then, signals a profound ethical release into the presence of the other. Through this erasure-testimony preaching becomes a passive and passionate act of *signing* that reveals an unknowable, but signifying infinity (of welcome/love). By moving back onto the (abysmal) ground of the glory of the Infinite, of proximity, something dangerous in the *said* is erased, or *crossed-through* in its *saying* (witness, *martureō).* Something, perhaps everything in the homiletic theme, image, or narrative, is erased, not merely rhetorically countered or re-framed, by moving onto the ground of its "other."

The Word as Perfectly Open Sign

It is now time to see if it is possible to extend this double negation at the heart of testimonial communication toward a deepened understanding of Christ as the Word of God for preaching. It is here that Rebecca Chopp's theology of Jesus Christ as the Word of God becomes a serious conversation partner. For Chopp, the Word that Christians proclaim is a "perfectly open sign."[41] In *The Power to Speak: Feminism, Language, God,* Chopp also makes use of Ricoeur's reinterpretation of Levinas's idea of testimony. Similar to Brueggemann's interaction between core testimony and countertestimony, Chopp acknowledges the same relationship between what she calls testimony as "words" and testimony as "life." She calls testimony as life "confession." Confession has a countertestimonial quality that moves it closer to Levinas's "saying." She calls it "the confession of faith of the testifier . . . the confession . . . of one's life, even the acceptance of suffering and death, martyrdom, for the testimony." Testimony as life (confession) resists closure and deconstructs testimony as narration, in order to keep testimony open and renewable. She shows how, in the relationship between life and words, "words open up life, life opens up words, but always in relation to the visions produced by the relation between narration and confession" (61).

In the last analysis, however, Chopp remains unsettled about the relationship between the Word as perfectly open sign and this interaction between nar-

41. Rebecca S. Chopp, *The Power to Speak: Feminism, Language, God* (New York: Crossroad, 1991), pp. 30-47. Subsequent page references are given parenthetically in the text. This Word is "the Word of creation and transformation" (30). It "is the sign of all signs, connected, embodied, open, multivalent, all the things as sign can most perfectly be, but the Word/God is this in the perfection of all perfection and thus, in full openness, creativity and gracefulness creates, sustains, and redeems all words in their ongoing process of signification" (31-32).

ration and confession within testimony. On the one hand, she asserts that "the Word as perfectly open sign is testified to in the very act of testimony itself, for in prophetic testimony the open play of confession and narration are productive of aesthetic visions of human flourishing" (61-62). In other words there seems to be something in the logic of transformation that occurs between narration and confession (cf. Brueggemann's core testimony and counter-testimony) that at least brings the Word as perfectly open sign into view. For Chopp, it is as if the logic of aesthetic transformation, which she calls "abductive logic," actually "suggests" that the Word as perfectly open sign "may be" available, or indeed, actively at work (38).

On the other hand, she asserts that we must be cautious about too closely identifying the Word as perfectly open sign with this aesthetic process. Neither the core testimony (narration), nor the life of the witness (confession), nor the courtroom of listeners who sit in judgment, nor any rhythm between these things, should be grounds for assuming any closure on this Word itself. It is impermissible, therefore, to say that these aesthetic, rhetorical, and forensic-fiduciary testimonies *become revelation* in any but the most tentative sense. She concludes that:

> testimony is a rhetorical act, an act that moves to judgment. If on one side of proclamation we have testimony, in which the proclaimer's life is sealed to her testimony of freedom, on the other side we have those who hear, who must in turn receive the truth and power of both testimony and proclamation. *But at the end of this passage the power and truth of even our testimony in proclamation cannot and will not close the openness of the Word of God.* (62; italics added)

For Chopp, therefore, there seems to be a still more radical "openness" to the other that takes place in the process of ethical transformation and redemptive speech. This opening to others is accomplished when our lives, which are already "sealed to these narrated and confessed desires of freedom," are, at the same time, sealed to a still more radically other-directed sign, the Word that Jesus incarnates, whereby "all may be questioned, rejected, or crucified, precisely when the meaning is grasped" (66).

Chopp, it seems, is mindful that the Word as perfectly open sign requires that all of our dialectics of transformation, even emancipatory transformation, must be erased — in her language, "crucified" (i.e., torn up) by the Word, by its perfect openness. This is done to ensure that our testimony does not *keep us from others.* Once again, a "transformation of transformation," to use Loder's language, is required, in order to make sure that neither our confession (testimony as life) nor our proclamation (testimony as words) nor their richly textured relationship ultimately keeps us from the other — and thus keeps us from love.

Erasure Testimony and the Transformation of Ethical Transformation

We are now at a point where we can inquire whether, in proclamation, Levinas's "glory of the Infinite," Chopp's "Word as perfectly open sign," and Loder's "cruciform Holy Spirit" might have anything in common. In all three instances, we can identify a permutational union of (1) *negation* and (2) *negation of negation.* The *negation* is represented by the *infinity,* the perfect *openness,* and by the *cruciform* Spirit of Jesus Christ, who in Loder's terms "has plunged into the abyss."[42] In all instances, nothing short of a negating ethical and existential *erasure* or crossing-through/out/over, is adequate to open up the ground of love — to lead one beyond the wily defense tactics of the ego and of hegemonic speech.

The *negation of negation* is indicated by the *glory* of the Infinite, the *perfection* of the openness of the Word/sign, and the *holiness* of the Spirit that fills the void. At the heart of erasure, within the abysmal "letting go" of infinity, openness, and the void there is encountered the glorious *trace* (glory, perfection, holiness) of God who is Otherwise than Being.[43] The transformation of ethical transformation, therefore, is a permutational logic that requires a co-mixture of an extreme negation of "totality," "closure" and "ego-defenses" *and* a negation of that negation by the glory of the Infinite, perfect freedom, or the filling by the Holy Spirit. In short, four-dimensional ethical transformation in proclamation involves a union of *erasure-as-negation* and *erasure-as-trace* (negation and negation of negation) in which speech, and perhaps even the human semiotic function itself, are transformed, *at the very moment that preaching moves onto the far ground of love.*

42. *Transforming Moment,* p. 122.

43. Erasure as trace or erasure-trace signifies that this trace is not of some ontological Being-as-God, but of God who is ultimately untraceable — so erasure and trace are reflexive as well as co-extensive. The erasure is necessary because, as Levinas puts it, the trace is "the subversion of essence into substitution. . . . Its distance from a theme, its reclusion, its holiness, is not its way to effect its being (since its past is anachronous and anarchic, leaving *a trace which is not the trace of any presence*), but is its glory, quite different from being and knowing. It makes the Word God be pronounced, without letting 'divinity' be said" (italics mine). *Otherwise than Being,* pp. 161-162. Levinas locates this trace in the glory of God that "passes by" in Exodus 33. See *Collected Philosophical Papers,* trans. Alphonso Lingis (Dordrecht, The Netherlands: Martinus Nijhoff, 1987), pp. 106-107.

Loder speaks of this in developmental terms as the self that begins to "let flourish."[44] According to Loder,

> The self is itself when it expresses the nature of being-itself as that which "lets be" or "lets flourish." The self is grounded in the power that posits it when it lets the being of others flourish. In less abstract terminology, the self is truly itself in *the ongoing act of giving love.*[45]

The "self as conscience" *crosses through* (erases) its ethical re-scripting of reality and becomes "truly itself" in the act of giving love. The "way of love," therefore, erases and re-posits both the malignant defenses of the self, and the self's entire mode of "signifying" or scripting reality. In Loder's words, "the self *composes* the 'world' in a new way. 'Thou' is transformed from threat to privilege or gift, and the self becomes a 'thou' even where there is no 'I' responding."[46]

Preaching and the Way of Love

How can preachers discover, share in, and learn to express this "way of love"? This question, asked and answered in a variety of ways, seems to be occupying the thinking of several homileticians in this generation.[47] In each instance, as homileticians attempt to answer this question, preaching is embedded within some form of mutual speaking-listening, face-to-face interaction (proximity) with others.

Some of these homileticians encourage preachers to make more pronounced efforts to listen to persons with marginalized experiences. This is seen as one way to begin to move preaching onto the ground of the "others" in our midst on Sunday morning. In *Preaching as Weeping, Confession, and Resistance,*[48] for instance, Christine Smith encourages preachers to consider the testimonies of persons with disabilities, the elderly, gays and lesbians, racial ethnic minorities, and victims of classism in their preaching. In *A Healing Homiletic,*[49]

44. *Transforming Moment,* pp. 65, 77-78, 80, 92, 156, 185.

45. *Transforming Moment,* pp. 77-78; italics added.

46. *Transforming Moment,* p. 78; italics added.

47. For a summary of the movement toward this emphasis in preaching, and for an in-depth exploration of its types and prospects, see John S. McClure, *Other-wise Preaching: A Postmodern Ethic for Homiletics* (St. Louis: Chalice Press, 2001).

48. Christine Smith, *Preaching as Weeping, Confession, and Resistance: Radical Responses to Radical Evil* (Louisville: Westminster John Knox Press, 1992).

49. Kathy Black, *A Healing Homiletic: Preaching and Disability* (Nashville: Abingdon Press, 1996).

Kathy Black asks preachers to attend carefully to persons with disabilities. She carefully reconsiders biblical texts having to do with blindness, sickness, disease, cure and healing, deafness and hearing loss, paralysis, leprosy and chronic illness, and mental illness. In *Telling the Truth: Preaching about Sexual and Domestic Violence,*[50] several scholars encourage preachers to keep in mind the likelihood that many of their hearers have experienced the trauma of sexual and domestic violence. In *Sharing the Word: Preaching in the Roundtable Church,* Lucy Atkinson Rose wants preachers "to make spacious room for the experiences of others, specifically those who hover at the margins of one's known reality."[51] In *Preaching as Local Theology and Folk Art,*[52] Leonora Tubbs Tisdale invites preachers to be keenly aware of the unique and often strange lives of the people around them, to appreciate their very particular folkways, and to learn to "dance" with each listener in ways that go far beyond the usual forms of pastoral identification.

In *The Roundtable Pulpit: Where Preaching and Leadership Meet,*[53] I offer "collaborative preaching" as another option to help preachers move into closer proximity to "others" in their preaching. In pre-sermon inductive Bible studies (roundtables) and then, by extension, in their sermons, preachers act as *hosts* who welcome strangers into teaching-learning conversations. These collaborative conversations include explicit "topic-setting" dynamics (Who will establish the sermon's theme?), interpretation dynamics (Whose meaning will prevail?), "empowerment dynamics" (Who has a testimony to offer?), "coming-to-terms" dynamics (How can this sermon stand *with* and stand *for* our community?), and "practice" dynamics (How can ideas become daily practices of Christian faith?). As they piece together sermons that grow out of roundtable discussions preachers prepare sermons within the context of an actual embodied experience of face-to-face struggles for meaning within and beyond the church.

In *The Word on the Street: Performing the Scriptures in the Urban Context,* Stanley P. Saunders and Charles Campbell take the concern for the engagement between preachers and others a step further. Saunders and Campbell invite preachers to participate in the ministry of the Open Door Community in Atlanta, Georgia, entering into face-to-face relationships with the men, women, and children who live on Atlanta's streets. Campbell and Saunders develop

50. John S. McClure and Nancy Ramsay, eds., *Telling the Truth: Preaching about Sexual and Domestic Violence* (Cleveland: United Church Press, 1999).

51. *Sharing the Word: Preaching in the Roundtable Church* (Louisville: Westminster John Knox Press, 1997), p. 129.

52. *Preaching As Local Theology and Folk Art* (Minneapolis: Fortress Press, 1997).

53. *The Roundtable Pulpit: Where Preaching and Leadership Meet* (Nashville: Abingdon Press, 1995).

from this a theology of "the powers" and a homiletic of resistance and hope. Preachers are encouraged "to become apprentices to those who are poor, homeless, imprisoned, or abused."[54]

Going a step beyond those just listed, for whom the countertestimony of "life" (confession) is central, Anna Carter Florence encourages a more pronounced move toward testimony as "erasure." Florence appeals for another form of testimonial preaching, one in which "our lives are not the testimony, and our lives do not prove the testimony; rather, our lives are *sealed* to the testimony, sealed to the narrated and confessed *freedom* the testimony proclaims: the Word as perfectly open sign."[55] Making use of Rebecca Chopp's theology of the Word, Florence de-essentializes testimony and *seals* it to the absolute freedom from the hegemony of the discourse situation that is expressed in the Word as a "perfectly open sign."

It is precisely this rupture of hegemonic experience by the "perfectly open sign," and the absolute freedom that issues from hearing this Word that mark the "celebration" of much of African-American preaching. According to Henry Mitchell, celebration emerges from a deep "internalization" of and "saturation" by God's liberating Word[56] (cf. Florence's "sealing"). This internalization becomes what Warren H. Stewart calls "an awareness that God is involved in one's holistic liberation."[57] Olin P. Moyd relates this directly to "earthly deliverances" that involve freedom from bondage to the entire set of options assumed to exist for "black folk" in society. This deliverance is experienced as literally *unstoppable,* sending the hearer of the Word into ecstatic celebration.[58] Like Florence's testimony, therefore, much of African-American preaching is proclamation that is sealed to this perfectly open sign, sealed to the task of rupturing the totality of hegemonic speech with the infinity of possible positions that remain always other to that totality.

Most if not all of these homileticians encourage preachers *to make a mutual speaking-listening, face-to-face encounter with others an essential aspect of the preaching process.* In each case, a re-scripting of reality through a dialectic between testimony (same) and countertestimony (other) is very important. Ul-

54. Stanley P. Saunders and Charles L. Campbell, *The Word on the Street: Performing the Scriptures in the Urban Context* (Grand Rapids: Eerdmans, 2000), p. 72.

55. Anna Carter Florence, *Preaching as Testimony, Towards a Women's Preaching Tradition and New Homiletic Models* (Ph.D. diss., Princeton Theological Seminary, 2000), p. 168.

56. *The Recovery of Preaching* (New York: Harper & Row, 1977), p. 37.

57. *Interpreting God's Word in Black Preaching* (Valley Forge, PA: Judson Press, 1984), p. 47.

58. *The Sacred Art: Preaching and Theology in the African American Tradition* (Valley Forge, PA: Judson Press, 1995), p. 106.

timately, however, it is not enough. Something more is being sought, through heightened awareness of proximity, through increased interaction before and after preaching, and through sealing preaching to the otherness and openness of the Word itself. This something is beginning to look like the "way of love."

* * *

In summary, homileticians and preachers interested in the relationship between testimony and ethical proclamation can learn at least two things from James Loder. In the first place, Loder recognized the power and centrality of the logic of transformation across all arenas of human life, including especially the esthetic, rhetorical, therapeutic, developmental, mythic, and ritualistic. It appears that testimonial speech bears within it the same grammar or logic of transformation. Preachers can learn to attend to the ways in which testimony and countertestimony can introduce the logic of transformation into their preaching. This will help them to discover ways to esthetically script and re-script reality for their listeners. The writings of Walter Brueggemann will be tremendously helpful for this project.

In the second place Loder was profoundly aware that all of these transformations are, in the last analysis, analogues of the transformation of all things by the *Spiritus Creator.* Because of this, these transformations require transformation by God's Spirit, the Spirit incarnate in the person and work of Jesus Christ. Ultimately, *it is the way of love itself that testifies to this final transformation.*[59] It is *testified to* by the movement into the space where the "other" is found, into the face-to-face nexus where erasure as negation and trace are conjoined.

All of this suggests that preachers have done only part of their ethical work when they provide an esthetic and rhetorical re-scripting of reality, as important as that may be. It suggests that love, an emergence onto the ground of the other, into the glory of the Infinite in the face of the other, is the central thing that will concern the ethical preacher. All re-scripting will be unredeemed speech, displays of transformational rhetorical power, unless transformed by and for the "way of love," *unless the preacher is preaching face-to-face in the deepest and most profound sense.*

Four-dimensional ethical preaching begins and ends in a testimony of erasure through which the preacher moves into proximity to others, becomes a "signing" to others, a "saying" of our proximity, our mutual exposure, the "one-for-the-other." In this way, the logic of ethical transformation in preaching is it-

59. According to Loder, "When it [the human spirit] testifies with the Holy Spirit, its transformations are themselves transformed." *The Logic of the Spirit,* p. 36.

self transformed, displaying traces of the *shekinah* Glory of the God of infinite justice, of the perfectly open Word of God incarnate in Jesus of Nazareth, and of the cruciform Holy Spirit that fills the void that separates human beings from each other and from God.

4. Transforming Encounter in the Borderlands: A Study of Matthew 15:21-28

Daniel S. Schipani

In his classic book, *The Transforming Moment,* James E. Loder suggests that it would be "intriguing and helpful to pursue tranformational logic as a key to biblical narrative." The suggestion appears in the preface to Loder's use of Luke 24:13-35 to illustrate transformational logic transposed into four dimensions (self, lived world, the void, and the Holy) under the authorship and mediation of Jesus as the Christ.[1]

In this essay honoring my former Princeton mentor, I seek to demonstrate that, indeed, the "logic of transformation"[2] can be profitably employed as a key hermeneutical device in the study of other biblical stories, such as the captivating account found in Matthew 15:21-28. I will do so by using that key in the interpretation process within an overall inductive approach to the study of the gospel text. Further, I will show that such logic also illumines the dynamics and the pattern of creativity which defines the study of Scripture as a spiritual discipline.

Throughout the centuries Christians have interpreted and used the story of Jesus' encounter with the Syrophoenician/Canaanite woman in many ways. In recent years writings from a variety of perspectives reflect renewed interest in this fascinating story.[3] This essay reports my own work with this gospel nar-

1. James E. Loder, *The Transforming Moment,* 2nd ed. (Colorado Springs: Helmers & Howard, 1989), pp. 97-120.

2. Loder defines the "logic of transformation" as a patterned process consisting of the systematic interconnection of the following five steps: (1) conflict in a context of rapport; (2) interlude for scanning; (3) insight felt with intuitive force; (4) release of energy and repatterning; and (5) interpretation and verification.

3. Elisabeth Schüssler Fiorenza took the title of her book, *But She Said: Feminist Practices of Biblical Interpretation* (Boston: Beacon Press, 1992), from the story of the Syrophoenician-Canaanite woman. In her view, the story "represents the biblical-theological voice of women, which has been excluded, repressed, or marginalized in Christian discourse" (p. 11).

rative in Bible study and in conversation and collaboration with others in the settings of church and academy. Working with a practical theological perspective, I will address two interrelated questions: How may this unique story be illumined by Loder's contribution? How may this biblical text become foundational for faith and ministry?[4]

I will follow the familiar movements of an inductive study process, in popularized Latin American terms: *seeing, judging,* and *acting.* I assume that study of any biblical text should happen within the context of a Spirit-led faith community that prayerfully seeks to become wiser in the light of God in formative and transformative ways. And I also assume that one always brings perspectives, agendas, biases, and other sensitivities to any Bible study, while needing to welcome others' readings and contributions critically as well as creatively.[5]

First, we will take a close look at the biblical passage, trying to grasp its meaning afresh. Second, we will ponder its significance, keeping in mind the social and cultural context. Finally, we will draw implications for our embodiment of the message in truthful and fruitful ways.

4. As a practical theologian, I use the term "foundational" deliberately and precisely. For me, the Bible is foundational in at least four interrelated ways: (a) It informs my normative framework and perspective for practice and reflection, especially regarding wisdom (knowing how to live in the light of God); (b) it offers key content disclosed in the teachings, narratives, and other materials (poetic, prophetic, apocalyptic, etc.) which express the written Word in ways that illumine and address our human condition; (c) it calls for engagement in an interpretive process for the sake of discernment and wise living; and (d) it grounds my own spirituality as a man of faith and as a ministering person (teacher and pastoral counselor), theological educator, and theologian.

5. My personal story includes growing up in Argentina right before Vatican II, when the Roman Catholic Church was the official state church and discrimination against Protestants was widespread. My parents were active members of the local Mennonite church, so I developed a strong separate religious identity. I learned to read the Bible and to live out and reflect on the Christian faith as a member of a marginal community. As an immigrant in the United States I find myself not fully belonging in this country and being reminded frequently of my "otherness" because of my accent, appearance, and certain social and cultural characteristics. I now feel that I no longer fully belong in Argentina either, though I keep close contact and collaborative ties in my country as well as in other parts of Latin America and the Caribbean. In sum, I have become one of the millions of "hybrid" people living in the United States, and my unique way of being Latin American conditions the way I read the Bible today. Finally, I am blessed with opportunities to teach and work in several contexts, including Europe. I increasingly appreciate perspectives and contributions of countless others with different cultural and ethnic backgrounds and from a variety of Christian traditions — especially Reformed and Roman Catholic — even as my own Anabaptist convictions have been shared, tested, and enriched.

The Meaning of the Text: *Seeing*

This story appears only in the Gospels according to Mark and Matthew. In fact, Mark chapter 7 and Matthew chapter 15 are remarkably parallel as far as narrative content and sequencing are concerned. Nevertheless, we note some significant differences between the two accounts of Jesus' encounter with a foreign woman.[6] These dissimilarities suggest that Matthew has an interest in underscoring and intensifying some features of the story. For this reason, I have chosen to focus on its narrative.

A Comparative Reading

Jesus left that place and went away to the district of Tyre and Sidon. Just then a Canaanite woman from that region came out and started shouting, "Have mercy on me, Lord, Son of David; my daughter is tormented by a demon." But he did not answer her at all. And his disciples came and urged him, saying, "Send her away, for she keeps shouting after us." He answered, "I was sent only to the lost sheep of the house of Israel." But she came and knelt before him, saying, "Lord, help me." He answered, "It is not fair to take the children's food and throw it to the dogs." She said, "Yes, Lord, yet even the dogs eat the crumbs that fall from their masters' table." Then Jesus answered her, "Woman, great is your faith! Let it be done for you as you wish." And her daughter was healed instantly.

(Matt. 15:21-28, NRSV)

From there he set out and went away to the region of Tyre. He entered a house and did not want anyone to know he was there. Yet he could not escape notice, but a woman whose little daughter had an unclean spirit immediately heard about him, and she came and bowed down at his feet. Now the woman was a Gentile, of Syrophoenician origin. She begged him to cast the demon out of her daughter. He said to her, "Let the children be fed first, for it is not fair to take the children's food and throw it to the dogs." But she an-

6. One is inclined to think that the narrative would also fit well in Luke's Gospel, given what we know about Luke, a Gentile writing to Gentiles, who gives women a significant place in his telling of the gospel. According to Elisabeth Schüssler Fiorenza, Luke does not include the story because he puts Paul and Peter at the center of the debate about the mission to the Gentiles: "This Lukan historical model has no room for a story about an educated Greek woman, who as a religious and ethnic outsider argues with Jesus for the Gentiles' share in the power of well-being" (Fiorenza, *But She Said*, p. 97).

> *swered him, "Sir, even the dogs under the table eat the children's crumbs." Then he said to her, "For saying that, you may go — the demon has left your daughter." So she went home, found the child lying on the bed, and the demon gone.*
>
> (Mark 7:24-30, NRSV)

I will succinctly highlight four variations in the two accounts. We recognize first a puzzling ambiguity about the location of the encounter, especially in Matthew's account: Had Jesus entered the region of Sidon and Tyre, or simply approached it — as suggested in many scholarly interpretations? Had the woman left that area for Jewish territory and only then encountered Jesus?[7]

Second, while Mark identifies the woman as a Gentile (a Greek), of Syrophoenician origin (or, by race a Phoenician from Syria), in Matthew the woman is "a Canaanite woman from that region." The latter account implies that she is unclean and pagan, and possibly poor, perhaps a peasant. According to Matthew's version, a demon possessed and tormented the woman's daughter; this characterization suggests great evil and danger. Further, "Canaanite" evokes an adversarial relationship, dating from the divinely-sanctioned conquest of the Canaanites' land by the Israelites, who were taught to view themselves as "chosen . . . out of all the peoples on earth to be God's people and treasured possession" (Deut. 7:1-6).

Third, Matthew's account includes not just Tyre but Sidon. "Tyre and Sidon," cities located on the Mediterranean coast, traditionally designated the Gentile/pagan region northwest of Jewish territory. Earlier in the Gospel, Jesus characterized Tyre and Sidon as more open to the gospel than were the Galilean cities of Chorazin and Bethsaida: "If the deeds of power done in you had been done in Tyre and Sidon, they would have repented long ago" (11:20-21).

Fourth, in Matthew's version of the story, the conversation is more involved and the disciples take part. In verse 23, they ambiguously advise Jesus to "dismiss her." Surprisingly, the woman addresses Jesus in the language of Israel's faith, "Lord, Son of David," and lays her need at his feet. In Matthew, not only does she address Jesus directly, but she is the first woman to speak in the

7. See, for instance, Daniel J. Harrington: "It is possible to envision the Matthean episode as having taken place on Jewish soil, with the pagan woman coming forth from her own land to meet Jesus who was travelling in the direction of Tyre and Sídon. This scenario involves translating *eis* in Matt 15:21 as 'to' or 'toward,' not 'into,' and subordinating the prepositional phrase 'from those regions' (15:22) to the participle 'came forth.' The scenario would be consistent with Jesus' directive to his disciples to confine their mission to the lost sheep of Israel (see Matt 10:5-6)" (Daniel J. Harrington: *The Gospel of Matthew,* Sacra Pagina Series, 1 [Collegeville, MN: Liturgical Press, 1991], p. 235).

Gospel. Correspondingly, in the end Jesus praises the Canaanite woman for her faith, and the whole incident thus becomes a special instance of "praying faith."

Having thus highlighted four variations in the two accounts, it is also necessary for us to keep in mind that our story is placed in a particular context in both Matthew 15 and Mark 7. First, we learn about a serious controversy involving Pharisees and scribes concerning the "tradition of the elders" on the question of eating with defiled hands. Jesus responds by accusing them of breaking the commandment of God and making void the word of God for the sake of their tradition, including a damning quote from the prophet Isaiah (Matt. 15:1-9; Mark 7:1-13). Then we are told that Jesus engages in authoritative teaching about the spiritual implications of his position. In fact, he does this by using both direct and indirect language, that is, parabolic communication which requires further explanation (Matt. 15:10-20; Mark 7:14-23). Finally, after the story of the encounter with the Syrophoenician/Canaanite woman, the gospel writers portray Jesus involved in ministry with admirable compassion and power (Matt. 15:29-39; Mark 7:31-37).

It is significant that, before encountering the foreign woman, Jesus has been engaged in a very serious conflict situation. His adversaries put the controversy in terms of socio-religious, cultural adaptation, that is, the conventional wisdom of needing to follow the tradition of the elders. In other words, the gospel accounts suggest that the nature of their argument betrays a two-dimensional vision: they understand holiness in terms of conformity to the precepts and practices handed down through religious teachings and socialization. Observance of the tradition, then, defines one's belonging to the chosen people of Israel. Jesus, on the other hand, views the struggle four-dimensionally:[8] for him, the real problem lies in accommodating to tradition while disobeying the will of God, as in the case of the commandment to honor father and mother. In that light, Jesus contends that the very worship of God has been compromised. So, for Jesus, the transformation of the tradition of the elders itself is a necessary outcome of radical trust in and obedience to the living God of Israel. Radical obedience is for him the way to life in lieu of those fruitless endeavors to gain divine acceptance and favor in the face of the threat of evil and condemnation.

It is also interesting to visualize Jesus speaking firmly, with certainty and authority, about the way of authentic spirituality right before he meets the

8. This is a direct allusion to Loder's view of the "fourfold knowing event" — which involves the lived world, the self, the void, and the Holy. See *The Transforming Moment*, chap. 3. Loder writes that "being human entails environment, selfhood, the possibilty of nonbeing, and the possibility of new being. All four dimensions are essential, and none of them can be ignored without decisive loss to our understanding of what is essentially human" (p. 69).

woman in the borderlands and faces a seemingly different kind of conflict. Indeed, it may be argued that Jesus still needed to process more deeply, both existentially and theologically, the very meaning and implications of "tradition" being confronted by divine grace. Could it be that a difficult scanning process requiring the collaboration of such a special stranger would eventually lead Jesus to further light, that is, to a transformative learning that would translate into deeper caring and liberating power, and to a clearer sense of vocation? With such a question in mind we now turn to that eventful encounter.

Focus on the Encounter: Highlights of a Stunning Confrontation

A plain reading of the story presents a clear and unique instance in which Jesus yields. One could argue that here he is bested in an argument. The most striking and problematic part of the story is, of course, Jesus' initial responses to the request of the woman: first a deafening silence, then an uncharacteristic affirmation of boundaries, followed by parabolic refusal. At that moment he appears to regard the woman's request as inappropriate, even as outrageously *out of place!* Only in this gospel story does Jesus clearly ignore a supplicant, place the barrier of ethnicity before a plea for help, and then use offensive language to reiterate the barrier. Without question, "dog" is a disdainful metaphor, though Jesus uses a diminutive form ("puppy," "little bitch"). The implication, of course, is that the Gentiles/dogs have no place at the table. The woman, however, appears to play along with that harsh image and simply urges Jesus to take it one step further. She appeals to him as "Lord," asserts her claim, and demonstrates her faith by arguing that at the very least both children (Jews) and dogs (Gentiles) are under the same caring, compassionate authority.

One need not infer that the woman agrees with the Gentile/dog analogy. Nor do we need to conclude that she considers herself unworthy and less than human, or that she identifies herself as a dog. On the contrary, we may assume that she is requesting that she and her daughter be included, that she hopes for a place at the table and challenges Israel's excluding ideology. When she says, "Yes, Lord . . . ," she agrees with Jesus that it would be wrong to throw the children's bread to the dogs. But she also reminds Jesus that if even dogs may eat what their masters waste, she and her daughter should receive bread, too. The Canaanite woman understands the grave meaning and the implications of Jesus' initial response, but she proceeds wisely and daringly to reframe and recast it. Jesus' original challenge to the woman merely restates the status quo of gender, ethnic, cultural, religious, and political division. Her counter-challenge calls him to look to the place of new possibilities across and beyond the established boundaries. Instead of accepting the dichotomy of children (insiders/receive food) versus dogs (outsiders/no food), she imagines that both the children and the dogs can be graciously fed inside, within the same household and from the same table.[9] Stated in other terms, the foreign woman is standing at the void as she faces the painful reality of her daughter's torment, and begs for mercy. Jesus, however, initially appears to cling to the very two-dimensionality that he had earlier rejected. He seems to be pushed to face the possibility of his own faithlessness and abandonment of God at this point and, thereby, to come face to face with the holiness of God "beyond the boundaries" at the prompting of the foreign woman.

The dramatic import of this encounter in the borderlands is heightened as we recall its historical and textual background. "Show them no mercy," Moses had said to the people of Israel (Deut. 7:2). "Have mercy on me, Lord, Son of David," the Canaanite woman implores the New Moses of Israel. This Canaanite woman thus shatters the lingering image of wicked Canaanites, who presumably offer their children in sacrifice to their gods; she pleads on behalf of her daughter, who cannot speak for herself.[10] Well aware of his people's position and privilege as "chosen," Jesus initially reasserts the exclusiveness of his mission. But in the end, he welcomes the woman, and she receives what she had sought with passion, courage, and determination.

Finally, this story parallels that of the Roman centurion, in Matthew 8:5-13. These are the only two healings in this Gospel explicitly involving Gentiles and accomplished from a distance. In both cases Jesus deems the people worthy of the gift of healing. In fascinating reversals, both Gentiles even become exemplary figures. Most commentators indicate that although Matthew's final word on mission to the Gentiles does not come until the last chapter of the Gospel (28:16-20), in these and related episodes the theme emerges that ethnicity does not define the people of God. Intertextual comparative studies indicate that Matthew's positive portrait of Jesus' response to the Gentiles constitutes a partial reversal of the Exodus tradition by focusing on the missional goal of bringing outsiders to the knowledge of the God of Israel.[11] God's purposes include

9. Elaine M. Wainwright lucidly argues this point in *Shall We Look for Another? A Feminist Rereading of the Matthean Jesus* (Maryknoll, NY: Orbis Books, 1998), pp. 86-92.

10. For this way of restating the meaning of the encounter, I am indebted to my former student Leticia A. Guardiola-Sáenz, who shared with me a paper written during her doctoral work at Vanderbilt University (summer 1998), "Jesus' Encounter with the Canaanite Woman: The 'Hybrid Moment' of the Matthean Community."

11. Willard M. Swartley makes this point in *Israel's Scripture Traditions and the Synoptic Gospels: Story Shaping Story* (Peabody, MA: Hendrickson, 1994), p. 70.

Gentiles, and Jesus the Jew is the agent of divine grace on their behalf.[12] Transformation will happen in the borderlands.

The Significance of the Text: *Judging*

We raise above the question whether Jesus, as a ministering person, needed to undergo a difficult "scanning" process requiring the collaboration of a foreign woman in the borderlands, in order to further discern the nature and contours of divine grace. Earlier in the gospel text we saw him responding with clarity and certainty in the face of the challenge by Pharisees and scribes. Now he is treading unfamiliar territory and the "context of rapport" of his circle of disciples does not seem to be particularly helpful.

The text before us suggests and calls for several kinds of stretching. Geographic, ethnic, gender, religious, theological, sociocultural, moral, and political dimensions are involved. No wonder, then, that the intrusion of the woman into his life and sense of vocation and ministry stunned Jesus. Because this narrative has much spatial and contextual import, it is fitting that our interpretation underscores that this marginal Canaanite woman emerges as the center of the story! In fact, the story is primarily her story. We observe a surprising, transforming reversal: Jesus comes to acknowledge that she has *great* faith. This Gospel uses that adjective to describe faith only once. The woman's faith encompasses her persistent demand for inclusion in the face of Jesus' resistance; her challenge to the gender, ethnic, religious, political, and economic barriers; her recognition of Jesus' authority over demons; and her reliance on his power.[13]

12. See, for instance, the fine commentary by Warren Carter, *Matthew and the Margins: A Sociopolitical and Religious Reading* (Maryknoll, NY: Orbis Books, 2000), pp. 320ff. Other recent biblical studies done with a "decolonizing" interest and perspective present a different picture as they attempt to unveil and deconstruct certain perceived biases in the biblical text. See, for example, Musa W. Dube, "A Postcolonial Feminist Reading of Matthew 15:21-28," part 3 of *Postcolonial Feminist Interpretation of the Bible* (St. Louis: Chalice Press, 2000). For this African scholar, "the divergent receptions accorded to the centurion and the Canaanite woman reflect the imperial and patriarchal currents at work in Matthew. . . . No doubt, the implied author, writing in the post–70 C.E. period, wishes to present the Matthean community as a nonsubversive community" (pp. 132-133). Dube's work includes serious critiques of the work of several white, western, middle-class feminist writers on this text (pp. 169-184). Her thesis and overall discussion are provocative; nevertheless, my appraisal is that she and other authors with similar perspectives often neglect to acknowledge inherent tensions and dialectical import within biblical texts, and thus fail to appreciate one key aspect of their liberating and transformative potential.

13. Carter, *Matthew and the Margins*, pp. 324-325.

Perhaps Jesus' praise includes a realization we can appreciate today as well: in that encounter in the borderlands, the Canaanite woman became a prophetic and wise teacher. Out of her desire for healing for her daughter, she acted and spoke counter-culturally and counter-politically as she reminded Jesus of the larger vision of the reign of God. And she did so in a way consistent with the converging prophetic and wisdom traditions with which Jesus/Wisdom (Sophia) is interpreted in the Gospel of Matthew.[14]

Put in other words, the Syrophoenician/Canaanite woman had approached Jesus seeking help on behalf of her daughter; in the process of her encounter with Jesus, she also ministered to him by eventually focusing on *negating the negation* involved in the dog-Gentile analogy traditionally used by the Jews. In terms of transformational logic, her bisociating insight indeed amounted to a constructive act of the imagination[15] which eventually resonated with Jesus' own imaginative work. The encounter itself — the unique relationality linking Jesus and the foreign woman — was transformed: confrontation became a kind of collaborative work. And while the disciples seemed to fade in the background, the foreign woman became spiritually closer to Jesus.[16]

The most vexing question for us is, of course, why Jesus would act as he initially did in this encounter. An answer requires that we maintain the tension between two historical realities pertaining to his *lived world.* On the one hand, we must assume that Jesus had been socialized into the conventional wisdom of his time and dominant culture. According to such socialization, prudence involved keeping clear boundaries; adhering to certain criteria of what is proper, clean, normal, and appropriate; and holding to right categories and patterns of perception, thought, relationships. This socialization was undoubtedly part of Jesus' identity as a first-century Jew. From a human science perspective, we do not expect that Jesus would have been exempt from dealing with prejudice. Neither do we expect that he would have spontaneously developed the kind of understanding enabling him to readily appreciate and communicate with the

14. Wainwright, *Shall We Look for Another?* p. 88.

15. According to James Loder's own definitions, "bisociation" denotes "the surprising convergence of two incompatible frames of reference to compose an original and meaningful unity. Bisociation is the basic unit of an insight, which may include several bisociations to form a complex new meaning." And "constructive acts of imagination" are those "[i]nsights, intuitions, or visions that appear — usually with convincing force — in the borderline area between consciousness and unconsciousness. They convey, in a form readily available to consciousness, the essence of a conflict resolution." Loder, *The Transforming Moment,* p. 222.

16. A formal definition of when it is appropriate to identify change as *transformation* is in order. According to Loder, "transformation occurs whenever, within a given frame of reference or experience, hidden orders of coherence and meaning emerge to replace or alter the axioms of the given frame and reorder its elements accordingly." *The Transforming Moment,* p. 229.

woman across vast social and cultural differences. On the other hand, we must also recognize that Jesus of Nazareth was himself a marginal person.[17] He was rejected by the dominant groups and became a friend of marginalized people — tax-collectors, outcasts, women, the poor and oppressed, "sinners," and Gentiles. In other words, Jesus related abnormally well to those people, and was accepted by them, because he was himself an outsider, a homeless person (Matt. 8:20) living in two worlds without fully belonging to either.[18] In sum, from a theological perspective, whenever we look at Jesus the Christ we should see that the historical and existential reality of the incarnation is not only about "body" *(sōma)*, but is also about "soul" *(psychē)* and "spirit" *(pneuma)*. In other words, we propose to take seriously the New Testament references which point to a wholistic anthropology, including a distinction between the soul and the human spirit.[19]

An outsider, a multiply-marginal person, challenged Jesus to relate and minister across and beyond those boundaries. She gave him an opportunity to respond in tune with God's alternative wisdom expressed in an ethic and politics of compassion and radical inclusiveness. It is fitting to conclude that Jesus faced a major conflict and temptation, indeed a temptation from within, and that eventually he chose wisely, even as he was creatively challenged by the foreign woman. This conclusion need not compromise the christological conviction about the nature and work of Jesus as Christ. As Hebrews 4:15 puts it, "We do not have a high priest who is unable to sympathize with our weaknesses, but we have one who in every respect has been tested as we are, yet without sin." If

17. For a scholarly treatment of the marginality of Jesus, see John P. Meier, *A Marginal Jew: Rethinking the Historical Jesus* (New York: Doubleday, 1991).

18. Jung Young Lee has insightfully discussed the question of Jesus and marginality in *Marginality: The Key to a Multicultural Theology* (Minneapolis: Fortress Press, 1995). Writing from an Asian (Korean) American perspective, Lee proposes "a new theology based on marginality, which serves not only as a hermeneutical paradigm but as a key to the substance of the Christian faith" (p. 1).

19. Consider, for instance, the blessing in 1 Thessalonians 5:23, "May the God of peace himself sanctify you entirely; and may your spirit and soul and body be kept sound [complete] and blameless at the coming of our Lord Jesus Christ." The distinction between the soul and the human spirit, as found in Hebrews 4:12-13, is particularly significant in light of our discussion: "Indeed, the word of God is living and active, sharper than any two-edged sword, piercing until it divides soul from spirit, joints from marrow; it is able to judge the thoughts and intentions of the heart. And before him no creature is hidden, but all are naked and laid bare to the eyes of the one to whom we must render an account." See James E. Loder's foundational essay, written as an interpretative response to that Hebrew text, "Incisions from a Two-Edged Sword: The Incarnation and the Soul/Spirit Relationship," in *The Treasure of Earthen Vessels: Explorations in Theological Anthropology*, ed. Brian H. Childs and David W. Waanders (Louisville: Westminster John Knox, 1994), pp. 151-173.

we accept this interpretation, we must reject three other interpretations: (a) that Jesus was testing (playing games with) the woman while knowing all along what he should and would do, (b) that he wanted to teach the disciples a dramatic lesson about loving enemies or, as proposed by some radical feminists, (c) that Jesus had to be converted (repent from sin). The biblical text supports none of these interpretations. On the contrary, it is our view that the text implies the triumph of Jesus' (and the foreign woman's) spirit grounded and sustained by the Spirit of God. In fact, in addition to pertinent christological consideration, in James Loder's terms this gospel story illumines the question of how the spiritual life can become transcendent and at the same time preserve its immanent integrity in the context of human experience. Loder asserts,

> in keeping with the pervasive Christ-centered transformational view of the Divine Spirit in the book of Hebrews, we can conclude that the Divine Spirit calls forth the human spirit, disembedding it from its captivity to the psychic economy and making itself, the Divine Spirit, determinative of the spiritual life of the individual. No longer does the ego-centered psychic economy contain and govern the spirit in human life. Rather, the human spirit, although still in reciprocity with that psychic economy, is governed by the Spirit of God. This makes possible any number of behaviors that are not strictly consistent with the reality principle, such as returning good for evil, forgiving those who persecute, and rejoicing in suffering. Such behaviors, which must be ascribed to pathology of the ego in the psychological model, are the norm for those who "walk in the spirit." Indeed, without a spiritual transformation of the psychic economy, such behavior may well be expressive of masochistic or oppressed personality types. However, the *metamorphē* of the psychic life yields up a new being sustained by the birthing of the human spirit from within its containment in the psyche to communion with the Divine Spirit. Thus, "born of the Spirit," the person finds his or her soul at "rest" in the life of God. . . . Thus [Christ's] nature, not primarily the reality principle of the ego, becomes the new norm by which life is to be conducted.

He continues,

> This in no way eliminates the ego or the reality principle, but it makes the relationality between the ego and its tacit sense of wholeness much richer and less defensive. As this reciprocity increases in depth and intensity, the psyche becomes increasingly aware of itself as spiritual in the larger context of a Divine Spirit who is its origin and ultimate ground beyond any ultimacy or groundedness implicit in the psyche per se. On the other hand,

> the ego-centered psyche continues to bring language and intelligence to bear upon this intrinsically spiritual situation, but these now serve primarily as means to adaptation, not so much to the natural or social environment, but to the Divine Spirit. What the Divine Spirit is doing in the world to convict, to transform, and to conform the world to the nature of Christ becomes the new environment of the ego-centered soul.[20]

As Jesus appropriated the woman's insight significantly expanding the contours of compassion and care, energy was released (he praised the woman in unusual terms, her daughter was healed, and then more miracles took place), and Jesus further engaged in interpretation and ministry in the light of God's reign. The personal drama and the behavior of the Syrophoenician/Canaanite woman became a kind of catalyst of the multifaceted transforming encounter in the borderlands: many barriers broke down, temptation was overcome, understandings were deepened, faith was affirmed, and a child was healed. Ultimately, however, the Mediator of transformation was not the woman but the very Spirit of Christ.[21]

The story as it unfolds makes clear that both the woman and Jesus became boundary walkers and boundary breakers. By eventually choosing to relate and to minister "out of place," Jesus and the woman pointed the way to God's utopia. "Utopia" means literally "no place," not in the sense of never-never land, illusion, or fantasy, but as in the stuff of prophetic dreams. From a biblical perspective, utopias are places that are not yet, not because they are mere ideals beyond reach, but because evil and sinful structures and behaviors resist and contradict God's will for ethnic and racial justice and reconciliation.

Finally, as we judge this text, we must realize its significance in light of the social and existential realities of the Matthean community. On the one hand, we recognize that the Gospel according to Matthew was written from the perspective of the chosen people of Israel, beginning with "Jesus the Messiah, the son of David, the son of Abraham" (Matt. 1:1). The author writes from the center of the tradition, and from a typically "centralist" point of view.[22] Within this framework Jesus instructs the disciples, "Go nowhere among the Gentiles . . . ,

20. Loder, "Incisions from a Two-Edged Sword," p. 168. For a systematic discussion of the relationality between the human spirit and the divine, see James E. Loder and W. Jim Neidhart, *The Knight's Move: The Relational Logic of the Spirit in Theology and Science* (Colorado Springs: Helmers & Howard, 1992), especially sections I and III. See also James E. Loder, *The Logic of the Spirit: Human Development in Theological Perspective* (San Francisco: Jossey-Bass, 1998), pp. 17-45.

21. I agree with Loder that only Jesus Christ is the ontological Mediator of fourfold transformation events.

22. Lee, *Marginality*, p. 116.

but go rather to the lost sheep of the house of Israel" (Matt. 10:5-6). The latter expression is unique to Matthew and repeated in our text. The author leaves no doubt about Israel's priority in salvation history. On the other hand, the story of the Canaanite woman can help undermine and even dismantle chosenness as ideology, as justification for excluding and discriminating against the other, the stranger, the foreigner. A powerful paradox is at work here!

We surmise that the early readers of Matthew were Jewish Christians separated from the synagogue and relating both to a largely Gentile Christian movement and to the Jewish community. The story must have aided them to understand their new place and role in God's plan and reign. This story may also have helped free them from the ideology of chosenness so they could be transformed into a more liberating and inclusive faith community. Perhaps they were already beginning to experience such a community, but were unsure about how to cope with, legitimate, and reflect on it.[23] This transition and transformation of the Matthean community would have been crucial for their sense of identity as well as for the mission to the Gentiles. The new community — where there is no longer Jew or Greek, slave or free, male and female, for all are one in Christ (Gal. 3:28) — is thus called to celebrate, embody, and be an agent of the coming reign of God, the future in which God is making all things new. Transformation will indeed happen in the borderlands!

Embodying the Text: *Acting*

In this final section we must focus on application. We will do that in light of the twofold purpose for writing this essay, as stated at the beginning with the questions: (1) How may this unique story be illumined by James Loder's contribution? and (2) How may this biblical text become foundational for faith and ministry?

Interpretation Dynamics: Guidelines for Reading the Text as a Creative Process

In the previous pages we shared a relatively smooth account of the results of our study of Jesus' encounter with a Syrophoenician/Canaanite woman. The actual study of the Gospel account in personal and group study settings, how-

23. See Leticia A. Guardiola-Sáenz's helpful discussion of this question in "Borderless Women and Borderless Texts: A Cultural Reading of Matthew 15:21-28," *Semeia* 78 (1997): 69-81.

ever, has been richer but also more complex and problematic. Indeed, one of the most interesting and helpful realizations concerning the dynamics of Bible study has been that there exists a fundamental analogy between the "logic of transformation" as a hermeneutical key to biblical narrative and as a pattern of creativity that defines the study of Scripture as a truly spiritual discipline. In other words, the content of the first and second section of this essay represents the summarized results of our having read the text in the mode of an unfolding creative process. The actual interpretation dynamics included, as suggested by James Loder, a number of learning tasks that can be readily identified and connected with the five steps of that transformational pattern, as briefly illustrated below.[24] Together with Loder, it is our claim that those learning tasks must be intentionally fostered and must be viewed as interrelated, completing and supplementing each other.

First of all, there is the identification of and focus on the dissonance and even conflict resulting from a text that appears to contradict our common understanding of Jesus' grace-filled disposition on behalf of the stranger and marginated people. Within the kind of *context of rapport* that fosters trust and welcomes questioning and the patient search for truth, we can learn to face and embrace the conflict, and we commit ourselves to careful discernment with perseverance. It is essential, therefore, that we see and value conflict, engagement and complexity as occasions for transformative learning and spiritual growth. In other words, we must be aware of our impulses to master, or preemptively domesticate, the text. Such a disposition will allow us to experience the next movement.

Second, we engage in the Bible study version of *interlude for scanning*. Thus, instead of prematurely settling for easy answers (such as those of many [male] commentators who rush to defend Jesus by proposing resolutions not supported by the text itself), we must struggle with the text while prayerfully seeking the guidance of the Spirit. We are thus free to participate in a potentially transformative and empowering hermeneutical process. So, learning to search and to explore with expectancy and hope is another learning task intentionally fostered. It includes not only careful observation but also sensitive listening to external as well as internal messages. We thus experience the adventure of exploration at diverse levels (conscious and unconscious, personal and communal) made possible by the stance of openness and longing for revelation and truth as a welcome gift.

24. See James E. Loder, "Transformation in Christian Education," in *Religious Education* 76 (March-April 1981): 204-221. See also Daniel Schipani, *Religious Education Encounters Liberation Theology* (Birmingham: Religious Education Press, 1988), pp. 48-55.

Third, we find ourselves led to appropriate discoveries connected with the initial sense of dissonance and conflict and with our quest for knowledge and truth, such as those reported in the second part of this essay. This is the movement characterized by *intuition and insight* in the "logic of transformation" that defines the creativity paradigm that may be fittingly applied to Bible study. Hence, for the learning task of receiving hospitably, the gifts of insight that come with intuitive force will depend on having nurtured the inclination to attend to, value, and trust those constructive acts of the imagination. In the prayerful, worshipful setting of Bible study, those insights may be received and processed as the stuff of the collaborative engagement of our spirits with the Spirit whose guidance has been sought and honored from the beginning of the process.

Fourth, insights experienced with intuitive and convincing force are normally followed by *release of tension and transformation of energy* bound up with the original existential and theological conflict situation. Tensions associated with the problems being confronted (for instance, on the level of Christology) tend to be dissolved with a pleasant sense of meaning and value, and anticipated freedom and transformation. The celebration of learning and knowing that tends to take place spontaneously can be further affirmed and refocused in terms of learning to celebrate worshipfully. Further, we may begin to visualize possible ramifications and applications of the new knowledge and related learning.

Finally, the transformational sequence of creative Bible study calls for further *interpretation and verification.* Critical interpretation is necessary for understanding the connections between insights (e.g., regarding Jesus' inner struggle and "temptation from within") and the initial dissonance (the caring Jesus resists the request of a needy, faithful foreign woman) and for probing their correspondence with the public context of those conflicts. In our case, such probing included further consultation with biblical scholars and theologians seeking to ascertain the soundness and pertinence of our findings. The correlated, main learning task to be fostered is interpretive reflection and responsible action in an ongoing process that nurtures both faith and ministry, as indicated below.

Substantive Content: Guidelines for Faith and Ministry

We may realize the creative and liberating potential of this story in many ways on personal and communal levels. The following interrelated guidelines illustrate how this text has become foundational for me and other Bible study partners, how the text has ministered to us so that we can minister to others, so to speak. Without trivializing the import of this wonderful story, one can think of ways our text foundationally illumines specific principles — dependable guides to practice — for faith and ministry. For example, much could be said about multicultural communication and hermeneutics, evangelization and mission, education for peace and justice, care and counseling, among others.[25] I have chosen to highlight just three general guidelines in the following paragraphs.

First, contrary to what dominant cultures hold, the borderlands can become privileged places for the blessings of transformative learning, and for personal and communal growth and creativity. Conventional and pragmatic wisdom favors the safe havens of familiar territory, the shrewd and sensible stance of "playing it safe." The story of the Canaanite woman who confronts Jesus helps us realize that we can see reality better at places of marginality and vulnerability, and from the vantage point available to us at the borders. Our vision may thus be transformed. Hence, we are called to creative "willful contextual dislocations." This story asks us to move deliberately beyond our comfort zones, either by going out to, or by welcoming into our midst, the stranger, the alien, or the different other.[26] By moving from the center to the margins, we will find our perspectives significantly changed: we will become aware of the lenses through which we view the world, and our cultural and ideological captivities will be unveiled. We will be open to see better how God wants us to live and act in creative, redeeming, and empowering ways wherever we are.

A second guideline suggested by our study is that situations of conflict and suffering can become opportunities for transformation, for renewal and healing, and for witnessing God's amazing grace. People who hunger and thirst for wholeness, justice, freedom, and peace are especially close to the heart of God, because their desire reflects God's own longing for all people. For this reason they are blessed (Matt. 5:3-11). For this reason the Canaanite woman was blessed. That is the meaning of the claim of liberation theologies, that God has

25. For instance, in multicultural and anti-racism education we might focus on the reality of our perspectives, ideological captivities, and incomplete personal visions; dynamics of openness to the stranger and hospitality; embracing and dealing creatively with conflict on different levels; affirmation and transformation of identities; reconciliation and community building.

26. I have described the notion of willful (or voluntary) dislocation in several places; see, for instance, Daniel S. Schipani, "Liberation Theology and Religious Education," in *Theologies of Religious Education*, ed. Randolph Crump Miller (Birmingham: Religious Education Press, 1995), pp. 308-310; and "Educating for Social Transformation," in *Mapping Christian Education: Approaches to Congregational Learning*, ed. Jack L. Seymour (Nashville: Abingdon Press, 1997), pp. 37-38.

a preferential option for the poor and oppressed, for the victim and the weak. Jesus not only taught about this preference, he also showed concretely what it involves. In our story, the demonstration happened in a context of conflict and against his human inclinations! The church is sent to continue his ministry and to embrace the suffering neighbor seeking healing and hope. As we respond, our hearts will be nurtured and transformed. Places of pain become places of grace as we are led and empowered to practice the virtues essential for caring as representatives of Christ: humility, hospitality, love, compassion, patience, hope, generosity, and courage.

Third, as Jesus himself may have experienced, ministry at its best is a two-way street, a mutual practice and process. For us in North America, the center of the center in the ongoing globalization process, this kind of ministry poses special challenges. To become missional churches our faith communities will need to undergo a conversion to the margins. Many of us Christians need to shed our own ideology of chosenness to better attend to our deepest yearnings, limitations, and needs, as well as to the potential of others. We bless and we are in turn blessed, sometimes the hard way, in spite of our blinders and shortcomings. Often we will unexpectedly find ourselves being ministered to. In fact, we cannot truly participate in other people's liberation and healing without allowing them to participate in our own liberation and healing. In this process our common human vocation in the light of God is reconfirmed and sustained. And for us today, this blessing includes an additional realization: Serving and being served in the borderlands, across and against boundaries, again and again becomes the sacred experience of encountering Christ and loving him anew. In due time, it will be revealed to us, as in the eschatological parable of Matthew 25:31-46:[27] "Truly I tell you, just as you did it to one of the least of these who are members of my family, you did it to me."

27. Matthew's judgment scene in 25:31-46 is the culmination of a two-chapter eschatological discourse, and it has been interpreted in diverse ways. In any event, two things should be kept in mind. First, for Matthew, Jesus is identified with the (marginalized) community of disciples, and he is present with them as they engage in mission to communicate the gospel (18:20; 28:20). Second, in this text Jesus praises the actions of the righteous from "all the nations" (presumably Gentiles as well as Jews and Christians) because they have lived out the gospel by caring for the poor, oppressed, and marginalized; the actions of these "sheep" blessed by the Father are the practices of service expected of gospel bearers, followers of Jesus Christ.

5. Leadership and Serendipitous Discipleship: A Case Study of Congregational Transformation

Robert K. Martin

The key to the survival and health of the church, it is said, is leadership.[1] Almost a century ago, church statesman John R. Mott proclaimed a sentiment that is often repeated today: "Wherever the Church has proved inadequate it has been due to inadequate leadership."[2] To a great many ecclesiastical commentators, the current situation in the mainline churches is a crisis of declining membership and influence. Cries for greater leadership have echoed throughout the ages, but at present, the focus on leadership is intense. Yet, as Thomas Frank, professor of church administration and congregational life at Candler School of Theology, instructs us, "often the turn to 'leadership' has brought with it a framework of assumptions unsuited to the nature and purpose of churches as communities of witness and service."[3]

This essay will explore the nature of Christian leadership by contrasting one particularly dominant image of leadership in the church with a case study of a congregation whose life was transformed by bearing its cross faithfully. This case will be viewed through the lens of James E. Loder's transformational logic

1. E.g., Herb Miller, *Leadership Is the Key: Unlocking Your Effectiveness in Ministry* (Nashville: Abingdon Press, 1997).

2. John R. Mott, *The Future Leadership of the Church* (New York: YMCA, 1908), p. 4. As the General Secretary of the World's Student Christian Federation at the turn of the century, Mott had a particularly broad vantage point from which to view the future of leadership for the church. He was most concerned about the need for "men of ability rather than upon the need for greater numbers," for "more ministers of large caliber and possessing gifts of leadership." He continues: "As the progress of the Christian religion is of the most fundamental and vital interest, it must not be committed to the charge of incompetent hands" (pp. 10-11).

3. Thomas E. Frank, "The Discourse of Leadership and the Practice of Administration," *Journal of Religious Leadership* 1, 1 (Spring 2002): 7.

I wish to thank Rev. Harold Backus for reading and commenting on this essay.

and its theological framework. A great many persons have found Loder's work on transformation to be illuminative of human personality and of the individual's journey of self-transcendence to greater faithfulness by way of transformational patterns of knowing. Yet, perhaps because Loder concentrated mostly on transformations of the human personality, his theory of transformational logic has not been widely used to understand group dynamics: for example, how transformational patterns can be found in congregations or other groups. But in my teaching I have found transformational logic to be essential to the preparation of leaders for the church. In this essay, we will explore how transformational logic illumines the work of the Spirit in a particular congregation, and we will come to discover key insights into the nature and function of leadership for the church. But first, let us examine a common image of church and pastor born out of the traditional understanding of "effective" leadership.

The Corporate Model of the Church

While we might agree with some church observers that "effective congregations" always have effective pastoral leadership,[4] I wonder what is meant by effective. Effective *how?* Effective at *what?* In a landmark study of business management, effectiveness is characterized as the ability to get things done and the exercise of power over others in order to get things done.[5] Uncomfortable with the rather Machiavellian tone of that definition, many studies of leadership and power have recently taken a cue from Robert Greenleaf's theme of "servant-leadership" in which effective leaders are the ones who "empower" others in the organization to fulfill the vision and mission through productive and meaningful labor.[6] But still, whether it entails exercising power "over" or "with" others, the notion of effectiveness has mainly to do with having the *capacity to accomplish the tasks that further the interests of a particular group.*

It is common today to view the community of faith as being in the business of promoting the gospel and "making disciples" and to view the pastor as the church's CEO in all matters spiritual and administrative. It is a seductive image, imported from the business world and buttressed by the ideology of

4. Cf. "Pivotal Leadership" by L. Gregory Jones and Susan Pendleton, *The Christian Century*, September 12-19, 2001, pp. 24-28.

5. J. R. P. French and B. Raven, "The Bases of Social Power," in *Studies in Social Power*, ed. D. Cartwright (Ann Arbor, MI: Institute for Social Research, 1959), pp. 150-167.

6. Cf. Robert K. Greenleaf, *On Becoming a Servant Leader* (San Francisco: Jossey-Bass, 1996), and Robert K. Greenleaf, *Servant Leadership: A Journey into the Nature of Legitimate Power and Greatness* (New York: Paulist Press, 1977).

"technological society."[7] The multiple ways that churches have uncritically adopted capitalist ideology and strategies resembles "institutional cross-dressing, in which churches and big corporations can't wait to run around in each other's clothes, each trying to pass for the other."[8] In a recent lecture at Duke Divinity School, United Methodist Bishop Ken Carder bemoaned the acquiescence of churches to the dominant paradigms in society, namely the corporation of the church seen especially in the commodification of faith.

> The most pervasive logic or vision for ministry today is shaped by the market and the values of consumerism rather than by the gospel of Jesus Christ. The myths, rituals, and methods of the consumerist driven market have now invaded the church, been baptized by the church, ritualized by the church until the message of the gospel is so filtered through the consumerism of the global market that the Gospel of Jesus Christ itself has become another commodity to be exchanged for self-fulfillment, personal success, institutional advancement, and now even national security.[9]

Richard H. Roberts associates the corporatization of the church with the emergence of a new form of modern managerialism called "enterprise culture."[10] Enterprise culture, identified with the rise of Thatcherism in Great Britain and Reaganism in the United States, extends the reach of managerial control and routinization to all sectors of society through what François Lyotard has called the "performative absolute," the measurement and evaluation of labor in terms of objective and impersonal standards. Seeking to reverse declining numbers and ethos and to reign in rogue clergy, denominations strive to "normalize" their clergy by emphasizing "effectiveness" (meaning the power to get things done) and "quality" (implying established standards of performance) and by employing bureaucratic procedures to assess effectiveness and

7. Cf. Jacques Ellul, *The Technological Society*, trans. John Wilkinson (New York: Alfred A. Knopf, 1970). For Loder it is important to distinguish between genuine science as a basic quest of the human spirit to dwell in reality more fully and its technological distortion, that is, the attempt to control and manipulate the created order without asking about the essential meaning and ultimate purpose of the attempt itself. Cf. James E. Loder and W. Jim Neidhardt, *The Knight's Move: The Relational Logic of the Spirit in Theology and Science* (Colorado Springs: Helmers & Howard, 1992), pp. 3-7.

8. Michael L. Budde and Robert W. Brimlow, *Christianity Incorporated: How Big Business Is Buying the Church* (Grand Rapids: Brazos Press, 2002), p. 7.

9. Ken Carder, "Market and Mission: Competing Visions for Transforming Ministry," Hickman Lecture, Duke Divinity School, October 16, 2001. http://www.pulpitandpew.duke.edu/publications.html.

10. Richard H. Roberts, *Religion, Theology and the Human Sciences* (Cambridge: Cambridge University Press, 2002).

quality. To further confuse the matter, quantitative measurement of professional performance is often disguised as outreach, service, and evangelism. Carder forcefully diagnoses the church's capitulation this way: "Leadership in the church now is defined in terms of institutional management and advancement, rather than as a serendipity of discipleship of Jesus Christ."[11]

Unless explicitly trying to resist managerial control and routinization, the very tools we use to increase quality in leadership — for example, leadership development literature, workshops, and assessment tools — may very well cultivate in pastors a therapeutic, self-regulatory constriction of self. A closed loop of self-interrogation makes leaders apprehensive and anxious; it saps passion and undercuts conviction, leading to what Edwin Friedman has diagnosed as a "failure of nerve" and an inability to be a non-anxious presence in the midst of an anxiety-ridden society.[12] A therapeutic gaze fixated upon the self closes the self upon itself and narrows its worldview to one of immediacy and pragmatism. To be preoccupied with self and with all the possible outcomes of one's actions fosters a "claustrophobic closure of opportunities for liminality and transcendent possibility."[13]

At risk in the closure of transcendence is the very potentiality for Christians to mature into discipleship and for congregations and other ecclesial bodies to be the church. Without over-identifying particular ecclesial organizations with the fullness of what the church is, still we can affirm that ecclesial bodies, such as congregations, can be more or less the church as their members gather together in Christ's name to practice the presence of God and become the body of Christ for the sake of the world. It is the very nature and purpose of the church to manifest Christ's life in the world. But, to share in the divine life means that we will continually undergo a process of death and resurrection, of baptism into a new way of being. Transformation names this process by which we transcend our present state and find our lives grounded ever more deeply in the divine reality.

It could be argued (convincingly, I think) that the highly programmed, rigidly hierarchical, achievement-oriented corporate model of the church stifles the communal ministry of Christ. It blocks the transformation of ecclesial bodies into the likeness of Christ by preoccupying us with social roles, personal qualities, pragmatic exigencies, thereby diverting our attention away from transcendent possibilities.[14] Beyond that, however, the plain truth is that for plenty

11. Carder, "Market and Mission."

12. Edwin H. Friedman, *A Failure of Nerve: Leadership in the Age of the Quick Fix,* ed. Edward W. Beal and Margaret M. Treadwell (Bethesda, MD: Edwin Friedman Estate/Trust, 1999).

13. Roberts, *Religion, Theology and the Human Sciences,* p. 178.

14. To understand how managerialism and routinization overshadow the incarnate presence and work of God, representing what Loder calls an "Eikonic eclipse," see James E. Loder, *The Transforming Moment,* 2nd ed. (Colorado Springs: Helmers & Howard, 1989), p. 26.

of congregations, the corporate model of leadership and organization simply does not work. In most small-member rural and urban-core congregations, achievement-orientation, bureaucratic administration, and highly structured programs are at odds with a more familial, organic, and less calculative way of life.[15] Yet, we can acknowledge that there are also those suburban congregations who want off the performative treadmill and are seeking something other than a programmed, compartmentalized life.[16]

Auburn United Methodist Church: A Case Study in Serendipitous Discipleship

Let me introduce you to one of those all-too-ordinary congregations for whom the corporate model is ill-fitting. Because the story of Auburn United Methodist Church of Auburn, Nebraska, is not particularly unusual, it may not seem to warrant close inspection. Yet, perhaps because of its ordinariness, because its story will sound familiar — and hopeful — to the vast majority of Christian congregations who do not have a charismatic leader and who could never follow the corporatized, mega-church model, we should pay close attention and give it a practical theological interpretation.[17] This is not a story of explosive growth in membership or of a particularly effective "program." From the outside, the congregation looks much the same, and many of the members are not able to specify what happened. But as pastor Harold Backus sums it up, "Everything is different." "Serendipity of discipleship" is an apt description of what has emerged at Auburn UMC. Although there are many aspects of their story to which we could attend, our focus will be upon the nature of congregational transformation and the role and power of leadership in the process.

Newly appointed to Auburn UMC in June 2001, twenty-plus-year veteran pastor Harold Backus took up his post and began his ministry there as he had many times elsewhere in the Midwest and on the East Coast. He was pleasantly surprised when he arrived to find a healthy, stable, friendly, even a bit sleepy

15. Cf. the description of small-membership congregational life in Carl Dudley, *Making the Small Church Effective* (Nashville: Abingdon Press, 1978).

16. For an example of a very interesting and successful experiment in starting regional congregations within a larger congregation, see Randy Frazee, *The Connecting Church: Beyond Small Groups to Authentic Community* (Grand Rapids: Zondervan, 2001).

17. Cf. Edward Farley's characterization of practical theology as the interpretation of situations in "Interpreting Situations: An Inquiry into the Nature of Practical Theology," in *Formation and Reflection: The Promise of Practical Theology*, ed. Lewis S. Mudge and James N. Poling (Philadelphia: Fortress Press, 1987).

and comfortable congregation of about 350 members, which is considered to be a large church in a small agricultural town. Reflecting the decreasing population across the region, many of the congregations in the area are either in decline or have closed their doors.

Beginning his appointment in July, Harold proceeded to lead the congregation as he had done so many times before: to gently nudge it into a bit more active ministry. An unexpected turn in the story occurred on a cool, crisp day in late October when Harold was pushing his grandson on a swing in the park. As Harold gave a particularly vigorous push and his grandson squealed and squirmed with glee, Harold lost his balance and fell into the swing, gashing his forehead just above the left eye. Not too long after that, Harold noticed problems in his vision. An examination diagnosed a detached retina, and Harold immediately underwent a series of major surgeries, the odds of which were not favorable for saving the eye. For weeks on end he had to lie perfectly still, face down, racked with pain, oscillating between panicked fear of losing his eye and abject boredom.

It was not long until it was apparent that Harold would be out of commission for an extended time, and something would need to be done about meeting pastoral responsibilities. Luckily (or perhaps providentially), in the years preceding this crisis, five persons had been trained as lay speakers, and they took turns preaching and leading worship. Others volunteered to visit the hospitals and to carry on the general work of the church during the most hectic time of the church year from Thanksgiving through Christmas and into the New Year. Much to everyone's surprise, the church thrived. Worship attendance and contributions remained high despite Harold's absence. The most surprising change that Susan, the lay leader, noticed was that people stopped complaining during those months, and for reasons unknown the negativity has not resumed.

As Harold's medical crisis continued, neither Harold nor the congregation could ignore the greater existential challenges that were to come. As Harold lay motionless in his darkened room, several things haunted him. He was afraid he would lose his eye. He was also afraid that the congregation would not want an invalid for a pastor, and he assumed that they would request the bishop to appoint a new pastor. More than this, however, the agreement to distribute pastoral responsibilities to the laity weighed heavily upon him. For as he lay incapacitated and isolated in his room, reports of the church's smooth operation without him stung like salt in an open wound. Demons of despair visited him and suggested that if he were unable to function as a pastor, this would render him in-valid and worthless as a person. As the congregation learned of Harold's depression, fissures in their own sense of safety and comfort appeared. Demons of doubt and fear visited them, as well. They imagined that once Harold recovered, he would want to make a completely fresh start somewhere else, putting the whole mess of the pastoral appointment behind him. To be without a pastor would mean that they would be leaderless, and without a leader, the congregation could not possibly withstand the forces of dissolution that were closing so many other churches in the area. Without pastoral leadership, the congregation feared it would wither and die.

Throughout December, as the church celebrated the Advent eruption of the true Light in a darkened and troubled world, both Harold and the congregation were anxiously experiencing something of a dark night of the soul, exigencies from which they could not extricate themselves. If there was ever an "aha!" moment of illumination in this story, when shadows were dispelled by divine grace, it was during the Christmas Eve service. On that day, Harold ventured forth from his shrouded and solitary room to join the congregation for worship. All the windows had to be covered and the lights extinguished, although a few candles were lit to read scripture and sing hymns. For everyone the moment of Harold's entrance was electric. As he slowly proceeded into the sanctuary, it is reported by several members that the eyes of all were riveted upon him, aware of his every belabored move. Anxiety was palpable, each fearing abandonment by the other.

But the service proceeded with its familiar rhythm; no announcement of resignation came, and anxieties gradually subsided. At the close of the service, the people swarmed around Harold, greeting him enthusiastically. Feeling the press of welcome and gladness, Harold felt enveloped by the congregation's outpouring of affection. The congregation, in turn, felt reassured that he would remain their pastor. As they welcomed and embraced him and he them, as each demonstrated commitment and love to the other, their identity as a congregation and his identity as pastor seemed to quicken. That moment of mutual regard and love was a point of contagion, "a tipping point," when a seemingly small action has great effect upon the system as a whole. They became more of a family, more of a caring community, more of the Body of Christ. It is a moment, as Malcolm Gladwell writes, when "everything can [and does] change all at once."[18]

In the weeks that followed, Harold made his way to each Sunday morning service, and people eagerly anticipated his arrival, preparing the way by darkening the sanctuary and awaiting his slow but steady procession into their midst. Only when Harold arrived could the service begin. Membership and giving continued its gradual advance upward as a sign of the faith community's health

18. Malcolm Gladwell, *The Tipping Point: How Little Things Can Make a Big Difference* (Boston: Little, Brown, 2000), p. 9.

and sense of well-being. Harold was most surprised by the increasing energy and activity of ministry by new, as well as long-term, members. Because of their involvement in preaching and leading worship, two of the lay speakers experienced personal transformation and discerned a call into full-time ministry. But perhaps the pastor experienced the most dramatic transformation of all. As Harold describes it, his entire understanding and practice of pastoral ministry changed. Having gone through the crucible of self-doubt about his vocational calling, he emerged a more humble and yet energetic pastor. He understands his leadership very differently now. Rather than giving the answers and directing things to happen, he has begun to trust the uncertainty, the chaos, the imbalance, for in the bustling disequilibrium of congregational life, growth can occur and new ways of being church together can emerge. His pastoral style has shifted from being a rescuer, protector, and caretaker to trusting that the Holy Spirit is already there, already in the situation, leading.

The Logic of Congregational Transformation

Predominant theories of ministerial leadership are unable to explain organizational transformation in a situation that lacks powerful and effective leadership. What can possibly explain the emergence of new life and vitality in Auburn UMC and give us guidance in other settings? Are we left at the level of mystery? Is there anything we can derive from this situation that might help reorient us and our congregations to the Spirit of Christ who indwells the church? To begin to answer those questions, we turn to the work of James E. Loder and the pattern of transformation. In doing so, we certainly do not want to dispel a sense of mystery and awe at the divine presence and activity in and among God's people. Yet, the spiritual journey of intensified discipleship need not be completely unintelligible. For more than thirty years, Loder has served as a guide and mentor for many who yearn to understand how human beings are conformed to the Spirit of Christ and so become disciples who together constitute the Body of Christ.

Before we begin an analysis of the case study, several preliminary remarks are needed to set the stage. First we should ask, "What is transformation?" Acknowledging that most of the essays in this volume set out to answer that question in one way or another, suffice it to say here that transformation is not only a religious process. Transformation is a universal and generic process of structural change that occurs in every context of nature and human life whenever, as Loder defines it, "within a given frame of reference or experience, hidden orders of coherence and meaning emerge to replace or alter the axioms of the given frame and reorder its elements accordingly."[19] It may be helpful to think about transformation as distinct from incremental change within a system whereby things are added to or subtracted from a given system without structurally reordering it.

With that definition in place, let us consider why transformation is so crucial to being human. Drawing critically upon Wolfhart Pannenberg's theological anthropology, Loder identifies two major themes at the core of what is involved in being human: the image of God and sin. To agree with the Hebraic affirmation that human beings are created in the image of God is to affirm the uniqueness of human beings in the natural order of creation and their closeness to the divine life. This is to say that there pertains an analogous relation between the ecstatic creativity of the triune God — in which the three divine Persons in communion continually bear forth and sustain the creation as "other" than God — and the way human beings grow and mature by transcending their present state in a multitude of ways: biological reproduction, psychological development, sociocultural development, etc.[20] In fact, to be self-transcending and self-giving is, for Loder, the meaning of "spirit" as the human spirit expresses the nature of the ever-creating God, who is the ground and source and destiny of all life.

Sin, according to Loder, is the "de facto separation from God of human beings whose true destiny is union with God."[21] Rather than living transcendently, with an openness to our ultimate source and destiny and an openness to other creatures and the world at large, human sin represents "the perversion or turning inward of the human spirit," which cuts us off from both the divine and creaturely references of our contingency. To be alienated from our very nature as contingent beings produces internal and external conflict, individual and collective anxiety, and self- and other-destructive behavior.[22]

Because the ego's primary aim is to "adapt to the physical, social, and cultural environment so as to maximize satisfaction and ensure survival,"[23] the

19. *The Knight's Move,* p. 316. From Loder's many examples of transformation, we offer here only two to demonstrate the fact that transformation is indeed transposed across the entire range of natural and human existence: the change in form as a caterpillar changes into a butterfly; the redirection of entropy in open systems. Cf. *The Transforming Moment,* p. 42, and *The Logic of the Spirit: Human Development in Theological Perspective* (San Francisco: Jossey-Bass, 1998), p. 248.

20. *The Logic of the Spirit,* p. 28.

21. *The Logic of the Spirit,* p. 28.

22. *The Logic of the Spirit,* p. 29. The meaning behind Pannenberg's term "exocentric centeredness" is helpfully discussed and diagrammed in *The Logic of the Spirit,* pp. 74-77.

23. *The Logic of the Spirit,* p. 72.

ego is essentially a conservative psychosocial force that constructs "self" and "world" without respect to its absolute dependence. To face squarely its own contingency would amount to coming face to face with finitude, with its own mortality, with the void at the center of existence. Existential void comes to us in many guises during the course of life, but none as ultimately threatening as death itself, against which the ego has no power. The harder the ego strives to protect itself from the void, the more it has to rely upon repressive strategies which, in turn, cut it off even further from the transcendent Ground of Being, to which we are meant to be open and oriented. For the defenses of the ego to be relaxed into an openness to that which transcends and undergirds it requires intervention from beyond the self, beyond even the reaches of death and annihilation. "If the self is to remain authentic," writes Loder, "it must be, as Kierkegaard says, 'transparently grounded in the Power that posits it.'"[24] Yet, to be grounded transparently in the One in whom we "live, move, and have our being" requires that the defensive posture of the ego (individual or communal) to maintain and protect itself be negated and transformed. This the ego cannot do by itself. Transformation is at the heart of the matter, according to Loder, because the replacement of the ego as its own ground by a reorientation and openness to the Source of all Being requires changes, not only incrementally in various aspects and characteristics of our lives, but most importantly, it involves a systemic reconstruction of identity in Christ.

To be raised to new life in Christ necessitates a transformation, a transfiguration from one form of existence to another. Orthodox theologian John Zizioulas describes it as a change from a "biological existence" (hypostasis) — in which the ego's yearning for eternal, unique, unrepeatable individuality is ultimately obliterated by death — to an "ecclesial existence" (hypostasis) that reconstitutes human existence within God's eternal life and liberates it from the necessity of death and oblivion. In this respect, self-transcendence characterizes the process through which congregations (and the members) are transformed into what they are meant to be, which is as Karl Barth writes: "Christ's own earthly-historical form of existence, the one Holy Catholic and Apostolic Church."[25]

Loder clarified five interrelated stages that together constitute the transformational process. It is probably easiest to think of the stages as sequentially ordered, but as Loder has shown, one can enter at any point and complete the transformational process. This is so because the inherent human drive to-

24. *The Transforming Moment,* p. 84.

25. Karl Barth, *Church Dogmatics,* IV/1, trans. G. W. Bromiley (Edinburgh: T&T Clark, 1956), p. 643.

ward resolution draws one through the sequence as a whole no matter how the process was initiated.[26] If the apex of transformation seems to be the resolution of a problem, then it makes sense to locate the first step of the process in the initial sense of rupture, disequilibrium, or conflict in the lived world. In Harold's case, disequilibrium began literally as he was knocked off-balance by the unexpected movement of his grandson. As his medical crisis developed and his eyesight was seriously threatened, the transformational process was well under way.

For Auburn UMC, Harold's medical crisis offered an initial opportunity to explore new possibilities of ministry and a new sense of self.[27] Certainly, Harold's infirmity posed a problem for the congregation to address, but it was one they took up without much anxiety. However, the existential crisis in the congregation began in some earnest when the possibility arose that they might lose their pastor. These folks were undoubtedly aware of the shortage of capable, qualified leadership who are available for appointment in rural communities. Compounding the problem, in the United Methodist itinerancy pastors are appointed by the bishop, many times without in-depth consultation with the congregation. The likelihood of receiving another pastor as qualified as Harold was slim at best. In an environment of congregational decline, they would at least tacitly question their institutional viability. That realization kindled a desire — an interest — in seeking creative resolution to the problem that went well beyond what they were able to do among themselves.

To search for clues to resolution is the next stage of the process of transformation. According to Loder the "interlude for scanning" "is the step of waiting, wondering, following hunches, and exhausting possibilities."[28] We scan all of our resources for ways to lessen the disequilibrium we feel and the disruption of our normal way of living. The human ego tries its best to search among readily available options that will not call into question its place at the center of the personality. However, when the problem cannot be resolved by reference to the context itself, and when none of the typical ego functions ease the sense of disruption, one becomes more open for answers to come from beyond the con-

26. *The Transforming Moment*, p. 43.

27. Although it may seem a bit odd, we will refer to the "self" of the congregation as a way to name the common identity that accrues to an organization over time. Well-known organization theorist Margaret Wheatley puts it this way: "At the heart of every organization is a self reaching out to new possibilities." Margaret J. Wheatley and Myron Kellner-Rogers, *A Simpler Way* (San Francisco: Berrett-Koehler Publishers, 1996), p. 56.

28. *The Transforming Moment*, p. 38. Michael Polanyi calls this a period of "Incubation": "that curious persistence of heuristic tension through long periods of time, during which the problem is not consciously entertained." *Personal Knowledge: Towards a Post-Critical Philosophy* (Chicago: University of Chicago Press, 1958, 1962), pp. 121-122.

text; that is, one begins to think outside the box, by allowing insight to come from beyond psychological and sociological constructions of self and world.

But if resolution cannot be found within the normal defensive patterns of the ego's strivings, then where else might it come from? To answer this question, Loder would point us to the dimensions of life that are just beyond the ego's constructions. We have already mentioned that the ego (whether individual or collective) is the psychic agency that defends the self from existential negation, "the potential and eventually inevitable absence of one's being." Loder uses the term "void" to connote the "ultimate telos toward which all experiences of nothingness point."[29] Yet, if we are surrounded by the threat of nothingness, why do people continue to construct meaning; why do they keep on living? The answer, responds Loder, "is intrinsic to our selfhood."

> We continue to live precisely because in the center of the self, for all of its potential perversity, we experience again and again the reversal of those influences that invite despair and drive toward void. Kierkegaard repeatedly insisted with bewildering brilliance that the faces of the void become the faces of God.[30]

The conviction that life is truly upheld in God, that ultimately nothing can separate us from the love of God, is an insight that comes only by facing that which most threatens us. This entails confronting, even indwelling, the very negation we are trying to avoid. For example, Harold ventured from his solitary confinement without knowing how he would be received or if his strength could last the hour. Likewise, the congregation gave themselves to the process as they prepared the way for Harold's arrival. In this case, both Harold and the congregation risked rejection and abandonment from each other to find that they belonged to each other. This case illustrates that the process of transformation is exactly the opposite of a flight of fancy that takes one out of the world. Rather, analogous to the redemptive work of the Spirit, transformational knowing is characterized by an incarnational principle, which is, as T. F. Torrance forcefully argues, the "supreme principle of God's action."[31] It immerses persons more and more deeply into the world and into their assumptions about it so that they can participate in the world in a new and redeemed way.

It is interesting to note that in the scanning phase, not all of the mind's effort to resolve the problem is intentional or explicit. In fact, much of the ex-

29. *The Transforming Moment,* p. 73.

30. *The Transforming Moment,* p. 90.

31. T. F. Torrance, *The Trinitarian Faith: The Evangelical Theology of the Ancient Catholic Church* (Edinburgh: T&T Clark, 1988), p. 3.

ploratory process is tacit, happening in the back of one's mind while one's attention is focused elsewhere. In this case, it is no mere accident that the resolution arose in and through worship, which was pregnant with symbolic and concrete reminders of the life they shared in Christ. In one sense, the worship service intensified the sense of the problem as the membership and pastor gathered in one space. As Harold walked into the sanctuary, members reported that the level of anxiety increased palpably. But later, the practices of worship distracted their conscious minds from the problem as such. Loder avers that such a distraction is an essential component in the transformational process; all acts of discovery are founded upon and arise within the tacit workings of the imagination. He writes,

> Knowing anything is to indwell it and to reconstruct it in one's own terms without losing the essence of what is being indwelt. Indwelling is preparatory; as we shall see, it winds the mainspring of the imaginative leap in which subjective involvement and objective provocation combine to constitute a spontaneous image, the crux of the knowing event.[32]

The great gift and truth of worship is that it points beyond itself to the ultimate Ground from which new life springs. Worship brought them together from their daily routines to a new space and new opportunity to encounter once again the One who transcends all they can think or say, but who nevertheless deigns to pitch tent among them. Worship focused their collective attention beyond social norms and customs that constitute self and world to the empty manger that will, in due time, bear God incarnate. This refocusing allowed their collective imagination to begin reimagining reality outside the predominant conventions.

The third stage in the transformational pattern is the "constructive act of the imagination" in which an insight or vision conveys the essence of the resolution. This is the moment of awareness that we have mentioned above when an insight is felt convincingly, and the conflict or the lack of "fit" we once felt is replaced by a feeling of congruence, of fit, of integration. As Loder writes, "It is this third step, the construction of insight sensed with convincing force, that

32. *The Transforming Moment,* p. 24. In fact, as Michael Polanyi, on whom Loder depends for his understanding of tacit knowing, has shown, a bit of mystery is crucial to discovery and the emergence of insight in every field of human endeavor. Having things too explicit can subvert the process of knowing by relegating too much power to the ego so that it responds defensively to the constructive acts of the unconscious. If knowing is too explicit, too intentional, it can paralyze and reduce the scope of knowing. Cf. *The Transforming Moment,* p. 26; Michael Polanyi, *The Tacit Dimension* (Gloucester, MA: Peter Smith, 1983), especially chap. 1.

constitutes the turning point of the knowing event. It is by this central act that the elements of the ruptured situation are *transformed*, and a new perception, perspective, or world view is bestowed on the knower."[33] For the Auburn congregation, the most dramatic moment of insight came during the Christmas Eve service when the great anxiety between Harold and the congregation dissolved into a mutual embrace and commitment. Could it be that in that pregnant moment of mutual regard between Harold and the congregation — as they saw him broken and suffering, as they embraced him unreservedly — the congregation came to know more truly who they were? Perhaps in their loving care for the one most broken, God's call to the congregation was embodied and made explicit. Perhaps in the congregation's embrace, Harold's broken spirit experienced redemption and healing. Each discovered in the other more of what it means to be the Body of Christ giving sacrificially to the other, and in so doing, making the space between them sacred and holy.

In the fourth stage, as a result of the constructed resolution, much of the psychic energy that was bound up in the problem is released, and the knower senses a kind of liberation and relief. Freed from the burden of holding together relatively incoherent parts of a problem and elated with the power of a wonderful idea or a life-giving experience, the self opens to associations and implications stretching further than the elements of the original conflict. In the case of Auburn UMC, the discharge of creative energy can be perceived in the absence of negativity in the congregation, on the one hand, as well as in increased participation of members in discipleship practices, such as volunteering in ministries and enrolling in Bible study and prayer groups. The change in Harold is just as apparent. Typically soft-spoken and somewhat reserved, so thankful and joyful was he that it was initially difficult for him to talk about the experience without becoming emotionally overwhelmed.

This brings us to the fifth stage of the transformational pattern: "*interpretation* of the imaginative solution into the behavioral and/or symbolically constructed world of the original context."[34] Interpretation is oriented, according to Loder, to the past and to the present, as a means of opening up possibilities for the future. This is vividly demonstrated in our case. After a period of convalescence, Harold rejoined his studies in a Doctor of Ministry program with surprising vigor and urgency as a means of understanding the nature and call of his pastoral leadership in light of his experience. With respect to the congregation, when I asked various members about the Christmas Eve illumination, each of them could narrate the experience, but none could put in theological

33. *The Transforming Moment*, p. 39.
34. *The Transforming Moment*, p. 40.

terms exactly what liberated them from their anxiety. They knew, however, that the ethos and activity in the congregation was very different from that day on, but the reasons for the change were shrouded in mystery. When I first talked with Harold about it, his grasp of the experience was also mostly intuitive. But through his reflection and study, Harold has become quite articulate about the christological identity that they together discovered. Consequently, he is able to clarify for the congregation through the proclamatory ministries of preaching and teaching what they know experientially so that they can more intentionally live into that identity.

However, it still remains unclear how and to what extent the congregation will live into its discovery of greater communion in Christ. Given what they now know and experience, Harold is leading them into a period of discernment and exploration of ministry opportunities with the very representations of what they feared most: declining rural congregations. The great hope is that they will accept the implications of their new life in Christ and live into them more fully; however, the end of this chapter in their common life has not yet been written, and we wait prayerfully their response to the leading of the Spirit. Yet, whatever they choose as a congregation, however they decide to respond to their common calling, they will not have completed the transformational process, so as to end it. Rather, they are together thrust ever deeper into the very matrix of existence where, as Loder says, "the dynamics of change become the vital center of mutual interaction, not merely the means to higher order stability. . . . Theologically, this means actualization by the presence of the Holy Spirit of the trinitarian image of God through Jesus Christ."[35]

Analyzing the case of Auburn UMC vis-à-vis the four dimensions of life in God (self, world, void, and holy) and through the five stages of transformation demonstrates the applicability of the model to both individual and organizational life. As we delved into congregational dynamics, we held in tensive balance the individual journey of the pastor as well as that of the congregation as a whole. For both, the initial conditions of the problematic situation were met with the protective, defensive strategies of the ego. This is, of course, the "normal" course in human development. However, one of the unmistakable conclusions to be drawn is that spiritual transformation, whereby the human spirit finds its ground in the divine Spirit, does not detract from ego functioning. On the contrary, spiritual development sets the ego free of its adaptive preoccupations and repressive strategies to enable greater love, forgiveness, self-sacrifice and other behaviors that are in service to life in Christ. As it became more and more difficult to sustain ego competence in light of encroaching existential ne-

35. *The Knight's Move,* pp. 305-306.

gation, anxiety increased and both Harold and the congregation were opened to a resolution that could negate the negation of the void and so disclose the redemptive presence of God. In the Christmas Eve worship service, a spontaneous eruption of love between pastor and congregation not only resolved the tension between them but also disclosed more fully their true christological identity as the nature and purpose of their fellowship and mission. Subsequently, as the conflict was resolved, greater energy was available to invest in their common life and ministry. Also, as the tacit insight, which was the basis of the resolution, has become more explicit and to the extent that they have chosen for it, the relationality of their common life has come to reflect to a greater degree the "communion-creating activity of the Holy Spirit."[36]

Transforming Leadership

Thus far, we have problematized one of the dominant paradigms of leadership in the church — the professionalized, corporate model. Moreover, we have questioned the common assumption that the fortunes of the church rise and fall on the power and capacities of its leadership. Despite the clamor around developing "quality" leadership for the church's survival, our study of Auburn UMC has led to the conclusion that leadership is not the "key" to the church's life; new life in Christ is. Whether or not some are pushed or pulled by others into the "New Being" (Tillich) is far less important than the fact that they are indeed made new. Whether leadership is helpful to and evocative of transformation is an important issue, but it is secondary to the content and consequence of transformations themselves. Indeed, the development of spiritual maturity in Christ is the true foundation from which church leadership should arise. Distinct from one's skill set or expertise, regardless of whether one is charismatic and articulate, the fundamental mark of a true Christian leader is whether she or he is a follower, a disciple of Christ. William Willimon puts the matter this way, "[Christian] Leadership begins in the mind of God, as a gracious inclusion of humanity into the plan and purposes of God. . . . God's choice tells us more about the quality of God than the positive qualities of the people who are called to lead."[37]

This reordering of priorities puts leadership in a new light. Certainly, we are not arguing that leaders should not be concerned about the power they ex-

36. T. F. Torrance, as quoted in *The Knight's Move,* p. 305.

37. William H. Willimon, "Back to the Burning Bush," *Christian Century,* April 24–May 1, 2002, p. 7.

ercise or the capacities and skills upon which they draw. Rather, these matters are reframed. If living more fully in the communion of the Spirit is the church's true vocation, then it is our primary responsibility to faithfully prepare ourselves for the Spirit's visitation. This raises a crucial question regarding leadership and the transformation and renewal of the church: "how might leaders better prepare the way?"

The present study yields four conclusions about transformation that include three implications for a practical theological reconstruction of leadership in the church.

1. *Transformation cannot be predicted or controlled,* except to say that one can either resist and thwart the process or one can accept it and submit to it as an inherent dynamic within human development. Although transformation has a rhythm and order, that does not mean that leaders can control or predict when and how transformations will occur nor what the outcomes will be. Transformation refers to the spontaneous emergence of a hidden order within a system that reconstitutes it. Because the new order arises within the system, transformation cannot be imposed upon one by another. Therefore, leadership, as such, does not have the power to direct or control the transformational process. This should relieve leaders of the responsibility and compulsion to control congregational change and also of the guilt or shame or frustration leaders may feel if situations do not change in the ways hoped for. Leadership may plant and water, but only God makes the harvest.

2. *Transformation is a means to a more important end: conformity to Christ.* Just as the impulse to control the transformational process is mistaken, so too it is a mistake to elevate the process above the true goal. In other words, leaders should exhort communities of faith to live more fully, more transcendently in their particular corner of God's world so as to indwell the Spirit of Christ and to allow the Spirit to reciprocally indwell them. The mutual indwelling of Holy Spirit and human spirit is the true goal; transformation is the process whereby that indwelling is intensified and raised to new levels. There is a further reason why transformation as such should not become the preoccupation of our efforts: it is primarily a tacit operation of the spirit. In human development, transformative insight is a product of the tacit functioning of the imagination, and that happens in the back of one's mind. As Michael Polanyi, Loder's favorite epistemologist, has demonstrated, there is a point at which too much focal attention will subvert and paralyze the process of discovery, for the tacit workings of the mind, and thus imagination, require a bit of freedom to function properly.[38] Recall that during the

38. Michael Polanyi, *Knowing and Being,* ed. Marjorie Grene (Chicago: University of Chicago Press, 1969), p. 146.

Christmas Eve service, the liturgy diverted the attention of the congregation for a while from their anxious predicament. The diversion allowed the creative unconscious to generate the possibility for a resolution. This suggests that even if it were possible to predict or control the transformative process (which it is not), this type of egoistic activity would undoubtedly subvert and undermine the process by restricting the creative unconscious out of which the convictional insight emerges.

3. *Transformation is fundamentally a sacramental process of indwelling ever more deeply and manifesting ever more fully the divine life.* To caution leaders against trying to control transformation or trying to force transformation upon a congregation does not mean that there is nothing for leaders to do. Of course leadership is needed in ecclesial communities in more ways than I can enumerate here. Rather, it means that quality and activity of leadership should not be understood primarily as a set of skills, competencies, personal characteristics or any other functional criteria. What we normally take for granted as healthy ego development associated with "effective" leadership is actually "existentially and theologically maladaptive," according to Loder, if it gives "more or less a tacit consent to the status quo culture and blind historical influences. To put it more sharply, there is something existentially and theologically abnormal about functional normality."[39]

The Christian life of a cruciform ministry is a "walking sacrament,"[40] "a piece of weak, created, and fallible stuff in itself, but . . . a doorway into the life of the triune God."[41] As ecclesial institutions, congregations are called to live deeply and fully into their sacramental vocation: to be the ordinary means through which the extraordinary is manifest. It is the church's nature to be sacramental, to constitute the whole of its life as a liturgical enactment through which the world is transformed and redeemed through the inbreaking of the Kingdom. Emerging within the sacramental ecclesial life, Christian leadership leads people to indwell reality and its divine grounding more fully. Michael Jenkins puts the matter this way:

> The pastor like the prime suspect in a murder mystery has the means, the motive and the opportunity to commit a wondrous ministry, to point out to us the signs of God's presence, to take us to that place where the holy is found, to teach us how to live with reverence and serve with awe in the

39. *The Knight's Move,* p. 256.

40. Austin Farrar, *A Celebration of Faith* (London: Hodder and Stoughton, 1970), p. 110.

41. Paul S. Fiddes, *Participating in God: A Pastoral Doctrine of the Trinity* (Louisville: Westminster John Knox Press, 2000), p. 295.

house of the Lord. The pastor has this calling above all others to be an usher at the threshold of the holy.[42]

4. *Christian leadership should, therefore, be theologically reconstructed in light of the work of the Spirit and fashioned after the likeness of Christ.* A christocentric, trinitarian orientation in ministry produces, at the very least, three implications for a practical theological reconstruction of ecclesial leadership. First, *transformational leadership and discipleship is baptismal and cruciform.* Church leadership operates under a baptismal imperative whereby each person comes to indwell the fullness of God's incarnate reality through participating in the death and resurrection of Christ through the Holy Spirit. We prepare ourselves for an increasing awareness of God's presence and activity such that we respond by submitting to and participating in God's redemptive activity. We will help congregants to prepare for, to recognize, and to follow the movement of the Spirit not primarily through moralistic injunctions or admonitions to work and strive harder. Rather, as we orient *our* lives incarnationally — by allowing the Spirit to fill and lead us — our own lives will issue forth a call to others to respond faithfully to the Spirit in their lives. We are to be, as Loder urges us, "provocateurs of spirit."

Second, *transformational leadership and discipleship is eucharistic and communal.* As the body of Christ, the church is not an indivisible collective nor an association of discrete individuals. Rather the church is constituted by the Spirit to share in the communal existence of Christ with the "Father" in the Spirit. In ecclesial life, an incarnational, sacramental ministry of ecclesial leadership is constituted in communion and contributes to koinonia, the perichoretic (interpenetrative) sharing of life in Christ.[43] Practically, this means that the church's ministry will bear forth the ministry of Jesus as it was primarily oriented to the marginalized and oppressed in his society. Jesus was suspicious of the religious and political leaders of his day and instead sought out the lonely, outcast, infirmed, and despised to invite and include them in a community of faith. Obviously, this is rather antithetical to a corporate model of the church, but we are called to follow Jesus, not to imitate what society considers to be acceptable.

The third response of transformational leadership and discipleship is *kerygmatic and prophetic.* As leadership is oriented sacramentally to participate more fully in the divine life, that very life of God issues forth kerygmatically

42. Michael Jenkins, "Docents in the House of Wonder: Pastoral Leadership, Spiritual Transformation, and the Sacred Other," *Journal of Religious Leadership* 1, 2 (Fall 2002): 19.

43. Cf. especially *The Knight's Move,* pp. 304-306.

(incarnately) as a prophetic proclamation of the Word of God, calling each member as well as every institutional and societal system to repentance and conversion, to closer conformity to the trinitarian life of God, so as to be more fully a sacrament of the divine life in the world. Yet, as we embody and proclaim the call to greater discipleship, we remember that in an incarnational world in which the Spirit blows where it will, we cannot predict how ecclesial life will manifest itself. Indeed, it is more likely that the emergence of the divine life will surprise us and, in turn, call us to new understandings and ways of life that bear forth the Reign of God.

6. Youth, Passion, and Intimacy in the Context of *Koinonia:* James E. Loder's Contributions to a Practical Theology of *Imitatio Christi* for Youth Ministry

Dana R. Wright with Kenda Creasy Dean

The highest passion in a human being is faith.

Søren Kierkegaard

Introduction: James E. Loder, Adolescent Passion, and the Gospel

James Loder was a passionate man. He talked, taught, preached, and prayed passionately. He lived and loved with what Kierkegaard deemed "the highest passion in a human being" — faith. And as a result he remained undaunted by the adolescent passion that so often seems to unnerve the church. Instead, Loder recognized in adolescent passion a redemptive opening for the gospel. He taught about teenage passion without embarrassment as a key that unlocked the adolescent struggle for meaning and purpose. Sensitive to the human spirit's power to awaken young people (and all people) to their own mortality and to the possibility of their own non-being, Loder also trusted the adolescent longing for another possibility. As Kenda Creasy Dean has argued, adolescents seek something, *someone* "to die for," to use the slang of young people themselves; an Other beyond themselves who "seizes" them because this Lover alone is utterly worthy of their love, their dedication, and indeed the glad surrender of their entire lives. The Passion of Christ, notes Dean, is good news to adolescents not because Jesus suffers, but because Jesus *loves* so extravagantly, with such self-giving abandon, that young people find themselves and

---

This chapter began as a synthesis of several chapters from Kenda Creasy Dean's book *Practicing Passion: Youth and the Quest for a Passionate Church* (Grand Rapids: Eerdmans, 2004). I have developed and reinterpreted this synthesis for inclusion in this volume. — Dana R. Wright

their communities transformed in and through the story of God's *pathos* revealed in Jesus' life, death, and resurrection.[1] The *pathos* of God turns human passion inside out — redeeming, redirecting and reconstituting it according to the dimensions of Christ's self-giving love. Young people who have been awakened to the Holy Spirit's redeeming action experience their own lives as a passionate participation in the self-giving love of Jesus Christ, who is the source, the goal, and the dynamic structure of their humanity. Loder believed that adolescents, in their passionate demand for something truly real, reveal their potential for embodying God's call to the world to reflect the glory of its Creator. God calls young people, and all of us, to recover the *imago dei* by responding to the Gospel in faith and thereby to embody "life in the Spirit" as "the fellowship-creating reality of Jesus Christ" (Paul Lehmann), the *koinonia.* In the context of this passionate community where love, power, authority and freedom are to be patterned after the Passion of Christ — God's self-giving act of love — youth experience an alternative to the distortions of love, power, authority, and freedom promoted by a culture of death.[2] In this essay we make an interpretation of Loder's discussion of this transformation of adolescent passion into self-giving love in the context of *koinonia* as the basis for a vision of youth ministry, conceived as the call to *imitatio Christi.* After a section on "youth and the socialization of passion" to provide a conceptual summary of Loder's understanding of the central problem of youth experience, we will explore several interrelated dimensions of his vision of the redemptive transformation of youth — the theological dimension of adolescent identity crisis, the transformation of fidelity through convictional knowing as the experiential aim of atonement, the agonistic nature of convictional experience (Luther), the dialectical relational structure of convictional fidelity, intimacy as the relational essence of convictional knowing, *koinonia* as the corporate context of convictional fidelity, and *imitatio Christi* as the transformation of socialization into the "corporate" expression of convictional fidelity.

1. This is the thrust of Dean's thesis in *Practicing Passion.* In that book, her debt to Loder's thinking as it influenced her dissertation, "Youth Ministry as the Transformation of Passion" (Princeton Theological Seminary, 1996), is acknowledged, but less explicitly than in this chapter.

2. In his yet-to-be-published theory of Christian education entitled *Educational Ministry in the Logic of the Spirit,* Loder developed a theological theory of action based on a modification of the work of Talcott Parsons centered on "lifestyle" or the "fashioning of power over a lifetime" as a key conceptual thematic. In doing so he also developed a critique of American culture that argues that four distortive lifestyles of the human spirit tend to get socialized in American culture — achievement obsession (the distortion of love), authoritarianism (the distortion of power), oppressed lifestyles (the distortion of justice), and protean lifestyles (the distortion of freedom). Youth in particular rage against, even as they embody, these distortions.

Youth and the Socialization of Passion

To appreciate the depth of Loder's concern for transforming today's youth, we must first understand why he so severely criticized the dispassionate dishonesty and lack of integrity that passes for "maturity" in our culture and in our congregations and denominations under the power of socialization. He recognized that every embodiment of unredeemed culture is predicated on its ability to manage acceptable limits of human passion, to exploit others, and to deny still others (especially those passions that challenge dehumanized meanings and practices tolerated by a culture), all in the service of what he called, following Talcott Parsons, the "tension-reduction, pattern-maintenance" priority intrinsic to the social construction of reality.[3] He considered the church to be especially guilty of being consumed with upholding and securing a "pattern-maintenance status" and thus domesticating the church's potential for prophetic witness to society. Yet for all of his sharp critique of socialization and institutional power, he nonetheless affirmed the fact that socialization necessarily and legitimately exists as a regulative force in the formation and social ordering of human communities.[4] Passions must in some sense be legitimately curtailed or controlled in the interests of continuity and security, and socialization explains generally why order and not disorder marks our life together. Nonetheless, even sensitive sociologists like Peter Berger note that a kind of pathology operates in the passion-regulating power of socialization. "It is a regrettable fact of our cultural situation," Berger avers, "that capitulation to permanent dishonesty is often interpreted as a sign of 'maturity.'"[5] There is something "abnormal" about "normal" socialization-

3. See Loder, *Educational Ministry,* chaps. 1 and 2. On "the social construction of reality" see Peter Berger and Thomas Luckmann, *The Social Construction of Reality: A Treatise in the Sociology of Knowledge* (New York: Anchor Books, 1966). Loder argued that Parsons's understanding of human action under the power of socialization is implicitly definitional for all modern social theory. See his short discussion of John Milbank's opus *Theology and Social Theory* (Oxford: Blackwell, 1994) in Loder, *The Logic of the Spirit: Human Development in Theological Perspective* (San Francisco: Jossey-Bass, 1998), pp. 39-40. "Milbank recognizes that current leaders in the field of sociology of religion (Clifford Geertz, Peter Berger, Thomas Luckmann, Robert Bellah, and Niklas Luhmann) are fundamentally followers of Talcott Parsons's grand theory of social action, . . . even when it is denied" (*The Logic of the Spirit,* p. 39).

4. For Loder, socialization is a dialectical counterpoint to transformation, so that the "tension-reduction, pattern maintenance" movement of socialization implies a transformative movement in the other direction to reconstruct and expand the social construction of reality toward the embrace of greater complexity with greater simplicity. For Loder's most concise elaboration of these countermovements, see "The Crux of Christian Education" in *Educational Ministry,* chap. 1.

5. Peter L. Berger, *The Noise of the Solemn Assemblies: Christian Commitment and the Re-*

unto-maturity, and teenagers in particular detect it, even when they can't put their finger on what "it" is.

Therefore, for Berger as for Loder, adolescence in particular represents the "one moment in an individual's biography when questions of truth and authenticity are at least glimpsed" as a real possible alternative to the socialized distortions of maturity for which the young often capitulate under immense pressure from the older generation. Young people, confronted by a profound sense of non-being that threatens to expose the groundlessness of their impending adaptation to conventional order, may intuitively look beyond the socially constructed possibilities acceptable to adult culture for a transcendent meaning and purpose through which they discover the courage to be true to their deepest sense of themselves.[6] Astutely, Berger asserts that the refusal of some adolescents to "settle down" with these distortions of adult "maturity" becomes a sign, not of immaturity but rather that the teenager has reached a critical juncture in her life demanding the passionate engagement — implicitly or explicitly — with religious ways of being human in the world. Berger avers, therefore, that Christianity must be interpreted in light of an "intellectual passion" that stands in direct contradiction to the capitulation to social-dishonesty which so-called "mature" society upholds. Loder called this "intellectual passion" the human spirit, and he discerned "the logic of transformation" intrinsic to the human spirit's search for intimacy in the context of ultimacy. He further argued that under the aegis of *Spiritus Creator*, the logic of transformation itself is transformed to become what he called "convictional knowing," which is human knowing that approximates Christ's own knowing of the human situation, revealed to human beings Spirit-to-spirit, through the gospel by faith.[7] Apart from the convicting work of the Spirit, however, the human spirit inevitably capitulates to social dishonesty in the service of socialization. Thus, even more than Berger, Loder recognized that so-called "normal" social maturation (the goal of socialization) holds no necessary advantage in Christian experience.

> Spiritual development consists in increased access between the ego and the Divine center, not in ego development per se. Thus, the immature ego of

---

ligious Establishment in America (Garden City, NY: Doubleday, 1961), p. 10. For further discussion on the relationship between socialization, religious practices, and adolescent passion, see Dean, *Practicing Passion*.

6. Loder argued extensively that the whole human development, not just adolescent development, pushes us with ever-greater intensity to recognize our true groundedness beyond the social construction of reality. Human development seen theologically reflects a kind of tragic heroism driving us to recover a primal unity intuitively grasped, what Pannenberg called "the religious thematic" and what we might call "intimacy in the context of ultimacy."

7. Loder's groundbreaking study of convictional knowing was *The Transforming Moment* (San Francisco: Harper & Row, 1981).

> the child may have greater access to the center and be more spiritually mature than an adult ego with less access. However, the adult ego may be more articulate with less access than the child and so effectively confuse the issue, making it appear incorrectly that ego development is definitive of spiritual development.[8]

The socialized ego and the role structures and semiotic "worlds" it creates (the "worlds" we create and then thrust ourselves into) inevitably repress and negate the spiritual longing for transcendent connectedness underlying the adolescent demand to be loved and cherished in this ultimate way, and teenagers know this intuitively. As Loder never tired of saying, young people are "hard-wired" for being passionately self-related to both their creaturely surroundings and to ultimate reality. They feel this passionate longing in their bones, embody it in their hormones, enact it in their decisions, and deeply feel its power to make them fully alive and fully human.[9] Adolescent passion is not a modern "disease," nor a "barbarian invasion," as various theorists have claimed.[10] Rather, as Dean puts it, teenage passion serves as barometers of the human condition, indicators of rising and falling pressures on the human psyche. Indeed, there are no *youth* problems that are not also in fact *human* problems now "come to roost among the young."[11] In the words of sociologist Johan Fornas: "Young people's biological, psychodynamic, socially and culturally conditioned

8. Loder and Niedhardt, *The Knight's Move: The Relational Logic of the Spirit in Theology and Science* (Colorado Springs: Helmers & Howard, 1992), p. 284. Loder consistently emphasized that so-called "normal human development" and "normal ideals of maturity" in society shaped by socialization processes are "subnormal" from a convictional perspective. Both socially acceptable conformity enacted by so-called positive resolutions to the identity crises of youth (in Erikson, for example) and socially unacceptable nonconformity in teens who form negative identities, manifest distortions of their true nature when adolescent development is exposed christologically. See Loder's critique of the developmental project of James Fowler in *The Logic of the Spirit*, pp. 255-259. On the other hand, the classic case Loder cited to demonstrate truly convictional faith in children was Ruby Bridges, the young child who integrated Mississippi schools in the early 1960s and whose prayers to forgive her enemies (the racist crowds in her home town) confounded psychiatrist Robert Coles. See Coles, *The Story of Ruby Bridges* (New York: Scholastic, 1995).

9. The pervasive influence of Kierkegaard on Loder's thought, especially Kierkegaard's insistence on "subjectivity" in epistemology (participatory knowing), is captured by the metaphor of "hard-wired." See *The Knight's Move*, pp. 284-285.

10. On adolescence as a "disease" see Douglas Foster, "The Years of Living Dangerously," *Rolling Stone* 71 (December 9, 1993): 55. On adolescence as "a barbarian invasion" see the reference to Talcott Parsons in Loder, *The Logic of the Spirit*, p. 204.

11. Michael Warren's unpublished address to symposium, "Youth and the Evangelization of American Culture," Wesley Theological Seminary, Washington, D.C. (March 9, 1990).

flexibility [gives] them a strong, seismographic ability to register deep but hidden social movements and to express these in the clear language of style."[12] And while socialization ultimately seeks to domesticate or mute the existential impact of the "barometric" or "seismographic" sensibilities of the teenage spirit, most adolescents don't give up their passion for ultimate meaning without a fight. One way they fight social conformity to the church is by leaving spiritually domesticated congregations in droves.

Reconnecting Adolescent Passion to the Passion of Christ: A Core Concern for a Practical Theology of Youth Ministry

The hemorrhaging of adolescents from mainstream Protestantism[13] that began in the late 1950s had, by century's end, become a well-documented ecclesial crisis,[14] inspiring a virtual cottage industry of analysts who blamed young people's mass antipathy toward institutional Christianity on everything from insufficient leadership training, lack of denominational funding, sociological cycles, to the invasion of a predatory secular culture.[15] Meanwhile, denominations and congregations consistently evade the theological dimensions of the problem. Incredibly, as Dean's work points outs, most efforts to address the crisis showed a striking lack of interest in *theological* explanations of either the problem or its solutions. While adolescent passion remained a constant source of concern for parents, pastors, social scientists, and the media, the *theological* connection between the passion of youth and the Passion of Christ remained unexplored — except, perhaps, by young people themselves. As early as 1934, for example, twenty-eight-year-old Dietrich Bonhoeffer stood before the youth delegation of the Universal Christian Council for Life and Work to suggest that the "problem" of youth ministry could not be answered by youth ministry itself (i.e., by socially established programs and innovations), but only by the Word

12. Johan Fornas, "Youth, Culture and Modernity," in Fornas and Goran Olin, eds., *Youth Culture in Late Modernity* (London: Sage, 1995), p. 1.

13. "Mainline Protestantism" has become problematic as a descriptive term for denominations and congregations standing in the traditionally liberal trajectory of Protestantism in America representing the white middle class, or upper middle class associated with social and cultural power. We retain the use of this term for matters of convenience.

14. See W. C. Roof and Wm. McKinney, *American Mainline Religion* (New Brunswick, NJ: Rutgers University Press, 1987/1989), pp. 153-215.

15. Joy Dryfoos, *Adolescents At-Risk Prevalence and Prevention* (New York: Oxford University Press, 1990); Peter Benson and Carolyn Elkin, *Effective Christian Education: A National Study of Protestant Congregations* (Minneapolis: Search Institute, 1990).

of God: "The future of the church does not depend on youth but only on Jesus Christ," he noted. "The task of young people is not reorganization of the church but listening to God's Word: the church's task is not the conquest of young people, but the teaching of the Gospel."[16] To Bonhoeffer, only the church mattered, because only in Christ, who established and sustains the church by costly grace, does ministry become a matter of passion — that is, a matter of life and death as it witnesses to, and participates in, the Passion of God. Sadly, the absence or domestication of Christian passion *(heteropathos)* that largely describes mainline Protestant congregations today often betrays the efforts by these same congregations to maintain the orthodoxy and orthopraxy of Christian witness.[17] So many congregations seem to have forgotten that *Christian* faith is also a matter of *orthopathos* — that is, a matter of human participation in the Spirit-generated transformation of passion that gives rise to proper doctrine and practice.

Choosing life over death in light of the passionate redemptive action of God resounds throughout Scripture (cf. Deut. 30:19; Matt. 10:39; Luke 17:33) and in Christian writings from the earliest days of the church. The *Didache* (ca. 60 CE) — the first Christian curriculum we know of — declared: "There are two ways, one of life and one of death, and there is a great difference between the two ways."[18] This "two-way" tradition confronts adolescents with a radically different kind of curriculum than does postmodernity's endless array of "options." The Passion of Christ — enacted in the history of Jesus' life, death and resurrection — challenges young people to passionately conform their lives to the image of Christ in and through practices of self-giving love as witnesses to an alternative way to be human in "a spiritless generation."

Of course, employing passion as a theological starting point for youth ministry has risks, not the least of which is its "inconvenient" but necessary connection to the doctrine of the atonement, the source of some of the twentieth century's most shrill theological debates. As Dean points out, Christian history has often misused and misinterpreted atonement theories, employing

16. Dietrich Bonhoeffer, *Gesammelte Schriften,* Band III (Munich: Chr. Kaiser Verlag, 1960), pp. 292-293.

17. On the absence or domestication of Christian passion *(heteropathos)* in congregational life effectively rendering communities *heteropraxic* and *heterodoxic* in spite of every effort they may make to be properly orthodox in beliefs and/or practices, see Samuel Solivan, *The Spirit, Pathos and Liberation: Toward an Hispanic Pentecostal Theology* (Sheffield: Sheffield Academic Press, 1998). Solivan maintains that *orthopathos (right passions)* is the crucial link between orthodoxy and orthopraxis.

18. *Didache,* in *The Apostolic Fathers: An American Translation,* trans. E. Goodspeed (New York: Harper and Brothers, 1950), p. 11.

them as blunt instruments to legitimize suffering, oppression or abuse, or to engender moral passivity and the worst forms of religious reductionism.[19] Yet *without* the atoning Christ (revealed in the cross and communicated through the Holy Spirit) at the center of Christian self-understanding, the ground upon which the church challenges the dominant culture's ideologies of entitlement, self-fulfillment, and greed evaporates, leaving teenagers — like the rest of us — even more vulnerable to distortion.[20] For his part, Loder envisioned a relational way of "recasting" the impact of atonement on adolescent development in light of the Christomorphic structure and dynamism of the *Spiritus Creator* acting convictingly on teenagers. That is, he recognized in the generative but proximate pattern of the human spirit transforming human development itself (i.e., in the stage transition process) an *analogia relationis* to the ultimately generative and definitive pattern of divine-human relations (at-one-ment) revealed in Jesus Christ through the power of the Holy Spirit. Loder maintained that "in the God-man, as in the stage-transitional dynamics, we have a relational reality — a bipolar, asymmetrical, reciprocal relationship" that atones by revealing to the human spirit that the living ground of human transformation is a christological actuality. He wrote:

> The hierarchies of the created order [are turned] inside out [by Christ's nature], revealing that their ground and purpose is hidden in the tacit dynamics that give rise to them. The God-man has redefined history and all its inherent patterns as a created and redeemed order; this order can then be recognized as the external side of an internal covenantal relationship between God and humanity. Thus, all the great antitheses that mark the created order and give rise to hierarchical accounts of that order get their definition from the relationality of that covenant. Particularity and universality, transcendence and immanence, life and death — indeed, all the classical antitheses that characterize the extremities of human nature, includ-

19. The most intense criticisms have come from feminist theologians. Carter Heyward represents much of the feminist critique in her declaration that "A Christology of passion has no place in atonement," as well as Beverly Harrison's judgment on Anselm's atonement theory as "the sadomasochism of Christian teaching at its most transparent." See Heyward, "Suffering, Redemption and Christ," *Christianity and Crisis* 49 (Dec. 11, 1989): 384, and Harrison and Heyward in *Christianity, Patriarchy, and Abuse: A Feminist Critique,* ed. J. C. Brown and C. R. Bohn (New York: Pilgrim Press, 1989), p. 153.

20. Dean suggests that historically in American mainline Protestantism the cross has indeed been downplayed or even ignored, causing the churches also to eliminate a relevant theory of atonement and its accompanying doctrine of sin. The result has been an insipid enculturated Christianity devoid of passion because devoid of the urgency of repentance, sacrificial love, and prophetic protest. See Dean, *Practicing Passion.*

> ing the contingent relation between the Creator and the creature — are now recast according to the definitive relationship given us in the God-man, Jesus Christ.[21]

Recasting human development in relation to the nature and action of christomorphic relationality through the Holy Spirit was central to Loder's practical theological vision of atonement, communicated to a scientific culture. And no group demonstrated more transparently humanity's hunger for such a relational grounding (at-one-ment) than teenagers. What are the theo-anthropological dimensions of the redemptive transformation of adolescents?

Adolescence as a Theological Identity Crisis

Loder elaborated his own version of the "two ways" in relation to youth development in two successive chapters in *The Logic of the Spirit: Human Development in Theological Perspective* — "Adolescence in Psychological Perspective" (chapter 9) and "Adolescence in Theological Perspective" (chapter 10). Undergirding his discussions were four themes that organized Loder's understanding of human development as a whole: (1) the inevitability of order (or hierarchy), (2) the inevitable dissipation of order toward disorder, (3) the possibility of new order arising out of, but transcending, the old disorder, and (4) the relationality underlying the whole process.[22] He described the emergence of these four themes at a new level of intensity and meaning in adolescence, first noting that prior to adolescence

> the human spirit, primarily through its construction of the ego and the superego, has consistently created forms of order designed to sustain the developing person in the face of incipient destruction. However, all of these forms of order were compromises and half-adequate solutions, trapping the human spirit behind the lines of its own defenses. The spirit, restless with its limited successes and its corresponding failure to liberate itself without entailing further entrapment, now breaks free in the strange new powers of adolescence. In effect, all previous solutions to the major issues of the first ten years of life undergo an upheaval that thrusts the developing person into the abyss of nothingness underlying the ego, and calls that person into transformation. For better or for worse, both the ultimate empti-

21. Loder, *The Knight's Move,* p. 197. See also Loder, "The Place of Science in Practical Theology: The Human Factor," *International Journal of Practical Theology* 4, 1 (2000): 22-41.

22. Loder, *The Logic of the Spirit,* pp. 7-8 and 203; and "The Human Factor," pp. 36-38.

> ness and the possibility of new order and meaning are imposed on the developing person at this time. What begins now is a conscious and intentional quest for the adolescent to put it all together in a new and more comprehensive way in the ever-threatening context of potential meaninglessness . . . multidimensional relationality is the context out of which the human spirit generates new forms of order and meaning. Adolescents . . . get a grip on their own many-sided potential for both entropic destruction and new order.[23]

As we have noted, Loder understood adolescents to exhibit behaviors that "disclose in bold type and vivid colors the latent patterns of social disorganization that lurk always under the surface of polite society." Thus, their so-called "social nonconformity is often a dramatization of the [dehumanized] underside of large-scale social conformity."[24] For Loder, social nonconformity often arose in adolescents because the inevitable orders into which they were socialized provided no satisfactory answer to the "Why?" question in the face of the "abyss of nothingness."

Teens tend to perceive themselves in a kind of "lost" state between the fading glory of childhood and the terrifying emptiness and awful meaninglessness of the adult "world" stretched out in front of them. In this awakening of teenagers to "fierce (inner and outer) landscapes" and the "divine indifference" to all things human that *seems* to reign there, Loder saw evidence of the "triumph of negation" in developmental history inevitably revealed to the teenager when she confronted, now with adult-like meaning-making capacities, the full existential impact of "the presence of an absence" at the center of her life, what Loder called "the Void."[25] Loder believed that young people awakened to this deep, pervasive

23. Loder, *The Logic of the Spirit*, pp. 203-204.

24. Loder, *The Logic of the Spirit*, p. 205.

25. The developmental origins of the human experience of the "triumph of negation" are discussed in *The Transforming Moment*, pp. 161-165, and in part 2 of *The Logic of the Spirit*, "The Triumph of Negation." Loder argued that the rise of "object permanence" in infancy allows the developing child to recognize that the face of the mother, the cosmic source of integration for the infant, actually goes away, leaving her alone. This experience of the loss of the face as the infant's existential awareness of nothing (the void) produces deep anxiety which in turn ushers in a "reaction formation" by the child's spirit, who refuses to be left alone. The result of this experience of existential negation at the loss of the face of the mother is the ego, upon which all cultural and social orders are built. In the creation of the ego, the developmental recapitulation of original sin occurs in every person. The full impact of the meaning of human development of these early experiences of negation through encounter with the void emerges in adolescence when the ego is again confronted by the inner and outer meaninglessness. Beldon Lane recalled his own experience of awakening to the void in "Fierce Landscapes and the Indifference of God," *Christian Century* 106, 29 (1989): 907-910. See also Lane's *The Solace of Fierce Landscapes*

"black hole" at the center of their personal reality also awakened to the groundlessness of the "plastic world" being offered them by the official propaganda of the dominant society.[26] The teenage spirit discerns that so-called "reality" constructed by a socialized ego, and the ego itself, are built on nothing more than the empty promises and inadequate solutions — social and personal — to the existential threats of abandonment on the one hand and/or absorption on the other. Adolescents often feel caught between the false yet urgent-sounding call toward social conformity precipitated by culture (the source of their fear of absorption) and their own inner longing to resist conformity vehemently so as not to lose themselves to mass society or kinship structures (the source of their fear of abandonment).[27] Sadly, many adolescents finally lose touch with their passionate longing for transcendent meaning and vitality, and either (1) capitulate to the adult "world" of false intimacies and tame pseudo-ultimacies, becoming in the process willing disciples of what Douglas John Hall called America's "officially optimistic society,"[28] or (2) die trying to resist such conformity.

For Loder, the experiental upshot of this unredeemed adolescent confrontation with the void was a profound, even debilitating sense of loneliness, isolation and cynicism, masquerading as "being grown up." The adolescent loses touch with her unique sense of selfhood, her longing for relational integrity with herself, others and God, her deep desire to give and receive love sacrificially. And in so doing, teenagers replay the infant experience of primal abandonment from the face of the mother, but now with a growing existential, if tacit awareness, of the ultimate implications of the loss.[29] For Loder, only the "self-confirming

(New York: Oxford, 1998). For a powerful fictional description of pervasive negation in young people see Ron Moody's biting novel, *Garden State* (Boston: Little Bay Books, 1992).

26. Recall the movie *The Graduate*, in which Benjamin, the Ivy League graduate, is offered, in hushed tones befitting religious revelation, "Plastics" as the key to adult success in life.

27. There are several modes through which young persons navigate adolescence in relation to identity formation that can be linked to Loder's work. Adams, Abraham, and Markstrom identified four identity categories vis-à-vis adolescence: (1) *diffusion* (corresponding to Loder's distortion of freedom in protean lifestyle; (2) *foreclosure* (similar to Loder's distortion of authority in authoritarian lifestyle); (3) *moratorium* (identity in conflict but not resolved, possibly connected to Loder's oppressive lifestyle as the distortion of justice); and (4) *achievement* (corresponding to Loder's achievement lifestyle as the distortion of love). Loder's point is that whatever lifestyle identity is chosen tends to repress the sense of the void underlying every social construction of reality, and finally calls out for a theological reading of reality. See G. Adams, K. Abraham, and C. Markstrom, "The Relations Among Identity Development, Self-Consciousness, and Self-Focusing During Middle and Late Adolescence," in *Adolescent Development: The Essential Readings*, ed. G. Adams (Malden, MA: Blackwell Publishers, 2000), pp. 72-82.

28. D. J. Hall, *Lighten Our Darkness: Toward an Indigenous Theology of the Cross* (Philadelphia: Westminster, 1976), chap. 1, pp. 43-59.

29. Loder, *The Logic of the Spirit*, p. 219. Tragically, the adolescent desire for experiences

Presence of a loving Other" stronger than death itself can redemptively confront this void and put death to death, conscripting every proximate form of death, and death itself, into the service of Life.[30] Only the One who comes to us from beyond the social construction of reality can "negate the negation" threatened by existential abandonment or the absorption of mass culture and free the adolescent from her bondage to the fear of death (Heb. 2:15). The gospel calls teenagers, confronted by the power of non-being, to embrace their being-embraced by a relational reality more powerful than the void, authorizing in them a "bounded liberty" or "liberative boundedness" that they recognize through faith as their true vocation.[31] In this experience of what David Ford calls the "overflowing soteriology of abundance,"[32] teenage "nobodies" become confident "somebodies," "created in Christ Jesus from before the beginning of the world" with an identity that cannot be taken away from them.[33]

Thus, Loder posits a new, re-centered identity for adolescents grounded in the Reality of Christ. In the crucified and raised Messiah, God has filled the "black hole" of non-being itself with life-giving power of God's presence, in relation to which adolescents find the true matrix of abundant life "in the Spirit." Instead of being divided by unconverted and domesticated passions

---

of affiliation, sexual contact, and fulfillment, and the potential for intimacy, are stretched thin over time as the negation hidden in the recesses of the social construction of reality continues to assert its powerful hold over every relationship. Every aspect of the young person's identity-constructing initiatives — an emerging adult body, an ideology that orients one's hopes, an affiliative community that mentors, potential love relationships that share dreams, a vocation that means something, an internalized sense of authority — all of which they hope can give them a meaningful place in the world, now bear the dreadful traces of the threat of non-being at the heart of human development. Every effort of the unredeemed human spirit to create structures to secure intimacy in the context of ultimacy inevitably leads to a deeper immersion in false orders of intimacy and hollow claims of ultimacy that promise so much and deliver so little, ever concealing the whole truth that tacitly undergirds them.

30. On the death of death see Russell Haitch's essay in this volume, Chapter 1.

31. On "vocation" as a mode of human being in the world see Walter Brueggemann, "Covenanting as Human Vocation," *Interpretation* 2 (1977): 115-129; and also James Fowler, *Becoming Adult, Becoming Human* (San Francisco: Harper & Row, 1984), chap. 4.

32. David Ford, *Self and Salvation: Being Transformed* (Cambridge: Cambridge University Press, 1999), pp. 113-114, 117, 119-120.

33. Womanist theologian Jacqueline Grant describes the formation of "somebodiness" over against "nobodiness" as the goal of youth ministry for African-American adolescents, and bases her analysis on the dehumanizing history of American Blacks. This analysis supports the general call of adolescence in America for a theological identity not determined by the pronouncements of those in power, regardless of race, creed, sex, or color. See Charles Foster and Grant Shockley, *Working with Black Youth: Opportunities for Christian Ministry* (Nashville: Abingdon Press, 1989), pp. 55-76.

managed by socialization, or conquered by uncontrolled passions in rebellion against socialization, the redeemed or convicted self (or community) conforms itself to a liberated identity grounded in Christ's passionate enfolding of it. Loder's insights on the ground of human identity in Christ supports Moltmann's conviction that "Christian identity can be understood only as an act of identification with the crucified Christ, to the extent to which one has accepted the proclamation that in him God has identified [God's] self with the godless and those abandoned by God, to whom one belongs. If Christian identity comes into being by this double process of theological identification, then it is clear that such identity cannot be described in terms of human faith alone, nor can it be protected against decay by correct doctrinal formulae, repeatable rituals and set patterns of moral behavior."[34] That is, identification with Christ's Passion is not first of all a human attainment but rather a trinitarian achievement in the making.[35]

Being Astonished by Being: The Transformation of Fidelity as the Experiential Aim of Atonement in Adolescence

Christ makes the person a new creation by engrafting her through the Spirit into Christ's body, justifying, sanctifying, and calling her according to the elective initiative of God revealed in the cross. Young people awaken to what Abraham Heschel called the "divine attentiveness and concern" for them, so that their place in the world does not finally depend upon them but upon the divine willingness to bear them up redemptively into God's *pathos*. Heschel called this generative concern for the beloved other the "ultimate significance of (divine) *pathos*."

> Pathos in all its forms reveals the extreme pertinence of man to God, His world-directness, attentiveness, and concern. God "looks at" the world and

34. Jürgen Moltmann, *The Crucified God* (Minneapolis: Fortress, 1993), p. 19. In a theological perspective this identification with Christ is not an achievement of the human ego but a work of radical grace.

35. As Barth recognized, "The jolt by which man is wakened and at which he awakens . . . is not the work of one of the creaturely factors, co-efficients and agencies which are there at work and can be seen, but of the will and act of God who uses these factors and Himself makes the co-efficients and agencies for this purpose, setting them in motion as such in the meaning and direction which He has appointed. We are thus forced to say that this awakening is both wholly creaturely and wholly divine. Yet the initial shock comes from God." Barth, *Church Dogmatics*, IV/2 (Edinburgh: T&T Clark, 1958), p. 557, quoted in Loder, *Transforming Moment*, p. 116.

> is affected by what happens in it; man is the object of His concern and judgment. The basic feature of pathos . . . is a *divine attentiveness and concern.*[36]

Like Loder, Heschel maintained that we experience the divine *pathos* revealed by God's personal (Subjective to subject) relationship to Israel and to all humankind (Loder would add, "in Christ through the Spirit") when we turn to God passionately in response to God's passionate coming to us. Christians therefore come to experience *pathos* radically, not merely as an emotion at the psychological level but as the theological experience of being "undone" or "overwhelmed" into a new creation by the divine Lover.[37] Similarly, Reinhard Hütter understands Luther's theology of the Cross to reflect a "pathic" ontology of radical Grace that "astonishes" us into being when Christ reveals to us our "being-determined" nature as creatures. Hütter finds this "pathos of astonishment" articulated by the psalmist, who asked in astonishment, "What are humans that you [YHWH] are mindful of them?" (Psalm 8).[38]

Loder developed his understanding of human development "astonished" into Christo-pathic dimensions through the Spirit in both *The Transforming Moment* (chapters 5 & 6) and *The Logic of the Spirit* (*passim*, but focused on adolescence in chapter 10, "Adolescence from a Theological Perspective"). In the former book he argued that in convictional experiences (those that convince us

36. Abraham Heschel, *The Prophets*, vol. 2 (New York: Harper & Row, 1962), p. 263. This ultimate attentiveness and concern marks the difference between pagan and prophetic insight about passion, maintains Heschel. Judeo-Christian history "associated passion with love out of freedom for others and those who were different, and taught an understanding of the meaning of the suffering of love from the history of the passion of Israel and of Christ." See Moltmann, *The Crucified God*, p. 270.

37. Thus, passion refers to God's historical "undoing" in Christ on our behalf which provided the basis for our own "undoing" from sin and from the conforming powers of the world. By identifying with the One who is God's undoing we are ourselves undone and re-fashioned into the new creation. "Once you were not a people, but now you are God's people; once you had not received mercy, but now you have received mercy" (1 Peter 2:10). On the notion of being "overwhelmed" by life and especially by God's grace, see David Ford, *The Shape of Living: Spiritual Directions for Everyday Life* (Grand Rapids: Baker, 1998); and Reinhard Hütter, *Suffering Divine Things: Theology as Church Practice* (Grand Rapids: Eerdmans, 2000), pp. 30-31.

38. Hütter, *Suffering Divine Things*, pp. 30-31. He writes: "God's specific action here, namely, that he is mindful of human beings, 'determines' the believing psalmist in Psalm 8 and, with him, all human beings *qua* creatures. The quality of a certain 'determination' which a person's being acquired before God and from God (as creature, as sinner, and as new creation) is the pathos characterizing the core of Christian experience." Heschel also noted that awareness of the divine being begins with wonder or "radical amazement" at reality. See *God in Search of Man* (New York: Harper & Row, 1966), p. 46.

we are Christ's), the Spirit works to make the gospel meaningful to us, throwing us into

> a conflict of immense proportions. The Spirit of Holiness makes us sinners, the enlightenment makes us blind, dimensions of the Holy call into play the threats of evil, annihilation, and damnation. The self and all its "worlds" are exposed as alienated from each other and within themselves. This is the intention of the Spirit in Luther — to convict through conflict and then to overthrow the conflict through the Word of the Gospel.[39]

Loder in essence argued that human development itself, under conviction by the Spirit, becomes intelligible as a "law" (like Luther's "first use of Law") that drives us to Christ.[40] He noted: "there is an innate structure in human development that responds to transformation wherever it appears," but in convictional experience these transformations become significant beyond themselves. Loder cited the experience of C. S. Lewis, who was "mysteriously moved" in his study of mythic transformations to see them as "proximate forms" of transformation in Christ.

> If one's defenses against the deeper-than-ego structure of personality have been loosened, broken down, or opened up, then there may be a greater readiness to respond personally to transformational structure written out in historical terms by the action of God in Christ. . . . [Lewis] was able to see himself and those other proximate forms as inside and a replication of the transformation of all things. Thus, his own transformation became fully Christocentric and Eucharistic. . . . [Lewis] is saying that 'the actual incarnation, crucifixion, and resurrection' constitute the most adequate possible expression of God's word to humankind. All of our efforts to restate the actuality behind scripture, doctrine, or any Christian literature are 'less true' than the actuality itself. Yet as described by the early church, the Christ event resonates with the transformational potential in every personality and enables us to comprehend obscure historical actualities, contemporary personal transformations, and the overall transformation of history under his initiative.[41]

39. Loder, *Transforming Moment*, p. 115. Loder draws on Regin Prenter's work on Luther (see below).

40. Loder argued that when a young person journeys through adolescence and awakens in astonishment to the One who passionately loves her, and when that Lover is the Creator of the universe, "one has the making of *homo religiosus* transformed and transfigured by the Spiritual Presence of Christ." Loder, *The Logic of the Spirit*, p. 233.

41. Loder, *Transforming Moment*, p. 152. Loder's references to Lewis here probably come

Conviction means becoming passionate about this Actuality, and it is captured well by Moltmann: "The word 'passion' . . . is well suited to express the central truth of Christian faith. Christian faith lives from the suffering of a great passion, and is itself the passion for life which is prepared for suffering."[42] We might call humanity re-created in these pathic dimensions *homo testans* — the transfiguration of the adolescent capacity for ego fidelity (Erikson's description of ego strength in young people) now reconstituted in four dimensions according to the work of *Spiritus Creator*, who "bears witness" to Jesus Christ. Under conviction, persons bear witness to, and embody, the sacrificial vocation of being human according to the nature of Christ. Loder noted that

> because of their totalism, their deep ideological hunger, their heightened awareness of their potential nonbeing, and their sense of urgency about the meaning of life, adolescents are especially capable of the kind of commitment and 'fidelity' in self-sacrifice that life in the Spirit calls for. . . . Given clarity about the object of faith, Jesus Christ, and the transformational work of his spirit [sic], the struggle to work out who one is only in relation to why one exists at all forges an identity of theological proportions.[43]

When the human spirit in all its proximate transformations is now ultimately grounded as spirit in God's Spirit, young people experience "the glorious liberty of the children of God"[44] and the "experiential aim of the atonement."[45] Now the center of the personality becomes "invested with God's Presence," so that "the ego's anguish at absence and abandonment is dissipated, and its de-

---

from *The Weight of Glory*. The point is that for Loder, human development, theologically discerned, makes sense because "the patterns and dynamics of human development are prototypically related to basic theological concepts; such patterns and dynamics are original but deficient expressions of ultimate categories of meaning" (p. 174).

42. Moltmann, *Trinity and the Kingdom: The Doctrine of God*, trans. M. Kohl (New York: Harper & Row, 1981), pp. 22-23. Thus, the connecting thought among Heschel, Luther, Hütter, Loder, and Moltmann is passivity — not according to its common connotation as disinterestedness or indifference, but rather the opposite — suffering divine things according to the courage engendered from being loved infinitely and completely so as to inspire loving others passionately.

43. Loder, *The Logic of the Spirit*, p. 248. In convictional experience of Christ the objective truth of *Deus pro nobis* is no longer just perceived as a "truth" among other possible truths, but an existential awakening to Christ's knowing of us.

44. Loder, *The Logic of the Spirit*, p. 248.

45. Loder, *The Logic of the Spirit*, p. 268. Through the incarnation-atonement "God in Christ made love the definitive power in and over all creation" because "the conflict between God and humanity has been so profoundly resolved that all creation has been transformed through him" (p. 269).

fensive energies . . . poured into its competencies."[46] Let us consider these matters further by looking at Loder's fullest discussion of adolescent development in theological perspective in *The Logic of the Spirit,* his reconstruction of Erik Erikson's famous psycho-historical analysis of Luther in *Young Man Luther.*[47]

Luther and the Agonistic Nature of Convictional Transformation in Adolescence

Loder's discussion of Luther's experience of passionate transfiguration turns on his (Loder's) four heuristic themes of order, disorder, new order, and relationality. In Erikson's account of Luther's experience, which Loder reinterpreted theologically, Luther was a product of German patriarchal culture and an ambitious father, Hans Luther, who set young Martin on a course to become a lawyer. His father had sacrificed a great deal to make this vocation happen in order to afford his son the potential for enjoying considerable privilege in the reordering of society that was emerging out of the Renaissance. But at the age of twenty-one, young Martin, on his way to law school, was nearly struck by lightning and almost killed. This experience became so traumatic and powerful for disordering his place in his father's constructed "world" that Luther could only fathom a life-and-death (i.e., a theological) solution to his vocation, in spite of efforts by mentors like Staupitz to reduce Luther's crisis to the dimensions of German society governed by a socially constructed conscience. Luther had been so "overwhelmed" by the event of the threat of death and damnation at the hands of God that his whole life became the excruciating experience of "suffering divine things" (Hütter). Entering a monastery, he became a priest, only to suffer a second trauma serving his first communion. What Loder discerned in Erikson's discussion was the eruption of an existential disorder in Luther's carefully constructed "world," which was not "new" but rather "the exposure of an unseen crisis tacitly known from birth" which had now come to the

46. Loder, *Transforming Moment,* p. 167. One could even say with Loder that the redeemed spirit now has the capacity to intentionally transcend normal competencies (like returning good for evil, forgiving our enemies, rejoicing in suffering) because the energy invested in defensive patterns that keep the autonomous spirit alert to securing itself is now redirected to the deeper longing to give and receive love. See Loder, "Incisions from a Two-Edged Sword: The Incarnation and the Soul/Spirit Relationship," in *The Treasure of Earthen Vessels: Explorations in Theological Anthropology, in Honor of James N. Lapsley,* ed. B. H. Childs and D. W. Waanders (Louisville: John Knox/Westminster, 1994), p. 168.

47. Erik Erikson, *Young Man Luther: A Study in Psychoanalysis and History* (New York: Norton & Co., 1958).

surface to demand resolution.[48] Loder noted that Erikson, working from a psychoanalytic perspective, described how through identity crisis "a young man became a great man."[49]

However, Loder argued that from a theological perspective (which was Luther's own perspective), this psycho-dynamic explanation did not do justice to the nature of Luther's experience, nor to the power underlying the generative force of that experience. Luther understood his experience as having originated in the work of the Holy Spirit, not the human spirit. In the adolescent totalism typical of youth, Luther demonstrated the profound means by which young persons can be awakened to a theological ultimacy that requires a struggle of immense proportions *(Anfechtungen)* to flesh out. This struggle, which cannot be reduced to psychological categories alone, pushes young people to confront the limits of their meaning-making capacities at the boundaries of human creatureliness, and places their whole existence under radical question. Loder averred, "In effect, in Luther's struggle there could be no satisfactory solution to the *anfechtungen* [sic] that did not deal with the whole of the life span, from birth to death, from beginning to end." Even as Erikson admitted, "Luther had to know not only *who* he was, but *why* he was, and he had to have the why before he could accept the who."[50]

48. Loder, *The Logic of the Spirit,* p. 240.

49. Erikson argues that Luther is traumatized by these series of events because of the ambivalence intrinsic to his decision, against his father's wishes, to embark on a vocation without the approval of his father. His conformity to his father's expectations (mirroring and supporting society's expectations) comes apart as the "near-death" experience requires Luther himself to rethink his identity from the standpoint of its endpoint in death. For Erikson, Luther is divided from his father's plans for him by the lightning bolt, which brings the whole structure of his ego up for reexamination — taking seriously the sense of judgment and dread surrounding him both theologically (in relation to God) and psychologically (in relation to the father and culture). Luther survives the trauma by "splitting the ambivalence" he has to his father, whom he now both loves and hates. Later, in the famous tower experience, Erikson noted that Luther affirms Jesus Christ as the face of God, which allows him to complete his psychic resolution by projecting justification and approval onto the heavenly father and by projecting judgment and death associated with the evil father onto the devil and the pope. Luther, having formerly been undone in his succession of traumas (the lightning, communion, and the "fit in the choir"), learns to stand firm on his conviction that God is for him, and for us. He identifies with Christ as the good son, through Scripture as related to the nurturing mother, and launches the Protestant protest as a result.

50. Loder, *The Logic of the Spirit,* p. 243. In terms of Erikson's epigenetic scheme, Luther demanded a solution to the last conflict with death, which amounted to "an answer to the meaning of his entire existence if he were to affirm his identity," and this prolonged crisis to find a theological solution demonstrates for Loder "normal" human development transformed into redemptive human development.

Thus, theologically what happened in Luther was that his descent into the abyss of nothingness underlying the social construction of reality triumphed by negation in order to discern from there the ground of his humanity in the presence of God more powerful than death and hell. This "profound move into the nothingness" is initiated by the Holy Spirit, not the human spirit, and may be understood as the "crucifying" Spirit pushing the boundaries of human experience through "inner conflict" to their penultimate destiny in death *(mortificatio)*, out of which conflict alone one receives illumination *(illuminatio)* in the Presence of God and awakens to newness of life *(vivificatio)*.[51] To paraphrase Luther's well-known adage, "convicted adolescents are not made by reading and studying but by living and dying and being damned." This death-to-life movement of the Holy Spirit's convicting work human-ward (order → disorder → new order) has psychological and theological dimensions, both of which are important, but finally the theological dimensions must be decisive if transformation is to be redemptive and our understanding of it adequate to the nature of convictional experience.[52] The premier sign of redemptive transformation is *Anfechtungen*, or

> the mortification of conviction and the way the Spirit begins a work in our lives. Developmentally, conviction takes place with respect to the lost face, not anything else or any other standard. The anguish that follows is the struggle to work back through one's developmental history to deal with law and love, with the hidden and the revealed, with the alien and the proper, with the cross and the glory; this is all to work out the significance of the inner conflict of guilt inflicted by the Spirit in an act of conviction. In Luther these are the temptations, the *anfechtungen* [sic], the struggles with God.[53]

51. Loder drew upon the work of Regin Prenter to discern the "logic of the Holy Spirit" in relation to the human experience of inner conflict. Commenting on "inner conflict" as central to Luther's understanding of Christian faith, and not just biographical to Luther's own experience, Prenter wrote:

> inner conflict is not merely of biographical interest or of interest in the care of souls but is closely connected with the very heart of [Luther's] whole conception of Christianity. *Wenn ich noch eine Weile leben sollt, wollt ich ein Buch von Anfechtungen schreiben, ohn welche kann kein Mensch weder die Schrift verstehen noch Gottesfurcht und Liebe erkennen, ja, er kann nicht wissen, was Geist ist.* In this passage, which Vogelsang used as the theme of his book about the Christ of inner conflict in Luther, it is also stated that inner conflict is of special significance in the understanding of what spirit is. It is in inner conflict and only there that the Spirit's work is understood. (Regin Prenter, *Spiritus Creator* [Philadelphia: Muhlenberg, 1953], pp. 13-14, italics in the original)

52. Loder spells out psychological and theological implications of convictional experience in *The Transforming Moment*, chap. 7, pp. 183-210.

53. Loder, *The Logic of the Spirit*, p. 244. Prenter followed up his assessment of Luther's

Dialectical Identity as the Reconciled Relational Structure of Convictional Fidelity

The Spirit pushes us to the extremities of human experience in order to redeem us, because only awakening to the full force of our existential condition and living in that awareness day to day gives us motivation to look beyond ourselves and others for our identity-in-convictional-fidelity. Conviction originates and continues through the hearing of the Word from the other side, which announces the Good News that the nothingness we apperceive underlying the social construction of reality and the violence we deem necessary to suppress it are not final or ultimate.[54] The relational nature of convictional identity is brought out by Hütter in his discussion of the "hearing of faith" centered in worship.

> The notion of *audire* (hearing) as the actualization mode of pathos points directly to the decisive element of pathos within the theological context, namely, the surrender to God's presence such that this presence defines or determines us and in so doing inevitably defines or determines our theological [identity]. . . . Not only does God's action "determine" human beings qualitatively . . . it also creates them as both creature and as new creation. This human pathos . . . corresponds to God's own *poiesis,* the *poiesis* of the Holy Spirit to which all theology is subjected and which is presented to theology in a quite specific way.[55]

This transformation of adolescent "lostness" into convictional fidelity (the ego strength in "normal" adolescent development identified by Erikson as fidelity,

---

understanding of "inner conflict" cited above by stating, "For Luther, inner conflict is not a psychologically abnormal state, a disease of mind which the pastor should try to remove if possible, but it is a means in the hands of God, man's state under the wrath of God. Inner conflict is a common condition, for the Christian it is even inevitable." Prenter, *Spiritus Creator,* p. 14.

54. Milbank, in *Theology and Social Theory,* argues that modernity (as well as ancient philosophy) has tended to assume an ontology of violence as ultimate. From a Christian standpoint, however, a deeper reality still is "the ontology of harmonious difference" (The Trinity).

55. Hütter, *Suffering Divine Things,* p. 31 (text modified). While Hütter is referring to the impact of the Spirit on the practice of theology, his insights can be expanded to include convictional experience. Thus, we experience Christ convictionally as an "alien" presence awakening us from beyond human powers and competencies by calling us into new existence. "I hear, or I am called, therefore, I am." We awaken to God's mindfulness of us when we are "compelled to freely respond" to One who is both Lord and Life. God no longer remains for us an object for idle intellectual speculations, nor an excuse for liminal intoxication, nor a moral accountant of our debits and credits, but a living presence in whose passionate awareness of us we find the courage to live passionately and freely even in the face of death.

now transformed) made possible through God's accommodating to us in Christ through the Spirit, is liberating because the young person now knows her own identity (and her relations with others) henceforth as radical gift.[56] The relational form of the human experience accommodated in Christ is dialectical — "I yet not I but Christ" ("we yet not we but Christ") — which for Loder is Paul's "highly condensed version of the inner structure of faith" established by grace "across the fundamental abyss that separates the human from the divine" at all levels of personal, interpersonal, and intersocial and intercultural experience. One moves from embodying "negation incorporated" to embodying "life in the Spirit." The central place (and practical implications) of this dialectical identity is made explicit in Loder's critique of James Fowler's *Stages of Faith.*

> The grace of God in Jesus Christ has, by the power of the Creator Spirit working in us, transformed the human ego, setting it free from the negation that underlies it, negating that negation and simultaneously recentering the psyche on the indwelling presence of Christ. The ego, now free *from* its defensive posture, can be free *for* the full exercise of its competencies. It is the expansion of competencies that Fowler's work seeks to describe, but the essence of faith resides in the divine-human relationship, not in the developing competencies of the ego.[57]

We can now ask: What is the essence of convictional identity (fidelity transformed through convictional experience)?

56. Loder draws on George Hendry's insight that the incarnation of Christ has two constitutive aspects, *condescension* and *accommodation.* "However, the Reformers' position so overstressed condescension that it overlooked accommodation. The aim of the incarnation . . . must accommodate to human nature, transform it, and restore it to its origins in God" ("Incisions from a Two-Edged Sword," p. 160). Loder argued that "the restoration of human nature as spiritual" results from the accommodation intrinsic to the Spirit-to-spirit relation established with believers by the work of the Spirit. "God accommodates to human beings by recapitulating in human experience the relationality between divine and human natures in Christ" (pp. 160-161).

57. Loder, *The Logic of the Spirit,* p. 267. This living, grounded relationship produces in the heart what Calvin called "that steady and sure knowledge of Divine benevolence toward us . . . revealed to our minds and confirmed to our hearts, by the Holy Spirit." In this benevolent relation we find a "proper confidence" in the One who neither absorbs nor abandons the other. We in essence recapitulate the Chalcedonian reality in our own experience as dialectical relationality. In Christ, the "full exercise of one's competencies" is the ability to give and receive love as "non-possessive delight in the particularity of the other," or "receiving the other as a gift."

Intimacy in the Context of Ultimacy: The Essential Motivation of Convictional Knowing

For Loder, the convictional courage that arises from the transformative work of the Holy Spirit initiates the believer into an ever-deepening intimacy with the Source of being itself, the true Ground of the human spirit's creative competencies. *Spiritus Creator* works in human experience as purifying holy love at the level of an "intimacy . . . running deeper than [any experience of dehumanization imaginable] and [with] immense restorative power" to release the energy of "perfect love" to cast out the fears that bind us from our true vocation.[58] The intimacy of the Spirit satisfies

> the deepest longing for the Face, the Face that will not go away. This satisfaction occurs at a level deeper than psychological *intimus*, the innermost being of a person. At the very point where I know what it is for me to be me, I discover that it is the spiritual presence of Christ that knows better than I do what it is for me to be me. This realization produces the potential for freedom for intimacy at other levels. This new potential occurs because the recentering of the psyche on the Face or the Face representation, the presence of God, overcomes the two main threats to loving: the fear of absorption and the fear of death or annihilation. This transformation works to free the person to give love because now one does not need anyone else to be that Face. One does not need anyone to satisfy that longing.[59]

From Loder's perspective, then, the redemptive transformation of adolescent experience according to this intimate, dialectical relationality reveals the true nature and telos of human development. That is, the natural developmental drive of the human spirit for order out of disorder to new order exhausts itself when confronted with the existential inadequacies of its own powers — and those from culture — to secure a generative intimacy in individual and corporate existence.[60] We might call this intimacy, born out of our

58. Loder, *The Logic of the Spirit*, p. 265.

59. Loder, *The Logic of the Spirit*, p. 265. Loder is not saying that people and the church community are not needed or not important. He is rather insisting that this intimacy as a work of the Creator Spirit within creaturely life is the generative source for life in the *koinonia*, "the fellowship-creating reality of Jesus Christ" (Paul Lehmann) who vivifies and determines ecclesial practices as the multifaceted practice of love.

60. The awareness of our need for faith (but not faith itself) is built into human development, such that the navigation of psycho-social conflicts outlined in Erikson's epigenetic schedule provides something like the developmental raw materials for exposing us to the groundlessness of our lives so that we might awaken to our true and only destiny in Christ. The deep search

experience of justification by grace through faith, the constitutive dimension of "life in the Spirit," which for Loder motivates the courage to live out of ascriptive worth rather than achieved worth, in this achievement-addicted culture.[61] Our experience of the justification of Christ requires a mode of Spirit-to-spirit relational being-in-the-world that participates transparently (intimately) in the God-man structure of reality, which is a communion-creating Reality. Loder described this intimate communion as "the essence of convictional knowing."

> The essence of convictional knowing is the intimacy of the self with its Source. The breakdown of the eternal distance between them, the establishment of the internal dialogue, the illumination of Christ, the shared joy of Christ and the thrust into the people and culture of Christ, together constitute the shape of that intimacy. This is the form of the ongoing spiritual communion into which convictional experiences call the believer, not once but again and again throughout life.[62]

Thus, in the intimacy born of redemptive transformation, in which we are called to "learn Christ," the burning holiness of the divine love continues to purge us of the experiential manifestations of the barriers to communion Christ has already overcome in the world through the cross. All human efforts to establish communion on other grounds (i.e., the human spirit in all of its constructive capacities and creations under the power of socialization) are exposed as "truth producing errors" that come short of redemptive transformation. The "communion creating reality of Jesus Christ" purifies because it participates in the holy love revealed on the Cross.

> What seems evident from the standpoint of the dialectical identity as moral agent is that agape is not the highest form of love *because* it is self-sacrificial

---

for a self-confirming presence, repressed in the "normal" course of human development and social formation and neutralized by the practitioners of consumption, hedonism, and egotism who thrive in our spiritually adrift culture, pushes young people to despair or to resignation.

61. Loder, *The Logic of the Spirit,* p. 174. See also Serene Jones, "Graced Practices: Excellence and Freedom in the Christian Life," in *Practicing Theology: Belief and Practices in the Christian Life,* ed. M. Volf and D. Bass (Grand Rapids: Eerdmans, 2002), pp. 51-77. Jones avers that courage comes from our liberation from achieved worth grounded in our election in Christ, as "one begins to see that what one does and who one becomes in the messy unfolding of our daily lives are not finally determinative of who we are. . . . our salvation rests in [God's elective] decision and not in the penultimate decisions that constitute the texture of our day-to-day existence" (p. 64).

62. Loder, *The Transforming Moment,* p. 122.

> but because it is *holy* and *pure* and has the power of purity in its encounter with the impurities of creation, including death. Thus, the transforming power of love has its integrity not in sacrifice but in purification of any context where the impurities of human existence have stifled the human spirit, choking off the prospect for experiencing the communion-creating presence of Jesus Christ.[63]

Loder's understanding of the purifying love of the communion-creating Presence of Christ cannot be reduced to psychological dimensions and privatized in the interior of the psyche, for the Spirit seeks to fashion life styles that reflect the public reconstitution of the personal and communal nature of life in communion with the Mediator. In the purifying intimacy with Christ the young person develops "a practice of love through the deepening of spiritual intimacy over time" that "cancels the ultimate isolation of human existence from its source in God's love," including every distortion of unregenerate development woven into the warp and woof of communal life. Reversing the power of the "re-enactment of original sin" at the origins of ego development, which permeate the social construction of reality, the Spirit of Christ takes up the young person's developmental history, and the history of the community of support, and begins to crucify the accrued defensiveness of the spirit bound in sin and to "burn it away" so that our deepest longing to love and be loved finds its generative Source, authorizing a different way of being human in the world with others. *Spiritus Creator* teaches us "the practice of love in the Spirit of Christ, the reappropriation of the developmental history of the 'I' in the dialectical identity bestowed upon the believer in faith."[64] Loder wrote: "such a love is comprehensible only as one practices it in a purifying relation to the other one and to the ground of that love — that is, only as one practices the deepening of intimacy at the one point where intimacy is of ultimate significance in the koinonia."[65]

63. Loder, *The Logic of the Spirit,* p. 270.

64. Loder, *The Logic of the Spirit,* pp. 272ff. Loder drew upon Irenaeus's theology of atonement as recapitulation and Charles Hampton Turner's generic model of the dynamics of mutuality to develop an understanding of the Spirit of Christ working back into the whole developmental history of the convicted person and community through the intensification of intimacy worked out in the context of *koinonia.* For a critique of Loder's view of "progress" in sanctification from a sympathetic Lutheran, see the essay in this volume by Margaret Krych, chapter 10.

65. Loder, *The Logic of the Spirit,* p. 277. Human nature governed by the Spirit of Christ makes possible, according to Loder, "any number of behaviors that are not strictly consistent with the reality principle, such as returning good for evil, forgiving those who persecute, and rejoicing in suffering." See "Incisions from a Two-Edged Sword," p. 168.

Therefore, if the "what" and/or "how" of redemptive transformation in adolescent development is the negation of negation by the Spirit-to-spirit "intimacy (transparency) of the self with its Source," leading to the transformation of fidelity, then the "why" of redemptive transformation is to fulfill the deep longing we have to give and receive love. This "way of love" is precisely what adolescents long for and even demand from congregations that claim to know something about the astonishment of our being known and loved by God this way. Thus, in the remainder of this essay we want to connect these themes of convictional knowing, dialectical identity, and intimacy to an ecclesiology of Christian practices, and to do so under the theme of *imitatio Christi.* But first a short foray into ecclesiology itself is warranted.

Perichoretic Possibilities for Ecclesial Practices: The *Koinonia* as the Context and Goal of Fidelity Transformed

In her practical theology of youth ministry, Kenda Creasy Dean locates "the practice of passion" in an ecology of core practices of the Christian community that together embody corporate life in the Spirit. For Loder, what made these constitutive practices passionate according to the nature of Christ was their grounding in the inner life of the Trinitarian being, which he took to be a perichoretic relational dynamism at the heart of his ecclesiology.[66] In the Trinity, divine persons "mutually indwell one another without changing their identities." God "exists" as a "dynamic dance" of identity-in-mutuality, the simultaneous affirmation of both unity and distinction, such that the "unity is the relationality" in motion and the "relationality is the unity" in motion.[67] Into this kinetic, relational, perichoretic reality, through a kind of "miracle of transubstantiation" (not of elements but of people), the Spirit creates and sustains communion with the church *(koinonia),* our "shared human participation in the very life of God," in spite of human sinfulness *(simul iustus et peccator).*[68] In this miracle of "holiness acting upon sin as grace" (P. T. Forsyth) the communion-creating reality of Jesus Christ "sets the reality of the church as (the justified) body of Christ into dialectical relationship with the church as sinful institution." Christ's Spirit creates and maintains the congregation in this tensive relationality. Loder quoted Barth on the matter.

66. Loder, *The Logic of the Spirit,* p. 276; *The Knight's Move,* chap. 13; "The Human Factor," p. 40.

67. Loder, *The Logic of the Spirit,* pp. 195, 226.

68. Loder, *The Knight's Move,* pp. 300-304.

> The work of the Holy Spirit . . . is to bring and hold together that which is different and therefore, as it would seem, necessarily and irresistibly disruptive in the relationship of Jesus Christ to His community, namely, the divine working, being and action on the one side and the human on the other, the creative freedom and act on the one side and the creaturely on the other, the eternal reality and possibility on the one side and the temporal on the other. His work is to bring and hold them together, not to identify, intermingle or confound them, not to change the one into the other, not to merge the one into the other, but to co-ordinate them, to make them parallel, to bring them into harmony and therefore to bind them into a true unity (which is the unity of the church as the body of Christ).[69]

Thus, the relation of "life in the Spirit" *(koinonia)* to the institution (ecology of practices) is tensive and Christomorphic in a Chalcedonian sense. This means that the practices cannot be simply identified with life in the Spirit (because of the triumph of negation in all human practice), nor separated from it (which would negate the theological intention to transform them). Furthermore, the relation is asymmetrical according to the dual nature of Christ, meaning that the interaction or interplay between divine and human action in the practice must participate in the Spirit's transforming movement to negate socialized order (bearer of negation) and reorder it according to the dynamic christomorophic relationality. Therefore, congregations that "hand over" their practices (even orthodox ones) to the power of unredeemed socialization grieve the Spirit and drain those practices of their passionate purpose and meaning. *Koinonia* is constituted only through the Holy Spirit, and as such, we might say that ecclesial practices become redemptive when the christomorphic relationality of the Holy Spirit becomes the "positive third term" of our convictional praxis. The language of "positive third term" is from Kierkegaard, and has to do with his view that relationality "takes on a life of its own" in the power of the Holy Spirit that mediates the integrity of the bi-polar interchange. In the Spirit the polarities of a relation are "now differentiated out of the positive relational unity" revealed in Christ and experienced through faith. Loder stated: "This positive unity is the spiritual Presence of God in the life of the believer, but true to its Christological nature it holds finite and infinite, immanent and transcendent, together after the pattern of the God-man. However, this is not just a new organization of the personality, but it is the person 'in the power of the Spirit'; that is, the dynamic inner nature of this third term means that a

69. *Church Dogmatics,* IV/2, p. 761. See Loder, *The Knight's Move,* p. 52; also "Normativity and Context in Practical Theology," in *Practical Theology: International Perspectives,* ed. F. Schweitzer and J. A. Van der Ven (Frankfurt am Main: Peter Lang, 1999), p. 373.

person's response to the world, to other persons, and to God is an open-ended and kinetic encounter and embrace."[70] For Loder, the relational transformation of co-humanity in the *koinonia* means that all "normal" relationships (including those embodied in socialized religious practices and family role structures) must be affirmed, crucified and resurrected. The reality of Christ's presence and the pattern of Christ's reality now become the living relational structure through which human experience itself becomes meaningful theologically. We no longer seek to secure our life in Christ by "hanging on" to our practices, beliefs, commitments, et al., for through conviction the Spirit already places us "inside" our practices, beliefs, and commitments and from there calls us to "work out our salvation with fear and trembling" (Phil. 2:12). We participate in the generative Source that gives rise to doctrines, beliefs, narratives, and practices and that continues to render them meaningful to us and through us to the world. We will call this participatory practice the *imitatio Christi.* But to understand what we mean by *imitatio* we must proceed carefully in order to avoid moralistic and naïve or common-sense understandings of the term.[71]

Imitatio Christi: The Convictional Transformation of Socialization as the Corporate Form of Convictional Fidelity

According to Dean, the word "imitation" here is taken from the Greek term *mimesis,* which generally means to acquire what the other has, or to become what the other is. John's Gospel underscores the need to identify with Christ in something like a mimetic way with its frequent use of the particle *kathōs,* such as in his exhortation to his followers, "As I . . . so also you" (John 13:34; 15:12). Although in English we translate *kathōs* as "as," merely suggesting a rough equivalent or a similarity of intention, the Greek connotation is much stronger: "exactly as" or "to the exact same degree and extent as." The implication here is more than moral imitation, or simulation, or copying. *Mimesis* has to do with enactment, embodiment, even *methexis* or participation. Jesus is not asking his

70. *The Knight's Move,* p. 144.

71. We are not concerned here with supporting programs of moral strenuousness advocated in years past and present like "What would Jesus do?" campaigns, the spiritual counterpart to Nancy Reagan's famous "Just say no!" campaign against drugs. Such efforts may signify a psychological naiveté that assumes that to tell young people what to do and to point them to moral exemplars satisfies their deep-seated longing for meaning and purpose. Kenda Dean expands on this point in *Practicing Passion.* Her discussion there is indebted to Erich Auerbach's classic study *"Mimesis": The Representation of Reality in Western Literature,* trans. W. R. Track (Princeton: Princeton University Press, 1953).

disciples to "ape" his behavior — as if life, death, and resurrection could be "aped" — but to be incorporated (in-bodied) into a living-dying-rising communion of the Holy Spirit in which learning to love in the power of the Spirit is central. The community responds to the Spirit by creating "forms of excellence" (ecclesial practices) that give christomorphic pattern to human experience grounded in God's passionate delight in God's people.[72] The justified and sanctified community comes to expression in ecclesial life in passionate participation in practices like prayer, worship, fellowship, friendship, study, meditation, service, etc. However, these and other practices have no redemptive power in and of themselves apart from the communion-creating Spirit of Christ vivifying human actions "not once but again and again throughout life."[73] Practices, like other constructs of the human spirit — ego, role structures, identities, institutions, ideologies, human development, culture, language — always incorporate and transmit existential negation apart from this kinetic participation in the work of the Holy Spirit.

For Loder, all of these transformative practices, beliefs, commitments "bear a figural or 'sacramental' relationship to the ultimate transformation" in Christ, "who is to come as the climax of the history of transformations and as the finisher of all unfinished transformations."[74] Speaking of this transforming judgment of Christ on all kinship structures resident in the celebration of the Eucharist, for example, Loder wrote:

> At the Lord's Supper [we are] put into a new bloodline. It is a judgment on kinship. You are not finally a member of your family. You do not belong to them. You belong to Christ. Christ separates you from your family and so

72. Serene Jones, "Graced Practices." The incarnation is not simply a movement of solidarity with humanity — it is also an atonement and reconciliation and reconstruction of humanity according to the nature of Christ. The objective of salvation is so share in Christ's nature in every sphere of human action, the nature of which is love. Of course, the decision to love always implies a willingness to suffer with and for the beloved. The suffering of Christ is grounded in God's passionate delight in creation; it is not intended to demonstrate the merits of self-sacrifice. Church historian Roberta Bondi observes:

> The early church does not teach that the most basic quality of God's love is a suffering self-sacrifice. What first engages God with us is not a duty of need or self-sacrifice or obligation or the need to be right or good but delight in us as the beloved. . . . Delight makes the lover extravagantly eager to make sacrifices for the beloved. The cross, which is the occasion for God's own terrible pain, is very real, but it is God's delight in and desire for us that calls God to do it. (Roberta Bondi, *To Pray and to Love: Conversations on Prayer with the Early Church* [Minneapolis: Fortress, 1991], pp. 121-122)

73. Loder, *Transforming Moment,* p. 122.

74. Loder, *Transforming Moment,* p. 120.

> enables you to really love them. The reason we have to be separated from family is because it is where you learn ego patterns and role structures. As long as the Lord's Supper sacralizes ego patterns and role structures, it is taken to your condemnation. . . . So if you take it rightly, it separates you from your family, it separates you from your kinship so that you can re-enter those relationships on the strength of who Christ is . . . a communion creating reality.[75]

Here is the redemptive transformation of practice: the crucifixion of socially established human actions and the raising of them to participate in the perichoretic power of trinitarian relations.

Although Loder taught that transformed youth do indeed go in search of a community of love and faith (the *koinonia*) to support their own Spirit-led "journey of intensification" to create a Christian style of life, his concern to expose socialization as the inevitable bearer of "negation incorporated" in the corporate life may have muted his efforts to elaborate how the core practices that make up the *koinonia's* embodiment of "life in the Spirit" can be understood to participate in, and to give shape to, corporate experiences of convictional fidelity.[76] We may ask, "Does Loder have a communal analogue to the journey of intensification?" He offered a clue for making this analogical connection in the twelfth lecture from ED 105, "Worship as Paradigm for Education." Here he argued that the repeated practice of worship *(leitourgia)* functioned like a fourth type of learning theory he called "paradigmatic learning."[77] Paradigmatic learning takes place through "the spontaneous emergence of a new grammar or logic by which all previous symbols and symbolic systems are simultaneously reconstructed." Drawing on an unpublished dissertation by one

75. Loder, *Educational Ministry,* p. 106. The reason dialectical identity and the intensification of intimacy need practices to incarnate love is that the Spirit of Christ, the Spirit of holiness, must accommodate to the other in order to love the other. The Spirit seeks a medium through which to communicate the Spirit's own nature, so to speak — first in Christ and then in the church. But church practices as the media of the Spirit no longer "exist" outside the transformed personality as "objects" within the ego's domain, for the whole ego-matrix has been decentered and re-centered according to the relational (dialectical) identity established in Christ.

76. Generally, Christian or religious educators recognize a core ecology of practices that make up the "curriculum" of the church. These generally consist of larger categories of worship, fellowship, preaching, teaching, service, and witness. See Maria Harris, *Fashion Me a People: Curriculum in the Church* (Louisville: Westminster/John Knox, 1989), and Robert Pazmino, *Principles and Practices of Christian Education: An Evangelical Perspective* (Grand Rapids: Baker, 1992), for different ways of articulating these ecologies of practice.

77. The other three learning types were (1) classical conditioning, (2) operant conditioning (behavior modification), (3) symbolic learning. See *Educational Ministry,* pp. 225ff.

of his students, John S. McClure, Loder outlined the power of the liturgy of the Word to effect a paradigmatic theological transformation among congregants.[78] He then argued that the liturgy "works" transformation "because (as the basic structure of reality) it discloses and celebrates the hidden order of all creation and redemption into which we are baptized," which is "the pattern of Christ" (Phil. 2:5-11). Through the worship of God in passionate faith, the Spirit negates every false form (Greek *schēma*) of unredeemed human existence and calls us to participate together in the true form (Greek *morphē*) of humanity defined by Christ. The "pattern of Christ . . . the underlying grammar of the liturgy . . . is designed to break down schematic assumptions of the marketplace and transform them via a step by step deepening of our conformation to Christ and his pattern for the redemption of the world." Four times in the liturgy the pattern is enacted, so that

> the pattern here is not primarily socialization, but primarily transformation. The holistic pattern of Christ which is embedded in us through our baptism into his nature, emerges for the worshipper like the configurations of a photograph emerge from the negative exposure by being repeatedly immersed in an appropriate chemical process. Socialization and related forms of learning are all involved but they are all gathered up under the larger pattern of Christ which transforms us and all creation into the life of God. Learnings of all sorts are designed to give rise to the new grammar in the liturgy. In turn, then, all such learning needs re-interpretation in light of the vision of Christ, according to whose nature all things are destined to be transformed to the glory of God.[79]

Loder seemed to be arguing here that we "learn Christ" through a faithful immersion over time in the pattern of Christ embodied in dynamic, four-dimensional practices (paradigmatically the practice of worship). In this corporate practice, the negation-negating and intimacy-creating power of the Spirit engages us in a *corporate* "journey of intensification" out of which an uncommon life-style emerges that reflects (in partial yet nonetheless authentic ways) the nature of Christ in the corporate life. Liturgy, then, is the paradigmatic expression of our embodiment of the *imago Christi* — the goal and des-

78. First, the liturgy draws worshipers out of the marketplace and into the "strange world of God's presence." Second, worshipers enter the "strange world of the Bible" through the reading of Scripture. Third, the sermon bears the Word of God using ordinary language, so that the marketplace is claimed as the arena of God's action. And fourth, the congregation becomes the bearer of the divine mission toward the world. See *Educational Ministry,* pp. 229-230.

79. *Educational Ministry,* p. 233.

tiny of human creation. The practices themselves (liturgy and by extension all core practices), as they participate passionately in the life of Christ, can be conceived from this perspective as *imitatio Christi.* Crucial to the *imitatio Christi* conceived as communal practices on the corporate journey of intensification is the re-tension of (i.e., keeping the tensiveness of) the bipolar relationality that makes up the practices (divine and human action in christomorphic relationality). These practices must embody the tensiveness that Luther captured at the heart of his soteriological imagination: *simul iustus et peccator.* In Loder's metaphor of a congregation's "repeated immersion" in a "chemical process" that transforms it, the ingredients in kinetic tension *(simul)* are human action bearing negation *(peccator)* and divine action actualizing transformation *(iustus).* This metaphor complements Sarah Coakley's notion of the "hidden efficacy" at work in the "handing over" of Christ's body to the world through long-term immersion in faithful practice. We conclude, then, with a short conversation between Coakley and Loder on "deepening practices" as a way to talk about *imitatio Christi* as the "corporate journey of intensification" central to youth ministry.[80]

Drawing upon the work of Anglican W. H. Vanstone, Coakley helpfully places her discussion of Christian practices in the context of the "long haul" (using Vanstone's metaphor of moving from the shallow end to the deep end of a swimming pool) to argue that the work of the Spirit in and through ecclesial practices functions as "the handing over" of Christ's body to the world in a process that often bears only "hidden efficacy." As a "peculiarly active form of passivity" (what we mean by *imitatio Christi*) that embodies both the means and ends of redemptive transformation, this "handing over" of Christ's body is the process that reveals Christ over the "long haul" of repeated (and qualitatively distinct yet integrated) practices of faithfulness.[81] Ancient theologians, according to Coakley, discerned in the repetition of Christian practices over time a purification movement that (1) initially embodies what we might call *purgative*

80. Sarah Coakley, "Deepening Practices: Perspectives from Ascetical and Mystical Theology," in M. Volf and D. Bass, eds., *Practicing Theology,* pp. 78-93. Dean bases her description of youth ministry as *imitatio Christi* on the classical categories of practice outlined by Coakley. See Dean, *Practicing Passion.*

81. Coakley wants to complexify our understanding of practices by attending to how "the logical relation of beliefs to practices may shift in different circumstances and in different stages of a Christian person's growth to spiritual maturity . . . the 'deepening' of practices . . . allows forms of belief to emerge that could not otherwise be accessed" ("Deepening Practices," p. 78). She draws on pre-Reformation Catholic theology's discernment of different manifestations of grace to discern "the way in which human responsiveness to the divine could have different shades or depths through a lifetime of graced interaction with divine love" (p. 79).

imitatio (i.e., the intentional setting of life in Christ over against the former life defined by the world);[82] (2) moves through a stage we might call *illuminative imitatio* (i.e., a more habituated imitation that results in the indirect or subconscious enlargement of the heart toward genuine creaturehood);[83] and finally (3) arrives at *unitive imitatio* (i.e., transparent incorporation into the life of the Trinity, what Loder called the "mundane ecstasy" of transparency);[84] Coakley then argues that in this last stage the means of *imitatio Christi* (Christian practices) and the end of *imitatio Christi* (communion) converge, so that what is revealed as *unitive imitatio* in maturity has actually been the tacit or underlying truth of the whole journey of faith from beginning to end.

> Clearly something crucial has occurred to the notion of practice in thus charting different levels of appropriation and relation to beliefs. At the third level . . . an approach to the Trinity is hazarded that, it is claimed by the contemplatives involved, can only be the epistemological preserve of those already transformed by divine grace itself to the point of "spiritual marriage." But what culminates in "union" has been sustained throughout . . . by God's providence; even the ostensibly trivial acts of Christian self-definition in the neophyte (like forsaking wearing jewelry) . . . but the goal is a progressive purification of the self so as to become transparent to the divine.[85]

Coakley's discussion complements Loder's suggestive interpretation of the

82. Young persons who forsake jewelry, commit themselves to chastity before marriage, or burn their stereo equipment to demonstrate their conviction may be engaging in *imitatio Christi* at the purgative level.

83. "In the second level . . . the 'over-and-againstness' of Christian identity secured in the first level is more subtle. . . . [Christian practices] are to be followed in order that, over a lifetime, there may be a habituating of love, an imitation in a more than extrinsic way of the life of Christ . . . practices will re-modulate beliefs, . . . they will cause us to find Christ . . . in new and unexpected places" (Coakley, "Deepening Practices," p. 86).

84. The transforming union actualized in our incorporation into the life of the Trinity is, according to Coakley's understanding of the mystics, "corporeal" in that it does not depend on "intense psychological ecstasies" but rather takes place in "the ordinary" as a "permanent incarnational reality" ("Deepening Practices," p. 89). This emphasis recalls Loder's theme of "mundane ecstasy." Loder wrote, "In the ecstasy of Christian experience, one perceives the world of common experience in a new way; one becomes absorbent of almost more 'mundaneness' than can be contained. One is beside oneself in the perception of particularity and the essential goodness of being itself" (*Transforming Moment*, p. 109). Loder continued, "such an ecstasy is an affront to those personal, social, and cultural systems that are built on the systematic repression of the void and of the Holy" (p. 110).

85. Coakley, "Deepening Practices," p. 90.

efficacy of liturgical practice "in the Spirit" as we think about our relationship to supposedly low levels of spiritual maturity — that is, in young people. Her work suggests that the *imitatio Christi* can take "adolescent form" as *"purgative imitatio"* and yet be affirmed as participating in *unitive imitatio* nonetheless. Adolescents who have awakened to the reality of Christ's Presence in their lives (who have come into the tension of the *simul*) bear the traces of Christ's nature even when their general behavior remains uncomfortably *adolescent* on the surface. Thus, communities of faith can fully rejoice over, and delight in, the particularity of the teenager who has entered passionately into the "shallow end" of a very long marathon swim and who may struggle for years to find her "stroke." Youth leaders "in the Spirit" will rejoice in this spiritual tadpole and passionately love her further into the deeper waters of faith, through which she will finally be transformed into the princess she already is in Christ. And she in turn will hold the community accountable to its best theological identity by insisting (even demanding) to be loved this way. The *simul peccator* side of the tension in *imitatio Christi* is realized when young people are loved unconditionally like this.

On the other hand, Loder helps deepen Coakley's insight into the legitimacy of adolescent practices by his insistence, cited earlier, that so-called normal human development under the *aegis* of the ego represents no necessary advantage for, and may in fact be a liability to, spiritual maturity defined as increased access of the human spirit to the Holy Spirit.[86] The communion-creating nature of the work of the Spirit means that practices reflect their transparent grounding in the power that posits them, the redemptive relationality established from the divine side human-ward by the Christ event. Communities of faith are called to embody this relationality as they entrust themselves to a faithful Creator who works over "the long haul" to redeem us all, and teenagers may actually be light-years ahead of adults when it comes to living out this intimate relationality Spirit-to-spirit. "Unless you become like a child you shall have no part of me." The capacity for spiritual integrity, even prophetic witness, in and through young people reflects perhaps the impact of the *simul iustus* side of the tension of *imitatio Christi* for youth alive in the Spirit.

Conclusion: Reclaiming a Passionate *Imitatio Christi* for Youth Ministry

Will mainline Protestant congregations reclaim the Passion of Christ as the ground and structure of their theological identity? Will they take up the risky

86. See note 8 above.

way of love that imitates Christ by learning to live "in the Spirit"? We don't know. But we are convinced that the youth of today and tomorrow will continue to demand that congregations embody the *imitatio Christi* (the corporate journey of intensification) in terms similar to those outlined in this essay. They will do so because it is in them to demand it. And when they don't find "the real thing" in congregations, teens will continue to act out in violent, anti-social behavior until and unless we either shame them into spirit-depleting conformity to the "plastic worlds" of false imitations we have created, or until they destroy themselves by "looking for love in all the wrong places." Either way, they will not darken the door of a passionless church in which the so-called imitation of Christ looks suspiciously more like an imitation *from* culture than *of* Christ. Loder challenged passionless Christianity to repent of its spiritual tepidity and to forsake its grieving of the Spirit's presence, because he knew so much more had been promised to us. He called upon the Spirit to breathe new passion into the church, so that she might fulfill she marturological vocation in the world "to give and receive love." Loder bet his life that young people, and all people, would die to be part of a community that loved so passionately. We believe he was on to something crucial, a *crux* or cross for the church to bear that she dare not fail to take up with passion.

II. Redemptive Transformation *of* Practical Theology

7. Remembering the Poor: Transforming Christian Practice

Susanne Johnson

They asked only one thing, that we remember the poor. . . .

Galatians 2:10

This chapter is a critical inquiry, from the standpoint of a practical theologian and Christian educator, into *remembering the poor* as a "practice" constitutive of Christian faith and life; more specifically, it is inquiry into the contemporary church's engagement in that practice. The chapter is laid out in four parts. In section one I set forth a way to understand the notion of "practice," especially as related to the Christian practice of remembering the poor. In section two, I offer some critical observation of how our prevailing economic choices as a nation are institutionalizing gross inequities between the rich and the poor, and perpetuating unprecedented levels of poverty and suffering — despite touts of economic progress and development in the U.S. and around the globe. In section three I explore the contemporary church's conventional response to the poor — a *service paradigm* — finding it to be inadequate, both in terms of the demands of the gospel and the demands of contemporary socioeconomic realities. Folded into this section I also name, in a variety of ways, theological grounds of our hope and freedom as believers to resist injustice, and to make choices more in keeping with our own distinctive Christian Story and Vision. In section four, in skeletal fashion I briefly outline a *faith-based community revitalization paradigm,* an approach I consider to be especially fitting to the church's call, and privilege, to participate in God's own missionary activity in the world in remembering the poor and renewing all things in Christ Jesus.

Because there exists an appalling and ever-widening gap between the have-*nots* and have-*lots* in the U.S. and around the globe, and because *remembering the poor* is one of the practices most fundamentally constitutive of the

Christian witness of faith, there is tremendous need today for a radical rethinking of its nature as such, and its potential impact on the shape and scope both of practical theology and Christian education in the twenty-first century. In light of the virtual stampede toward urban ministry and the fevered academic interest in *economic globalization* sweeping through theological education today, the need is all the greater for a fresh consideration of the ancient practice of remembering the poor, and for an articulation of its connection to the contemporary theological agenda. What is the real impetus for urban ministry anyway? And why should we concern ourselves with a topic that seems so remote and removed as economic globalization? We need a renewed theological vision and conceptualization that brings these disparate but related dynamics into clearer connection and perspective, affording us the possibility of more faithful, creative participation in, and public witness to, God's own missionary work in the world, and God's own special concern for remembering the poor.

The Christian Faith: A Rich Tapestry of Practices

Among a growing number of scholars today, there is an emerging consensus that — in terms of its lived expression — the Christian faith can best be understood as a rich tapestry of practices that form a dynamic Way of living in the world. Speaking of faith in these terms serves as a reminder that faith is not so much something we *have* as it is something we *do*. Faith is a verb, not a noun.

Some theorists of human development posit faith as an innate construct of the human personality — a genetic endowment — thus interpreting faith as the "organ" by and through which human beings make meaning. Rather than construing faith as an innate, developmental competency of the human ego — as the structural school of thought contends — in *The Logic of the Spirit* James Loder rightly claims that faith is best understood biblically as a dynamic, active participation in the power and purposes of God in and for the sake of the world. Faith arises or comes forth in, and depends on, relational encounters with witnesses of faith, preeminently an encounter with Jesus. There is an "event" quality to faith as it is always played out — *practiced* — in historical, concrete situations where repeatedly it proves and authenticates itself as faithfulness to God's own creative and transformative work in the world.[1]

It is the perspective on faith as a participation in the power and purposes of

1. James E. Loder, *The Logic of the Spirit: Human Development in Theological Perspective* (San Francisco: Jossey-Bass Publishers, 1998), pp. 257-258. Loder acknowledges his indebtedness to Gerhard Ebeling for many of his insights regarding faith.

God for the life of the world that I assume in this chapter. Having both a divine and human side — on the human, subjective side, faith is something we human beings *do.* Faith is something we *practice* in light of and in response to our discernment of God's active presence in and for the sake of the whole created order.

Much of the recent work on the notion of Christian faith practice is informed by Alasdair MacIntyre's influential book *After Virtue: A Study in Moral Theory.*[2] Rather than the more familiar and traditional language of spiritual disciplines or means of grace, the terminology of "practice" is widely used today in hopes of helping believers think in fresh new ways about older traditions in the church. In this present chapter, I use practice in MacIntyre's sense to refer to a coherent and complex form of socially established human activity that addresses some particular, fundamental human need, and that includes an ongoing tradition and designated practitioners.

Given our individualistic approach to Christian faith and spirituality, when we talk about Christian practice we likely call to mind images such as an individual actor off alone somewhere engaged in meditation and prayer. But notice that "practice" as defined here embraces activity shared by and within communities; it is a *cooperative* human enterprise. The actions of persons become "practice" only when engaged in as participation in the larger practice of a community into which the "practitioners" have been initiated, and by which they are held accountable according to standards internal to the practice. Law, medicine, and social work, for example, reflect this understanding of practice.

Communities shape their practices in distinctive ways. But practices also shape communities and individual members therein particular ways, giving practices epistemological and moral weight. Through lifelong engagement in practices we come into awareness of certain realities — we come *to see* and *to know* and even *to be* things — that apart from such participation would otherwise remain beyond our ken. There are certain goods, values, and virtues internal to particular practices that can be acquired only from the inside out, through sustained participation in practicing communities. Through cooperative engagement over time, intersubjectively and communally we form a *habitus,* understood as a predisposition to be a particular kind of community, and a particular kind of person within the community. Formation of a distinctly Christian, therefore also a theological, *habitus* involves sustained, lifelong communal participation in practices constitutive to the Christian faith and life. Though we are prone to view our engagement in certain practices — such as remembering the poor — as the *consequence* of our faith in God, scrip-

2. Alisdair MacIntyre, *After Virtue: A Study in Moral Theory,* 2nd ed. (Notre Dame: University of Notre Dame Press, 1984).

tures often reverse this logic, claiming some practices as the *precondition* for authentic worship, praise, and participation in the life of God. According to Gospel writers Luke and Matthew, remembering the poor is precisely such a practice. In these gospels, remembering the poor is seen as the precondition for our capacity to recognize and respond to our living Lord: the Spirit of Jesus who *today* is present with the poor, the hungry, the homeless, the least and last.

Christian practice, thus, can be understood as a rich tapestry of historically mediated, identity-forming, patterned actions through which the church itself attempts faithful witness to and participation in God's own active presence in and for the sake of the world. These inherited actions should be seen in dynamic not static ways because, as they are handed on from one generation to the next, practices are continuously shaped and reshaped through the ongoing dialogue we orchestrate between present sociocultural circumstances and the historic Christian witness of faith.

Christian practices are the patterned, cooperative, and informed ways that our lives as Christians are caught up into the things that God is doing in the world *already.* Appreciation for God's prior initiative is a reminder that, ultimately, the focus or referent of any Christian practice is not on what we humans are doing to change ourselves (spiritual formation) or to change the world (social justice) — these are misleading distinctions in the first place. Instead, through our engagement in given practices, we pay, or at least try to pay, unyielding attention to *what God is doing in the world through Jesus Christ to transform all the created order.*

Hence, rather than referring to the church's mission in the world, we speak instead of *missio Dei,* God's own mission in the world in and through Jesus Christ. By so doing we avoid the specter of works righteousness, or trying to earn our way into salvation. Because salvation is already given to us *proleptically* as a free gift of grace through Jesus Christ, God sets us free to actualize the effects of grace and salvation into the total matrix of life in all its interrelated, contingent dimensions: personal, interpersonal, social, economic, and political.

Speaking from within this general framework for understanding Christian practice, my contention is that the historic practice *most* in need of fresh consideration by practical theologians and Christian educators today — precisely because too many people are disappearing into the underside of history, caught in the undertow of unfettered free market forces — is the very practice receiving the *least* amount of attention: that of *remembering the poor.* By this biblical phrase (Gal. 2:10) obviously I do not mean some sort of sentimental feeling or existential angst that the poor are in fact poor. Remembering the poor is a concrete, historical practice with a long, varied and rich tradition, grounded in and shaped by faith communities across many centuries.[3] As Christian *practice*, remembering the poor is bodily, concrete, experiential, relational, communal, even political; and as *Christian* practice, is biblical, liturgical, theological, and sacramental.

Canaries Have Stopped Singing

September 11, 2001, will long be remembered as a day of horrific national tragedy in the U.S., sending shock waves around the globe. America is still reeling at the magnitude of loss. September 11 will long be remembered as a *day of death.*

For some 30,000 children around the globe under the age of five, *every* day is a day of death.[4] This is the number of children who die *daily* of starvation or from preventable infectious diseases that we have both the money and the know-how but not the moral compunction to prevent.[5] This is the number of children who die daily from direct consequences of being raised — forlorn and forgotten — in abject poverty.

On the day following the unspeakable slaughter of innocents, President Bush declared war on terrorism, and since then has repeatedly reminded the American public that "such a campaign will be long and difficult, will require time and resolve, and may take years to root out. We will rally the world. We will be patient. We will be focused. And we will be steadfast in our determination," he said. Over time, public leaders have cobbled together sentiments such as these and stylized them into a national liturgy of sorts, that both expresses and that shapes, on a tacit yet daily basis, our sense of the world and our place in it.

What if, in this living liturgy — along with our laments for the 3,000 who died on 9/11 — we were to include lamentation for the some 30,000 who die daily of poverty-related causes? What if we were to echo the indelible wails that

3. In her book *The Gospel in History: Portrait of a Teaching Church* (New York: Paulist Press, 1988), Marianne Sawicki names and traces three major ways the church proclaims and communicates the reign of God in the world. One of the three is "ministries of service," a notion similar to what I mean by *remembering the poor.* Ministries of service consist, she says, of "efforts to secure the physical, economic, social, and psychological welfare of disadvantaged people; and whatever is done in Jesus' name to relieve the suffering of his sisters and brothers." See Sawicki, *The Gospel in History,* p. 36.

4. So began Joerg Rieger in his chapel sermon on Tuesday morning, September 12, 2001.

5. For further information see: *Human Development Report 2002: Deepening Democracy in a Fragmented World,* United Nations Development Programme. http://www.undp.org/hdr2002.

"thousands of lives have been ended by evil" and "the pictures of suffering fill us with disbelief, terrible sadness, and a quiet, unyielding anger"? What if we were to "rally the world's attention" on the pain and suffering of those excluded from the technological and economic progress of the twenty-first century? What if we were to become "steadfast in our determination" to promote the full flourishing of all God's creatures and creation? What if the deaths of the masses "living below" were to be equally horrific to us as the deaths of the elites "living above" on the top floors of this world?

In his book, *Raising Children in a Socially Toxic Environment,* James Garbarino decries how the socioeconomic context in which we raise children and youth today — in the U.S. and around the globe — poisons their development and puts them at great developmental risk.[6] Garbarino recalls that in the days before coal mining became high tech, it was customary for miners to bring caged canaries into the mines with them. They hung the caged birds from the roof beams of the tunnels. When the canaries stopped singing and died, the miners were warned that the caverns were filling up with toxic, deadly gasses. Similarly, Garbarino suggests, our most vulnerable youth serve as weather vanes and indicators of what is going on in our world today; they are our canaries.

Coal miners paid very close attention when their canaries stopped singing and died. They heeded the warning. But how about us? To what do we pay close attention? What does the daily death of 30,000 children around the globe tell us? That "caverns" elsewhere are toxic, but not ours? To my mind, these deaths are nothing less than clear signals of toxic wastes — social, economic, environmental, political — being left behind by corporate-driven capitalism as it wafts its way around the world like a traveling Chernobyl. The specters that daily sneak around and snatch away 30,000 vulnerable children are the selfsame ones putting at risk *all* women, men, and children in the U.S. and abroad, whether they live on the upper or lower decks of our Earth Home. Even our Home itself is at risk. While the toxins kill some people outright, they kill others of us in slow motion; but all the same — they snuff out the life God intends for us and for the entire created order.

According to Loder's *interactional* perspective on human development, children and youth grow up in an ecology where systems remote to them nonetheless have a direct impact on them and their families. A child's development is the result of a complex interplay among immediate family systems and the wider social, political, and economic systems within which children and families negotiate their lives. *All* these systems are now co-opted and compromised

6. James Garbarino, *Raising Children in a Socially Toxic Environment* (San Francisco: Jossey-Bass Publishers, 1999).

by consumer-oriented corporate-driven capitalism and the quasi-religious way of life promoted by it. In and through his writings, Loder consistently decried the propensity of American culture to construct, to perpetuate, and to lavishly reward as "normal" a prototypical lifestyle that is, in fact, killing us right and left. For all its economic achievements, the United States has *more poverty* and *lower life expectancy* than any other major advanced nation. Males in Costa Rica have a longer life expectancy than males in the U.S.! On nearly every index or indicator of well-being, such as infant mortality, child poverty, homelessness, health care, nutrition, education, teen pregnancy, life expectancy, child care, family income, rates of imprisonment, the U.S. comes off worse than most other industrialized nations.

We live in a society predicated on the assumption that normative human development — and the socioeconomic environment required to optimize and sustain it — is best driven forward by ever-escalating competition, consumption, ambition, addiction, achievement, and acquisition. For free-market forces to do what economic theory suggests they must do in order to float all boats, these must be the driving forces. This precisely is why Gordon Gekko in the movie *Wall Street* could say without guile "greed, for lack of a better word, is good. Greed is right. Greed works." Loder repeatedly said that the attitudes and behaviors considered "normal" and "normative" in American society actually should be seen as socially constructed, mutually reinforced, culturally applauded, historically accelerated *patterns of human self-destruction.*

In light of Loder's voice, along with a growing chorus of scholars, the underlying thesis of this chapter seems, in some respects, not entirely new, yet bears repeating nonetheless. That is to say, in our ordinary daily existence, both as persons and congregations, we mainline Christians in North America are much more profoundly influenced and shaped by values of the "free market model" of neo-liberal economic thought than we are by our own distinctive set of faith practices and beliefs. The most potent and persuasive initiation of our children and youth today is not into a countercultural vision of flourishing for all creatures and creation, but rather is into a culture born and bred by free-market, consumer-oriented, corporate-driven capitalism that advantages the few at the expense of the many. *Children and youth know early in life whether they've been assigned to the few or to the many,* and they begin equally as early to score their whole lives accordingly.

The effort of the church to initiate believers into a distinctive set of countercultural practices does not take place in a vacuum; there is no clean slate anywhere. Anything and everything we do is culturally compromised because we ourselves are compromised by a culture of consumer and corporate capitalism. Whatever we think we can see of this actually is only the proverbial tip of the iceberg. My additional thesis here is that we cannot fully appreciate the sheer magnitude of what is happening unless and until we begin to keep company with those grassroots communities where families are clinging to life in the undertow of globalized economic forces — and hear firsthand from them their history and their story, their pain, and their hopes and dreams for the world and for the future of their children in it.

On these points, Joyce Ann Mercer and I share similar perspectives: "With Craig Dykstra, Dorothy Bass, and others focusing on participation in the practices of faith as the way young people take on Christian identity and vocation," she says, "I can affirm in a general sense that this faith and this calling are probably 'more caught than taught.'"[7] Notwithstanding, she observes there to be a certain naiveté in the movement. Discussion proceeds, Mercer laments, "as if none of these communities or theologies exists in captivity to the cultures through which they are expressed; as if these communities are all equally well equipped to be adequate mentors of Christian faith practices; as if the needs and interests of marginalized persons will be automatically protected by communities rather than subsumed into them."[8]

Christian Practice in a Gilded Age

Paul Krugman is right when he asserts that we "can't understand what's happening in America today without understanding the extent, causes and consequences of the vast increase in economic and political inequality that has taken place over the last three decades, and in particular the astonishing concentration of income and wealth in just a few hands."[9] Although America has *higher per capita income* than other advanced countries, it turns out that that's mainly because our rich are much richer. We have spawned a capitalism wherein the wealth of the wealthiest 1 percent of Americans exceeds what 95 percent of other Americans have to live on, and a globalized economy where the world's 200 richest people own assets greater than the combined income of the world's 2.5 billion poorest people. *Economic globalization* is better seen as *corporate-driven capitalism:* the top 200 multinationals have total annual sales greater than the annual output of the United States economy. Of the 100 largest econo-

7. Joyce Ann Mercer, "Call Forwarding: Putting Vocation in the Present Tense with Youth," *Compass Points: Navigating Vocation: The 2002 Princeton Lectures on Youth, Church, and Culture* (Princeton: The Institute for Youth Ministry, 2002), p. 37.

8. Mercer, "Call Forwarding," pp. 37-38.

9. Paul Krugman, "For Richer: How the Permissive Capitalism of the Boom Destroyed American Equality," *New York Times Magazine,* October 20, 2002, p. 64.

mies in the world 51 percent are corporations, only 49 are countries. Mitsubishi is larger than Indonesia; Toyota is bigger than Norway.[10]

"We are now living in a new Gilded Age, as extravagant as the original," says Krugman.[11] Income inequality in America has returned to the levels of the 1920s, when 12 percent of all American families controlled close to 86 percent of the nation's wealth.[12] The economic reality Krugman talks about as the *new Gilded Age,* other writers dub as a *plutocracy* (rule by the rich) or *kleptocracy* (rich steal from the poor — unconsciously, compulsively, obsessively).

The Invisible Guiding Hand: Leading Us Where?

We are all members of a society and a culture, now global in scope, whose very fabric is knit together by neo-liberal tenets of market capitalism, today the most influential ideology in the world. Capitalism, as an economic paradigm, is rooted in neo-liberal economic theory dating back to the eighteenth-century Scottish economist Adam Smith who, in 1776, published his classic *An Inquiry into the Nature and Causes of the Wealth of Nations.* This work represents the emergence of economic liberalism. Smith believed that free trade, without government intervention, promises the best path to economic growth for a nation. Now known as *neo*-liberalism, the model is based on the principle that pursuit of private or individual self-interests in an unfettered, unregulated market is the most efficient means to produce economic growth which eventually will benefit all members and institutions in a given society.

Because people today understand the market to be neutral or value-free, beyond categories of good and evil, they thereby believe individuals should pursue private interests according to their own particular values and purposes. What individuals will achieve depends on what they bring to and invest in the market, such as individual effort, hard work, diligence, perseverance, intelligence, personal ambition, competitiveness, a spirit of risk, single-minded pursuit of individual rights, self-interests, and achievement. The more these characteristics are present, the more the market will thrive; within this framework, indeed "greed is good." Greed motivates. Under the guidance of the "invisible hand" of the market, over the long haul outcomes will be produced that are beneficial not only to individuals *qua* individuals, but also to the common

10. For further information see: http://www.just-international.org.

11. Krugman, "For Richer," p. 63.

12. Robert D. Kaplan, "Was Democracy Just a Moment?" *The Atlantic Monthly* 280, 6 (Dec. 1997): 55-80.

good. Therefore the market is best left to follow its own internal logic even if nations or groups must go through untoward periods of economic adjustment and readjustment.

Perhaps the more fundamental problem today should not be located in the market *per se,* but rather in the fact that the American public (and the church) has allowed free-market philosophy — in unbridled fashion — to pervade more and more sectors of public life and public policy and, worse yet, to jump out of the public sphere and into private life where its logic *was never intended to belong.* As Duncan Forrester points out, according to classical economic thought the market and its procedures and processes were to be associated with only one part of life. The health of a society could not totally revolve around the market, but was to depend fundamentally on a moral and social order (civil society) in which it was situated and on which it depended for vitality. Each sphere of the social order was understood to operate according to different and sometimes even contrasting principles.[13]

But today, by some measures, free-market capitalism and the globalized economy it spawns have, for countless numbers of people, become like a religion. In his classic essay "Religion as a Cultural System," Clifford Geertz defined religion in *cultural-linguistic* terms as a system of symbols formulating a picture of the way things *are* — with such an aura of authority and facticity that it instills in people pervasive, powerful, and long-lasting moods and motivations.[14] According to Geertz's definition, a religion provides and induces in adherents both a *model of* and a *model for* living according to a conception of "the really real." In other words, religion not only *expresses* one's sense of reality, it also *shapes* it, thereby forming in persons and groups a distinctive style of life in ordinary, everyday comings and goings, and in habitual dispositions and behaviors (a *habitus*).

There is a major difference, however, between this "religion" and the religious traditions to which believers become conscious adherents. While believers today — whether attending a mosque, a church, a temple, or other house of worship — have at least *some* opportunity consciously to think about the vision and values promoted by their tradition, the worldview promoted by the market model gathers its force by the very fact that we are never asked to examine and explore its features. It simply exists as an invisible fact of life — like the air we breathe — and so we dwell in it as fish in water never knowing anything differ-

13. Duncan B. Forrester, *Christian Justice and Public Policy* (Cambridge: Cambridge University Press, 1997), pp. 159-160.

14. Clifford Geertz, "Religion as a Cultural System," in *The Religious Situation,* ed. Donald R. Culter (Boston: Beacon Press, 1968), p. 664.

ent even exists. Insofar as we dwell in this system even as this system dwells in us without notice, our engagement in Christian practices is influenced in unknown and unseen ways.

What currently is happening, laments William Coats, is the creation of a *world society* dominated by large capitalists in which inequality and exploitation are now institutionalized via free market mechanisms, even as widespread human misery increases. Coats worries that while the working class feels too overwhelmed and powerless, the middle class feels too comfortable and complacent to mount up any significant protest against present economic arrangements. From a Christian standpoint, writes Coats, one can hardly think of "an uglier configuration" than the institutionalization of inequality and a world dominated by a small capitalist class.[15]

Congregations: America's Hidden "Safety Net" of Services?

According to H. Richard Niebuhr, it is crucial — before one proceeds to ask *what shall we do?* — first to ask *what is going on?* While in the previous section we explored some of what is going on, there is yet another aspect: this has do with what the church presently is doing to remember the poor, based on perceptions, past and present, of "what is going on." That question is the focus of this section.

To bolster the case that U.S. churches are in a position to expand their role in caring for poor children and families — in light of welfare reform (1996) and the Bush administration "faith-based" initiatives — several major studies attempted to gauge the church's present and historical involvement in social services. On the basis of research findings, Ram Cnaan, professor of social work at the University of Pennsylvania, now celebrates the mainline church in North America as our national "hidden safety net." The studies reveal that at least the simple majority of the 353,000 congregations in the U.S. are involved, directly or indirectly, in addressing one or more immediate, emergency needs of persons and families for food, clothing, or shelter.

Cnaan, along with the vast majority of mainline congregations in North America, apparently accepts as pre-given a *service-delivery paradigm* as the primary, normative strategy for how the church should go about remembering the poor. I wish to make the case, however, that the so-called *servanthood* model — translated into *service delivery* regarding ministry with the poor — is grounded

15. William R. Coats, *God in Public: Political Theology Beyond Niebuhr* (Grand Rapids: Eerdmans, 1974), p. 82.

neither in solid biblical-theological foundations nor in a perceptive analysis (and spiritual discernment) of how best to be *stewards* (housekeepers and managers) of our manifold God-given resources.

In this section, in order better to understand the servanthood model — or at least one version of it — I shall reflect on the hermeneutic of service propounded by Craig Dykstra in his book *Vision and Character: A Christian Educator's Alternative to Kohlberg.*[16] In his critique of Lawrence Kohlberg's developmental theory of moral development, Dykstra proposes *Christian service* as an alternative pathway to Christian moral growth. As I examine his model, it may begin to appear to readers that my aim is to offer "a Christian educator's alternative to Dykstra's alternative to Kohlberg," but that is not my primary concern. Dykstra's book warrants lengthy exploration precisely because it makes explicit the otherwise implicit model of ministry operative in the majority of mainline congregations in the U.S. today. When the covers are pulled back, the model he explicates appears to be virtually the same one mainline congregations use when they give an account of *why* and *how* they go about remembering the poor — namely, the Bible says that we Christians are called to "serve" the needy (and we can do it without hauling in "politics"). By getting inside Dykstra's proposed logic of Christian service, we are able to see from the inside-out how many mainline, middle-class congregations go about construing their praxis with the poor.

Having reflected at great length on Dykstra's proposed model of Christian service, I am convinced — I regret having to acknowledge — that to a great extent it mirrors mainline, middle-class piety which itself is riddled with unseen, unacknowledged class interests, ideologies, and distorted views of power and authority. Upon close analysis of Dykstra's project, it becomes apparent that he merely moves from a conventional conception of justice (dominated by the mechanics of structural-developmental theory) to a conventional conception of service (dominated by the mechanics of psychodynamic theory). Juridical ethics (Kohlberg) depends on *cognitive* processes while visional ethics (Dykstra) depends on *imaginal* and intuitive processes. Other scholars fortunately, such as Carol Gilligan, have found ways to overcome such binary thinking — but that is not my focus here. My concern is that in his fascination with the mechanics of *how we see* (he depends heavily on the conflict-creativity paradigm of James Loder, as well as on the philosophy of Simone Weil and Iris Murdoch) he forgets the overriding concern of biblical writers for *what we see.* H. Richard Niebuhr, one of Dykstra's resources, noticed it makes all the differ-

16. Craig Dykstra, *Vision and Character: A Christian Educator's Alternative to Kohlberg* (New York: Paulist, 1981).

ence in the world whether, as Christians, we seek *to be loving* or whether we seek *to love our neighbor.* By the same token, it matters a great deal — as least biblically speaking it does — as to whether we attempt in some generic way to *see reality* or whether we attempt *to see the reality of the poor from the perspective of the poor.* Dykstra never considers this viewpoint.

Though Dykstra does not demonstrate for the reader his exegesis of the texts on which he rests his claims about Christian service, there is evidence that he de-historicizes and de-contextualizes them to the point that he removes their theological bite and eschatological sting. For this reason, in his explication of "service" he lapses into the conventional morality of the white middle-class church in America. As we will see, his approach puts the emphasis on service as *interpersonal,* ignoring socioeconomic and political dimensions of how we address (and also how we locate) human pain and suffering. Though in a footnote he acknowledges that "service has a political and prophetic dimension" he says he chose not to deal with these dimensions because space did not permit (odd, given the brevity of the book at only 143 pages). This demurral is problematic for at least five reasons. First, it assumes we can understand and give proper care to persons apart from their specific socioeconomic or political context. In today's globalized, pluralistic world, we can do no such thing. Second, it assumes (actually, he outright asserts) that later on we can "add and stir" *structural, institutional,* or *political* dimensions without having to reconstruct or rethink his current definitions. This is peculiar given that his definition of service requires denunciation of power from the outset. Third — and this is most troublesome — his methodology *privileges service over justice,* which is exactly what the white, mainline, middle-class church in North America has done all along and continues to do. Fourth, it ignores the fact that injustices embedded in contexts where service is given undercut and distort Christian service from the outset. Fifth, it fails to explain why a book that sets out to critique a notion of justice instead replaces it with a notion of service — rather than with a revised notion of justice.[17]

In *Vision and Character,* Dykstra's stated purpose is to critique Lawrence Kohlberg's structural-developmental theory of justice (juridical ethics) that puts individual rights, along with principles of fairness, at center stage. Dykstra proposes an alternative quasi-developmental model of "visional ethics." According to Dykstra's critique, Kohlberg depicts *character* essentially as a "disconnected bag of virtues." Dykstra wants to claim, to the contrary, that character is a coher-

17. Though this book appears early in Dykstra's career, there is little in later writings to suggest that his theological framework overall, or important constructs related to it, have altered in any significant ways.

ent dynamic that gains unity based on "what we see" rather than "what we do." In ethics, he maintains, vision has (or should have) primacy over action. Vision, he says, occasions conduct. *True* vision occasions *true* conduct. Particular actions, virtues, decisions, and choices, therefore, are not the first and foremost consideration in visional ethics. The uppermost concern, rather, is with *what we see,* and *what enables us to see.* "For visional ethics, action follows vision; and vision depends on character."[18] And character, in turn, does not merely "develop" according to genetically-given stages (Kohlberg). Rather, character is instilled by and through communities that provide us with a moral compass, owing to the vocabulary, the narratives and discourses, and all the actions and rituals that influence our perceptions, values, and ways of being in the world.

However, "visional ethics" *per se* does not set *Christian* formation apart from formation by and in other communities. Distinctive communities instill distinctive ethics. The distinguishing element for Christians lies in three core disciplines: service, repentance, prayer. *Christian service,* along with interrelated disciplines of *repentance* and *prayer,* provides for Christians an alternative to Kohlberg's conception of the moral life: we must make *service* the prominent practice of the Christian moral life. In constructing his alternative model, Dykstra here makes his decisive methodological turn, for there is nothing in the unfolding logic of his argument that would have prevented him from proposing *justice,* biblically defined — rather than *service* — as the prominent practice of the Christian moral life. Precisely at this point is where hidden ideologies of class and white privilege come into play. Let us see how this is so.

Dykstra defines Christian service as "a discipline through which care, concern, and aid are given by one person to another in a particular way, in a way that is shaped by *presence* — vulnerable, just, compassionate, and committed."[19] Dykstra's argument for the centrality of service is rooted in a selection of biblical passages that mention service and allude to servanthood. Whenever the disciples argued about who would be nearest to Jesus in the coming Reign, for example, Jesus answered by saying it would be "servants." An even more powerful image of service and servanthood in the Bible, however, says Dykstra, is Jesus bending over to wash the feet of his disciples (John 13:1-17).

In order for our service to be authentically biblical and Christian, Dykstra avers, we must avoid two common tendencies found in the ordinary practice of service: one is making "effectiveness" a primary goal, and the second is garnering power in order to make service effective. Service has to do with the "foolishness" of the Christian gospel, Dykstra says, because it means "*renouncing power*

18. Dykstra, *Vision and Character,* p. 59.
19. Dykstra, *Vision and Character,* p. 59.

in order to be present with others in vulnerability, equality, and compassion."[20] In place of *effectiveness* or *power,* at the heart of a biblical model of service is the dynamic of *personal presence.*

From this point on, Dykstra directs attention to *interpersonal* and *intersubjective* relationships — diverting attention away from how systems and ideologies (such as white privilege and class bias) often play a profound role in shaping and structuring, allowing and disallowing, certain relationships in the first place. The way Dykstra defends his intersubjective bent reveals the binary way he sees the world. For him, ethics is based *either* on "objective and publicly articulable needs of persons" (Kohlberg) *or* on "the realm of intersubjective relationships where it matters who in particular is making the claim, who in particular the claim is being made of"[21] (visional ethics). He chooses the latter because he believes that "a very great portion of the situations that make up our moral lives are of the intersubjective rather than the objective kind."[22] How we negotiate our everyday lives "has a great deal to do with who we are as moral beings," he says.[23] What we learn, what we do, how we think, how we feel within the context of our ordinary, everyday, intersubjective world determine how we will face and deal with dilemmas of a more public nature.[24] This sounds wonderful until you consider how much time we spend in our class-ridden enclaves. Does this model mean that people on top floors of our society are being morally equipped in ways similar to those who live in the middle or on the lowest floors? In "visional ethics" does it matter whether one views a moral dilemma from the bottom of the heap rather than from the top?

In rendering Christian service, according to Dykstra, we should *renounce power,* but not because power is evil in and of itself. Rather, when we deliberately collect power in order to be "effective" in our service, Dykstra assumes that *we ourselves must predetermine* the criteria of effectiveness and decide what will become of needy people when our service has accomplished its purposes. Whenever we seek to make our service "effective," he believes, we only end up defining for others what health and strength should look like. It never occurs to him that this could be done as a collaborative, cooperative endeavor, carried out interpersonally (and better yet, collectively). It never occurs to him that there are many uses to which power can be put, even in interpersonal situations, other than aiming to be "effective."

Dykstra worries that we might unduly run the risk of accumulating

20. Dykstra, *Vision and Character,* p. 103.

21. Dykstra, *Vision and Character,* pp. 14-15.

22. Dykstra, *Vision and Character,* p. 15.

23. Dykstra, *Vision and Character,* p. 15.

24. Dykstra, *Vision and Character,* p. 15.

power simply for the sake of *having* power rather than for the sake of serving others with and through the use of power. Certainly, to gather and use power is to run risks — *big* ones. But should the Christian moral life be predicated on neuroses about — and worse yet, avoidance of — taking risks? I challenge Dykstra's assumption that the only way to avoid abusing power is to renounce power. And I especially challenge his assumption that Jesus himself calls followers to renounce power. And finally, I challenge his lack of self-awareness regarding the impact of social location on perceptions of power. It strikes me that only an individual (white male) born into and living an entire lifetime in the upper echelons of white privilege — a hidden hierarchy that *daily* and *from the outset* confers unequal power and advantage — could be so disingenuous about the need for *and divine gift of* power in order to contribute to and participate in human flourishing. *Only persons already over-privileged by power can pretend its unimportance.* Persons like myself (white female) — born into a poor working-class family located on the lower socioeconomic rungs of a class-ridden society — can ill afford the luxury of such pretense.

As I read scriptures, I hear Jesus asking us to denounce power *used abusively* — in ways that are self-referential, repressive, imperialistic, and unilateral. This has been the unfortunate legacy of American expansionism and colonialism carried out under the guise of Christian missionary witness. Dykstra's comments imply that his one and only conception of power is a picture or model of power used in this way. But there's another option. Jesus asks us to embrace "the other" and — in mutuality and partnership with "the other" — to exercise power in collaborative, creative, communal, relational, constructive ways in order to build up the common good and to promote human flourishing. As people "called out" *to be stewards* of God's own household (the created order itself, not simply the church), we cannot afford to repudiate an essential dimension of our moral agency as Christian persons: the capacity to use power judiciously and creatively (on all levels: interpersonal, social, political) to resist and restrain evil, to reduce institutionalized forms of injustice, and to promote the full flourishing of all God's creatures and creation.

The Bible Tells Us So?

To my mind, Dykstra's alternative construction of the Christian moral life depends, in part, on the veracity of his claim that "the theme of service is a prominent one in the Bible, and particularly in the Gospels."[25] The five biblical pas-

25. Dykstra, *Vision and Character,* p. 98.

sages — which, in Dykstra's estimation, commend a service-oriented model for ministry and for Christian moral life overall — deserve a fresh reading. We will begin with Mark 10:35-44. In this story — which occurs on the journey toward Jerusalem — the disciples James and John approach Jesus, imploring him to *privilege* them in a particular way. Upon hearing about this incident, the other disciples get angry, and so Jesus calls them all together to discuss the matter. He points out to them how the prevailing Gentile rulers were using power (actually *force*) to lord it over others, and how leaders considered great were acting in oppressive, abusive ways. "It will not be so among you," Jesus insists.

In Mark 10:35-44, as in the other passages to which Dykstra refers, Jesus does not explicitly use the word "power" which, in and of itself, is a neutral notion. The word for power in Spanish is *poder,* meaning "to be able." Because we are beings created in the image and likeness of a triune God — bestowing to us a relational and communal nature, and giving to us a generous participation in who God is and what God does — *we are able,* that is, we have God-given power, to create conditions (including economic, social, political, religious) under which "the other" (and we ourselves) may flourish in ways that contribute to, rather than detract from, the flourishing of all creatures and creation. The only condition under which we do not or cannot use power to influence reality is called *death.*

While it is true that — as beings prone to distort our image and likeness to God — we sometimes use power abusively, it is also true that under the impress of ongoing healing and transformation — grounded in who God is and what God is doing — relatively we are *freed from* self-serving use of power and relatively *freed for* self-giving (but not self-abnegating) use of it. One of the definitive aspects of *metanoia* — an ongoing dimension of the Christian moral life — is our turn from power used destructively to power used creatively and constructively — in order to contribute to and participate in human flourishing (understood as grounded in God's active presence in and for the world). This is core to "living in the Spirit."

Luke (22:24-27) locates the interchange about greatness as part of the fellowship and dialogue among disciples shared around the table following the Last Supper — giving Jesus' comments an eschatological perspective. During this conversation, Jesus insists that — in contrast to Gentile leaders who use power and authority to abuse or to exclude — among his followers the greatest must become *like the youngest,* and the leader *like ones who serve.* In the same breath, Jesus says: "I confer on you, just as my Father has conferred on me, a kingdom, so that you may eat and drink at my table" (Luke 22:29-30). Ordinarily, *slaves* — bought, sold, traded on the auction block (or even homegrown) — are ones who serve the table; and so Jesus here calls attention to two of the most excluded, non-person groups in that social context, the *children* (the youngest) and the slaves. What's more, he identifies himself with these excluded groups! "I am among you as one who serves" (as one of the excluded slaves) (verse 27). Even further, he confers on the excluded groups a kingdom, so that they may eat and drink "at the table." In contrast to the dominant status quo, where authority is located among those *already* at the table, in his allusion to the eschatological reversal, Jesus relocates authority, along with dignity and respect, among and within persons presently excluded — now *they* "may eat and drink at my table" (verse 30).

As in Mark, the Gospel of Matthew locates the incident with James and John on the journey toward Jerusalem (their mother is now in the picture) (Matt. 20:20-28). The stories between which Matthew situates the "greatness" incident add potential new insights into it. Immediately prior to the story about James and John, Matthew recalls an incident in which Peter points out to Jesus that because he and others had given up all their possessions — unlike the rich young ruler — they should reap extra rewards. Jesus answers by telling a parable about day laborers who all receive the same wages, though some worked all day while others worked only one hour. Among the early-birds there arises bitter resentment that the ones who arrived last *were made equal to* those who were there first.

Jesus uses this occasion to talk about the sheer generosity of God, and about God's completely gratuitous love. Because of the generous character of God, in the inbreaking reign (Matthew says "at the renewal of all things") there are great reversals as to who counts and who does not, who is first and who is last. God remembers and is generous to those silenced at the margins, to those ignored at the front gate, to those excluded from the table, to those beaten up and tossed to the side of the road, to those who suffer pain and poverty, to those born on the bottom rungs, to those who show up last — whether "deserving" or not — simply and only because God is God.

Another biblical text identified by Dykstra is Matthew 23:11: "the greatest among you will be your servant." The context here is extremely important (because the statement may, in fact, be an eschatological indicative rather than an ethical imperative). Speaking to the masses of the working poor, Jesus directs their attention to "mainline" religious leaders (like us), humming along in their capacity as authority figures, interpreting and teaching the theological tradition. Jesus commends the crowds and the disciples to follow these teachings. In terms of their financial giving, Jesus points out that leaders were lavishly generous and set extraordinarily high standards by what they gave (Matt. 23:23). But Jesus suddenly unleashes seven harsh woes on those very leaders. So what is the problem? *Jesus names and criticizes what was being concealed by and underneath mainline piety.* Widows, for instance, were being evicted from their homes, and the mainline leaders were not lifting a finger to help them (Matt. 23:4, 14). Jesus told the masses that because their religious leaders do, in fact, handle the theological traditions of Moses, they should pay attention to *those* teachings but those teachings *only* (Matt. 23:3). The working class people, otherwise, should be wary, Jesus warned, of *all* the other practices of the mainline leaders, because those practices are laden with economic, political, social, and spiritual neglect and abuse.

Within the wider (and proper) setting of the text (Matt. 23:1-39) — and not simply Dykstra's decontextualized verse (23:11) — we see how Jesus educates and sensitizes masses of working poor people to a system that exploits and disadvantages them, whie it overprivileges an elite few (Matt. 23:1-11). Jesus intimates to the poor: though this society — in social, economic, political, and even religious ways — treats you as non-persons, in terms of the Reign of God you are already great. (*This* radical grace is the real foolishness of the gospel — *not,* as Dykstra would have it, the renunciation of power.) In verses 7-8, Jesus points out how the incumbent religious leaders bask in the deference paid to them, both in the "secular" marketplace and in their seats of religious authority. These leaders loved the power and status conferred by the title "Master." "Do not ever allow anyone to call you that," says Jesus, *"for all of you are on the same level . . ."* (Matt. 23:7-10). Aside from the implied eschatology, Jesus teaches resistance to imposed inequality. He teaches poor people how to spot and to resist those systems that overprivilege the few at the expense of the many. This resistance has a twofold dynamic: resistance against *being dominated,* and resistance against *dominating others.* In other words, Jesus teaches the proper uses of power and authority. He does not blip these issues off the radar screen.

Jesus has a different set of warnings (seven woes!) for those advantaged by systems at the expense of those who are disadvantaged (Matt. 23:13-39). The spiritual foofaraw of the elites made it possible for them to conceal their neglect of *what matters most:* the practices of justice, and of faith, and of mercy (Matt. 23:23). These things you ought to be doing, says Jesus to the leaders, while not neglecting other routine ministries, like teaching, giving money, and conducting rituals. Jesus makes it clear that it does not matter to what extent or how well a congregation is practicing other forms of piety (like "service"??). *If they do not practice justice they are about as life-giving as a mausoleum* (Matt. 23:27).

The final passage to which Dykstra appeals is Mark 9:33-35. Dykstra chops off the text right after Jesus says to the twelve, "Whoever wants to be first must be last of all and servant of all." It is important to notice that the full pericope includes two other verses *key* to its meaning (9:36-37). Jesus places a little child in the disciples' midst, then takes the child into his own arms, saying: "Whoever welcomes one such child in my name welcomes me, and whoever welcomes me welcomes not me but the one who sent me" (Mark 9:37). The scholarly consensus, according to James Bailey, is that Mark 9:33-37 and Mark 10:13-16 must be understood in light of each other, and that both passages must be understood in light of the historical frame of reference out of which Jesus spoke: *the extremely marginalized social status of children in the first-century world.*[26] When Jesus places the child in the disciples' midst, and then takes the child into his own embrace, he introduces the child as among "the least ones" in the society who need actively to be sought, received, and embraced. So far, the disciples have been too dense to understand that being drawn near to Jesus means being drawn near to the excluded, to the least and last. *To show respect for the poor and the excluded is to show respect for God!*

The implications of all these various passages cannot be distilled into only one narrow message — written, as they were, by different authors speaking to different audiences. A fresh reading of the texts reveals a rich mosaic of motifs, metaphors, and images. Many of these are concerned not so much with a denunciation of power as with an *alternative construction of power* (to be used relationally, communally, collaboratively) and a *relocation of power and authority* (to be distributed among and between ordinary persons, including "the least ones"). By no stretch can these texts be boiled down to the theme of *service* or *servanthood.* To claim or even imply that the flow of logic here is predominantly about the middle-class "serving the needy" is to take the world-altering, cosmos-changing eschatological power of Jesus' message and squeeze it into a conventional, class-bound cultural container.

Within the rich mosaic rendered by these texts, there are *many* practices relevant to Christian moral agency — some of which require our engagement on simultaneous levels (interpersonal, social, structural) — such as resisting, renewing, reversing, respecting, reciprocating, recognizing, restructuring, restraining, including, critiquing, discerning, deconstructing, dismantling. Jesus recommended, modeled, and implied our engagement in such practices as a way of life that stands over against a life shaped by coercing, concealing, oppressing, co-opting, controlling, lording, excluding, abusing, and dominating. To boil down the richness of these texts to the theme of "service" is an exercise in reductionism.

According to Dykstra's Christology, Jesus did not come to bring an end to suffering but rather to be with us in our suffering; this is the meaning of the incarnation, he believes. Jesus himself practiced *service as presence;* so should we.

26. James L. Bailey, "Experiencing the Kingdom as a Little Child: A Rereading of Mark 10:13-16," *Word and World* 15, 1 (Winter 1995): 58-67.

Besides, says Dykstra, "when we are suffering, our deepest need is *not* the alleviation of our suffering but the knowledge that our suffering does not annihilate us."[27] Aside from the misleading binary thinking here — not to mention the insensitivity to inscrutable forms of suffering and pain in our world today — to my mind Dykstra proposes a Christology *sans* eschatology. A more perceptive theological view is that "the gospel of God's suffering love in Christ is inseparable from the gospel of hope."[28] According to Christiaan Beker, the predominating claim of scriptural writers is that faith offers us "a meaningful integration of suffering and hope" and so *both* "must be embodied and concretized by the 'hopeful' suffering of the church at the hands of the powers of injustice."[29] As persons who are grounded in eschatological hope, we know our suffering ultimately will not annihilate us, for we are given reassurance of this, says James Loder, through the Spirit, in whom "the flow of time is from the future into the present to change, heal, restore, or transform the past for the sake of the coming future."[30] Hence, "the church, the new creation of God in the midst of the old creation, is called not only to *endure suffering* but also *to engage* suffering, *to relieve* the suffering caused by the world's injustice and idolatry."[31]

We still suffer and we still die, to be sure. But God is overthrowing not only the power suffering has over us existentially, but also the sources of suffering (physical, emotional, spiritual, economic, social, environmental, political). "God's final triumph is already casting its rays into our present, however opaque those rays often are and however much they seem contradicted by the empirical reality of our present world."[32] At every turn, around every corner, on every page of the Gospels, in and through the person and work of Jesus we see suffering *actively* being defeated by God: the lame are made to walk; lepers are cleansed; deaf are given hearing; the dead are raised; oppressed are freed; sinners are forgiven; broken-hearted are healed; the entombed are unbound; captives are released; the blind are given sight; prisoners are visited; the downcast

27. Dykstra, *Vision and Character,* p. 103.

28. J. Christiaan Beker, *Suffering and Hope: The Biblical Vision of the Human Predicament* (Grand Rapids: Eerdmans, 1994), p. 97. Beker is a clear example of how autobiography and social location influence the doing of theology. His theology of suffering and of hope is deeply rooted in the dehumanizing experience of being carted off to a Berlin forced labor camp by the German occupation, where all around him he saw innocent people tortured, gassed, murdered, and slaughtered. Perhaps this is a reason why his work offers a nuanced analysis of how suffering and hope creatively can be intertwined in the life of Christian believers.

29. Beker, *Suffering and Hope,* p. 89.

30. Loder, *The Logic of the Spirit,* p. 110.

31. Beker, *Suffering and Hope,* p. 86.

32. J. Christiaan Beker, *Paul's Apocalyptic Gospel: The Coming Triumph of God* (Philadelphia: Fortress, 1982), p. 58.

are given hope; enemies are embraced; strangers are welcomed; women are made socially equal; the lost are found; the hungry are fed; the thirsty are given drink; the naked are clothed; the homeless are taken in; the bent over are straightened; the tyrants are toppled; the excluded are included. Not only then — but also *now.*

The possibility of fullness of life in all its varied expressions (and institutional forms), lived in praise of God through mutuality with, and equal regard for, all that God creates and loves, is the good news Jesus brought and still brings. And nothing, in the final analysis, can destroy this possibility and this news, though many human beings are giving it a good heave-ho, the cross being the symbol of the ugliest attempts to do so. Through the proleptic reality of God's eschatological triumph, we not only can embrace and endure our own suffering, and be compassionate to the suffering of others, we also can participate — provisionally, partially, in ways appropriate to our finitude — in the power and purposes of God in human history to overthrow evil, to alleviate human misery and suffering, and to renew and restore human flourishing. *Not* to so participate is to refuse our human call and vocation.

In his suspicion of power and his claim that we humans have too high a view of our power, Dykstra is reminiscent of the long line of theologians, such as Reinhold Niebuhr, who associate sin with self-pride, with humans claiming too much, grasping too much, thinking too highly of themselves. While this may be the case for many people — especially those who are most privileged and advantaged by their society — it is not a theologically accurate description of what constitutes sin for all people in all times and places and stations of life. Persons who have grown up beaten down, persons mired in misery on the margins on account of race, gender, or class, often have internalized a false, negative sense of self that includes a sense of powerlessness. Sin in this world owes as much to powerlessness as it does to *hubris* and gluttony for power, especially given that asymmetries of power are so broadly institutionalized and enforced today. The other side of *hubris* or pride, declares Moltmann, is hopelessness, resignation, weariness, timidity — which all amount to falling away from the living hope that God promises. In Moltmann's understanding, *the sin that most profoundly threatens us* is not the evil we perpetrate with power, but rather the good that we do not do with the power we have.[33]

Dykstra argues that Kohlberg's understanding of justice (and moral agency) is far too conventional and far too limited to be useful to the moral life of Christians. By the same token, by the time he is finished with his critique and reconstruction — though acclaimed for his beautiful prose — Dykstra essen-

33. Jürgen Moltmann, *Theology of Hope* (New York: Harper & Row, 1967), pp. 22-23.

tially has morphed justice into an understanding of service that itself is far too conventional and far too limited to be theologically and morally useful to the church's contemporary practice of remembering the poor, or even to Christian moral agency overall. In that we are asked to renounce power as inappropriate to service, our moral agency is shrunk. But so is the agency of the ones we are "to serve." In Dykstra's equation, it is as though the ones receiving Christian service have no moral agency, no power, no creativity of their own — only "need." Despite the potential of "visional ethics," everything about Christian service is said, done, thought, conceived from the point of view of the one who serves, *never* from the point of view of the ones being served. Moreover, despite warnings about determining what is healthy for others, service remains defined as that which we, as middle- or upper-class Christians, unilaterally *give* or *do to* and *do for* another person. This is a one-way street in which the agency of "the other" disappears into thin air. The servant relationship, says Dykstra, "provides opportunity for a person in need to feed off of the powers of the servant"[34] — as if other persons have no powers of their own.

Some people will want to argue that service is one foot of remembering the poor, and justice is the other. But all this view has ever done is hobble the church and hobble the poor. Justice is the core of the Christian moral life, and justice has two feet. Some people say we need to balance giving people fish for a day by teaching them how to fish for a lifetime; these are people who want to obscure their ownership of the ponds in the first place, and their control of who gets to fish in which pond. Some people will ask: what about the long tradition of *diakonia?* Today, there is no *diakonia* not already embedded in and tainted by vast economic and power inequities of corporate-driven consumer-oriented capitalism.

"June Cleaver, allow me to introduce you to Maria Santos"

It is interesting to note what Dykstra himself "sees" (and even scarier, what he does *not*) as he looks out through his "service" lens over the landscape of moral pain and moral dilemma in our world today. In his looking, he must have been living in Lake Wobegon. Aside from brief mention of the Detroit race riots in 1967,[35] the worst case scenario with which Dykstra deals in his book is a wife

34. Dykstra, *Vision and Character,* p. 103.

35. In the midst of the 1967 Detroit race riots, Dykstra's home church (Presbyterian) helped to organize the "New Detroit Committee" to bring white people and black people together in efforts to rebuild the city. Dykstra does not notice the class-ridden, white-privileged irony that a big-wig male from a big-wig church in upper-middle-class Grosse Pointe was sent in to chair the committee.

who "feels she is being used." When she finally cries to her husband that he is not paying enough attention to her, he retorts, "What do you want from me? I have given you everything. Time, a house, children, money — everything I have is yours!"[36] (This woman must be June Cleaver upset with Ward on a bad hair day.) The class-bound nature of this scenario speaks for itself, as does the never-never land where the Cleavers reside.

Consider alternatively the following scenario. After a short absence from attending church due to personal turmoil, Maria Santos shows up in a new congregation. She is fleeing an abusive marriage, and is suffering spiritually, emotionally, as well as economically, and also, in less obvious ways, socially and politically. She has little work experience, no college education, few job skills, no self-confidence, no money, very little family support, a broken spirit, a broken marriage, a guilty conscience, and three young children to feed, clothe, house, school, and otherwise properly care for. Maria spent years bent over, washing feet and washing clothes, renouncing her own power, and serving nothing but the needs of her husband, because that's what she heard the church telling her to do. Now she's bent under a burden of guilt for leaving. She has no immediate hope of receiving child support payments since her husband lost his job — and she lost out on a potential place of employment — when another industry in town closed and moved to Mexico for cheap labor and cheap materials (leaving several thousand local people jobless, mostly low-skilled Latina women with little education). While Maria receives welfare assistance she must spend full-time looking for gainful employment. Despite the fact that poverty rates are cut in half for single ethnic mothers who achieve even just one year of post-secondary education, her own state's welfare policy makes no provisions in that regard. And Maria has neither the time nor the money to attend college at night — besides, by evening she's way too exhausted, and who would care for her children? When Maria leaves the rolls of the welfare poor, she will join the ranks of the working poor. This is virtually guaranteed, given that the poverty rate in 2000 for families who stopped receiving welfare assistance and began working full-time ranged between an estimated 41 and 58 percent. Working full-time at minimum pay, Maria's income will not lift her above the poverty threshold, because in the U.S. *minimum wage is not a living wage.* To boot, she likely will have no health benefits through her job, and also she likely will have to work odd hours and be forced to pay high costs even for *sub*standard child care. (Quality child care in most U.S. states is more than public college tuition.) Gender injustice will compound the harsh reality of the official poverty in which she now lives (if women were given equal pay for equal work, the poverty

36. Dykstra, *Vision and Character,* p. 14.

rate of single-parent mothers in the U.S. would be cut in half). The condition of poverty will begin to dictate the options that are and are not available to her. This will be especially true for her children, now put at great developmental risk (poverty is the single most powerful factor that can negatively influence brain development). Because of the blighted neighborhood where the family now is doomed to live, the children will be exposed to environmental toxins, increased violence, lowered quality of child care, lack of quality schools, lack of primary supports needed by young people in order to navigate into responsible, caring adulthood. Research reveals further strong links between poverty and place: weak job information networks, lack of adequate public transit, deteriorated infrastructure, lack of decent, affordable housing.

Pour all this into the conventional impersonal service paradigm and then ask: what, thereby, do we *best* see, and what do we *not* see? Within any given ethical framework, before we can assist anyone we must first see the real nature of the need. Through the lens of Christian service given to us by Dykstra, the self-same lens through which practically the entire church today sees and remembers the poor, consider the vast parts of Maria's story we will ignore. Consider how various interlocking systems — religious, interpersonal, social, economic, global — are inextricably woven together into the fabric of Maria's life. Consider how the service paradigm functions to repress things we prefer not to notice anyway: realities that intimidate us because they seem unmanageable and overwhelming. In Christian service with Maria, Dykstra lays down the precondition that we renounce power. But he overlooks the tremendous *power of definition.* Within this paradigm, vast parts of Maria's story — her past, her present, and her future — will remain unattended to because *within the service paradigm, we are taught not to see or address them.* By renouncing power (or pretending to), we have exercised the greatest power of all: the power to conceal, the power to define, the power not to question the status quo, the power to determine the agenda.

Remembering the Poor: A New Paradigm

Fortunately, there are scores of grassroots, common-sense communities of practical theology all over the globe that are ignoring the pretensions and concealments of the middle-class, mainline piety of "Christian service." These communities have a vision of ordinary Christians — poor and non-poor alike — working together as partners in mutual resistance against "the ugly configuration" of institutionalized inequality and *de facto* rule by the rich, in the U.S. and in places around the globe where economic globalization is taking root.

Hope for the future is appearing in dramatic and stunning ways. The world over, there are groups of people who are organizing and living toward an alternative vision of a global economic order (they have spun a movement called "glocalization"). In their countercultural vision, the wealth of a few is not bought by the impoverishment of the many and of the Earth itself. With imaginations inspired by the inexhaustible resources of Christian faith and hope in God's Reign, these groups craft ways for the whole household of God — all of God's created order, the human and non-human that both need and give life — to flourish and fulfill their God-given vocation. Though there does not exist a ready-made model of "Christian economics," these groups are drawing on a wealth of theological resources which, when brought into dialogue with economic theories and options, give significant insights into the ongoing reconstruction of an economy more radically inclusive of the least and last among us. Instead of the *consumer* society, we can pursue a vision of the *just* society.

In these communities, primacy is not given to generic "vision"; primacy is given to the poor and to their voice and to their perspective on reality. Primacy is given not to middle-class presence, primacy is given to the presence of the poor in history, and to God's own special presence in and concern for the poor. Concern for power is defined by what the have-nots don't have: *power,* not just money. In these grassroots communities, there is no false ideological divide between the personal, the interpersonal, the social, and the structural. Within these settings, persons are provided with a sacred, safe setting wherein they are invited to pour out and to share their personal, private pain, and along with others, translate collective pain into redemptive, public action for the common good. Here, pain, suffering, and anger are given epistemological and moral weight, for they illumine how and where the old order is groaning and manifesting transformational potential under God's renewing of all things in Christ.

In small supportive grassroots groups — which, by the way, emphasize interpersonal and intersubjective presence without curtailing concern for the systemic — persons pour out their pain, anger, and suffering; their stories become the basis for *collective critique of ideology.* Biblical faith, says Walter Brueggemann, instills the capacity to discern clearly the destructive powers of the dominant culture, and to claim the freedom to act apart from, or over against, those unjust structures. Public outcry and *public processing of pain* generate moral energy that helps people refuse to conform to present social and economic arrangements that benefit the few on the backs of the many. As Moltmann underscores, God creates in those who practice hope the energy to fight what is *eschatologically doomed,* and the energy to establish here and now anticipations of what is *eschatologically destined.*

Participants in these grassroots groups are members of a large movement of the welfare and working poor who, in partnership with middle class Christians who join with them in common cause, are claiming a place at the table in their communities where decisions are made that affect their children, their families, and their daily lives. Through strategies associated with *faith-based community revitalization,* their foremost concern is to engage together in the context of local, distressed neighborhoods — where economic globalization shows itself in very concrete, tangible ways — and, with the help of the wider community, build healthier environments in which to raise children and youth. Faith-based community revitalization represents a convergence of themes and practices, old and new alike, which can be depicted as a three-legged stool. The three "legs" that together comprise this approach are the three interrelated strategies of *community organizing, community building,* and *community developing,* as explicitly faith-based, theologically informed practices.[37] As "universities of public theology," faith-based community organizations help grassroots people understand the public policies and public programs that bear on their local situation. Local residents identify the assets they presently have, as well as the resources they need in order to begin the process of community revitalization, redevelopment, and reinvestment.

In these communities, the people exercising mature moral agency and "visional ethics" commensurable with the Christian story and vision are the so-called "needy" ones themselves. The tables have been turned. These grassroots, commonsense communities of practical theology ought to be our primary mentors in the task of reconstructing notions of moral agency and Christian justice — not so-called experts whose only view of the world is from the top floors down.

37. Traditionally, these three practices have been seen as separate traditions, but in the paradigm I propose they are brought together. See Susanne Johnson, *Suffer the Little Ones: Children, Poverty, and the Church* (St. Louis: Chalice Press, forthcoming).

8. Paradigmatic Madness and Redemptive Creativity in Practical Theology: A Biblical Interpretation of the Theological and Methodological Significance of James E. Loder's Neo-Chalcedonian Science for the Postmodern Context

Dana R. Wright

> *It is possible to be mad and to be unblest; but it is not possible to get the blessing without madness; it is not possible to get the illumination without the derangement.*
>
> Norman O. Brown

Introduction: Paradigmatic Madness in Practical Theology

James E. Loder Jr. never served as a minister of Christian or religious education in a congregation. In forty years of teaching classes at Princeton Seminary he focused relatively little attention on the craft of Christian education — the rules of art that govern curriculum development, lesson planning, teaching the Bible, administration of educational programming, recruitment and training of teachers, and the like. He never developed a course on the vocation of the Christian educator. His designation as the Mary Synnott Professor of the *Philosophy* of Christian Education testified to his dominant concern for the *theoretical* dimensions of practical theology and Christian education. When in 1962 Loder confessed to his senior colleague at Princeton, D. Campbell Wyckoff, that he had no real experience in practical Christian education, Wyckoff assured the young scholar not to worry, for teaching the craft of Christian education was Wyckoff's forte. Relieved, Loder went to work on getting the theory right and never looked back.[1]

1. The emphasis upon the significance and priority of theory in the whole of Loder's efforts to reconstruct the theological and interdisciplinary integrity of practical theology and Christian education cannot be overstated. Against the general tendency in the academic study of practical theology, Loder argued for the inevitable priority of theory over praxis or experience. Quoting Einstein, Loder maintained that in the necessary reciprocity between theory and praxis theory has priority because "it is theory that decides what we can observe." Loder be-

I will argue in this essay in honor of him that, in spite of his lack of attention to the craft and rules of art in Christian education (or maybe because of it!), he generated innovative, potentially revolutionary interdisciplinary metatheoretical resources out of which practical theologians and Christian educators might learn to orient the postmodern church and culture to what he called "the hidden orders of intelligibility" that give ultimate meaning to, and generate redemptive creativity within and beyond, the social construction of reality. Loder's forty-year effort to "get the theory right" resulted in a compelling vision of the content and dynamics of divine-human relations discerned within every dimension of human action — organic, psychic, social, and cultural — out of which human experience as participation in the logic of the Holy Spirit comes sharply into view.[2] Loder's mature theoretical vision can be understood as neo-Chalcedonian analytic practical theological science,[3] conceived in dynamic critical-confessional (fiduciary) and relational terms.[4] This innovative science

---

lieved that the priority of theory is inevitable because some theory is tacitly present with every observation or experience. The good scientist always make her theory as explicit as necessary in order to indwell the phenomenon at hand, risking both changing the theory in relation to new observations and having the theory change the facts being observed. "Good theory is a comprehensive point of view which can be provisionally articulated as a set of mutually consistent, corrective, and enhancing principles . . . from the matrix of experience viewed by the theory, but also from the highest Truth to which they are finally accountable. . . . Good theory in Christian education . . . is an on-going disclosure and articulation of a hidden created order of things in relation to and in light of the Truth of God's self-revelation." See his unpublished volume *Educational Ministry in the Logic of the Spirit,* chap. 1, pp. 1-10.

2. The work that makes Loder's vision most explicit is the unpublished volume mentioned above, *Educational Ministry in the Logic of the Spirit.* This book, which is available in various "editions" in the Loder archive, needs to be studied before the full breadth and depth of Loder's work can be discerned by the wider academic and ecclesial community. For an outline of the content of this book, see Chapter 11 in this present volume by Russell Haitch.

3. Loder's colleague Richard Osmer identified Loder's position as "postfoundational science" in his "mapping" of rationality in the field of practical theology. See "Rationality in Practical Theology: A Map of the Emerging Discussion," *International Journal of Practical Theology* 1, 1 (1997): 34 n. 73. Osmer also identified Loder's model of interdisciplinarity as "Chalcedonian." See R. Osmer and F. Schweitzer, *Religious Education between Modernization and Globalization: New Perspectives on the United States and Germany* (Grand Rapids: Eerdmans, 2003), p. 236.

4. LeRon Shults has argued that interdisciplinary practical theology in a "critical-confessional" form, what he calls "postmodern fiduciary structure," must be understood relationally within a kinetic or "figure-ground" dynamic structure in which theological actualities interact with human potentialities, and the priority for ordering theology and the human sciences is always given to the relationality made possible from the divine side. Shults writes:

> A postmodern fiduciary structure . . . takes the relational reality of the subject-object in the knowing event as a bipolar tensional unity that hermeneutically precedes the de-

described the nature of human participation Spirit-to-spirit in what Paul Lehmann called "the God-man structure of reality."[5] For Loder, the "God-man structure of reality" defined the tacit power and pattern of God's eschatological rule underlying every dimension of contingent reality, which became explicit in the church's witness to the gospel through faith. Thus, for example, in his unique study *The Logic of the Spirit: Human Development in Theological Perspective,* Loder reconceived the life span in terms of a "dynamic christomorphic relationality" that reconstitutes human identity in Christ as a dialectical actuality experienced through faith in the power of the Holy Spirit.

> Jesus becomes the Face of God for us only through faith and by the power of the Spirit . . . for Jesus to become our contemporary means that the very

---

> scription of the poles. "*Ab intra* relationality" is my way of describing the way a person with this underlying fiduciary structure . . . will tend to the relation of psychology and theology. An interdisciplinarian with this type of methodological faith can recognize the contextual, provisional nature of the subject pole, but simultaneously affirm the real, objective existence of the object pole, because knowledge is constructed out of the relationality itself. In the theology-psychology relation, figure and ground are reversed: interdisciplinary method is turned inside out. In this way of thinking the interdisciplinary relationality helps us to understand the disciplines, which can only be fully explained by accounting for their being-in-relation. This emphasis on the field that constitutes the tensionality of the fields can ultimately result in a mutually enhanced understanding of both disciplines.

See LeRon Shults, "'Holding On' to the Theology-Psychology Relationship: The Underlying Fiduciary Structures of Interdisciplinary Method," *Journal of Psychology and Theology* 25, 3 (1997): 329-340. In another place I have called this form of practical theology (following Claude Welsh's analysis of Barth's doctrine of the Trinity) "kerygmatic-analytic" practical theology. See Dana Wright, "*Ecclesial Theatrics*" (diss., Princeton Theological Seminary, 1999), pp. 204ff. Also see D. Wright, "The Contemporary Renaissance in Practical Theology in the United States: The Past, Present and Future of a Discipline in Creative Ferment," *International Journal of Practical Theology* 6, 2 (2002): 288-319, in which I call this fiduciary form of practical theology "comic/kerygmatic-analytic practical theology" to distinguish it from "tragic/apologetic-synthetic practical theology."

5. "The life and death, the resurrection and ascension, of Jesus Messiah disclose the God-man structure of reality that is experienced whenever and wherever time gives shape to space, people to things, persons to processes, and providence to history" (Paul Lehmann, *The Transfiguration of Politics: The Presence and Power of Jesus of Nazareth in and over Human Affairs* [New York: Harper & Row, 1975], p. 279). Following Lehmann, Barry Harvey wrote that in the Messiah, Jesus of Nazareth, "the power and pattern of God's eschatological rule, 'the God-man structure of reality,'" have broken in upon the present. Consequently, the inauguration of the messianic politics of God in the life, death, resurrection and ascension of Jesus forms the center and criterion of life in the *koinonia.* See B. Harvey, *The Politics of the Theological* (New York: Peter Lang, 1995), p. 128.

> form of his bipolar person becomes the structure of our own identity. In spiritual language, the relationality between the Divine Spirit and the human spirit in us has to become Christomorphic. He remains captive of history, culture, or the religious imagination until he comes into us Spirit-to-spirit. For him to come out of history into the fullness of the present time means that our spirits and all their creations are transformed, so we want this dynamic Christomorphism to define us. . . . He must dwell in us by virtue of the spirit-to-Spirit dialectic that replicates in us and beyond us the Chalcedonian bipolar relational unity that characterizes two natures in one person. This issues for us in a dialectical identity in which we say "I — yet not I — but Christ." . . . From this identity, we live out the *analogia spiritus.*[6]

In a risky exercise of pattern recognition, I want to argue here that Loder's articulation of a fiduciary framework for practical theology to contemporize the God-man structure of reality, constructed over a forty-year engagement with Scripture, Kierkegaard, the Reformed tradition, Luther, and the requisite human and physical sciences (and motivated out of his own powerful convictional experiences of Christ), "repeats" in a startling way the practical theological vision of that deutero-Pauline, pre-Chalcedonian, and pre-scientific interpretation of God-human relationality known as Ephesians. Ephesians enshrines a canonical vision that offered the early church a fiduciary framework for contemporizing Christ-church-culture relations during a crucial era when ecclesial identity in the world had become radically uncertain in post-apostolic times. In essence, I argue that the kind of fiduciary concern that created canonical Ephesians — the crisis of how to orient congregations in Asia Minor within the messianic blessedness of *Christus praesens* — is discernable as well in Loder's neo-Chalcedonian science, which he developed in response to the crisis he indwelt — that is, the loss of, and need to reclaim, a dynamic christological relationality at the center of the church's life and witness in a radically uncertain postmodern world. In Ephesians, the theme of *plērōma* functions as the author's master metaphor for the fullness of Christ's powerful presence transforming human life. In relation to the fullness of Christ, congregations were called to "improvise" their identity in every sphere of life, what we might call "*pleromic* improvisation" in witness to the Empire.[7]

6. Loder, *The Logic of the Spirit* (San Francisco: Jossey-Bass, 1998), p. 120.

7. For discussions of the theme of *plērōma* in Old Testament and New Testament and in Ephesians, see R. Schippers, "*Plērōma,*" in *New International Dictionary of New Testament Theology,* ed. Colin Brown (Grand Rapids: Zondervan, 1975), vol. 1, pp. 733-741, and the discussions in critical commentaries, including Andrew Lincoln, *Ephesians,* Word Biblical Commentary (Dallas: Word

Loder's life-long project, what he once called "paradigmatic madness," was to imagine, *in scientific terms,* the structure and dynamics of christomorphic relationality transforming human life, calling the church to discover and to enact her identity-witness through a creative process he finally understood as redemptive transformation according to the logic of the Holy Spirit. To make this convictional connection between "*pleromic* improvisation" in Ephesians and "redemptive creativity" in service of transformation in Loder's science more explicit, I first attend to Ephesians —

1. *To develop a theological interpretation of Ephesians that highlights its author's concern to situate Roman culture in relation to the gospel, rather than the other way around.* In essence, Ephesians calls congregations in Rome to order their life together in the Empire according to the eschatological politics revealed in Christ, and thereby to testify to the Empire to the way things really are, christologically discerned.
2. *To show that in this theological interpretation the author does not obliterate, or succumb to, the reality principle governing ordinary life in Rome but affirms, crucifies and resurrects it in the service of the gospel's reconciling power.* I argue that this visionary orientation of Ephesians is not conceived to support christological imperialism but to bear witness that Jesus Christ is "dying to be revealed" in reconciling power through the church to the world.
3. *To argue that the* plērōma *theme in Ephesians signifies that the dynamic relational structure of divine-human interaction christologically determined has turned ecclesial life "odd" according to the nature of Christ.* God has

---

Books, 1990), and Peter O'Brien, *The Letter to the Ephesians,* Pillar New Testament Commentary (Grand Rapids: Eerdmans/Leicester, UK: Apollos, 1999). Generally speaking I take the author's development of the metaphor of "*plērōma*" in Ephesians to connect (1) the Old Testament assertion that the glory of Yahweh "fills heaven and earth" (Jer. 23:23, 24 LXX, where *plērōma* is not used but the idea is unmistakable), (2) the Gnostic use of *pleroma* to designate the divine Spirit who fills and unifies the entire cosmos, in which the author has eradicated the radical dualism between the earthly and the heavenly which Gnosticism assumed, and (3) Paul's use of *plērōma* in Colossians in reference to the "fullness of deity" which dwells in Christ. In Ephesians the "fullness" of Christ is seen to have filled or completed the church. Lincoln writes: "Yes, Christ is the head over all things, but as head over all he has been given to the Church, and only the Church *is* his body. And yes, Christ is filling all things in terms of his sovereign rule, but he fills the Church in a special sense with his Spirit, grace, and gifts . . . so that only the Church *is* his fullness. The writer's consistent approach, like that of Paul, is that humanity is to be viewed from the vantage point of what has happened to Christ. . . . The importance of the Church, for the writer, is that as Christ's fullness it provides the present focus for and demonstration of that presence which now fills the cosmos in a hidden way but which will do so openly and completely" (Lincoln, *Ephesians,* p. 80).

filled reality with Christ's presence so that the practices of everyday life in Christian churches in Rome are called to actualize themselves according to the blessed power of this Christological Presence through the Holy Spirit. Congregations "discover Christ anew" when they become obedient to this *pleromic* Presence in the ordinary circumstances of day-to-day living.

I then turn to Loder's project —

4. *To elucidate the early work of Loder on the imaginative dynamic structure of "born again consciousness" in religious experience as "reality-restoring."* Loder's unlikely integration of Freud and Kierkegaard identified how religious experience, when it is healthy, exposes the "insanity" of "normal" secularized adaptation and restores our "sane" capacity to care according to the pattern of Christ.
5. *To explicate how Loder, in a 1969 lecture, taught us to provoke "the paradigmatic radicalization of the reality principle" through a therapeutic process of creativity according to the pattern of care in Christ.* In what amounts to an exegesis of Ephesians 6:1-4, Loder argued that the "generation gap" tearing apart American culture in the radical 1960s constituted a "crisis of care" resulting from the neurotic entrapment of parents and young people in conflicted roles — anti-role structure expectations that quenched the spirit of mutual regard and left them unreconciled. To meet the crisis, Christian educators require a reality-restoring therapeutic process patterned according to Christ's healing nature.
6. *To argue that Loder's early work on the dynamics of reality-restoring consciousness laid the groundwork to develop his version of the* Anknüpfungspunkt *or "point of contact"*[8] *for discerning the critical core of divine-human interaction — what he called the "analogia spiritus."* While Loder's early paradigm on the imaginative structure of reality-restoring consciousness

8. The possibility and problems associated with *Anknüpfungspunkt* find their classic articulation in the Barth-Brunner exchange. See the discussion in Garrett Green, *Imagining God: Theology and Religious Imagination* (San Francisco: Harper & Row, 1989), especially chaps. 2 and 3. I am arguing here that Loder's *analogia spiritus* represents a dynamic *Anknüpfungspunkt* that illuminates the nature of the relationality between divine and human action portrayed in Ephesians. I will in particular pay attention to Loder's early development of this scientific *Anknüpfungspunkt* in his formative years at Harvard and Princeton, during which he focused on an integration of the dynamics of reality consciousness in Freud and Kierkegaard that laid the groundwork for his interdisciplinary and scientific method in practical theology and the eventual transformation of that early conceptual effort after 1970. My hope is that this discussion of the pre-1970 origins of Loder's work will illuminate the theo-anthropological significance of his overall practical theological project.

remained theologically reductionistic prior to 1970, important aspects of this formal structure were essentially retained even after the paradigm itself was reconceived after 1970 according to a fuller accounting of its participation in the redemptive transformation of the Holy Spirit.

7. *Finally, to argue that Loder ultimately sought to understand and to make known the God-man as the ontological ground of all divine-human and human-human relations, calling for the creative redemption of human experience.*[9] In effect, this "analogic" of Spirit-to-spirit relations according to the God-man structure of reality can be understood as Loder's postmodern attempt to provide the contemporary church with a scientifically credible, Ephesians-like vision that places human action within the *pleromic* dynamism of life in the Spirit.

For Loder, the church's participation in the God-man structure of reality through the power of the Holy Spirit (whether in the ancient world or in the postmodern world) was the central issue, the "core generative problematic," for practical theological science.[10]

Ephesians as Canonical Exemplar and Warrant for "Pleromic Improvisation" in the Context of Empire

In the epigraph to this chapter I quoted Norman O. Brown: "It is possible to be mad and to be unblest; but it is not possible to get the blessing without madness; it is not possible to get the illumination without the derangement."[11] This quote, which Loder actually cited in the 1969 address to describe his practical theological

9. From the outset of his work at Harvard, Loder was concerned about "the nature of human participation in religious experience." He wanted to overcome sloppiness of thinking and lack of precision in the field of practical theology. In his dissertation he wrote: "The purpose of this thesis is to work toward a sounder integration between theoretical points of view in the fields of religion and psychiatry" ("The Nature of Religious Consciousness in the Writings of Sigmund Freud and Søren Kierkegaard" [diss., Harvard University, 1962]). He differentiated his perspective from Roman Catholicism, fundamentalism, liberalism, ad hoc correlations focused on pragmatic outcomes (Hiltner), phenomenological perspectives, and, perhaps most significantly, Paul Tillich's correlation method, which seeks to develop a third-term philosophical ground to mediate the relation between the two domains *(tertium quid)*. Loder wanted to articulate with great precision how one could understand the dynamics of human participation in religious experience.

10. See the Introduction to this volume for a discussion of "core generative problematic."

11. Norman O. Brown, quoted in Loder, "Adults in Crisis," reprinted in *The Princeton Seminary Bulletin* LXIII, 1 (old series), pp. 32-41 (quotation on p. 39).

method, interprets for me the counterintuitive significance of the letter to the Ephesians, which explodes with blessed madness from the outset (1:3-14), prays for the illumination of the derangement (1:15-23; 3:14-19), and calls congregations within the Roman Empire to embody the blessedness that now determines divine-human relations (4:1-3) so that congregations might "be filled to the measure of all the fullness of God" (3:19) and live out their vocation of being human according to the nature of Christ. Therefore, I want to take Ephesians, a familiar text to Christian educators, as a canonical exemplar of "paradigmatic madness" constructed as a persuasive encyclical to orient small, struggling outposts of Christian *koinonia* to "the God-man structure of reality." Ephesians encourages congregations to rediscover their Christ-determined-life-in-the-Spirit identity in changing circumstances — that is, the extension of their historical existence in the "alien" territory of the *Pax Romana.*[12] In other words, I take Ephesians to be a proto-trinitarian,[13] pre-Chalcedonian improvisation making explicit the hidden orders of intelligibility now revealed to the Roman world as the *Pax Christi* (Eph. 3:1-10). These hidden orders determine and define Christian identity-practice in everyday life in witness to the Roman Empire. David Ford suggests this coming to new self-understanding in Christ in the context of Roman culture requires enormously inventive modes of persuasive speech, or *parrhēsia,* so that Ephesians enshrines a "classic communication movement" through which the author

> takes up themes that had been communicated, prayed through, debated and applied in various situations, and improvising upon them to make a fresh and probably unprecedented synthesis. It is . . . an example of what I would see happening in other classics of Christian thinking down through the centuries: immersion in a multifaceted tradition of worship, belief, community living and action helping to generate the continuities and innovations needed for the present and future. Paul had long been doing this

12. I date Ephesians about A.D. 85 or 90, written by a disciple of Paul as the Christian movement entered an important phase between charisma and institution (Max Weber), fostered by the unexpected delay of the Parousia. The crisis of the church is its identity in relation to competing claims of ultimacy offered according to the *Pax Romana* on the one hand and to the gospel's claims of the *Pax Christi* on the other. Faced with the dying off of the apostles, the the living link to Jesus Christ, the church was forced to improvise its identity, grounded in the Jewish messiah who is Lord of the cosmos. See David Ford, *Self and Salvation* (Cambridge: Cambridge University Press, 1999), chap. 5. Ford draws on Andrew Lincoln, especially Lincoln and A. J. M. Wedderburn, *The Theology of the Later Pauline Letters* (Cambridge: Cambridge University Press, 1993).

13. Several commentators have noted the proto-trinitarian features of the epistle. See F. Martin, "Pauline Trinitarian Formulae and Christian Unity," *Catholic Biblical Quarterly* 30 (1968): 199-219.

> in his mission (i.e. Colossians) . . . and Ephesians does it partly by improvising on Paul's letters and on Colossians. Ephesians eventually entered the canonical repertoire of works that have since been continually 'performed' and have helped to shape various Christian identities. I am now trying out yet another improvisatory performance.[14]

Our concern here is to interpret Ephesians *theo-anthropologically* if we are to avoid the danger of misreading it as a kind of *tour de force* propagandizing to justify a kind of christological *(pleromic)* triumphalism that simply obliterates or ignores all things human and cultural in the name of the crucified (unblessed madness to be sure![15]). On this kind of false reading any potential for establishing a truly reconciled relationship between gospel reality and Roman reality, especially at the level of face-to-face relations, is eliminated.[16] Against *"pleromic" triumphalism* we argue that Ephesians calls churches to take up a nuanced stance vis-à-vis Rome that is truly relational and redemptive, one that calls for *"'pleromic' improvisation."* On the one hand, congregations are to "stand firm" against the illusory and idolatrous ultimacy-claims and legitimation propaganda of the Empire itself (6:10-20) so as not to "learn (improvise) Christ" according to the enculturating patterns of Roman *esprit de corps* corrupted by sin (4:17ff.). Congregations are to be filled with Christ's reconciling Spirit, not the spirit of Rome.[17] On the other hand, congregations also need to take seriously (penultimately) what today the psychoanalytic tradition calls "the reality principle" shaping Roman society — that nexus of motivational en-

14. Ford, *Self and Salvation,* pp. 111-112. Ford calls Ephesians an "explosion of fresh communication, of *parrhesia* in relation to God, towards the whole world and within the community, a dynamic which is meant to pervade ordinary living, thinking, feeling and action. The most fundamental purpose of the community is fulfilled and enjoyed through this constantly new improvisation of *parrhesia*" (p. 110). Ford also describes Ephesians as a "prose equivalent of the Psalms" in that, like the Psalms, which "take up most of the main Old Testament genres — narrative, law, prophecy, lament, hymn, liturgy, wisdom, blessing, curse — into the overall movement of praise, so Ephesians interweaves its source genres into a letter whose overall thrust is to shape a community of singers of the glory of God" (p. 112).

15. One hardly needs to mention the demonic nature of religious triumphalism in mad pursuit of "un-blessing" the world.

16. Ford's consistent emphasis on "face-to-face" relations as the core of Christian blessedness was very helpful for thinking through the significance of Ephesians as an interpretation of the meaning of Loder's work. Ford's examination of Ephesians in *Self and Salvation,* chap. 5, encouraged me immensely in the writing of this essay to recognize Loder in Ephesians and Ephesians in Loder, something I had mused about for quite some time and about which I had a discussion with Dr. Loder himself.

17. Loder's constant concern was that Christian faith always had to be learned in the right spirit if it was to be truly learned at all. This truth he learned from Kierkegaard.

ergy, psychic ambivalence, institutional expectation, and cultural ethos that constitutes a viable social order.[18] Ephesians implicitly affirms and engages (even establishes, albeit in qualified terms) Rome's reality-regulative institutions (marriage, family, slavery) and conventional face-to-face social norms (Ephesians 5:25–6:9) in its ecclesial vision as penultimate (not epiphenomenal!) concerns, even as it calls them to be crucified and transformed by their participation in the *pleromic* blessedness of Christ's presence.

Andrew Lincoln describes this qualified affirmation of Roman culture implicit in Ephesians' vision by making a non-triumphalistic interpretation of *plērōma* that discerns an important continuity between creation and redemption in Christ.

> [I]t is in the fellowship of the Church that the fullness of Christ's presence is to be experienced. . . . Christ's fullness . . . provides the focus for and demonstration of that presence which now fills the cosmos in a hidden way but which will do so openly and completely. Although the paraenesis in particular draws a clear ethical distinction between believers and surrounding society . . . the perspective here is not one in which the Church and the rest of creation are two entities fixed in a state of permanent opposition and alienation. Rather, because the Church's head is head over all, and because the one who fills the Church is filling all things, there is now a continuity between the realm of salvation and the realm of creation . . . between the Church and the world. The whole created reality becomes the Church's legitimate concern, and the Church symbolizes the realization of the possibilities inherent in God's purpose in Christ for all creation.[19]

This (ultimately) positive relation that the *pleromic* Presence of Christ establishes with the reality principle embodied in Roman society is never from the human side in this vision, and never can be, even as it requires a full human re-

18. In *Religious Pathology and Christian Faith* (Philadelphia: Westminster, 1966), Loder defined the reality principle as "an endopsychic demand for agreement between the external world as it is perceived, conceptualized, judged, and/or reproduced in consciousness, and the power of the psyche which both energizes those conscious processes and at the same time demands, through the introduction of tension which is felt as mental 'pain,' the ultimate cooperation of those conscious processes in its own self-expression. When an individual himself becomes real, i.e. when the reality principle is the immanent law of his psychic nature, then he seeks pleasure in such a way that the power which underlies and energizes consciousness finds *valid expression* in the external world through the operation of conscious functions" (p. 122).

19. Lincoln, *Ephesians*, pp. 80-81. For a winsome expression of the connection of salvation and human culture see Richard Mouw, *When the Kings Come Marching In: Isaiah and the New Jerusalem*, 2nd ed. (Grand Rapids: Eerdmans, 2002).

sponse (Eph. 2:1-11). Ephesians recognizes an ontological and soteriological divide separating human orders from divine reality, a divide that only the gospel can, and has, bridged.[20] Thus, in light of the gospel these affirmed socialized patterns of motivation, ambivalence, institution and ethos governing "reality" in Rome are also exposed as the bearers of the entropic power of sin and death unless and until they are "turned odd" in proximity to the transforming power of the Kingdom which has "leeched" itself into Roman reality and filled it with Christ's Presence.[21] Missiologist Andrew Walls suggests that Christianity's turning culture "odd," with its combination of affirmation and judgment-unto-transformation, is grounded in the gospel's "bewildering paradox" revealed in the Incarnation and throughout the missionary history of the church.

> The bewildering paradox at the heart of the Christian confession is not just the obvious one of the divine humanity; it is the twofold affirmation of the utter Jewishness of Jesus and of the boundless universality of the Divine Son. The paradox is necessary to the business of making sense of the history of the Christian faith. On the one hand it is a seemingly infinite series of cultural specificities — each in principle as locally specific as utterly Jewish Jesus. On the other hand, in a historical view, the different specificities belong together. They have a certain coherence and interdependence in the coherence and interdependence of total humanity in the One who made humanity his own.[22]

20. The earlier work of Loder's that we will look at in the second half of this essay supports this statement only implicitly. But Loder came to embrace this essentially Barthian position in his work that unfolded after 1970. I have argued elsewhere that Loder's project after 1970 can be understood as a critical neo-Barthian form of practical theology. See Wright, "The Contemporary Renaissance in Practical Theology in the United States," esp. pp. 288-295, 315-319.

21. Theologian Katherine Tanner argues that the church functioned "parasitically" in relation to the dominant culture. The church did not invent a "finished" identity over and against culture but rather engaged the cultural values, symbols, and images that reigned in various contexts and "turned them odd" according to the nature of Christ. Christianity could be construed as a social movement that seeped into the warp and woof of Roman society and "leeched" itself onto the cultural artifacts, practices, and images upon which Roman society constructed itself, but filled them with Christ. See *Theories of Culture: A New Agenda for Theology* (Minneapolis: Fortress, 1997), esp. pp. 110-119. We should mention here that Loder understood and worked out these "parasitic" and "turning-odd" dynamics in great detail according to his analogy of the spirit and Chalcedonian framework in all of his post-1970 writings, and especially in what might be considered his practical theological trilogy, *The Transforming Moment*, 2nd ed. (Colorado Springs: Helmers & Howard, 1989), *The Logic of the Spirit* (San Francisco: Jossey-Bass, 1998), and *Education Ministry in the Logic of the Spirit* (not yet published). We will come back to Loder's more mature understanding at the end of this essay.

22. Andrew Walls, *The Missionary Movement in Christian History* (Maryknoll, NY: Orbis,

Thus, in Ephesians, a canonical depiction of God making humanity God's own in Jesus Christ, the "certain coherence and interdependence" of the cultural specificities through which Roman society was ordered (what we might call the "liturgy" of the Empire)[23] is implicitly affirmed, especially in the paraenetic section's often close correspondence with, and even borrowing from, extant Jewish, Stoic, Roman and Persian ethical sources and "household codes" for governing social behavior (Eph. 5:22–6:9).[24] But these specificities are then oddly subjected (crucified) unto liberation (transformation) "in the coherence and interdependence of total humanity in the One who made humanity his own" (life ordered according to the *pleromic* "liturgy" of the *Pax Christi* testified to in Ephesians). We see this liturgical "subjection" unto liberated blessedness expressed (1) in the author's appropriation of the Hebrew *Berakah* (1:3-14) to depict human reality redeemed in the "blessed mindfulness" of God revealed in Jesus Christ;[25] (2) in the depiction of Jesus Christ as the New David (New Adam) (1:19b-23) who orders a reconciled style of life grounded in forgiveness and equal access for all to the worship of God (Eph. 2);[26] (3) in the

2001), p. xvi. For insight into how Loder understood the work of God in Christ through history in terms that are perhaps similar to Walls's see chap. 2 of *Educational Ministry in the Logic of the Spirit,* entitled "Socialization and Transformation: A Brief History." I wish to thank Tom Hastings for this connection of Walls to Ephesians and to Loder.

23. For a description of empire as "liturgy" see Daniel Bell, *Liberation Theology after the End of History: The Refusal to Cease Suffering* (London: Routledge, 2001), p. 4.

24. Much of the scholarly consensus on Ephesians supports this view that the writer of Ephesians may have drawn from contemporary sources which contained raw materials from the culture to be "turned odd" in relation to Christ. The Christian church, facing the delay of the Parousia, had to figure out how to go on living in Roman society as well as "in Christ." See Pheme Perkins, *Ephesians,* Abingdon New Testament Commentary (Nashville: Abingdon, 1997), pp. 126-131, and Martin Kitchen, *Ephesians* (New York: Routledge, 1994), pp. 94-96.

25. The *Berakah* is a Hebrew liturgical form demonstrated in Psalms 105, 106, and 108, in which the history of Israel is depicted according to the astonishing providence and mercy of God. *Berakah,* the Hebrew word for "blessing," recalls human life "in a state of favor and wholeness that is not grounded in anything originating with human beings but in the promise of God." Blessing is also linked closely with the notion of "glory" and of God's "face." In Numbers 6:24-26, the basis for our benedictions, we find the idea of Yahweh's face being "turned towards Israel" so that the glory of Yahweh became the environment within which Israel was called to live. Yahweh does not "hide his face" from Israel but "turns his face toward Israel" and Israel lives and prospers. In Ephesians 1:3-14, the outworking of God's foundational "yes" to Israel has now become God's "yes" to all humankind (Jew and Gentile) through Jesus Christ. In Jesus Christ the "face" of God turns "yes-ward" to us finally and irrevocably (2 Cor. 3:12–4:6). The emphasis here is that the blessedness revealed in Christ requires redemption (Eph. 1:7-8; 2). Those familiar with Loder's work on "the face" will recognize a connection to the *Berakah* in Ephesians.

26. The New David imagery is taken from Psalm 110, which is alluded to in Eph. 1:20-21, but which also recalls Genesis 1:26-27 and, by implication, Psalm 8 (connecting "mindfulness"

two prayers (1:15-19a and 3:14-19) and the benediction (3:20-21) that call the community to permanent *metanoia* as its basic mode of existence in Christ;[27] (4) in the epistle's depiction of the "practice of everyday life" in Rome now relocated in the soteriological spaciousness designated "in Christ";[28] (5) in the call to "learn Christ" (i.e., "to put off the old self [and] to be made new in the attitude of your minds . . . to put on the new self, created to be like God") (4:22-24); and finally, (6) in the *plērōma* theme.

Regarding this last theme, reading Ephesians *"pleromically"* (i.e., human reality filled with the redeeming, reconciling Presence of Christ in witness to Rome) recalls how George Hunsinger taught us to read Karl Barth's reading of reality christologically. Hunsinger presents the "prismic" or even "holographic" structure of Barth's imagination when he relates true "secular words" (i.e., "secular parables") to revelation in volume IV/3 of the *Church Dogmatics.*[29] In Barth, the relation of "true secular words" to the Word (as for example, the relation of analogues from Roman culture in the paraenetic section of Ephesians to the *Pax Christi*) is the relation of "periphery to center" (a radical and scandalous "de-centering" of Roman ultimacy claims). Instead of a commonsense or "linear" understanding of this relation, Barth, according to Hunsinger, champions a "dialectical intensification and deepening" of it so that "the truth of the one Word of God is not only identified with 'the center of the circle,' but also with 'the whole periphery constituted by it.'" Secular words "at the periphery" do not speak partial truth but "total" truth when they are placed in the service of (subjected to) the Word. Barth's "holographic" imagination is Christological and relational in a very specific sense that

---

of God to the *imago dei*). In the ancient world, an "image" of the conquering king was placed at the boundaries to make known to all who entered that the land belonged to this sovereign. David epitomized the image of a king of Israel who ordered life around the worship of God. Yet David failed in this calling, and a New David was needed. In the New David's ordering of life around the worship of God, all persons have "equal access" to the Father and therefore the boundaries of privilege and presumption have been relativized to serve reconciliation. On David see Walter Brueggemann, *In Man We Trust: The Neglected Side of Biblical Faith* (Richmond, VA: John Knox Press, 1973), *passim.*

27. Ephesians portrays a "being-realized" eschatology in that the Spirit's inspiration of the community's "*pleromic* improvisation" connects the church's present experience to the eschatological politics of God (the already–not yet). In the Spirit the community's improvisation of its identity both embodies and requires prayer.

28. Ford, *Self and Salvation,* pp. 117-120. I take "in Christ" to be theological shorthand for what we have called human participation in the "God-man structure of reality."

29. George Hunsinger, *How to Read Karl Barth: The Shape of His Theology* (New York: Oxford University Press, 1991), pp. 260-263, 292 n. 7.

> "the one truth of Jesus Christ is indivisible." Human words at the periphery cannot and do not fragment this truth. "They express the one and total truth from a particular angle, and to that extent only implicitly and not explicitly in its unity and totality." In other words, the truth of the center in its unity and totality is always implicitly present in any of its manifestations at the periphery. The whole as a differentiated unity is always implicitly present as such in the part without either of them losing its identity or becoming superfluous. True human words — whether from the Bible, the church, or the world — are all in essentially the same situation. Insofar as they are true, they are holistic manifestations of "the one light of the one truth." From a particular standpoint they are a holistic refraction of "the one light." Each in its own "particular and individual way" reflects and reproduces the truth of Jesus Christ in its totality. As each word is "enlightened by the truth of the one Word itself," it both draws upon and manifests this light in "its fullness."

Hunsinger then continues with language reminiscent of the *plērōma* theme in Ephesians:

> The mode of relatedness which emerges might therefore be stated like this: whereas the truth of the periphery imparts itself to the center by participating in and manifesting the totality which the center has established, the truth of the center imparts itself to the periphery by filling it and endowing it, at each and every point, with the fullness of uncreated light. Center and periphery are thus related by a mutuality of self-impartation. They are mutually (though differently) implicated in each other through a pattern of reciprocal coinherence.[30]

Important here is Hunsinger's qualification of his use of the hologram image by emphasizing, like Ephesians, the ontological and soteriological divide between culture and Creator that the dissimilarity in the analogical relation between them must uphold.[31] To be faithful to revelation the relation of the

30. Hunsinger, *How to Read Karl Barth*, pp. 261-262. Quotes in this paragraph are from Barth, *CD* IV/3, p. 123. Hunsinger here also draws upon *The Holographic Paradigm and Other Paradoxes: Exploring the Leading Edge of Science*, ed. Ken Wilbur (Boulder: Shambala Publications, 1982).

31. One of the keys to understanding Loder's work is his careful attention to analogical predication in terms of both the requisite similarity and dissimilarity integral to all true analogies. Loder's analogical predication is always carefully constructed to preserve the integrity of divine-human relations according to the nature of Christ. His book with Niedhardt, *The Knight's Move: The Relational Logic of the Spirit in Theology and Science* (Colorado Springs: Helmers & Howard, 1992), is an expansive elaboration of a powerful disclosure analogy.

christological *plērōma* to the cultural particularity must be governed by both (1) the asymmetrical differentiation-in-unity between the center and the periphery according to the nature of Jesus Christ (Chalcedonian pattern) and (2) the relational inclusion of the truth of the center coming to expression in the periphery (perichoretic pattern).[32] Hunsinger explains,

> It is evident that two familiar formal patterns are in the background of this conception of the circle with its center and periphery. The differentiated unity of center and periphery suggests the Chalcedonian pattern. The connection between the two is indissoluble . . . yet it retains its distinctive identity . . . and one is primary and formative and the other is secondary and derivative. Moreover, the dialectical inclusion of the truth of the center in the forms at the periphery further suggests the trinitarian pattern of coinherence . . . for human words to be true, the truth of the Word "must dwell within them," and . . . in their own way these words will "say the same thing."[33]

In Ephesians, traces of these Chalcedonian and perichoretic patterns of "reciprocal coinherence" can be inferred from what we have thus far described as the *plērōma* theme. For example, in relation to Christ the Lord, Roman imperial claims of ultimacy and power have been relativized to the periphery not center, so that the "totalizing" claims of the Empire are granted "a wholesome limitation to soteriologically charged expectations of politics" (Eph. 4:17-24).[34] Further, the humbled church receives from culture important forms and structures for her common life, so that Ephesians also grants "a wholesome limitation" to the soteriologically charged expectations of *ecclesial* politics as well (contra *pleromic* triumphalism). Here it should be noted that when the *pleromic* presence of Christ, acting through the "dynamic christomorphism" of the Spirit, interpenetrates the life-experience of congregations within the cultural matrix of Asia Minor and calls them to faithfulness according to Christ's nature, "the soteriology of abundance" revealed in Christ "is enacted primarily in face to face relationships in daily life which require attention to their sup-

32. Hunsinger, *How to Read Karl Barth*, p. 292 n. 7.

33. Hunsinger, *How to Read Karl Barth*, p. 261.

34. Bernd Wannenwetsch described the "de-totalization of politics" in that "Worship interrupts the course of the world over and over again . . . not only labor and production, but also politics, witnessing that the world is sustained not by human politics, but by the politics of God celebrated in worship. Therefore, worship stands not only against this or that totalitarian regime, but against the totalisation of politics in general — granting a wholesome limitation to soteriologically charged expectations of politics." See "The Political Worship of the Church: A Critical and Empowering Practice," *Modern Theology* 12, 3 (July 1996): 279.

porting institutions, such as marriage." Marriage is affirmed yet reconstituted perichoretically by the filling of the Spirit and takes hold as a "cruciform" call to "be subject to one another out of reverence for Christ (5:21) . . . the new self in ordinary life, year after year with the same person."[35] Amazingly, then, ordinary married relations filled with the Spirit of Christ become "holograms" of christomorphic relationality. Indeed, "in the Spirit" every ordinary conversation, face-to-face commitment, social and economic interchange, act of care and responsibility, etc., is called to embody "holographic" witness to the fullness of reconciled life that has come in Jesus Christ.[36] David Ford captures the nature of the impact of the *pleromic* presence of Christ in ordinary social intercourse as a kind of subjection to liberation unto reconciliation.

> The blood, the death, the cross of Christ are prominent in the first two chapters, and the main interpretation of them is in terms of love and peacemaking. . . . To have this crucified and risen person as the location of the community's identity should, in the light of what the rest of the letter says, have consequences such as: giving testimony in ways which suffer rather than coerce; refusing to claim any overview of the extent, subtleties and surprises of the love of Christ . . . ; being open to radical reconceptions of one's boundaries, comparable in significance to those the recipients of the letter were having to cope with; and, above all, giving up any idea of being in control of a *pleroma* that works in unimaginably generous, gentle and understanding ways.[37]

35. Ford, *Self and Salvation,* p. 119. Ford's interpretation agrees generally with the commentary on Ephesians by Markus Barth, who interpreted the instructions concerning marriage, parenting, and slave-master as examples of the programmatic call to be "filled with the Spirit" and therefore to be "subject to one another." See M. Barth, *Ephesians,* vol. 2, Anchor Bible Commentary (Garden City, NY: Doubleday, 1974), pp. 608ff.

36. In more scientific terms, Christ "fills" ordinary relationships, socio-culturally constructed ego defenses, role structures, and cultural imaginings with the soteriological meaning and power of his reconciling nature so that these former normative mediators of human relatedness in Roman society are crucified and transformed in order to bear the new quality of reconciled relationality Ephesians calls the new humanity. Every dimension of human action — the bodily, the psychic, the social, and the cultural — and every institution that orders social life in Rome becomes now "in Christ" through the power of the Spirit a testimony to, and a bearer of, the reconciled relatedness to which Christ has determined human history through the cross (Eph. 2:11-22).

37. Ford, *Self and Salvation,* pp. 132-133. Those who know the work of James Loder will recognize that the force of this passage resonates with his understanding of the impact of the Spirit of Christ on human life, biologically, psychologically, socially, and culturally. For another compelling account of how Christ sponsors the radical reconsideration of the nature of identity in terms of inclusive cultural boundaries in Christ, especially in international relations, see

To summarize, the author of Ephesians has "improvised" Paul's interpretation of the *plērōma* of Jesus Christ, the fullness of the Godhead bodily (Colossians) by extending it in relation to ordinary Roman time and space, "weaving together God, Christ, church, Christian living and the whole cosmos into a dynamic (and Christ-transforming) soteriology of abundance."[38] Furthermore, Ford recognizes how the writer integrates a realized and a being-realized eschatology to communicate his portrayal of the new humanity caught up in the *pleromic* "perfecting of perfection" of Christ making humanity God's own.[39]

> One way of seeing the link between these [paradoxical eschatologies] is by the idea of pleroma . . . an abundance already there but also endlessly generative. In the way this letter talks of completeness there is no sense of a full stop, of ending. It is better conceived through the notion of overflow linked with pleroma. In linguistic terms it is found in such notions as blessing, praise, thanks . . . the very act of thanks shows that there is more beyond . . . the act of praise paradoxically perfects the perfection (implicit in the praiseworthy referent) . . . a distinctive form of completeness [is] indicated by Ephesians.[40]

To be caught up in this *pleromic* paradox revealed in Christ in the context of the Empire requires "conversion" or "permanent revolution" from the human side, facilitated by an enormously creative and persuasive linguistic environment. Moreover, Ephesians' call to the "endless generativity" (conversion) through the medium of imaginative *parrhēsia* also points implicitly to the constituent conditions for discovering who Christ is in each generation. Andrew Walls uses the metaphor "translation" (roughly what Ford means by "improvisation") to argue that the distinctive nature of Christ's impact on the social construction of reality becomes manifest precisely wherever the church engages culture creatively to translate God's redemptive mission in cultural terms. In such engagements

---

Miroslav Volf, *Exclusion and Embrace: A Theological Exploration of Identity, Otherness, and Reconciliation* (Nashville: Abingdon Press, 1996). See also the essay in this volume by John McClure, chapter 3.

38. Ford, *Self and Salvation*, p. 114.

39. On the one hand, he takes up the theme of the expansion of boundaries conformed to the new humanity that has already been established in Christ, breaking down all religious, social, and cultural barriers between God and humanity and among human communities. But on the other hand, he prepares his community for the long haul by instructing them to pay attention to social institutions, roles, and responsibilities "turned odd" in relation to Christ's transforming power (Hunsinger's "reciprocal coinherence").

40. Ford, *Self and Salvation*, p. 115.

> a new conceptual vocabulary had to be constructed. Elements of vocabulary already existing in that world had to be commandeered and turned towards Christ [so that] people began to see Christ in their own terms . . . the process was hugely enriching; *it proved to be a discovery of the Christ . . . as though Christ himself actually grows through the work of mission. . . . the divine saving activity can be understood in terms of translation.* Divinity is translated into humanity, but into specific humanity, at home in specific segments of social reality. If the Incarnation of the Son represents a divine act of translation, it is a prelude to repeated acts of re-translation as Christ fills the Pleroma again — other aspects of social reality. And the proper response to such activity is conversion.[41]

The connection of *pleroma* to conversion through translation in mission is startling, especially in light of Walls's suggestion that ever-fresh discoveries of the reality of Christ's *pleromic* presence wait, at least in part, upon the church's perspicuous obedience (and perhaps the world's as well!) in diverse sociocultural contexts. Ephesians suggests that ever-deeper dimensions of the *Pax Christi* are discovered through acts of "*pleromic* improvisation" (redemptive creativity) — human experience "turned odd" through obedient participation in the dynamic christomorphic power of the Spirit. Amazingly, Christ becomes both the "prisoner and liberator of culture" as he condescends to enter the distortions and depravities woven into human existence (Eph. 4:17-19) with the fullness of forgiving grace and through his Spirit accommodates to human existence to orchestrate a reconciling obedience through our coming-to-identity, over and over again, in him.[42] Paul Lehmann vividly describes the inner psychic tension of living creatively where the *pleromic* presence of Christ's Spirit engages the reality principle in socialized experience. We live, said Lehmann, at "that delicate conjunction of the inner springs of human motivation and of human judgment" which designates "that pivotal personal center of man's total response to the dynamics, direction, and personal thrust of the di-

41. Walls, *The Missionary Movement in Christian History,* pp. xvi-xvii; emphasis added.

42. For Walls, the gospel embodies an "indigenizing principle" (Christ in solidarity with particular cultures and peoples) and a "pilgrim principle" (Christ transforming particular cultures and peoples). Congregations as centers of theological improvisation enact and embody "provisional" yet "true-enough" interpretations of the faith in dialogue with Scripture, tradition, and cultural contexts. The fullness of Jesus Christ "comes to fullness" in particular locations as redemptive creativity. Walls's insights here correspond to those of George Hendry, who understood the impact of the incarnation in terms of both *condescension* (Walls's indigenizing principle) and *accommodation* (pilgrim principle). Hendry's book *The Holy Spirit in Christian Theology* (Philadelphia: Westminster, 1961) was enormously influential on Loder's development of the *analogia spiritus.*

vine claims made upon [humanity]." Christ is "the living link between the order by which human life is sustained and the personal response of obedience to that order [which enables us] to discern in, with, and under the concrete course of human events the presence and power of God at work giving shape to human life, providing specific knowledge of what God expects of humanity and what humanity owes to God."[43]

From the standpoint of Ephesians, God alone establishes the parameters of the correspondence between God and humanity, and these parameters conform to the "liturgical situating" of human reality by Jesus Christ the Lord, calling humanity to the obedient vocation of being human according to the nature of Christ.[44] Ephesians locates Roman life in the context of the givenness of things divine and human in Christ, and the redemptive transformation of all things Roman as liberating limit (christomorphic limitation as the freedom of creaturehood fully accepted and embraced and repentant).[45] Ephesians imagines an ecclesial identity in the world that testifies convictionally that "the new reality brought about in Jesus Christ *is* reality."[46] Ephesians makes known the Agent of this "new reality [which] is reality," an Agent of "lavish generosity in blessing, loving, revealing and reconciling . . . an inexhaustible, dynamic and personal source of abundance and glory with an all-inclusive, universal scope of operation,"[47] who holds himself captive to the host cultural context in order to liberate it according to his own nature. This is neither christological imperialism from the ecclesial side nor the domestication of Christ from the culture

43. Paul Lehmann, *Ethics in a Christian Context* (New York: Harper & Row, 1963), p. 316.

44. Karl Barth could well have had Ephesians in mind when he argued that "the human situation [is] universally altered and redetermined by the act and Word of God, by the existence and work of Christ; this statement concerning the status of every [person and community], even the uncalled, that [we] stand already in the light of life, has to be ventured as a dogmatic tenet because it forms the indispensable presupposition . . . of the doctrine of [humanity's] vocation to be a Christian." *Church Dogmatics,* IV/3, second half (Edinburgh: T&T Clark, 1962), section 71, p. 490.

45. On the subject of human life as de-limited by the nature of Christ rather than as an exercise in unlimited potential, see Walter Lowe, "Prospects for Postmodern Christian Theology: Apocalyptic without Reserve," *Modern Theology* 15, 1 (Jan. 1999): 22. See also Lawrence Richards's important discussion of limitation in *A Theology of Christian Education* (Grand Rapids: Zondervan, 1975), chap. 7, "A Discipling Purpose," pp. 70-79.

46. John Webster, speaking of theologies of hope, argued that "a Christian theology of hope will be disoriented from the outset unless it is securely anchored to an account of the grace of God as constitutive of created being and action. . . . If we are to make some headway . . . it will have to be by taking with great seriousness the Christian Confession that the new reality brought about in Jesus Christ is reality." See Webster, *Barth's Moral Theology: Human Action in Barth's Thought* (Grand Rapids: Eerdmans, 1998), p. 95.

47. Ford, *Self and Salvation,* p. 113.

side, but Jesus Christ "dying to be discovered" in every age as the power who enables "the glorious liberty of the children of God" to come to expression as life in the Spirit fashioned from the raw materials of Roman cultural praxis.

We can now appreciate the significance of the prominent place that the writer of Ephesians gave to the practical theological vocations of preacher, pastor-teacher, evangelist, and apostolic missionary (4:11ff.) at the dawning post-apostolic age. The author locates these vocations precisely where the task of *pleromic* improvisation becomes urgent, where messianic actualities (articulated out of Hebrew and Christian, especially Pauline sources — Eph. 1–3) intersect perichoretically with the Roman reality principle governing the practice of everyday life (Eph. 4–6), to call out for improvised identity-speech-practices (imaginative preaching, teaching, counseling, caring, serving, administrating unto obedience), the human medium for the rediscovery of Christ in every age.[48] Ephesians envisions a christomorphic way of being human in the world that affirms, crucifies and transforms the reality principle governing the "practice of everyday life" by reconstituting it relationally according to the God-man structure of reality. Thus, the author calls forth gifted persons like himself — evangelists, preachers, pastor-teachers, etc. — to provoke *pleromic* improvisation from the congregations of Asia Minor toward the purpose of redeeming every realm of human action *coram Deo* (Eph. 4:1-24).

Of course, it is one thing to interpret Ephesians as a canonical exemplar and warrant calling for *pleromic* impovisation unto the discovery of Christian identity in the context of the prescientific *Pax Romana,* and quite another to contemporize this vision in relation to the scientific culture of the twenty-first century *Pax Americana.* In the next section of this essay I want to discern in the early work of James Loder his initial efforts to do just that — contemporize Christian identity by indwelling and describing the dynamics of "reality-restoring" consciousness for a secularized, scientific culture. Loder wrote in 1965 of the aim of education as the

48. Lincoln, *Ephesians,* pp. 232-233. "So the issues of church life that the writer of Ephesians is addressing are how, without the apostle [Paul], the Pauline churches can remain unified and how, without the apostle, they can remain apostolic. . . . In response to the latter issue, he underlies the significance of the bearers of the tradition of the Pauline gospel, who, along with the foundational apostles and prophets, now include evangelists, pastors and teachers. These ministers are to be seen as no less than gifts of the exalted Christ to his Church, who will play a vital role both in the maintenance of its unity and in the preservation of its true teaching, the apostolic tradition of the Gospel of Christ. . . . Since the writer to the Ephesians himself attempts such a role, he presumably views himself as a teacher in the Church and the perspective of this passage would therefore also function, like the device of pseudonymity, to lend authority to his own application of the Pauline gospel" (p. 233).

expansion of the boundaries of paradigmatic freedom [which] is a fusion of content and process; indeed, it is precisely in the fusion that consciousness is created. At their origins Biblical knowledge and creedal formulations are the creative resolutions to psychological, sociological, and cultural conflicts of the eras in which they appeared . . . that is precisely how they are learned today, i.e. as solutions to current issues, but the intention behind their contemporary appropriation is nothing like the intentions that created them in the first place. Both intentions are valid, but their identity can never be assumed; each "meaning" is extracted from a different body-environment matrix.[49]

In this passage Loder makes "born-again consciousness" underlying religious creativity in the service of therapeutic reality-restoration analogous to the creativity that generated expressions of biblical and creedal formulations (i.e., like Ephesians).[50] This insight laid the analytical foundations for his development, after 1970, of the *analogia spiritus,* his understanding of the dynamic and living *Anknüpfungspunkt* in which the Spirit-to-spirit transformation of all things human according to the nature of Christ is discerned in everyday life. By examining this early work in religious consciousness and creativity in the service of restoring mental health we gain important clues into the significance of his later work to bring Christian reality and cultural realities into redemptively creative relations, analogous to the *pleromic* connection the author of Ephesians makes to interrelate the *Pax Christi* and the *Pax Romana.*[51]

49. Loder, *Religious Pathology and Christian Faith,* p. 224.

50. Loder makes this connection between classic texts and the human spirit's development under the power of the Spirit explicit in *The Knight's Move* in a chapter on "the journey of intensification." In the journey of intensification, a "journey into the depth of particularity that yields final universality," there is a "drive toward establishing *inner coherence* between the *Divine Presence,* the *accompanying vision,* the *consuming passion,* and the *public world of ego equilibration*" which is "far stronger than socialization" and is "the backbone of true prophecy. . . . [And] if David Tracy is correct, then intensification is also the power behind the creation of all the classics in art, poetry, music, and theology" (emphasis Loder's). From this standpoint, the task of the congregation under the journey of intensification is to become a "classic" expression of Christomorphic relationality. See *The Knight's Move,* pp. 274-275. See also Tracy's discussion of "classic texts" in *The Analogical Imagination* (New York: Crossroads, 1981), pp. 133f.

51. "Creativity" is for Loder the best theme for describing the generative quality of the human spirit at work in human development, scientific discovery, therapeutic healing, artistic creativity, and religious conversion. In Loder's earlier work (prior to 1970), the creativity of the human spirit is central to his practical theological science, but it is only tacitly redemptive because he had not connected it analogically to the redemptive work of *Spiritus Creator.* For the difference between "reality-restoring" therapeutic knowing such as characterized Loder's early

Loder's Paradigmatic Madness and the Structure of Born-Again Consciousness: Reality Restoration within a Therapeutic Framework

Recall that in the Introduction to this volume we mentioned Loder's powerful experience of the presence of Jesus Christ at the death of his father during his matriculation at Princeton Theological Seminary in 1957. This experience of the assurance of Christ's love for his father and for himself compelled the young philosopher to return to Princeton in search of a way to make sense of it all. Under the direction of Hans Hofmann, Loder turned to Kierkegaard for answers, and then accompanied Hofmann to Harvard under a grant to study the relation of religion to mental health. At Harvard, Loder sought to connect religious experience to the human sciences in a way that articulated psychoanalytically and functionally the dynamic structure of his own experience of Christ, what might be called a psychic archaeology of born-again consciousness. His initial effort to discern Christian realities in relation to scientific culture is illumined for us in his 1962 dissertation, "The Nature of Religious Consciousness in the Writings of Sigmund Freud and Søren Kierkegaard," and from an interpretation of this work by one of his early doctoral students, C. Daniel Batson.[52] Batson, in his own dissertation "Creativity and Religious Development" (1971), described the "hypnagogic paradigm," Loder's pre-1970 construct of the structure and dynamics of reality-restoring consciousness as follows:

> The religious behavior of the psyche by which one's consciousness is transformed from a pathological state into a criterional one is described as "the hypnagogic paradigm." According to this paradigm consciousness moves through the following sequence: endopsychic conflict, a movement of belief in an "image"; resolution of the conflict; bestowal of the criterional state of consciousness; anagogic analysis of the image presented. This sequence characterizes Kierkegaard's description of conversion by the God-man as well as reconstructive and converting phantasies described by Freud.[53]

---

work and "four-dimensional" convictional knowing that characterized his mature thought, see *The Transforming Moment,* esp. chaps. 2 and 3.

52. Loder, "The Nature of Religious Consciousness in the Writings of Sigmund Freud and Søren Kierkegaard" (Ph.D. diss., Harvard University, 1962), and C. Daniel Batson, "Creativity and Religious Development" (Th.D. diss., Princeton Theological Seminary, 1971). Loder's concern here is to develop a paradigm for psychology as a sub-discipline of epistemology toward "a systematic approach to practical theology."

53. Loder, "The Nature of Religious Consciousness," p. 5, quoted in Batson, "Creativity and Religious Development," p. 84. This quote outlines an early form of Loder's "logic of the spirit," which he developed after 1970, what he called "the logic of transformation." Over several years the original paradigm's structure evolved into a five-stage dynamic process: (1) conflict in

The underlying question Loder sought to answer here is: "What were the psychosocial dynamics of human consciousness Freud and Kierkegaard observed when the experiences they were observing were understood by the individuals being observed to be religious in nature?" Loder wanted to compare and contrast the perceptive insights of these two exemplary observers of the inwardness of human consciousness.[54] Through an exhaustive analysis of the functional role of the imagination in both Freud and Kierkegaard to restore mental health, Loder first identified modes of religious consciousness that bred non-creative, neurotic or reality-repressing outcomes (i.e., Freud's compulsive-obsessive religion) and cultural conformity (i.e., Kierkegaard's description of Aesthetic, Ethical, and Religiousness A within Danish Christendom). He then described a reality-restoring mode of consciousness discernable in both Freud and in Kierkegaard (Religiousness B). Loder argued that "Kierkegaard's concern to understand the 'how of the proclamation' of Christianity was extended by Freud in a non-reductive fashion" through the dynamics of criterional consciousness — Freud's hypnagogic paradigm — a paradigm Freud did not understand to be "religious" but that Loder saw in Kierkegaard was central to human participation in redemptive religious transformation (Religiousness B). Batson commented on Loder's project to connect religious experience to reality-restoring knowledge in terms of the imaginative dynamics of criterional consciousness in both Freud and Kierkegaard.

> The "reconstructive phantasies" upon which Loder bases much of his analysis are those of "Little Hans" (cf. Freud's "Analysis of a Phobia in a Five-Year-Old Boy," 1909). The reader may think it strange to attempt a constructive analysis of religious growth through analysis of Freud's treatment of the change process. Loder's concern here and in subsequent writings is not to ig-

---

context, (2) subconscious scanning for resolution, (3) the inbreaking of an intuitive insight that reconstructs the framework of the original conflict, (4) a release of energy bound up with the conflict, and (5) verification. For descriptions of this "logic" by two of Loder's earlier students, see Craig Dykstra, *Vision and Character: A Christian Educator's Alternative to Kohlberg* (New York: Paulist Press, 1981), and Margaret Krych, *Teaching the Gospel Today: A Guide for Education in the Congregation* (Minneapolis: Augsburg, 1987), chaps. 4 and 5. See also the discussions of this pattern in several essays in this volume.

54. Loder sought integrity in his integration of religion and psychoanalysis for describing the "new birth" by taking a clue from Clarence I. Lewis's classic work, *Mind and World Order: Outline of a Theory of Knowledge* (New York, Chicago: Charles Scribner & Sons, 1929). Loder argued that the most constructive potential for correlating the disciplines comes at Lewis's second level of understanding — the interpretative. That is, he will bracket out commonsense correlations based on naive realism (level 1) as well as correlations at the metaphysical level which preclude integration (level 3), and attempt to discern how psychiatry (Freud) and religion (Kierkegaard) actually interpret the data they observe of persons who claim to participate in religious experience.

> nore the import of Freud's critique of religion but to see this critique as applied to religious pathology and to ask if this need be the only form religion can take. Thus, for example, in *The Future of an Illusion* (1927) Freud juxtaposes socializing religious training to "education to reality" (p. 81). Loder challenges the necessity of this juxtaposition, attempting to explore creative religious thought which is also "education to reality" in a more profound but no less pragmatic sense than Freud's realist assumption can recognize.[55]

To make his argument Loder discerned the positive religious importance of the hypnagogic paradigm for restoring mental health.[56] From Freud he learned the psycho-dynamic power of the hypnagogic imagination to resolve hidden psychic conflicts, thereby giving psychoanalytic nuance to the insights of Kierkegaard on the restorative power of imagination in religious experience. From Kierkegaard he learned that the deepest manifestation of hypnagogic imagination is the God-Man image, Jesus Christ, in relation to whom Kierkegaard corrected Freud's axiomatic reduction of religion itself to neurosis.[57] In his surpris-

55. Batson, "Creativity and Religious Development," pp. 84-85 n. 138. Loder worked out an analogy between creativity and religious development to provoke healthy personal and social functioning as liberation. In Batson, P. Schoenrade, and W. Larry Ventis, *Religion and the Individual: A Social-Psychological Perspective* (New York: Oxford University Press, 1982/1993), Batson elaborated nine assumptions about this analogy that undoubtedly reflect his mentor's early assumptions: (1) reality is constructed, (2) constructs are grounded in cognitive structures, (3) structures have a hierarchical complexity, (4) creativity involves an improvement of one's cognitive organization, (5) the creative process has an identifiable grammar, (6) it may have physiological origins, (7) a similar process structures personal problem solving, (8) a similar structure occurs in many profound religious experiences, and (9) religious experiences may be neurotic as well as creative (pp. 88-109).

56. This paradigm grew over the course of Loder's ministry in its extraordinary generative power to illuminate the relation of divine to human action at the deepest and broadest limits of human experience.

57. Loder, *Religious Pathology and Christian Faith*, pp. 223-229. Loder rejected the necessity to interpret religion pathologically (illusion — Freud; opiate — Marx; lie — Kierkegaard), using Kierkegaard's *Stages Along Life's Way* to make his case. After comparing aesthetic consciousness (Kierkegaard) and religion as "obsessive-compulsive neurosis" (Freud), Loder found support for describing the way in which the introspective human spirit awakens to its nature as a "dynamic relational unity" of immanence and transcendence ever in need of transparent grounding in the power that posits it (p. 107). In the transformed life Kierkegaard called Religiousness B, "the historical and actual Absolute Paradox drives a decisive wedge between thought and being" (a source of dread) and thereby supplies for sinful humanity "an actual unity between eternity and time" from the divine side (the God-man structure). "Transparency in the individual occurs when the Paradox, as the historical determinant of existentiality itself in the self, categorically eliminates a fixed unity of thought and being, and thereby makes psychic 'movement' — the direct expression of the Power that posits the self — the cardinal aspect

ing correlation of Freud and Kierkegaard a dynamic anagogic paradigm of the human spirit uses imagination as the medium through which to restore reality consciousness to the self. In essence Loder created out of this correlation a dynamic, structural-functionalist model of psychic processes using the powers and limitations of imagination as a medium for human creativity that empowers human beings to choose for a "delimited freedom" according to the image of the God-Man. He called this psychic functioning "paradigmatic madness" (Kierkegaardian irony!), and he regarded it as the normative means by which the individual restores herself to sanity in a world gone collectively out of its mind by either "fossilizing" the reality principle or rejecting it. Against the tendency and drive of socialization to conform persons to false consciousness under the guise of preserving "normalcy" ("fossilizing") Loder argued that congregations must instead become "reality restoring" according to the pattern of choosing to care in a manner inspired by Jesus Christ. Against the tendency to abandon the reality principle by those who fear absorption into the system, Loder counseled sensitivity to the *hubris* implied in such a stance. Thus, congregations obedient to the creative possibility bestowed in the God-Man image practice an "education to reality" that overcomes the "insane" confinement of religion by the "normal" ("fossilizing" the reality principle), and the "insane" abandonment of all norms through *hubris* (rejecting the reality principle), in order to "radicalize" the reality principle and liberate persons and congregations from their bondage to care-lessness. This concern for "radicalized" reality practice dominates the 1969 Bonnell lecture in which Loder placed spiritual creativity and human sciences in the service of reconciling the generations according to the pattern of Christ.

Paradigmatic Madness in Therapeutic-Educative Action: Loder as a Provocateur of Sanity-Restoring Education to Reality

Loder's lecture "Adults in Crisis" (1969) can be read simultaneously as a provocative commentary on Ephesians 6:1-4 (Loder's scientific interpretation of

---

of psychic life" (p. 115). "Criterional human reality is that joyful state of existence in which one finds all the power and movement which underlay his thought and being so relate him to his existential environment that he is capable of being independent of its categories, but at the same time capable of having, through his understanding, a direct and effective influence upon them" (p. 126). Loder then noted that in Freud's work there is movement from more deterministic understandings of somatic-libido energy conceptions to more "mobile" "ego-libido" conceptions that are close to Kierkegaard's distinction between power and "movement." "On this point," Loder observes, "Freud and Kierkegaard have clearly observed the same phenomenon" (pp. 145-146). See also Dykstra, *Vision and Character,* pp. 81-87.

"*pleromic* improvisation" regarding parent-child relations) and as a demonstration of his early practical theological method.[58] In this lecture, Loder sought to confront broken parent-child relations with a process of reality-restoring creativity. One could say that Loder entered the depth dimensions of the neurotic cycle of blame and irresponsibility at the heart of the generation gap, and, using resources from psychology and religion, he reframed the boundaries of the conflict according to a vision of Christian care and reconciliation. Loder proposed a solution to generational alienation by imagining a different way to know parent-child relations creatively within the Christ-defined contours of obedient practice.[59] "Generation gap" symbolized a crisis of trust and care among generations assaulting American society in the 1960s. Accepting the basic psycho-social framework of Erik Erikson regarding youth and adulthood, Loder argued that "demands for the blessing" by rebellious youth to determine their own way in a society created by their parents, who gave up so much for them, is more than the older generation can tolerate, and has locked the generations into a neurotic cycle of confrontation and miscommunication. On the one hand, youth manifest an "ambivalence of openness" created by their demand for an "unrestricted right just to be worth something without having to achieve it." They "protest against the Protestant ethic as unethical," and they ride the high moral purpose "to open up and liberate the 'establishment' from their hypocrisy." Youth thus reveal their deep-seated fear or anxiety of being enslaved to social patterning of any kind. Yet their demand for an "unpatterned pattern" (i.e., unrestricted openness) blinds them to the *hubris* embedded in the oppressiveness of their demand, so that their ambivalence manifests itself as "close-minded openness."[60]

58. James E. Loder, "Adults in Crisis," pp. 32-41. References in this essay are taken from the pamphlet published by Fifth Avenue Presbyterian Church, New York City.

59. Note again that the author of Ephesians makes a similar move. He incorporates ethical norms that any Roman citizen would recognize as appropriate behavior yet filled with conflict ("Children, obey your parents"), areas of life in which the potential for breaking faith exists. But by treating children as responsible members of society with important responsibilities, and calling them to take their faith "in the Lord" seriously, the writer expands the boundaries of Roman convention regarding parent-child relations and transforms them according to the presence of Christ. For an illuminating discussion of the meaning of this passage as both conventionally "Roman" and creatively "Christian" see Judith Gundry-Volf, "The Least and the Greatest: Children in the New Testament," in *The Child in Christian Thought,* ed. Marcia J. Bunge (Grand Rapids: Eerdmans, 2001), esp. pp. 53-58.

60. Loder, "Adults in Crisis," pp. 3-7. The "youth seem to be claiming and living out the very things which the 'establishment' has denied itself in order to get ahead; . . . youth seem to be latently reflecting a desire to be the establishment as evidenced by their own ambivalence, particularly their covert oppressiveness" (pp. 5-6).

On the other hand, the older generation embodies a neurotic "ambivalence of closure" that (1) betrays an authoritarian consciousness whose fear of the loss of social control creates an ethos of making scapegoats of the young, and (2) supports the "establishment" obsession with achievement at all costs which suppresses the longing for ascriptive worth in both generations, resulting in a profound lack of love. The prolongation of this crisis reinforces the polarization as both generations lose sight of the less ambivalent, postwar era when culture seemed invincible, sure of itself, and generative. Such a polarized neurotic cycle of non-care reveals a failure of generativity on a massive scale.[61] Loder wanted to expose the psycho-social dynamics of this massive distortion of relationships so that the image of the God-Man might be called upon to engender a new practice of conciliatory sanity in personal and social existence.

Loder provocatively framed his discussion of the religious dimension of this crisis of care around the themes of "sanity" and "canonicity" as determined by the rise in reductionistic secularism that defined reality in America in instrumental and pragmatic terms.[62] Reductionistic secularism ushers in a massive "governing of the soul" in which "the triumph of the reality principle" depends upon maintaining "a well-structured, de-centered or objectified view of space and time within the ego." According to Loder, "This well-structured ego pattern recognizes and adopts established social and institutional patterns — and roles within those patterns — by means of which the pain associated with spontaneity and affect can be avoided or controlled," resulting in "the philosophically dubious but nevertheless functional assumption that a good fit between established patterns and this structured ego is the norm of sanity."

> The secularization process may then be described as the reduction of Christian beliefs and practices to conformity with the reality principle. In the secularization mind-set we want a sane religion; in the face of neurotic interaction among the generations we want to sacralize sanity — to preserve sanity somehow. We want a religion that is in principle predictable and in which conformity to well-established socialized religious patterns is canonical.[63]

61. Loder, "Adults in Crisis," p. 7. This theme, the lack of love and the need to enable love, pervades Loder's work.

62. Loder anticipated the cultural criticism of later postmodern thinkers. For example, Barry Harvey calls the "supervision" of religion by the "normal" in culture the "panoptic confinement of religion" by liberal democratic society, taking his cue from Foucault's allegorization of Jeremy Bentham's famous Panopticon, a prison designed to supervise all inmates from one central tower. See Harvey, "Insanity, Theocracy, and the Public Realm: Public Theology, the Church, and the Politics of Liberal Democracy," *Modern Theology* 10, 1 (January 1994): 29.

63. Loder, "Adults in Crisis," p. 8.

Averring that it is impossible to get the blessing without the madness, the illumination without the derangement, Loder pointed to the double bind of a society bent on suppressing creativity in the name of "normalcy," thereby reproducing the dehumanizing effects of care-less-ness under the illusion of taking responsibility. Essentially Loder exposed the insanity of a culture caught between two absurds *vis-à-vis* religion — the absurdity of sacralizing the reality principle or demonizing it.[64] What is needed instead is a "radicalization of the reality principle by positive religion" in which the neurotic cycle is broken through a restorative process that empowers the Christian community to care rather than to control or to criticize. To care is to know reality, and therefore, to re-create reality according to the way it is known in the vision of Christian care, by an "education to reality."

Loder illustrated the "radicalization of the reality principle by positive religion" by recalling an experience of his former professor, John Bonnell (the namesake of the lecture series), who interceded for a woman contemplating suicide by sensing from a distance her troubled state and calling her on the telephone to avert a tragedy. Loder noted that the "reality principle" governed by Euclidean/Newtonian time and space was "radicalized" in this intercession by Bonnell's act of faith. In essence Bonnell repeated the radicalization of Jewish time and space by Jesus Christ through the incarnation when he entered from afar the "lived space" of the despairing woman, ripped open the "monotonous rhythm" of chronological time, and acted in "the fullness of time" *(plērōma!)* for her restoration to sanity according to the power of the image of the God-Man. Bonnell enacted the creative "absurdity" of a Christian view of reality in which "life-space is not strictly bound by objective or practical space," and in which "correct time" has been relativized by "know[ing] what time it is in the lives of men [sic]."[65]

64. The logic of totally secularized religion is (obviously) absurd, because no one really wants (or could construct) a machine-like religious consciousness that "programs the intrinsically human" and routs out all the "inherent claims of novelty" that make religious faith a living reality. But the abandonment of the reality principle itself is also absurd, for the truth of the reality principle binds us to each other and makes our institutions generative. What is needed is a "religious education to reality." Loder, "Adults in Crisis," p. 9.

65. Loder, "Adults in Crisis," p. 11. Loder argued that in the incarnation "we have the perfect paradigm for space and time thrown into radical perspective." Jesus "revealed the timeless, unlimitable faceless Yahweh within the limits of a man's height, starting in the even more diminished space of a womb." He "extended into the unlimited life-space of God, claiming that he was at one with the Father," allowing him the "capacity to expand or extend himself almost without limit into the lived-space of other people. . . . When the right time came, 'his time' he called it, he shrank to the dimensions of a dead body, and then he completely disappeared, but only to re-appear in a fashion which permitted him to occupy the lived-space of others with or without the objective space so basic to the reality principle" (pp. 10-11).

Uptight parents and the young, who "demand behavior" from one another based on coercion, cannot generate the freedom to care for the other that is needed. Reconciliation requires an expansion of the "boundaries of paradigmatic freedom" by a creative act of imaginative religious care coming to power in human relations.[66]

Thus, Christian faith offers to culture caught in the grip of "absurdities" another Absurd, according to Loder. Jesus Christ is the "paradigmatic radicalization of the reality principle," not merely as a "theological construct" but also as "actually formative of our own lived-space [and] time."[67] Essentially, the "mind of Christ" engenders a new "live option" that calls the church to overcome the non-creative powers of socialized moral necessity (rigid role expectations) or its abandonment (the rejection of role expectations) in order to liberate Christians to enact a radical ethic of care that overcomes the polarization of the generations by the "insanity" of Christian love. Loder summarized:

> We have seen that the adult crisis of our time [is] a crisis of caring, and we have said that the crisis feeds on the secularization of the Christian faith, a reduction of its claims to the terms of the reality principle. On the other hand, we have seen that the *self-understanding* of the Christian faith, revealed paradigmatically in the caring, curing person of Jesus Christ, radicalizes the reality principle, transforming it from a necessity to a live option. Such radicalization means for us that once we are blest, the dimensions of existence can be radically re-composed according to the caring, curing mind of Christ. "Let this mind be in you. . . ."[68]

Loder's solution to the crisis of care assaulting American society in 1969 is grounded in the paradoxical call to *expand* the imaginative boundaries of liberation according to the paradigmatic (delimited) *expression* of those boundaries in Jesus Christ. Loder called us to enter the crises we face and to re-create (expand and delimit) them in christological terms. He called the church to appropriate her imaginative resources to empower care across the generations, and to create the conditions for supporting such care. Thus, we save ourselves from the

66. Loder, *Religious Pathology and Christian Faith,* pp. 223ff.

67. Loder, "Adults in Crisis," p. 12.

68. Loder, "Adults in Crisis," p. 13. Loder called on congregations to enable the radicalization of the reality principle by creating the conditions necessary for liberation from the neurotic cycles of uncaring, that is, to (1) "disavow any complete submission to authority" so as to foster relations of respectfulness, to (2) "sustain a concern for complexity" and resist scapegoating, to (3) maintain a measure of hopefulness, to (4) "accept non-rational aspects" of human life, and to (5) "accept and live with wide divergences among persons" (pp. 14-15).

"absurd sanity" that inflicts us by taking more seriously the riskier absurdity — the "insanity" of caring according to our self-understanding in Christ. Loder sought to provoke his hearers, in the call of Christian education, to a life of Christian care according to the pattern of Christ.

Conclusion: From Reality-Restoring Therapy to Redemptive Creativity in the Spirit

If Andrew Walls is right, "the distinctive nature of the Christian faith becomes manifest in its developing dialogue with culture" when "a new conceptual vocabulary" constructed out of culture elements is "commandeered and turned towards Christ . . . so that people begin to see Christ in their own terms" through a process so "enriching" that it "proved to be a discovery of Christ . . . as though Christ himself actually grows through the work of mission." We discerned something like this improvisational process-unto-discovery revealed in canonical form in Ephesians. But what can we make of the early practical theological improvisations of James Loder in relation to the discovery of Christ? At the end of his reworked dissertation, entitled *Religious Pathology and Christian Faith,* Loder revealed the underlying concern of his initial project as follows:

> the boundaries of Christian education theory are to be set by the demands of paradigmatic freedom. The future of the paradigm lies in its being transactionally related to social theory, theological language, and institutional practice. The development of such a set of relationships might be conceived as a systematic approach to practical theology.[69]

The theoretical impetus lying behind his concern to connect paradigmatic freedom systematically and comprehensively to scientific understanding appears to have been inspired, at least in part, by Talcott Parsons, the great American philosopher of theoretical sociology, with whom Loder studied at Harvard.[70] Ap-

69. Loder, *Religious Pathology and Christian Faith,* pp. 228-229. Critics who discern in Loder only an interest in conversion experiences, the human imagination in crisis situations, or transformational events fail to grasp that his deeper intent from the beginning was a systematic and comprehensive approach to practical theology.

70. In conversations with Loder he told me that he believed Talcott Parsons's paradigmatic work in sociology actually predated and anticipated Thomas Kuhn's more famous *The Structure of Scientific Revolution* (Chicago: University of Chicago Press, 1970). Loder, it seems to me, derived his vision of "paradigmatic madness" from Parsons just as much as from Kierkegaard and Freud. See his discussion of Kuhn's paradigmatic learning theory in relation to

parently inspired from the beginning by Parsons's grand vision for theoretical sociology, Loder envisioned practical theology theoretically as a scientific discourse with enormous potential for illuminating the power of religious experience to transform human relations in every dimension of human action.[71] Loder's "Parsonian" vision for theory in practical theology becomes vivid if we take license to interpolate Peter Hamilton's description of Parsons's contribution to theory in sociology by substituting "Loder" for "Parsons" and "theo-anthropology" or "practical theology" for "sociology" or "social theory." Thus, like Parsons, of Loder it could be said that one is

> struck by the scale of the contributions . . . Loder made to the development of practical theology. . . . [He] reformulated the nature of practical theological inquiry . . . gave it a direction, a theo-anthropological program. . . . Loder concerned himself almost wholeheartedly with practical theological theory, in the belief that by doing so he could provide practical theology with a coherent method of progressing as a science — presenting both a general theo-anthropology and . . . the conceptualization of a distinctively practical theological subject matter. . . . In directing his efforts toward the production of a general theo-anthropology, a total view of theo-anthropological reality which could provide the practical theologian with theoretical tools for formulating any area of research, he was tempted to employ a language all his own. . . . At least part of the difficulties Loderian prose presents to the reader can be traced to his aim in developing a particular language of concepts related to his theoretical concern with "theo-anthropology" and "practical theological vision."[72]

This "fanciful" interpolation of Parsons's sociological imagination into Loder's systematic approach to practical theology captures the significance and scope of what later became Loder's neo-Chalcedonian analytic practical theological science. Interpreters of Loder should recognize that he set out from the beginning

---

worship in chapter 10 of *Educational Ministry in the Logic of the Spirit,* pp. 227-228. See also his criticism of Kuhn in *The Knight's Move,* p. 31 n. 22, and his affirmation of John Milbank's interpretation of the formative influence of Parsons on all modern social theory, "even when it is denied," in *The Logic of the Spirit,* pp. 39-40.

71. My interest here is not to articulate the specific contribution Parsons makes to Loder's theoretical understanding, which is implicitly described in *Educational Ministry in the Logic of the Spirit.* Rather, I want to identify the less direct influence of Parsons on Loder in that it seems plausible that Loder imbibed from Parsons a general way to envision the field of practical theology theoretically as science.

72. Peter Hamilton, *Talcott Parsons,* Key Sociologists series (London: Routledge, 1983), pp. 13-14.

(1) to "reformulate the nature of practical theological inquiry, giving it direction";[73]
(2) to "provide practical theology with a coherent method of progressing as a science";[74]
(3) to articulate "a total view of theo-anthropological reality which could provide the practical theologian with theoretical tools for formulating any area of research";[75] and
(4) to create "a language all his own . . . a language of concepts related to his theoretical concern with 'theo-anthropology' and 'practical theological vision.'"[76]

On his way to mature thought, Loder relentlessly worked out a scientific practical theology that addressed itself to the two crises he felt compelled to address — the crisis of science (bringing faith and knowledge into their proper relation) and the crisis of spirit (the search of the human spirit for its generative ground).[77] By addressing himself to the task of connecting Christ's reality in relation to the depths of human reality in the context of a scientific culture, Loder envisioned practical theology as a "process . . . hugely enriching" and promising to be "a discovery of the Christ" anew (Walls) for our scientific age.

However, we must remember that according to Loder's own understanding, his early vision for a Parsonian-sized practical theological theory of "reality-restoring" therapeutic creativity *finally proved inadequate for himself as a discovery of Christ!* Only after his 1970 reawakening to the living presence of

73. As I mentioned in the Introduction to this volume, Loder sought to ground practical theology, both content and method, in the Chalcedonian reality that reveals the definitive nature of the relationality between Creator and creation. See his *Logic of the Spirit* for a summary statement of his work, pp. 36ff., and his stated "theological premise" that "relationality is revealed to us definitively in the inner nature of Jesus Christ," *The Knight's Move*, p. 13.

74. For Loder, a "coherent method" must avoid introducing a *tertium quid* to hold theology and the other sciences in their proper relation, since *tertium quids* "divide the reality that is held together by Christ into fragments held together by nothing more than the speculative preference of the interpreter" (*Logic*, p. 37).

75. In my view, Loder has effectively shifted practical theological discourse to center on theo-anthropology as it has been determined and revealed in Christ. Loder's whole project can be interpreted as an elaborate, interdisciplinary "exegesis" of the formula "God is God *pro nobis*" and the difference it makes to us that God is God this way.

76. Loder's creation of his own "language system" outside traditional theological categories (so frustrating for his students) testifies to his abiding concern to relate Christ to scientific culture so as to "discover Christ." How effective Loder has been in retaining integrity between theological discourse and scientific discourse remains an important concern of his future critics and interpreters.

77. Loder articulated these two concerns to me in my interview with him in April of 2001.

the God-Man through the accident that nearly took his life did Loder come to see that the therapeutic process he had understood so well in psychoanalytic and religious terms fundamentally lacked the power to restore reality when reality itself confronts us at the boundaries of human existence where the presence of Nothingness and the power of death claim supremacy. Indeed, the powers of human creativity alone come pathetically short of enabling reconciliation with God and/or others in the face of the void. Therefore, the human spirit inevitably calls out for its generative source from beyond the social construction of reality — *Spiritus Creator.*[78] When asked in 2001 about what changed in his practical theological project after 1970, Loder responded by emphasizing the profound theo-anthropological difference between therapeutic creativity and redemptive transformation.

> Before [1970] I was [working] in a basic psychoanalytic model, that conflict learning is basic to psychoanalysis. So I was upgrading psychoanalysis a little bit. . . . After [1970], when I realized it was the Spirit of God who creates the problem . . . the whole convictional picture in four dimensions began to become a way for me to talk about what I know had happened, and what could happen. And so, it was still conflictual, but now it had shifted into a much bigger perspective. And the dynamics involved were not just limited to the human spirit but were also part of divine redemptive action.[79]

This existential crisis confronted Loder at the height of his powers with the palpable sense of the close proximity to his own non-being and the non-being underlying everything he had worked on for fifteen years. His life and his vocation came under radical question, perhaps not unlike the radical question the author of Ephesians faced when the dying-off of the apostles and the imperial shadow of the *Pax Romana* threatened the very survival of Christian identity in the ancient world. Indeed, the gracious presence that attended him throughout this brush with death also convinced him that human creativity itself had to be "turned inside out" (affirmed → crucified → resurrected) and placed in the service of the redemptive initiative of *Spiritus Creator* if human life and vocation were to bear witness to the God-man structure of reality. Affirmed, crucified, and resurrected into life in the Spirit, Loder set forth to investigate, understand, and describe the dynamic

78. The discovery of Christ comes to us only through the power of Christ's Spirit, because only a power stronger than death itself can convince us that death itself has been relativized to penultimate rather than determinative status in our lives.

79. Interview with Dana Wright in April of 2001.

transformative structure of human participation Spirit-to-spirit in this *pleromic* actuality. He sought to place the work of the Spirit of Christ more fully at the center of "a systematic approach to practical theological." He identified crucial points of contact in Spirit-to-spirit relations (the formation of the ego [psychological], the development of role structures [social], the ability for semiotic function [cultural]) where the Spirit must work redemptively to transform the distortions of the human spirit that enslave us. One can discern in the unfolding of his vision, corresponding to his major publications, his deepening and broadening grasp of crucial dimensions of divine-human relationality:

1. *The imaginative, psycho-dynamic and reality-restoring structure of born-again consciousness.* As we have seen, Loder attempted to discern psychoanalytically the function of imagination in therapeutic and religious consciousness that restores persons to a more realistic life-practice against the insanity of secularized society (*Religious Pathology and Christian Faith,* 1966).
2. *The analogic pattern of Spirit-to-spirit relations revealed through convictional experience.* He argued that convictional experiences were events initiated by the Spirit that awaken us to live in the light of the God-man structure of reality by the power of the Spirit. Convictional knowing transforms everyday patterns of adaptative and defensive meaning-making into "faith seeking understanding" in the service of sacrificial love (*The Transforming Moment,* 1981).
3. *The Spirit's transformational work in culture and the history of culture.* He argued that the God-man structure of reality revealed in convictional experience is nothing less than the hidden order of creation itself, the ultimate subject-matter of scientists and theologians alike, and the ultimate ground of all transformation to which they both try to give account (*The Knight's Move,* 1995).
4. *The "logic of the Spirit" governing psycho-social development itself.* Loder showed how the Spirit works in, with, and through epigenetic transformations of the human spirit to reconstitute human development itself (body, ego, role structure, and semiotic function) according to the nature of Christ — the redemptive transformation of functional human transformations into "life in the Spirit" (*The Logic of the Spirit,* 1998).
5. *The Spirit's transformation of transformation in every realm of human action.* Loder developed a neo-Parsonian action theory in theological dimensions that showed the illuminative power of his understanding of the work of the Holy Spirit in every realm of human action — bodily, psy-

chological, social, and cultural (*Educational Ministry in the Logic of the Spirit* (unpublished).[80]

Loder's spiritual and intellectual journey of faith seeking understanding in pursuit of "a systematic approach to practical theology" represents a life and vocation "turned odd" under the initiative of *Spiritus Creator.* One might say that the same kind of fiduciary passion that inspired the author of Ephesians to connect the reality principle of Roman society redemptively to the *pleromic* blessedness of *Christus Praesens* inspired Loder to indwell the God-man structure of reality revealed in Christ in search of conceptual resources that connect what the Spirit of Christ is doing in the world to make and keep human life human (Paul Lehmann) within the powerful forces of modernization and globalization that distort the human spirit's generative capacities and make the world such a dangerous place.[81] His critical confessional practical theological science affirmed us in our personal, social and cultural particularities as being central to the economics and politics of grace, and yet called us to participate in "the fullness of time" so that our lives might manifest the redemptive power of *pleromic* blessedness that surrounds us and interpenetrates all that is. Whether Loder's "discovery of Christ" and the neo-Chalcedonian science of Spirit-to-spirit relations inspired by it someday proves compelling for practical theolo-

80. In summarizing these concerns we tentatively posit another possible connection of Loder to Parsons. Peter Hamilton suggested that Parsons developed his meta-theory for sociology in three phases: an initial phase in which he worked out the dynamic function and structure of an action unit; a second phase in which he went beyond the structural-functionalist dynamic to develop a general theory of action; and finally a third phase in which he developed a cybernetic model of social systems. See Hamilton, *Talcott Parsons,* pp. 19-20. Loder, I believe, also developed his theory of practical theology in three general phases: initial work prior to 1970 in which he perfected his understanding of an "action unit" within human consciousness called "the hypnagogic paradigm"; a second phase in which he reworked this paradigm theologically in terms of a dynamic analogy between the human spirit and the Holy Spirit (1970-1985); and a third phase in which he made his practical theological understanding more explictly christomorphic in relation to Chalcedonian dimensions of reality (1985-2001).

81. On the importance of recognizing the context of religious education (and, by extension, practical theology) "between modernization and globalization," see Richard Osmer and Friedrich Schweitzer, *Religious Education between Modernization and Globalization: New Perspectives on the United States and Germany* (Grand Rapids: Eerdmans, 2003). Loder identified four lifestyles in this context that distorted the human spirit: (1) oppressive, the distortion of justice, (2) achievement, the distortion of love, (3) authoritarian, the distortion of power, and (4) protean, the distortion of freedom. My sense is that one could make a case that there are modernized and globalized expressions of each of these lifestyles, but the essential nature of the distortion to which each contributes is the distortion of the reconciling relationality among God, human beings, and the earth that the Spirit seeks to actualize.

gians, religious educators, and/or cultural architects of the "brave new world" remains to be seen. This biblical interpretation of the potentially radical significance of his efforts to orient postmodern culture to the *Pax Christi* argues that he, like the ancient author of Ephesians, offered us a compelling and imaginative resource for the best minds in practical theology, Christian education, and scientific culture to ponder for quite some time to come.

9. George Lindbeck and Thomas F. Torrance on Christian Language and the Knowledge of God

Thomas John Hastings

> *Because of this many of the disciples turned back and no longer went with him. So Jesus asked the twelve, "Do you also wish to go away?" Simon Peter answered him, "Lord, to whom can we go? You have the words of eternal life. We have come to believe and know that you are the Holy One of God."*
>
> John 6:66-69

Introduction

An examination of a local congregation's teaching ministry reveals much about how that congregation understands the relationship between the God revealed in Jesus Christ, the Scriptures of the Old and New Testament, Christian doctrine, and the contemporary witness of personal and corporate Christian life. While the complex, inherent relations that exist between God, Christian language, and our knowledge of God is relevant across the entire theological encyclopedia, practical theologians in the subdiscipline of Christian education have a particular interest here since they have been entrusted with the theoretical and practical tasks of describing the dynamics of Christian transformation and formation and suggesting rules of art for guiding the actual pedagogical practices of congregations. When we consider the variety of contemporary approaches to the teaching ministry found in the Protestant churches, we find a striking lack of consensus on the question of how Scripture and doctrine mediate the knowledge of God in Christ and the corollary question of the church's proper modality of reception of and response to this particular knowledge.

The fragmenting drift of postmodern Protestantism into the competing options of orthodoxy, experientialism, and activism shows up nowhere as clearly as in the teaching ministry of the churches. Three general tendencies present themselves when considering the various modes of reception and transmission of the knowledge of God in Christ found within and across the churches of the Reformation today. Orthodox Protestants have privileged the cognitive/propositional modality, liberal, evangelical, Pentecostal, and charismatic Protestants the affective/experiential modality, and socially progressive Protestants the volitional/active modality in their reception and transmission of the Christian knowledge of God mediated by Scripture and doctrine. While these differing emphases reflect complex historical developments, the lack of integration among the cognitive, affective, and volitional dimensions in the reception and transmission of the Christian knowledge of God is also deeply linked to the way we interpret the relation between God, Christian language (in Scripture and doctrine), and Christian life. Given the tragically splintered state of contemporary Protestantism, one of the core tasks for practical theology must be to attempt to articulate an integrated epistemology which accounts for the divine/human relationality consonant with this particular field of investigation.

Of course, this concern to overcome the fragmenting drift of modern Protestantism within a rich christocentric and trinitarian theological framework animated Dr. Loder's work. I believe that his work represents the most comprehensive post-1960s "epistemological excavation" of this field's core problems among theorists in the United States. As this *Festschrift* attests, his theory of transformational logic, which attempts to account for divine agency across the various fields of human action, and his transformational/Chalcedonian model of practical theology are helping to move the discussion in this field beyond some of the hardened dualisms of our enlightenment heritage. I want to express my gratitude to the Lord for Dr. Loder's sanctified mind and loving guidance during our many conversations between 1992 and 2001. He always gave his strong encouragement to the direction in which I was moving, or as he would characteristically put it, the direction in which the Spirit was moving me. In the present essay which was, in its original form, written for my final doctoral course with Dr. Loder *(The Theology of T. F. Torrance)* during the spring semester, 2001, I feel that I am simply continuing to press the practical theological questions that he so graciously helped me to freely imagine and frame in light of the ecumenical church's faith, a close reading of the human sciences, and my personal experience of God's grace in Jesus Christ.

In providing an account for human formation and transformation in Christ which, under the gracious power and powerful grace of the Triune God, takes place within the divine/human praxis of justification and sanctification in Christ, the *inherent constitutive relations*[1] among God, Christian language, and

1. This phrase expresses one of Torrance's key epistemological principles.

life in Christ need careful consideration. In *The Mediation of Christ,* T. F. Torrance speaks of an epistemological circularity which necessarily pertains in post-critical inquiries in science and theology.

> We develop a form of inquiry in which we allow some field of reality to disclose itself to us in the complex of its internal relations or its latent structure, and thus seek to understand it in the light of its own intrinsic intelligibility or *logos.* As we do that we come up with a significant clue in the light of which all evidence is then reexamined and reinterpreted and found to fall into a coherent pattern of order. Thus we seek to understand something, not by schematising it to an external or alien framework of thought, but by operating with a framework of thought appropriate to it, one which it suggests to us out of its inherent constitutive relations and which we are rationally constrained to adopt in faithful understanding and interpretation of it.[2]

On the one hand, what distinguishes Christian language is its claim to witness, albeit indirectly or analogically,[3] to the act and being of the eternal God as revealed within the radical continuity and discontinuity of the history of the covenant people of Israel and, in the fulfillment of that divine/human relationality, in the life, death, resurrection, ascension, and promised coming at the end of the age of a first-century Jew named Jesus of Nazareth who is also confessed as Messiah or Christ, the Word of God, the eternal Son of the Father. On the other hand, what distinguishes life in Christ is its contingent relationality, spirit to Spirit, to the divine/human person of Jesus Christ inaugurated in the mystery of the incarnation and fulfilled in the mystery of the eschaton. Under the mediation of the Holy Spirit, Scripture and doctrine, which are themselves built up from the church's careful hearing of the witness to Jesus Christ in Scripture,[4] function as the fecund life-long matrix of the justified and sanctified new humanity in Christ. In book 4 of the *Institutes* entitled "The External Means or Aids by Which God Invites Us into the Society of Christ and Holds Us Therein," Calvin draws on Cyprian's metaphor of the church as Mother to describe this life-long spiritual nurture.

2. T. F. Torrance, *The Mediation of Christ* (Colorado Springs: Helmers & Howard, 1992), pp. 3-4.

3. "A witness is not absolutely identical with that to which it witnesses. This corresponds with the facts upon which the truth of the whole proposition is based. In the Bible we meet with human words in human speech, and in those words, and therefore by means of them, we hear of the lordship of the Triune God. Therefore when we have to do with the Bible, we have to do primarily with this means, with these words, with the witness, which as such is not itself revelation, but only — and this is the limitation — the witness to it." Karl Barth, *Church Dogmatics,* I/2, ed. Geoffrey W. Bromiley and Thomas F. Torrance (Edinburgh: T&T Clark, 1956), p. 463.

4. A clear example of the above-mentioned "necessary circularity."

> For there is no other way to enter into life unless this mother conceive us in her womb, give us birth, nourish us at her breast, and lastly, unless she keep us under her care and guidance until, putting off mortal flesh, we become like angels [Matt. 22:30]. Our weakness does not allow us to be dismissed from her school until we have been pupils all our lives.[5]

Rather than engaging in the kind of painstaking inquiry which might open up the "internal relations" or "latent structure" of the ecclesial practices of formation which serve the transformational dynamics of reception by, participation in, and communion with Jesus Christ,[6] practical theologians, perhaps succumbing too quickly to pressures to guide the practices of the churches, have often imposed distortive and alien noetic categories on a discipline which is, in its core, also theological and not just concerned with practical applications and techniques. To find a way beyond the fractured Protestant epistemologies of "objectivism," "subjectivism," and "volitionalism," practical theology must seriously address the dimension of divine agency if it is to provide an adequate account for the knowledge particular to Christian faith which Paul calls "the knowledge of the glory of God in the face of Jesus Christ" (2 Cor. 4:6b). Of course, a key limiting aspect of the "face to face" knowledge of God and humanity in Jesus Christ is its eschatological character. "For now we see in a mirror, dimly, but then we will see face to face. Now I know only in part; then I will know fully, even as I have been fully known" (1 Cor. 13:12). When we take seriously the ground and fulfillment of this divine/human knowledge, we come up against the decisive and permanent priority of the "Object," or more properly, the incarnate Subject of faith over the human consciousness of faith and, indeed, even over the apostolic witness to that Subject in Scripture. From beginning to end, our reception by, participation in, and communion with Christ is contingent upon the hypostatic union of the divine Word and human word in Jesus Christ. Without losing sight of its responsibility for guiding the practices of the church, practical theology also needs to engage in serious conversa-

5. *Institutes,* IV.1.4.

6. In an unpublished article entitled "The Dimension of Depth: Thomas F. Torrance on the Sacraments of Baptism and the Lord's Supper," George Hunsinger describes how these three benefits are imparted in baptism by the vicarious humanity of Jesus Christ on our behalf. "In our baptism, then, the risen Christ's saving obedience unto death (perfect tense) and his self-communication (present tense) bring us not only to the point of reception and participation but also into living communion. Again, the perfect tense is the dimension of depth in the present tense; his finished work *pro nobis* is the content, reality and power of his self-communication. Christ's self-communication involves at least three things simultaneously: our receiving *of him* into our hearts, our participating *in him* personally, and our communing *with him* eternally."

tion with biblical, systematic, and historical theology in order to properly address the divine/human problematic of its field.

Among the current approaches to the question of how to move the Protestant churches beyond their current divisions, none has received as much attention, at least in "mainline" and even in certain evangelical circles, as the proposal of American Lutheran theologian George Lindbeck. Lindbeck's *The Nature of Doctrine: Religion and Theology in a Postliberal Age* addresses the problem of the relation between Christian doctrine and Christian life, an issue of vital importance both for Christian education and practical theology as a whole. In this essay, I will examine Lindbeck's cultural-linguistic proposal in critical conversation with Scottish Reformed theologian Thomas F. Torrance.[7] I will begin with a brief introduction to Lindbeck's methodology.

The Methodological Ambiguity of Postliberalism

While *The Nature of Doctrine* offers a trenchant phenomenological description and critique of the dead ends of theological objectivism and subjectivism,

7. Specifically, I will consider *The Nature of Doctrine* in dialogue with Torrance's *The School of Faith* (1959) and other representative works, including *Theological Science* (1969), *Space, Time and Resurrection* (1976), *The Ground and Grammar of Theology* (1980), *Reality and Evangelical Theology: The Realism of Christian Revelation* (1982), *The Mediation of Christ* (1983) and *Transformation and Convergence in the Frame of Knowledge: Explorations in the Interrelations of Scientific and Theological Enterprise* (1998).

While the theological methodologies and conclusions of Lindbeck and Torrance are very different and, I will argue, incommensurate in some basic ways, their academic work has been animated, in part, by two similar personal passions. First, both theologians have engaged in serious ecumenical discussions on doctrinal issues: Lindbeck in the Lutheran–Roman Catholic dialogue on justification and Torrance in the Reformed-Orthodox discussions on the Trinity. Second, both are concerned to move contemporary theology beyond the mutually exclusive modernist polarities of orthodox fundamentalism and neo-Protestant liberalism and to restore the churches to what Lesslie Newbigin has called a "proper Christian confidence" without retreating into some romantic repristination of tradition.

Further, both Torrance and Lindbeck have aroused the interest of practical theologians who have a vested interest in the vital question of the relation of Christian doctrine to life in Christ. While Torrance has directly addressed the subject of reformed catechesis in his classic introduction to *The School of Faith*, the implicit catechetical possibilities of Lindbeck's proposal have been drawn out, for example, by Gregory Higgins in a short article entitled "The Significance of Postliberalism for Religious Education," in J. A. Astley et al., *Theological Perspectives on Christian Education: A Reader on Theology and Christian Education* (Grand Rapids: Eerdmans, 1996). However, rather than focus specifically on catechesis in this essay, I will examine and compare the methodologies of Lindbeck and Torrance and their proposals for Postliberalism and Theological Science.

Lindbeck's cultural-linguistic proposal remains wrapped in methodological ambiguity. Is this systematic theology, practical theology, or pragmatic ground rules for ecumenical dialogue? In the foreword to *The Nature of Doctrine*, Lindbeck states the method and goals of his project.

> Although the *focus* of this book is on intra-Christian theological and ecumenical issues, the *theory of religion and religious doctrine* that it proposes is not specifically ecumenical, nor Christian, nor theological. It rather derives from philosophical and social-scientific approaches; and yet, so I shall argue, it has advantages, not only for the nontheological study of religion but also for Christian — and perhaps also non-Christian — ecumenical and theological *purposes*. What is new about the present work, in short, is not its theory of religion, but the use of this theory in the conceptualization of doctrine, and the contention that this conceptualization is fruitful for theology and ecumenism. The range of arguments extends uncomfortably far beyond the ecumenical concerns that prompted it, but this is inescapable. A theory of religion and doctrine cannot be ecumenically useful unless it is nonecumenically plausible.[8]

I have italicized three key words and phrases from this paragraph to help unpack the methodological problems with Lindbeck's approach.

1. Subject Under Investigation *(Focus):* "intra-Christian theological and ecumenical issues" (Lindbeck's personal passion)
2. Methodology *(Theory of religion and religious doctrine):* "philosophical and social-scientific" (primarily, Wittgenstein and Geertz)
3. Desired Outcomes *(Purposes):* (a) "the nontheological study of religion," (b) "Christian ecumenical and theological purposes," and (c) perhaps non-Christian ecumenical and theological purposes"

If we take Lindbeck at his word, he claims to investigate "internal" issues by means of a "third-party" theory for the purpose of addressing both "internal" and "external" issues. I will return to the basic epistemological problems with this approach later on. For now, I want to point out that Lindbeck's ambitious project has not necessarily been appreciated in terms of his desired outcomes.

Systematic theologian and Barth scholar George Hunsinger, whose association with Lindbeck and Hans Frei goes back to his student days at Yale, has diplomatically, but seriously challenged Lindbeck's theory of truth which adjudicates

8. George Lindbeck, *The Nature of Doctrine: Religion and Theology in a Postliberal Age* (Philadelphia: Westminster, 1984), pp. 7-8.

the status of theological sentences solely on the basis of performance. Refuting David Tracy's characterization of postliberalism as "a methodologically sophisticated version of Barthian confessionalism," Hunsinger argues that Lindbeck's view on the "conditions for cognitive truth" actually has a closer theological affinity with Thomas Aquinas than Karl Barth.[9] Focusing on Lindbeck's hypothetical crusader who shouts *"Christus est Dominus!"* while lopping off an infidel's head in the heat of battle, Hunsinger carefully outlines the cultural-linguistic theory of truth and distinguishes it from Barth's more nuanced theological approach. Though his prose is polite, Hunsinger brings the theologically suspect "anthropocentricism" of the cultural-linguistic model into clear relief.[10]

If the cultural-linguistic model doesn't suffice as *Reformed* systematic theology, how does it fare as practical theology? Here again we encounter possibilities and problems of which Lindbeck himself seems to be aware. At the close of a conference which brought postliberal and evangelical scholars together to discuss their similarities and differences, Lindbeck offered the following characterization of postliberalism. "Postliberals happen to be a collection of individuals engaged in what scientists call a research program. . . . Second, the particular research program that postliberals are engaged in can be characterized as an attempt to recover premodern scriptural interpretation in contemporary form."[11] Here, postliberalism is made to sound more like a practical theological ecclesial program than a constructive theory of doctrine.[12] Lindbeck does offer a strong, pragmatic rationale for rigorous teaching and learning the language of Christian faith. Indeed, in the final chapter of *The Nature of Doctrine* entitled "Toward a Postliberal Theology," Lindbeck says

9. George Hunsinger, *Disruptive Grace: Studies in the Theology of Karl Barth* (Grand Rapids: Eerdmans, 2000), pp. 306, 318.

10. Hunsinger, *Disruptive Grace,* p. 318. Reinhard Hütter offers this helpful response to Hunsinger's critique of Lindbeck's theory of truth claims: "Although Hunsinger's objection is indeed justified, it transcends the capacity and intention of Lindbeck's model, which Hunsinger no longer understands analogically but rather as an explicit theological truth claim itself! Although his criticism does not really do justice to the intention and status of Lindbeck's model, it does uncover problems inhering within that model. . . . Lindbeck's model cannot address his substantively theological argumentation because Lindbeck does not explicitly understand his model as being a part of theological discourse as church practice, and thus cannot bring the *theological* point of his own formalism to bear against Hunsinger." Hütter, *Suffering Divine Things: Theology as Church Practice* (Grand Rapids: Eerdmans, 2000), pp. 51-56.

11. George Lindbeck et al., *The Nature of Confession: Evangelicals and Postliberals in Conversation* (Downers Grove: InterVarsity Press, 1996), p. 246.

12. Lindbeck has endorsed Reinhard Hütter's critical revision of postliberalism along more ecclesiological and pneumatological lines as the most convincing systematic theological reflection on his work to date.

that "This method resembles ancient catechesis more than modern translation. Instead of redescribing the faith in new concepts, it seeks to teach the language and practices of the religion to potential adherents."[13] At the same time, Lindbeck is gravely pessimistic about any practical application of his proposal in the current sociocultural situation.

> Western culture is now at an intermediate stage, however, where socialization is ineffective, catechesis impossible, and translation a tempting alternative. . . . The intertextual intelligibility that postliberalism emphasizes may not fit the needs of religions such as Christianity when they are in the awkward intermediate stage of having once been culturally established but are not yet clearly disestablished.[14]

Thus, Lindbeck leaves the reader with the paradoxical (Lutheran?) conclusion that, while postliberalism has a family resemblance to the catechesis of the early church, a renewal of catechesis today is ruled out because the churches today are so completely enculturated. "In the present situation, unlike periods of missionary expansion, the churches primarily accommodate to the prevailing culture rather than shape it."[15]

In spite of the implicit "Law-Gospel pattern" in Lindbeck's thought,[16] postliberalism's cross-disciplinarity does appear to be more at home among the company of Western practical theologians who, over the past twenty years, have employed various human science and philosophical arguments in trying to unravel the conundrum of the interdisciplinary relation of theory and practice or theology and the human sciences: in Lindbeck's case, utilizing Wittgenstein's correlation of "language games" and "forms of life." When discussing with Dr. Loder the possibilities of utilizing Lindbeck's approach to doctrine as a practical theological grounds to press for a revival of contemporary Protestant catechesis, he said, "In *The Nature of Doctrine,* Lindbeck is doing anthropology, not theology."[17]

13. "Translation" here is, of course, a reference to the correlation and revised correlation methodologies of Tillich and Tracy which Lindbeck sees as mired in the subjectivity of experiential expressivism. See *The Nature of Doctrine,* p. 132.

14. Lindbeck, *The Nature of Doctrine,* p. 133.

15. We have already mentioned that when he wrote *The Nature of Doctrine,* in 1984, Lindbeck was rather pessimistic, given the cultural context, about the church's ability to rise to the task. See *The Nature of Doctrine,* p. 133. It is worth noting that, since *The Nature of Doctrine,* the interest in catechesis among Protestant churches has grown markedly, as evidenced, e.g., in the approval of *The First Catechism* and *Study Catechism* by the PC(USA)'s General Assembly in 1998.

16. This perceptive idea was suggested by George Hunsinger in conversation.

17. Loder's intuitive reservations about Lindbeck remind me of how postliberalism has

Lindbeck's Typology and Pragmatic Proposal for Ecumenical Dialogue

Following Wittgenstein, Lindbeck sees religions as "comprehensive interpretive schemes, usually embodied in myths or narratives and heavily ritualized, which structure human experience and understanding of self and world."[18] He begins by offering a typology of what he sees as "the most familiar theological theories of religion and doctrine."[19] His first three types are described in terms of their normative view of language and experience. While Lindbeck ultimately hopes to overcome the hopeless subjectivity he sees in the liberalism of "mainline" Protestantism — hence the self-conscious label "postliberalism" — he also wants to carefully distinguish his project from traditional orthodoxy.

Type One: Cognitive/Propositional (Traditional Orthodoxy)

According to Lindbeck, orthodoxy "emphasizes the cognitive aspects of religion and stresses the ways in which church doctrines function as informative propositions or truth claims about objective realities."[20] He critiques what may be called Orthodoxy's doctrinal positivism: "if a doctrine is once true, it is al-

been greeted by Western-trained Japanese Protestant theologians. While Lindbeck's basic methodological move, which utilizes a theory drawn from philosophy and the human sciences to treat basic theological questions, seems not to have caused too much consternation among theologians in North America and Europe (with the exception of Loder), the reaction of my Japanese colleagues at Tokyo Union Theological Seminary is noteworthy, especially given Lindbeck's hopeful claim that his theory of religion and doctrine will help to encourage ecumenical discussion and cooperation. While confessing a pragmatic attraction to the "cultural-linguistic" proposal over against orthodoxy's "cognitive/propositionalism" and liberalism's "experiential/expressivism," my colleagues, whose theology continues to be guided by Barth and his most formidable Japanese interpreter Kumano Yoshitaka, wonder how what they see as essentially a "religious studies argument" could have created such a huge sensation among theologians in North America and Europe. Among the older generation of Japanese Barthians, some wonder if postliberalism is yet another sign that the Japanese church has little to gain and potentially much to lose from further theological or ecumenical dialogue with what they perceive as the theologically confused churches of the deconstructionist, postmodern West. Thus, in spite of Lindbeck's claim to focus on "intra-Christian theological and ecumenical issues," postliberalism has been greeted with a profound ambivalence in one tenaciously Barthian non-Western Protestant church. They are puzzled how a subject such as doctrine could be treated adequately by a thoroughly nontheological theory.

18. Lindbeck, *The Nature of Doctrine,* p. 32.
19. Lindbeck, *The Nature of Doctrine,* p. 16.
20. Lindbeck, *The Nature of Doctrine,* p. 16.

ways true, and if it is false, it is always false."[21] Lindbeck suggests a historical family resemblance between orthodoxy's propositionalism and "modern Anglo-American analytic philosophy with its preoccupation with the cognitive or informational meaningfulness of religious utterances."[22] Borrowing from Bernard Longeran, Lindbeck finds orthodoxy's Achilles' heel in what may be called its *structuralist correspondence theory of truth.*

> Those who are to some degree traditionally orthodox understand the propositional truth that they attribute to religious statements as a function of the ontological correspondence or "isomorphism" of the "structure of knowing and the structure of the known." Each proposition or act of judgment corresponds or does not correspond, is eternally true or false: there are no degrees or variations in propositional truth.[23]

Type Two: Experiential/Expressive (Protestant Liberalism)

Lindbeck now turns his critical gaze on his chief adversary: liberalism's type of religion "which interprets doctrines as noninformative and nondiscursive symbols of inner feelings, attitudes, or existential orientations."[24] In contrast with the settled objectivity of claims to truth and falsity in propositionalism, expressivism sees doctrines as "polyvalent in import and therefore subject to changes of meaning or even to a total loss of meaningfulness, to what Tillich calls their death."[25] Commenting on Lindbeck's typology, Hütter says, whereas the orthodox model "understood religion in analogy to metaphysics, the liberal model understands it in analogy to aesthetics."[26] Lindbeck decries this affinity between subjective religious and aesthetic experience. Not surprisingly, he finds the emergence of this theory of religion and doctrine in "continental developments that began with Schleiermacher."[27]

> Whatever the variations, thinkers of this tradition all locate ultimately significant contact with whatever is finally important to religion in the prereflective experiential depths of the self and regard the public or outer

21. Lindbeck, *The Nature of Doctrine,* p. 16.
22. Lindbeck, *The Nature of Doctrine,* p. 16.
23. Lindbeck, *The Nature of Doctrine,* p. 47; the quote within the quote is from Bernard Lonergan, *Insight* (New York: Harper & Row, 1978), p. 399.
24. Lindbeck, *The Nature of Doctrine,* p. 16.
25. Lindbeck, *The Nature of Doctrine,* p. 17.
26. Hütter, *Suffering Divine Things,* p. 43.
27. Lindbeck, *The Nature of Doctrine,* p. 16.

> features of religion as expressive and evocative (i.e., nondiscursive symbols) of internal experience.[28]

It is not difficult to see how this completely individualistic approach would, according to Hütter, be "useless for ecumenical dialogue."[29]

Lindbeck's Proposal: Cultural-Linguistic (Postliberalism)

Now we come to Lindbeck's cultural-linguistic model, which aims to subvert liberalism's subjective approach to religious language and experience. Since it is a novel construction and not a phenomenological description of a historical theological movement, it technically does not function as a type. In place of the liberal emphasis on the subject's expression of some encounter with the transcendent, Lindbeck's proposal puts language prior to experience.

> It remains true, therefore, that the most easily pictured of the contrasts between a linguistic-cultural model of religion and an experiential-expressive one is that the former reverses the relation of the inner and the outer. Instead of deriving external features of a religion from inner experience, it is the inner experiences which are viewed as derivative.[30]

This basic and controversial philosophical claim that "public linguistic categories shape even preexperiential activity"[31] derives from Wittgenstein's correlation of language games with forms of life. I will quote at some length Lindbeck's most succinct description of his research project.

> [A] religion can be viewed as a kind of cultural and/or linguistic framework or medium that shapes the entirety of life and thought. It functions somewhat like a Kantian *a priori*, although in this case the *a priori* is a set of acquired skills that could be different. It is not primarily an array of beliefs about the true and the good (though it may involve these), or a symbolism

28. Lindbeck, *The Nature of Doctrine*, p. 21.

29. Hütter, *Suffering Divine Things*, p. 44. Lindbeck also briefly suggests a third type, which he calls "Ecumenically-inclined Roman Catholics," represented by Roman Catholic theologians like Rahner and Lonergan, which essentially combines the cognitive-propositional and experience-expressive models of types one and two. "Like many hybrids, this outlook has advantages over one-dimensional alternatives, but for our purposes it will generally be subsumed under the earlier approaches." *The Nature of Doctrine*, p. 16.

30. Lindbeck, *The Nature of Doctrine*, p. 34.

31. Lindbeck, *The Nature of Doctrine*, p. 37.

> expressive of basic attitudes, feelings, or sentiments (though these will be generated). Rather, it is similar to an idiom that makes possible the description of realities, the formulations of beliefs, and the experiencing of inner attitudes, feelings and sentiments. Like a culture or language, it is a communal phenomenon that shapes the subjectivities of individuals rather than being primarily a manifestation of those subjectivities. It comprises a vocabulary of discursive and nondiscursive symbols together with a distinctive logic or grammar in terms of which this vocabulary can be meaningfully deployed. Lastly, just as a language (or "language game," to use Wittgenstein's phrase) is correlated with a form of life, and just as a culture has both cognitive and behavioral dimensions, so it is also in the case of a religious tradition. Its doctrines, cosmic stories or myths, and ethical directives are integrally related to the rituals it practices, the sentiments or experiences it evokes, the actions it recommends, and the institutional forms it develops. All this is involved in comparing a religion to a cultural-linguistic system.[32]

What does this proposal mean for the relation between Christian doctrine and personal or corporate life in Christ? Instead of seeing either objective linguistic truth claims (a la propositionalism) or subjective nondiscursive aesthetic experience (a la expressivism) as "first-order" discourse, this model sees "use" or "performance" of religious language, what Lindbeck calls "liturgical, kerygmatic and ethical modes of speech and action,"[33] as primary, and official church doctrine or theology as "second-order discourse about first-intentional uses of religious language."[34] The attempt here is to subsume both the propositional and expressive aspects of the premodern and modern views under Wittgenstein's philosophical epistemology. Now, both proposition and expression, rather than being prior to performance, are reconstrued as deriving from the primary cultural-linguistic idiom of performance. In other words, religious life is described as a primal, internal dimension, not an external extension of its particular language. This correlation of language and life comes from Wittgenstein's insightful claim that language games are not a bridge between "the internal life of persons" and "some external reality" but are themselves the idiom of the world, inhabited by thinking and embodied persons. Since language games have no "outside," no *externum verbi,* it follows that religious beliefs and ritual are *sui generis* with no ground beyond themselves. They do not operate as fact, knowledge or reason and cannot be sub-

32. Lindbeck, *The Nature of Doctrine,* p. 33.
33. Lindbeck, *The Nature of Doctrine,* p. 69.
34. Lindbeck, *The Nature of Doctrine,* p. 69.

stantiated or refuted by fact, knowledge or reason.[35] Hütter describes Lindbeck's intention well:

> The cultural-linguistic model intends to overcome the dichotomy between subject and object so typical of modernity, a dichotomy between the strict affirmation and strict negation of the allegedly correspondential truth of theological statements. Both the subject and object are now part of a matrix constituted by distinct practices; this matrix is reproduced intersubjectively, and within the framework of specific practices accompanying it a person becomes the "subject," perceives "objects," and has "experiences."[36]

It is not difficult to imagine how this distinction between the primal language game and the subordinate, second-order speech about the language game, if accepted, would encourage the ecumenical dialogue to which Lindbeck is committed.

> Here, in contrast to the common supposition, one rarely if ever succeeds in making affirmations with ontological import, but rather engages in explaining, defending, analyzing, and regulating the liturgical, kerygmatic, and ethical modes of speech and action within which such affirmations from time to time occur. Just as grammar by itself affirms nothing either true or false regarding the world in which language is used, but only about language, so theology and doctrine, to the extent that they are second-order activities, assert nothing either true or false about God and his relation to creatures, but only speak about such assertions.[37]

I will suggest later that precisely this philosophical distinction between first- and second-order language is the Achilles' heel of postliberalism.

Now I will turn to a brief consideration of Torrance's theological methodology.

"Theological Science"

While Torrance's approach, which he calls "theological science," owes much of its theological substance to Barth, it is his work in the dialogue between theology and contemporary science and in Greek patristics that has moved him be-

35. Henry Leroy Finch, *Wittgenstein — The Later Philosophy: An Exposition of the "Philosophical Investigations"* (Atlantic Highlands: Humanities, 1977), p. 202.

36. Hütter, *Suffering Divine Things*, p. 46.

37. Lindbeck, *The Nature of Doctrine*, p. 69.

yond Barth, perhaps most notably in his strong emphasis on the doctrine of the *vicarious humanity* of Jesus Christ and his reconception of natural theology. Torrance emphasizes that it is only in the vicarious humanity of Jesus Christ that the Word of God empowers us to make the "decision against ourselves" over and over. "Strictly speaking then, for Christians, the real text with which we have to do in the New Testament Scriptures is the *humanity* of Jesus Christ, for it is in the humanity of the Word of God incarnate in him, that we meet and are addressed by the Word of the living God."[38]

In the preface to *Theological Science,* Torrance writes about the receptive or *pathic* disposition with which we properly begin our inquiry into the knowledge of God.

> A. E. Taylor called for the locating of authority, neither in individualism nor in some institutional seat, but in a reality which is wholly given and trans-subjective, and simply and absolutely authoritative in its givenness. If knowledge is to be more than personal opinion, he argued, there must be control of our personal intellectual constructions by something which is not constructed but *received.* In our human knowledge of God this is humbly to acknowledge that what is genuinely given has unquestionable right to control our thinking and acting, just because it is so utterly given to us and not made by us.[39]

Considered from the standpoint of the givenness of divine self-revelation in the incarnation, faith "in Christ," or perhaps more appropriately, the vicarious faith "of Christ," in which the Christians of all of the divided churches participate, can not be parsed into the mutually exclusive categories of "objective propositionalism," "subjective expressivism" and "volitional activism" without seriously undermining the integrity of the full humanity which Jesus Christ himself bears, redeems, and sanctifies. From the singularity of the *assumptio carnis,* Christian faith is more properly viewed as a unity of the cognitive, affective and volitional aspects of human being initiated, sustained, and fulfilled by divine/human agency in the person of Jesus Christ himself. From its beginning to its fulfillment, our human knowledge of God in Christ, or "God for us," subsists in the joyful and grateful consciousness of its contingent relation to the act and being of the eternal Son of God who, in his birth, life, death, resurrection, and ascension presents a whole and redeemed humanity to the Father and yet ever promises to remain "God with us" by the power of the Holy Spirit.

38. T. F. Torrance, *Divine Meaning: Studies in Patristic Hermeneutics* (Edinburgh: T&T Clark, 1995), p. 7.

39. T. F. Torrance, *Theological Science* (Edinburgh: T&T Clark, 1969), p. viii.

How does Torrance reconceive of natural theology without losing Barth's radical emphasis on the otherness of God? Torrance fully supports Barth's rejection of any *theologia naturalis* conceived of as a "revelation-independent" knowledge of God which is considered to be generically accessible to human reason.

> It seems evident, then, that Barth's opposition to the traditional type of natural theology, which is pursued as an independent system on its own, antecedent to positive or revealed theology, rests upon a radical rejection of its dualistic basis and constitutes a return to the kind of unitary thinking we find in classical Christian theology as exemplified by Athanasius, in which theology is committed to one coherent framework of thought that arises within the unitary interaction of God with our world in creation and incarnation, and in which we are unable to make any separation between a natural and a supernatural knowledge of God.[40]

Torrance reconceives of natural theology as "*natural* both to theological and natural science" when both disciplines are comprehended "within their common sharing of the rational structures of space and time conferred on the universe by God in his creating of it, and within their common sharing in the basic conceptions of the unitary rationality of the universe, its contingent intelligibility and contingent freedom."[41]

While the investigational trajectories of natural science are obviously distinct from those of theology, Torrance emphasizes that both human inquiries take place within the same "field limitations" of the *unitary rationality of the universe*, its *contingent intelligibility*, and *contingent freedom*. Torrance tries to make the historical case that these three pivotal ideas, which cohere in both science and theology, did not and could not have arisen either from natural science or Greek philosophy. Rather, he claims that it was the church's theological reflection on God's self-revelation in the incarnation of the divine/human Jesus Christ and the relation of that singular revelation to the doctrine of creation *ex nihilo* which was the historical impetus for the rational, scientific investigation of the created universe.

Torrance goes to great lengths to show how theology has been threatened in the ancient, medieval, and modern periods by a variety of philosophical dualisms that have, in one way or another, undermined this unitary approach to theoretical and empirical knowledge. He says that "revelation-independent" natural theology thrived during times when the church lapsed into dualistic

40. Thomas F. Torrance, *The Ground and Grammar of Theology* (Charlottesville: University of Virginia Press, 1980), p. 93.

41. Torrance, *Ground and Grammar*, p. 94.

modes of thought wherein "knowledge was allegedly derived by way of abstraction from sense experience or deductions from observations."[42] Contrary to those approaches which are centered in human experience and logic, Torrance claims that the universe's order is not grounded in some immanent *logos* but in the "uncreated and creative Logos, in whose image, by the grace of God, we ourselves have been created, so that as we contemplate the rational order in the creation, we are directed above and beyond ourselves to the one God, the Lord of creation."[43]

By means of an analogy to the reconstrual of geometry as four-dimensional within the unitary view of the universe in Einsteinian physics, Torrance seeks to reclaim a proper place for natural theology within the unified field of revelation opened up under the Incarnation of the eternal Son of God. "If natural theology is to have a viable reconstruction, it can only be on the basis of a restored ontology in which our thought operates with a fundamental unity of concept and experience, or of form and being, within a contingent but inherently intelligible and open-structured universe."[44] Within this unified field of inquiry, natural theology finds "its proper place and status within the area of overlap between natural science and theological science, that is, within the overlapping of created and uncreated intelligibility where natural science presses its inquiries in one direction and theological science presses its inquiries in another direction."[45]

Thus, Torrance rejects what he sees as the disastrous split in modernity between theoretical and empirical knowledge and goes to great lengths to carefully

42. Torrance, *Ground and Grammar,* p. 76.

43. Torrance, *Ground and Grammar,* p. 77.

44. Torrance, *Ground and Grammar,* pp. 86-87.

45. T. F. Torrance, *Reality and Evangelical Theology* (Downers Grove: InterVarsity Press, 1982), p. 31.

In the preface to *Space, Time and Resurrection,* Torrance recounts his last meeting with Barth a few weeks before Barth's death in 1968. He described to Barth how he was trying to move natural theology beyond its objectionable status as a "*praeambula fidei*" or "an independent conceptual system antecedent to actual knowledge of God." Torrance then gave him an example from the *Church Dogmatics* in which Barth himself had transposed natural theology "into the material content of theology where in a changed form it constitutes the epistemological structure of our knowledege of God." Torrance reports that Barth "expressed full agreement with my interpretation of his thought, and said, rather characteristically, of the relation of geometry to physics, 'I must have been a blind hen not to have seen the analogy before.'" T. F. Torrance, *Space, Time and Resurrection* (Grand Rapids: Eerdmans, 1976), pp. ix-x.

See also Thomas F. Torrance, "The Transformation of Natural Theology," in *Ground and Grammar,* pp. 75-109; and "Natural Theology in the Thought of Karl Barth," in *Transformation and Convergence in the Frame of Knowledge: Explorations in the Interrelations of Scientific and Theological Enterprise* (Eugene: Wipf and Stock, 1980), pp. 285-302.

show how the emergence of scientific inquiry in the West is actually rooted in the early Christian struggle "to break through the pagan outlook upon the world with its identification of cosmology and theology, and often the identification of God and the world."[46] The pressing issue for the early church in its missional encounter with conflicting accounts of God and the world was how to give adequate rational articulation to the relation between the doctrines of Creation *ex nihilo* and incarnation. According to Torrance's reading of this history, the ancient church's struggle with regnant cultural conceptions has been erroneously caricatured as an intra-ecclesial move to enforce doctrinal conformity as a way of consolidating its institutional power. On the contrary, he asserts, the precarious history of the Nicean-Constantinopolitan formulation and reaffirmation of the *homoousion* had epochal public epistemological consequences, issuing in "a radical reconstruction of the foundations of ancient philosophy, science and culture."[47] Torrance says that the *homoousion* shattered "the dualistic structures of the ancient world, with their bifurcation between what is real and eternal and changeless and what is unreal, apparent, and evanescent. . . . There was a head-on clash at essential points in the basic structures of thought."[48] The result of this clash between gospel and culture was a unitary conception of the universe where the intelligible order and freedom of creation is understood to be in contingent relationality to divine intelligibility and freedom.

This brings us to a core apologetic conviction which infuses Torrance's entire *corpus*. He is convinced of a felicitous analogy between the unitary view of the universe constructed under the restraint of the truth of the gospel in the early church and the contemporary search for a unified theory of the physical universe opened up (but not closed) by Einstein's theory of relativity. While his argument for a deeper dialogue between science and theology is resolutely theological and apologetic, Torrance does not reduce theology to science or science to theology. Following Barth, Torrance is faithful to the Chalcedonian Christology that confesses Jesus Christ as "one person in two natures, without separation or division and without confusion or change." For Torrance, the divine/human relationality which coheres perfectly in Jesus Christ alone func-

46. Torrance, *Ground and Grammar,* p. 46.

47. Torrance, *Ground and Grammar,* p. 47. Actually, the history between Nicea and Constantinople shows that Arianism was not easily defeated. Given the large number of Arian-tending bishops, if the church had been interested only in institutional benefits, the compromise of the *homoiousios* ("similar substance") over the *homoousios* ("same substance") would have won the day. Cf. Frances Young, *From Nicea to Chalcedon* (Philadelphia: Fortress, 1983), and Donald McKim, *Theological Turning Points: Major Issues in Christian Thought* (Atlanta: John Knox, 1988).

48. Torrance, *Ground and Grammar,* pp. 46-47.

tions as the "constitutive" and "regulative" ground[49] for the analogy between natural science and theological science. In an analogy to this mystery, the competing spheres of human rationality are reconceived within this deeper, more comprehensive unity without losing their individual integrity and distinctions.

> However we consider it, it seems clear that theological science and natural science operate within the medium of space and time, which are the bearers of contingent order or intelligibility in which all created realities share. Within that medium, natural science is concerned to explore the stratified structures of contingent existence, and theological science inquires of God their Creator who reveals himself through them.[50]

In articulating the epistemology for theological science, Torrance discovers that science and theology share two basic criteria which he learned from his reading of Barth and Michael Polanyi. The first is the criterion of an *a posteriori objective realism.* As in Barth, all speculative attempts to get in front of, above or behind the given "datum of revelation" are rejected. While this realism or actualism is the point where Barth's theology appears to invite the charges of a "positivism, objectivism or foundationalism of revelation," Torrance defends this approach, with the help of Polanyi, as epistemologically more consonant with contemporary science. Since the "object" of inquiry may be known only according to its own inherent intelligibility and not from any external, independent, or disinterested ground, the inquirer must always resist the temptation to impose some alien theory or frame of reference onto the "object." Torrance sees Barth as a towering exemplar of this *a posteriori objective realism.*[51]

The second shared epistemological criterion in science and theology is what I call *pathic self-investment.* Because the self-disclosure of the "object" al-

49. These terms are borrowed from George Hunsinger's careful description of the Chalcedonian Christology in "Karl Barth's Christology," in *Disruptive Grace,* pp. 131-133.

50. Torrance, *Reality and Evangelical Theology,* p. 30.

51. To repeat, the conviction here is that any field under investigation will disclose its inner intelligibility only when it is apprehended in ways appropriate to its actual nature. The "object" exercises a definitive marginal control in the knowing event. Put another way, the inquirer's questions must first be rigorously *directed by* an object under investigation before they may properly be *directed to* that object. By acknowledging the epistemological priority of the object over the knower, Torrance is seeking to get below the surface to what he calls a field's "being-constituting relations or 'onto-relations.'" This approach "leads to a form of inquiry in which we probe into their internal relations in order to allow them to disclose to us their inherent organisation or structures so that we can understand them in their intrinsic significance or *logos* which controls our interpretation and description of them." Torrance, *The Mediation of Christ,* p. 47.

ways exercises a primary, marginal control in any epistemic event, there is an inescapable dimension of *pathos,* in the sense of an "undergoing," "suffering" or "bearing with" on the part of the inquirer which cannot be circumvented on the way to new discovery and insight.[52] In terms of Loder's logic of transformation, *pathic self-investment* is potentially brought to a new depth and intensity in the second movement, the *interlude for scanning,* where new insight or discovery is waiting to break in upon the knower, but also where the downward psychic drive toward adaptation is often overpowering.[53]

Pathic self-investment is the attitude of one who has freely submitted him or herself in service to the "object" which, because of freedom and contingency, is always open to be more fully known. Characterized by trust, risk, meditative patience, and intuitive alertness, pathic knowing events necessarily embrace the entire epistemic repertory of cognition, affect, and action. This integrated disposition is evident in the work of theologians and scientists who approach their inquiries with an attitude of passionate and attentive receptivity (in Polanyi's terms, by "indwelling" the phenomena), conscious that new insight and discovery is contingent upon the field's self-disclosure of its own inherent intelligibility. Polyani says that all instances of human knowing are self-investing and involve tacit, emotional, and fiduciary dimensions.[54]

Thus, Torrance's theological science combines a strong Reformed theo-

52. This description of *pathos* is informed by Walter Brueggemann's description of prophecy as "the sense of fracture and abrasion between what is at hand and what is promised" in *The Creative Word — Canon as a Model for Biblical Education* (Philadelphia: Fortress, 1982), p. 12, and Reinhard Hütter's definition in *Suffering Divine Things,* pp. 29-32.

53. Cf. James E. Loder, *The Transforming Moment,* 2nd ed. (Colorado Springs: Helmers & Howard, 1989). Since, as Freud rightly claimed, ego and culture conspire to maximize pleasure and minimize pain for the individual and the collectivity, much inquiry is short-circuited at this crucial point. Thus, in many contemporary educational contexts in and outside of the church, an *ethos* which values quick, easy and painless "answers" subverts the kind of investigation which is "unto transformation."

54. In speaking of the passions of the scientist, Polanyi says, "From the start of this book I have had occasion, in various contexts, to refer to the overwhelming elation felt by scientists at the moment of discovery, an elation of a kind which only a scientist can feel and which science alone can evoke in him. . . . I quoted the famous passage in which Kepler announced the discovery of his Third Law: '. . . nothing holds me; I will indulge my sacred fury. . . .' The outbreak of such emotions in the course of discovery is well known, but they are not thought to affect the outcome of discovery. Science is regarded as objectively established in spite of its passionate origins. It should be clear by this time that I dissent from that belief; and I have come to the point at which I want to deal explicitly with passions in science. I want to show that scientific passions are no mere psychological by-product, but have a logical function which contributes an indispensable element to science." Michael Polanyi, *Personal Knowing* (Chicago: University of Chicago Press, 1958), p. 134.

logical tradition, mediated via Calvin and Barth, with a deep appreciation for the hard-won doctrinal substance of the ancient catholic church within an epistemology that is equally consonant in ecumenical theology and post-Einsteinian science.

Now, in order to distinguish more clearly between the proposals of Torrance and Lindbeck, I will turn to a more in-depth look at *Space, Time and Resurrection,* in which Torrance distinguishes his scientific approach to Scripture and dogma from "logical propositionalism" (Lindbeck's *type one*) and what he calls "neo-Protestantism" (Lindbeck's *type two*).

Beyond the Fatal Deistic Disjunction between God and the World

Torrance, like all post-Barthian theologians, including Lindbeck, constructs his theology in opposition both to liberalism and fundamentalism. Whereas Lindbeck is committed to the pragmatic goal of deeper ecumenical dialogue between the churches, Torrance's far more ambitious purpose is to move theology beyond what he calls the "fatal deistic disjunction between God and the world."[55] Like Barth, Torrance makes no apology for beginning with the givenness or actuality of revelation, saying,

> If God really is God, the Creator of all things visible and invisible and the Source of all rational order in the universe, I find it absurd to think that he does not actively reveal himself to us but remains aloof, so that we are left to grope about in the dark for possible intimations and clues to his reality which we may use in trying to establish arguments for his existence. I do not deny that there is a proper place for rational argumentation in what is traditionally known as "natural theology," for I find it contradictory to operate with a deistic disjunction between God and the universe, which presupposes belief in the existence of God but assumes at the same time that he is utterly detached and unknowable.[56]

I have already mentioned Torrance's concern to restore to theological thinking a unitary conception of the universe wherein theoretical and empirical aspects of human knowledge cohere within the authoritative actuality of the vicarious humanity of the incarnation of the divine/human Word and to reconstruct natural theology upon the ground of that revelation. On the basis of the doc-

55. Torrance, *Space, Time and Resurrection,* p. 2.
56. Torrance, *Space, Time and Resurrection,* p. 1.

trine of the Incarnation, Torrance attacks the modernist dualism "between subject and object on the one hand and between God and the world on the other hand,"[57] which has, in fundamentalism, engendered the ironically modernist reduction of the Word of God in Jesus Christ to the human witness to that Word in Holy Scripture and, in liberalism, the facile acceptance of the fatal distinctions between *Geschichte* and *Historie, kerygma* and *didache* or the Jesus of history and the Christ of faith.

Because God in Jesus Christ has entered the very space and time in which we live and has fully assumed our humanity, the "intelligible structures" of space and time have been decisively transformed or opened up to our rational minds to reveal their contingent intelligibility and freedom in relation to the Creator. In other words, in the vicarious humanity of Jesus Christ, real knowledge of God has really been communicated within the epistemic limits of human experience.

> If God really is God, the living Creator of us all, not only is he intelligibly accessible to our understanding but actively at work within the world in revealing himself in cognitive ways to those whom he has made for communion with himself.[58]

Torrance contrasts this approach which grounds our knowledge of God in divine agency with modernist approaches to the New Testament witness which cut a deep gulf between our knowledge of God and knowledge of God in himself. These reductionistic approaches leave us with what Torrance calls a

> non-cognitive revelation, detached from the intelligible structures and the objectivities of space and time within which the Word was made flesh in Jesus Christ. . . . Since it declines to accept any objectively grounded revelation of God or any knowledge of God objectively grounded in himself, biblical and theological interpretation of this kind is regularly trapped within the fallacies of *socio-cultural relativism* and *linguistic nominalism*.[59]

For Torrance, what is at stake here is nothing less than the truth claims of the gospel and whether or not the biblical writings can in any way "be regarded as conveying a real Word from God." Denouncing the demythologizing turn that biblical studies took following Bultmann, Torrance suggests what he calls a more scientific approach to Scripture and doctrine, proper both for biblical

57. Torrance, *Transformation and Convergence*, p. 6.
58. Torrance, *Space, Time and Resurrection*, pp. 1-2.
59. Torrance, *Space, Time and Resurrection*, p. 2; italics added.

scholars and theologians, which "does not automatically exclude the ontological unity of form and being, or of structure and material content, in their investigation and interpretation of the Holy Scriptures."[60]

He begins by distinguishing this "more scientific" approach from Roman Catholicism and Protestant fundamentalism which both make the fatal mistake of constructing doctrines from a "logical propositionalist" reading of Scripture.

> This has the effect of putting the Scriptures themselves, with the conceptions they enshrine, into the position of providing the direct objects to which the mind of the interpreter or theologian attends, thereby obscuring the actual realities beyond to which he is referred through them. Here we have implied a view of the biblical language as bearing upon conceptions rather than upon the objective realities through conceptions, and a view of truth in which the truth of statement is identified with the truth of being and logical relations are equated with objectively real relations.[61]

At first glance, Torrance's characterization of propositionalism sounds just like Lindbeck's *type one.* However, when they move from description to prescription, we discern a decisive parting of the ways, with Lindbeck taking his direction from philosophy and Torrance from theology. Lindbeck's entire proposal rests upon Wittgenstein's reduction of *signum* and *res* to a particular language game's mutually agreed upon rules. Such an approach denies the possibility of any external referent or objective ground beyond the inherent performative rules of a particular language game or form of life. By sharp contrast, the crux of Torrance's critique is the way Roman Catholic institutionalism and Protestant biblicism obscure the objective actuality of God's self-communication, as *res,* to which Scripture, as *signum,* refers, albeit indirectly and analogically. "Understanding and interpretation of the Scriptures does [*sic*] not focus myopically, as it were, upon the words and statements themselves, but through them on the truths and realities they indicate beyond themselves."[62] To reiterate, Torrance rejects Roman Catholic and fundamentalist propositionalism and offers his "more scientific" approach on decidedly theological, not philosophical grounds.

Next, Torrance turns his critique on the experiential approach of liberal "Neo-Protestantism" which he sees as mired in the outmoded epistemology of science and history that continues to dominate critical biblical studies. He rejects the view that doctrine or dogmas are constructed "by a process of deduc-

60. Torrance, *Space, Time and Resurrection,* p. 7.
61. Torrance, *Space, Time and Resurrection,* p. 8.
62. Torrance, *Reality and Evangelical Theology,* p. 64.

tion from observational data, regarded as the 'raw' or 'uninterpreted' facts of experience. This is the view that has admittedly prevailed in Neo-Protestantism, and is as such the by-product of the 'observationalist' view of scientific activity dating back to Newton's claim that he did not invent hypotheses but deduced them from appearances or phenomena."[63] While Torrance does not dismiss the important findings of historico-critical approaches to the biblical sources, he rejects as patently unscientific the view that we can somehow penetrate to the theological depths by observing surface phenomena.[64]

Theology must penetrate "into the interior connections of the field," which means that the theologian "operates with the whole apostolic tradition in its stratified depth in order to allow himself to be directed from all sides to the objective realities under the creative impact of which all the apostolic tradition incorporated into the New Testament took its rise and shape in the primitive Church."[65] Elsewhere, Torrance quotes Einstein's dictum that "God does not wear his heart on his sleeve" to illustrate that serious inquiry in science and theology must "penetrate into the underlying ontological structure of the ordered regularity of things, to which the phenomenal patterns of that regularity are coordinated, and by which they are controlled, and in reference to which they may be accounted for."[66] In other words, the theologian must "indwell" the biblical witness with the same level of passionate intensity and commitment with which a neuro-biologist examines the human brain. "Hence, what the theologian does, and must do, is to make himself dwell in the semantic focus of the many-layered memory or tradition embodied in the New Testament. In this way his mind gradually becomes assimilated to the integration of the different strata in their bearing upon the objective events and realities they intend, and as it falls under the intelligible power of those events and realities there arises a structural kinship between his knowing and what he seeks to know."[67]

Thus, for Torrance, the knowledge which is mediated by Scripture is always contingent upon "the self-revelation and self-communication of God through Jesus Christ and in the Holy Spirit." Our human knowledge of God in the hearing of Scripture is initiated, sustained and fulfilled by divine agency. "In so far as Scripture . . . may prove to be an opaque medium, historico-critical and theologico-critical elucidation may help, as it were, to cleanse the lens, but what really makes Scripture a transparent medium is the divine light that

63. Torrance, *Space, Time and Resurrection,* p. 8.

64. Loder would say this kind of thinking that dominates biblical studies reflects the common confusion between science and technology.

65. Torrance, *Space, Time and Resurrection,* p. 10.

66. Torrance, *Ground and Grammar,* p. 119.

67. Torrance, *Space, Time and Resurrection,* p. 11.

shines through it from the face of Jesus Christ into our hearts."[68] While we might say that, from our side, the words of Scripture are an iconic witness through which faith apprehends the Word of God, we should also remember that the very possibility of our human apprehension is permanently contingent on the agency of the God who, in Jesus Christ, initiates, sustains, and fulfills the saving knowledge of God himself and is in need of no other witness.

> The real text with which we are concerned is not the letter of the Scriptures as such but the Humanity of Christ including His historical Life and Work, that is, the actual way in which the Word of God has objectified Himself for us within our human modes of existence in space and time, and has revealed Himself within our human speech and thought.[69]

Concluding Remarks

We have already mentioned that Torrance claims Barth as a model of the *a posteriori objective realism* which is at the heart of his own approach to theological science. It is worth noting that Lindbeck also tries to claim Barth as an "exemplar" of his cultural-linguistic approach because of his rejection of liberalism's "turn to the subject."[70] Though the insights of great theologians are often claimed by people with differing theological agendas, I think we can fairly adjudicate these claims by considering how philosophy is viewed by Barth in comparison with Lindbeck and Torrance.

Torrance offers Barth's "scientific" approach to philosophy as an example of how this *a posteriori objective realism* operates in his thought.

> Whenever Barth engages in polemical debate with "philosophy," he is not concerned in any way to dispute the necessity or relevance of logic and metaphysics, but to attack the erection of an independent (and naturalistically grounded) *Weltanschauung* within which, it is claimed, Christianity must be interpreted if it is to become understandable in the modern world, and more frequently, to attack the erection of a masterful epistemology, elaborated independently of actual theological inquiry, which is then to be applied prescriptively to knowledge of God. In his rejection of this kind of "philosophy" Barth stands shoulder to shoulder with every proper scientist who insists on the freedom to develop scientific methods appropriate to the

68. Torrance, *Space, Time and Resurrection*, p. 12.
69. Torrance, *Theological Science*, p. 193.
70. Lindbeck, *The Nature of Doctrine*, p. 24.

field of his inquiry and to elaborate epistemological structures under the compulsion of the nature of things as it becomes disclosed to him in the progress of his investigation, all untrammeled by *a priori* assumptions of any kind. *A posteriori* science involves rigorous methodological questioning of all preconceptions and presuppositions and of all structures of thought independent of and antecedent to its own processes of discovery.[71]

In this passage, we find Torrance's characteristic rejection of any epistemology which is "elaborated independently of actual theological inquiry." The field of inquiry for the theologian is not the same as that which interests the philosopher. While he does not reject philosophy out-of-hand, Barth's thinking is directed by the authoritative givenness of revelation. "Theology is not philosophical argumentation for the knowability of God, because God has already given us real knowledge of himself in Jesus Christ."[72] If philosophy helps give clearer articulation to the christocentric, trinitarian field of theological inquiry, the theologian is free to utilize its categories *ad hoc,* as, for example, when Barth uses Hegel or Kant and Torrance uses Polanyi and Wittgenstein.

By contrast, Lindbeck's claim that Barth is a proto-postliberal is less than convincing. First of all, his scant and selective use of Barth is problematic. For example, Lindbeck's *type one* takes up the negative aspect of Barth's critique of traditional orthodoxy while completely passing over his positive appraisal. In his critique of the orthodox view of Scripture, for example, Barth writes,

The weakness of orthodoxy is not the supernatural element in the Bible; on the contrary, in that lies its strength. It is rather the fact that orthodoxy has a way of regarding some objective description of an element, such as the word "God," as if it were the element itself.[73]

Further, Lindbeck says that, "on the specifically theological side, Karl Barth's exegetical emphasis on narrative has been at second hand a chief source of my notion of intertextuality as an appropriate way of doing theology in a fashion consistent with a cultural-linguistic understanding of religion and a regulative view of doctrine."[74] Unfortunately, he says nothing beyond this about Barth's alleged "exegetical emphasis on narrative" and *how* it is "consistent with a cultural-linguistic understanding of religion and a regulative view of doctrine." Thus, his claim that Barth should be read as an exemplar of the cultural-

71. Torrance, *Transformation and Convergence,* pp. 292-293.

72. Torrance, *Reality and Evangelical Theology,* p. xiv.

73. Barth, *Church Dogmatics,* I/1 (Edinburgh: T&T Clark, 1955), p. x.

74. Lindbeck, *The Nature of Doctrine,* p. 135.

linguistic model is empty and, as I tried to show by referring to Hunsinger and my Japanese colleagues, not necessarily accepted by Barth scholars.

In spite of his protests to the contrary, Lindbeck's entire project is unstable as a theory of Christian doctrine precisely because it is thoroughly grounded methodologically and epistemologically in the non-theological, philosophical discourse of Wittgenstein's correlation of language and performance. By the standards of Torrance's theological science, postliberalism represents the imposition of an external and alien framework of intelligibility on the particular *inherent constitutive relations* which pertain to a field whose parameters are directed by the self-revelation of God in Jesus Christ. Even by the standards of Wittgenstein's language games, hasn't Lindbeck forced the alien "language games" of philosophy and anthropology onto the "language game" of Christian theology? Further, given the high degree of cultural and linguistic pluralism that characterizes our electronic age, one may legitimately wonder about the actual existence of the kind of sequestered Christian communities posited by Lindbeck's Wittgensteinian view of doctrine.[75]

Most decisively, the projects of Lindbeck and Torrance part ways in their differing understanding of the locus of first-order discourse. Lindbeck, following his reading of Wittgenstein, makes a distinction between "abiding doctrinal grammar and variable theological vocabulary."[76] In another place, he describes this difference in more detail. The "abiding doctrinal grammar" is correlated with the religious community's "liturgical, kerygmatic and ethical modes of speech and action,"[77] while the "variable theological vocabulary" is correlated with official church doctrine or theology as "second-order discourse about first-intentional uses of religious language."[78] To repeat, *first-order discourse* is limited to the "liturgical, kerygmatic and ethical" modalities of language and action and *second-order discourse* to reflection on those modalities. Thus, within the philosophical parameters of Lindbeck's cultural-linguistic view of doctrine, do we really find any room for an objective, transcendent theological referent?

By contrast, in Lindbeck's terms, Torrance sees Jesus Christ himself, the incarnate Son of God, as the "first-order discourse," or "abiding doctrinal grammar" of Christian faith. To use an analogy from science, as matter and en-

75. Given the present situation of high modernity or postmodernity in which many of us in the church spend our daily lives trying to negotiate our exposure to the mind-boggling plurality of particular language games with incongruent cultural linguistic rules, one also needs to ask Lindbeck where in North America the churches exist today in which doctrine actually functions in the way he has claimed.

76. Lindbeck, *The Nature of Doctrine*, p. 113.

77. Lindbeck, *The Nature of Doctrine*, p. 69.

78. Lindbeck, *The Nature of Doctrine*, p. 69.

ergy are correlated to the singular constant of the speed of light in Einstein's theory of relativity, the Church's liturgical, kerygmatic and ethical modes of speech and action and its theological vocabulary are all correlated to the epistemological singularity of Jesus Christ who

> is confessed to be God of God, of one and the Same Being with God, the very one who for us men and our salvation was made man. The *homoousion,* then, to refer to it in its more abstract form, is of staggering significance. It crystallizes the conviction that while the incarnation falls within the structures of our spatio-temporal humanity in this world, it also falls within the Life and Being of God. Jesus Christ is thus not a mere symbol, some representation of God detached from God, but God in his own Being and Act come among us, expressing in our human form the Word which he is eternally in himself, so that in our relations with Jesus Christ we have to do directly with the ultimate Reality of God.[79]

Lindbeck invites the suspicion that he has too quickly surrendered his clerical robes for an academic hood. If ecumenical dialogue is possible only when theology is reconceived as the handmaiden of linguistic philosophy and cultural anthropology, we run the risk of an even further distantiation of Christian language from its divine referent which can have only disastrous results for the educational ministry of the church.

79. Torrance, *The Ground and Grammar of Theology,* p. 160.

10. Transformational Narrative in a Non-Transformational Tradition

Margaret A. Krych

One of the interesting and practical implications of James Loder's theory of transformation is his use of transformational narrative in Christian education. Loder particularly deals with this approach in *The Transforming Moment*[1] but also refers to it in *The Logic of the Spirit.*[2] He holds that the prototype transformational process inherent in human developmental stage transition[3] is transposed with effectiveness first to the level of intentional acts of creation in spheres where the absence of established frames of reference calls for the employment of transformational logic, and then to the level of fictive time in the plot of transformational narratives.[4] Such narrative form can be used therapeutically to heal depression and neuroses. The logic can be used in stories that "tell us who we are, why we are, and what is our destiny" (132).

Transformational Logic

Loder defines "transformation" as "a change in form from lower to higher orders of life along a continuous line of intention of development" (38). He delineates the steps in transformational logic as: conflict, an apparent rupture in the

1. James Loder, *The Transforming Moment: Understanding Convictional Experiences* (San Francisco: Harper & Row, 1981).

2. James Loder, *The Logic of the Spirit* (San Francisco: Jossey-Bass, 1998), pp. 198-199, 247.

3. Loder, *The Transforming Moment,* pp. 128-131. See also James E. Loder, "Negation and Transformation: A Study in Theology and Human Development," in *Toward Moral and Religious Maturity: The First International Conference on Moral and Religious Development,* convened by Christiane Brusselmans (Morristown, NJ: Silver Burdett Co., 1980), pp. 166-190.

4. Loder, *The Transforming Moment,* p. 131. Subsequent page references will be given parenthetically in the text.

knowing context which initiates the knowing response (31); an interlude for scanning in which the knower searches out possible solutions, takes apart errors, keeps parts and discards others (32); the constructive act of the imagination, in which insight or intuition or vision conveys the essence of the resolution (32); a fourth step marked in two ways — first, by the "release of energy bound up in sustaining the conflict" and second, "by an opening of the knower to him- or herself and the contextual situation" (33); and finally, "interpretation of the imaginative solution into the behavioral and/or symbolically constructed world of the original context." Interpretation works backward (by making congruent connections from the structures of the imaginative construct back into the original conditions of the problem situation) and forward (by examining the imaginative construct for its correspondence to a consensual view of the world) (34).[5]

It is the third step, "the construction of insight sensed with convincing force, that constitutes the turning point of the knowing event. It is by this central act that the elements of the ruptured situation are *transformed,* and a new perception, perspective, or world view is bestowed on the knower" (33). This sequence is one of continuity and discontinuity. The knower's built-in intention to complete the knowing acts constitutes the continuity, while discontinuity is due to the mediating image, intuition, vision, or insight (36). Such mediating discontinuity is a mystery that surprises us. It has the quality of gift. "When the resolution is given, self-transcendence (consciousness of being conscious or freedom to choose) springs into being spontaneously like a still heart suddenly resuscitated" (36).

Such discontinuity "suggests intentionally cooperative intervention from a realm of reality beyond consciousness itself," and this discontinuity is what makes transformation possible. Mediation through the imaginative construct begins from the point of engagement with the dissonance of the conflicted situation, but then the transformed construction actually emerges from outside of the conflicted situation, giving new interpretation, a liberating sense of resolution, and a gain in knowledge (36).

Such transformational logic is the grammar of the knowing event. One may enter at any one of the five points in the sequence of this transformational process, thus on either side of the middle step of transformation or at that actual middle step (37). But in any case, the sequence remains as the structure or grammar through which transformation occurs.

5. The transformational pattern is also elucidated in James E. Loder and W. Jim Neidhardt: *The Knight's Move: The Relational Logic of the Spirit in Theology and Science* (Colorado Springs: Helmers & Howard, 1992), p. 266.

Loder's central contention is that human transformations must themselves be transformed in encounter with Christ for redemptive transformation to occur (61). The conflicts that lead to deep spiritual transformation are conflicts that bring us face to face with non-being or the void which Loder says "has many faces such as absence, loss, shame, guilt, hatred, loneliness, and the demonic" (83). Such conflicts issue in transformation only by the transforming work of the Holy Spirit, the Creator Spirit, who brings us to conviction in faith. "At the heart of convictional knowing is a radical figure-ground shift that is not merely perceptual but existential, in which the truth of Christ's revelation transforms the subject from a knower into one who is fully known and comprehended by what he or she first knew" (122-123). Such logic is not only the grammar of the knowing event, but convictional knowing is also the "grammar" of the Holy Spirit (115). The logic of the human spirit and the logic of the divine Spirit in fact have an analogical relationship. Loder believes that the Holy Spirit manifests its inner life to the eyes of faith. We know the Holy Spirit only through the human self as spirit, by analogy (92).[6] Anything analogous shows both likeness and difference; for Loder the likeness between the human spirit and the Holy Spirit is due to the pattern of transformational logic that applies to both, "making the human spirit transformable to the Holy Spirit and the Holy Spirit intelligible to the human" (93). It is in Christ, both human and divine, that the analogy becomes actual and historical.

Transformational Narrative

Transformational narrative has the structure or grammar of transformational logic in story form. The narrative begins with conflict and scanning steps. Then, the third, fourth, and fifth steps of the transformational pattern include radical intervention by an agent from outside of the original situation. This intervention negates the void and leads to new self-understanding and the convictional knowing of faith. A critical role is played by the "code-breaking semantic mediator," the outside agent by whose intervention the void is negated and convictional knowing is brought about.

Anthropological structuralists Elli Köngäs Maranda and Pierre Maranda built on the work of Claude Lévi-Strauss by analyzing structures in folklore and mythology. They examined the grouping of elementary constituents in

6. On the analogy between the human spirit and the Holy Spirit, see also Loder, *The Logic of the Spirit*, pp. 35-36.

narratives[7] and arrived at a set of four models of narratives, one of which exhibits the transformational pattern and is therefore helpful in developing transformational narratives to communicate the gospel message in Christian education. This model begins, as in Loder's pattern, with a problem situation. An agent (A) seeks a solution to the problem, but uses inadequate means and so fails to solve the problem. Then, agent B (the semantic mediator) seeks a solution to the same problem, but, unlike A, uses an adequate means to bring about the solution. B thus participates in the function that A tried to accomplish, but B does so in a successful way that achieves what A could not do. This in turn reverses the situation for A, who is now enabled to participate in the successful solution provided by B. The final solution actually turns out to be a gain for A, and the outcome is greater than simply a mere reversal of the problem.[8]

Expressing it even more simply, the transformational narrative structure involves a pair of opposites and a "semantic mediator" capable of including them. The structure as structure is neutral, and can be used in many ways with many different kinds of content. (Maranda and Maranda, for example, were dealing with folktales, not the gospel.) However, the structure lends itself well to patterning a narrative that communicates the gospel in Christian education.

To put it more closely in terms of Loder's transformational pattern: first, there is a seeking or scanning phase by A that fails to produce a solution. Then follows the intervention of an outside agent, B, in which the solution is given by B's successful participation in A's function. This results in A's perceiving the situation in a new way — actually, perceiving the solution and participating in it. In a final phase, A recognizes and operates in light of the solution. In this scheme, B may be called the "code-breaking semantic mediator," the agent by which the solution is accomplished.[9] Such narrative has a crossover or chiasmic (from the Greek letter X) pattern in that B takes over and does for A what A tries in vain to accomplish, and in so doing lifts A to a new plane.[10]

Loder holds that the structure of transformational narrative bears the pattern or "grammar" of the Holy Spirit who transforms our situation, negates

7. Elli Köngäs Maranda and Pierre Maranda, *Structural Models in Folklore and Transformational Essays*, Approaches to Semiotics No. 10, ed. Thomas A. Sebeok (The Hague, Paris: Mouton, 1971), pp. 21-22. Elli Köngäs Maranda found that children were able to conserve this structure of narrative even in quite complex narratives.

8. Margaret A. Krych, *Teaching the Gospel Today* (Minneapolis: Augsburg, 1987), p. 77.

9. For an extended treatment of this narrative form, see Krych, *Teaching the Gospel Today*, chap. 5.

10. It surely is no accident that the figure of the "strange loop" that Loder uses to summarize the relation of the human spirit to the Holy Spirit in *The Knight's Move*, p. 121, is a variant of a looped chi(x).

our negation or the void, and brings us to the convictional knowing of faith. Such convictional knowing involves a new understanding of who we are. It also involves a new way of being and living. And, the structure or pattern of the narrative actually points beyond itself to the message being conveyed.[11]

In communicating the gospel through transformationally structured narrative, the "semantic mediator" is also understood as the theological mediator, Jesus Christ, who does for us humans what we attempt but cannot ever do for ourselves by obtaining salvation and bringing us into a right relationship with God. The chiasmic pattern is reflective of biblical passages such as 2 Corinthians 5:21 ("For our sake he made him to be sin who knew no sin, so that in him we might become the righteousness of God," NRSV). Through the cross, sinful humanity's situation is changed by the divine-human agent, changed from condemnation to reconciliation and eternal life, and so the outcome is far greater than anything humanity could have hoped to accomplish.

As Loder describes it, "the structure of the transforming intuition works as follows. Human intention, self-defeating in its negation of the divine initiative, is negated by divine intention. Cancellation is the result of this double negation such that human intention is now left free to choose for the Author of the cancellation. Thus the nature of the divine bestows itself through the freedom of human choice made in the context of grace" (*Transforming Moment*, 104). Loder says that in the Emmaus story, Christ "as Mediator implicitly identifies himself as the source of the transformational process by which the Emmaus travelers (representing the early church and potentially all people) come under conviction" (106).

Loder understands Martin Luther as supporting a view of transformational logic as the "grammar" of the Holy Spirit (115). Transformational logic is in fact the pattern or grammar of human spirit and of the human developmental process as well as that of the Holy Spirit. The Holy Spirit's pattern of action is recognizable as that of transformation yet also shows discontinuity in the surprising newness of power that makes us a new creation. All transformations on the human level of spirit must themselves be radically transformed by the Holy Spirit. For the gospel to be meaningful, the Spirit throws us into inner conflict by having our situation of alienation radically exposed; the Spirit convicts through conflict and exposes our brokenness. But the Spirit also restores us as gift; "the destiny of his regenerative work is a sanctifying unity with Christ in worship and in his ongoing redemption of the world" (116). So, the origin and destiny of human transformation in personality are transformed by the Spirit, and the intertwining of ultimate continuity with ultimate discontinuity

11. Krych, *Teaching the Gospel Today*, p. 81.

becomes a personal stance of the Word of God, a conversion or awakening to sanctification (117). Such conversion is into the transformation of all things since the Spirit transposes the logic expressed in personal conversion and extends it to the whole created realm. Loder places the Eucharist at the center of transformation, in which the human spirit itself is turned inside out, the Eucharist becoming the lens through which one's own being and being itself is viewed (118-119).

Convictional experiences then are initiated by Christ, and are characterized by sacrificial love in the one transformed (190-191). Because they are from Christ, transforming moments seek objective expressions about Christ. They are essentially breakthrough experiences from the future which call for communal experiences of Word and sacrament (196-197). And, since in convictional experiences the Spirit transforms all other transformations, "convictional knowing is primarily a free and gracious act of love" (185). Transformational narrative must witness to this gift-character of God's work through Christ.

"Upward" Movement

Transformational narrative essentially has a characteristic theological hopefulness built into it. The narrative exposes the human situation of conflict, but always ends with the person transformed to a new plane by the work of the Spirit. In fact, it would seem that there is an upward, or perhaps spirally upward, trend to the succession of convictional experiences that might be expressed through transformationally structured narratives. The narrative never ends full circle back at the beginning, but rather always ends with agent A, through the work of agent B, in a greater state or a higher level than even the state that agent A had originally sought.

For example, in transformational structure, the story of Zaccheus begins with Zaccheus putting himself and his needs at the center of his life, which renders him unacceptable to those around him. But, perhaps barely conscious, there is conflict that drives Zaccheus to want to see Jesus whose lifestyle condemns self-centeredness and who is centered in the needs of others, including the needs of Zaccheus. Zaccheus is alienated from the self he wishes to be just as he is alienated from the populace. This scanning phase is followed by the appearance of Jesus as mediator, who shows acceptance of Zaccheus who is unacceptable, and, as he does so, Jesus becomes the one who is criticized, who is unacceptable to the crowd. And Zaccheus experiences grace as gift, free acceptance in spite of who he is and what he has done. Zaccheus's life is turned around and he now seeks in generosity to reverse the deep wrongs he has done to others. Jesus' presence and acceptance expose to Zaccheus who he truly is and at the same time provide the transformation into other-centeredness and restoration.[12]

Similarly, in the story of Peter's denial and restoration (John 13:36-38; 18:15-18, 25-27; 21:15-19), the void opens before Peter as he denies Jesus and then realizes what he has done. Peter cannot restore himself. But the crucified and risen Lord, who identifies with sinful denying humanity, comes to Peter after the resurrection and, in a three-fold restoration, both forgives Peter and gives him a commission to care for those with faith.

Many biblical and other faith stories can be similarly structured, and remain true to the original biblical narrative. In each one, it will be Jesus, crucified and risen, who is the mediator (semantic and theological) who brings about transformation, so that the agent who began the episode in conflict and void finally becomes the one lifted up onto a higher plane through the work of Christ.

Given the conclusion always on a higher plane, the transformational logic pattern seems particularly appropriate for use in a tradition that has an understanding of sanctification as transformation, as real change of life that includes an "upward" movement away from sin and increasing conformity to the life of Jesus. In the transformational narrative, each experience ends by the mediator lifting one to a higher state — the final state of the person being better than the beginning one before the conflict.

Note that there is no suggestion here that humanity is initiating the onward and upward movement. Loder is very clear that the outside agent — the semantic and indeed theological mediator — is key to the change brought about in the life of the person who has the convictional experience. The Spirit is sole worker in this change. So clearly the transformational narrative is a narrative of grace. But it may be seen as a narrative of "onward and upward," of ascending movement.

Such a structure works well with an understanding of the work of the Holy Spirit as genuine transformation of the person, a gradual process of change in which the person becomes more like Christ and progressively less and less sinful. In such an approach, each transformational experience would move one along in the process. An onward and upward pattern of "progressive sanctification" would be reflected in the series of transformations. Appropriate images would be those of sin being "rooted out" of one's life, of becoming more like Christ, of daily growth toward perfection. Loder himself characterizes the mission of the Creator Spirit as "transformation into conformity with Christ as

12. For a much longer and detailed account, see Krych, *Teaching the Gospel Today,* pp. 84-86.

the restored image of God and mediator of the redemption of all creation."[13] Paul Tillich sees Calvinism as an example of this approach: "In Calvinism sanctification proceeds in a slowly upward-turning line; both faith and love are progressively actualized. The power of the divine Spirit in the individual increases. Perfection is approached, though never reached."[14] One might expect that transformational narrative would readily be appropriated in such a tradition.

In a Non-Transformational Tradition

But can transformational narrative be used — or in what way might it be used — in traditions in which sanctification is viewed less as transformation and more as a daily return to the good Word of justification, of God's mercy in forgiving sin? Lutheranism, for example, understands sanctification very differently from a progressive upward movement. In fact, it eschews a progressive movement in the Spirit's work. "In Lutheranism the emphasis on the paradoxical element in the experience of the New Being was so predominant that sanctification could not be interpreted in terms of a line moving upward toward perfection."[15] Rather, sanctification is seen as an up-and-down movement of faith and unbelief, of being justified and sinful simultaneously *(simil iustus et peccator)*. This paradoxical experience is not temporary but continues throughout life. Only beyond death is the work of the Spirit complete and the individual released from sin and given perfect holiness. Christians need forgiveness constantly in this life because we are never without sin, hence the importance of Word and sacraments to give the comfort of the gospel of forgiveness of sin. Every day we need the benefits of Christ's atonement; every day therefore is a return to the Word of proclamation of the forgiveness of sins, a return to our baptism.

Does all of this mean that, in a tradition such as the Lutheran tradition, one cannot use transformational narrative? I would argue that indeed transformational narrative can be used, but with certain emphases highlighted and with certain adaptations made.

13. Loder, *The Logic of the Spirit*, p. 41.

14. Paul Tillich, *Systematic Theology*, vol. 3 (Chicago: University of Chicago Press, 1963), p. 230.

15. Tillich, *Systematic Theology*, vol. 3, p. 230. Is there no "process" in the Christian life? Tillich suggests there are four principles of process: increasing awareness of sin; increasing freedom from the law; increasing relatedness to others, self, and God; and increasing prayer. But never increasing toward perfection (pp. 231-237).

Sin

First, the matter of conflict, the initial situation of agent A, will be seen as a situation of alienation, hostility, and rebellion, which continues daily throughout life, even as the grace-filled answer is given daily. The Lutheran Reformation insisted that, while human beings are both creatures of God and sinners at the same time, sin is indeed a very serious matter. All persons are sinners, and sin is a continual inclination of our nature that permeates all that we do. Sin is therefore no mere external impediment nor a developmental characteristic but a deep corruption of our entire human nature, a matter of being turned in on ourselves, or elevating ourselves to the place of God. Sin is estrangement from God, others, and ourselves as we were meant to be. It is contempt of and hostility toward God, unbelief, a lack of trust in God. It is our personal responsibility; we are culpable.

Throughout Loder's writing there seems to be a swing back and forth on the culpability issue. The depth of seriousness of the void, of negation, sometimes more than others, conveys the sense of personal responsibility. The void's faces include absence, loss, shame, guilt, hatred, loneliness, and the demonic.[16] Not all of these carry the same culpability. Where Loder borrows from Regin Prenter's treatment of Luther in *Spiritus Creator*, he acknowledges Luther's emphasis on the gracious work of the Spirit in convicting of sin, bestowing the alien righteousness of Christ, justifying, bringing salvation, and creating anew.[17] Here he is closest to Luther. But perhaps it is when Loder then makes his immediate move to developmental transitions that the tone changes and the ego is seen more as tragic hero with a fatal flaw[18] than as rebellious unbeliever who bears personal responsibility before God. Loder's understanding of sin is basically separation of the human spirit from its grounding in the Spirit of God, a wandering, blundering brilliance, a loose cannon of creativity.[19]

Now, this is not to say that Loder does not have complexity in his understanding of the human situation. First, he builds in complexity in his stage structures of the ego — the interplay of structures and process is not a simple one like James Fowler's in which stage structure is the controlling factor. Rather, in Loder, "the process can be exercised in a variety of ways to call forth structural resources from the substrata of the psyche in order to meet a great variety of conflictual situations, whether governed by or embedded in the develop-

16. Loder, *Transforming Moment*, p. 83.
17. E.g., Loder, *The Logic of the Spirit*, pp. 114-118.
18. Loder, *The Logic of the Spirit*, p. 115.
19. Loder, *The Logic of the Spirit*, p. 10.

mental sequence or not."[20] The transformational process may actually leap over developmental stages or incorporate them in an order of its own.[21] Second, there is no question that Loder allows for more ambiguity and tension than Fowler and others who have an "upward" movement in human development (albeit "spiral" for Fowler[22]). Loder argues against Fowler's understanding[23] and insists on struggle and negation in human development. Ultimately the struggle requires the solution of the negation of this negation by the divine Spirit. In *The Knight's Move,*[24] Loder emphasizes that, left to itself, ego development is rooted in negation and death; only the Spirit can bring about the negation of developmental negation, and the Spirit does so in terms of relationship, of access between the ego and the divine center, while outside the developmental process itself.

Nevertheless, at the heart of Loder's understanding of humanity there lingers a certain anthropological optimism. He decries in both Pannenberg and Barth the tendency to depreciate the distinctive significance of the human spirit.[25] He emphasizes the inherent creativity of the human spirit, the expansive self-transcending power of the human spirit that drives towards transformation of obstacles in life.[26] This is a somewhat different emphasis from that of the Lutheran Reformers who focus more on the depth of human sinfulness, the bondage of the will, and human nature that is culpable and guilty and needs radical forgiveness and atonement.

In a Lutheran tradition, then, the first step in transformational narrative will emphasize a conflict for which the agent is seriously and personally responsible and guilty (however clearly or poorly that may be understood or expressed by the agent himself or herself).

20. Loder, *Transforming Moment,* p. 137.

21. Loder, *Transforming Moment,* p. 138.

22. James W. Fowler, *Stages of Faith* (San Francisco: Harper & Row, 1981), p. 289.

23. Loder commends Fowler for his "insightful study of the ego's competence in structuring meaning" but says that Fowler's study is only potentially but not necessarily related to faith in a biblical and theological sense, and that Fowler's development in faith "seems to reflect rather than correct the 'ritualization of progress' in an achievement obsessed society." James W. Fowler and James E. Loder, "Conversations on Fowler's *Stages of Faith* and Loder's *Transforming Moment,*" *Religious Education* 77, 2 (March-April 1982): 135, 137.

24. Loder, *The Knight's Move,* p. 284.

25. Loder, *The Logic of the Spirit,* p. 34.

26. Loder, *The Logic of the Spirit,* pp. 33, 35.

Centrality of the Crucified Christ

Second, strong emphasis in the narrative will be placed right where Loder insists that it be placed — on the work of Jesus Christ as Mediator, and on the centrality of the cross. Lutheran confessional documents emphasize that we can do nothing to make ourselves right with God, but Christ as Mediator brings us salvation as a merciful gift. The reconciliation of humanity to God is due solely to the work of Christ, who, in his obedience and suffering on the cross, provides the means for our forgiveness. The Reformers emphasized the cross and suffering of Christ as obedience in perfectly keeping God's law so that God reckons his righteousness to us and forgives our sins, treating us as if we were righteous even though we are not. Because Christ was truly God, his obedience can be reckoned to us as righteousness; and because Christ was truly human his righteousness is reckoned as our righteousness. And this righteousness is appropriated and accepted by faith, which is itself a gift from God. Such a dealing with sin does not overlook sin but takes it very seriously and deals with it in the most costly way. Good works that serve the neighbor then become a response of thanks for God's forgiveness. So does the desire to share the gospel with others. Because we remain sinful, even though saved, we need daily to return to the good word of forgiveness by God's grace through faith. The Lord's Supper (Eucharist) for Lutherans is essentially a proclamation of the forgiveness of sin.

In communicating the gospel, the developer/communicator of transformational narrative must be sure that the role of Christ is primary. If agent A is understood as humanity, and agent B as Jesus the Christ, then humanity in the situation of sin attempts many solutions to get right with God and fails miserably on all counts. The answer to our human predicament comes from outside the human situation through the work of Jesus Christ, agent B, who does for us what we cannot do for ourselves, by offering himself on the cross for our salvation. Because of his solution to our human problem of sin, we are then, through the Spirit, able by faith to participate in the benefits obtained through his work and so share in eternal life. This pattern reflects Paul's image in Romans 8:3: "For God has done what the law, weakened by the flesh, could not do: by sending his own Son in the likeness of sinful flesh, and to deal with sin, he condemned sin in the flesh" (NRSV). Therefore, the just requirement of the law has now been fulfilled in us, and we walk according to the Spirit and have eternal life. The final outcome is not simply lack of condemnation but also restored relationship, indwelling by the Spirit, new life, a new creation.

While the centrality of the mediator is in fact built into any transformational narrative as a matter of structure, in a Lutheran tradition this will be the step in the sequence that is most emphasized, on which the teller lingers, rather than hurrying through it to put the main emphasis on the final situation of agent A who is now on a higher plane. The linkage will be made clear between that final story ending and the cruciform narrative. The Chi pattern will be highlighted.

For such an emphasis, Loder has every sympathy. He has a characteristic christocentricity to his theology and insists on Christ's divine and human natures as necessary for salvation.[27] He strongly emphasizes that justification is solely a matter of God's grace, never our own works.[28] He also emphasizes that "apart from the Spirit-to-spirit communication of the mind of God, the attempt of the human mind to know itself, to say nothing of knowing the mind of God, is utter foolishness,"[29] so there is no question that the solution to the human condition is to be found in the One who is other than we are.[30]

In his Emmaus Road narrative (*Transforming Moment*, 96ff.), Loder certainly lingers on Christ's work. As Loder interprets the narrative, the void has opened up before Simon and Cleopas as the crucifixion has destroyed their hopes, although they have some glimmer of hope in the light of the women's story of the empty tomb. The first step of the transformational process is conflict. Jesus' death exposes the conflict by showing that their hopes for Israel were too small, a conflict they already brought into their relationship with Christ. The disciples cannot transcend or recompose or escape their situation. As Christ expounds the Scriptures, they engage in the interlude for scanning (the second step in the transformational process). Christ is the guide in this scanning process; it is the Spirit working deeply within the disciples that prepares the spirit to turn to the Holy beyond the self (96-102). The transforming intuition of Christ comes into play in the breaking of the bread, when, "in the broken bread, his brokenness is united with theirs, and theirs is united with his as they are invited to take it into themselves. . . . It is a union of brokenness embraced and upheld by his resurrected Presence, which is now theirs to incorporate" (103). The Holy transforms the void, exposing the men's false hope and brokenness, and presenting a new reality, a new way of looking at things. "Human intention, self-defeating in its negation of divine initiative, is negated by divine intention. Cancellation is the result of this double negation such that human intention is now left free to choose for the Author of the cancellation" (104), free to choose for itself as spirit. Loder speaks of a four-dimensional inte-

27. Loder, *The Knight's Move*, pp. 82-87, 142-143.

28. Loder, *The Logic of the Spirit*, p. 166.

29. Loder, *The Logic of the Spirit*, p. 11.

30. Loder, *The Logic of the Spirit*, p. 12.

gration and transformation in the dimensions of environment, selfhood, the void, and the Holy (104; see also 66-68).

Loder refers to Luther's explanation of 2 Corinthians 5:21 as a good example of convictional knowing, of the double negation — the sinless Christ became sin so that my sin might be condemned yet no longer accuse and condemn me; Christ gives a death that crucifies and swallows up the death of the flesh, the condemnation of sin. Christ is the initiator and the one who carries out the process, which is essentially a relational process — we humans are not absorbed by Christ, but given a relationship to him in virtue of what he has already done for us. "It is Christ's World that the self creates out of the freedom that Christ's grace has made possible. Thus, while the self, world, void, and the Holy are reconstellated by his nature, the self is freed within that very context — the context of his nature — to choose for or against him" (106).

Christ himself as truly human and divine is the epitome of the relation between the self and the Holy. He is intimately related to the Father, and composes the world "in accordance with the Father's composition of the World" (107). So, Jesus reveals what it means to be truly human. Yet, by doing what the Father was doing, he also reveals the nature of God. "Thus for the self the consequence of transformation at the hands of the Mediating Christ is to be led into conflict with all other 'worlds' and into a sacrificial love for the World which the Father composes and sustains" (107). For the disciples at Emmaus, this experience releases a new self-understanding, a release of tension, a joy that gives new insight and experiencing the world in a new way (108-109). Loder terms this mundane ecstasy — perceiving the world of common experience in a new way, coming into Christ's world, "awakening to one's own particularity and goodness as given by grace" (109).

Justification and Sanctification as Unity

Third, the cyclical nature or repetitive nature of transformational narrative will be emphasized. The Lutheran understanding is that sanctification is simply the other side of justification — the daily return to baptism, the daily forgiveness of sin, the daily hearing of the Word of God's gracious justifying activity. There is no process as in "first justification, then sanctification." Rather, sanctification is the ongoing work of the Spirit daily bringing again the Word of forgiveness of sins to the believer who constantly needs to hear it.

Gerhard Forde argues that, if justification is followed by a process of sanctification, then sanctification becomes the primary reality, and justification then fades into the background as a presupposition for the real work of sanctification.[31] Instead, Forde holds that justification-and-sanctification is a unity. "Justification by faith means the death of the old and the resurrection of the new. Sanctification is what results when that is done to us."[32] *Simul iustus et peccator* implies that there is no growth, no progress in sanctification. Believers stand as sinners, knowing that Christ alone is their hope and giving God the glory.[33] Thus, if there is a "movement" in sanctification, it is the movement "from that which one has and is in oneself to that which one has and is in Christ."[34] Each moment is a start and finish, a beginning and an ending. When there is a proclamation of forgiveness of sin by grace through faith, there is the death of the old and the rebirth of the new. Such justification explodes in acts of love and service to the neighbor. "Sanctification is what happens when the unconditional and eschatological event of justification breaks into one's life. Sanctification is what happens when one acts out of faith in the gift of total and complete righteousness," and such faith issues in good works done for the sake of the other.[35]

In this approach, the primary work of the Spirit is to call forth faith through the Word. Robert Jenson suggests that the verbs that specify the work of the Spirit as that which calls, illumines, converts, justifies, renovates, unites with Christ, and sanctifies are actually instructions to preachers, liturgical leaders, teachers, and advisers.[36] They are accomplished in the act of gospel-speaking itself. "Conversion is a change in the communication situation within which every person lives; a proper sermon or baptism liturgy or penance liturgy just *is* that change."[37] So, the proclamation of absolution is the conversion of the penitent's life from the old situation to a new situation. Such proclamation clearly happens again and again, week after week and day after day.

It may be helpful to pause here and reflect in more detail on Loder's understanding of the work of the Spirit. Loder's overall enterprise is to consider "the whole scheme of human development . . . from a theological vantage point."[38] He believes that upheavals in the lifespan are upheavals of the nega-

31. Gerhard O. Forde, "Eleventh Locus: The Christian Life," in *Christian Dogmatics*, ed. Carl E. Braaten and Robert W. Jenson, vol. 2 (Philadelphia: Fortress, 1984), p. 429.

32. Forde, "Eleventh Locus," p. 430.

33. Forde, "Eleventh Locus," p. 431.

34. Forde, "Eleventh Locus," p. 431.

35. Forde, "Eleventh Locus," p. 437.

36. Robert W. Jenson, "Eighth Locus: The Holy Spirit," in *Christian Dogmatics*, vol. 2, pp. 130-134.

37. Jenson, "Eighth Locus," p. 134.

38. Loder, *The Logic of the Spirit*, p. 232. Subsequent page references will be given parenthetically in the text.

tion at the base of the ego "and a spiritual cry to behold the face, the Face of God," with each upheaval directing us "away from partial, inadequate, adaptational solutions towards knowing and being known by the Author, the One who made it all" (*Logic of the Spirit,* 232). While Loder refers to upheaval throughout the lifespan, and the work of the Spirit in turning toward the Author, there is something decisive about the way in which he speaks of the Spirit's work in conversion — a genuine newness that has lifelong consequences, a change and transformation that begins a trajectory. For example, the role of the divine Spirit in Kierkegaard's conversion is to gather up Kierkegaard's past and transform it and set a course for the future, a christomorphic experience in which the Spirit conforms Kierkegaard to Christ (234-237). "It was an act of God's Spirit that reaches its culmination only in this transforming moment when the human spirit and all its previous struggles are so permeated by the Divine Spirit that the two become one in 'the transparency' that eliminates despair and grounds the self in faith" (238).

Loder makes a similar claim of a decisive turning point in the life of Luther. He is critical of Erikson's view which understands Luther's "tower experience" as an affirmation of Jesus Christ as the face of God, splitting the ambivalence that Luther has toward his father while recognizing Luther's bond with Scripture as a reunion with his mother (238-242). Loder finds the analysis helpful from a positive point of illumination of the human spirit, but he critiques Erikson for failing to take note of the *Anfechtungen,* the anxiety, guilt, and death, the struggles with God that plagued Luther. Luther needed an answer in terms of the whole lifespan, including confronting his own death, and therefore in terms of the *Spiritus Creator* who heightens the dichotomy between life and death, convicts of sin, and puts one in relationship with God. "This is the mortification of conviction and the way the Spirit begins a work in our lives" (244). Loder takes account of the anguish that accompanies the struggle of working through one's developmental history, dealing with law and love, hidden and revealed, cross and glory, inner conflict of guilt. "The Spirit mortifies in order to redeem by the Word" and the experience is decidedly one in which Luther is passive and God's Spirit is the active agent through the Word of God that brings the presence of Christ and justification (245). The transforming power of the Spirit grasps Luther so that he sees God's face open toward him, Christ present in the Word and in the church. Luther's sense of damnation is reversed by the power of the *Spiritus Creator* (244-245).[39] Loder then goes on to describe the new action that results from this transformation — Luther's writings, the German Reformation, and a transformational logic that transforms the whole life

39. See also Loder, *Transforming Moment,* pp. 144-146.

span. All subsequent stages of Luther's ego development "are now going to be interpreted in the light of the ultimate transformation that has brought Luther's total life under the power of the Spirit" (247).

Loder is inclined to understand Luther's tower experience as the beginning of a totally new way of looking at things, a dramatic change. While in one sense this may be true, theologically it would be helpful if Loder would rather emphasize the ongoing nature of the work of the Spirit as proclamation of the forgiveness of sin, of return to the Word of justification alone. What happened daily for Luther (and for Lutherans today) was not transformation and progression, but rather an up-and-down cycle of dying and being raised to new life, of constantly hearing a Word event in which one is killed and made alive, of being daily restored to relationship with Christ, a proclamation that is ongoing, and that ends only when the work of the Spirit is completed on the other side of death.

For Loder, the relationship with Christ leads to an actual change, transformation, "awakening to one's own particularity and goodness as given by grace" — by grace, to be sure, but genuine goodness. The Christ event calls forth and gives historical concreteness "to the transformational potential of the personality. To put it succinctly, the Christ event is the historical paradigm of transformation."[40] For Luther, the relationship has little to do with awakening to one's own particularity and goodness, and everything to do with clinging to the Word of God's mercy in spite of our lack of goodness — the surprising daily word of forgiveness of sin rooted in the hiddenness of God on the cross for justification. Luther's focus is always on *simul iustus et peccator* — which, in *The Knight's Move,* Loder acknowledges in critique. He correctly complains that, in Luther's theology, the work of the Spirit "is never able to move the believer beyond the persistent paradox that pertains between sinful humanity and the convicting holiness of God's Spirit . . . the Christian is always *simul iustus et peccator.*"[41] Precisely. Hence Luther's view of the Spirit brings Christ and culture into paradox. Loder points out that Calvin does have a genuine transformation role for the Spirit that Luther does not have — Calvin's interpretation of the Holy Spirit as the transforming and unifying link between Christ and all creation, moves us beyond Luther's paradoxical view, and makes Christ the transformer of culture.[42]

Loder wants to find a "kinetic" link that takes into account the dialectical logic of the incarnation, of crucifixion and resurrection, of criticizing and reshaping, in relation to culture. Loder suggests that Kierkegaard breaks out of

40. Loder, *Transforming Moment,* p. 152.

41. Loder, *The Knight's Move,* p. 27.

42. Loder, *The Knight's Move,* pp. 27-28.

the Niebuhrian typologies of paradox and transformer to transcend both.[43] In this, he seems to be attempting to get beyond the traditional Lutheran-Calvinist distinctions.

In any event, there is no question that Loder stands firmly in the Reformation tradition in believing that it is not the work of human beings that enables them to move in the progressive pattern — this indeed is the work of the Spirit and therefore a matter of God's gracious activity. This gift quality of the work of the Spirit and a relational interpretation of the Spirit are warmly appreciated by Lutherans. However, the latter become nervous at a pattern of spiritual development that "moves from *awakening* to *purgation* to *illumination* to *unification,* and at each stage access to the Divine center is enhanced as ego anxiety and strategies of the defense subside."[44] True, in the subsiding of strategies of defense Loder continues to emphasize the relationality, the access of the ego to the divine center, and the centrality of Christology. But he does believe that "spiritual development may be conceived as a way of life in which one increasingly appropriates the bipolar coherence of Christ into one's own nature," recentering the ego to the One who, in his nature, completely holds the mutual indwelling of the divine and the human.[45]

In the last analysis, it is on the issue of *simul iustus et peccator* that the difference from Loder's approach is most notable. In many of Loder's illustrative examples from life and from counseling, the transformational process ends with the agent having a permanent life-changing experience. Conflicted Kay, for example, sees the Christ-like figure, after which her whole life is remarkably and permanently changed.[46] Willa and the young Roman Catholic woman likewise undergo a permanent change/healing.[47] Norma struggles with the loss of her grandmother and with questions of death and non-being, but she is transformed in therapy, and her "voices" never return after the transforming experience.[48] Transformational narratives such as these with a permanent change do not work well in a framework where sanctification has an up-and-down pattern, a daily dying to sin and rising to new life, a need every moment to be killed and raised by the Word.

43. Loder, *The Knight's Move,* p. 65.

44. Loder, *The Knight's Move,* p. 284.

45. Loder, *The Knight's Move,* p. 284.

46. Loder, *The Logic of the Spirit,* pp. 228-229.

47. Loder, *The Logic of the Spirit,* pp. 264-265.

48. Loder, *Transforming Moment,* pp. 175-177. And we could go on with Rita who completed her seminary career and managed to make a break with her boyfriend, pp. 198-199, and Luis who found new life, pp. 204-205, and Kendrick who was able to relate to his mother, pp. 206-207.

Therefore, in any Lutheran tradition, transformational narrative will have this up-and-down quality. While the semantic mediator, B, will indeed change the situation for agent A, and A will indeed be raised to a higher plane, the same pattern will need to be repeated daily, hourly, constantly. Transformational narrative will have a necessarily repetitive or cyclical quality.

Cross and Suffering

Fourth, the final state of agent A will be cruciform. Lutherans hold that the daily pattern of life is one under the cross. Christ's own cross is paradox — the all-powerful God is helpless and seemingly defeated, but to the eyes of faith, here is God's great defeat of sin. God's true nature is revealed in Jesus Christ and yet we recognize God hidden in Christ's humility and suffering. So, too, the Christian life is paradox — we are righteous and yet sinners, ours is a hidden righteousness by faith. We are called to participate daily in cross and suffering for the sake of the gospel and for the sake of other persons and for the world.

This means that in the narrative the final state of agent A may not always be a "happy" higher plane. Certainly Christ, agent B, has won for us a new life and salvation. But the final state will always be one also of cross and suffering. The story may have quite a sober joy or joyful soberness about it. The ending also will not dwell only on the solving of the original conflict, as though the whole point of the narrative is the eventual state of agent A. In fact, we might say that the point of the narrative is actually the work of agent B, and also the call of agent B to agent A to engage the world in speaking the Word, in service, and in prayer. The end of the narrative is really a beginning, on into service of the neighbor.

Finally, in a non-transformational tradition, the purpose for developing and using transformational narratives will be less for the purpose of change and growth in the believer and more for the purpose of proclamation and reassurance of mercy. It will be the repeated message that constitutes what is "new" each day. Transformational narratives will be used for the comfort of those whose conscience troubles them, and who fear the judgment of God. The narratives will be used for the purpose of proclaiming the gospel itself, to speak a good Word of the forgiveness of sin by grace through faith.

Conclusion

With these guidelines, transformational narrative can indeed be used as a valuable tool in Christian education, even in traditions that normally avoid the term "transformation" in their theological discourse. The narrative structure is able to be grasped and retained by age levels and persons who otherwise may not be able to appropriate the gospel readily.[49] It can be used in pastoral care, as Loder so well testifies. It is an excellent teaching tool by which to communicate clearly a grace-centered, Christ-centered message of the gospel for all age levels.

49. Krych, *Teaching the Gospel Today,* chap. 4.

11. A Summary of James E. Loder's Theory of Christian Education

Russell Haitch

This essay summarizes James Loder's theory of education. It explains his critique of approaches based on socialization and his proposal that education "in the logic of the Spirit" must become *transformational, four dimensional,* and *christocentric.*

After Forty Years

After teaching Christian education for nearly forty years, Loder began turning his lecture notes into his first book directly on this field. While his previously published work on the dynamics of transformation had cast significant light on educational ministry, the manuscript on which he worked in his final days was to make his theory and convictions more explicit. It was not fully ready for publication when he died, nor were many of us — his students, friends, and colleagues — ready to end our conversation with him. However, one theme he had often stressed was the need to allow *kairos,* God's fullness of time, to redefine *chronos,* sequential clock time. From that perspective, perhaps the frustration of unfinished creation testifies both to the hope that God will bring all things to completion and to a ready reliance on the Spirit who helps us in our weakness.

The editors of this volume asked me to sum up, within the limits of a single essay, the basic ideas and movements of the unpublished book. I have already implied the most important thing: that for Loder, the Spirit of Christ is both center and circumference of Christian education. He says that educational ministry ought to be done according to the "logic of the Spirit,"[1] and that such

1. The working title of his book is *Educational Ministry in the Logic of the Spirit.*

education will be *transformational, four dimensional,* and *christocentric.* I will now try to explain what he means.

Nearly forty years ago, back in 1965, Edward Farley wrote two articles for *Religious Education,* both entitled: "Does Christian Education Need the Holy Spirit?" Farley's arch response was: No. First, he noted a bad tendency in the field to confuse the process of "instruction" with that of "nurture." This confusion was not detrimental for those religious educators in the nineteenth and early twentieth centuries who held humanistic goals, because for them both processes tended toward the same end — formation of character and development of human powers. But in his day, said Farley, nurture proponents tended also to be theologically neo-orthodox, and so their goal was divine salvation and sanctification. Toward this end they summoned the Holy Spirit. Here "the formula seems to be, Christian education plus Holy Spirit equals salvation or sanctification. When this is the case the Holy Spirit becomes a kind of *explanation* for the X-factor in salvation not covered by human efforts."[2] Yet this sort of explanation explains nothing about the process of education. It is like trying to explain the process of farming by saying the farmer's goal is to glorify God, or that the farmer relies on the Holy Spirit. Granted that church instruction is not identical with instruction outside the church, still one can name worthy *educational* goals, such as intellectual development and understanding Christian faith, and for these goals "the Holy Spirit is simply superfluous in the program of Church education."[3]

Various rejoinders ensued from veterans in the field who felt impugned by young Farley. For young Loder, however, the charges had some merit. If "Christian education" were to be more than instruction, then the Holy Spirit needed to be seen as more than a nebulous "X-factor" called in to bless and grant success to an otherwise human-centered approach. From the very start, thinking about education needed to be grounded in thinking about the Holy Spirit. This Spirit-centered approach was the Copernican revolution Loder envisioned. The relationality between Holy Spirit and human spirit would then become the crux of education. But that path meant Loder could not offer a theory of education without first making theological and anthropological preparations. It also meant pursuing a different agenda. Educators at this time were often busy weighing the first concern Farley named: Should "education" be understood as church school instruction or as the overall formation of a Christian way of life? The question continues, and the answer is usually some form of

2. Edward Farley, "Does Christian Education Need the Holy Spirit?" *Religious Education* 60, 6 (Nov.-Dec. 1965): 430.

3. Farley, "Does Christian Education Need the Holy Spirit?" p. 431.

both — education means both instruction (e.g., promoting biblical literacy) and an ongoing process of socialization, enculturation, or nurture into the life of faith. In short, it is both information and formation. But Loder was concerned with *transformation.* For this is the word that expressed for him how the Holy Spirit and human spirit work. (Loder did not employ this trio of words — information, formation, and transformation — as I have here; I hope that it is heuristic.)

Was Loder's approach thus akin to those of earlier revivalists and evangelists? Clearly personal "regeneration" epitomizes transformation.[4] At the same time, he eschews any approach that is "individualistic" or "isolationist,"[5] because the aim is for humanity to participate in God's transformation of all creation, in a way that includes physical, psychical, social and cultural dimensions.[6] Further, Loder objects to what he calls "socialized evangelism," the intentional attempt to bring about conversion "through natural means."[7] As a paramount concern, therefore, he wants to distinguish socialization from transformation. His theory's leitmotif is the "dynamic interaction" of these "two great powers of human experience."[8]

Socialization and Death

Concerning socialization and transformation, he builds his case with care. In C. Ellis Nelson's influential book, *Where Faith Begins* (1967), Loder finds a theory of education that is socialization par excellence. Nelson understands that instruction should not be confused with nurture, but he still wants to keep education large in goal and broad in scope. He says the aim of Christian education is to engender a Christian lifestyle, where "lifestyle" refers not to the fashion section of a magazine, but rather (following A. N. Whitehead's notion of style as the fashioning of power) to how all the energy of a human lifetime is directed. Loder agrees with this aim and claims it as his own. The telos of education is not just passing on information, or even instilling values, but rather creating a whole way of life. Nelson contends this creation can occur through socialization. After all, socialization was what happened in biblical times, when people wrote the law on doorposts and highway stones, when parents told their children about God at bedtime. Through the social sciences, today's educators

4. Manuscript (hereafter MS), chap. 9, p. 9; cf. chap. 9, p. 3.

5. MS, chap. 6, p. 2.

6. MS, chap. 9, p. 9.

7. MS, chap. 1, p. 18.

8. MS, chap. 1, p. 3.

can understand the socialization process better and manipulate it to advantage. Here Loder strongly disagrees. To be sure, socialization does occur all the time, for good or ill, as educators need be aware; when speaking of youth education, for example, it is vital to include parents in the picture. The problem, however, is that overall the forces of socialization are both more powerful and deadly than people realize.

Loder makes this point with both logic and anecdote. Following P. Berger and T. Luckman, "socialization" may be defined as all the processes, both conscious and unconscious, both interpersonal and socio-cultural, by which people become inducted and inculcated into the larger contexts of society.[9] In these processes of interaction between organism and environment, the drive is toward balanced functioning, pattern maintenance, tension reduction — equilibrium. Thinking it through to logical conclusion, how shall we depict this quiescence? The image may come to mind of a person sitting calmly, breathing steadily in and out, in and then out; but really one must go further, to the image of a flat line on the heart monitor. Socialization, if it drives toward equilibration, drives toward death, and, in the largest context of the natural order, toward entropy and death of the universe. This is the cosmic backdrop to Loder's claim that socialization incorporates death.

In the near term, the power of "death" at work in socialization is witnessed in sundry ways. It was evident to Loder from social science research into the authoritarian personality. This was the sort of research that tried to demonstrate how ordinary people could become good Nazis — what H. Arendt called the "banality of evil." Consider, for example, Stanley Milgram's research at Yale University.[10] Milgram asked for volunteers from the New Haven area to participate in a "learning" experiment. They were paid $4.50 (in the late 1950s, a fair sum) and told they would be contributing to the cause of learning at Yale. Money, science, and learning were all potent social attractors. The experimental paradigm involved having these participants administer what they thought were extremely painful electric shocks to another volunteer. In fact, the other person was an actor and the shocks were mild, but the participants did not know this up front; to them he was simply another volunteer, a cordial man about fifty years old who mentioned something about a heart condition, but was willing to go along with the procedure. In their social role as "teachers," the participants were told to punish errors made by the "learner" (actor), by ad-

9. Peter L. Berger and Thomas Luckman, *The Social Construction of Reality: A Treatise in the Sociology of Knowledge* (New York: Doubleday, 1967), pp. 130-131.

10. The following description of this experiment is based on Philip G. Zimbardo and Richard Gerrig, *Psychology and Life* (New York: Longman, 1999), pp. 793-799.

ministering the shocks. They were told that this experiment would test how pain influences a person's ability to learn. Of course something else was really being tested.

The would-be learner was strapped to an "electric chair" in the next room and communicated with the teacher via intercom. Each teacher was given a sample shock of 45 volts. Then the testing began. The learner's task was to memorize pairs of words; for example, "when I say *blue,* you say *sky;* when I say *tree,* you say *leaf.*" As P. Zimbardo and R. Gerrig recount: "The learner soon began making errors, according to a prearranged schedule, and the teacher began shocking the learner. The protests of the victim rose with the shock level. At 75 volts, he began to moan and grunt; at 150 volts he demanded to be released . . . ; at 180 volts, he cried out that he could not stand the pain any longer. At 300 volts, he insisted that he would not take part in the experiment any longer and must be freed. He yelled out about his heart condition and screamed. If a teacher hesitated or protested delivering the next shock, the experimenter said, 'The experiment requires that you continue' or 'You have no other choice; you *must* go on.'"[11]

A panel of psychiatrists was asked to estimate, prior to the experiment, how far the "teachers" would go in giving volts to someone for missing questions. The scale on the voltmeter went up to 450 volts. The psychiatrists predicted that fewer than 4 percent would comply at 300 volts, and only about 0.1 percent would go all the way to 450 volts, potentially killing the learner. But what happened? How many people went up to 300 volts with the learner crying, "I've got a heart condition, get me out of here!" One hundred percent. No one quit below 300 volts, 78 percent went beyond 300, and 65 (*not* 0.1) percent went all the way to 450 volts. As Loder put it, "all because the learner could not remember the connection between blue and sky. All because Stanley Milgram stands over there in a white coat and says, 'I will take responsibility.' *In the name of science, Yale and $4.50, go ahead — electrocute him!* That's the power of socialization in a scientific culture."[12]

Countless other illustrations could be given; the basic point is that the prevailing socio-cultural milieux also permeate and shape the empirical church. The forces of socialization engulf educators' feeble efforts to manipulate them. Church leaders may think they are running the socialization machine, when actually it is running them. Instead of creating a "Christian lifestyle," a church may be reinforcing various death-dealing lifestyles of society in the name of Christianity. In the original write-up of his experiment, Milgram

11. Zimbardo and Gerrig, *Psychology and Life,* p. 794.

12. MS, chap. 2.

suggested that the subjects might have capitulated because they lacked a language of nonconformity. But here he was looking for a cultural solution. One participant was a graduate of Princeton Theological Seminary, who presumably had been well schooled in the Christian language of nonconformity. Nevertheless, he decided to administer 450 volts. The dynamics of socialization are more insistent than human words. For this reason, the "challenging" and "prophetic" Sunday morning sermon can become a cathartic experience that inoculates listeners against a real encounter with God, returning them safely to the current social order.[13]

Adapting the social theory of T. Parsons, Loder mapped out the entire field of human action in terms of four isomorphic and interrelated processes of socialization: organic, psychical, social, and cultural (see fig. 1 on p. 304). By drawing on a range of other theorists, and through poignant real-life vignettes, he explained the socialized lifestyles of Western culture that can come to dominate churches, correlating these lifestyles with the neo-Parsonian quadrants. There was, and is, the *achievement-oriented lifestyle,* which gets obsessed with goal-getting and earning love; second, the *authoritarian lifestyle,* which engenders forced conformity to external social standards; third, the *protean lifestyle* generated by postmodern cultural diffusion, whereby the flood of images and fluidity of values give rise to a restless but cynical search for meaning; and fourth, the *oppressed lifestyle,* where initiative and creativity are squelched as the organic drive for survival saps all energy. None of these is a Christian lifestyle. Rather, they represent, respectively, a perversion of love, power, freedom, and self-control; they all distort or outright contradict the gospel. Yet Loder emphasized that this is the path of socialization, and the course of church education when it follows that path.

Loder watched an ironic drama unfold in his own field, as year after year he lectured students on the imposing power of socialization. A new trend was taking place: increasingly and with enthusiasm, educators and theologians began speaking of "transformation," the very word he had championed from long

13. Further examples of socialization's power can be found in this volume. In his essay, John McClure draws on the theories of J. Derrida and E. Levinas to say how the preacher's "counterscript" (W. Brueggemann's term) may work to co-opt the "other." The sermon's putative "social unraveling" is actually determined in terms of the social bond and serves to reinforce it.

In his essay, Robert Martin draws on the theory of F. Lyotard to describe how notions of "effective" church leadership are determined by prevailing business paradigms, since there is a tendency for churches uncritically to adopt capitalist ideology and strategies. These former students of Loder have put his critique of socialization into conversation with streams of postmodern theory.

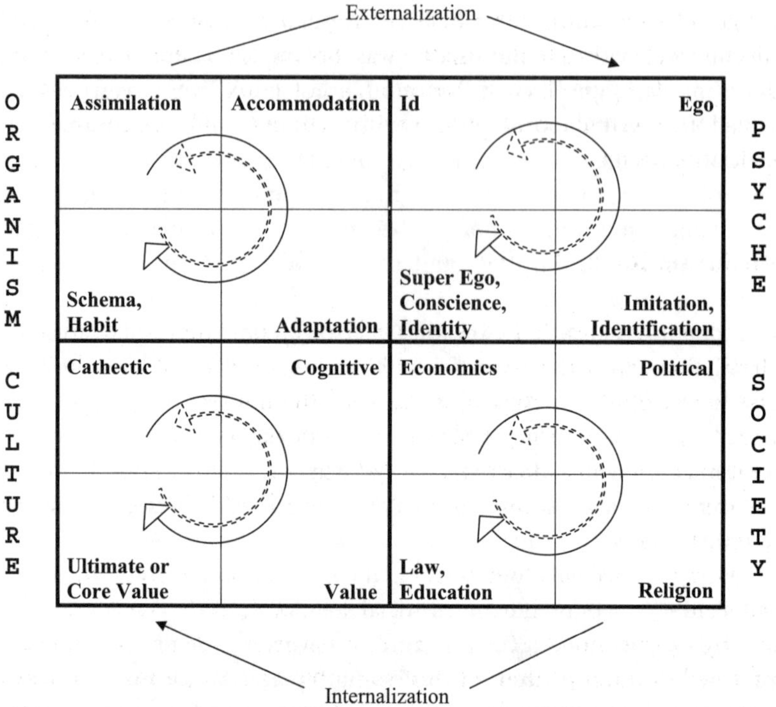

Figure 1: This diagram comes from the social theory of T. Parsons. It depicts all human action in terms of four systems that work together (simultaneously): organism, psyche, society and culture. The four systems are isomorphic, each being a miniature of the whole. The circular arrows show how: (a) raw, restless needs and striving . . . (b) come into contact with external constrictions . . . (c) and out of this interaction, an equilibrium emerges . . . (d) giving rise to patterns of reinforcement. The dotted line arrows show there is feedback.

ago. However, the irony was that transformation often became merely a new name for the old socialization approaches. Transformation meant simply change in a positive direction;[14] and religious educators often proposed that one could arrive at the desired transformation by way of socialization — by a process of nurture, formation, or enculturation into the faith (for example,

14. In MS, chap. 2, Loder points to M. Sawicki *(The Gospel in History)*, A. Moore *(Religious Education as Social Transformation)*, and D. Browning *(A Fundamental Practical Theology)* as examples of theologians who emphasize the centrality of transformation. He adds: "At the same time, there is no corresponding emphasis upon the presence and power of the Holy Spirit or upon the human spirit by which transformation must be understood if it is to mean anything more than a crypto-Hegelian move in a positive direction."

through reflective engagement in churchly practices). Hence the power of socialization was evident in the putative way it could digest and excrete "transformation" as its by-product. In writing his last book, Loder said part of his agenda was to save the concept of transformation from being co-opted by the socialization camp.

Transformation and Spirit

I have spent some time in this essay sketching out the problem Loder sought to address, although if this were one of his courses we would be at it for some weeks longer. With M. Polyani, he believed that indwelling the problem was propaedeutic to discovering a solution, even one mapped out ahead of time. Yet once it has been seen sufficiently how and why socialization fails, the next steps are to explain (1) transformation and (2) the relationship between socialization and transformation.

Why is transformation so good? One could turn directly to Scripture, where Paul says, "do not be conformed to this world, but be transformed by the renewing of your mind" (Rom. 12:2). In other words, do not be socialized or conformed to sinful patterns of this world, but be transformed into new creation. Granted the importance of this text, Loder wanted also to explain transformation in terms of human science. Even here scriptural language gives a pointer: the Greek word for transformation entails change in the *morphē* or essential form of something, as opposed to change in its *schēma* or perceptual form. (This language is not meant to impel an idealist or essentialist philosophy; the "essential forms" may be, and for Loder certainly are, inherently relational.) Thus Loder notes that the purpose of transformation is the emergence of new essential forms, and "the process of transformation is governed by the desire to discover hidden orders of meaning within a given frame of reference that have the power to redefine and reconstruct that frame of reference."[15] The priority of transformation was evident to him everywhere in the natural order, and especially through psychology. Take any developmental stages you like, he offered — whether those of Piaget, Erikson, Levinson, Kohlberg, Gilligan, or Fowler — and you will find that the real action resides not in the stages themselves, but in the transformative movement from one stage to the next. As soon

15. James Loder and Russell Haitch, "ED 105 Educational Ministry: Overview" (course syllabus, Spring 2000). Cf. MS, chap. 4, p. 7: "we would define transformation as follows: Within a given frame of knowledge [and experience], transformation is a patterned process whereby hidden, internally coherent orders of meaning are awakened and empowered to reconstruct that original frame of knowledge and experience."

as a person reaches any stage, she or he starts moving toward the next. This dynamism, which Piaget recognized, has received more recent attention, leading some scholars to insert intermediate stages into old paradigms, and others to question the concept of stages altogether. The basic point here is that transformation is even more definitive of the human spirit than socialization.

And here we hit bedrock: ultimately Loder's case for transformation rests on its relatedness to spirit, and hence to relationality, creativity, and the *imago dei.* I will try to chart the movements of his case as I see them. First, we begin in God, who is Spirit, and with the theological premise that the Holy Spirit is the Teacher: "It is the Holy Spirit by whom the Scriptures become the Word of God. It is the Holy Spirit who brings Jesus Christ out of the remoteness of history, creating faith through grace. This is our epistemology. For all that pertains to teaching and learning in the Christian context, our fundamental epistemology and guiding assumption has to be: The Holy Spirit leads us into all Truth."[16]

Second, human beings, created in God's image, are also spirit. This is his fundamental anthropology. After working as his teaching assistant one semester, I met with Dr. Loder before the final preceptorials, to ask him: "What is the most important thing you hope students will have learned in this course?" He replied: "To see themselves as spirit." For as he saw it, humans are spirit more than they are reason, consciousness, or even experience. He tried to teach this truth not propositionally, but through experiences of puzzlement and discovery.

What, then, is "spirit"? The human spirit is best characterized as *creativity.* In his survey of the human spirit in Western thought, G. Thomas finds that the spirit has been equated with reason, love (particularly eros), personality, universality, freedom, and creativity. Loder chooses the last as the mode that includes the others and more. If we press further to ask, But what is creativity? then I think we must come to Loder's emphasis on *relationality.* Human creativity resides in the spirit's inherent relationality. We are not only egocentric, self-relating, but also exocentric, relating to what is beyond us. Thus in *The Logic of the Spirit,* Loder suggests that "human spirit" is well characterized as "openness to the world and self-transcendence."[17] Meanwhile in *The Knight's Move,* he says ("with a debt of gratitude to W. Pannenberg") that the human spirit is "a dynamic tension between 'centeredness' and 'openness.'"[18] To define

16. MS, chap. 5, pp. 1-2. (See John 16:13.)

17. *The Logic of the Spirit: Human Development in Theological Perspective* (San Francisco: Jossey-Bass, 1998), p. 5. The term "exocentricity" is used by W. Pannenberg; Loder commends his discussion of the human spirit, but notes that he, like Hegel, mistakenly conflates Holy Spirit and human spirit.

18. With W. Jim Neidhardt, *The Knight's Move: The Relational Logic of the Spirit in Theology and Science* (Colorado Springs: Helmers & Howard, 1992), p. 53.

the spirit in words may be like trying to catch the wind in a net, so let the present congeries suffice: the human spirit has or is creativity, relationality, exocentricity, openness, self-transcendence. Now the further take-away idea here is that humanity, spirit, and transformation go together. The dynamics of transformation point to spirit, and spirit points back to the fact that transformation is even more definitive of what it means to be human than is socialization. Further, Loder asserts, this fact can be established through human and hard sciences, even without recourse to theology.

Third, the "starting point" of Loder's constructive proposal for Christian education, and for all of practical theology, thus becomes an "analogy of the Spirit."[19] Here he turns back to Scripture, finding that humanity's creation "in the image of God" (Gen. 1:27) can be said to indicate that the human spirit is the image of the divine Spirit. Even more explicitly, an analogy is seen where Paul likens the Spirit of God who searches the deep things of God to the spirit of the person who searches the deep things of the person (1 Cor. 2:10-11). Then too, in Romans, Paul writes, "It is the Spirit bearing witness with our spirit that we are children of God" (8:16); and in Philippians, "work out your salvation with fear and trembling for God is at work in you" (2:12-13). Loder explicates such passages in terms of Reformed concepts of "analogy" rather than Eastern Orthodox concepts of "synergism"; but regarding the latter, he does speak of humanity's vocation as participation in the divine life. In the end, there is to be not just an analogy between human spirit and Holy Spirit, but an intense and intimate relationality. The ultimate goal of Christian education is a Christian lifestyle, but such a lifestyle entails nothing less than the transformation of daily life into an act of worship.[20]

Fourth, between the starting point and this end there falls the human condition. Created in the image of God, people are inherently and consumingly creative. But separated from the Spirit of God, the human spirit becomes "a kind of loose cannon of creativity."[21] Unaided human ingenuity can propagate amazing changes, as seen, for instance, in the scientific and technological explosion. We can invent vaccines to cure diseases, or methods of germ warfare to spread them. We can devise plans to help the poor or schemes to exploit them. We can transform a wilderness into a vibrant city or a city into an unwholesome site of various forms of violence. If socialization processes tend toward death, while transformational attempts so easily backfire or fall prey to blind spots, then one is confronted with the need for a pretty stringent doctrine of

19. MS, chap. 5, p. 1.
20. "ED 105 Educational Ministry: Overview" (course syllabus, Spring 2000).
21. *The Logic of the Spirit,* p. 36.

human sin as a basic element of Christian education. However, before rallying to some predictable "Reformed" or "neo-orthodox" position, one does well to reflect that from Loder's perspective the ambiguity of human creativity is genuine, as is his desire to esteem the human spirit's ingenuity. Doctrines of sin can themselves become sinful when they fail to heighten our appreciation for the human spirit's God-given capacities — capacities that in sum point to the underlying capacity for creativity and relationality.

Loder witnessed the human spirit at work in the times of therapeutic counseling that became integral to his educational research. As a psychologist, he had the psychologist's respect for neurosis, for the way that it evinces the human spirit's remarkable creativity, its ability to call forth solutions to the most intractable of problems, the most horrendous of traumas — solutions that so often are intelligent, even poetic, in form, at the same time they careen toward self-destruction. The neurosis is not without rhyme or reason, and therapeutic understanding does in some measure yield power to choose for or against it. Still, a long-term, realistic appraisal must take note that ultimately the self can choose only between formats of self-destruction. Neurosis and sin are not the same thing, but both point to fissures of relationality and to the inability of the self to ground itself in the face of death, whether that death is ontic, moral, or spiritual. There are problems even the human spirit, for all its creativity, cannot conquer.

The Christomorphic Pattern of Relationality

Given the foregoing understanding of transformation, it is important now to reintroduce the concept of socialization, to see how the two processes are related. It should be quite evident that Loder is not saying that one process is all good, the other all bad; for both are ambiguous. Transformation can fall prey to evil, and socialization, it must be acknowledged, is needed for survival. Through processes of socialization people learn behavioral patterns, social roles, and ego strengths. Schools and factories, farms and governments all run on socialization power — the ability to induct and inculcate new members into adaptational patterns of thinking and doing. Moreover, it needs to be seen how the processes of transformation and socialization are quite inseparable. There is no socialization that does not call upon transformations, and no transformation that does not presuppose some base of socialization.[22] New forms (trans-

22. MS, chap. 2, p. 2. These statements refer to people, since God can transform nothing, creating *ex nihilo*.

formation) are premised on previous patterns of adaptation (socialization); while equilibrium (socialization) requires the ability to create new order (transformation).

Socialization and transformation, and their interrelation, can be illustrated in many ways, but I may as well explain Loder's idea by retelling one of his favorite stories. Right after the birth of his second daughter, the infant became exceedingly active, waving her arms, kicking her feet, and screaming at the top of her lungs, to the point that even the nurse became disconcerted. Then the baby was given back to the mother, who said softly: "Hi, there" — and all at once the crying stopped. The child was accustomed to this voice, having heard it many times within the womb, and now this familiar sound enabled her to cope with a radically upsetting personal situation, namely the trauma of being born. The maternal voice was a socializing force engendering equilibrium. So entrenched is the process of socialization that it begins before birth. The success of the process, however, depends on the organism's ability for transformation. Here the voice in the womb was associated with the voice in the world, and this association of two previously-unrelated frames of reference, womb and world, is a creative act of transformation. The speechless infant, as if sensing, "I can be at home here for the moment," finds calm equilibrium. The maternal voice is a socializing force, but its appropriation a transformative action.[23]

Now what happens if we step back and look at such experiences from a structural standpoint? First, there is an inseparable unity between socialization and transformation. At the same time, there is an indissoluble difference — they are polar opposites, united but not to be confused. Third, the relationship between the two is asymmetrical, in that transformation has conceptual priority (being more basic to the human spirit). By now the student of theology may have had an "aha!" moment. Especially if the student has studied the early Councils, or drank deeply from the wells of Kierkegaard or Barth, it becomes apparent that the relationship of transformation and socialization resembles *in pattern* the description of Christ's divine and human natures given by the Council of Chalcedon in 451.

Any reader of Loder becomes quickly aware how central this pattern is to his thinking. He finds this christomorphic pattern at every intellectual turn (see figure 2 on p. 310). For example, as a psychologist he is an interactionist: in the questions of nature versus nurture, organism versus environment, the answer is both — but the real question is how in the relationality between the two does development occur? This relationality he understood as a bipolar, asymmetri-

23. While Loder would tell this story to demonstrate the power of socialization, I have added to the interpretation to evince the organism's innate power of transformation.

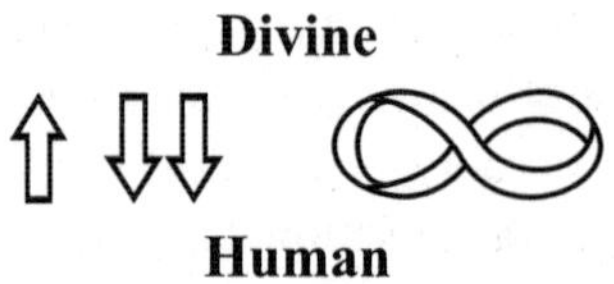

Christian Transformation Theory

Education Socialization Practice

Figure 2: In these illustrations of bipolar, asymmetrical relational unity, the arrows point in both directions to show dynamic relationality. The two arrows on one side show that the structure is asymmetrical, while the Moebius band [to be inserted] shows it is a unity (even as the band itself has only one side).

cal unity. Transformation and socialization are also, as we have just said, a bipolar, asymmetrical, relational unity. Mind and body are a bipolar, asymmetrical, relational unity (where perhaps the spirit who relates the two is itself relationality personified, yielding a trinitarian anthropology).[24] Holy Spirit and human spirit (in, e.g., Romans 8) can likewise be seen as a bipolar, asymmetrical, relational unity. The eternal Church and empirical church are in bipolar, asymmetrical, relational unity. In preaching, God's Word and biblical texts become a bipolar, asymmetrical, relational unity. In physics, wave theory and particle theory comprise a bipolar, asymmetrical, relational unity. In every field, theory and practice form a bipolar, asymmetrical, relational unity. On and on the pattern reverberates, and at some point in class lectures or personal conversation, Loder would exclaim: the reality *is relationality!* He was wedded to this conviction and urged it on all to accept the basic insight that relationality is reality, even if they did not right away embrace either the Chalcedonian descrip-

24. Cf. 1 Thess. 5:23. Loder's anthropology often resembled a Reformed body-and-soul duality, though I am suggesting that a Byzantine "trichotomist" (or better put, "trinitarian") anthropology is more consistent with his approach; our conversation on this matter was unfinished. As a further footnote, the word "mind" in Loder's theory may refer to the "soul" as distinct from the "body," whereas in Byzantine writings *nous* can be translated as either mind or spirit; in the latter case, the trinitarian scheme would be one of spirit, soul, and body. Cf. John Meyendorf, *Byzantine Theology* (New York: Fordham University Press, 1979), p. 141: "a majority of Byzantine theologians describe man in terms of a trichotomist scheme: spirit (or mind), soul, body. Their trichotomism is very directly connected with the notion of participation in God as the basis of anthropology."

tion of Christ or its specific pattern of relationality. While foremost a Christian, Loder was also immersed in the currents of postmodern thought. Thus, in moving away from seeing reality in terms of "substances," he tended to use the term "relationality" rather than relationship when wishing to connote dynamic interplay and coinherence — consistent with Byzantine notions of *perichoresis, circumincessio* and *koinonia,* as well as scientific field theories.[25] For that reason, in each of the examples just cited, one could speak either of a "relational unity" or a "unified relationality," just as in trinitarian theology one may focus on either the unity of the Godhead or the distinctness of the Persons.

I would add a word about the term "asymmetrical" in this pattern. Especially to those concerned for an ethic of equality, it may sound as if the pattern invites dominance. But returning to the Chalcedonian depiction, we recall that Jesus Christ is fully human as well as fully God. Though in respects the two natures are polar opposites — for example, divine is infinite, human is finite — still they are unified. They are asymmetrical in that the "divine" has priority. The "divine" certainly does not oppress or squelch the "human"; yet an orthodox Christology requires that one start with the divinity of Jesus to know his humanity. If one starts with humanity and evaluates within his social context such claims as "I and the Father are one," then one may conclude that he is deranged, or a blasphemer; but starting from the other direction one can see that his divinity defines, or redefines, what it means to be truly human, reflecting God's image.

This christomorphic pattern recurs often in Loder's thought and has direct bearing on his educational theory. His final unpublished book can be seen as part of a trilogy on the "logic of the Spirit."[26] In *The Knight's Move,* his topic is the large sphere of science and theology, viewed through the logic of the Spirit. Next he moves to the realm of human science, addressing psychological development in the logic of the Spirit; and finally turns to the specific agenda of educational ministry in the logic of the Spirit. The focus shifts, but the "logic" stays consistent: in each case, the creative and relational human spirit comes to fulfillment in its relationality with the Holy Spirit. And in each case the pattern of this Holy Spirit and human spirit relationality is christomorphic — a bipolar, asymmetrical unity. Thus pneumatological and christological dimensions converge.

In returning now to educational ministry, it may be said that "Christian" and "education" also represent a bipolar, asymmetrical, relational unity. Were it

25. For a review of "substance" and "relationality" in Western philosophy, see F. LeRon Shults's essay in this volume. See also Loder, *The Knight's Move,* chap. 13.

26. I thank Dana Wright for prompting me to underscore this point.

not so, then from our foregoing discussion it would certainly appear that "Christian education" is an oxymoron. For what is "education" but deliberate formalized socialization? Society educates in order to induct and inculcate, so that people become well-adjusted, successfully functioning members of the social order. But what is "Christian" if not transformation? To be "Christian" means not to be conformed to predetermined patterns of this world (Rom. 12:2), but transformed by a "new mind" that creates new forms, new order reflecting God's reign. The bipolar opposition of socialization and transformation, and thus of "education" and "Christian," is seen also in the way that one process drives toward stasis — the reduction of tension within a system and maintenance of predetermined adaptational patterns; while the other drives toward re-creation — the emergence of new patterns and new essential forms, even at the cost of conflict, heightened tension, and greater intensity.

The paradox is resolved through the pattern of relationality just named, where much hinges on its being asymmetrical. Will transformations of the human spirit become co-opted by forces of socialization, or will socialization become the basis for godly transformation? That is, will there be transformation unto socialization, or socialization unto transformation? It must be the latter, if we are to have *Christian* education. But if it is to be Christian education, then the transformation must involve more than the human spirit. For human transformations, it has been pointed out, are ambiguous, allotropic, sinful. Therefore, transformations of the human spirit *must themselves be transformed* through the Holy Spirit. This is what Loder means when he says that Christian education must become "four dimensional." Having established the *transformational* aspect of Loder's theory, let me make more explicit this second assertion — that education is to be *four dimensional.*

"Four Dimensional" and "Christocentric"

The first two dimensions are "self" and "lived world." The self is social, cultural, biological, and psychological. In its interactions, the human spirit achieves remarkable transformations, including the seminal creation of an "ego," which balances psychical reality over against environmental reality. However, the ego is based on negation of the "other" and repression of the longing to love. In saying "I," the ego says, "not you" and "not You." The negation and repression seen in ego development is but one example of, one pointer toward, the third dimension of human existence — the void. The "void" refers to absence of being. Its faces include death, loneliness, and despair. As the third dimension of existence, the void negates the first two. The void is manifest *within* human transformations, in the "double binds" created by the psyche's ego defenses, society's role structures, and culture's root metaphors or master images: in each case, they are needed for survival, but they drive toward death. Ultimately the void issues a blanket negation *of* human transformations, negating the human spirit's attempt to ground life in self and world.

However, there is a fourth dimension — the Holy. The Holy negates and transforms the void. In Loder's writings, "the Holy" can refer both to God and human encounters with God; both to the Hebrew *qādôsh,* separateness from the mundane world, and (following R. Otto) to the fascination and mystery of supramundane experience. Certainly the Holy exceeds the bounds of human religious expressions. Likewise, from the perspective Loder offers, it would be futile to postulate that the Holy can be found in all or even most of the world's religions; this idea might seem reasonable, but the Holy shows up to shatter human ideas of reasonableness. Thus the Holy is to be apprehended not primarily in terms of human ideas about religion, but through God's self-revelation, and so ultimately the Holy refers to the Holy Spirit. Nor is the Holy Spirit ever a "generic" spirit, but always the Spirit of Christ, who unites the universal and the particular. The Holy is thus a proper noun.

In the realm of experience, the Holy receives its sharpest and clearest definition in the context of the void: "when the Holy appears in the context of the void, you know you had nothing to do with it."[27] Grace is recognized as thoroughly gracious, and in this way even the void itself becomes gracious. In this way too, negation itself is supremely transformed. Thus, to take the case of ego development, the negation inherent in the ego's creation needs in turn to be negated, so that the ego can be transformed into dialectical identity with God. When Christ mediates this negation and transformation, one can say as Paul did, "I, not I, but Christ" (Gal. 2:20). The self is not swallowed up (for Paul goes on to depict a dialectical identity: "the life *I* live in the body"), but is rather freed to receive and give love.[28]

Here we come to Loder's assertion that Christian education must become not only *transformational* and *four dimensional,* but also *christocentric.* In one respect, this assertion is patent, since we are talking about *Christian* education. But more should be said, since Loder's theory runs counter to those who would foster interfaith commonality by treating Christian education as a subset of religious education. Perhaps many mainline theorists might follow Loder to the

27. MS, chap. 5, p. 23.

28. For a fuller discussion of these dynamics of negation and transformation, see my previous essay in this volume, "'Trampling Down Death by Death': Double Negation in Developmental Theory and Baptismal Theology."

point of agreeing that education must be transformational and four dimensional and that the Holy Spirit is the Teacher — but then object to this final assertion, that the Holy Spirit is the Spirit of Jesus Christ, and therefore education, to be truly redemptive, must be christocentric. By this assertion Loder does not mean that the subject matter is always explicitly Christ, but rather that "subject matter of even the most secular sort will yield to the four dimensional, transformational perspective of Christ."[29] Nevertheless, in an ethos of postmodernism and relativism, this christocentric constancy seems destined to cause conflict. If a stumbling block, still it is integral to his theory. As further clarification, however, it was evident from Loder's lectures that his focus was not on attacking the world's religions, but instead on calling churches, especially mainline ones, to a kind of repentance. For them a lack of Christ-centeredness may manifest the church's attempt to adapt to society's ethos of relativism; however, he warns, "a church immersed in . . . adaptation to main stream society is foredoomed to extinction."[30]

I think Loder's case for christocentricity has what might be called both a "pattern" trajectory and a "power" trajectory, even as structuralist and charismatic concerns coalesced in his mind. The "pattern trajectory" moves from trinitarian to christomorphic, and then from christomorphic to christocentric. Science has discovered relationality, but relationality is found in theology long before, in the perichoresis of the Trinity, and the relationality of Christ's divine and human natures. Contemporary society may presume that science has also, since Einstein, discovered that everything is relative, but Loder notes how Einstein's theory of relativity makes the speed of light an invariant and universal constant. (Einstein may have preferred his theory be called the *Invarianz-Theorie,* to avoid "philosophical misunderstandings.")[31] Moving from the created light of Einstein to the uncreated light of God, Loder reasons that the logic of the Spirit revealed in Jesus Christ is the universal constant in human affairs. How are we to understand the relationality of transformation and socialization? According to the pattern of Christ's divine and human natures. How are we to understand four-dimensional transformation, in which the negative element in human transformation is itself negated and positively reconstituted? According to the pattern of Christ's death-defeating death and resurrection. Now if one comes to the conviction that these patterns are not just abstractions, but actualities, then one's approach moves from being christomorphic to christocentric.

29. MS, chap. 9, p. 10.

30. MS, chap. 7, p. 3.

31. See *The Knight's Move,* p. 31.

The "power trajectory" starts with recalling the nearly insuperable power of socialization. In all the literature, Loder says, the theory of Thomas Groome most closely parallels his own. In *Christian Religious Education: Sharing Our Story and Vision,* Groome proposes a way for human freedom to be transformed into freedom in and with God. Loder commends Groome's emphasis on social praxis; like Groome, he is concerned with both individual and community, both theory and practice. However, when Groome writes, "our religious education must promote a critical reflective activity,"[32] here Loder detects what he calls "potentially the major weakness in Groome's approach." For "usually critical consciousness is not enough to transcend the dynamics of socialization."[33] It is not enough to put the story and vision of the faith tradition into critical correlation with the story and vision of the contemporary faith community. The power of socialization will overwhelm the power of critical reflection.[34] If, for example, an authoritarian lifestyle governs the community, then these dynamics will thwart or distort the community's development of critical consciousness. A power greater than the community is needed, which means that education needs to take place not just in the context of story-telling and vision-sharing, but in the locus of prayer and worship, where the power of the Holy Spirit is consciously invoked. Moreover, people must see themselves not just as free agents, but as "spirit" able to respond to this Spirit. Here we return to the earlier point, that this Spirit is not generic, but the Spirit of Christ (who mediates universal and particular, transcendent and immanent), and thus Christian education must be christocentric to receive power enough to enact God's reign.

Implications for Practical Theology and Educational Practice

At this point, I will try to draw out some concluding implications of Loder's thinking for Christian education and practical theology. Given that the Holy Spirit is the Teacher who transforms, we might ask: What is left for human teachers to do? How shall they enter into and do the works of the Spirit? Is it simply a matter of praying before, after, and during education? Certainly prayer is not to be disparaged. As a teacher, Loder himself became convicted, and went from being a professor who never prayed in class to one who always

32. Thomas Groome, *Christian Religious Education* (San Francisco: Harper & Row, 1980), p. 108.

33. MS, chap. 10, p. 16.

34. Perhaps it could be said that if "critical consciousness" is analogous to cognitive therapy, then Loder as clinical psychologist saw the intractability of sinful social patterns.

did. Nor was this praying perfunctory. It caught his attention that so often alumni would recall these prayers with gratitude — and sometimes, he noted, that was all they could recall. After weeks of intricately argued, tightly compressed lectures, years later the praying is what stood out. But the lectures were good ideas, and many of us who listened think his theory has yet to receive its due.

As one observation, then, I would say that in the current praxis-oriented climate Loder's theory teaches us to honor the worth of "theory." If there is anxiety in society, then there is anxiety in the church, which comes to roost in Christian education as an anxious pragmatism that demands: Give us a program, any program, that will work. And give us some plan that will work for young people. The notion of "workability" is seldom deeply probed. Most crassly, the aim becomes bringing more bodies into the church, when instead it ought to be for the church to embody the Spirit of Christ in the world. If the "church" is to live in the power of the Spirit, not die under the forces of socialization, then teachers must attend to the hidden theories already embedded in the church's thought, word, and deed. Besides anxious pragmatism, another concern is false liberation. The church may cry "liberation," but if the cry is entrenched in patterns of socialization, then it may express only a desire to see the oppressed attain the lifestyle of oppressors. Or if truly it means more than that, it may lack the power to enact the vision; or else the revolution, once unleashed, may unleash violence equal to the first oppression. So theory is needed to critique the church's facile appropriation of the world's theories; and, one might add, it needs to be theory that admits outright the insufficiency of human critique and theory, as well as human liberating praxis. Perhaps Loder is espousing a self-abnegating theory, one that invites the Spirit to critique and implement it.

Loder establishes this need for humility by drawing on H.-G. Gadamer's analysis of *theoria* in ancient Athens. There the term applied to observation and celebration of what the gods were doing — in this way pointing to the notion that theory seeks a vision of higher and hidden order. Theory is thus exalted, but Loder also stresses that the word "theory" is *not* derived from *theos,* which should remind us that theories do not enable people to play God. Loder well recognizes how theories, hardened into ideologies, have been oppressive; he agrees with the desire to correct this problem through careful attention to observable human conditions. What he advocates is a reciprocal relation between *theoria* and *praxis,* one that is mutually illuminating. Since practice is theory being indwelt or made incarnate, theory and practice may be seen as a bipolar, asymmetrical, relational unity. Theory has conceptual priority and exercises "marginal control," because it is the tacit dimension, often hidden from view, but still guiding how practitioners view "observable" reality.[35] (Here "theory," in its broad and unformulated sense, is similar to the "pre-understanding" denoted by J. Habermas as "interests" and Gadamer as "prejudices.") Thus Loder's project exhorts the church to bring its theory into the light of God. His manifest agenda is to offer a theory of Christian education. His tacit agenda is to articulate a broader theory of practical theology, one that approaches each field of human action from the standpoint of God's power to transform it.

As a second observation, I would say that Loder's thinking inclines us to honor and do justice to the human spirit. He used the phrase "logic of the Spirit" in two connected senses, to refer both to the logic of the human spirit's creativity, and to the logic of the relationality of Holy Spirit and human spirit. (In both cases "logic" refers to pattern, structure, or grammar.) The logic of the relationality between Holy Spirit and human spirit is, as we have said, the christomorphic pattern of bipolar, asymmetrical unity. The logic of the human spirit's creativity is a five-fold pattern of transformation that Loder elucidated in his earlier book, *The Transforming Moment.* In the unpublished manuscript we have been summarizing he offers guidelines for educational ministry based on this pattern, intending to honor the spirit's creativity. In so far as these guidelines are grounded in the human spirit, they could apply to teaching and learning in any arena. The five-fold pattern of transformation has been adumbrated in previous essays in this volume, and the salient guidelines were given as early as 1980, in Loder's inaugural address at Princeton.[36] Very helpfully do they connect the logic of the human spirit's creativity with specific teaching and learning tasks, so I will mention them briefly.

In the five-fold pattern, the first stage is *conflict,* a rupture in equilibrium. Whether conflict occurs in interpersonal relations or scientific research, we honor the human spirit's creativity at this stage when we see how the goal is not just resolving conflict quickly for the sake of socialization, but rather learning to *face and embrace appropriate conflict with perseverance.* This task entails both figuring out which conflicts are really worth such energy and teaching people to care enough to persevere. Here, for example, is where teaching about oppression and social justice begins.

If the conflict is embraced, then there follows an *interlude for scanning,* the second stage of transformation. The related teaching task is inviting people

35. "Marginal control" is a term Loder uses often, appropriating it from the writings of M. Polanyi (e.g., *Personal Knowledge: Toward a Post-Critical Philosophy* [Chicago: University of Chicago Press, 1958]). In the relationality of "tacit" and "explicit" dimensions of thinking, the tacit is hidden from view but exercises marginal control because it supplies the source of new discovery.

36. See "Transformation in Christian Education," *Princeton Seminary Bulletin* 3, 1 (1980).

to engage in what might be called *contemplative wondering.* From a socialization standpoint, it may not be efficient or cost effective to explore infinite connections and combinations, but we do justice to the human spirit when we provide free space for such wonderment, supporting the learner's inner guidance rather than supplying ready-made answers. In time, as the problem is indwelt, there comes *insight,* the third stage of transformation. Insight reveals the human spirit in flight, creatively apprehending and constructing reality. The insight is felt with intuitive force: it is not irrational, but it is the spirit reaching beyond reason's confines. The more creative the insight, the more potentially disruptive it will be of established patterns, so socialization tends to suppress its power. When insight includes all four dimensions, it can become the sort of "convictional experience" that deeply change people and their world from the inside out. Hence the educational task (now referring explicitly to Christian education) is *learning from convictional experiences and insights that have convictional significance.* Here the effort is not to manufacture such experiences through human means, or to make them the membership ticket into the group, but rather to do them justice — to give them the valuation they deserve, and to learn from them, by seeing them as a gift not just to individuals but the community as a whole.

Following insight, the fourth stage in the pattern of transformation is a *release of energy* (the energy initially bound up in the conflict) *and new openness* of knowers to themselves and the world around them. The educational task corresponding to this stage is *teaching people to celebrate.* There is joy as well as struggle in learning, and the human spirit rightly rejoices in new creation, when it can see that it is good. The fifth stage of transformation is *verification* or truth testing. Does the insight cohere with everything else one knows to be the case? If not, one may need to rethink the insight — or else start to rethink everything else. Does it correspond to what is known publicly? If not, one may well doubt the insight — or perhaps decide to become a prophet, or a martyr. In working through these verifications, the educational task is *teaching people interpretation and responsible action.* Though last in the sequence, this task is often first in the classroom, because it connects most readily to the cause of socialization. It is true, we do want people to come away with certain conclusions and habits of good behavior, for these also are consonant with the human spirit's creativity. However, the main point is that teaching and learning do justice to the human spirit when they attend not just to one of the five tasks just named, but to all of them together, for together they embody the grammar of creativity.

As a third and final observation, I would say that Loder's theory encourages us to honor the Holy Spirit, especially in the relationality of Holy Spirit and human spirit. Did openness to the Holy Spirit in scholarship originate with

Loder, or is his the only theory it has reached? Of course not. Adherents of Nelson's work on socialization, Groome's work on liberative praxis, or James Fowler's work on faith and human development could all say that the power of the Holy Spirit is implicit in these approaches — and even is self-evidently the most important thing. Loder's continual refrain was: well then, let us start with what is most important and reason from there. Thus his desire was not to jettison the work of colleagues but to reconceive it in light of the Holy Spirit–human spirit relationality. For apart from such reconception the work of the Holy Spirit too easily becomes divorced conceptually from the rest of the approach, akin to Farley's nebulous "X-factor"; and even more serious, apart from life-giving relationality to the Holy Spirit, human socialization, human development, and human praxis all tend toward, and end in, death.[37]

37. It may be pointed out that James Fowler also writes about "transformation," as well as divine-human relationality, which he calls "partnership with God" and "synergy with Spirit" (see esp. *Becoming Adult, Becoming Christian: Adult Development and Christian Faith* [San Francisco: Jossey-Bass, 2000], pp. 57-75, 115-116). Without giving a full comparison of Fowler and Loder, I can indicate why I think their approaches differ significantly. To refer to Loder's rubric, Fowler's approach in *Becoming Adult, Becoming Christian* is not "transformational" in the sense of its also being "four dimensional" and "christocentric."

For Loder, transformation to becoming Christian is cruciform: two-dimensional existence (of self and world) is negated by the void (third dimension) and is resurrected and newly constituted in relation to the Spirit of Christ (fourth dimension). At the level of the psyche, the ego is negated and reconstituted in relation to Christ, who mediates this transformation. In like manner, social, cultural, and even organic life is negated and reconstituted in relation to Christ. In this way Christian transformation is four dimensional and christocentric.

For Fowler, becoming Christian is but one way to fulfill the "human vocation" (p. 75; cf. p. 57), and this "transformation" is more akin to a developmental process of socialization. While Fowler says that this "transformation toward vocation . . . requires not only development but also *conversion*," he goes on to describe conversion in ways that make it sound very much like another process of development: "by conversion I mean an ongoing process . . . *through which people (or a group) gradually bring the lived story of their lives into congruence with the core story of the Christian faith*. . . . Conversion, then, is not so much a negation of our human development as it is a transformation and fulfillment of it" (115; italics his). While this "transformation" — sans negation — does, in Fowler's depiction, involve a decentering of the self and recentering of passion, it is a decentering and recentering that the self undertakes to accomplish in stages of development, by coupling "social action" with a "strong mystical dimension" (58). For the latter, any number of religious "traditions" may suffice (e.g., Hindu, Buddhist, Christian, or Jewish), provided the "person or community continually experiences the availability of Spirit and its power for transformation" (60).

But what does Fowler mean by the latter phrase? In places his pneumatology means that the Spirit's presence may in fact entail a kind of "negation" or at least "relativizing" of the lived world (59), but more importantly he separates pneumatology from christology, keeping with the cause of reducing interfaith conflict, but perhaps in the process reducing the Spirit to an impersonal force or "energy field" (69). Fowler says the Spirit lures and calls people (55), he says

Loder declares: "I as teacher am a socialized human being, yet I am uniquely and profoundly spirit."[38] To live as spirit is to become a participant with God in the transformation of creation, "by the power of the One whose nature is given to us in Jesus Christ."[39] The ways in which Loder himself chose to participate were unique. As an academic guild member, he was not always the presenter of papers, but more often the thoughtful critic whose presence was respected.[40] His thinking was frequently outside the mainstream, but not at all parochial, and in fact its influence may be wider than is commonly recognized. Christian students from diverse cultural contexts, from countries in Asia and Africa, often find his theory, with its openness to the Holy Spirit, applies more precisely to their social location than some other theories that aim more intentionally at becoming "multicultural" yet lack such explicit pneumatological and christological dimensions.

Loder's participation in the divine transformation of creation involved his creative labor to transform human science understandings, in order to honor the scope of the Holy Spirit's activity in each social location and across the full range

---

the Spirit mingles with human capacities (115), but he does not, so far as I can see, say why (to quote Farley) Christian education needs the Spirit — since the Spirit is generally, ineluctably and ineffably operative, outside the church as well as within. To be sure, his attention here is not on the church as Christ's body, but on the earth as "God's body," and for him an education unto partnership with God, or synergy with Spirit, entails a process of nurture, socialization, and enculturation: "Whether by biological parenting or the investment of care in the children and youth of our common trust, [partnership with God] means . . . the nurturing of persons toward wholeness and richness of contribution to the common good. Entering into partnership with God the Creator . . . includes both care for the earth, including the quality of the physical environment — God's body — and also care for the environment of *spirit* — culture" (72; italics his). Here Fowler does not distinguish "spirit" as "culture" from Spirit (of Christ).

Though Fowler means to appropriate the Eastern Orthodox notion of *synergy* to depict human partnership with God, I think Loder's idea of divine-human *relationality* is actually closer to Orthodox *synergy* than is Fowler's *partnership* — because the Eastern Orthodox understanding of synergy is so ecclesial, personal, and christocentric. As G. Florovsky says, the church as social and charismatic community exists "in direct and immediate union with Christ and His Father." He adds: "This is the chief reason why we should prefer a christological orientation in the theology of the Church rather than a pneumatological. For . . . the Church, as a whole, has her *personal centre* only in Christ; she is not an incarnation of the Holy Spirit, nor is she merely a Spirit-being community, but precisely the Body of Christ, the Incarnate Lord. This saves us from impersonalism without committing us to any humanistic personification" (*Bible, Church, Tradition: An Eastern Orthodox View,* vol. 1 in *The Collected Works of Georges Florovsky* [Belmont, MA: Nordland, 1972-], p. 67; italics his).

38. MS, chap. 9, p. 8.

39. MS, chap. 9, p. 8.

40. I thank Donald Miller for this and other recollections, which stretch back to the days when he and James Loder were graduate students together at Harvard.

of human action. With reference to the four Parsonian quadrants, he depicted how the psyche is transformed through conversion, so that in Christ one is fired back into the world with new velocity to love; society is transformed through *koinonia,* so that corporate life is lived in the communion-creating reality of Christ; culture is transformed through the Word of God, so that root images, symbols, and value systems become transparent bearers of Christ's presence; and even the organic body is transformed through resurrection hope, so that the imperious drive for survival can relax into a love of life that is yet willing to embrace sacrifice for God's sake: therefore (since God is so merciful), we are to present our bodies as living sacrifices, being not conformed to this world, but transformed by the renewal of the mind (Rom. 12:1-2). For James Loder, renewal of the mind led him to desire the renewal of practical theology, a cause to which he gave himself. He gave (as he often said love gives) sacrificially and with integrity.

III. Redemptive Transformation *beyond* Practical Theology

12 The Philosophical Turn to Relationality and the Responsibility of Practical Theology

F. LeRon Shults

The theme of "relationality" pervaded James Loder's writings, as well as his pedagogical and therapeutic practice. His passion was to lead others into a deeper understanding of the illuminative and transformative power of the ultimate relationality between God and humanity revealed in Jesus Christ. Loder's goal was not merely to engender an abstract understanding about christological relationality, but to facilitate the passionate self-involvement of the reader or listener so that she might participate more intensely in this relation to God made possible by the Spirit of Christ. In one of his last articles, he argued that practical theology should be guided by an explicit theological position, namely

> the Chalcedonian formulation of the relationality between the Divine and the human natures in the one person of Jesus Christ. This relationality is characterized in Barthian terms as "indissoluble differentiation," "inseparable unity" and "indestructible (asymmetrical) order." More succinctly, this constellation of factors is designated as asymmetrical, bipolar, relational unity which is self-involving through faith.[1]

In other words, the relational logic of incarnation and redemption should be at the heart of practical theology, both methodologically and materially.

Why is understanding the *philosophical* turn to relationality important? Why not simply talk about incarnation and redemption? As Professor of the *Philosophy* of Christian Education at Princeton Theological Seminary, Loder often dealt with the epistemological, ethical, and metaphysical issues that underlie various models of the dynamics of redemptive transformation. Although he did not publish extensively on the philosophical concept of relationality, he

1. James Loder, "The Place of Science in Practical Theology: The Human Factor," *International Journal of Practical Theology* 4, 1 (2000): 22-41, at 23.

did deal with it indirectly and implicitly in his various treatments of Kierkegaard, Bohr, Piaget, Polanyi, and others.[2] Loder refused to immunize his view of theological relationality from critique, but engaged in rigorous interdisciplinary dialogue, identifying proximate patterns of relationality in other fields of study such as physics and psychology, patterns that he believed pointed toward the ultimate relationality revealed in Jesus Christ. In physics, Loder was particularly interested in the relationality depicted in the Copenhagen interpretation of the quantum reality of light, commonly called "complementarity."[3] In psychology, he focused on the dynamics of relationality that characterize the process of human development, building on the work of Piaget and others as he outlined an ontology of relationships that could account for our experience of spiritual transformation.[4] Loder showed us the valuable mutual enhancement that can occur when we transgress the boundaries of the traditional disciplines of theology, physics, and psychology.

I have tried to explicate and appropriate Loder's relational model elsewhere,[5] but I am aware that many readers are not familiar with the general philosophical issues that lie behind his fascination with the concept of relationality. The purpose of this essay is to illuminate the broader trajectory in the history of philosophy in which Loder's interdisciplinary efforts were tacitly embedded. In this limited space, I can identify only some of the key pivotal points in what I call the philosophical "turn to relationality."[6] The focus will be on some of the key thinkers who participated in the shift from "substance" and toward "relationality" as a dominant hermeneutical category. The first two sections outline the philosophical turn to relationality in two stages: from Aristotle

2. Loder spells out his understanding of relationality in greatest detail in *The Knight's Move: The Relational Logic of the Spirit* (Colorado Springs: Helmers & Howard, 1992), co-authored with physicist W. Jim Neidhardt. An implicit treatment of philosophical relationality was already present in the book based on his dissertation, *Religious Pathology and Christian Faith* (Philadelphia: Westminster, 1966).

3. See esp. *The Knight's Move* and his later "Barth, Bohr and Dialectic," in *Religion and Science: History, Method, Dialogue*, ed. W. Mark Richardson and Wesley J. Wildman (New York: Routledge, 1996), pp. 271-289.

4. See esp. *The Logic of the Spirit: Human Development in Theological Perspective* (San Francisco: Jossey-Bass, 1998).

5. See *The Postfoundationalist Task of Theology* (Grand Rapids: Eerdmans, 1999), chap. 4.

6. Much of the following material overlaps with my treatment of relationality in *Reforming Theological Anthropology: After the Philosophical Turn to Relationality* (Grand Rapids: Eerdmans, 2003), chap. 1. For an exploration of the implications of the turn to relationality for the doctrines of soteriology and ecclesiology, see chaps. 4 and 5 in F. LeRon Shults and Steven J. Sandage, *The Faces of Forgiveness: Searching for Wholeness and Salvation* (Grand Rapids: Baker Academic, 2003).

to Kant, and from Hegel to Levinas. I will defend my decision for including particular thinkers and movements as we go along. In a concluding section, I briefly explore the responsibility of practical theology, which now operates in a cultural context that has been radically altered by late modern philosophical reflection.

Relationality from Aristotle to Kant

Most of the pre-Socratic Greek philosophers focused less on the relation of things to each other and more on the question of the essence of things. What "substance" stays the same beneath all the changes that we see in the world? They offered a diversity of answers, including water (Thales), air (Anaximenes) and fire (Heraclitus). This debate about being and becoming was in the background when Plato (428-347 B.C.E.) proposed a metaphysical dualism between an immaterial realm of unchanging Forms or Ideas and a material realm of temporal change. In several of Plato's dialogues (e.g., *Theaetetus* and *Philebus*) the difference between the unchanging substance of a thing and its changing accidental qualities is presupposed, but it was his student Aristotle (384-322 B.C.E.) who developed a full theory of predication that carefully distinguished substance from accidents. Here we find the root of the western philosophical privileging of substance over relationality.

In an early work called the *Categories,* Aristotle was interested in understanding how we *say* what a thing is (τὸ ἔστιν?). Sometimes we simply speak of a thing itself (e.g., "the man" or "running"). At other times, as when we make a statement, we speak of a thing in combination with some other thing (e.g., "the man is running"). In other words, we say "things" about things and things are said about "things." This is hardly shocking. Aristotle wants to go further and determine what types of "things" we say about things, and to clarify the nature of the "things" about which other things are said. He argues that things that are said (simply, not in combination with other things) fall into ten categories: "each signifies either substance or quantity or qualification or a relative or where or when or being-in-a-position or having or doing or being-affected" (1^b25).[7] The term "substance" is not only first on his list, but also takes ontological priority because a substance must be included in any predication. That is, to make an affirmation (or negation) requires combining a substance, such as "the man," with a predicate that fits into one of the other categories, such as "running" (doing).

7. Quotations and references are from *The Complete Works of Aristotle,* ed. Jonathan Barnes, 2 vols. (Princeton: Princeton University Press, 1984).

This is where Aristotle introduces his influential distinction between "primary" and "secondary" substances. Primary substances are particular things like an individual person. Secondary substances are the species and genera to which the particular thing belongs, which in the case of an individual person would be "rational" and "animal." The more concrete the more substantial, argues Aristotle, for "of the secondary substances the species is more a substance than the genus, since it is nearer to the primary substance" (2^b7). All of the other categories are said of primary or secondary substances. Aristotle clearly gives the category of substance (οὐσία) priority over the fourth category, which is the category of relation, i.e., the "toward something" (πρός τι) of a thing. What we might call a thing's "towardness" does not really get at its "whatness" for Aristotle. As illustrations of the category of relation, Aristotle offers the terms "half," "double," and "greater." He suggests "we call *relatives* all such things as are said to be just what they are, *of* or *than* other things, or in some other way *in relation to* something else" (6^a37). Already in this early work we sense that he views the category of relatives as somehow farther from substantiality than the other categories. Yet Aristotle expresses a nagging feeling that he is missing something.

> Now if the definition of relatives given above was adequate, it is either exceedingly difficult or impossible to reach the solution that no substance is spoken of as a relative. But if it was not adequate, and if those things are relatives from which *being is the same as being somehow related to something,* then perhaps some answer may be found. . . . It is perhaps hard to make firm statements on such questions without having examined them many times. (8^a29, 8^b22)

In his later writings, Aristotle overcomes this hesitation; he is less reserved and explicitly argues that relatives are accidental and less real. In the *Metaphysics,* he explains that "the great and the small, and the like, must be relative to something; but the relative is *least of all things a real thing or substance,* and is posterior to quality and quantity; and the relatives are accidents of quantity" (1088^a21-25; emphasis added).[8]

Notice that each of his examples for "relatives" in the *Categories* implied a *quantitative* ratio and presupposed susceptibility of mathematical measurement. Here in the *Metaphysics,* "relation" is now explicitly an accident of "quantity." Although relatives are singled out, he seems to think of all of the other categories (except substance) as relative in a broad sense, and so accidental. The

8. Cf. *Posterior Analytics* (83^a15-24).

substance of a thing, as the "substratum" that underlies it, is "that which is not predicated of a subject, but of which all else is predicated" (1029^a8). Only substances can exist independently; relatives, like the other categories, cannot. While debate continues among Aristotle interpreters over his precise intentions here, the important point for our purposes is not controversial: his model led to a hard distinction between "substances" and "accidents" (including relations) in which the latter are not essential to what a thing is, and so less real. It came to be orthodoxy in Western philosophy that the relations of a thing to other things are not essential to defining or knowing what that thing is.

During the centuries that followed, Aristotle's list of ten categories was not universally followed.[9] The Stoics typically had a shorter list of four "generic" concepts: substratum (or subject), quality (or essential attribute), state (or accidental condition), and relation. Much more influential, however, was the emergence of Neoplatonism, and especially the contribution of Plotinus (205-270 C.E.). He rejected both the Stoic and the Aristotelian lists, and took the five "kinds" in Plato's *Sophist* as the ultimate categories: Being, Motion, Stability, Difference, and Identity (*Enneads,* VI.1-2). Plotinus begins with "Being," which he takes to be obviously a primary genus, but then argues that the other four are not merely modifications of Substance (Real Being), nor are they distinct from Substance; they are "constituents" of Substance. Immediately following his exposition of these five primary genera, Plotinus goes out of his way to stress that the term "Relation" is "remote from Being." He asks: "As for Relation, manifestly an offshoot, how can it be included among primaries? Relation is of thing ranged against thing; it is not self-pivoted, but looks outward."[10]

In the early Middle Ages we find a mixture of Neoplatonic and Aristotelian influences in the theological appropriation of the categories of substance and accidents.[11] Plotinus had insisted that one cannot apply the same categories in the same way to both the intelligible and sensible worlds, and he explored the *way* in which these "kinds" existed. Porphyry, who was a pupil of

9. This was exacerbated by the fact that he is internally inconsistent, offering different lists in various writings. The ten of the *Categories,* however, are usually considered the "Aristotelian" list. For a treatment of this background and a general historical overview see H.-G. Steiner, "Relation," in *Historisches Wörterbuch der Philosophie,* vol. 8, ed. Joachim Ritter and Karlfried Gründer (Basel: Schwabe & Co., 1992), pp. 578-611.

10. Ennead VI.2.16. In *Plotinus: The Enneads,* trans. Stephen MacKenna, new ed. (Burdett, NY: Larson, 1992), p. 553.

11. For analysis of an example of a theological anthropology that adapts elements from both streams, see my treatment of Leontius of Byzantium in chap. 7 of *Reforming Theological Anthropology.*

Plotinus, accepted the ten Aristotelian categories in his *Isagogue,* but asked very Plotinian questions about them. Do genera and species exist only in the understanding or also outside of it? If the latter, are these categories corporeal or incorporeal? Are they separable from, or do they only reside in, sensible things? When Boethius, who was deeply influenced by Augustine, translated the *Isagogue* into Latin in the sixth century, he also offered his own answers to these questions. This set the stage for the debate over "universals" that dominated the high Middle Ages. Whether the answer is the moderate realism of Thomas Aquinas[12] or the nominalism of William of Ockham, the question is the same; Christian theologians for the most part accept the validity of Porphyry's way of formulating the issue, which presupposes the basic distinction between substance and (accidental) relations.

As early modern science arises out of the Renaissance, we see a slow but revolutionary shift in the understanding and use of categories. For Aristotle, the "generic" *qualities* of a thing (like its being "white" or "bovine") are very real; in fact, they are more real than the *quantitative* predicates that we apply to it like "large" or "half" (which are merely "relations"). As the mathematical models of Copernicus, Galileo, and others came to explain more and more of the world, philosophers began to think that quantitative analysis may get us closer to the "whatness" (or substantiality) of a thing than does a description of its qualities. The latter, after all, appears more subjective than the former. Perhaps the only "real" description of nature is provided by objective mathematical measurement. This bias was further strengthened by the increasing popularity of nominalism, which used Ockham's razor to cut off what appeared to

12. Thomas's reliance on Aristotelian distinctions, including the categories of substance and accident, is well known. Because he accepted the idea that relations are not essential to a thing, he had difficulty thinking about the trinitarian relations as essential to the divine nature. It is interesting, however, that Thomas resists giving up on the importance of relationality, which he believes is built into the nature of theology: "Now all things are dealt with in holy teaching in terms of God [*sub ratione Dei*], either because they are God himself or because they are relative to him as their origin and end. . . . All these indeed are dwelt on by this science, yet as held in their relationship to God [*ordinem ad Deum*]. . . . All other things that are settled in Holy Scripture are embraced in God, not that they are parts of him — such as essential components or accidents — but because they are somehow related to him." *Summa Theologiae,* Blackfriars edition, vol. 1 (New York: McGraw-Hill, 1964), p. 27 (I, Q. 1, Art. 7; cf. I, Q.8, Art 1). Despite his inability to fit them into the categories of his Aristotelian substance/accident metaphysic, Thomas could not give up on the central Christian intuitions about relationality in God (Trinity) and the relation of God to creatures. This tension was also evident in Augustine; while he generally relied on substance metaphysics, his reflection on his own relation to the *trinitarian* God led him to recognize that when "things" are "said" about God "according to relation," these relations are not accidental (*De Trinitate,* 5.5.6).

be the unnecessary hypothesis of universal generic qualities; this supported the growing scientific interest in dissecting and naming particular phenomena. By the seventeenth century, we find a rigorous debate on the nature and distinction between "primary" and "secondary" qualities. In his *Meditations on First Philosophy* (1641) Descartes argued for a radical dualism between two types of substance: "extended thing" *(res extensa)* and "thinking thing" *(res cogitans)*. In this way, he could protect the reality of secondary qualities like color and sound, but the price for this was segregating them in the subjective realm of *res cogitans*. Spinoza exemplifies the other extreme; he proposes a monism in which all that exists is Absolute Substance *(Deus sive Natura)*. In his *Ethics*, which was published soon after his death in 1677, he tried to maintain an infinite plurality of attributes of the one substance, although each attribute also expresses the essence of the one substance. The tension between these two philosophical extremes is still with us today.

During this era the sciences that we now call "physics" and "astronomy" were encompassed by the term "natural philosophy." The title of Newton's influential *Philosophiae Naturalis Principia Mathematica* (1687) underscores the important relation between science and philosophy. It also illustrates the growing faith in the explanatory power of mathematics. Here we have a picture of the universe in which bodies (material substances) move around absolute (static) space and bump into each other. Mathematics measures quantities and ratios that operate in accordance with the laws of inertial force. As the world of "subjective" qualities which the human mind perceives was made secondary to the "objective" qualities of nature, people began to feel like aliens, "unrelated" to the cosmos.[13] Since that time, scientists have come to emphasize relationality much more radically. Einstein himself was aware of the philosophical underpinnings of mechanistic science, and even in his explanation of the theory of "relativity," he felt it was important to point to developments such as the nineteenth-century field theories of Faraday and Maxwell that led to understandings of reality not as "particles" of matter in the traditional sense, but as fields of energy.[14] With discoveries and developments in quantum theory, we find further outworking of relational thinking; particle physics is not really about "particles" anymore but about relationships — interpenetrating and mu-

13. Partially for religious reasons, Robert Boyle tried to remind his scientific contemporaries of the *de facto* existence of human subjects and insisted on the equal reality of "secondary" qualities. For a history of this development, see E. A. Burtt, *The Metaphysical Foundations of Modern Science* (Atlantic Highlands, NJ: Humanities Press, 1932).

14. See Appendix V in Albert Einstein, *Relativity: The Special and General Theory* (New York: Crown, 1961). Cf. Einstein, "The Mechanics of Newton," reprinted in *Ideas and Opinions* (New York: Bonanza, 1954).

tually binding energy fields.[15] After the emergence of "chaos theory" in the late twentieth century, most physicists agree that units and relations are distinct but interdependent: "for an interaction to be real, the 'nature' of the related things must derive from these relations, while at the same time the relations must derive from the 'nature' of the things."[16]

Back in the early modern period, however, substance metaphysics was thriving, albeit in new dualist and empiricist forms. Its survival would require philosophical clarification on the issue of the distinct types of qualities. The distinction found its classical formulation in John Locke's *An Essay Concerning Human Understanding* (1689). He explains that the primary qualities of "Body" that produce simple ideas in us are Solidity, Extension, Figure, Motion or Rest, and Number. Among secondary qualities, which "in truth are nothing in the Objects themselves, but Powers to produce various Sensations in us," he includes colors, sounds, and tastes (II.7.9-10). For our purposes, the more important point is Locke's argument that the ideas of Substance and Accidents are not of much use in philosophy, because we do not know what substance is, except it is that which supports accidents; we have no idea of what it is, only an obscure and confused idea of what it does (II.13.19). Further, when he does treat of "Relation," he notes that "though it be not contained in the real existence of Things . . . yet the *Ideas* which relative Words stand for, are often clearer, and more distinct, than those Substances to which they belong" (II.25.8). So secondary qualities like smell and sound, which we might "subjectively" call beautiful or good, are merely powers in an extended thing that produce a certain *sensum* with which the mind forms an Idea. The primary qualities measure the "objective" world.

In the eighteenth century, David Hume tried to follow out the logic of Locke's position, which he believed led to skepticism. If Locke's "substance" (or substratum) is merely a "something we know not what" then we cannot predicate anything of it, or know anything about it. In his *Enquiry Concerning Human Understanding* (1748), Hume argues that anything we do say about substances is merely habit or convention, because we cannot know or say what the thing *is*. This skepticism applies not only to substances but also to the connections (relations) we habitually associate between substances, relations such as cause and effect. Hume was clearly aiming at Christian theology here. In 1710, Leibniz had

15. For introductions to these developments in physics and their theological implications, see Ian Barbour, *Religion in an Age of Science* (San Francisco: HarperCollins, 1990), pp. 95-124; and Arthur Peacocke, *Theology for a Scientific Age: Being and Becoming — Natural, Divine and Human* (Minneapolis: Fortress, 1993), pp. 29-43.

16. Ilya Prigogine and Isabelle Stengers, *Order out of Chaos: Man's New Dialogue with Nature* (New York: Bantam, 1984), p. 95.

published his famous *Theodicy* in which he argued that this is the best of all possible worlds, a world caused by a God who is perfectly good.[17] Hume was not impressed by this defense, as he makes clear in the *Dialogues Concerning Natural Religion* (not published until after his death in 1776). For our purposes, however, the important point is his devastating critique of the very idea of a "substance" that can be separated from all of its accidents. By the time of Hume, many theologians had hitched their theological carts to the philosophical horse of substance metaphysics. Unlike the early Reformers, for whom relationality was a key concept for articulating (for example) a doctrine of the whole person as the image of God,[18] their followers were surprisingly quick to revert to Aristotelian categories, which they borrowed from the medieval Scholastic discussion.[19] Not surprisingly, the doctrine of the Trinity became less central during this period, and attention was turned to proving the existence of God as an Immaterial Substance that was the First Cause of the world.[20]

Immanuel Kant credited Hume with waking him from his "dogmatic slumbers." Like most of us, he was resting peacefully in his assumption that he could know and speak of a thing as it really is. Kant's "critical" philosophy is a call to question such assumptions. He argues that we can speak of things as they appear to us (phenomena) but not of things in themselves (noumena). This is the main point of his critique of pure (theoretical) reason: showing its limits to "make room for faith." Kant believed that the time was ripe for revisiting the Aristotelian categories and the relative importance of the concepts of substance and relation. In Book I of the Transcendental Analytic in his influential *Critique of Pure Reason* (1787), Kant provides his own Table of Categories. The importance of this shift justifies our portrayal (Figure 1) of these "predicables," which he calls the concepts of pure understanding.[21]

17. Like Spinoza, Leibniz had made the concept of substance fundamental to his system, but rather than a single substance he proposed a multiplicity of "monads." These are simple immaterial substances that exhibit a pre-established harmony created by God.

18. For Luther, the justification-relation is the key category through which all human understanding is judged. For Calvin, the key is that the whole person is called to be united to Christ by the Spirit.

19. Both Strigel on the Lutheran side and Bucanus on the Reformed side differentiated between the substance of the "image" of God and the accident of "likeness" to God.

20. As Michael Buckley, S.J., has shown, atheism itself arose as a negation of modern "theism," which itself emerged when theologians turned away from the particularity of the Christian belief in incarnation and Trinity and toward abstract philosophical categories as the basis of their attempts to defend the existence of God. *At the Origins of Modern Atheism* (New Haven: Yale University Press, 1987).

21. Kant, *Critique of Pure Reason*, trans. Norman Kemp Smith (New York: St. Martin's Press, 1965), p. 113 (B106).

I
Of Quantity
Unity
Plurality
Totality

II
Of Quality
Reality
Negation
Limitation

III
Of Relation
Of Inherence and Subsistence
(substantia et accidens)
Of Causality and Dependence
(cause and effect)
Of Community (reciprocity
between agent and patient)

IV
Of Modality
Possibility — Impossibility
Existence — Non-existence
Necessity — Contingency

Figure 1: Kant's Table of Categories

The most obvious discontinuity between the Western tradition up to this point and Kant's proposal is the latter's "Copernican revolution" in which he reverses the importance of human "subjectivity" and the "objective" world. Instead of beginning with the claim that an external (or noumenal) objective reality contains structures that are grasped by the mind, he proposes that the human subject itself provides the structural categories by which "objects" that appear (as phenomena) in human consciousness are "thought." The transcendental structures of human reason yield intuitions by means of sensibility and give rise to concepts through the understanding — these have purchase only in the realm of phenomena, or in the "appearance" of things in the mind. So he treats the categories not as realities or distinctions of "things in themselves" but as *a priori* categories of the understanding. This means that the categories "Of Relation" are forms through which the human subject understands a "thoroughgoing reciprocity" in the field of *phenomena.*

Two key points about Kant's table are relevant for our historical survey of the philosophical turn to relationality. First, notice that Kant explicitly makes "substance and accident" a subcategory of Category III — "Of Relation." This is a major adjustment and sets the stage for the radical developments we will trace below in the next section of this essay. In addition to his radical elevation of the category of relation, Kant's second major contribution was his unleashing of relationality from Category I, "Of Quantity," to which it had been tied since Aristotle. Later, Kant defines a system of "principles" of pure understanding that are correlated to the "categories." These principles are applied *mathematically* for Categories I and II, but are applied *dynamically* for Categories III and IV.[22] The "analogies of experience," which are the principles derived from Category III ("Of Relation"), provide Kant with a way of maintaining the importance of the categories of dynamic human experience in transcendental analysis, without subordinating them to quantitative or mathematical categories.

Despite his otherwise radical revisions, Kant still viewed substance in terms of permanence, and alteration as occurring only through the changing of accidents, described with the categories of cause and effect. Community (the third subcategory under "Of Relation") is, Kant argues, simply the combination of the second subcategory with the first, that is, "the causality of substances reciprocally determining one another."[23] This important point of continuity with the Aristotelian substance tradition would be challenged by many who came after Kant, as we will see below. However, Kant's explicit critique of Aristotle's treatment of relationality provided the impulse for a series of philosophical developments that would open conceptual space for the rapid advancement of dynamic relational hypotheses in physics, psychology, and the other sciences that shape our contemporary culture.

Relationality from Hegel to Levinas

G. W. F. Hegel (1770-1831) contributed to the history of the concept of relationality in many ways, but three aspects of his work have been particularly influential: (1) challenging the basic separation of the category of accident from the category of substance, (2) insisting that the phenomena of relationality and process are essential not only to the reflective movement of knowing but also to being itself, which is self-related, and (3) emphasizing that the ultimate or absolute relation cannot adequately be defined by speaking of the Infinite over against the finite because the "true" Infinite must somehow embrace the finite while transcending it. Hegel was by no means the first to make these claims, but he did articulate them in a way that has set the tone for much of the philosophi-

22. Cf. *Critique*, pp. 196ff. This separation plays a key role in his proposed solution to the antinomies of pure reason later in the book (pp. 462ff. [A529]).

23. *Critique*, p. 116 (B111).

cal discussion over the last two centuries. For this reason, it makes sense to use Hegel as a kind of historical marker for an important pivot in the turn to relationality. After briefly outlining these three Hegelian emphases, I will point to some of the key thinkers since Hegel who have shaped attitudes about relationality in Western philosophy.

First, Hegel challenged the basic separation between the categories of substance and accident, which most of the thinkers discussed above, including Aristotle and Kant, had taken for granted.[24] We can find the core of Hegel's argument expressed in two closely related sections of his *Science of Logic:* "The Absolute Relation," which is the final chapter of Volume I (Objective Logic, 1812), and "The Notion," which is the first chapter of Volume II (Subjective Logic, 1819).[25] Like Kant, substance and accidents are brought under the category of "relation," but in a more radical way. For Hegel, both substantiality and accidentality refer to determinations of the totality or the whole; this "whole" is neither "being" nor "essence," however, but their dialectical unity in the reflective movement of the *"absolute relation,"* which is the highest category in the objective logic. "Substance, as this identity of the reflective movement, is the totality of the whole and embraces accidentality within it, and accidentality is the whole substance itself." Hegel speaks of an "immediate identity" and a "unity" of substance and accidents; here again, these are manifestations of the movement of the absolute relation. The extremes of accidentality and substantiality have no subsistence on their own. Accidentality is "*in itself* indeed substance," but as the "actuosity" of substance coming forth of itself; and substantiality is not substance "as substance," for it "has only accidentality for its shape or positedness."[26] This dialectical unity of substantiality and accidentality flows from Hegel's rejection of the hard distinction between form and content. For Kant, as for Aristotle, the logical categories were "forms" of reasoning and could be abstracted from "content." For Hegel, form and content are inseparable in the dialectical process of logic, and method cannot be so easily separated from being: "The method is the pure Notion that relates itself only to itself; it is therefore the *simple self-relation* that is *being*."[27]

This allusion to a self-relating "Notion" *(Begriff)* brings us to the second of Hegel's themes that bear on the turn to relationality: his insistence that *process* is essential not only to reflection but also to being. Here substance is linked not

24. The substance-accident distinction was not as central to the Platonic tradition, as we saw in Plotinus, although "Relation" was still separated from substance.

25. Published together in *Hegel's Science of Logic,* trans. A. V. Miller, ed. H. D. Lewis (Amherst, NY: Humanity Books, 1999).

26. All of these quotes are on pp. 555-556 of *Hegel's Science of Logic.*

27. *Hegel's Science of Logic,* p. 842.

only to relation, but also to movement: "Substance as this unity of being and reflection is essentially the *reflective movement* and *positedness* of itself. This reflective movement is the reflective movement that is *self-related,* and it is thus that it *is.*[28] In his earlier *Phenomenology of Spirit* (1807), Hegel had argued that the cognition of the individual is participation in the Absolute Knowing of the Spirit, by which the Spirit becomes what it is in self-consciousness; substance is objectified and becomes Self in this process.[29] In the "Subjective Logic," Hegel explicitly critiques Spinoza for stopping with the notion of Absolute Substance. This halt had left Spinoza with the problem of necessity that flowed naturally from his monism (pantheism). Hegel argues that we should recognize the moment of truth in Spinoza but go further. It is not Substance but "Subject" that is Absolute; as the self-comprehending pure Notion, the Spirit (as Subject) consummates Spinoza's concept of substance by sublating its necessity into the freedom of the Notion.[30] In Hegel's philosophy, subjectivity becomes a higher category than substance, and "becoming" is radically incorporated into "being." Hegel's "phenomenology," which held together the forms of thought and the content of being, was therefore an attempt to overcome the Kantian dualism between noumena (things in themselves) and phenomena (things as they appear).

The third Hegelian contribution was his rigorous reflection on the ultimate relationality, the relation between the Infinite and the finite. One might even argue that it was this reflection that led him to emphasize relationality and process in his understanding of phenomena. Finite things are finite because they are defined over against that which they are not. This limitation constitutes their finitude. The idea of the "In-finite" suggests that which is not-finite. Hegel points out that if the Infinite and the finite are thought together in such a way that they are merely opposed to each other, then the Infinite is determined by the finite. The Infinite is limited by the finite if it is defined simply as that which is not-finite. If we speak of Infinity in this way, which Hegel calls the "spurious" or "bad" infinite, then in fact we have *two* determinatenesses, two mutually limited worlds. In the relation between them, "the infinite is only the *limit* of the finite and is thus only a determinate infinite, an *infinite which is itself finite.*"[31] The "true" Infinite embraces both itself and finitude; it is a process that raises its difference from itself into the affirmation of itself, and through

28. *Hegel's Science of Logic,* p. 555.

29. Hegel, *Phenomenology of Spirit,* trans. A. V. Miller (Oxford: Oxford University Press, 1977), pp. 479-493.

30. *Hegel's Science of Logic,* pp. 580-582. The term "sublating" refers to Hegel's well-known use of the German word *aufheben* to describe the negation as well as elevation of one idea or process into another.

31. *Hegel's Science of Logic,* p. 140.

this mediation is becoming itself. Here it is important to distinguish between two clusters of ideas about the Infinite in the history of philosophy; what we might call the "mathematical" cluster thinks of infinity in terms of endlessness, immeasurability, or unlimitedness, while the "metaphysical" cluster of ideas emphasizes the Infinite as wholeness, absoluteness, or perfection. Kant had separated "Of Relation" from "Of Quantity," but Hegel went further not only by making Relation an even more dominant category, but also by explicitly tying it to *Quality,* which he then privileged over *Quantity.*[32] The mathematical (quantitative) infinite had dominated early modern consciousness; Hegel vigorously argued for a vision of the metaphysical Infinite as a self-related Absolute that could include finitude without being limited by it.

Like most Christian thinkers since that time, Søren Kierkegaard did not find Hegel's way of trying to solve the question of true infinity compelling. On the one hand, it seems to vitiate the transcendence of God and, on the other, it threatens the particularity of individual finite creatures who seem to be absorbed into an all-encompassing Subject. Kierkegaard's insistence on the "infinite qualitative distinction" between God and creatures was a response to both concerns. His whole authorship was driven by the question of the relation of the individual to the Infinite (or Eternal, or Unknown). Kierkegaard's pseudonymous writings can be understood as attempts to lead the reader through a process of intensification; the *Stages On Life's Way* (1845) are existence-spheres, or ways of relating to the self, the world, and God, through which readers are (indirectly) called to move. Despite his resistance to Hegel on so many other fronts, for Kierkegaard, too, "relationality" was a key concept. We may point, for example, to Kierkegaard's definition of the self in his 1849 *The Sickness Unto Death* as "a relation that relates itself to itself or is the relation's relating itself to itself in the relation; the self is not the relation but is the relation's relating itself to itself."[33] Many of the influential scholars associated with "postmodernity" were shaped by and contributed to the twentieth-century revival of Kierkegaard scholarship.[34]

32. *Hegel's Science of Logic,* p. 79. Hegel explicitly criticizes Kant in this context.

33. Kierkegaard, *The Sickness Unto Death,* trans. Howard V. and Edna H. Hong (Princeton: Princeton University Press, 1980), p. 13. In *Kierkegaard as Humanist* and *Kierkegaard as Theologian,* Arnold Come argues that the brief section in which this quote appears is the key to interpreting the whole Kierkegaardian corpus (London: McGill-Queen's University Press, 1995 and 1997).

34. This is particularly evident in the work of Jacques Derrida, whose well-known emphasis on the category of *différance* has been so influential. For an example of his treatment of Kierkegaard, see his *The Gift of Death,* trans. David Wills (Chicago: University of Chicago Press, 1995). For Kierkegaard's influence on other postmodern scholars, see the essays in *Kierkegaard in Post/Modernity,* ed. Martin J. Matuštík and Merold Westphal (Bloomington: Indiana University Press, 1995).

Later in the nineteenth century, the American philosopher Charles Sanders Peirce took up the question of "relations" and developed his own "New List" of categories in 1867. At this early stage, he had five categories; a major division between substance and being, with the latter having the subcategories of Quality, Relation, and Representation.[35] Later these subcategories would become dominant, and he would give them names only a philosopher could love: Firstness, Secondness, and Thirdness.[36] Formally he called these the three "classes of relations" (monadic, dyadic, triadic). Materially, Firstness was linked to the *Quality* of Feeling, the "suchness" of immediate phenomenal experience; Secondness to the *Reaction* to some First, the "thisness" (haecceity) element of the phenomenon experienced in its "upagainstness"; and Thirdness to the *Representation* in thought that mediates the relation or "betweenness" of a Second to its First. These categories also led him to divide philosophy into three departments: "Phenomenology," which treats the qualities of phenomena in their Firstness; "Normative Science," which treats the laws and relations of phenomena in their Secondness; and "Metaphysics," which treats phenomena in terms of their Thirdness. Peirce's fascination with relationality is also evident in his suggestion that we may overcome idealism, dualism, and materialism with "synechism," the doctrine that everything is continuous.

The concept of "relation" was significantly affected by the divergence of two philosophical streams in the late nineteenth and early twentieth centuries. The first stream, which is commonly called the "analytic" tradition, has focused on relations in logic and language. Since Aristotle, logic had been limited to one-place categories (e.g., the man) and two-place predication (e.g., the man runs). Throughout the Middle Ages this had led to logical difficulties when dealing with relations between more than two categories; for example, the man runs at the cow, or the man bears the "is running toward" relation to the cow. This weakness in Aristotle's approach to logic was overcome by Cantor's work in set theory[37] and Frege's development of what is now called quantification

35. Peirce, "On a New List of Categories," in *The Essential Peirce,* vol. 1, ed. Nathan Houser and Christian Kloesel (Bloomington: Indiana University Press, 1992), p. 6. At this early stage, he called the latter three intermediate categories "accidents," but this terminology faded from importance in his mature work.

36. For an introduction to these categories, see Peirce's Harvard Lectures on Pragmatism, reprinted in *The Essential Peirce,* vol. 2 (Bloomington: Indiana University Press, 1998). Broadly speaking, these categories were related to pure possibility, actual existence, and real generality, respectively. His emphasis on Thirdness was an attempt to overcome the nominalism that had dominated science.

37. As he developed set theory, which is still the basis of contemporary mathematics, Cantor was led to postulate the idea of an "Absolute Infinite," which is clearly a theological idea.

theory. These tools allow logicians to signify and discuss the relations between multiple categories and sets of categories. In the analytic tradition, one of the most important debates has been over the issue of "internal" and "external" relations. Some relations seem to be essential (or internal) to a thing's being what it is — for instance, my being "younger" than my grandfather. Other relations appear to be external to the essence of a thing — for example, my living east of the Mississippi River. Many philosophers have challenged the validity of this hard distinction for two reasons: first, ideas about which relations are "internal" or essential are gradational rather than absolute; and second, judgments about which relations are internal (essential) are relativized by the interests of the one making the distinction.[38] Nevertheless, such distinctions are helpful for the purposes of logical or linguistic analyses, which operate within the defining mechanisms of predication.

The second stream emerged out of a quite different understanding of language and of the task of philosophy. Although commonly called the "continental" tradition or "speculative" philosophy, for our purposes here we might risk the ambiguous appellation "phenomenology" for this stream of thought. Hegel's use of the term "phenomenology" was taken up and modified by a variety of nineteenth-century philosophers; we think immediately of Marx, who argued that the dialectical process of historical phenomena was material rather than spiritual, and of Dilthey, whose reflection on the relation between parts and whole in human understanding shaped the rise of historicist hermeneutics. In the twentieth century, however, "phenomenology" has been associated especially with the methodology of Husserl and those influenced by him.[39] In this school the focus is on *categorial intentionality,* the establishing of a categorial object by human consciousness. We may distinguish three aspects of this process. First, we have the passive perception of a thing, such as a man in a barnyard scene. Second, a particular element of the whole comes to the foreground — for example, a kerosene lamp knocked into the hay by a cow. Finally, we have the registering of the relation between the whole and part, the simultaneous articulation of a state of affairs: a man is running toward a cow in order to put out a fire. This achievement of a categorial intuition comes all at once, but we may still distinguish the parts, the whole, and the relation between them in the phenomena. Notice that the interest here is not so much on listing types of categories, but on understanding the types of relations or distinctions that appear in consciousness.

38. See the influential article by Timothy Sprigge, "Internal and External Properties," *Mind* 71 (1962): 197-212.

39. For a more detailed treatment of the following issues, see Robert Sokolowski, *Introduction to Phenomenology* (Cambridge: Cambridge University Press, 2000).

Two of the most important philosophers of the twentieth century, Heidegger and Sartre, struggled with the relations inherent in being, although they interpreted it differently insofar as they focused on the phenomena of time and nothingness, respectively. Heidegger's thematic analysis of *Dasein* (being-there) led him to emphasize a whole host of relational distinctions including being-with, being-in, and his famous being-towards-death.[40] Sartre argued that the reciprocal relation of "being-seen-by-another" and "seeing-the-other" is an irreducible and fundamental relation that appears in consciousness; this relation of being-with and being-for-other *is* the self's being, or is the self as the apprehension of being. He was most well known for his emphasis on the existential anxiety that emerges from the inability to control the inherent negation of these relations.[41]

The most important twentieth-century American philosopher who contributed to the growing dissatisfaction with Aristotelian substance metaphysics, and its denigration of the category of relation, was Alfred North Whitehead. In *Modes of Thought,* he criticizes Aristotle's attempt to draw clear lines of division among genera and species. Nature is not so neatly divided. Tracing developments in the sciences, especially physics and biology, Whitehead argued that the fundamental concepts by which we understand the world are activity and process.[42] In *Process and Reality,* he set out his own eight "categories of existence" — these are Actual Entities (actual occasions), Prehensions, Nexus, Subjective Forms, Eternal Objects, Propositions, Multiplicities, and Contrasts. For our purposes, the key point is Whitehead's prioritization: "Among the eight categories of existence, actual entities and eternal objects stand out with a certain extreme finality" while the others have an "intermediate character."[43] He explicitly rejects the Aristotelian idea of "individual substances, each with its private world of qualities and sensations,"[44] and criticizes what he calls the "substance-quality" doctrine of actuality. In its place, Whitehead proposes a doctrine of "actual occasions" or "societies" in which reality is described in essentially dynamic and relational terms. Unlike Descartes (and others) for whom a physical body has the *attribute* of extension, for Whitehead physical "occasions" have the primary *relationship* of extensive connection to all things. To be an actual

40. Martin Heidegger, *Being and Time,* trans. J. Macquarrie and E. Robinson (San Francisco: HarperCollins, 1962).

41. Jean-Paul Sartre, *Being and Nothingness,* trans. Hazel E. Barnes (New York: Philosophical Library, 1956). See esp. the section on "The Look" and the conclusion.

42. *Modes of Thought* (New York: Capricorn Books, 1938), p. 191.

43. *Process and Reality,* corrected edition, ed. David Ray Griffin and Donald W. Sherburne (New York: Free Press, 1978), p. 22.

44. *Process and Reality,* p. 160.

occasion (or entity) in the nexus of the physical world is to be a *relatum* in this fundamentally organic extensive scheme.[45]

Process thought has had a tremendous impact on the way in which both philosophers and theologians think about the category of relation. The process concept of God and the God-world relation is unacceptable to most Christian theologians because it tends to subsume God and the world under a larger whole or totality, a tendency already evident in Hegel. Nevertheless, the emphasis on relationality as essential to reality has contributed to a renewed interest in the doctrine of Trinity,[46] as well as to new attempts to overcome the problems in the early modern understanding of the God-world relation.[47] Debate continues among process thinkers over the way in which relations to past occasions are *constitutive* of present occasions, an idea that David Ray Griffin calls one of the "core doctrines" of process theology.[48] Lewis S. Ford believes that the future, too, must be conceptualized as a source of creativity in relation to present occasions, and not merely the past or present as most process thinkers have argued.[49] One of the most important (sympathetic) critics of process philosophy is Robert Neville, who has underscored the necessity of the integrity of *relata* as well as the reality of relations themselves in cosmology.[50] In response to Whitehead's idea that God must be the highest exemplification of our metaphysical categories, Neville also represents the classical insistence in Christian theology that created categories are not capable of completely explaining divine creativity.[51]

The philosophical turn to relationality has shaped not only the way we think about knowing and being but also our understanding of human acting. In the early modern period human (free) agency had been dualistically sepa-

45. *Process and Reality,* p. 288.

46. See, e.g., Joseph A. Bracken, S.J., and Marjorie Hewitt Suchocki, eds., *Trinity in Process: A Relational Theology of God* (New York: Continuum, 1997).

47. See, e.g., Philip Clayton, *The Problem of God in Modern Thought* (Grand Rapids: Eerdmans, 2000).

48. Griffin, "Process Theology and the Christian Good News," in *Searching for an Adequate God,* ed. John B. Cobb Jr. and Clark H. Pinnock (Grand Rapids: Eerdmans, 2000), p. 5.

49. Ford, *Transforming Process Theism* (Albany: State University of New York, 2000).

50. "If things have no essential features over against their conditional features, they are reduced to their various relations with other things. But then it is the relations that are real, and the things are merely perspectives on the relations." Robert Neville, *Eternity and Time's Flow* (Albany: State University of New York, 1993), p. 73. He concludes that "things are harmonies of both conditional and essential features, conditional ones in order to be determinately related to other things with respect to which they are determinate, and essential ones in order to be determinately different from those other things" (p. 75).

51. Neville, *Creativity and God: A Challenge to Process Theology* (Albany: State University of New York, 1995), p. 140.

rated from (mechanistically determined) nature, and this split registered its effect on anthropological theories. In contemporary psychology, and in the anthropological sciences generally, human persons and communities are more often described in ways that recognize that their *relations* are constitutive. A person is no longer defined as an "individual substance of a rational nature" (Boethius) or as a "punctual self" (Locke). Instead of autonomous subjects that stand over against the natural world and other subjects, today human self-consciousness is understood as always and already embedded in relations between self, other, and world. Twentieth-century philosophical anthropology played a crucial role in this development; we think, for example, of the "personalism" of philosophers like Martin Buber, for whom the "between" of I and Thou is constitutive for personhood.[52]

In psychology proper, the turn is most obvious in "object relations" theory,[53] where the agential relation of a person to objects is essential to his or her developmental identity. These relations are not accidental or irrelevant but in some sense constitutive of the person. In the psychoanalytic tradition as well we find scholars who have recognized the centrality of the concept of relationality for understanding and helping persons.[54] Similar insights have arisen out of research in evolutionary biology in general and the neurosciences in particular, which are illustrations of the blurring of boundaries between the "natural" and the "human" sciences. Today human acting is rarely described in terms of a substantial soul with abstract faculties (or powers) to influence the material world, but more often in terms of a dynamic self-in-community.[55]

It seems appropriate to end this brief survey with Emmanuel Levinas, not only because he so well illustrates the postmodern fascination with Infinity, but also because he provides us with an example of the impact of the turn on ethics. First, Levinas is aware of Hegel's criterion of true infinity, and although he rejects the idealist solution, he accepts the need to move beyond "bad" infinity. For Levinas the "in" of in-finity signifies both "non" and "within." The Infinite's "very in-finity, its difference from the finite, is already its nonindifference to the

52. For some contemporary proposals in theological anthropology that have tried to account for these phenomena, see Stanley J. Grenz, *The Social God and the Relational Self* (Louisville: Westminster John Knox, 2001), and Alistair I. McFadyen, *The Call to Personhood: A Christian Theory of the Individual in Social Relationships* (Cambridge: Cambridge University Press, 1990).

53. See, e.g., Robert Kegan, *The Evolving Self* (Cambridge: Harvard University Press, 1982).

54. See, e.g., Stephen A. Mitchell, *Relationality: From Attachment to Intersubjectivity* (Hillsdale, NJ: Analytic Press, 2000).

55. Cf. *Reforming Theological Anthropology*, part 3.

finite."[56] For Levinas the Infinite produces the "primordial" relation between the I and the Other, which as an ethical (rather than an ontological or epistemological) relationship precedes and subtends discourse and being. In face-to-face relations, we find ourselves called by and obligated to the other; in and through these relations we are also confronted with the presence of the absolutely Other, the Infinite. The Infinite is essentially beyond the grasp of the I, who cannot comprehend it, but its transcendent presence is mediated through the ethical relation to the other — precisely as that which is beyond essence.[57] This primordial relation, then, has become an overarching or underlying category. Rather, as Levinas would probably say, it is not a category at all, but beyond categorization — this is an even more radical prioritization of relationality. We have come a long way since Aristotle.[58]

The Responsibility of Practical Theology

This brief overview of the philosophical turn to relationality should convince us that Loder's interest in the concept was not merely idiosyncratic. As we saw in the quote with which this essay began, Loder's own way of conceiving relationality was deeply influenced by Karl Barth, the most important Reformed theologian of the twentieth century. Barth's own theology focused on the revelation of the Word of God in Jesus Christ; and his understanding of that revelation was inherently relational, both materially (as is evident in, e.g., his doctrine of the Trinity) and formally (as is evident in his commitment to *analogia relationis*). The philosophical theologian who most impacted Loder's view of relationality was Søren Kierkegaard; this influence is implicit in the reference above to self-involvement through faith,[59] but is made explicit in several of his works — from his dissertation on Kierkegaard and Freud to *The Knight's*

56. "God and Philosophy," in *Emmanuel Levinas: Basic Philosophical Writings,* ed. A. T. Peperzak et al. (Bloomington: Indiana University Press, 1996), p. 138.

57. For elaboration of these themes, see Levinas, *Totality and Infinity: An Essay on Exteriority,* trans. Alphonso Lingis (Pittsburgh: Duquesne, 1969), and *Otherwise than Being or Beyond Essence,* trans. Alphonso Lingis (Pittsburgh: Duquesne, 1981).

58. Most contemporary interpreters of Aristotle agree that today his view of substance must be expanded to incorporate the importance of a thing's relations. Aristotle was right that we say things about things, but we should also say that the relations of things are essential to their being thingy. See the essays in M. L. O'Hara, *Substances and Things: Aristotle's Doctrine of Physical Substance in Recent Essays* (Washington, DC: University Press of America, 1982), and D. M. MacKinnon, "Aristotle's Conception of Substance" in *New Essays on Plato and Aristotle,* ed. Renford Bambrough (New York: Humanities Press, 1965), pp. 97-119.

59. Loder, "The Place of Science in Practical Theology," p. 23.

Move. Like Kierkegaard, Loder believed that the relationality disclosed in the "God-man" is a basic hermeneutical category and that each individual is called to appropriate this relationality existentially through inward passion.

Reflecting on the historical development of the philosophical turn just outlined and on Loder's own engagement within it, we may identify at least two aspects of the responsibility of practical theology vis-à-vis the late modern interest in relationality. First, in some ways practical theology is responsible *for* the turn. Before the general separation of the natural and human sciences in the Enlightenment and before the development of the "encyclopedia" model of theological education, all theology was in a sense "practical" theology. In the patristic and Reformation eras especially we find that rigorous theoretical reflection was always and already embedded in the practical work of pastors and church leaders. Inherently relational doctrines, such as the incarnation, the Trinity, and the sanctifying presence of the Spirit, emerged out of inherently relational experiences of redemptive transformation in community. Hegel's worry about "bad" infinity was anticipated already in early church theologians like Gregory of Nyssa and in medieval theologians like Nicholas of Cusa. Such thinkers fought against the Greek view of *apeiron* as negative infinity and insisted that divine infinity suggests something positive — the perfection of unlimited superabundance. It was through Hegel's struggle with Christian ideas about incarnation, Trinity, and Spirit that he was led to link relationality and essence, and we should not let the fact that his constructive proposals are problematic cloud our recognition of this philosophical contribution. Loder himself often noted that the relational Christian intuitions of nineteenth-century scientists like James Clerk Maxwell and Michael Faraday contributed to their new ways of conceptualizing physical reality primarily in terms of fields rather than substances.

Theology is responsible in another sense — not only *for* but also *to* the philosophical turn to relationality. Retrieving the relational thought-forms of the biblical tradition can help us respond to late modern anthropological self-understandings that are open to the categorical and existential significance of relationality. Practical theology, which is intrinsically interdisciplinary and oriented toward the integral relation of praxis to theory, is in a unique position to contribute to this task. All of the sub-disciplines of theology ought to be aware of the way in which philosophical and cultural context shapes and is shaped by Christian speech about God, but practical theology is particularly focused on this hermeneutical reciprocity at the intersection of faith and *contemporary* culture. Loder's transgression of disciplinary boundaries and passionate incursion into nontheological fields of inquiry that have struggled with the agonistic and ecstatic relations of human becoming offer us an example of a practical theologian who was responsible to the divine call to participate in the reconciliation of persons. Although the philosophical turn to relationality may require a more critical evaluation of some traditional doctrinal formulations that were overly shaped by ancient Greek or early modern substance metaphysics, the general elevation of dynamic relationality over static substance should be a happy occasion for Christian theology and praxis. James Loder was among those who have seen that these philosophical developments provide an opportunity for a fresh clarification of the theological relationality at the heart of Christian belief and praxis: the redemptive transformation made possible by the incarnation and Pentecost.

13. The Heidegger in Loder (or, How the Nothing Became the Void): Provoking Wonder in Education

John D. Kuentzel

Anyone familiar with James Loder's work will know that one of the central concepts in his ontology is that of the void. Within that ontology, he also articulates the meaning of self, world, and the Holy,[1] but void experiences are crucial in his understanding of transformation. Void is the conflict that sets human knowing on its way toward transformation; it is the conflict that makes possible transformation in four dimensions when one is open, through faith, to the working of the Holy Spirit in one's life.

Although the connection is not at first apparent, one of the readings Loder used to assign the students taking his Philosophy of Education class was Martin Heidegger's "What Is Metaphysics?" That essay — originally his inaugural lecture at the University of Freiburg in the summer of 1929 — represents Heidegger's most sustained elaboration of the problem of the nothing. There can be little doubt that this essay has exercised its influence in Loder's understanding of the four dimensions of Being, and specifically that dimension he called the void.[2] In what follows, we will provide an overview of the salient points in "What Is Metaphysics?" making reference as appropriate to relevant passages in *Being and Time* and other works of Heidegger, and try to show the way in which Loder's conception of the void was influenced by Heidegger at

1. See James E. Loder, *The Transforming Moment*, 2nd ed. (Colorado Springs: Helmers & Howard, 1989), pp. 67ff.

2. See *Transforming Moment*, pp. 80ff. A reference to "What Is Metaphysics?" occurs in the discussion of "negation" in its calculative mode in the glossary; see *Transforming Moment*, p. 226. Heidegger's thought does, of course, get mediated to Loder in part through the work of the Scottish theologian John Macquarrie; see *Transforming Moment*, p. 68 n. 1. Yet Macquarrie, one of the two translators of the first English version of *Being and Time*, was himself deeply influenced by Heidegger, and so it will not be inappropriate to reach back to Heidegger himself, whom Loder had also read, to examine the influences at work in his notion of the void.

various points. This is in no way to diminish the fact that Loder's own void experiences, of which he gives an account at several points in *The Transforming Moment*,[3] made their own contribution to his understanding of the term, but there is a clear sense in which Heidegger also gave him a language with which to make sense of these experiences.

For Loder, of course, the void is to be understood as encompassing any of the experiences of evil one might endure in a lifetime. It shows its many faces in such experiences as loneliness, guilt, shame, despair, alienation, loss, conflict, and suffering of virtually any sort. It is present in the multiple negations that become the basis of ego strength. Uncovering the Heidegger in Loder, however, will allow us to reclaim the positive connotations in this notion. This will be done partly through the experience of wonder, the implications of which we will explore for education.

Heidegger and Loder: From the Nothing to the Void and Beyond

Heidegger's approach in seeking an answer to the question "What Is Metaphysics?" is unapologetically phenomenological. Because it is an inaugural lecture, Heidegger will take the sciences, which are any of the fields of study one may find in the university, as his point of departure in seeking to discern what is metaphysically essential to every mode of human knowing. He introduces the essay with a dual characterization of the task of metaphysical inquiry. First, "every metaphysical question encompasses the whole range of metaphysical problems. Each question is itself already the whole."[4] On a first reading, this can seem an extremely obscure claim to one not acquainted with Heidegger's work. When one remembers that Heidegger was preoccupied first and foremost with fundamental ontology, that is, with the question of Being itself,[5] some clarity

3. See, e.g., *Transforming Moment*, pp. 9ff., 87-88.

4. Martin Heidegger, *Basic Writings*, ed. David Farrell Krell (San Francisco: HarperCollins, 1993), p. 93. What is not under consideration here are an afterword and an introduction added by Heidegger in 1943 and 1949 respectively. In the afterword, he attempted to respond to a number of the criticisms that had been raised with respect to his notions of the nothing, anxiety, and logic.

5. Fundamental ontology had already become Heidegger's preeminent concern by the time of the writing of his *magnum opus*, published two years prior to the inaugural lecture; see *Being and Time*, trans. John Macquarrie and Edward Robinson (San Francisco: HarperCollins, 1962), p. 1. Here it is the question about the *meaning* of being that is uppermost, and an understanding of the being of *Dasein*, the human being, is the way toward a first answer.

may begin to dawn. For Heidegger, the essence of metaphysical inquiry is this question about Being itself, which term signifies a totality which is not itself one kind of being among others. As he says near the end of the lecture, metaphysics is "inquiry beyond or over beings, which aims to recover them as such and as a whole for our grasp."[6] Every question about Being itself, then, is a question about the whole. This first characterization accords most nearly with what is commonly understood to be metaphysical inquiry in that it is something like a transcendental conception of Being that is sought.

A second characterization follows on the first as its corollary: "every metaphysical question can be asked only in such a way that the questioner as such is present together with the question, that is, is placed in question."[7] Belonging to that totality which is being itself, the human questioner, too, is brought into question. This is the non-conventional dimension in metaphysical questioning, the dimension that finally denies the adequacy of any characterization of Heidegger's approach to metaphysics as "transcendental." This human dimension is what has gotten consistently overlooked in this mode of inquiry. Although one can detect the beginnings of a shift taking place in Heidegger's thought from a focus on the *Dasein* who can ask about the meaning of Being — as in *Being and Time* — to the place of the *Dasein* who questions within the whole of being, one still hears an echo in this second characterization of the earlier insistence that precisely that being who can raise the question about Being is the proper (phenomenological) point of departure for a fundamental ontology.[8] The fact that Loder, too, puts the question about what it means most essentially to be human together with the question about Being mirrors this early conviction of Heidegger's.[9] As Loder says, "the two are not separate investigations, because the most immediate, and I would argue the most necessary, avenue to the essense of Being-itself is through human being."[10]

Because it belongs in its original form to the genre of the inaugural lec-

6. *Basic Writings*, p. 106.

7. *Basic Writings*, p. 93.

8. *Being and Time*, p. 27. In the "Letter on Humanism," Heidegger suggests that a "turning" *(Kehre)* has taken place in his thought after *Being and Time* — although precisely what the term means and to what point in the development of his work it refers are much debated issues. If Heidegger is allowed this self-characterization of his work, one would not be entirely remiss if one were to trace at least the origin of the "turn" to the inaugural lecture, for here Being itself — *inclusive* of the being of the questioner — is in question. Whether or not the idea of a "turn" is adequate, however, the point being made is that Heidegger has a much larger domain, the totality that is Being itself, in view in "What Is Metaphysics?" in a way that shows both continuity and discontinuity with the earlier *Being and Time.*

9. See *Being and Time*, p. 34.

10. *Transforming Moment*, p. 69.

ture, one should not be surprised that Heidegger early takes up what he sees to be the problem of the sciences. These varied disciplines have become such diverse specialties that the only thing that can be said about their unity is that it lies in "the technical organization of universities and faculties . . . the practical establishment of goals by each discipline provides the only meaningful source of unity."[11] The conclusion he draws from this is that "the rootedness of the sciences in their essential ground has atrophied."[12]

We are now drawn into a fully phenomenological investigation as we encounter Heidegger's opening sallies into the matter. Heidegger wishes to probe beneath the common assumptions that are held by and about the sciences in order to discern their "essential ground." Put differently, Heidegger wants to allow the sciences, by way of an eidetic analysis,[13] to reveal what is most basic to them, and this with the being who is able to conduct scientific research fully in view. In the words of an earlier formulation, Heidegger wants to "let that which shows itself be seen from itself in the very way in which it shows itself from itself."[14] Or, in those of a later formulation, Heidegger says: "Thinking . . . lets itself be claimed by Being so that it can say the truth of Being."[15] One already sees presaged in these methodological formulations the later notion of a "letting be" *(Gelassenheit)*, which became a significant aspect of John Macquarrie's thought in *Principles of Christian Theology* and which Loder recast as "letting flourish" in *The Transforming Moment.*[16]

Noting that the existence of all those present at the lecture is determined by the practice of science in the academic context, Heidegger asks: "What happens to us, essentially, in the grounds of our existence, when science becomes our passion?"[17] This then becomes the question that will allow "the unfolding of a metaphysical question" in the first section of the lecture. If we take seriously "their most proper intention, in all the sciences we relate ourselves to beings themselves."[18] Science has taken as its task the investigation of these beings — or, more accurately, a prescribed segment of these beings and their specific,

11. *Basic Writings,* p. 94.

12. *Basic Writings,* p. 94.

13. The term "eidetic analysis" identifies more precisely the method of phenomenological investigation. The word "eidetic" comes from the Greek εἶδος, which means "form" or "outward appearance." The eidetic analysis — or eidetic reduction, as it is sometimes called — involves the probing beneath the outward appearance of a thing in order to determine the thing in its essence.

14. *Being and Time,* p. 58.

15. *Basic Writings,* p. 218.

16. *Transforming Moment,* pp. 68, 79-80.

17. *Basic Writings,* p. 94.

18. *Basic Writings,* p. 94.

lawful modes of being in relation to one another — and this puts the scientist *in relation to* beings according to science's own most proper definition of its task.

Moreover, the scientist is properly guided by a canon that insists on impartiality in the research; adequate results cannot be attained in scientific inquiry, according to this canon, if personal bias interferes significantly in the processes and outcomes of the research. Thus, there is a kind of *submission* of *Dasein* as scientist to the beings under investigation. As Heidegger puts it, "In such impartiality of inquiring, determining, and grounding, a peculiarly delineated submission to beings themselves obtains, in order that they may reveal themselves."[19]

However, for Heidegger this submission cannot mean the submersion or disappearance of the human being. If, as he has already indicated, every metaphysical question has to do with the whole of beings, and if, for that reason, the place of the human being as questioner in this whole cannot be overlooked, Heidegger, in a further characterization of *Dasein*'s scientific existence, describes it as an irruption into the whole of beings:

> Man — one being among others — "pursues science." In this "pursuit" nothing less transpires than the irruption by one being called "man" into the whole of beings, indeed in such a way that in and through this irruption beings break open and show what they are and how they are. The irruption that breaks open, in its way, helps beings above all to themselves.[20]

This irruption is an unequivocally phenomenological concept for Heidegger, inasmuch as it is an irruption that "helps beings to themselves." The human being, one kind of being among many other kinds of being, is the only being to whom something like an "essential nature" of the beings under investigation can appear. Apart from human being, no beings at all are revealed as beings. Thus, the irruption signifies that the human being is capable, in an act of transcendence, of apprehending a being as what it is within a field of other beings which includes her or his own being.

We might note at this point that Loder has a notion of the self's involvement in scientific research that appears to echo Heidegger's sentiments on this:

> When in any given frame of knowledge reason reaches its intrinsic limit, not just for this or that problem but *the limit in itself* with respect to its object of investigation, it is not just a matter of too little information or insuf-

19. *Basic Writings*, pp. 94-95.
20. *Basic Writings*, p. 95.

> ficient technology. It is finally because reason has ignored the reasoner. When this is accounted for, then, a wider frame of knowing must be conceived which includes both reason and the reasoner in a relationality that is pertinent to the field of inquiry involved.[21]

If we remember that this text reflects primarily the influence of Kierkegaard and Polanyi,[22] we may be permitted the conjecture that Heidegger, too, stands behind this formulation of the self-involvement of the researcher — even if somewhat remotely. At the very least, Loder's notion of "relationality" in this text, although directed explicitly at the various fields of scientific inquiry, could easily stand in for Heidegger's understanding that every metaphysical question takes in the whole of beings including the being of the *Dasein* who asks the question about Being.

Heidegger sums up the discussion of the human involvement in scientific inquiry by saying that it entails a *relation to the world* in which *Dasein,* too, has its being, an *attitude* toward that world which involves the impartiality of *Dasein's* submission, and the *irruption* of *Dasein* into that world such that beings are disclosed as what they are — that is, show themselves from themselves, as it were. Then, as if once again to stress the proper role of science, Heidegger insists: "What should be examined are beings only, and besides that — nothing; beings alone, and further — nothing; solely beings, and beyond that — nothing."[23]

Having followed the argument thus far, the reader might be inclined to regard Heidegger's characterization of science as a fairly conventional account. Is not the investigation of beings precisely what the scientist attempts to accomplish? And does not the impartiality of the scientist's submission to beings serve the purposes of the investigation? Is this not what the culture of science attempts to inculcate in all those who enter the rank and file of researchers in the various disciplines? What has been sought is the suppression of those passions that might bias the results through a submission to beings such that they will disclose themselves in their own being. What more is needed? But what Heidegger wants to engage is that "nothing" which appears at first almost as an afterthought. Denying that it is a bare tautology, a mere rhetorical flourish to justify science's place in the modern world, he notes that science rejects "the nothing" as beyond the proper domain of its investigation. "Against it science

21. *Transforming Moment,* p. 54.

22. See, e.g., Søren Kierkegaard, *The Sickness Unto Death: A Christian Psychological Exposition for Upbuilding and Awakening,* ed. and trans. H. V. Hong and E. H. Hong (Princeton: Princeton University Press, 1980); and Michael Polanyi, *Personal Knowledge: Towards a Post-critical Philosophy* (Chicago: University of Chicago Press, 1958).

23. *Basic Writings,* p. 95.

must now reassert its seriousness and soberness of mind, insisting that it is concerned solely with beings." Yet precisely in abandoning it in this way, the nothing is admitted: "science wishes to know nothing of the nothing. Ultimately this is the scientifically rigorous conception of the nothing. We know it, the nothing, in that we wish to know nothing about it." Thus, when science seeks to define itself and its tasks, "it calls upon the nothing for help."[24]

In this way, Heidegger arrives at the nothing which, as the argument proceeds, will be seen as the reason why the scientist can have beings to investigate in the first place. Indeed, the old substance metaphysic, the tradition passed on by Descartes to modernity, in which one undertakes the questioning of particular beings, is being superseded by what Heidegger considers the more encompassing reality: the nothing. Although the investigation of beings may be said to be what scientists in fact do, it is not the most basic way of characterizing their endeavor, according to Heidegger. Science has failed to be philosophically rigorous about what it is up to. Loder, of course, also argued this view about the *human* sciences, although he acknowledged that some in the field were more aware of this problem than others.

Heidegger now attempts some clarification of this phenomenon of the nothing and the way in which it is apprehended in an "elaboration of the question" about metaphysics in a second section. Yet we are immediately confronted with a problem. If we postulate the nothing in our thinking or speech, "we posit it as a being. But that is exactly what it is not. Interrogating the nothing — asking what and how it, the nothing, is — turns what is interrogated into its opposite."[25] This means also that any of our attempts to provide an *answer* to this conundrum about the nothing are equally absurd, because they assume that the nothing somehow exists. Every question and answer concerning the nothing makes what is not objectifiable into something objective. The influence of Heidegger in Loder is seen perhaps most perspicuously at the point when, in *The Transforming Moment,* we read: "Any talk of 'void' is of course a semantic anomaly; it seems to be speaking of nothing as if it were presence; nonbeing as if it were being."[26]

What Heidegger will call for, then, is a way of thinking — by its nature always thinking about something in particular — that runs counter to its essence when it gets the nothing "in view."

Logic, of course, might propose that "the nothing is the negation of the to-

24. *Basic Writings,* p. 96. To get a circumscribed field of beings in view for the purposes of scientific research is to put the nothing in abeyance; yet this putting the nothing in abeyance has precisely the effect of "helping beings to themselves"!

25. *Basic Writings,* p. 96.

26. *Transforming Moment,* p. 80.

tality of beings."[27] One might try to think the totality of beings by way of an idea, upon which one would then perform a negation, thus substantiating the nothing through this logical operation. But a problem already emerges here in that human beings are finite creatures for whom the intellectual penetration of the totality of beings is not possible.[28] Moreover, while such an operation might give us the formal (hypothetical) concept of the nothing, it cannot give us the nothing itself. Thus, logic fails the enterprise. It cannot overcome the problem it has itself posed regarding the absurdity of thinking about the nothing, for even as a formal concept it has distinguished something, that is, made *some thing* of the nothing.

This analysis of logic leads Heidegger to pose all sorts of questions about the priority of logic and the intellect — and these implicitly serve a larger goal stated early in his career: the destruction of the history of ontology.[29] In turn, this line of questioning leads to and concludes with the query whether the negation of the intellect is what gives the nothing or rather the nothing which gives the possibility of negation. Heidegger asserts unequivocally that it is the latter: "the nothing is more original than the 'not' and negation."[30] The nothing precedes the negation of the logician; indeed, the nothing is its very ground. "How could negation [of the logician] produce the not from itself when it can make denials only when something deniable is granted to it?"

How then is one to think about the nothing if logic fails us (by presuming so much as to explain its own ground)? Here, Heidegger poses another set of questions that in part recall Socrates' epistemological paradox.[31]

> Where shall we seek the nothing? Where will we find the nothing? In order to find something must we not already know in general that it is there? Indeed! At first and for the most part man can seek only when he has anticipated the being at hand of what he is looking for. Now the nothing is what we are seeking. Is there ultimately such a thing as a search without that anticipation, a search to which pure discovery belongs?[32]

The claim implied in the questioning here is that the nothing must be "given beforehand" — which is to say, it must be encounterable — if we are to get our bearings on it. This explains how it is given in "anticipation," although the anticipation is full of the paradoxes we have already encountered in the nothing.

27. *Basic Writings*, p. 97.
28. *Basic Writings*, pp. 98-99.
29. Cf. *Being and Time*, pp. 41ff.
30. *Basic Writings*, p. 97.
31. See Plato, *Meno*, trans. Benjamin Jowett (New York: Macmillan, 1949), p. 36.
32. *Basic Writings*, p. 98.

What Loder seems to have gotten from Heidegger on this point is that despite the human inability to talk meaningfully about the void, it is something experienceable and something that can be made sense of in terms of its manifestation in human loneliness, isolation, conflict, and death. Thus, he insists that

> it is part of the uniqueness of human being that negation is meaningfully included in the composition of our "lived worlds" and in our sense of "self." Many people live not only on the near side of the limit [the void], but in a real sense beyond it as they choose to enact self-destructive patterns of behavior. . . . Void is the ultimate aim of all proximate forms of nothingness; the implicit aim of conflict, absence, loneliness, and death is void.[33]

Here, Loder assumes (with Heidegger) that the void "is not beyond human experience."

To put all of this another way, the "totality of beings must be given in advance so as to be able to fall prey straightway to negation — in which the nothing itself would then be manifest." Yet is this not the very strategy of the logician? How can the "totality of beings" be anything other than an idea of it? What is Heidegger proposing here that is any different from the approach of logic? If we keep in mind that Heidegger is working as the consummate phenomenologist, we will see that what he has characterized as the approach to the question of the nothing made by logic is in fact the essence of any proper approach to the nothing. Furthermore, one must read these notions of the "totality of beings" and "negation" in light of what is coming into view for Heidegger. To be sure, we cannot comprehend the whole of beings in themselves, but "we certainly do find ourselves stationed in the midst of beings that are revealed somehow as a whole."

> In the end an essential distinction prevails between *comprehending* the whole of beings in themselves and *finding oneself in the midst of* beings as a whole. The former is impossible in principle. The latter happens all the time in our existence. . . . No matter how fragmented our everyday existence may appear to be, . . . it always deals with beings in a unity of the whole, if only in a shadowy way.[34]

What Heidegger appears to have in mind in this notion of "beings in a unity of the whole" is something like his earlier notion in *Being and Time* of the

33. *Transforming Moment*, p. 81.
34. *Basic Writings*, p. 99; italics added.

"worldhood of the world," that referential totality which belongs essentially to *Dasein* in that it is composed by *Dasein*.[35] Heidegger actually posits four meanings of the term "world" there, but the third and fourth meanings are the ones that concern us for now. An ontical meaning describes "world" as the *"wherein"* of *Dasein*'s encounters; this refers to the understanding of world as a circumscribed structure of meaning which gives significance to *Dasein*'s role functions within that "world," so that one can speak, for example, of the teacher's "world" or the carpenter's "world." This world is beyond any complete objectivization; indeed, we humans live in these worlds *mostly circumspectively* — that is, beings become manifest as what they are within a field of other beings which tacitly define the context, and moreover they become manifest not so much to reflection but to use.

An ontico-ontological meaning renders "world" that structure — again, non-objectifiable — belonging essentially to *Dasein* as Being-in-the-world which makes possible the world construction of the first definition just given. It is important to emphasize here that this latter notion is not itself the meaning structure *per se*, but is rather its possibility. Taking them together, which Heidegger himself does when he speaks of the "worldhood of the world," we might go so far as to say that the two terms are what gives a culture; the "worldhood of the world" is what allows human beings to participate in the making and re-making of culture. The "worldhood of the world" is what makes it possible for the human being to take on the role of teacher or carpenter and interact meaningfully with the people and things that occupy the worlds of the teacher or the carpenter, and even to set in motion processes that will transform those worlds when something problematic is encountered. In these two notions of world, we encounter what Loder would come to call our "composed 'worlds.'"[36] This notion of "beings as a whole," then, signals a totality which is not, however, an *idea* of the whole, but is rather a localized reality which itself constitutes a *mostly circumspective* meaning of totality. And it is by way of mood or attunement *(Stimmung)* that one finds oneself situated among this totality of beings.

Heidegger comments briefly on the way boredom can do this. The boredom of which he speaks is *not* in view when one says, for example, "I'm bored with this book," or "I'm bored with this game." In saying this, one makes reference more to a quality of the entity encountered — so that one could just as well say this book or that game is boring — than to the fact that one is bored oneself. "Boredom is still distant" in these instances. What is in view here is not a boredom with some thing in particular but rather the more primal experience

35. See *Being and Time*, p. 93.

36. *Transforming Moment*, p. 69.

that "one is bored." Heidegger's way of characterizing this is poignant: "Profound boredom, drifting here and there in the abysses of our existence like a muffling fog, removes all things and human beings and oneself along with them into a remarkable indifference. This boredom reveals beings as a whole."[37] In the same place, Heidegger suggests that the mood of joy at being in love can also reveal beings as a whole. He does not say how this happens, but one can imagine again that what is not in view is a joy in something particular — the joy that comes with getting married or over the birth of a child — but rather an all-pervasive joy which gets infused into all of one's encounters and all of one's doings. In either case, beings as a whole are revealed — in the totalizing indifference of boredom or in the fullness of joy. Yet these moods, even as they disclose beings as a whole, at the same are said to "conceal the nothing" from us.

The mood, however, which originally and most decisively reveals beings as a whole, and therewith the nothing, is anxiety. Here, Heidegger appears to be recapitulating an earlier account of the matter in *Being and Time.* This anxiety is said to be rare and occurs only momentarily when it is experienced at all.[38] As in the matter of boredom, Heidegger rejects the common view of anxiety which reduces it to fearfulness. We are always afraid of some thing in particular; we become fearful "in the face of" this or that particular threat posed by some concrete entity or event. But anxiety is a different matter: "a peculiar calm pervades it. Anxiety is indeed anxiety in the face of . . . , but not in the face of this or that thing. . . . The indeterminateness of that in the face of which and for which we become anxious is no mere lack of determination but rather the essential impossibility of determining it."[39] As long as it is remembered that Heidegger's is a phenomenology of being as mediated in social practices rather than of individual consciousness (Husserl, Sartre),[40] we might note that John Macquarrie, in his *Principles of Christian Theology,* helpfully characterizes this anxiety as a "mode of awareness" rather than a subjective emotion[41] — not something we apprehend directly so much as simply a way of apprehending. The English word "attunement" communicates this sense perhaps better than "mood" does. Thus, anxiety becomes a way of *being*-in-the-world. Yet, in the words "the essential impossibility of determining," we already encounter the first sign of the nothing, the source of original anxiety, beginning to emerge.

37. *Basic Writings,* p. 99.

38. *Basic Writings,* p. 100; cf. *Being and Time,* pp. 233-234.

39. *Basic Writings,* pp. 100-101; cf. *Being and Time,* pp. 230-231.

40. This point is cogently argued by Hubert L. Dreyfuss in his study of Division One of *Being and Time* in *Being-in-the-World* (Cambridge: MIT Press, 1991), pp. 13-14.

41. John Macquarrie, *Principles of Christian Theology* (New York: Charles Scribner's Sons, 1977), p. 86.

In a further characterization of the experience of anxiety, Heidegger says: "*es ist einem unheimlich.*" Krell has adequately translated this as, "one feels ill at ease." Yet this does not quite communicate the rich sense of the word *unheimlich.* Heidegger himself pointed out in *Being and Time* that, from an etymological point of view, the German word *unheimlich* means "not-being-at-home." In experiencing being as uncanny, one feels dislocated, a stranger in one's place. "Everyday familiarity collapses."[42] A sense of meaninglessness prevails. As was said of boredom, "All things and we ourselves sink into indifference."[43]

Let us be perfectly clear that this sinking into indifference does not signify in any way that beings disappear. If we can keep in mind the phenomenological frame of reference out of which Heidegger is working, we may have less difficulty with his assertion that while beings in anxiety are seen as receding from us, they are at the same time experienced as turning back toward us.[44] This peculiar claim signifies what we have already met with: the meaning structures by which we encounter entities in our worlds have collapsed so that beings, just in their being-ness, are all that is left to us in the moment when anxiety is felt most acutely. Thus, in anxiety the child will see the chalk and the chalkboard, the desks, computers, and so forth — all still there as objects — but they no longer possess the circumspective significance they had only moments before in the world of the child as student; the hammers, saws, nails, and the partially completed building are all still there in anxiety, but they no longer constitute the meaning-structure they once did in the world of the carpenter. The entities, just as entities — that is, devoid of any relational significance — is what remains in each case.

Heidegger sees this anxiety as a profoundly ambivalent reality. If, in the receding of beings as a whole, beings as the mere entities they are turn back toward us in their receding, our being amongst these beings becomes burdensome to us.[45] In the closing in of the beings that are receding, "anxiety oppresses us." At the same time, in anxiety our experience is that we "can get no hold on things. In the slipping away of beings, only this 'no hold on things' comes over us and remains."[46] The "no hold on things" signifies the existential dimension of the loss of the significance of the beings within-a-world.

It is in this receding of beings which at the same time come oppressively near that the negation of the totality of beings occurs which is the experience of

42. *Being and Time,* p. 233.

43. *Basic Writings,* p. 101.

44. *Basic Writings,* p. 101.

45. In *Being and Time,* Heidegger discusses this sense of the burdensomeness under the broader category of mood; cf. *Being and Time,* pp. 172ff.

46. *Basic Writings,* p. 101.

nothingness. In a few terse words, Heidegger says, "Anxiety discloses the nothing." It takes speech away; "in the face of anxiety, all utterance of the 'is' falls silent." As Loder used to say on occasion, we can never say what it is that makes us feel this way, so that when we are asked what we feel anxious about, and we say, "It's nothing," we have spoken the truth. If the experience of crisis may be said to have a kinship to — in that it is the "offspring" of — this original anxiety, those with a measure of experience in pastoral care will know that when it occurs death often leaves people speechless, and they will know too that often it is best to keep silence with the family in the face of this event. And they will know as well that medical professionals who encounter it on a regular basis are often given over to compulsive talk to conceal the awe-fulness of it when it occurs. Anxiety also robs one of one's self; even "we ourselves — we humans who are in being — in the midst of beings slip away from ourselves."[47] Again, there is no other experience like the experience of the loss of a loved one that can bring out feelings of being "out of touch with" oneself. Part of the grieving process is figuring out how to re-situate oneself among the entities of a once familiar environment following the death of a spouse, a child, or even a parent.

From this, it will be obvious how the experience of crisis can bring one to an encounter with the nothing. And I think this obviousness has led many of Heidegger's critics to assume therefore that his notions of anxiety and the nothing have no more than negative, possibly even nihilistic, connotations. I would vigorously contest any claim that this is all there is to these matters. Indeed, all Heidegger will say about these negatives is consequential to a claim that were the negation of the logician the source and ground of the nothing, then the human experience of evil would be a trifling matter at best. Yet,

> Unyielding antagonism and stinging rebuke have a more abysmal source than the measured negation of thought. Galling failure and merciless prohibition require some deeper answer. Bitter privation is more burdensome.[48]

Here, he is simply trying to make the point that the experience of the nothing is fundamental — more fundamental than the logician's negation. Beyond this, a close reading of Heidegger will reveal the positive dimension in this way of thinking as well. I want to suggest that for Heidegger the nothing is the dynamic that underlies all human transformation. Indeed, the negation that a creative scientist experiences when encountering phenomena that cannot be accounted for under a traditional theoretical paradigm (as when inconsisten-

47. *Basic Writings*, p. 101.
48. *Basic Writings*, p. 105.

cies in the measurement of particles began to be observed prior to the emergence of quantum theory) is hardly to be characterized as nihilism; it in fact propels the scientist into an active scanning process out of which new theoretical insights may emerge.

If we might step back for a moment and define the temporal structure of *Dasein,* this will set the stage for seeing more clearly the dynamic in the nothing. The origin of the word *Dasein* in the German has been variously traced to *Da-sein* (signifying something like "there-[is-]being" or "being there") and *Das-sein* (from medieval philosophy signifying the more primordial "that-being" as opposed to the "what-being" [*Was-sein*] which is the product of a reflection). The differences between the two terms is not, in my judgment, substantive with respect to Heidegger's intentions; they would in either case point to that fundamental human reality that we have not chosen our Being-in-the-world and yet we each one of us has our being as an issue for us — or, as Heidegger puts it, "The 'essence' of Dasein lies in its existence."[49] We are, in our human essence, a temporally projected Being-possible as also thrown. In that openness which is the human Being-possible, we do not escape the givenness of our "is" which we did not choose, and yet we are possessed of the freedom (and responsibility) to make of ourselves what we are yet "to be" within the givenness of our "is." The confluence of the "is" and the "to be" in *Being and Time* is the issue of what Heidegger will call the nothing in "What Is Metaphysics?" In other words, *Dasein* emerges from the nothing and is continually re-creating itself out of this nothing — and characterizing this becomes the burden of the fuller "answer to the question" in the third section of "What Is Metaphysics?"

To this end, Heidegger states the implication of what has already been said up to this point in the lecture: "in anxiety the nothing is encountered at one with beings as a whole." Raising the question of what "at one with" might mean, he begins to probe the dynamic nature of the nothing: "the nothing makes itself known with beings and in beings expressly as a slipping away of the whole."[50] A further characterization of the nothing follows:

> In anxiety there occurs a shrinking back before . . . that is surely not any sort of flight but rather a kind of bewildered calm. This "back before" takes its departure from the nothing. The nothing does not attract; it is essentially repelling. . . . *This wholly repelling gesture toward beings that are in retreat as a whole, which is the action of the nothing that oppresses Dasein in anxiety, is the essence of the nothing:* nihilation.[51]

49. *Being and Time,* p. 67.
50. *Basic Writings,* p. 102.
51. *Basic Writings,* pp. 102-103; italics added.

This is Heidegger's most explicit, if seemingly paradoxical, articulation of what the nothing "is." Indeed, to say that the nothing "is" will be on Heidegger's terms to say no more than that the nothing repels.

Ontologically the nothing as repelling gesture must be seen as the very dynamic by which human transformation is set on its way, including transformation in human knowing. We have already seen that it belongs essentially to the experience and "perception" of *Dasein.* It is not something "out there" to which the thoughts of *Dasein* must somehow correspond; indeed, it lacks all objectivity whatsoever.[52] And yet, the nothing in its repellent force is "at one with" beings as a whole. Phenomenologically, it is encountered in that movement of anxiety which is at once the receding from and the closing in on *Dasein* of beings as a whole. This repelling or nihilating nothing is what "makes possible in advance the revelation of beings in general." It is, in other words, that from which beings emerge. "[A]s the repelling gesture toward the retreating whole of beings, it discloses these beings in their full but heretofore concealed strangeness as what is radically other — with respect to the nothing."[53] Thus, the nihilating nothing is the *ground* of being.

What can this possibly mean? Heidegger gives a clue — but only a clue — when he says, "In the clear night of the nothing of anxiety the original openness of beings as such arises: that they are beings — and not nothing." This, of course, is the central issue for metaphysics and the issue that drives the entire thought-project in the lecture. In the closing lines of the lecture, he will call for a willingness to let ourselves be held in the suspense of the nothing so that we can experience that most "*basic question of metaphysics* which the nothing compels: why are there beings at all, and why not rather nothing?"[54] And in the opening lines of *Introduction to Metaphysics* (a lecture course delivered in the summer semester of 1935 at Freiburg), he likewise poses the question, "Why are there beings [*Seiende*] rather than nothing?" In this later text, he calls it "the first of all questions" which most people never encounter directly: "And yet each of us is grazed at least once, perhaps more than once, by the hidden power of this question. . . . The question looms in moments of great despair, when things tend to lose all their weight and all meaning becomes obscured."[55] This most basic question of metaphysics, then, is always implicit in anxiety's primordial encounter with the nothing, and this is what makes metaphysics "the basic occurrence of Dasein."[56] Metaphysics, in

52. *Basic Writings,* p. 104.

53. *Basic Writings,* p. 103.

54. *Basic Writings,* p. 110; italics added.

55. See Martin Heidegger, *Introduction to Metaphysics,* trans. Ralph Manheim (New Haven: Yale University Press, 1987), p. 1.

56. *Basic Writings,* p. 109.

other words, is what human being by nature does as *Dasein.* In the nothing encountered in anxiety, we are "transposed directly into metaphysics."

Yet we are less concerned with the implications of the nothing for metaphysics than we are with the transformational potential the experience gives, and the phrase, "the original openness of beings arises," already suggests a dynamism into which we have only partially tapped with that notion of the "repelling gesture" which is the nihilating of the nothing. The argument moves apace here. In the experience of the nothing, *Dasein* gets brought, as if for the first time, before beings as such, and this is to be understood as including *Dasein's* own being. As Heidegger puts it, "since existence in its essence relates itself to beings — those which it is not and that which it is — it emerges as such existence in each case from the nothing already revealed."[57] What we have in these words is an account of human transcendence. Even more explicitly, Heidegger will say: "Da-sein means: being held out into the nothing."

> Holding itself out into the nothing, Dasein is in each case already beyond beings as a whole. This being beyond beings we call "transcendence."[58]

In part, what Heidegger is saying here is that the essence of *Dasein* is transcendence. What this means further is that in the absence of the encounter with the nothing, the human being would lack the capacity to relate itself to beings as beings within-the-world or even to itself as one being within the whole. In a terse formulation, Heidegger insists that apart from the experience of the nothing, there is "no selfhood and no freedom."[59]

It is, of course, well known that for Loder too the ego is constructed on a series of negations. As he puts it, "The ego autonomy emerges as an outgrowth of the child's learning to function as the agent rather than the victim of negation. Thus negation creates the foundation of the autonomous ego and the personality is thereafter effectively divided."[60] (Here again, one gets the impression that void signifies the experience of evil in Loder's thought.)

In order to grasp transformation in Heidegger, it is imperative that we see these notions of the "openness of beings" and "transcendence" together. In Heidegger's thought, these two conceptions cannot stand in opposition to one another, but are, rather, completely intertwined in human consciousness. Beings have their openness only in human transcendence, which is the human's freedom; human transcendence is what it is in the openness of beings. The two

57. *Basic Writings,* p. 103.
58. *Basic Writings,* p. 103.
59. *Basic Writings,* p. 103.
60. *Transforming Moment,* pp. 164-165.

cannot be separated. What Heidegger clearly wants to say here is that human encounters with beings (including encounters with itself) and human perceptions of those encounters are fluid and ever-changing. If, as the analysis in *Being and Time* would seem to require, beings are always encountered as beings within-the-world, the significance structure within that referential totality which is the world is always fluid and the relevance of particular beings within that structure always changing. The "openness of being" as grounded in the nothing and "transcendence" thus gives us Heidegger's account of transformation. In Heidegger's terms, the transformation of the being of *Dasein* would necessarily entail the transformation of beings, and vice versa. The two cannot be divided because that with which we have to do is beings as a whole. Heidegger's is a thoroughly relational notion of the human being in this account, which is a likely reason why his work had its appeal to Loder. To recast what is essentially the same thing in Loder's terms, we can say that transformations of self, the first dimension of being, necessarily entail transformations of the lived world, the second dimension of being, inasmuch as the self-world is an indivisible, relational unit; moreover, these processes will of necessity take place on the social level as well as the individual, for, in Loder's terms, "The body is magnificently transposed and extended into personal, social, and cultural 'worlds' by the common genius of the imagination and the symbolic process."[61] The transformation of this self that is always "taking in" and "getting into" things (to use Loder's language) necessarily involves the constructing and reconstructing of the lived world as well.

For Heidegger's part, he comments on the dynamism involved when he says: "The nothing does not merely serve as the counterconcept of beings; rather, it originally belongs to their essential unfolding as such. In the Being of beings the nihilation of the nothing occurs."[62] It is what gives beings their stark otherness with respect to the nothing. And this then becomes the ground for *Dasein*'s creative engagement with beings. Human transcendence, which is holding oneself out into the nothing, is that by which we recognize beings in their pure beingness and that in which the possibility of new interpretations of these beings is opened to us such that they can become beings for us in new ways.

Some important questions naturally emerge from this account of transformation, and Heidegger acknowledges this when, putting himself in the place of an imagined interlocutor, he asks: If we have to hold ourselves out into the nothing in order to be related to beings, and if anxiety is what originally dis-

61. *Transforming Moment*, p. 71.
62. *Basic Writings*, p. 104.

closes the nothing, do we not then have to hold ourselves in the suspense of anxiety constantly in order to relate to beings, including our own being? And how does this happen if anxiety is said to be rare? Moreover, do not people relate to beings without this anxiety? So how can this anxiety and the nothing it supposedly points to be anything more than a fiction, "a flight of fancy"?[63] In response to these questions, Heidegger points out that what it means to say, "the original anxiety occurs in rare moments," is that the nothing "is at first and for the most part distorted with respect to its originality." Our normal disposition in our day-to-day existence is an orientation toward beings. Yet, "[t]he more we turn toward beings in our preoccupations the less we let beings as a whole slip away as such and the more we turn away from the nothing. Just as surely do we hasten into the public superficies of existence." Although the statement reveals more the influence of Kierkegaard than it does Heidegger, Loder too says: "There is no positive self in this posture; it is only negatively or implicitly present as the person makes an ongoing series of culturally absorbed choices." The self, in other words, is inauthentically other-determined in the constant turning away from the direct encounter with the nihilating nothing. Here Heidegger and Loder, no doubt, both reflect the influence of Kierkegaard who defined anxiety as "the dizziness of freedom" which "gazes down into its own possibility, grasping at finiteness to sustain itself."[64] At the same time,

> this constant if ambiguous turning away from the nothing accords, within certain limits, with the most proper significance of the nothing. In its nihilation the nothing directs us precisely toward beings. The nothing nihilates incessantly without our really knowing of this occurrence in the manner of our everyday knowledge.[65]

If repelling is the most basic significance of the nothing, then *Dasein*'s turning away from it and toward beings is a movement that follows its most natural inclination in the matter. Yet *Dasein* does this out of the ubiquity of the nothing in human existence. We do not have to be held constantly in anxiety in order for the nothing to be doing its work of making entities manifest as the beings they are. The essence of being human is transcendence, holding oneself out into the nothing, and it happens all the time, even in the most mundane of activities. If Heidegger's is a more descriptive account of the turning away from the

63. *Basic Writings*, p. 104.

64. See Søren Kierkegaard, *The Concept of Dread: A Simple Psychological Deliberation Oriented in the Direction of the Dogmatic Problem of Original Sin*, trans. Walter Lowrie (Princeton: Princeton University Press, 1957), p. 55.

65. *Basic Writings*, p. 104.

nothing, Loder's is more pastoral, and this is partly because of the evil that belongs to the experience of the void. Discussing the inevitability of death — the intransigence of human finitude — as pointing to the void, Loder says, "It is small wonder that we screen this inevitable fact out of our minds and out of the 'worlds' we create."[66] The awareness of death potentially makes life meaningless, and so this awareness is avoided.

Yet for Loder the encounter with the void also initiates transformational knowing. In the second chapter of *The Transforming Moment,* Loder had articulated a five-step pattern in transformational knowing in which there is "an apparent rupture in the knowing context"[67] — a conflict — that sets human reflection in motion. Here an important anthropological presupposition of Loder's emerges: the human being is possessed of a fundamental need to compose an ordered environment in which to live. He asserts that "the generative sources of human intelligence abhor a vacuum. Beneath our educated and scholarly ways of knowing, another dynamic moves to explore 'the deep things of the person,' and to generate from hidden resources new, and sometimes powerful insights that transform the horizons of intelligibility."[68] The human experience of conflict/void thus represents "a need on the part of the ungrounded self to recompose the lived 'world' in some imaginative way so as to remove the intrusive threat of nothingness."[69] In one very clear sense, this characterization of transformation nicely parallels Heidegger's own account of the dynamic in the "openness of beings" and "transcendence," where being might be construed as an always fluid "principle of order" for Heidegger. Indeed, we could surmise that this is something of what Heidegger has in mind when he calls metaphysics "the basic occurrence of Dasein."[70] Then in the third chapter of *The Transforming Moment,* Loder insists that void "is the 'conflict' that moves transformational knowing into action."[71]

66. *Transforming Moment,* p. 84.

67. *Transforming Moment,* p. 37.

68. *Transforming Moment,* p. 2.

69. *Transforming Moment,* p. 81.

70. Although Heidegger clearly had metaphysics in an academic sense in mind in the lecture, any of the ordering activities of a self-transcending consciousness — a self holding itself out into the nothing — could, it seems to me, be comprehended by the rubric of metaphysics determined as the "basic occurrence of Dasein."

71. *Transforming Moment,* p. 81. In another contribution to this volume, Russell Haitch — also an important conversation partner in the writing of this essay — rightly notes that we do Loder an injustice if we think of void only as the experience of crisis. If the void is the conflict that initiates transformational knowing, and if conflict is the first step in a pattern of transformational knowing that has applicability to a wide range of ways of knowing (as Loder more than adequately demonstrates in the second chapter of *The Transforming Moment*), then

This discussion of the influence of Heidegger in Loder would be incomplete were we to overlook the critical perspective that Loder's ontology in *The Transforming Moment* brings to bear on Heidegger's understanding of human being. One of the things that conclusively distinguishes Loder's view from Heidegger's is that Loder is concerned first and foremost with defining what it means to be human as a way of comprehending transformation in the fullness of its four dimensions. And with that dimension he calls the Holy, Loder intimates that not the metaphysical, but the theological perspective is what gives the more adequate conception of human being and human transformation. For the Heidegger of *Being and Time,* the meaning of being was preeminent and it emerged as one apprehended the totality of one's existence as bounded only by birth and death in an authentic awareness of one's death. Resoluteness was the issue of this awareness; that human transcendence also opens one to an encounter with God was not considered.[72] It is probably for this reason that Loder said to me on several occasions that Heidegger's human being is a mostly aesthetic being (Kierkegaard). And it is true that on Loder's terms Heidegger's nothing gives us what amounts to only the two-dimensional transformation of the self-world unity. Encounter with the nothing for Heidegger does not prompt questions about ultimate realities as it does for (Macquarrie and) Loder.

For Loder, on the other hand, the encounter with the Holy is absolutely crucial in comprehending the fullness of four-dimensional transformation.

---

we need not take his discussion of void as having reference to existential crisis alone. The scientist whose interest is aroused by the perception of a problem in a theoretical paradigm and who musters all of the resources of his or her imagination to the resolution of the problem has encountered the void — however discreetly it makes its "appearance" in the problem. Moreover, Loder's discussion of the thoroughly mundane incident Sartre recounts in *Being and Nothingness* of waiting at the café for Pierre, who fails to appear as scheduled, should be enough to disabuse one of the notion that void has only to do with crisis. Yet this is not in any way to deny the reality of the void in the experiences of crisis. The simple fact is that the most visible faces of the void are such things as "absence, loss, shame, guilt, hatred, loneliness, and the demonic" (*Transforming Moment,* p. 84), and these all are the seeds of a potential transformation.

72. Theology was of concern to Heidegger in *Being and Time* only insofar as it had not yet gotten an ontologically rigorous perspective for the investigation of that realm of being which was its concern, the relation of the human being as *ens creatum* to God as the *ens increatum;* see *Being and Time,* pp. 30, 74. In "What Is Metaphysics?" the argument about theology is roughly the same, although in its abruptness his critique of it here appears somewhat more dismissive: "The questions of Being and of the nothing as such are not posed [in theology]. Therefore no one is bothered by the difficulty that if God creates out of nothing precisely He must be able to relate Himself to the nothing. But if God is God he cannot know the nothing, assuming that the 'Absolute' excludes all nothingness"; *Basic Writings,* pp. 107-108. Here too, it appears that if theology is to be taken seriously, it will have to become more metaphysically (ontologically) rigorous.

And it is the experience of the void that opens one to the transforming encounter with the Holy: "in the midst of the deepest extremity a sense of the Holy *in* us cries out for a manifestation of the Holy *beyond* us."[73] Macquarrie similarly asserts that the mood of anxiety

> may be said to constitute our capacity for receiving revelation. It predisposes us to recognize the approach of holy being. In other words, I am asserting a continuity between the quest for sense and grace that arises out of man's existence, and the directionally opposite *quest for man* to which experiences of grace and revelation bear witness.[74]

It is difficult to avoid the conclusion that Loder had this text, or one very much like it, in view when he formulated his own notion of how the experience of the void opens us to the experience of the Holy. In the experience of the receding of beings as a whole, such that just beings are what is encountered, lies the possibility of human creativity, no doubt; yet therein lies the possibility of the transforming encounter of human spirit with Holy Spirit also in what Loder calls a "negation of the negation."[75] This, of course, is the very concept that takes Loder beyond Heidegger, inasmuch as the negation of the negation is accomplished by a mediator in such a way that the original negation is taken up "as an essential element of the gain."[76] That the original negation as an existential encounter is taken up into the gain probably signifies what Loder had in mind when he would suggest from time to time, *à la* Kierkegaard, that transformation (as in Religiousness B) is not removal from one's concrete historical existence but is rather a relocation within that existence, based now upon the transparency of one's relationship to the Holy.[77] Void experiences are not brought to an end once and for all in the "negation of the negation"; rather, they are deprived of their power to determine and to dominate existence in the human encounter with the Holy.

In a sense that suggests Tillich's notion of the ultimate concern, Loder insists that even "those who would not agree that being is gracious implicitly live by that premiss with every affirmation of scientific discovery, esthetic intuition, or therapeutic success." In other words, they live by a faith in the orderliness of being. Yet for Loder the emergence of new orders of being in transformational knowing point beyond themselves to the generative power of being-itself. "[A]t

73. *Transforming Moment,* p. 86.
74. Macquarrie, *Principles of Christian Theology,* p. 87.
75. *Transforming Moment,* pp. 159-160; see also n. 1.
76. *Transforming Moment,* p. 160.
77. Cf. *Transforming Moment,* chap. 4.

the center of transformational knowing in science, esthetics, or therapy, the imaginative, constructive insight or vision is an undoing of nothingness; it is a proximate form of the ultimate manifestation of 'the Holy' in revelation."[78] In essence, for Loder the nothing does not have the central role that it does in Heidegger's thought. To restate the difference, whereas Heidegger makes the nothing the be-all and end-all of human transformation, Loder makes the encounter with the Holy ontologically most basic, the void being the dynamism in human transformation which has its own undoing assured as one encounters through it the face of God.

Heidegger and Loder: Provoking Wonder in the Education of the Child

As has already been noted, Loder sees a relationship between evil and the experience of the void, and this is made explicit when he suggests that void is "the 'goal' of evil." The relationship does not appear to be one of precise equivalence, however, for he immediately follows with the assertion, "Not every absence is evil," and the example he gives is the absence of pain. One could also note that the absence felt by the creative scientist in a theory that fails to account for all the phenomena is hardly to be characterized as evil. Moreover, at the beginning of the discussion of the Holy, Loder points out that "the faces of the void become the faces of God."[79] This, of course, can be seen as a phenomenological characterization of four-dimensional transformation. The evil Loder has in mind here is that which shows itself in human brokenness and prevents the realization of the self as spirit,[80] and it is a significant dimension of the experience of void. Void for Loder encompasses the experience of evil,[81] which is a substantial content of the void, but I want to suggest that void is not exhaustively defined by this experience.

Thus, it seems fair to probe behind Loder, to look at the Heidegger in Loder, in order to descry a positive aspect to this void or this nothing. In the light of Loder's qualification that not every absence is evil, it seems that we are justified in doing precisely this. Near the end of "What Is Metaphysics?"

78. *Transforming Moment,* p. 70.

79. *Transforming Moment,* p. 85.

80. *Transforming Moment,* p. 83.

81. In this text, however, the nothing appears as the source rather than the goal of these kinds of experienced evil, and this, of course, is fully consonant with Heidegger's insistence on the (metaphysical) priority of the nothing — a priority that Loder is not willing to give the void, as the discussion in the previous section suggests.

Heidegger says, "Only because the nothing is manifest in the ground of Dasein can the total strangeness of beings overwhelm us. Only when the strangeness of beings oppresses us does it arouse and evoke wonder."[82] For Heidegger, wonder gives rise to the scientific "why?" which itself generates the kinds of grounding for the beings that science is apt to give. Wonder by its grounding in the metaphysical nothing becomes an ontological determination of human existence. In Loder's perspective, however, the wonder that facilitates the scientist's "why?" would need to point through the void to being itself in which we encounter the Holy. Loder's appeal to that phenomenon which Rudolf Otto called the *mysterium tremendum et fascinans* would seem to allow this particular interpretation of wonder. As Loder puts it,

> The "*mysterium tremendum fascinans*" as manifest in the earthiness of human existence via the faces of new being retains Otherness and inflicts profound ambivalence. The experiential mark of the presence of the Holy is just this ambivalence that both draws and repels us, excites and overcomes us, intrigues and threatens us.[83]

Wonder is, of course, a basic determinant of virtually any sort of creative production; and in this sense it would seem to straddle the first two of Loder's steps in the transformational process: conflict and the interlude for scanning. Yet even in the situations where one is provoked to wonder — coming upon a vista while walking on a mountain trail, for example, or gazing at the gray swells in a stormy ocean — one realizes that here, too, the ordinary meaning structures by which one makes sense of things are not applicable in the encounter. One is at a loss for words; one finds that in the moment of encounter the "is" cannot be spoken. The self and its daily round of troubles fall away; indeed, the self almost merges with the reality encountered, and there is only being in its unspeakable majesty and grandeur. One is attuned by wonderment or awe toward "beings as a whole." The question, Why are there beings at all, and why not rather nothing? can be raised out of this sense of wonder, too. On Loder's terms, what will always be implicit in wonder is the possibility of the emergence of new orders of being.

We, of course, prefer the routine that establishes the familiarity of everyday existence. And particularly in times when chaos seems to threaten our lives, when options seem foreclosed and existence feels most uncanny, we are drawn even more urgently to that which is familiar. Wonder is always an ambivalent experience in that it sets before us possibilities that are strange. It gives us the openness

82. *Basic Writings*, p. 109.

83. *Transforming Moment*, p. 89.

of beings that are not always consigned to being what they are in the world of our present experience; the very *possibility* of being brings with it a measure of uncertainty, of ambivalence. We want outcomes that are suitably continuous with past experience, and yet we know full well that, in the encounter with possibility, the radically new may emerge, and this is profoundly threatening. This is precisely the ambivalence that afflicts us in wonder. This ambivalence/wonder is the phenomenological origin of creativity in any sort of endeavor.

Yet what needs to be stressed is that in being opened through wonder to being itself, one is also opened to the encounter with the Holy that suffuses all of being and yet is beyond beings as a whole. Beyond the possibility of new orders of being lies the divine reality that makes all transformation possible. Theologically, if anxiety delivers us over to the need for redemption, wonder can make us cognizant of creation as the work of God and of our own creativity as the proper of image of God in us. If anxiety makes manifest our finitude before the nothing, wonder gives us beings as created and contingent as well.

If wonder is a kind of void experience, then, and if void is the ground of all the creative transformations of the human spirit, is it not incumbent upon teachers to take seriously this human reality if they intend to give human spirit the attention it deserves in the educative process? How, then, can the teacher go about providing the stimuli to wonder?

I would suggest two general guidelines. (1) The teacher will need to allow wonder to become a part of her own life: she will need to get in touch with those significant experiences of awe, religious as well as nonreligious, that have shaped her own life world. She will need to acknowledge her own present experiences of wonder, and she will need to be willing to share these with her students — not just by word of mouth, but also by allowing her own wonder to come to life in the classroom, for she teaches as much by example as by content in this matter of wonder. Too often, teachers (especially in secondary and higher education) expect themselves and their students to put forward their thoughts in class as already well polished gems rather than as gems "in the rough." They overlook the fact that thinking is a process — as Heidegger's notion of the nothing powerfully suggests — and that those "finely polished gems" were themselves arrived at through a *process* of encountering a difficulty, inquiring into the conditions of the problem, reflecting on the possibilities for its resolution, and thinking it through to its (always open-ended) conclusion. For teachers who are serious about inculcating the spirit of inquiry in their students, what better way do they have to model the process than to begin in their own wonder about the topic? If we are guided by the root meaning of the word "educate," which is "a leading out" *(educare)*, the teacher needs to show the way into the process through her own wonder.

With this in mind, (2) the teacher will also need to provide opportunities for the students to experience wonder as well, and the effect these will have upon the students will depend in part on the teacher's own willingness to live into his own wonder. Wonder is that experience in which the imagination with all its promise is brought to life in children and youth. The educators who are the students in the graduate arts and humanities programs with which I am affiliated talk often of the ways in which education — in both the public school and in the religious classroom — can become an enterprise which deadens the human intellect rather than bringing insight to life. Indeed, offering up our thoughts as if they were well-polished gems needing little additional refinement will tend to do precisely this. Inspiring wonder, on the other hand, firing the imagination by providing experiences and even simple questions about readings, could counterbalance the deadening quality of that learning which occurs only by rote (e.g., multiplication tables, spelling bees, memorizing the Ten Commandments or the books of the Bible, lecturing, etc.).

For educators in the public realm, this could mean posing questions to older elementary students on a field trip to an aquarium, for example, about why some fish are brightly colored and others not, or during a music class how they feel when a particular passage of music they hear (e.g., Tchaikovsky's "Peter and the Wolf") is loud or soft, fast or slow. With respect to the first illustration, the teacher obviously avoids offering the quick answer (e.g., the bright colors may be related to aggressiveness)[84] but simply lets the question rest with the children as they gaze into the tank — lets it do its work of provoking wonder and stirring the beginnings of a conversation among the students and with the teacher that will continue when they return to the classroom. The work the children do in coming to some answer needs to be honored by the teacher. The theory about the relation of bright colors to aggressiveness may very well come to the fore in later classroom activities, but this again becomes the occasion further to stimulate wonder: "Why do you think aggression would be related to bright colors in the fish?" Again, the quick answer (e.g., the aggression may be related to the fact that brightly colored fish are more visible to each other) is avoided and allowed rather to emerge in the inquiry that gets constituted by the classroom activities. With regard to the second illustration, the teacher is, of course, bound to honor the feelings the children express; a theory of human emotions that connects it to neurological chemistry might be of relevance only

84. The very specific answers I suggest here represent only the vague memories of my reading the theory of Konrad Lorenz in his book *On Aggression* years ago, and are by no means intended to portray either the current state of a theoretical position that accounts for brightly colored fish or the theory that is finally to be represented to students by these answers in the classroom. The answers are simply illustrative.

to the teacher — and this marginally, at best — in this sort of learning context. What is of primary importance is that children are learning to own their feelings and to see themselves as related, through these feelings, to a world.

To return to that domain which was Loder's passion, provoking wonder for religious educators could mean posing questions about a conundrum in a story from Scripture: "God said he wanted Moses to be the leader of Israel in their journey through the wilderness. I wonder why Moses gave God so many excuses not to be the leader of the people?" (see Exod. 3). "Why do you think the priest and the Levite passed by the injured man on the other side of the road?" (Luke 10:29-37). Questions as simple as these start the wondering/scanning process and can lead children to significant insights. But in order for the process of mutual inquiry to get under way, the teacher again must avoid the quick answers (e.g., Moses lacked self-confidence, he didn't have enough trust in God, etc.; or the priest and the Levite were too proud, they were too bound to their tradition, etc.). Again, in a study of geography, in which one is showing slides of the rural countryside in Israel, the teacher could pose questions to middle school youth about why the people came to call this the promised land, "the land flowing with milk and honey," when it seems so barren, or why John the Baptist chose this wilderness where no one seemed to live to start preaching. The leader of a Christian youth group that has been invited to a *bar-* or *bat-mitzvah,* could, on the day of the visit, encourage the youth to sense the rhythmic quality of the chanting of the words of Scripture in a strange language, to feel the solemnity of the service, to taste the flavor of celebration in the meal and fellowship that follows — all of which have the potential to provoke wonder not only about the divine reality but also about other ways people have of worshiping God.

It is imperative that the teacher, whether a religious or a public educator, realize that the particular questions and the particular experiences will provoke wonder at different levels and in varying degrees in each of the students, and some may provoke no wonder at all. This is why it will be important to have many opportunities to experience wonder built into one's lesson plans. It is a shibboleth among teachers that the larger the class, the less attention can be given to individual children. My suspicion is that by providing many and varied opportunities in which children's wonder can be provoked, the teacher makes at least a beginning at addressing this problem of individualized attention, and, through thinking about education as in part provoking wonder, may find ways of connecting to the interests of a child who otherwise seems mostly disinterested in conventional educational settings. Is this not a way toward letting our children and youth flourish in the educative process?

14. Loder and Mystical Spirituality: Particularity, Universality, and Intelligence

Eolene Boyd-MacMillan

Introduction

This essay explores the relationship between Christian mystical spirituality and the transformation theory of James Loder through three assertions that structure the discussion. My first assertion is that the "heart" of Loder's transformational logic connects with mystical spirituality understood as "deep, transforming encounter with God." This phrase is my summary of contemporary investigations of classical texts in mystical theology representing three Christian traditions: Andrew Louth of Durham University (Orthodox), Bernard McGinn of the University of Chicago (Roman Catholic), Denys Turner of Cambridge University (Roman Catholic), and Mark McIntosh of Loyola University in Chicago (Anglo-Catholic).[1] Louth describes the mystics' "search for a sense of kin-

1. For their portrayals of mystical spirituality, I draw only from the following texts: A. Louth, *The Origins of the Christian Mystical Tradition: From Plato to Denys* (Oxford: Clarendon Paperbacks, 1981), see especially pp. xv, 195, 202-204. B. McGinn, *The Presence of God: A History of Western Christian Mysticism*, vol. 1: *The Foundation of Mysticism: Origins to the Fifth Century* (London: SCM Press, 1991); vol. 2: *The Growth of Mysticism: Gregory the Great through the Twelfth Century* (New York: Crossroad, 1994); vol. 3: *The Flowering of Mysticism: Men and Women in the New Mysticism, 1200-1350* (New York: Crossroad, 1998); vol. 4: *Continuity and Change in Western Mysticism* (not yet published); vol. 5: *The Crisis of Mysticism* (not yet published). I refer to each text by volume number. See esp. vol. 1, pp. xvii, xiv. D. Turner, *The Darkness of God: Negativity in Christian Mysticism* (Cambridge: Cambridge University Press, 1995), pp. 70, 268, 272-273. The apparent disagreement between Turner and McGinn is beyond the scope and space of this essay. However, Turner has reviewed and approved my synthesis statement of their understanding of mystical spirituality (personal conversation, 2002). M. McIntosh, *Mystical Theology: The Integrity of Spirituality and Theology* (Oxford: Blackwell Publishers, 1998), pp. 5-6, 8. Although Louth writes a negative review of McIntosh (see *Modern Theology* 16, 2 [April 2000]: 267-269), all four authors reject in the texts I have selected an "experientialist" account of mysticism,

ship with God."[2] "The mystic is not content to know *about* God, he longs for union with God."[3] McGinn describes his heuristic understanding of mystical spirituality as "beliefs and practices that concer[n] the preparation for, the consciousness of, and the reaction to what can be described as the immediate or direct presence of God."[4] Turner asserts that "from Augustine to John of the Cross . . . 'I' am in the last resort what I am in my deepest 'interiority' . . . in my deepest inwardness, I and God meet."[5] McIntosh presents spirituality as divine encounter[6] and mysticism as "the depth dimension of all spirituality," as "transforming knowledge of God."[7] Spirituality is *"the activity of being led by the Spirit into Christ's relationship with the Father."*[8] These statements accord with Loder's interdisciplinary theory of transformation that focuses on how a person knows herself drawn into the life of the Trinity through "deep, transforming encounter with God." Without denying the differences among all five authors, I assert this shared focus. My discussion of this assertion begins with an exploration of Loder's transformational logic and then its correspondences with mystical spirituality as depicted by the four authors. Although he does acknowledge the links, I implicitly criticize Loder for not probing these connections himself.

My second assertion is that Loder's theory can contribute to spirituality discourse about particularity and universality. In contemporary discourse on mystical spirituality, a debate focuses on the relationship between particularity and universality.[9] William James, Aldous Huxley, W. T. Stace, and Rudolf Otto each represent voices identified with the perennial philosophy or essentialist or universalist approach.[10] This approach translates or reduces all spiritualities into

---

not a rejection of experience as a part of mysticism, but a rejection of the assertion that mysticism is "nothing but" experience. Louth does not think that McIntosh succeeds in doing this, but I am unable to identify what exactly troubles Louth in McIntosh.

2. Louth, *Origins of the Christian Mystical Tradition,* p. 100.

3. Louth, *Origins of the Christian Mystical Tradition,* p. xv.

4. McGinn, *The Presence of God,* vol. 1, p. xvii.

5. Turner, *The Darkness of God,* p. 6.

6. McIntosh, *Mystical Theology,* pp. 5-6.

7. McIntosh, *Mystical Theology,* p. 8.

8. McIntosh, *Mystical Theology,* p. 152, italics original.

9. See E. Howells, "Mysticism and the Mystical: The Current Debate," *The Way,* Supplement 102 (2001): 15-27. See also S. Schneiders, "Spirituality in the Academy," *Theological Studies* 50 (1989): 676-697. These two articles provide some justification for the validity of this assertion on either side of the Atlantic (Howells — UK; Schneiders — U.S.).

10. W. James, *The Varieties of Religious Experience* (London: Longmans, Green & Co., 1902); A. Huxley, *The Doors of Perception* (London: Chatto and Windus, 1954); W. T. Stace, *Mysticism and Philosophy* (London: Macmillan, 1960); R. Otto, *Mysticism East and West* (New York: Macmillan, 1970). See discussion in Howells, "Mysticism and the Mystical." On placing the discussion of spirituality within the larger context of religion in general, see J. Bowker's comments

a core essence. Stephen Katz is often identified with the radical constructivist approach.[11] This approach insists that all spiritualities are so particular that they are unrelated and not translatable. While I have presented these approaches as extremes, in fact James (for example) and Katz, and most, if not all, theories of mystical spirituality represent some sort of integration of these extremes. These theories account for the particular distinctions of a mystical spirituality *and* for the universal or shared features.[12] Loder's transformation theory attends to spiritual and theoretical particularities while asserting their connection both on a human level and according to his theological commitments. I test the power of Loder's theory to account for particularity and universality by relating it to the ego-relativization theory of James Hillman. Loder's transformation theory in individual psychological terms requires ego-relativization.[13] Hillman's and Loder's theories contain impressive semantic and, to some degree, conceptual field overlap; however, the differences in their conceptual fields ultimately divide their theories, challenging the essentialist view of spirituality while affirming the transformational, relational, and imaginative capacities of human nature. This second section picks up the discussion of particularity and universality that closed the first section, placing it in the concrete assertions of one of the four authors, McIntosh, and his interactions with another investigator of spirituality, Sandra Schneiders, before describing Hillman's theory and relating it to Loder's.

My third assertion is that Loder's theory of transforming knowing concurs with the four contemporary investigators' portrayal of *knowing* in mystical spirituality. Louth, McGinn, Turner, and McIntosh all note the mysterious, intertwined relationship between love and knowledge (or understanding) in

---

in *The Sense of God: Sociological, Anthropological, and Psychological Approaches to the Origin of the Sense of God* (Oxford: Clarendon Press, 1973) regarding the untenable nature of the essentialist or perennial philosophy positions on religion in light of the diverse particularities within the universal phenomenon of religion (e.g., pp. 44-45, 141, 147-150).

11. S. Katz, "Language, Epistemology, and Mysticism," in *Mysticism and Philosophical Analysis* (London: Sheldon Press, 1978), pp. 22-74. See Howells, "Mysticism and the Mystical," for the argument that Katz is a modification of the Jamesian approach in his separation of experience from belief.

12. Both James *(Varieties of Religious Experience)* and Katz ("Language, Epistemology, and Mysticism") separate experience from belief, and both account for particularities through interpretative frameworks or thought systems. James accounts for universalities through the shared characteristics of experience; for mystical experience, he numbers the shared characteristics at four. Katz places universalities beyond human reach, although this placement is stated as a universal that Katz seems able to access. See Howells, "Mysticism and the Mystical."

13. J. Loder, *The Transforming Moment*, 2nd ed. (Colorado Springs: Helmers & Howard, 1989), pp. 140, 166-167; Loder, *The Logic of the Spirit: Human Development in Theological Perspective* (San Francisco: Jossey-Bass Publishers, 1998), p. 55.

mystical spirituality.[14] According to Turner, "the fulfillment of mystical theology, what brings about its goal of the intellect's union with God, and moves and stimulates its practice, is to be found in the soul's deepest love."[15] McIntosh contends that "[t]he soul's experience is not anti-noetic in the sense of implying that the quest for God demands an infamous sacrifice of the intellect, rather it is an awareness (with a very definite intellectual component) that the source of one's desire is beyond the grasp of the intellect."[16] Gregory the Great's famous maxim, *love itself is a knowing,*[17] summarizes the paradoxical relationship between love and knowing in mystical texts. Louth, McGinn, Turner, McIntosh, and Loder all agree that God is the "very condition for the possibility of knowing anything at all."[18] Accordingly, Loder's transformational logic challenges reductive accounts of knowing that separate knowing from relationality, and ultimately from loving, transforming human-divine relationship. The discussion in this section begins with Loder's analysis of all human knowing and its transformation through convictional knowing or deep, transforming encoun-

14. Louth, *The Origins of the Christian Mystical Tradition:* "it is beyond *theoria,* in the darkness of unknowing, that the soul penetrates more and more deeply into the knowledge and presence of God through love" (p. 97). McGinn, *The Presence of God:* "all Christian mystics" indicate that "love rather than knowledge or understanding leads to God, however much the latter contributes" (vol. 2, p. 390). Turner, *The Darkness of God:* "Denys [the Areopagite] . . . means that intellect is transported *as intellect* beyond what it can do by itself into its own dazzling darkness" (p. 131; italics original); "What Gallus has added to Denys' account is . . . 'knowing unknowing' in terms not of intellect's own self-transcendence, but in terms of a higher kind of knowing than that of intellect, the 'knowing of love'" (p. 193); "Hence at the point of breakthrough . . . the disciple can launch out on to the intellectually uncharted and unchartable seas of the knowing of love" (p. 199); McIntosh, see note 16 below.

15. Turner, *The Darkness of God,* p. 217.

16. McIntosh, *Mystical Theology,* p. 202. His thought continues: "That is not, therefore, a humanly diminishing mindlessness but a kind of amazement that is exhilarating and liberating for the whole person; drawn closer to God in this way, Gregory [of Nyssa] implies, the human self is invited into a realm of possibilities it would never have imagined."

17. *Amor ipse notitia est. Homilia in Evangelia* 27.4, *Patrologiae cursus completus.* Series latina, vol. 76 (1844-64), p. 1207. See A. Damasio, *The Feeling of What Happens: Body and Emotion in the Making of Consciousness* (New York: Harcourt Brace & Company, 1999), whose neurological research seems to support Gregory the Great's maxim.

18. McIntosh, *Mystical Theology,* p. 112. McIntosh associates this understanding with Joseph Maréchal and Karl Rahner. McIntosh (whose text appeared last among the four authors) understands McGinn to agree with this statement; indeed, McGinn identifies himself as agreeing with this aspect of Maréchal's and Rahner's ideas (*The Presence of God,* vol. 1, pp. 297-324). Turner uses a different phrase: the "exoteric dynamic *within* the ordinary" (*The Darkness of God,* p. 268; italics original) to express mystical encounter with creative immediacy, i.e., God's sustaining presence (p. 31). Louth is more implicit in his description of mystical apprehensions of God through Christ and the Holy Spirit (*Origins of the Christian Mystical Tradition,* p. xi).

ter with God. The discussion then emphasizes the inextricability of social and individual transformation illustrated through human knowing according to the logic of transformation. We turn now to my first assertion.

Loder's Logic and Mystical Spirituality

In Loder's understanding of human nature, all knowing manifests through the "logic of transformation."[19] Human beings function in their particular contexts according to this logic that characterizes the particularities of human lives: their artistic creations, scientific discoveries, and therapeutic insights.[20] The logic describes the operation of human knowing. Moreover, the logic characterizes human development itself. As we develop emotionally, socially, and cognitively, we follow this logic or pattern. Each developmental stage and stage transition follows this pattern. A five-phased pattern (conflict, scanning, insight, energy release, and interpretation/application),[21] the logic can occur in any sequence,[22] over many years or coalesced into an instant.[23] The "insight" brings together seemingly unrelated frames of reference without synthesis or reduction.[24]

Loder uses Archimedes as a paradigmatic example.[25] Archimedes needed to find out whether or not the king's crown was pure gold. He did not know how to do this. He became preoccupied with the problem, searching for a solution. One evening, as he stepped into his bath, the water rose and he had his insight. He could compare the water displacement of a pure gold crown with the water displacement of the crown in question! Two seemingly unrelated frames

19. Loder and Neidhardt, *The Knight's Move: The Relational Logic of the Spirit in Theology and Science* (Colorado Springs: Helmers & Howard, 1992), pp. 41-43, 232, 266; Loder, *Logic of the Spirit,* p. 12. Regarding the phrase the "logic of transformation," Loder notes that the "process of convictional knowing is taken up into classical theological categories as the 'grammar' of the Holy Spirit. . . . 'Grammar' may be translated into what I have designated as transformational logic, the unique sense of order that characterizes both the human spirit and the Holy Spirit" (Loder, *Transforming Moment,* p. 114). He cites Martin Luther's use of the term "grammar" (*Werke* [Weimar: H. Böhlau, n.d.], vol. 39, no. 2, pp. 104-105). See also Loder, *Logic of the Spirit,* p. 114.

20. See *Transforming Moment,* chaps. 2 and 5.

21. Loder, *Transforming Moment,* pp. 37-40; Loder and Neidhardt, *Knight's Move,* p. 266; Loder, *Logic of the Spirit,* p. 88.

22. J. Loder, "Transformation in Christian Education," *Religious Education* 76, 2 (1981): 208-209.

23. Loder, *Transforming Moment,* p. 112; Loder and Neidhardt, *Knight's Move,* p. 236; Loder, *Logic of the Spirit,* pp. 305-307.

24. Loder and Neidhardt, *Knight's Move,* pp. 96, 228.

25. For example, "Transformation in Christian Education," pp. 207-208, and *Knight's Move,* p. 266.

of reference, the crown and the bath, came together to form an insight. This insight can be understood as a bipolar relational unity.

The distinction between the transformation considered so far (e.g., Archimedes) and Christian transformation (or deep, transforming encounter with God) involves Loder's understanding of human existence. He asserts that human existence involves four dimensions: (1) the self, (2) the lived world, (3) the void, and (4) the Holy.[26] Loder engages analytical, object relations and other depth psychologies to explore formation and development of the self or selves.[27] The dimension "lived world" emphasizes that we are both *composers of* and *composed by* the world in which we live.[28] Negations such as repression, loneliness, rejection, and fear point to the "void"; the void points to death and alienation from the Holy, sin.[29] The "Holy" refers to the transcendent and immanent presence of God.[30]

The transformation exemplified in the Archimedes story can be understood as focusing on the first two dimensions. However, the void and the Holy are *tacitly* part of all transformations enacted by humans, developmental and creative. Physical death is always a reality of human life,[31] and the Holy is always enabling all that exists to exist, whether acknowledged or not.[32] The void and the Holy *become the focus* of transformation in Christian spirituality. That is, deep, transforming encounter with God (in a moment or over time) reveals God's sustaining presence on which all that exists, including the particular person, is dependent. As a person embraces God's offer of relationship, this deep encounter negates the "negations" riven through a person's life. Suffering remains, but a person now knows suffering four dimensionally, not in two or three dimensions. God is the focus of a person's existence. This encounter can also transform the operation of the transformational logic itself (the transformation of transformation) *from* maintaining self- or ego-centeredness *to* witnessing to human-divine relationality (more on this in the next section).

Loder's understanding of "deep, transforming encounter with God" fol-

26. Loder *The Transforming Moment*, pp. 69-70.

27. Loder *The Transforming Moment*, pp. 161-168; Loder, *Logic of the Spirit*, pp. 82, 90-95, 135.

28. Loder, *Transforming Moment*, pp. 70-75.

29. Loder, *Transforming Moment*, pp. 81, 82, 159; Loder *The Logic of the Spirit*, p. 94.

30. Loder, *Transforming Moment*, pp. 85-91.

31. ". . . human beings begin to die the moment they are born" (Loder, *Logic of the Spirit*, p. 73).

32. Loder uses T. F. Torrance's term "contingency" to refer to the dependence of all that exists on God's gracious sustaining will (Loder and Neidhardt, *Knight's Move*, pp. 50, 190, 197; Loder, *Logic of the Spirit*, p. 10).

lows the Chalcedonian articulation of the union of the divine and human natures in Christ;[33] that is, the union of human and divine natures in Christ models the dynamic of human-divine transforming encounter. Ultimately, Loder understands "deep, transforming encounter with God" to arise from the *perichoresis,* or well-choreographed "dance," of the Trinity.[34] The loving "relationality"[35] of the Trinity invites humans to participate in deep transforming encounter. All aspects of Loder's theory point to and flow from this central tenet: all that exists in time and space does so completely dependent or contingent upon God, while God's sustaining presence simultaneously offers in concrete historical ways deep, transforming human-divine relationships both in and beyond time and space.[36] The "concrete historical ways" involve the birth, life, death, resurrection, and ascension of Jesus Christ that transforms being and history in the spiritual presence of Christ *and* the birth, life, and death of "selves" composing and composed by the "lived world."[37] So far, I have presented a relatively uncontestable *précis* of these aspects of Loder's theory. What might be controversial is my assertion that they indicate a rich mystical spirituality at the heart of his theory.

In Loder's transformation theory, "deep, transforming encounter with God" — through Christ, in the power of the Holy Spirit — is (1) the generative source and *telos* of the insight of his five-phased logic of transformation in Christian transformation;[38] (2) the living referent of a transforming vision supported by the neurological intensification process;[39] and (3) the redemptive power underlying the classic four-fold pattern in Christian spirituality described by his transformational logic.[40] He refers explicitly to the operation of the transformational logic in "authentic religious experience" reported by the

33. Loder and Neidhardt, *Knight's Move,* pp. 82-87; Loder, *Logic of the Spirit,* p. 37. Fundamental to all his texts is Loder's engagement with the writings of Søren Kierkegaard in his exploration of paradox and "union in opposition" (bipolar relational unity) embodied in Christ as articulated by the Chalcedonian formula.

34. Loder and Neidhardt, *Knight's Move,* p. 52 n. 15, pp. 201-206; Loder, *Logic of the Spirit,* pp. 195, 276.

35. Loder distinguishes relationality from relationship. Relationality represents a relationship that assumes a life of its own. *Transforming Moment,* p. 78. See also Loder and Neidhardt, *Knight's Move,* pp. 36-59; Loder, *Logic of the Spirit,* pp. 13-14.

36. Loder and Neidhardt, *Knight's Move,* pp. 140, 216; Loder, *Logic of the Spirit,* p. 74.

37. Loder, *Transforming Moment,* pp. 69, 71-75, 147-153, 162-168.

38. Loder, *The Transforming Moment,* p. 146.

39. Loder and Neidhardt, *Knight's Move,* pp. 282-283.

40. Awakening, Purgation, Illumination, and Toward Unification. Loder and Neidhardt, *Knight's Move,* p. 284. I am grateful to John Kuentzel and Dana Wright for pointing me to this tetrad, and for their reading earlier versions of this essay.

"great mystics."[41] Such experience transforms the initiation and focus of the transformational logic itself, from the human ego to human-divine relationality. He names mystical authors whose texts illustrate the movement of this "transformation of transformation" in human-divine encounter. The "kind of *via negativa*" implicit in the "visions of God in St. Augustine, Hildegard, Teresa of Avila, Meister Eckhart, and others" describes the deep encounter with God that transforms the operation of the logic in a human being.[42] This deep, transforming encounter with God is understood and experienced neurologically through intensification.[43] Neurological intensification corresponds to the fourth element of union in the four-fold way.[44] As a person's imagination yields to the divine presence, she experiences: "(1) [an] *awakening* to God's presence . . . (2) the effort to purify oneself [*purgation*]. Here one is brought to an extremity where one's limits are reached and one's resources exhausted. Then and there one is met from 'the other side.' (3) *Illumination* follows . . . and [leads one] toward (4) *unification*."[45] Loder also uses the term "mystical" to refer to the experiences of people who have known the "transformation of transformation" in themselves.[46] Wary of the distortions to which

41. Loder and M. Laaser, "Authenticating Christian Experience: A Research Request," *Princeton Seminary Bulletin* LXVI, 1, old series (1973): 120-124.

42. Loder, *Logic of the Spirit,* p. 58.

43. Loder cites neurological support for his transformational logic in research by E. Gellhorn and his colleagues that explores the joint arousal of two brain systems during visionary or convictional moments (Loder and Neidhardt, *Knight's Move,* pp. 267-275). See recent research by Andrew Newberg who uses the term "neuro-theology." Newberg's former mentor and colleague is Eugene d'Aquili (see their co-authored books, *The Mystical Mind: Probing the Biology of Religious Experience* [Minneapolis: Fortress Press, 1999], and *Why God Won't Go Away: Brain Science and the Biology of Belief* [New York: Ballantine Books, 2001]). Loder quotes d'Aquili's description of the hyper-arousal of both brain systems as the brain's engagement with "the fundamental dichotomies of human existence," indicating neural correlates to figure-ground reversals that combine unrelated frames of reference without reduction (Loder and Neidhardt, *Knight's Move,* p. 271). See also *Logic of the Spirit,* pp. 59, 71.

44. Loder, *Logic of the Spirit,* p. 58. In the same text (the last major text published before his death), Loder uses the four-fold way to structure his discussion of a case study (chap. 3, pp. 46-78), and engages briefly with Augustine and Hildegard von Bingen (e.g., see pp. 34, 309). He also mentions mystical authors as providing examples of aspects of his theory (e.g., Teresa of Avila, pp. 58, 68, 312; John of the Cross, p. 312; Eckhart, pp. 58, 312; Richard of St. Victor, p. 313; Nicholas of Cusa, p. 313). He has mentioned some of these authors in earlier texts, but this last text draws on the greatest number of mystical authors for examples of his theory.

45. J. Loder, "Educational Ministry in the Logic of the Spirit" (Princeton Theological Seminary, unpublished manuscript, 2001), chap. 8, p. 15; italics added.

46. E.g., J. Loder, "Negation and Transformation: A Study in Theology and Human Development," in *Toward Moral and Religious Maturity,* convened by Christiane Brusselmans (Morristown, NJ: Silver Burdett Co., 1980), pp. 181, 185.

mystical spirituality is vulnerable,[47] he nevertheless draws upon mystical theological authors, terms, and patterns in the articulation of his own theory.

That Loder's theory arguably accords with the representations of mystical spirituality by the four authors is somewhat remarkable. Louth mentions the writing of a book called *The Protestant Mystics* in response to an assertion by W. T. Stace, "a Protestant," that "there are *no* Protestant mystics."[48] As the title indicates, the responding book by Anne Fremantle and W. H. Auden asserts the contrary. Similarly, McGinn remarks that "[s]ome modern Protestant theologians, beginning with Albrecht Ritschl, have judged the history of Christian mysticism to be at root nothing more than an invasion of the Christian faith by a fundamentally different and alien Hellenic religious element."[49] Thus, from the primarily Catholic and Orthodox "side" there seems to be concern that mysticism has been misunderstood and rejected. On the Protestant "side" there seems to be wariness about mysticism leading to distortions in spirituality — for example, rejection of the world. Despite this history, the focus of all four authors and Loder gathers around the movement of the Holy Spirit initiating "deep, transforming encounter with God" through Christ in the concrete lives of human beings.[50]

I am locating Loder's theory among those who have responded to God's transforming presence throughout the history of the church. Their shared attention to deep, transforming encounter with God is undeniable. This common focus reveals a "union despite differences" in the presence of One who is not confined or delimited by polarities. Loder's theory is part of the continued historic testimony to God's invitation to "deep, transforming encounter." Loder asserts that Christ unites and transcends polarities (e.g., life and death, beginning and end, divinity and humanity).[51] Surely a relationality is found among

47. E.g., Loder, *Transforming Moment,* p. 79, where he uses the phrase "world-denying mysticism."

48. Louth, *The Origins of the Christian Mystical Tradition,* p. xv, referring to Anne Fremantle and W. H. Auden who wrote *The Protestant Mystics* (London: Weidenfeld and Nicholson, 1962) and quoted W. T. Stace on p. vii; italics original.

49. McGinn, *The Presence of God,* vol. 1, p. 24. See his survey of theological, philosophical, and comparativist and psychological approaches to mysticism in the appendix titled "Theoretical Foundations: The Modern Study of Mysticism," vol. 1, pp. 265-343.

50. Loder self-identifies and his theology is identified as Reformed (see, e.g., R. Osmer, "James Fowler and the Reformed Tradition: An Exercise in Theological Reflection in Religious Education," *Religious Education* 85, 1 [1990]: 51-68).

51. Loder, *Transforming Moment,* p. 154. Loder refers to "the dialectical unity of existential opposites," asserting that "the Divine Presence is far more than a '*compositio oppositorum*'; as the face is beyond its flesh and bone, as the transfiguration is beyond the normal figure, so is his Presence beyond the oppositions united in him" (p. 154). Loder uses the term "opposition" in

the diverse Christian traditions as they seek to nurture and understand mystical spirituality. Hence the relationality among the theologians who write primarily from Reformed commitments and from Catholic or Orthodox commitments might represent the life that is the body of Christ. This relationality is larger than the four authors and Loder. The head is Christ, who embodies their union in polarity, whose presence is more than and beyond the polarities united in him.

If my assertions are valid about Loder's theory and mystical spirituality, then his theory will need to address major issues in mystical discourse. We turn to my second assertion that Loder's theory can contribute to spirituality discourse on particularity and universality. Before testing this assertion with the ego-relativization theory of James Hillman, consider the following history concerning particularity and universality in Loder's theory.

The first edition of *The Transforming Moment,* published in 1981, sparked some queries about the hospitality of Loder's theory to other faith positions. For example, James Fowler asked Loder to "acknowledge the power and truth of other religious apprehensions."[52] Similarly, in a review of the second edition (1989), Frank Rogers, a former student of Loder's, asked, "How does this Christocentric perspective allow for the Holy Spirit to work redemptively in other faith communities?"[53] Loder focuses on the relationship between universality and particularity in his next major text, *The Knight's Move* (1992), coauthored with physicist Jim Neidhardt.[54] There, he asserts that

> the dilemma of human *particularity* versus the *universality* of truth is *relationality* as the irreducible limit; beyond this no objectivating consciousness can speak without thereby saying less. The exhaustive and differentiated knowledge of the whole that includes the knower without remainder is only possible when the strange loop of self-inclusive relationality is bounded on one side by the mystery of the Divine Presence — in whom resides ultimate meaning and purpose — and on the other side by the human spirit in

the sense of existential opposites, such as life and death, sin and holiness, beginning and end, universality and particularity, humanity and divinity (p. 146). While diametrically different, the members of a contrasting pair are connected. He identifies "wholly creaturely and wholly divine" as "the extreme [example] in 'habitually incompatible frames of reference,'" noting "the impassable gulf of sin that would otherwise eternally separate all that is creaturely from the Divine Creator" (p. 116). Loder uses the term "separate" to refer to a person's unawareness of God's sustaining and convicting presence.

52. J. Loder and J. Fowler, "Conversations on Fowler's *Stages of Faith* and Loder's *The Transforming Moment,*" *Religious Education* 77, 2 (1982): 147.

53. F. Rogers, "Book Reviews," *Religious Education* 86 (1991): 325.

54. Loder and Neidhardt, *The Knight's Move,* pp. 188, 189.

> its drive to make all things intelligible. These two are not antithetical: in their relationality, they constitute the ultimate epistemological duality.[55]

This relationality between divine presence and human spirit is possible through the asymmetrical bipolar relational unity embodied in, but not definitive of, Christ's nature.[56] Ultimately, the transformational logic reflects the trinitarian movement of enfolding what is most polarized with God, as expressed on the cross.[57] Bipolar relational unity is a crucial part of Loder's interdisciplinary methodology rooted in the resolution of all polarities in Christ, whose nature is infinitely beyond these resolutions.

In his third major text on transformation, *The Logic of the Spirit,* Loder acknowledges that his methodology might be understood as christological imperialism.[58] He responds by asserting that a christological insight of relationality resolves rather than exacerbates interdisciplinary conflict. By focusing on the relationality, "the dynamism of exchange between these fields of inquiry" (human sciences and theology) as "the reality to be prized," his methodology enables direct relationship between seemingly polarizing disciplines and approaches.[59] In his estimation, other approaches use a third "thing" or field or discipline through which to relate disciplines and approaches.[60] Loder insists that direct relationship is possible and preferable. In the next section, I test his assertions. The section begins with a brief discussion of particularity and universality in spirituality discourse and then compares the transformation theory of Loder with the ego-relativization theory of James Hillman. Both decry egocentric lifestyles reinforced socially and culturally. But their portrayal of egocentricism and its antidote reveals the different conceptual fields of their theories.

Loder's Logic and Hillman's Ego-relativization Theory

The nature of spirituality discourse itself seems to require a conceptual framework that remains open to the possible reality, not simply the interpretative use,

55. Loder and Neidhardt, *The Knight's Move,* p. 189; italics original.

56. See note 33 above.

57. Note the agreement with Loder's understanding of God's movement from Rowan Williams, interacting with Martin Luther on mystical spirituality, in *The Wound of Knowledge: Christian Spirituality from the New Testament to St John of the Cross,* 2nd ed. (London: Darton, Longman & Todd, 1990), p. 149.

58. Loder, *Logic of the Spirit,* p. 37.

59. Loder, *Logic of the Spirit,* p. 41.

60. Loder, *Logic of the Spirit,* p. 37.

of divine initiative.[61] The *possibility* of divine agency as a required part of a conceptual framework of spirituality disallows a view of particularities (e.g., divine initiative or other) as add-ons or overlays to the "real" (accessible or inaccessible) spirituality being researched. Thus, McIntosh argues for the inclusion of God in the study of spirituality by interacting with three articles written by the founder and director of what he describes as one of America's leading graduate academic programs in the study of spirituality, Sandra Schneiders.[62] Schneiders asserts that a researcher must choose between a "view from above" and a "view from below."[63] She argues for a view from below, what she calls an "anthropological" approach. She justifies her selection as best facilitating interfaith and interdisciplinary discussion. This approach avoids the difficulties of particular "God-talk" and competing theologies.[64] It relates particularity to universality by focusing on a universal human trait of *self*-transcendence that particular religions address through their "spiritualities."

Schneiders acknowledges that an anthropological approach to spirituality can become so broad that "it is very difficult to achieve the clarity and distinction requisite for a useful definition."[65] But lack of clarity is not the only challenge. An anthropological focus can sideline the particularities of spiritualities in which God is understood and experienced as the primary agent. God might be appended to anthropological research into spirituality, but remain non-integral to the account of spiritual experience.[66] Explanatory and de-

61. Bowker concludes that the disciplines themselves "actually seem to demand a return to that possibility [reality of reference in the term 'God'] if sense is to be made of their own evidence" (*Sense of God*, p. 182). He suggests that interdisciplinary research (theologies and behavioral sciences) "endeavor to specify what would count as an effect of the claimed object of belief in their own case, and where such an effect can be discerned. Then . . . to the question of whether indeed God contributes to the sense of God."

62. Schneiders is a senior faculty member of the Graduate Theological Union, Berkeley, California. See the discussion of Schneiders in McIntosh, *Mystical Theology*, pp. 19-24. McIntosh interacts with three articles written by Schneiders (in order of publication): "Theology and Spirituality: Strangers, Rivals, or Partners?" *Horizons* 13, 2 (1986): 253-74; "Spirituality in the Academy," *Theological Studies* 50 (1989): 676-97; "Spirituality as an Academic Discipline: Reflections from Experience," *Christian Spirituality Bulletin* 1, 2 (1993): 10-15.

63. Schneiders, "Spirituality in the Academy," pp. 682, 683, 690-695.

64. Schneider's views contrast with Howells, who argues that "the study of mysticism *must* enter into a theological debate, including all the restrictions of context and perspective among competing theologies, rather than first seeking some purportedly universal discourse" ("Current Debate," p. 19).

65. Schneiders, "Spirituality in the Academy," p. 683.

66. Alistair McFadyen, psychiatric nurse and theologian, calls it the "Post-it" approach: God is tacked on to the end or beginning of research without making any difference or leaving

scriptive adequacy even on an anthropological, let alone any other, level can thereby be lost.

An approach to spirituality that allows for human-divine relationship as a starting point for human spiritual understanding and experience is *also* anthropological. "God-talk" is unavoidable even in a discussion that sets out to be "a view from below," because many human beings understand and experience God as the initiator in their spirituality.[67] Of course, a theological focus can sideline nontheistic spiritualities. Hence Schneiders asserts that there is no "generic" spirituality (or what I have called an essentialist approach).[68] Each spirituality itself accounts for human spirituality, theistic spirituality (if purely to explain it nontheistically), and relates the two.

From a Christian position, Loder insists that interdisciplinary research about human transformation must include a "view from above" (God) *as well as* a "view from below" (humanity).[69] The core of his theory explores the movements of the human spirit and then the transformation of the human spirit and the transformational logic by which it operates through deep, transforming encounter with God. By "spirit," he does not mean a vapor secreting from a person's pores, but a quality of relationality fundamental to human nature and the Trinity. In human nature, the spirit's quality of relationality is a paradoxical exocentric-centeredness that manifests the *imago dei* (a special correspondence between human and divine natures). Positing an analogous relationship between the human spirit and Holy Spirit, Loder contends that both operate ac-

---

any trace if lifted off. A. McFadyen, *Bound to Sin: Abuse, Holocaust and the Christian Doctrine of Sin* (Cambridge: Cambridge University Press, 2000), p. 11 n. 9.

67. This point was noted as the conclusion of Bowker in his interdisciplinary consideration of *The Sense of God* (see note 61 above). See D. Hay and L. Hunt, "The Spirituality of People Who Do Not Go to Church" (http://www.ctbi.org.uk/ccom/downloads.htm) for reports of those who do not claim any religious affiliation and yet understand their spiritual experience as having been at the initiative of something outside themselves.

68. "There is no such thing as generic spirituality or spirituality in general" (Schneiders, "Theology and Spirituality," p. 267).

69. Loder, *Logic of the Spirit*, p. 13. He acknowledges his dependence on Barth's "Christological position" (p. 30). "I accept the Chalcedonian model as a way of working (both methodologically and materially) from below and above at the same time, allowing the subjectivity of the revelation to deal transformatively with the objectivity of the sciences" (p. 33). See K. Barth, *Church Dogmatics* IV/3, first half (Edinburgh: T&T Clark, 1961), p. 63. However, Loder qualifies Barth on human spirit, the view from below. Loder understands Barth to give "no weight to [human spirit], consigning it to the realm of the unredeemed, the target of his famous '*Nein*'" (*Logic of the Spirit*, p. 34). Loder turns to G. Hendry's understanding of incarnational grace as involving divine condescension and accommodation, Holy Spirit to human spirit (*The Holy Spirit in Christian Theology* [Philadelphia: Westminster, 1976]); implicit in this accommodation is divine affirmation of the human spirit (*Logic of the Spirit*, pp. 33-35).

cording to the transformational logic.[70] He conceives of spirituality as a dialectical dynamic in which God both sustains and offers transforming relationship to human beings.[71] As a human-divine relationality, Christian spirituality can not be managed through techniques or strategies. But if spiritual experience is studied purely as a human trait, then spirituality can be reduced to another human trait that is managed through techniques and strategies.[72] "Human trait" spirituality can marginalize or devalue those spiritualities understood as dynamic response to divine initiative. Loder's theory aims to describe the movement of human knowing that is both particular to the concrete history of human individuals in particular social and cultural groups and universal in its understanding of human nature. His theory relates human knowing to transforming and transformed knowing that is particular to the concrete history of the triune God in human history as well as universal in its ontological claims for human-divine relationship.[73] We turn now to compare the theories of James Hillman and Loder. This comparison will test the handling of particularity and universality for spirituality discourse in Loder's theory as it aims to offer a view from below and above in a bipolar relational unity.

The archetypal psychologist, James Hillman, has been popularized by his protégé Thomas Moore through his best-selling books, such as *The Care of the Soul.*[74] Although Hillman does not self-identify as a writer on spirituality, his

70. Loder and Neidhardt, *Knight's Move,* pp. 48-50. Along with Hendry, Loder also draws on and qualifies W. Pannenberg's (*Knight's Move,* p. 166 n. 20; *Logic of the Spirit,* pp. 5, 33-34) and S. Kierkegaard's concepts of spirit (*Logic of the Spirit,* pp. xii-xiii). Loder argues "that the human spirit is to humanity what the Holy Spirit is to God (1 Corinthians 2.10), so these two are interrelated according to a bipolar relationality" (*Logic of the Spirit,* p. 35).

71. Spirituality is "not a leap *out* of time but a leap that releases time into human existence so the concreteness of *dunamis* of existence is lived out" (Loder and Neidhardt, *Knight's Move,* p. 198); "spirituality is an intimacy deeper than all the [other] dynamics" in which a person lives (Loder, *Logic of the Spirit,* p. 263).

72. Turner notes that this "managed" understanding of spirituality is something against which the mystical authors specifically write (*Darkness of God,* p. 4). Of course, those who affirm God as primary agent can also treat spirituality as techniques. See, e.g., David Benner's *Care of Souls: Revisioning Christian Nurture and Counsel* (Grand Rapids: Baker Books, 1998), pp. 91-92. See also note 138 below.

73. Of course the universal ontological claims about human nature within the Christian tradition (e.g., sin, the need for redemption) cannot be tested universally and therefore are nonfalsifiable as universal claims. I am suggesting as an extension of Loder that if a person accepts the Christian faith premises, then his theory may be a way of working out certain of those premises with regard to human anthropology and human-divine relationality in deep, transforming encounter with God (or mystical spirituality).

74. T. Moore, *Care of the Soul: How to Add Depth and Meaning to Your Everyday Life* (London: Piatkus, 1992).

theory of ego-relativization[75] parallels that of Loder in ways that enable an explorer of Hillman's theory to consider it as a kind of human "spirituality," archetypally understood.[76] He handles the particularity versus universality challenge through his concept of the world soul.

The world soul is a force or structure that guides and forms all that exists.[77] He refers to it also as the archetypal soul or *anima mundi.* He appropriates the concept from Heraclitus, Plato, Plotinus, Ficino, Vico, and Carl Jung.[78] All

75. Feminist theologians might suggest that the focus on ego-relativization by these two male theorists reflects the male problem, not a female problem (see, e.g., D. Hampson, *Theology and Feminism* [Oxford: Basil Blackwell, 1990], p. 155). However, Sarah Coakley suggests in *Powers and Submissions: Spirituality, Philosophy and Gender* (Oxford: Basil Blackwell, 2002) that "true divine 'empowerment' occurs most unimpededly in the context of a *special* form of human 'vulnerability'" (p. 32; italics original). She specifies prayer as one of these special forms, "especially the defenseless prayer of silent waiting on God" (p. 34). She asserts that a "danger to Christian feminism [is a] failure to confront issues of fragility, suffering or 'self-emptying' except in terms of victimology. . . . Only, I suggest, by facing — and giving new expression to — the paradoxes of 'losing one's life in order to save it,' can feminists hope to construct a vision of the Christic 'self' that transcends the gender stereotypes we are seeking to up-end" (p. 33). She notes the great personal risk involved in "contact of the thus disarmed self with God" (p. 35). In response to Coakley's suggestions and assertions, the following discussion on ego-relativization explores human vulnerability as ego-relativization in deep, transforming encounter with God.

76. Hillman carefully advocates a "downward" or "inward" movement that he identifies with "soul-making" over and against an "upward" or "outward" movement that he identifies with spirituality (see "Peaks and Vales: The Soul/Spirit Distinction as Basis for the Difference Between Psychotherapy and Spiritual Discipline," *Puer Papers* [Dallas: Spring Publications, 1979], pp. 64-65). Although he asserts that the soul and spirit exist as a "married" unity, the one operating to correct or balance the other, he insists on championing the soul over the spirit. His advocacy reflects his conviction that the Christian church has "killed" the soul. (See note 95 below.) My reference to Hillman's ego-relativization or transformation theory as a "spirituality" is as a non-theistic understanding of self-transcendence. Hillman himself somewhat facilitates this viewing, although not categorically. See Hillman, *Re-Visioning Psychology* (New York: Harper & Row, 1975), p. 168, where he states that he is talking psychologically and not religiously, although cf. his later comments: "psychology is a variety of religious experience" (p. 227) and "since [psychology's] inception it has been actively practicing religion" (p. 228). Elsewhere, he notes correspondences between his theory and the attentive posture encouraged in Christian mystical spirituality (*Myth of Analysis: Three Essays in Archetypal Psychology* [Evanston, IL: Northwestern University Press, 1972], p. 189; *Insearch: Psychology and Religion* [London: Hodder & Stoughton, 1967], pp. 20, 24-25, 30, 32). See note 89 below.

77. Hillman, *Re-Visioning Psychology,* p. xiii; Hillman, *Thought of the Heart and Soul of the World* (Woodstock, CT: Spring Publications, 1997), p. 101; Hillman, *The Soul's Code: In Search of Character and Calling* (London: Bantam Books, 1997), p. 258.

78. Hillman, "Plotinus, Ficino, and Vico as Precursors of Archetypal Psychology," in *Loose Ends: Primary Papers in Archetypal Psychology* (New York/Zurich: Spring Publications, 1975), p. 151; *Archetypal Psychology: A Brief Account* (Dallas: Spring Publications, 1983), pp. 1-5.

people, trees, animals, rocks, oceans, mountains — everything expresses the universal world soul.[79] This understanding of the world soul might appeal to people concerned about our ecological crisis. Understanding nature as an expression of the world soul encourages people to treat each other and everything else with respect. As an expression of a universal spiritual or "soul" force we might insist that all livestock live in free-range conditions, that all crops be cultivated organically, and that air and rivers not be polluted, full stop. For Hillman, the Christian focus on human salvation permeates his culture and society (in the U.S.) and has led to our reckless disregard for the sacredness of the cosmos.[80] Similarly, Christian monotheism has impoverished our self-understanding.[81]

People who feel oppressed by the need to be *one* self, always in control, find relief in Hillman's "spirituality." If we think that we need to be *one* self, then we are ruled by the "heroic ego."[82] But our dreams and fantasies reveal that we have many different selves.[83] By cultivating our dreams and fantasies, the world soul will relate the "heroic ego" to all our other selves.[84] Our many different selves express the many images in the world soul.[85] The "heroic ego" will fade in importance.[86] We will know ourselves as many different selves.[87] We will attend to the different selves in other people as well.[88]

As suggested, understanding human beings and the cosmos as manifesting the world soul creates a type of "human spirituality."[89] According to Hill-

79. Hillman, *Myth of Analysis,* pp. 189, 201.

80. Hillman, *Insearch,* pp. 135-141.

81. Hillman, *Archetypal Psychology,* pp. 33, 41-42.

82. Hillman, *Archetypal Psychology,* pp. 32-37.

83. Hillman, *Archetypal Psychology,* pp. 32-37.

84. Hillman, *Re-Visioning Psychology,* p. 55; *Myth of Analysis,* p. 5; *Insearch,* p. 58; "Peaks and Vales," p. 71.

85. Hillman, *Archetypal Psychology,* p. 14; *Re-Visioning Psychology,* p. 128.

86. Hillman, *Re-Visioning Psychology,* p. 41.

87. Hillman, *Myth of Analysis,* p. 186; "Peaks and Vales," p. 71.

88. Hillman, *Myth of Analysis,* p. 201; J. Hillman, *Anima: An Anatomy of a Personified Notion* (Dallas: Spring Publications, 1985), pp. 109, 111.

89. For example, note that Schneiders describes spirituality as referring to "(1) a fundamental dimension of the human being, (2) the lived experience which actualizes that dimension, and (3) the academic discipline which studies that experience" ("Spirituality in the Academy," p. 678). In an earlier article, she describes spirituality as the "human quest for meaning and integration" ("Theology and Spirituality," p. 268). Connecting Schneiders's words with Hillman's theory, one might say that the world soul represents a fundamental dimension of human being, soul-making the lived experience which actualizes that dimension, and archetypal psychology the discipline which studies that experience; the human quest for meaning and integration leads one to manifest the world soul. In this way, Hillman's theory can be understood as a type of "human spirituality." See note 76 above.

man, the world soul has an infinite variety of images or gods, with a small "g." He uses the term "god" to convey the power and force of these archetypal images that constitute the world soul.[90] Through the world soul, we can experience transformation out of an ego-centered life.[91] Living from the perspective of the world soul rather than the ego places human mortality on center stage in the individual and social psyche.[92] This transformation frees us from the tyranny of a "mono-theism" ("heroic" ego) that Hillman understands as insisting on unity at the expense of multiplicity.[93] The freedom of multiplicity enables us to appreciate the rich variety inherent to ourselves, other people, and nature without the oppressive unity represented by the Christian God.[94] However, all of our particularities come together (unite?) in the universal world soul.

As might be obvious from the preceding discussion on Loder's theory, Hillman has a particular understanding of Christianity, and many Christians might join him in his rejection of the Christianity that he portrays, However, his analytical support for his depiction of Christianity is arguably a misrepresentation of the Christian canon and church history.[95] However, he offers a valuable critical analysis of the modern mind-set that can be associated with the "Christian" West and that Loder would agree with in large part. The goals of Hillman's transformation theory agree with the aims of many belief systems (including Loder's understanding of Christian transformation). As described, movement away from egocentric living, connection with oneself/other people/ and the world, life lived in light of inevitable mortality — these are all the intended results of both Hillman's and Loder's transformation theories. More-

90. Hillman, *Myth of Analysis,* p. 265; *Healing Fiction* (Woodstock, CT: Spring Publications, 1983), pp. 59, 74-75.

91. Hillman, "Senex and Puer," *Puer Papers,* p. 14.

92. Hillman, "Senex and Puer," p. 27.

93. Hillman, *Myth of Analysis,* p. 265.

94. Hillman, *Archetypal Psychology,* p. 31.

95. Surveying the rulings of two church councils (Council of Nicea in 787 and Council of Constantinople in 869) and the Christian canon, Hillman holds the Christian church responsible for "killing the (archetypal) soul," denigrating imagery, and reinforcing egocentric living. See *Archetypal Psychology,* pp. 5, 41-42; *Puer Papers,* pp. 54-56; *Re-Visioning Psychology,* pp. 11, 169; *Insearch,* pp. 135-141. In his assertions he seems to misunderstand the council rulings and aspects of Hebrew thinking (see Hans Walter Wolff, *Anthropology of the Old Testament* [Philadelphia: Fortress Press, 1974], p. 8), and to miscount key terms in the Christian canon (cf. *The Dictionary of New Testament Theology*). Similar to J. A. Hall's analysis of Hillman regarding Jungian theory ("Differences Between Jung and Hillman," in *Essays on Jung and the Study of Religion,* ed. L. H. Martin and J. Goss [Lanham: University Press of America, 1985]), Hillman champions a soul supposedly neglected through the cultural influence of Christianity — one that the Christian canon and conciliar rulings have not actually neglected.

over, Hillman's exhortation to attend to one's dreams,[96] to interact with one's world respectfully without trying to dominate or control it,[97] to consider pathology as potentially indicative of an inner disconnection[98] — again, these attitudes can garner support from many disciplines and religions (including Loder's understanding of Christian transformation).

Yet Hillman could be understood as depersonalizing human nature: it seems that the uniqueness of each living thing is subsumed in its attachment to the world soul, which is a power or force. Loder predicts that a person will take on the characteristics of the transforming agent.[99] If the transforming agent is an impersonal power or force, then the transformation will create what seems to be an impersonal person.[100] Hillman's theory could also be understood as confusing epistemological with ontological structures.[101] For Loder, archetypes, if they exist, are structures of knowing, not being, and therefore are unable to address ontological questions of meaning and purpose. Hillman's theory viewed as a non-theistic "spirituality" sidesteps questions of meaning and purpose.[102] What is the meaning and purpose of understanding myself as expressing the world soul? Hillman dismisses this question as an attempt of the heroic ego to reassert control.[103] Particular people or other creatures matter since they manifest the universal world soul, but why is it valuable to do so?

Loder and Hillman both criticize cultural reinforcement of ego-centered living, identify routes for transformation through ego-relativization, and predict desirable consequences of ego-relativization for individuals and society. Yet Loder's spirituality could not be more opposite to Hillman's. Hillman's villain is Loder's solution, or the problem is the solution. Loder understands particularity and universality as united and transcended in the triune God. Quoting Karl Barth, Loder locates the value of multiplicity in the nature of Jesus Christ who

96. Hillman, *Insearch*, p. 112.

97. Hillman, *Insearch*, pp. 24-25; *Thought of the Heart and Soul of the World*, p. 116.

98. Hillman, *Archetypal Psychology*, p. 39.

99. Loder, *Transforming Moment*, p. 97.

100. As described below, Loder insists that a person is not subsumed in her attachment to God. Since God has individual (one God) and social (three persons) historic significance, so does the person — throughout life on the transformation journey.

101. Loder makes this point regarding Jung in *The Logic of the Spirit*, p. 307.

102. Like Loder (discussed further on in the body of this essay), Bowker contends that meaning and purpose questions "are legitimate in the search for causative explanations of human behavior." Bowker, *Is God a Virus? Genes, Culture and Religion* (London: SPCK, 1995), p. 101.

103. Another spirituality without God might address meaning and purpose questions or conclude that they are unanswerable. But an anthropological approach that disallows the *possibility* of divine agency would be inadequate for spiritualities that root meaning and purpose in human-divine relationality.

> is single, unitary, consistent and free from contradiction, yet for all His singularity and unity His form is inexhaustibly rich, so that it is not merely legitimate but obligatory that believers should continually see and understand it in new lights and aspects. For He Himself does not present Himself to them in one form but in many — indeed, He is not in Himself uniform but multiform. How can it be otherwise when He is . . . eternally rich?[104]

Loder ventures that this union of particularity and universality in both human and divine natures can be known through the "logic of transformation" and its role in concrete and historical human-divine relationality.

Loder asserts that, by nature, humans seek relationship with God.[105] He uses attachment theory to describe the expression of that desire through the face phenomenon. From birth, human beings seek a principal organizer for their worlds.[106] Babies seek and respond to a face, even a schematic diagram of a face, by following it with their eyes and smiling. They become agitated when the face leaves; its return calms the baby. The infant's reactions to the face indicate that she orients her world toward that face, that she longs for a face that will never leave.[107] Classic psychoanalytic theory on ego formation

104. Loder, *Logic of the Spirit,* p. 38, quoting from Barth's *Church Dogmatics,* IV/1 (Edinburgh: T&T Clark, 1956), p. 763. Loder refers to T. F. Torrance's "The Natural Theology of Karl Barth," chap. 9 in *Transformation and Convergence in the Frame of Knowledge* (Grand Rapids: Eerdmans, 1984). However, Loder notes that he modifies Barth and thereby avoids some of the "hierarchical" and "paternalistic" problems in Barth. "Incisions from a Two-Edged Sword: The Incarnation in Practical Theology and the Soul/Spirit Relationship," in *The Treasure of Earthen Vessels: Explorations in Theological Anthropology,* ed. B. Childs and D. Waanders (Louisville: Westminster/John Knox Press, 1994), pp. 151-173.

105. Loder, *Logic of the Spirit,* pp. 90-91. Again, this universal claim assumes Christian faith premises.

106. Loder draws on René Spitz, who makes this assertion in his books, *The First Year of Life* (New York: International Universities Press, 1965) and *No and Yes* (New York: International Universities Press, 1957). Loder notes that Spitz refers to S. Freud's essay on "Negation," *Collected Papers* (London: Hogarth Press, 1950), vol. 5. Loder also refers to D. W. Winnicott, *Playing and Reality* (New York: Basic Books, 1971) and A.-M. Rizzuto, *The Birth of the Living God: A Psychoanalytic Study* (Chicago: University of Chicago Press, 1979). See Loder, *Transforming Moment,* pp. 162, 163; *Logic of the Spirit,* pp. 83-94.

107. *Logic of the Spirit,* p. 95. Loder notes that "Erikson and others who have no particular theological axe to grind agree that this [the face phenomenon] has religious significance . . . this smiling response to the face or the consistent nurturing presence of another is a cosmic-ordering, self-confirming presence of a loving other. That is, to be human is implicitly to be religious" (p. 90). Understood thus, the face phenomenon illustrates the connection between religion and somatic exploration (Bowker, *Is God a Virus?* p. 152). Bowker notes that the research of d'Aquili (whom Loder also cites, see note 43 above) suggests that humans are prepared in the brain for God-recognizing behaviors (*Is God a Virus?* p. 62).

notes that by age two the child negotiates her environment through her ego, balancing her inner reality with her outer reality, organizing her world around herself via her ego.[108] She does this through "repression" or "negation," the mechanism by which we unconsciously forget some things so that we can remember or focus on others.[109] Using repression (or negation), the ego seeks to ensure survival and maximize pleasure. Buried in her negations is a continued desire for a face that will never leave; she continually negates that desire through her ego accomplishments and competencies, functioning two-dimensionally (self and world) in ways deemed as "normal" according to her society and culture.[110]

However, in feelings of loneliness or despair, during crises or quiet reflection, her secret desire for the face that will never leave "secrets," as Loder would say.[111] Somehow she faces her limited nature. The faces of the void loom large. She faces her own nothingness, the inevitable fact of her own non-existence, and on some level still seeks the face that will never leave. This facing and seeking opens her to an encounter.[112] She cannot cover over her inner void (repressions or negations) with her self-sufficiency. The emptiness of the void opens a space to reveal the fullness of God's sustaining presence that simultaneously offers transforming relationship. In a figure-ground reversal, God rather than the void becomes the focus.[113] As a person embraces the offer of transforming relationship, God negates the negation that guides a person's ego defensiveness and its social expressions. The presence of God becomes the insight that resolves the existential conflict between her life, her lived world, and the void (death, nothingness). The particular faces of the void give way to the presence of God through Christ in the power of the Holy Spirit, and a person's world becomes consciously four dimensional.[114] I face

108. Loder, *Logic of the Spirit*, pp. 92-95. Loder agrees with W. Pannenberg (*Anthropology in Theological Perspective* [Edinburgh: T&T Clark, 1985]) on this point (*Logic of the Spirit*, pp. 117-118) and mentions theological support from D. Bonhoeffer (Princeton Theological Seminary, audiotape no. 6329, 6 May 1997). In *Creation and Fall: A Theological Exposition of Genesis 1–3* (Dietrich Bonhoeffer Works [Minneapolis: Fortress Press, 1997], vol. 3) Bonhoeffer understands "to be an evil will that destroyed community by its 'general egoism [durchgängigen Egoismus]'" (*Communion of Saints*, 81 [*Dietrich Bonhoeffer Werke*, German edition 1:247], italics original).

109. For contemporary research validating early Freudian theory on repression (and assessing other aspects of Freudian theory), see B. Andrews and C. Brewin, "What Did Freud Get Right?" *The Psychologist* 13, 2 (2000): 605-623.

110. Loder and Neidhardt, *Knight's Move*, p. 256.

111. Loder, *Transforming Moment*, pp. 81, 159; *Logic of the Spirit*, pp. 115, 119, 244.

112. Loder, *Transforming Moment*, pp. 101, 115, 173; *Logic of the Spirit*, p. 115.

113. Loder, *Transforming Moment*, pp. 119, 121, 142, 170.

114. Loder, *Transforming Moment*, pp. 85, 168; *Logic of the Spirit*, p. 271. "To say that Jesus

God as I face other people and all of creation in ways that may not look "normal" to my society and culture.[115]

Deep, transforming face-to-face encounter can form a bipolar relational unity of particularity and universality in human and divine natures.[116] In this face-to-face encounter, human nature is not reduced to divine nature; a person is not simply an emanation of God. Neither is divine nature reduced to human nature; God is not simply a wish fulfillment. The particularity and universality of both the person and God enter into a non-reductive relationship as embodied in Christ and articulated in the Chalcedonian statement of Christ's two natures.[117] Citing Paul who wrote, "I, not I, but Christ," Loder notes that the reverse is true in this dialectical relationship, "Christ, not Christ, but I."[118] All of my selves are related to the infinite variety of Christ. Loder's theory of spiritual transformation with God totally affirms human existence. God does not subsume humanity into God's self, but affirms it historically and concretely by relating it directly to human nature through Jesus Christ in the power of the Holy Spirit. The bipolar relational unity is asymmetrical; the Creator has marginal priority over the creature, just as Jesus Christ's divinity has marginal priority over his humanity — or else he would not have risen from the dead.

Loder's understanding of Christian spirituality centers human meaning and purpose upon relating to God and upon living that relationship in historic particularities.[119] Paradigmatically, human-divine relationality liberates a person's ego competencies and accomplishments to attend to the other as other

---

Christ is the Face of God is to make reference to the long tradition and many-faceted metaphorical uses of 'the face' in Scripture to designate the personal presence of the holy God. In both Greek *(prosōpon)* and Hebrew *(pānîm)* the word for *face* also means 'presence'. However, the Face of God ceases to be metaphor and becomes historically and empirically concrete in the person of Jesus Christ. In him, the relation between God and humanity is full, complete, and actualized in the same spatiotemporal and historical context in which we also exist" (*Logic of the Spirit*, p. 119).

115. Loder, *Logic of the Spirit*, p. 232. Loder cites Bonhoeffer's "religionless Christianity."

116. In his book on transformation that focuses on facing, *Self and Salvation: Being Transformed* (Cambridge: Cambridge University Press, 1999), David Ford suggests seeing the "polarity of particularity and universality mediated through the face" (p. 19). The mediation or integration is the *relationality:* "The particular face has a capacity to *relate* to others that is in principle universal" (p. 19; italics added). For Ford, the Christian community is "concerned with the transformation of facing before the face of Christ" (p. 24). In Loder's terms, the transformation of facing before the face of Christ involves ego-relativization in face-to-face encounter with the spiritual Presence of Christ in the historic, concrete particularities of a person's lived world.

117. Loder and Neidhardt, *Knight's Move*, p. 96; Loder, *Logic of the Spirit*, p. 37.

118. Loder, *Logic of the Spirit*, p. 145.

119. Loder, *Transforming Moment*, p. 202; *Logic of the Spirit*, pp. 12, 73, 74, 267.

(respectful of particularity), to avoid reductive views of human nature (e.g., as knowing or intelligence), and to effect lasting social change (exposing social "normalcy" as the perpetuation of reality-denying negation).

In sum, Loder and Hillman use some of the same language. Both say that we should not live out of our egos. Both affirm infinite variety in a numerically single person. Both critique the social and cultural pressures that encourage ego-centered living. Both urge encounter. Both can motivate environmental and social justice action. But their theories do not translate each other; despite semantic overlap, their conceptual fields differ in crucial ways and ultimately their theories critique each other. Hillman's encounter is encounter with an impersonal world soul. Encountering the faces of the world soul is self-encounter since a person is really a shell for the world soul. Although Loder's Christian spirituality also insists on self-encounter,[120] the self-encounter of Hillman blends the particularities of the self with the universal archetypes of the world soul. The self-encounter of Loder relates a particular person directly to the particular face of God through Christ in the power of the Holy Spirit; a person is not a shell for God.[121] Human-divine encounter is with a mysterious Being, not an impersonal force. Loder "stress[es] the irreducibly personal nature of the Holy Spirit."[122] He "opposes . . . [the] view that the Spirit is an impersonal force emanating from God and detachable from God."[123]

As this brief comparison of Loder and Hillman suggests, an interdisciplinary approach that allows for the *possibility* that God initiates human transformation does not necessarily deny the dynamic significance of human nature. Loder insists that theology and the human sciences learn from one another.[124] Hillman's entire corpus explores the cultural roots of Western (particularly U.S.) cultural imagery and its concrete manifestation in and influence on people's lives, individually and socially. Loder's affirmation of images and the imagination concurs with Hillman's detailed attention to images; Hillman's

120. Loder, *Logic of the Spirit,* pp. 94, 95.

121. In the twelfth century, cosmologists, mystics, scientists, theologians, and philosophers all debated about translating the Holy Spirit as the *anima mundi.* In 1140, the Council of Sens ruled against this translation. See B. McGinn, "The Role of 'Anima Mundi' as Mediator Between the Divine and Created Realms in the Twelfth Century," in *Death, Ecstasy, and Other Worldly Journeys,* ed. John J. Collins and Michael Fishbane (Albany: State University of New York Press, 1995), pp. 289-319. The Council of Sens' concerns involved the implication that each person has two souls, the possible subordination of the Holy Spirit, and the risk of pantheism.

122. Loder and Neidhardt, *Knight's Move,* p. 23.

123. Loder and Neidhardt, *Knight's Move,* p. 23.

124. Loder, "Normativity and Context in Practical Theology," in *Practical Theology: International Perspectives,* ed. F. Schweitzer and J. A. van der Ven (Frankfurt am Main: Peter Lang, 1999), pp. 359-81.

work provides a valuable resource for Loder's theory. Ultimately, Loder's theory would relate Hillman's corpus to God and thus transform it from two dimensions to four, from human (or world soul) origins and destiny to human-divine relationality. However, in terms of interdisciplinary and inter-faith spirituality discourse, Loder's theory invites relationality without denying fundamental polarities; indeed, relationality arises from affirmation of the polarities, not removal of awkward and competing conceptual fields.

Having considered, first, that mystical spirituality is the heart of Loder's logic, and second, that Loder's logic can contribute to spirituality discourse about particularity and universality by comparing his ego-relativization theory to that of Hillman's, we turn now to the concurrence between Loder's portrayal of transforming and transformed *knowing* in mystical spirituality as depicted by the four contemporary investigators. The liberating impact of redemptive transformation on human competencies reveals love as central to the movement of intelligence. Intelligence as loving relationship, or love as itself a knowing, is central to mystical spirituality and to Loder's logic.

Loder's Transformational Logic as the Structure of Creative Intelligence

Loder's "logic of transformation" is an attempt to describe human knowing "in flight." He asserts that all human knowing is relational and transformational, that knowing is an event. By relational, transformational, and "event," he means that knowing involves the five phases of the transformational logic. These knowing events are situated, involving a person and her lived world in each phase. Moreover, the knower determines the knowing event. "It is previous theory, more or less latent, that determines *what* we observe and *how* we observe, and it is from the imaginative leap of the mind rooted in previously established theories that our new theories come."[125] A knower's assumptional world determines her understanding and value of new knowledge, while the insight of new knowledge represents a discontinuity with her assumptional world. "Discontinuity effected by an imaginative construct is the key and center of the knowing event; indeed, it is just this discontinuity that makes transformation possible."[126] New knowledge transforms a person's assumptions, her view of reality. The insight that performs a figure-ground reversal, that creates a bipolar relational unity, is the "leap of the imagination." He suggests a "new theory of er-

125. Loder, *Transforming Moment,* p. 29. My discussion draws from chaps. 1 and 2 of this text.
126. Loder, *Transforming Moment,* p. 41.

ror" that would reject as intellectual dissimulation any denial that a person's imagination had contributed to a new insight. "Rational processes can add no knowledge that is not first imagined."[127]

If people operate transformationally, according to this logic, then deep encounter with God affects (Loder says "transforms") the operation of the logic; the movement of transformation (the logic) is itself transformed through deep encounter with God. In this encounter, God, the source of all knowledge and wisdom, unites with the human knower, and their loving relationality may determine what is known. A person's assumptional world is now four dimensional (self, world, void, and Holy).

Loder's double use of the term "transformation" (like the double use of the term "negation") can make this part of his theory somewhat confusing. Loder describes human knowing as transformational and relational since he asserts that it operates according to the transformational logic. This human knowing is "proximate" to the knowing that issues from human-divine relationality. The latter he refers to as "convictional" knowing, knowing resulting from a convicted person's compulsion to reopen the question of reality in light of the Convictor and the convictional relationship of Christian transformation.[128] Human knowing participates "sacramentally" in "convictional" knowing (as visible signs of an invisible reality), potentially opening a person's awareness of God and pointing a person toward Christ's offer of deep, transforming relationship. Thus, in a sense, all human knowing is four dimensional, accepting Christian premises that God is the very condition for the possibility of knowing anything at all. But human knowing is reduced to two dimensions when explanations and interpretations do not include the void and God; the inclusion of God does not mean a superficial overlay, but relational embrace of God's loving involvement throughout the knowing event. The contrast is most evident in the comparison of human knowing (e.g., therapeutic, esthetic, and scientific) and convictional knowing.

For example, in therapeutic knowing a person experiences self-disclosure, and this also occurs in convictional knowing — a person becomes aware concretely of her limitations, of the void, of her fears and desires.[129] In esthetic knowing, a person transcends reductionistic, habitual

127. Loder, *Transforming Moment,* p. 33.

128. Loder, *Transforming Moment,* p. 14, citing Willem Zuurdeeg's *An Analytical Philosophy of Religion,* but noting his (Loder's) focus on the experience of conviction rather than the term's use in the philosophy of religion.

129. Loder goes so far as to suggest the possible greater tragedy of a person who tries to live without noticing the tragic nature of life "in the natural course of things" ("Educational Ministry," chap. 7, p. 7).

knowing, breaking out of "everydayness" to see the particulars of her lived world in a new way and this also occurs in convictional knowing — a person sees the ordinary as the bearer of the extraordinary grace of God. In scientific knowing, personal intuition and the creative unconscious, a visionary glimpse of some aspect of the universe, all work to counter the "creeping-conformist tendency toward technique," and this also occurs in convictional knowing — a person grasps imaginatively and rationally the mysterious, ineffable order of things as bestowed by God.[130] Outside of human-divine relationality (as differentiated from God's gracious sustaining presence or divine contingency), therapeutic, esthetic, and scientific knowing are two-dimensional; even though the void and the Holy are part of reality, the knower does not know relationally of their involvement.

Loder's logic focuses on the dependence of all knowing (the operation of human intelligence) on God for both its existence and transformation; as noted, Louth, McGinn, Turner, and McIntosh assert that mystical spirituality acknowledges God as the condition for knowing anything at all. Loder focuses on the sustaining presence of God who simultaneously offers to transform intelligence. If God is embraced, a person's understanding and experience are drawn into the life of the Trinity, moving from two dimensions to four.[131] This movement accords with Gregory the Great's maxim, cited earlier as a summary statement of the paradoxical relationship between love and knowing in mystical texts, that love itself is a knowing. As to the four contemporary authors and the classic mystical authors before them, Loder recognizes the implications of his reconceptualization of knowing and its operation as through human intelligence.[132] The role of the imagination and the personal assumptions that determine what is known and how knowing occurs require the personal engagement of the learner. Otherwise:

> One becomes a "good" learner, learning how to study but never how to generate his or her own thought, and one becomes a "good" practitioner but without thinking. In essence, the perversity is that interpretation is reduced to answers, albeit "good" ones, and practice is reduced to imitation and fol-

130. Loder, *Transforming Moment,* p. 46.

131. At stake is a view of who *can* be in relationship with God. Separating knowledge from experience can lead to the exclusion of those who are "disabled" on either side of the false dichotomy. See J. Swinton, "Restoring the Image: Spirituality, Faith, and Cognitive Disability," *Journal of Religion and Health* 36, 1 (1997): 21-27.

132. A critical historical survey of intelligence as it has been understood and tested appears in K. Danziger, "Putting Intelligence on the Map," chap. 5 of *Naming the Mind: How Psychology Found Its Language* (London: Sage Publications, 1997), pp. 66-84.

> lowing good advice, with the result that professionalism emerges in the wake of stagnant ideas and empty jargon.[133]

This description can apply to many contexts, disciplines, workplaces, and institutions. It indicates the social critique and inseparability of individual and social transformation inherent in Loder's theory.

Loder's logic both sustains and subverts the embeddedness of intelligence in society.[134] Regardless of how intelligence is understood, it operates according to transformational logic. The logic sustains the workings of human intelligence in academic cultures that reject it. Simultaneously, the very operation of the logic to produce creative new insights subverts reductive understandings of intelligence. Similarly, while providing the condition for people to know anything at all, God offers transforming relationship. Fundamentally, this constant offer questions our understandings of intelligence and human nature; it queries about meaning and purpose;[135] it reconceptualizes intelligence as transformational relationship rather than as mental speed.

How we understand intelligence affects our educational systems, our identification of talent, our promotion or demotion of individuals into positions of power, our understanding and reward of success or penalties for failure, our reward of competitive self-promotion, the very fabric of society.[136] Spiritualities or transformation theories that critique social and cultural norms inevitably support the very norms they critique *if* they affirm explicitly or implicitly the accepted understandings of knowing. This is one reason why Hillman's theory is a powerful resource for Loder's theory: Hillman critiques the accepted understandings of knowing as egocentric and emphasizes instead the role and multiplicity of images in knowing reality. Accepting Christian premises, his portrayal of human knowing remains two dimensional, but it is a valuable "view from below."

Understanding the knowing event as adaptation, intelligence as, for example, "what IQ tests test,"[137] truncates our understanding of human nature and thereby distorts spirituality. This distortion of intelligence renders spiritu-

133. Loder, "Transformation in Christian Education," pp. 217-218.

134. My assertion regarding Loder's logic in society parallels Loder's assertion that the church immersed in socialization and adaptation to mainstream society is foredoomed and yet has inherent resources for renewal ("Educational Ministry," chap. 7). As Loder asserts in his earlier text, *Religion in the Public Schools* (New York: Association Press, 1965), socialization and transformation are inextricably intertwined.

135. Loder and Neidhardt, *Knight's Move,* p. 197.

136. Loder, "Educational Ministry," chap. 7, p. 15.

137. As asserted by Harvard psychologist E. G. Boring in a 1923 interview published in the *New Republic.* There is some debate about whether he uttered those words facetiously or in all seriousness.

ality an adaptive technique or strategy inherent to human nature rather than a transforming movement initiated and superintended by God.[138] This very distortion of spirituality exercises the four authors. The four authors assert that the classic mystical authors themselves wrote against understanding spirituality as a set of techniques or strategies.[139] Although adaptation is relational and transforming in a sense, transformation differs from adaptation. A person (or group) adapts to her environment and thereby changes and is changed. Adaptive techniques or strategies manage change. A transforming movement initiated and superintended by God defies management. A person does not adapt to God. God lovingly sustains and transforms a person in both time and eternity, outside prediction.[140]

Conclusions

The agreement among James Loder and the four authorities on mystical spirituality, cited at the outset of this essay, with their shared focus on "deep, transforming encounter with God," occurred to me as a convictional insight, a "bipolar relational unity" enfolded in the life of the Trinity, in which I came to know these distinctive traditions relationally. This "bipolar relational unity" does not reduce all Christian traditions to the same thing.[141] Nor does it synthesize them into the same thing. Rather, the christological insight performs a figure-ground reversal, as predicted by Loder's transformational logic. That is, the focus shifts *from* the distinctions *to* God who gathers all polarities and sustains the body of

138. For an example of a presentation of mystical spirituality as an adaptive technique or strategy, see clinical and consulting psychologist David Benner's *Care of Souls: Revisioning Christian Nurture and Counsel* (Grand Rapids: Baker Books, 1998). He describes terms from Christian mystical spirituality, *kataphatic* and *apophatic*, as "techniques" and "classic approaches to meditation. Kataphatic spirituality is based on the active use of the imagination . . . apophatic spirituality is based on an emptying technique of meditation" (pp. 91-92). This is precisely what our four authors insist that *apophaticism* and *cataphaticism* are not! For example, Turner criticizes the contemporary "psychologizing" mind for thinking of the "mystical" in terms of "characterizing *experiences*" (*The Darkness of God*, p. 4; italics original). McIntosh gives the example that "[i]f a mystic said for example that, 'Darkness is the only way to God,' the experientialist interpreter takes this to mean that one must seek some inner state of 'darkness', rather than hearing it as a warning against reliance on particular beliefs, aspirations, feelings, or idols of any kind whatsoever in the encounter with the living God" (*Mystical Theology*, p. 23).

139. Turner, *The Darkness of God*, p. 4. See agreement with Turner: Louth, *Origins of the Christian Mystical Tradition*, pp. 183, 195, 200; McGinn, *The Presence of God*, vol. 1, p. xiv; vol. 2, pp. 140, 141; vol. 3, p. 24; McIntosh, *Mystical Theology*, pp. 9, 14, 21.

140. Loder and Neidhardt, *Knight's Move*, pp. 186, 235.

141. Loder and Neidhardt, *Knight's Move*, p. 228.

Christ,[142] relating distinct Christian traditions in the *perichoresis* of the Trinity.[143] Ultimately, such relationship transforms the traditions themselves.

Loder's logic contributes to spirituality discourse about particularity and universality in two ways. First, as a "view from below," the logic provides a conceptual framework for understanding the movement of the human knowing as creative, relational, and transformational; this movement can be understood as a human spirituality for the purposes of interdisciplinary and inter-faith discourse. Hence, Hillman's rejection of ego-centered living, affirmation of the richness of human nature and the world, critique of social and culture pressures that encourage egocentrism, insistence on encounter, and urging of environmental and social justice action all serve as a valuable resource on the particularities of human knowing. Second, as an approach to Christian spirituality, Loder's theory unites views "from below" and "from above" without reducing human participation to the passive reception of grace (the true test of the validity of my connection of Loder to mystical spirituality). Transformation transformed places all human knowing within a four-dimensional reality that transforms all particularities in human-divine relationality. The transformation theory of Loder can face the particularity of another theory to find the the triune God sustaining and yet offering transformation to all theories in the knowing of loving relationship.

Loder's logic describes the continuity and discontinuity between human knowing and knowing God, concurring with the depiction of loving knowing in mystical spirituality as presented by Louth, McGinn, Turner, and McIntosh. Paradoxically, Loder's logic of transformed intelligence has appeared within the academy, and the academy as the great American (and, I would argue other cultures') "factory" of socialization is integral to the structures that distort intelligence. The *perichoresis* of the Trinity may be most evident in what is most polarized from it, as displayed on the cross of Christ.[144] Reductive methodologies, disciplines, and transformation theories most polarized from deep, transforming encounter with God paradoxically reveal the gracious nature of God's sustaining presence as the condition of knowing anything at all.

As a transformed knower within the Christian tradition, James Loder paradoxically supported and challenged the seats of knowledge. In my view, that is a key insight into his legacy.

142. Loder, *Transforming Moment*, p. 194.

143. Loder, *Logic of the Spirit*, pp. 195, 276.

144. Williams, *The Wound of Knowledge*, p. 149; see also McIntosh: "[T]he role of God the Holy Spirit . . . has been to draw the Word further and further into creation, into what is 'not-God', precisely so that creation might be reconciled and drawn into fellowship with God" (*Mystical Theology*, p. 157).

AFTERWORD

The Potential Contribution of James E. Loder Jr. to Practical Theological Science

Dana R. Wright

> *It is, indeed, often misleading to talk . . . about choosing a model for imitation; what more often happens is that the model, by its sheer impressiveness, demands our imitation and in doing so not merely develops, but radically revises, our previous notions about what is worth imitating.*[1]

The impetus for this *Festschrift* arose from a conversation I had with Dr. Loder in April of 2001. While interviewing him for research I anticipated doing for a Talbot University–sponsored project entitled "Christian Educators of the 20th Century,"[2] I asked Dr. Loder if anyone had ever approached him about doing a *Festschrift* in his honor. When he replied "No," I then asked him how one gets such a project under way. He told me to talk with President Gillespie. Dr. Gillespie immediately supported the effort with enthusiasm, and he called William B. Eerdmans to assure him of Princeton Seminary's financial backing for the initial printing costs of the book. Assured of a publisher, I worked with Dr. Loder over the next few months to gain commitments from contributors, all of whom were secured by the end of the summer. Loder himself came up with the title *Redemptive Transformation in Practical Theology.* He also planned to write a response to the contributors' essays as the final chapter. I kept him updated on the progress of

1. Basil Mitchell, *Morality: Religious and Secular* (Oxford: Clarendon Press, 1980), p. 153.

2. Kevin Lawson, gen. ed., "Christian Educators of the 20th Century" (2001-2004). This database website project, developed in collaboration between Talbot University and the North American Professors of Christian Education, is being funded in part by a grant from the Lilly Endowment. This Afterword is a revision of the contribution essay I wrote for the James E. Loder Jr. entry to this project, completed in the Spring of 2004. Go to www.talbot.edu/ceacademic.

the project through that summer and into autumn. He was very grateful for all that was being done to honor him this way. He died that November.

During that same interview I had asked Dr. Loder if he was optimistic about the future of practical theology. He responded that he was optimistic, but he qualified his optimism as follows.

> I think it is absolutely crucial that practical theology flourish. But I think it has to be somewhat reconceived according to the great themes of the twenty-first century, which are on the one hand "science" and on the other hand "spirit." And it is not my idea that the twenty-first century should emphasize these things. But the practical theology that is going to last is going to show the relevance of those two themes to what we want to talk about in the church and in the teaching of pastors, and in theological seminaries. There is so much to be done in the interplay of those two driving forces. So, I am hopeful (a) because we need it and (b) because I think it is possible for practical theology to adapt to these emerging needs of the church put on it by the changing of culture. And "science" of course applies to technology, and "spirit" implies the Holy Spirit not just human spirit. But I think we will adapt to that. I mean we'll adapt [practical theology] to the transforming work of the Spirit.[3]

Loder believed that remarkable advances in our understanding of the nature of reality ("science") and of *homo poeta* as self-involved constructors of reality ("spirit") were compelling the church to reinvestigate the conceptual contours of her own self-understanding *vis-à-vis* the relationship of scientific culture to Christian revelation and tradition in the twenty-first century. Furthermore, he believed that the church possessed resources significantly attuned to, and indeed anticipatory of, these compelling developments in the natural and human sciences to fund a new level of dialogue that would foster a radical reconsideration of the relation of revelation to human meaning-making (divine action to human action) for a scientific context. Thus, on the one hand, a quick review of Loder's major published works, which includes (a) his convictional epistemology, conceived in *The Transforming Moment* as a truly scientific way of knowing, (b) his development of the *analogia spiritus* and disclosure models faithful to this analogy, especially his reconstruction with Neidhardt in *The Knight's Move* of a generic transfiguration of Bohr's model of complementarity called "the strange loop," (c) his reconsideration of human developmental insights under the "logic" of the Holy Spirit as a "journey of intensification" into reality *(The Logic of the Spirit),* (d) his insistence on "the human factor" (self-involvement)

3. Interview on April 20, 2001, with Dana Wright (text slightly modified).

in all true scientific knowing, and (e) the ontological precedence of relationality over rationality, reveals that Loder had set his own sights on reconceiving practical theology as a truly compelling scientific enterprise for a scientific context. Loder believed postmodern culture demanded that practical theologians work self-consciously as interdisciplinary scientists.

On the other hand, Loder wanted to center his interdisciplinary science on the work of the Holy Spirit human-ward, especially in relation to the dynamic creativity of the human spirit, a relation he conceived christologically. Loder believed that practical theology should conceive itself in relation to human participation in the very life of God revealed and lived "in the Spirit." Therefore, he directed most of his scholarly efforts to reconceiving the fundamental conceptual contours of practical theology as an interdisciplinary science grounded on the actuality of Spirit-to-spirit relations. For Loder, metatheoretical understandings in the natural and human sciences and theological understandings of Spirit-to-spirit relations might well converge to offer to the church and to culture powerful new models with explanatory power to discern the nature of reality *coram Deo.*[4]

After the *Festschrift* essays were submitted to Eerdmans, but before the proofs were issued for final editing, I came to suspect that Loder's self-understanding as a neo-Chalcedonian scientist, and of redemptive transformation in practical theology as a scientific enterprise, which were introduced in the biographical part of the Introduction, had faded somewhat from view. That is, I began to sense that references in the essays to Loder's inspiring work in practical theology perhaps understated the scientific claims Loder made for his own work. That he thought of himself as a scientist, and his own work as theoretical science of the highest order, even as he understood his work and his life under the *aegis* of the Holy Spirit, was not clearly discernable in the *Festschrift* as a whole. I began to believe that Loder's own response to the essays, had he lived to write it, might well have been to highlight the need for a truly scientific practical theology, a practical theological science of Spirit-to-spirit relations. So I decided to submit an Afterword on behalf of the collaborators, one that might reaffirm this crucial dimension of Loder's potential legacy to practical theology for readers of the *Festschrift.*[5]

4. Several if not most of Loder's publications after 1990, beginning with *The Knight's Move* (1992), reveal Loder's conviction that the signs of the times in both science and theology pointed to the potential for a renaissance in human understanding of the nature of reality that was promising for the witness of the gospel.

5. I want to thank John Kuentzel and F. LeRon Shults for their valuable feedback on this essay, given on short notice. Some of the contributors to the *Festschrift* may differ with me on my emphasis here. Nonetheless I am confident that all of us agree (along with others I have got-

Of course, this proximity of the word "science" to "Holy Spirit" should give any perceptive reader pause. We are not used to hearing this combination of words used coherently in the same sentence, and when we do we suspect immediately that something is afoul. We might expect any moment to see Gandolf appear over the next hill, riding his white steed Shadowfax and spouting some alchemic hocus pocus about Middle-Earth magic in the land of Mordor to a beguiled Frodo. From this standpoint we might conclude that Loder was simply beguiled himself, hoodwinked by some arcane demiurge deluding him to spend his years mixing things that are not permitted to be mixed. He in turn hoodwinked the hundreds of persons who flocked to his courses, or who streamed to Princeton to study under him or to receive his counsel, or who heard him lecture or preach in seminaries and congregations around the world. Or perhaps more reasonably, one might conclude that my claim that Loder was a scientist of Spirit-to-spirit relations teaching an entire generation of church leaders at the flagship Presbyterian seminary to do science "in the Spirit" is merely evidence of my own fideistic or absurdist reading of Loder's *oeuvres.*

But the "absurdity" squarely belongs to Loder, I am quite sure. Loder really believed that the integration of science and spirit came through the redeeming work of the Holy Spirit on the human spirit. He claimed to have identified a scientifically plausible understanding of the nature, structure, and dynamics of divine accommodation to human action through the Spirit — and to have touted the ability of this science to deepen human participation in the redemptive and re-creative power of the gospel as a basis for renewing human life in both congregation and culture. This claim is highly suspect in a culture that regards any transcendent mixing of "science" and "spirit" to be a lapse into mysticism or conjecture — or fideism of the worst sort. Thus, Loder's work remains a "hard sell" to those in the professional guild still operating largely under the *aegis* of the reality principle. Nevertheless, he sought to conform his practical theological science to the movement of the Holy Spirit in a scientific culture, a work he conceived to be both supremely orthodox and wholly scientific at the same time, while grounded beyond both theology and science in the trinitarian life of God. For Loder, practical theology "happened" in the Spirit, but it was no less scientific for that fact. And perhaps this is one reason Loder's work as a whole has not commanded the kind of scholarly attention it might otherwise inspire — it sounds like fantasy in a scientific culture still largely dominated by reduc-

ten to know and with whom I have spoken at some depth over the past few years) that Loder's work does indeed offer to the church and to the academy profoundly generative metatheoretical lenses for radically transforming our understanding of the nature of human participation in divine action for practical theology and Christian education, as well as for the relation of Christ to scientific culture, as we move into the next millennium.

tionistic forms of rationality and a dualistic split between "two cultures." That is, perhaps one reason Loder's work remains relatively "unknown" is that his project conjures up images of the hermetic alchemist working by himself in his secret laboratory on some arcane formula that promises to make gold out of lead, thus uniting elements that have no intrinsic common bond (like spirit and science, or faith and knowledge, or God and humanity) into a unified whole.[6]

Furthermore, his claims concerning the need for the christomorphic transformation of the knower herself in order to discern the nature of reality as contingent creation appears maddeningly *alchemical* to some who are committed to a more pluralistic and neutral or "objective" science modulated through a less confessional Christian witness. Loder opted to take seriously, for scientific investigation itself, Paul's assertion that natural intelligence and/or unredeemed rationality cannot discern the things of the Spirit until the human spirit as the generator of intelligence is reconstituted onto-relationally in christomorphic dimensions ("I, yet not I but Christ" taken as a scientific epistemological and hermeneutical principle!). Thus his claim that human knowing "in the Spirit" approximates how the Spirit of Christ knows the human condition sounds pretty farfetched to many theorists, and perhaps downright elitist to others. But Loder's insistence on the necessary transformation of the spirit of the mind of the practical theologian to "enlarge" the epistemological horizons of the human knower according to Christ's knowledge of them takes the control out of the theorist's own hands and places it squarely in the work of *Spiritus Creator*. Paradoxically, it demands at the same time even more rigor (and risk) from the practical theologian herself to learn how this intensive dialectical knowing in the Spirit effectively discerns hidden orders of intelligibility underlying a scientific culture that routinely suppresses the things of the Spirit. Simply put, Loder's practical theological science "in the Spirit" sounds too oddly *alchemical* to be true science, and too *scientific* to be alchemically transformative.

Actually, relatively few scholars seem to know what Loder was up to in all those years at Princeton, or to have discerned fully what his intentions really were for practical theology. Few established scholars have actually attempted a sustained analysis of his work as a whole that might help us render a credible judgment of any kind, positive or negative, as to the substance of

6. Several books of recent years have pointed to our inability in the United States to integrate faith and knowledge, conviction and science. See, e.g., Douglas Sloan, *Faith and Knowledge: Mainline Protestants and American Higher Education* (Louisville: Westminster/John Knox, 1994). See also Robert Benne, "The Crisis of Identity: A Clash over Faith and Learning," *The Christian Century*, Jan. 27, 2004, about the recent controversy at Baylor University surrounding the efforts there to create a research university within the context of a Baptist convictional stance.

his project.[7] Moreover, what interest he has generated has generally centered on only one, albeit vital, aspect of his total vision — the dynamic "grammar" of transformation he discerned in the context of convictional experiences, which he argued could be recognized as a pattern of the human spirit's creativity in various domains of human action and problem solving.[8] Even his former students have, with notable exceptions, appropriated only this single aspect of his work as his major contribution to practical theology — that is, as the "grammatical" key to identifying the power of the human spirit in profound religious experience and in generating creativity in various forms of ministerial *praxis.* Relatively few readers of Loder seem to have discerned that this "transformational grammar" requires radical reconsideration of many of the epistemological and ontological assumptions we bring to practical theology, not to mention those we bring to construct our understandings of the relation of faith to scientific culture in general. Furthermore, the dominance of critical correlation methodologies in practical theology, which tends to privilege apologetic criteria for judging theology's relevance *within* culture over the theological or prophetic challenge the gospel brings *to* culture, bends the ears of practical theologians away from the critical confessional science Loder developed.[9] No doubt, the failure of Loder to publish two significant

7. Loder's work as a whole has not received the critical attention it deserves from the practical theological guild, or from Christian and religious educators. Compare, for example, the scrutiny James Fowler's developmental paradigm has enjoyed since 1980 with the attention paid to Loder's redemptive transformational paradigm over that same time period. Both theorists, along with Thomas Groome, published a significant work with Harper & Row in the field of Christian education over twenty years ago — Fowler's *Stages of Faith* (1981), Groome's *Christian Religious Education* (1980), and Loder's *The Transforming Moment* (1981). Since that time, the developmental approach championed by Fowler has generated probably three times as much attention from practical theologians and Christian or religious educators as has Groome or Loder. Significantly, Fowler himself had a sense of this fundamental significance of *The Transforming Moment* in the summary of their debate, recorded in *Religious Education* in 1982. See J. Loder and J. Fowler, "Conversations on Fowler's *Stages of Faith* and Loder's *The Transforming Moment*," in *Religious Education* 77, 2 (1982): 133-148.

8. Three recent dissertations have focused on "larger" readings of Loder. The most comprehensive is probably Ken Kovac's dissertation, "The Relational Phenomenological Pneumatology of James E. Loder: Providing New Frameworks for the Christian Life" (St. Andrews University, 2003). See also the dissertations by Susan Buckles (2001) and Eolene Boyd-MacMillan (2004) listed in the bibliography. Interestingly, one of the more impressive reviews of Loder's work actually came very early in his career, after the publication of his dissertation in book form. Nelle Morton's review of Loder's *Religious Pathology and Christian Faith* discerned the vast scope of the implications of Loder's thinking for practical theology and theological education. One wonders if Morton herself followed Loder's work after 1970. I have found no evidence that she did.

9. See my essay, "The Contemporary Renaissance in Practical Theology in the United

works revealing his mature constructive approach to a practical theology of Christian education has contributed mightily to this lack of attention to his thought as a whole.[10] Ironically, his death makes his work more available than ever before, now that his papers are being catalogued at the Luce Archive on Princeton Seminary's campus.[11] Perhaps both established scholars and the next generation of practical theologians will take advantage of this archive to look more carefully at his fundamental proposals for an interdisciplinary science of practical theology grounded in the Holy Spirit. The question I will try to answer in this Afterword is, Why should they bother?[12]

My efforts here should not be seen as sour-grapes recriminations from one defending his dearly departed *Doktorvater* against the tyranny of neglect by an ignorant guild. Rather, my purpose arises from the consensus of all the contributors that Loder's work is, at the very least, as significant and/or even compelling as any other major practical theologian working at the meta-theoretical level during the past forty years.[13] As philosopher Basil Mitchell noted (quoted above in the epigraph), truly compelling work compels.

States: The Past, Present and Future of a Discipline in Creative Ferment," *International Journal of Practical Theology* 6, 3 (2002): 289-320.

10. *Educational Ministry in the Logic of the Spirit* and *Transformational Dynamics in Christian Education: A Study in Practical Theology* have not yet been published. These two works fill out the depth and breadth of Loder's conceptualization of Christian education at the meta-theoretical level of fundamental practical theology. There is some hope that these two works, or at least the first one, will one day be published. The latter work has not been fully located at the time of this essay. It would have been, in my judgment, Loder's *magnum opus* and perhaps the most influential book in practical theology of the past fifty years.

11. These papers were scheduled to be available in the summer of 2004.

12. Of course, part of the problem for assessing Loder's potential contribution to practical theology must be laid squarely at his own feet. Loder was a private man in many ways, who worked largely by himself and who did not seem to be in a hurry to get his work out into the public. He also showed a general disinterest in the organizational or institutional aspects of scholarship, those that necessarily impact the "marketing" of one's academic interests. Loder did not mix casually with others, nor was he comfortable attending professional gatherings to "network." He refused to jump on popular intellectual band-wagons or to take up particular academic concerns just because they were in vogue. And potential collaborations with other theorists rarely materialized, for one reason or another. His only truly collaborative relationship, a seven-year intellectual-spiritual harnessing with Jim Neidhardt, the physicist with whom he wrote *The Knight's Move,* ended when Neidhardt died prematurely in the early 1990s, just after their book came out. When I asked Dr. Loder in 2001 about his friendship with Neidhardt, he responded, with a wistful smile, that Neidhardt uniquely appreciated what he (Loder) was getting at. Loder had "something on his mind" that few others discerned fully, even to a large degree his own students.

13. Both Groome and Fowler seemed to have appreciated Loder's work at some level, as he did theirs.

> It is, indeed, often misleading to talk . . . about choosing a model for imitation; what more often happens is that the model, by its sheer impressiveness, demands our imitation and in doing so not merely develops, but radically revises, our previous notions about what is worth imitating.[14]

In this essay I want to try to articulate what I think compels us to look at Loder's work as a whole, by focusing on what I believe lies at the heart of his theoretical science of divine-human action, and from there to summarize its possible significance to practical theology as a generative science fit for the twenty-first century.

Why Bother with the Alchemist James E. Loder Jr.?

As we have already stated, few scholars have analyzed in depth the core themes and central concerns of Loder's overall science of practical theology, nor picked up on the larger implications of his vision for reconstructing the nature and dynamics of theory and practice in practical theology. Almost no one has identified a conceptual thread that "connects the dots" of his work in a way that brings his whole vision into view. Moreover, few have even attempted to assess his transformative understandings of the "dots" themselves. For example, few psychologists, educators, or researchers in the human sciences have studied his highly original critical reinterpretations of Freud, Piaget, Kohlberg, Erikson, Kegan, or Fowler, et al., leading to his convictional insights into the self-relating, self-transcendent nature of the human construction of experience.[15] Social theorists and theologians of culture remain largely ignorant of his reconstruction of classical Parsonian action theory in terms of the reciprocal relation of socialization and transformation as it expresses implicitly a "religious thematic" (Pannenberg) that pervades human experience at the tacit level within every domain of human action. Also ignored are his unique insights into (his theological and interdisciplinary reading of) the way in which existential negation gets incorporated into bodily existence and subsequently permeates intra-personal, inter-personal, communal and symbolic-religious dimensions of experience to generate pathological lifestyles or an ethos that dehumanizes and destroys the fabric of the body politic and that insulates us from the politics of God.[16]

14. Mitchell, *Morality,* p. 153.

15. Much of this material, scattered throughout his published works, is found in more compact form in his lecture notes for his Philosophy of Education course, located in the Loder archive.

16. These distortions are discussed in his unpublished work *Educational Ministry in the*

Furthermore, practical theologians have not appreciated fully the dramatic implications of Loder's single-minded devotion to discern and explicate the core problematic of the field, which he described as the persistent *theological* question as to why the field *is* a problem.[17] Nor have they considered the generative capacity of his generic models of relationality that he created to discern patterns of interrelations in different domains of scientific research according to the nature of Christ. Moreover, systematic theologians do not know about his persistent efforts to reconstruct the underdeveloped theology of the Holy Spirit in Christian tradition by attending to the self-relational structures intrinsic to, and constitutive of, spirit — not only the human spirit's movement outward but the Holy Spirit's own movement human-ward. The corollary of this concern is Loder's radical claim that participating in the Spirit requires a unique epistemology that conforms itself to the kinetic nature of the self-involved knower under conviction by the Self-involved Spirit.[18] Nor have theologians taken time to appreciate the depth of Loder's appropriation of Kierkegaard and Barth (through Torrance) for engaging the human and natural sciences, thereby challenging misguided stereotypes that prevent these two magisterial figures from having more impact on interdisciplinary constructive work in the West.[19] Finally, scientists know little of Loder's own efforts, building on Kierkegaard especially, to enhance the theology-science dialogue through his christological yet scientific reconstructions of (1) convictional epistemology (which includes a new proposal for overcoming "eikonic eclipse" in scientific method[20]), (2) the anthropic principle, (3) the theory of complementarity (his insistence on asymmetry in the complementary re-

---

Logic of the Spirit. This book, structured by Loder's reinterpretation of Parsonian action theory, develops substantial critiques of obsession with achievement (as in corporate [business] culture) as the distortion of love, protean relativism (as in Generation X) as the distortion of freedom, unreflective submissiveness to, or blind rage against, systemic oppression (like the oppression the once-oppressed inflict upon those they now rule) as the distortion of justice, and authoritarianism (as in fundamentalisms of the left or right) as the distortion of power. See Russell Haitch's essay in this volume, "A Summary of James E. Loder's Theory of Christian Education," for a review of the content of this book.

17. See Loder's article, "The Place of Science in Practical Theology: The Human Factor," *International Journal of Practical Theology* 4, 1 (2000): 22-41.

18. See Loder and Niedhardt, *The Knight's Move: The Relational Logic of the Spirit in Theology and Science* (Colorado Springs: Helmers & Howard, 1992), chap. 1.

19. For example, I argued in my dissertation that Loder's work helps the church recover a theological stance for developing critical confessional practical theology profound enough to initiate a "second Barthian reckoning" with religious education's emphasis on the human sciences. See "Ecclesial Theatrics" (diss., Princeton Theological Seminary, 1999).

20. Loder argued that imagination should be a prerequisite for determining falsifiability in science. See *The Transforming Moment: Understanding Convictional Experiences* (San Francisco: Harper & Row, 1982), pp. 31ff.

lation), and (4) the power of a Chalcedonian imagination to give structure to interdisciplinary work in a scientific culture at the level of spirit.

This rehearsal of the depth and breadth of Loder's intellectual horizons makes it obvious that Loder's uniqueness as a visionary practical theologian remains difficult to catalogue or classify, although Richard Osmer's designation of him as a post-foundationalist scientist is quite appropriate, I think, if not quite adequate.[21] Different taxonomies of the field of Christian education (Burgess, Seymour and Miller, Brueggemann, Boys)[22] and of practical theology (Mudge and Poling, Browning, Osmer)[23] are generally not comprehensive enough to do justice to the scope and complexity of Loder's imaginative enterprise, not only because Loder's emphasis on spirit tries to reach back into the generative source of conceptualization itself, but also because he tried to take full account of the impact of the Holy Spirit's work on the spirit of the one who conceptualizes. To my knowledge no other practical theologian takes the action of the Holy Spirit as seriously as Loder, with respect to both (a) reconstructing practical theology as a science of human participation in the pattern and power of the Spirit, and (b) for making this kind of radical theological, epistemological and ontological claim about the necessary convictional transformation of the nature of the knower by the Holy Spirit for reconceiving practical theological science according to the mind of Jesus Christ.[24]

So my intentionally provocative thesis is that Loder was indeed an alchemist in the service of *Spiritus Creator* seeking to persuade a skeptical scientific world that the epistemological key for gaining true knowledge of the human condition is Spirit-to-spirit relationality revealed convictionally to those reconstituted ontologically according to the nature of Christ. Loder's alchemic search for faith seeking understanding in a scientific culture fired him into the world of human experience and academic rigor under God with a velocity not his

21. Richard Osmer, "Rationality in Practical Theology: A Map of the Emerging Discussion," *International Journal of Practical Theology* 1, 1 (1997): 11-40; see n. 73 therein.

22. Harold W. Burgess, *An Invitation to Religious Education* (Mishawaka, IN: Religious Education Press, 1975); Jack L. Seymour and Donald E. Miller, eds., *Contemporary Approaches to Christian Education* (Nashville: Abingdon Press, 1982); Walter Brueggemann, *The Creative Word: Canon as a Model for Biblical Education* (Philadelphia: Fortress Press, 1982); Mary C. Boys, *Educating in Faith: Maps and Visions* (Kansas City: Sheed and Ward, 1989).

23. Lewis S. Mudge and James N. Poling, eds., *Formation and Reflection: The Promise of Practical Theology* (Philadelphia: Fortress Press, 1987); Don S. Browning, *A Fundamental Practical Theology: Descriptive and Strategic Proposals* (Minneapolis: Fortress Press, 1991).

24. I suspect that Osmer's characterization of Loder as post-foundational scientist needs to consider more fully Loder's emphasis upon the Spirit's redemptive transformation of the spirit of the practical theological scientist in convictional dimensions to get at the uniqueness of Loder's position as a science.

own, and allowed him, on analogy to the Word of God, "to pierce the division between soul and spirit" (Heb. 4:12) in order to be liberated from both the "spiritlessness" of so much scientific work in the contemporary world, especially manifest in the intellectual centers of our culture, and from the irrationality of so much contemporary spiritualism. One can discern his relentless commitment to know reality scientifically through the spirit of the mind on several levels.

First, Loder, like any good scientist, refused to rely on secondary sources, "textbook accounts" or popularizations of classical works in the scientific disciplines he studied. He wanted to get as close to the core generative insights of contemporary science as he could (his tremendous confidence in the human spirit to discern the nature of things — especially at the boundary conditions where the spirit reaches the intrinsic limits of inquiry and must reconstruct forms of rationality to account for the object being observed). He also wanted to avoid as much as possible the homogenizing effects of making the complex insights constructed by the human spirit more palatable for public consumption (his profound suspicion of the socializing impact on the integrity of the human spirit, what Frank Lentricchia called "the social grammar of confinement" pervasive in liberal societies).[25]

Second, he always tried to get to the underlying relational structure of concepts to critique them from the "inside out" (according to their explicit claims and tacit assumptions) and from "outside in" (i.e., according to their tacit or implicitly religious meanings). For example, when Loder began his work in the late 1950s and early 1960s, practical theology and religious education were caught in a major impasse, having failed to integrate psycho-social insights into the *process* of development (the great contribution of the liberal religious educators) and the theological claims centered around the *content* of divine-human relations (the equally great contribution of the crisis theologians). Loder intuited that this impasse could be addressed more successfully for practical theology by attending to the creative fusion of process and content underlying therapeutic and religious experiences that restores persons to mental and moral health, which he began to work out in scientific terms in his dissertation on Freud and Kierkegaard.

Third, Loder was ever alert to the problem of *tertium quid,* the introduction of "alien" conceptual frameworks (in this case, non-theological frameworks) that distort the relational integrity of interdisciplinary work in practical theology. Thus, for example, when socialization and enculturation theories came into vogue during the 1960s and 1970s, claiming to provide the language

25. Barry Harvey, following Frank Lentricchia, *The Politics of the Theological: Beyond the Piety and Power of a World Come of Age* (New York: Peter Lang, 1995).

and grammar of communal faith formation, Loder argued precisely why these unredeemed dynamics, representing the powers of death and entropy, could *not* finally be Christianized until and unless the death (negation) in them was itself negated by Christ's presence. When the developmental paradigm surged into prominence during the 1970s and 1980s, again Loder penetrated to the underlying structures of that theory and argued why "normal" human development could *not* be considered "normal" if we took Christ's presence in relation to human development as normative. He argued that the "negation in the 'normal'" had to be negated if human development was to be "normalized" (i.e., transformed) in the service of Christ's Spirit. When praxis modes of conceptualizing attracted the attention of theologians and educational theorists in the 1980s and 1990s, Loder proposed, against that trend, that theory must always have priority in relation to praxis when the relation is discerned theologically and scientifically. First, he reasoned that the relational unity of theory and practice is embodied in undifferentiated or primal wholeness in the infant's experience of the mother's face. This sense of wholeness translates into the tacit dimension that always precedes and generates differentiations like meaning, rationality, intelligence, and practice as the child interacts with her environment.[26] Second, he argued that the theoretic pole of the theory-praxis relationship always represents (tacitly if not explicitly) this prior relationality as the larger frame of reference required by intelligence, one that is tacitly religious. Finally, he averred that the relation of the divinity to the humanity of Christ reveals the definitive relational structure by which all other relational structures are finally determined, including the relation of theory to practice when discerned theologically. Loder tried to construct theoretical frames of reference that he thought bore proximate witness to the revealed nature of Jesus Christ under the redemptive transformation of the Holy Spirit, in a way that avoided the introduction of "alien" or non-theological constructs as the basis for interdisciplinary work. Of course, he himself may not have escaped the problem of *tertium quid* in his own work. Nonetheless, Loder sought out a theological version of postfoundational practical theological science, one that was grounded beyond all human foundations in the deep grammar of *Spiritus Creator,* who alone makes theoretical work (as well as human life and thought generally) redemptive. He ever sought to do fundamental practical theology "in the Spirit."[27]

26. His favorite example of this phenomenon was Helen Keller, whose initial grasp of the word "water" inspired her life-long search for the tacit wholeness her grasp of water signified and to which it pointed.

27. Loder's choice of dialogue partners needs to be mentioned here in light of his single-minded devotion to the alchemy of the Spirit-to-spirit relations revealed in Christ. Indeed, somewhat curiously, Loder really never deviated intellectually from the trusted interlocutors he

My selection of the metaphor of alchemist to describe Loder is provocative for another reason, related to the legacy of the Enlightenment and the so-called disenchantment of the world that came about in the West, arguably starting with Descartes, and its powerful hold on modern science (including practical theological science). Morris Berman argued in his book on the origins of modern consciousness called *The Reenchantment of the World* that "disenchantment" in the Western world (i.e., the separation of faith and knowledge, or, in Loder's terms, spirit and science) can be dramatically revealed in the psychic history of foundational thinkers like Isaac Newton who embodied the modern mind-set.[28] Berman argued that Newton's life and work in particular were motivated out of

---

had encountered early in his academic career whom he critically appropriated — the ever-present Kierkegaard in philosophical theology and psychology; Freud, Erikson, and Jung in depth and ego psychology; Piaget and Kegan in genetic epistemology and developmental psychology; Talcott Parsons in sociology; along with Einstein, Bohr, Polanyi, and Prigogine in the natural sciences. He also largely stayed theologically attuned to the neo-Reformed tradition of Brunner, Karl Barth, and Tillich, and, after 1970, to reconstructors of Barth's work, especially T. F. Torrance and Wolfhart Pannenberg. He distinguished his work from other reconstructors of orthodoxy, notably the post-liberals (Lindbeck et al.), and from the radical orthodoxy now associated with John Milbank. He also drank deeply from premodern sources — the Gospels and Paul, from the Greek Fathers (especially the magisterial work of Chalcedon) — and from Lutheran and Reformed understandings of *Spiritus Creator* (through Regin Prenter and George Hendry).

Here it must be noted that Loder did not fail to engage and learn from those with whom he disagreed. It is not that Loder believed that he was superior or that he could not learn from anyone. But like Bunyan's Pilgrim on the journey of faith seeking understanding, Loder maintained a vigilant course to reach the goal he had set for himself to get to the heart of practical theology at the level of spirit as a clue to getting at the nature and meaning of human participation in the divine life. He never wanted to be lured away from this singular concern to plumb the depths of divine-human relationality, the hidden orders of meaning and purpose that are revealed to the eyes of faith and to the well-prepared mind, because I think he believed that the gospel demanded nothing less from those who professed Christ, whether in academic settings or in ordinary life. His relentless christocentrism has opened him up to the charge of being too narrowly focused on the Christian tradition to be of any good for the pluralistic times in which we live. On his part, Loder believed that Jesus Christ scandalized all well-intentioned efforts to be relevant to the *Zeitgeist* by any other means than the Spirit of Christ.

28. Morris Berman, *The Reenchantment of the World* (Ithaca, NY: Cornell University Press, 1981), chap. 4. The idea that a pervasive existential anxiety motivated the Enlightenment and suppressed the human spirit in decisively dehumanizing ways is coming more and more to light. See Stephen Toulmin, *Cosmopolis: The Hidden Agenda of Modernity* (Chicago: University of Chicago Press, 1990); Richard Bernstein, *Beyond Objectivism and Relativism: Science, Hermeneutics and Praxis* (Philadelphia: University of Pennsylvania Press, 1983); Colin Gunton, *The One, the Three and the Many: God, Creation, and the Culture of Modernity* (Cambridge: Cambridge University Press, 1993); and William Placher, *The Domestication of Transcendence: How Modern Thinking about God Went Wrong* (Louisville: Westminster/John Knox, 1996).

an existential sense of absence originating from the tragic early loss of his father and the neglect that ensued thereafter from the inattention of his mother. Drawing on important studies of Newton by Frank Manuel and David Kubrin,[29] who showed the devastating impact of this parental absence on Newton's developmental history and on his work in science, Berman argued that Newton's true longing, buried under repression of this existential loss, was never to construct the mechanical universe in the absolutist dimensions for which he became immortalized in the annals of science, but rather to discover the arcane hermetic secrets integrating all knowledge in the universe, a destiny for which Newton felt himself to be uniquely chosen. That is, Newton was a closet alchemist all the time he was revered as a rational scientist![30]

Closer to our own concerns in this essay on the alchemist James Loder, one should recall that a similar reductionistic confinement of religious sensibilities by rational science (leading to the abandonment of a religious thematic in their work) took hold of two important figures in the history of religious education in the twentieth century. Both Jean Piaget and George Albert Coe, contemporary theorists whose works remain today sources of insight for practical theology and Christian/religious education, were "forced" to repress the impact of early religious experiences that initially motivated them to think about the world holistically, and to succumb to the seduction of the rational scientific ethos that surrounded them. Coe agonizingly sought a Methodist-styled conversion that would authorize his search for scientific understanding, while Piaget seriously considered a career as a theologian because of his early religious experience and the influence of reading August Sabatier and Henri Bergson.[31] But both of them finally repressed the "religious thematic" under-

29. Berman drew on Frank Manuel, *A Portrait of Isaac Newton* (Cambridge, MA: Harvard University Press, 1968), and David Kubrin, *How Isaac Newton Helped Restore Law 'n' Order to the West* (private printing available through the Library of Congress), and Kubrin's essay on Newton in *The Analytic Spirit*, ed. Harry Woolf (Ithaca, NY: Cornell University Press, 1981).

30. Manuel and Kubrin argue that Newton "cleaned himself up" for public consumption, having been seduced by the notoriety and enthusiasm his mechanistic views received from the Cartesian juggernaut that pervaded European culture at the time. Therefore, he was "forced" to abandon (at least in public) his alchemical enterprise in order to retain his reputation as a scientist in the scientific ethos of the times. Berman argues that the suppression of Hermeticists in Newton's day was vicious.

31. See Richard Osmer, "Practical Theology and Christian Education," vol. 1 (Ph.D. diss., Emory University, 1985) for the reference to Coe's religious struggles. See James Loder, *The Knight's Move*, p. 158 n.15 for the reference to Piaget. Loder had an extended conversation in 1968 with Piaget's successor at the University of Geneva, Jacque Van Esch, whose own doctoral student Ferdinand Vidal investigated the fundamental impact of religious experience on Piaget's life in a book entitled *Piaget Before Piaget* (1994). Loder argued that the religious thematic or

lying their work in order to keep faith with the scientific ethos that beckoned and rewarded them. For Piaget and Coe, as with Newton, the implicitly religious structure intrinsic to the human spirit's knowing of reality, out of which the subsidiary alchemical longing to connect religious wisdom *(Sapientia)* and scientific knowledge *(Scientia)* derives, was repressed in order to conform to the conditions of modernist scientific assumptions and to carve out a "reputable" vocation in the modern world. If we return to the Loder biography for a moment, we see that he struggled with the very same issue at a crucial time in his life.

Recall that Loder's religious experience at the death of his father motivated his initial search for faith seeking understanding at Princeton and Harvard. But seduced by the ethos of Harvard and science, he too constructed his early work within the framework of acceptable scientific limits defined by the academy, repressing the deeper spiritual motivation that launched his practical theological vocation in the first place. However, his second convictional experience, the accident in 1970, reawakened Loder's spirit to reinvestigate the meaning of the tacit religious thematic that shaped his early work, compelling him to reconsider the explicit theological link between spirit and science as revealed to faith. Loder's work on the transformational intelligence of the human spirit was itself transformed according to the transfiguration of Loder's own spirit by *Spiritus Creator.* Under conviction, Loder discerned that divine and human actions were inevitably linked together in what he called an "asymmetrical bipolar relational unity" grounded in Jesus Christ, who made the God-man structure of reality intelligible to Loder's own spirit. This convictional realization guided Loder's subsequent efforts to construct a science of Spirit-to-spirit relations in which the interrelation of spirit and science, proleptically unified and generative in the primal experience of the infant with the face of the mother, is ultimately unified and generative through convictional experience of the God-man, in the power of the Holy Spirit.

Scientists since Newton have been wary of the alchemical charge, and the dominant modern scientific ethos is ever vigilant to root out every potential lapse into mysticism. Though Loder was as careful a theoretical scientist as can be imagined, who always made his thought public through carefully crafted books, articles, and lectures, his christological convictions inevitably come up against a reigning apologetic ethos that recognizes only non-confessional base-

tacit sense of wholeness revealed to Piaget early in his life accounts for various "anomalies" in the "textbook" treatments of Piaget and his work that portray him as a rational scientist and atheist. See the lecture of December 6, 1993, that Loder gave to his Philosophy of Education class entitled "Structuralism and the 'Unknown' Piaget," in the Loder archive.

lines for doing interdisciplinary work. This resistance to confessional claims in scientific culture is voiced by theologians like Brian Gerrish, who answer "what kind of theology belongs to the academy" by arguing: "Anyone who believes that theology is possible and meaningful in the church alone, that it begins with God in his revelation in Jesus Christ, and that it is scientific just insofar as it corresponds to the word of God through obedience of faith, will need to come up with a quite different account of theology's credentials as a university discipline, or may prefer to pursue it somewhere else."[32] Loder, taking up just this challenge, was foolish enough to believe that "a quite different account of theology's credentials as a university discipline" was possible from a confessional stance, one that was compelling enough to speak with integrity to the modern university out of a christological concentration, despite the alchemical connotations such a position evokes in a scientific culture. In what follows I want to elaborate what I believe Loder was up to as an alchemist of spirit and science. Perhaps if we could get a tentative surmise of the direction and substance of Loder's alchemy as a whole we might yet be intrigued enough by what we see to guess also why he took the "alchemical" risk that so many like Newton, Piaget, and Coe abandoned.[33] I offer this surmise about the substance and direction of Loder's alchemy in the hope that it might inspire others to look again at Loder's work to discern its potential contribution toward developing a practical theological science for the times in which we live.

Loder's Fundamental Practical Theological Science of the Structure and Dynamics of Provident-Contingent Relations

Out of his reconstruction of the source, structure, and dynamics of convictional knowing according to what Paul Lehmann called "the God-man structure of reality," I think it can be argued that Loder forged a fundamental practical theological science of provident-contingent relations with the power to illuminate the nature, dynamic structure, and power of the actual relational Reality that holds all things together and apart according to the nature of Jesus Christ. Loder imagined that this asymmetrical but reciprocal relationality he constructed out of his neo-Chalcedonian integration of wisdom and science bore credible witness to certain essential dimensions of the

32. Brian Gerrish, *Continuing the Reformation: Essays on Modern Religious Thought* (Chicago: University of Chicago Press, 1993), p. 273.

33. Douglas Sloan gets at the problem I have characterized as alchemy in *Faith and Knowledge*. But his focus on imagination rather than spirit as a solution to the impasse between science and spirit prevents him from making a more convincing proposal.

actual Reality that bridges the incommensurable gap between divine and human action revealed through the church's deepest reflection on the incarnation. Loder created conceptual lenses and an interpretative framework for the church that he thought would "cut the world at its [relational] joints,"[34] so to speak, illuminating, for example:

(a) the perichoretic relational structure constituting trinitarian relations (the norm and generative source of all relationality)
(b) the cosmological structure inferred from the Big Bang (with its asymmetrical relation of gravity to energy that makes the life of the observer of the universe possible in the first place — the anthropic principle)
(c) the nature of light, the universal constant in science (wave and particle relationality)
(d) the bipolar structure of the social construction of reality, constituted by a reciprocal relationality of socialization-transformation
(e) the paradoxical structure of Israel and the church, both communal paradigms of *simul iustus et peccator* and the relation of *koinonia* to *ecclesia*
(f) the canonical relational structure of divine revelation in human words that constitutes Scripture
(g) the revelation of the Christ event (definitive relationality revealed to and accommodated within human experience)
(h) Chalcedon's doctrine of the *hypostatic union*
(i) the Reformed affirmation of a transformative relationality between Christ and culture
(j) the dis-relational impact of modernity (where relationality is pervasively distorted and in which faith and knowledge are split apart)
(k) the turn to relationality in postmodern science and theology
(l) the core generative experiences of all human development, in which the tacitly religious experience of the mother's face imprinting on the child prefigures the explicitly redemptive impact of the Spirit of Christ on human development
(m) the central generative relational reality in human existence, the human spirit, powerfully revealed when confronting the intrinsic limits of intelligibility at the quantum level (complementarity) or at the theological level (Chalcedon).

34. This metaphor of "cutting the world at its joints" is taken from Colin Gunton's discussion of metaphor in *The Actuality of Atonement: A Study of Metaphor, Rationality, and the Christian Tradition* (Grand Rapids: Eerdmans, 1989).

This relational structure of reality Loder sought to trace from the "big infinity" (his euphemism for cosmology) and beyond (the Trinity) to the "little infinity" (quantum reality) and beyond (the human spirit), characterizes, I believe, Loder's unifying theme and potential contribution to fundamental practical theological science on multiple levels.

I would argue here that Loder's fundamental practical theological science of provident-contingent relations responds to the call John Webster, an authority on Barth, gave to theologians of hope to elaborate the central structure of the ontology of grace revealed in Christ to contemporary culture.

> A Christian theology of hope will be disoriented from the outset unless it is securely anchored in an account of grace as constitutive of created being and action. Modern Christian thought . . . leaves us seriously deficient in this regard: eager to establish connections with worlds outside the gospel, it rarely takes the time to explore the primacy of grace in its ontological dimensions . . . modern Christian theology is rarely committed to articulating the ontologically definitive status of that which is confessed in the Christian credo. As a result, the descriptive force of Christian convictions is blunted. . . . If we are to make some headway . . . it will have to be by taking with great seriousness the Christian confession that *the new reality brought about in Jesus Christ is reality.*[35]

Loder's journey into the wilderness of scientific rationalism, postmodern relativity, and academic reductionism under the discipline of the Spirit in search of alchemic connections resulted in a body of work concerned (1) to discern and to articulate the relational structure of the ontology of grace that reveals at every level of human action contingent createdness as it participates in *Spiritus Creator,* and (2) to develop a convictional epistemology that allows human creatures transformed by grace to know their own lives *as creatures* and the natural universe *as creation.* This is a contingency that can be discerned only when the Spirit of God acts convictingly on the human spirit and reconstitutes the knower in her experience, so that in knowing the universe through convictional horizons we make the universe (including ourselves) understandable and articulate to itself as contingent creation sustained by grace. In a sense Loder's work becomes an extraordinarily complex commentary on Barth's dictum *"Covenant is the internal basis of creation"* while *"creation is the external basis of the covenant,"*[36] making Barth's core insight relevant to a scientific culture. What the

35. John Webster, *Barth's Moral Theology: Human Action in Barth's Thought* (Grand Rapids: Eerdmans, 1998), p. 95; emphasis added.

36. Karl Barth, *Church Dogmatics* (Edinburgh: T&T Clark, 1956-75), III/3, pp. 6, 7.

convictional experiences Loder suffered did for him was to "awaken" him to the ontology of grace and to the provident-contingent relationality revealed in Jesus Christ as the very structure of created reality, including the mind that grasps reality. To be known and to know contingently is to be able to trace this relational structure that stretches from the inner life of the Trinity to the spirit of the mind that grasps all things according to the Spirit of Christ as "inner teacher" (Calvin). In and through the mind of Christ revealed to the convicted knower, alchemy becomes a genuine possibility because Christ the Alchemist now teaches the human knower to discern his nature in all things that exist through his Spirit.

To attend to the generative source of human knowing (being known by God!)[37] and to learn to think out of that intimate connection is to be restored to the *imago dei* as "new creation in Christ." Out of this generativity one begins to integrate a lifestyle that participates (fallibly yet genuinely) in the perichoretic relationality that unites divine and human action, thus restoring oneself and one's community to "sanity," not by adapting to the religious conventions of cultures (which are finally "insane" in relation to the gospel's judgment of them) but by being reconstituted according to the trinitarian culture that is the ground of all being — including all social constructions of reality. Loder discerned the inner dynamic structure of contingent creation in relation to divine action according to his *analogia spiritus,* arguing that the contingent ontology to which the analogy points can be known only "Spirit to spirit." When we are known in the Spirit, we testify with that Spirit that we are children of God, in both personal and public spheres. Loder sought to extrapolate the diverse ways in which this testimony played out as practical theology in a scientific culture. His whole alchemic project can finally be understood as testimony, witness, or even evangelism in the form of convictional

37. This kinetic provident-contingent relationality revealed in the God-man structure of reality is not an impersonal field of force (Pannenberg, Welker) but a Subject in relation to whom we awaken. We live out of God's knowledge of us. In our acknowledgment of being known, we are changed, and in our knowing that arises out of being known, we make history according to God's provident care. Loder's work implies a theological anthropology of contingent creaturehood that I have characterized as *homo testans.* The implications of this construct are immense, because this theo-anthropological understanding places all human constructive capacities into the context of God's *pathos,* God's accommodating initiative that judges all human efforts to act in radical autonomy. Moreover, on analogy to the infant's experience of being "noticed" into existence motivating her development, the intimacy of being known Spirit to spirit provides the motivational clue for maturing according to provident-contingent relationality. Only in and through the power of the Spirit of Christ can human beings know what God is doing in the world to make and keep human life human (Paul Lehmann). Loder was on a quest to make God's knowledge of us the subject of scientific investigation.

science.[38] Loder sought to bear witness in a scientific culture to the One who holds all things together and apart according to the provident-contingent relationality revealed to the human spirit by *Spiritus Creator.* Perhaps Loder's effort to bear prophetic testimony to Jesus Christ through his practical theological science is controversial because, as an evangelist, he stayed so close to the Stone of Stumbling upon which all human reflectivity suffers shipwreck before it finds intellectual harbor.

If this is an adequate, if all too brief, description of the core theme of Loder's alchemic project, how might the potential significance of his work be delineated in terms of its implications for redemptive transformation in practical theology as a challenge to practical theologians and others?

Potential Challenges of Loder's Convictional Science to Practical Theology and Beyond

A. *Loder's work compels practical theologians to reconsider the meta-theoretical contours of their discipline as a science of Spirit-to-spirit relations, a reconsideration that is faithful to the trinitarian God of the gospel, to the postmodern turn in science toward relationality,*[39] *and to the dynamics of the human spirit.*

Loder loved the discipline of practical theology because it demands interdisciplinary work that tries to discern the nature and impact of redemptive transformation by the Spirit of Christ within virtually every dimension of human action, including the whole universe of discourse in a scientific culture. In his christomorphic reconstruction of the conceptual coordinates of these disciplines at the level of Spirit-to-spirit relations, Loder reached "inside" the core problematic of practical theology to discern what God was doing in the world to make and keep human life human (Paul Lehmann), and to articulate the nature of this relationality to a scientific world. If Loder has indeed brought fundamental insight into the true nature and structure of provident-contingent relations to describe the core dynamic of divine-human interaction, as well as to discern analogues of that provident-contingency in the human and natural sciences, then his work is significant because it requires a radical reconsideration of the meta-theoretical contours of this discipline according to the movement of the Holy Spirit human-ward. For Loder, both the content of faith and the process of faith

38. To be re-created in the Spirit so as to accept our contingent creaturehood as the central core of our humanity, what I call *homo testans,* is to participate fully in the true witness, Jesus Christ, and in the Spirit of his testimony to a world that can be known (and saved) only by grace.

39. On the "turn to relationality," see chapter 12 in this volume, by F. LeRon Shults.

are inextricably united according to the dynamics and structure of provident-contingent relations revealed in Christ. In classical theological terms, Loder's work reconfigures the debate over *Anknüpfungspunkt* (point of contact between the divine and the human) because it preserves divine initiative (the ontology of grace) without diminishing the full participation of the human knower in the process.[40] Loder showed how the Spirit's initiative in convictional experiences accommodates to the knower without destroying the integrity of the knower, transforming knowing itself to a higher level of integrative thinking, one demanded by the Object of her investigation. Furthermore, Loder addresses the point of contact issue by insisting that his efforts to integrate the disciplines of practical theology take place not through the "products" of the generative spirit (ego, rationality, intelligence, praxis, symbolism, imagination, etc.) but through the kinetic relational dynamics that give rise to these "products" — the generative human spirit in intense dialectical relation with the regenerating presence of Christ. By getting to the generative source of creativity constituted in the human spirit as the locus of the Holy Spirit's convicting work, transformation according to this provident-contingent relational pattern becomes redemptive transformation into the nature of Christ, the ontological basis for the scientific knowing of reality.

B. *Loder's convictional epistemology, unique in practical theology, lays the groundwork for offering to the church a compelling way to integrate insights into the human condition (both experiential and scientific) and revealed confessional commitments (tradition) through profound religious experiences that transform the meaning-making capacities of* homo poeta *into the faith seeking understanding of* homo testans, *which is self-involved knowing at the deepest level.*

Loder's fundamental work on the nature of spirit as a self-transcending and self-relating reality, which under the convictional impact of the self-knowing Spirit of God leads to human knowing of reality that approximates knowing according to the mind of Christ, is powerful because it unites being and thinking, process and content, spiritual passion for continuity with scientific attention to discontinuities, etc., in a way that gives certitude to existence while at the same time inspiring the courage to grasp meaning in an open universe. Thus, Loder's convictional epistemology provides an experiential basis not only for overcoming the dualism between faith and knowledge, or spirit and science, into which we are socialized and out of which we normally learn to

40. For the problem of *Anknüpfungspunkt,* see Garrett Green, *Imagining God: Theology and the Religious Imagination* (San Francisco: Harper & Row, 1989), and Dana Wright, "Ecclesial Theatrics," pp. 397-411.

think in a highly differentiated society, but also for recovering the intrinsically subjective nature of all serious objective thinking. Loder redefines objectivity and subjectivity in epistemology by placing both of them in the service of a relational continuum that is implicitly religious (and therefore calls out for ultimate intelligibility) and that becomes explicitly theological under conviction as the vital structure for knowing all things "in the Spirit."

C. Loder's analogia spiritus *and his "strange loop" model of complementarity, derived from and reflective of his convictional epistemology, demonstrate the power of convictional imagination to generate disclosure analogies as conceptual resources designed not only to overcome the dehumanizing dualisms in modern culture that separate faith and knowledge, spirit and science, imagination and rationality, etc., but also to overcome the equally dehumanizing monisms of popular spiritualities that collapse or confuse the divine and the human.*

Loder created uniquely generative models of relationality for theology, science, and human experience based on his convictional epistemology. As noted, these models of relationality compel us to discern that the crucial factor in knowing anything truly lies not in the mind of the knower (Kant) nor in the object of investigation (naïve realism) but in the relationality between them, especially when the nature of the knower as human is taken at full force. These models of relationality are particularly relevant to knowing that necessarily reaches beyond common sense and logical rationality, where the human spirit reaches its own intrinsic limits of intelligibility and is compelled to create qualitatively new modes of reason that are intrinsically relational and observer influenced, as in quantum physics or in Chalcedonian theology. Out of these "limit" situations the human spirit creates "classic" resources that reveal the hidden intelligibilities that hold polar opposites together and apart, like time and eternity (the finite and the infinite) in the structure of the human spirit (Kierkegaard), like particle and wave in the structure of the light (Bohr), or like divine and human in the structure of revelation (Chalcedon). Loder not only discerned the nature of convictional epistemology but he also demonstrated how the convicted imagination creates models of disclosure with tremendously generative power to make life intelligible.

D. Loder's work advocates reconstructing and deepening the church's understanding of the dogma of the Holy Spirit in onto-relational terms, according to the self-relational dimensions of the analogia spiritus, *with enormous implications for calling mainline, evangelical, and charismatic or Pentecostal traditions to consider a new basis for dialogue and mutual discovery of our common participation in the nature, power, and truth of the Holy Spirit.*

Loder's work on the relation of Holy Spirit to human spirit calls us to reconsider the dogma of the Holy Spirit at the creedal level, by taking into full account the self-relating nature of spirit on both sides of the *analogia spiritus.* In drawing upon the patristics (mostly the Greek fathers), the Reformers (Luther and Calvin), and their modern interpreters (Kierkegaard, Barth, Hendry, Prenter), Loder argued that the doctrine of the Holy Spirit in the Christian tradition requires a unique epistemology, grounded in revelation, to discern theologically the nature of human participation in the kinetic structure and power of God's self-knowing as it is accommodated to human reality. Thus, Loder's work could revolutionize the larger church's understanding of the Holy Spirit and in particular how the Holy Spirit works transformationally on the human spirit in order to make divine reality in relation to human reality knowable to human beings. The implications of this contribution are profound in terms of (1) the recovery of the Spirit in the life of evangelical and Reformed congregations that tend to intellectualize or moralize faith, and in terms of (2) correcting the excessive or sometimes reality-denying claims of charismatic and Pentecostal spiritualities. In relation to the tendencies of the former, Loder asserted that the Holy Spirit puts us into the life and mind of God in a way that resists objectifying faith morally or intellectually. In relation to the tendencies of the latter, Loder contended that the Holy Spirit puts us into the world and into the life of the mind in a way that overcomes the irrational fideism and escapism of so much that passes for spirituality today.

***E.** Loder's work addresses the historical impasse between the religious education movement and crisis theology out of which the current renaissance in practical theology and Christian or religious education had its origins. Loder offers a major meta-theoretical proposal for uniting a century's worth of scientific insight into the "What?" of human reality (the contribution of liberal theorists) with a near century's worth of convictional insight into the "Why?" of human reality* coram Deo *(the contribution of the Barthians), without compromising the integrity of either science or theology.*

Loder was on the ground floor of the renaissance in practical theology that continues today, including the near century-long debate about the theories that give order to religious or Christian or Christian-religious education practice.[41] He not only reenvisioned theologically a dynamic model for integrating the disciplines that inform practical theological science in general, but he also

41. See the recent comparative study of this history in Richard Osmer and Friedrich Schweitzer, *Religious Education between Modernization and Globalization: New Perspectives on the United States and Germany* (Grand Rapids: Eerdmans, 2003).

provided the conceptual resources to overcome specifically the century-long impasse in religious education theory that failed to adequately integrate liberal and neo-orthodox contributions to the discussion. He did this by directing his attention to the generative source of all creative thinking (liberal or conservative) — the human spirit — the power of which is released most fully when confronting realities that stretch the spirit's intense desire to know to its intrinsic limits. Out of these confrontations at the outer limits of human experience, limits that were not sufficiently appreciated by either liberal or neo-orthodox theorists, Loder's work places religious or Christian education theory under question at a new depth, even requiring theorists to construct radical new forms of rationality. Perhaps no other practical theologian of his generation has indwelt at such depth and breadth the core generative problematic at the heart of practical theology and religious education to discern the inner structural relations that hold divine and human action together and apart according to the nature of Jesus Christ and our best scientific readings of human reality known convictionally.

F. Loder's appropriation of the thought of Kierkegaard and Barth for a scientific cultural context provides an important and possibly revolutionary resource for developing a critical and confessional practical theological science of human participation in divine reality. Furthermore, Loder's work could lead even secular scholars to recover the crucial importance of these two programmatic thinkers for understanding the meaning of the postmodern world.

Loder's reconstruction of contemporary Reformed faith (Barth through Torrance) and especially his appropriation of Kierkegaard (in dialogue with Chalcedon, Pannenberg, and the human and natural sciences) serve as a major interpretation of the relevance of these two prophetic figures for a scientific world. In particular, the way Loder brings both Kierkegaard and Barth into dialogue with postmodern science is perhaps unparalleled in its potential contribution to the church's prophetic witness to a scientific culture, especially from a Reformed convictional stance. No other practical theologian has, to my knowledge, made such a comprehensive and compelling argument for critical confessional practical theology in the Reformed tradition, reconstructed through Kierkegaardian and Barthian (i.e., neo-Chalcedonian) lenses, with the potential for both deepening the insights of the secular academy and equipping the church in its prophetic witness to culture.

G. Loder's work offers up new conceptual coordinates for challenging and deepening the theoretical contours of evangelical Christian education and practical theology, especially in relation to his convictional epistemology (which resonates to the evangelical emphasis upon conversion). Loder's vision could compel evangelicals to discern the epistemological and ontological implications of conversion for life in the world, helping to overcome the ambiguity within evangelicalism concerning the Christ-culture relationship.

Loder's emphasis upon convictional experiences (his language for conversion) and the way in which he integrates his convictional epistemology into every domain of human action (organic, psychological, social, and cultural) offer to evangelical scholars a splendid and perhaps uniquely important resource for helping evangelical practical theology and Christian education theory to attain a higher level of complexity.[42] Loder's vision offers a significant conceptual reorientation to evangelical practical theologians and Christian educators that gives to them a more solid, nuanced, and generative understanding of the kinetic relation of Christ to culture revealed through convictional experience. Furthermore, the integration of process and content in Loder's thought helps overcome the tendency of evangelical practical theologians to focus primarily on pragmatic and applied concerns to the neglect and underdevelopment of hard thinking at the meta-theoretical, methodological, and interdisciplinary levels. The possible impact of Loder's vision for reconceiving the conceptual contours of evangelical practical theology and Christian education theory may be the most significant implication we can draw from this rehearsal of his potential relevance in the field, given the general failure of evangelical practical theologians to develop a convictional science that is adequate to illuminate conceptually the theological claims evangelicals make for the transformational power of the Holy Spirit in evangelical experience.

H. *Loder's understanding of the nature and dynamic movement of human development from a theological perspective and the journey of intensification that marks maturity in the faith offers a profound resource for practical theologians, educators, and those involved in spiritual direction or counseling, who depend on their ability to discern rightly the nature of the relationship between so-called "normal" human development (under the power of negation) and spiritual redevelopment in the Spirit of Christ.*

Loder's reconstruction of human development in theological perspective, which (1) placed emphasis on the dynamics of stage transition, not the stages themselves, (2) took seriously the recapitulation of the fall in unredeemed human development through the triumph of negation centered on the socialized

42. Evangelical practical theology remains largely insulated from the larger discussion in mainline circles. For example, there are very few practical theologians representing American evangelicalism in the International Academy of Practical Theology.

ego, (3) offered theological reinterpretations of classic theorists like Freud, Erikson, and Piaget to explicate a "thick" description of normal human development as a "truth producing error," and (4) accounted for the impact of the Holy Spirit's power to negate the negation of human development at any stage of development, is perhaps unrivaled in practical theological breadth and depth. Loder's account of human development in theological perspective is neither occasionalistic or conversionistic (God "zaps" persons only in remarkable experiences of discontinuity) nor reductionistic or Pelagian (God reduced to human dynamics "writ large"), but it is fully dialectical and intensive (God and human in a tensive dialectical relationality) in a way that takes both the human spirit and the Holy Spirit with utmost seriousness. In doing so Loder argues, in the tradition of Athanesius, that the glory of God is humanity fully alive.

I. Loder lays a non-foundationalist basis for theological anthropology by grounding it in a living actuality that reveals through convictional experiences the human condition coram Deo *as a four-dimensional reality (self, "world," the absence of being, and new being), calling the disciple community to live into the new being as the new being transforms the other three dimensions in the service of the politics of God.*

Ever since Calvin opined that the human knowledge of the divine and the divine knowledge of the human are the essential parameters of Christian understanding, one might argue that the central theological task has been to discern, between the "theology as anthropology" of Feuerbach and the "humanity of God" of Barth, an adequate ground for theological anthropology. Loder's work brings this search for a compelling ground into focus for a scientific culture by showing that the God-man structure of reality in relation to human reality is a living actuality that cannot be fully "captured" by comprehensive systems of thought or action, because such illusory "foundations" blind the thinker/actor to (a) the pervasive nothingness underlying all human constructions of reality, theoretical or practical, and to (b) the Spirit's power to overcome the nothingness through convictional experience. Loder is, in my judgment, one of the few practical theologians who take the third dimension of human experience — what he called "the void" — with *penultimate* seriousness in terms of both living and thinking "in the Spirit," and therefore he is one of the few practical theologians who take the fourth dimension — what he called "the Holy" — with *ultimate* seriousness.[43]

43. Loder's dictum "It takes the Trinity to raise a child" testifies to how seriously he took the Spirit.

***J.** Loder's transparent theological commitments and his penetrating insights into the hidden intelligibility underlying the human and natural sciences compel practical theologians and religious educators to "come clean" concerning their own theological assumptions, tacit or explicit.*

Loder's challenge to reconceive practical theology at the meta-theoretical level is analogous to John Milbank's challenge to theologians to overcome their "false humility" by seeking to understand and affirm theology properly as "metadiscourse." Milbank wrote that "an ultimate organizing logic" for theology "cannot be wished away," and if theology doesn't supply one self-consciously, some other discourse will.[44] Loder's forty-year effort to avoid the conscription of alien frameworks to integrate theology and the sciences (the problem of *tertium quid*) calls all practical theologians and Christian educators, as well as scientists, to be more conscientious about making their theoretical assumptions as explicit as necessary. Whether he himself successfully avoided the *tertium quid* or not, his concern to "come clean" with theological and meta-theoretical commitments is exemplary for practical theologians, Christian educators, and others.

***K.** Loder's work provides a meta-theoretical baseline for reconceiving the nature of theological education itself and its relation to secular culture, and for rethinking the place of theology in university discourse in a scientifically credible way. Loder's convictional science provides a powerful witness to the dominant culture for reconceiving the philosophical contours of culture itself as a proximate testimony to God in Christ.*

Loder's work is potentially powerful and sophisticated enough scientifically and conceptually to provide Christian scholars with resources for engaging the highest echelons of intellectual culture and for reconsidering the place of theology in culture. The pluralistic times in which we live are ripe for introducing comprehensive and credible proposals for discerning the nature and structure of reality from various viewpoints, and Loder's work could aid Christian scholars whose vocation is to witness to Christ in the intellectual centers of culture, like academia. Furthermore, Loder's work challenges the century-long hegemony of secular prophets (innovators like Freud, Piaget, Skinner, Erikson, Parsons, etc.) to determine the intellectual parameters of true science, parameters often grounded in reductionistic versions of rational science and limited imagination (what Loder called science under "eikonic eclipse"). Loder took seriously the lordship of Christ in relation to every challenge and alternative claim

44. John Milbank, *Theology and Social Theory: Beyond Secular Reasons* (Oxford: Blackwell, 1990), p. 1.

offered by culture, but he did so in a way that gave full if delimited play to contributions from culture.

L. *Loder's science provides resources for constructing a comprehensive critique of the social construction of reality, and especially of the ruling distortions of the human spirit that shape contemporary culture in dehumanizing and unjust ways.*

Loder's trenchant critiques of various lifestyles in the United States — obsession with achievement as the distortion of love, authoritarianism as the distortion of power, proteanism as the distortion of freedom, and oppression as the distortion of justice — are directed toward the fundamental distortion or dis-relationship in the human spirit: the triumph of negation or existential despair that permeates the social construction of reality. These distortions of the spirit plague not only culture but the church as well, destroying the integrity of the best efforts to teach and preach the faith (i.e., to teach right doctrine in an authoritarian or achievement spirit is to distort the doctrinal integrity as well as the pedagogical integrity of the process!). Loder's critique moves deeper than most approaches because he gets at the source of the distortion — the dis-relation in the unredeemed structure of the human spirit recapitulated through every dimension of the social construction of reality — not just the inevitable "manifestations" of this relational distortion in modern or postmodern forms.

M. *Loder's work has potential for reconceiving the relationship of* koinonia *(the body of Christ) to* ecclesia *(the church as institution) in a way that neither separates these dimensions of a unified reality nor confuses or conflates them, liberating the church to be a living demonstration of redeemed relations according to the nature of Jesus Christ.*

Loder's project is perhaps underdeveloped in terms of ecclesiology. Nevertheless, his fundamental insights into theological anthropology in terms of Spirit-to-spirit relations offers practical theologians a uniquely dynamic understanding of the core dialectical structure of the church in the world *(simul iustus et peccator)*. Loder argues that the church is a social reality that at the same time is not the product of socialization. The church in the power of the Spirit is one in which the socialization dynamics have been affirmed, crucified, and resurrected by the dynamic presence of Christ. In Loder's construction, the role structures that lie at the heart of socialized reality and that distort the intimacy that the Holy Spirit seeks to create must be transformed redemptively (the Spirit makes role structures reversible in Loder's theory) so that the role structures now serve, rather than distort, the intimacy of the Spirit. Loder's call for churches to live "in the Spirit" and to be centered beyond themselves through worship contains the seeds of recovering the church's prophetic and living vocation in a culture of despair — that is, to demonstrate *koinonia-ecclesia* as a visible enactment of, and witness to, trinitarian-human relations in a fallen world.

N. *Loder's understanding of the impact of the Holy Spirit on the body, on ego, on social roles, and on culture has implications not only for redeeming personal, interpersonal, and transpersonal relations within primary and secondary socialization of specific cultures but also for reconceiving international relations among cultures and ethnic groups.*

In a post–9/11 world in which relations are distorted at all levels of interchange, new understandings of inclusive identity that accept the otherness of the other are needed now more than ever. Loder's insights into the transformation of human action by the Holy Spirit in bodily, psychological, social, and cultural dimensions toward the restoration of relationality according to the nature of Christ provide valuable resources for reconceiving international relations as well under the impact of the Spirit. Loder's vision for redeemed relations complements recent proposals by philosophers like Emmanual Levinas and theologians like Miroslav Volf who address, in very different ways, how we might transform our understanding and practice of identity formation in order to overcome both the overly centrifugal forces of exclusion and the overly centripetal forces of inclusion that threaten life together in a globalized world community.[45] Here, Loder's definition of love as "the non-possessive delight in the particularity of the other" articulates the intended outcome of the Holy Spirit's work in every dimension of human life under God, including international relations.

O. *Loder's project provides conceptual resources for constructing a four-dimensional, convictional hermeneutic of divine-human relations, one that is interdisciplinary and can be used to "exegete" both written texts and living "texts" according to the nature of Jesus Christ.*

Loder's imaginative reconstruction of human action in relation to divine action through convictional experience provides a basis for developing a convictional hermeneutic, one that allows scriptural texts and congregational "texts" to be interpreted within a dynamic, four-dimensional framework that

45. For a survey of Levinas's thought on the "otherness of the other" see David Ford, *Self as Salvation: Being Transformed* (Cambridge: Cambridge University Press, 1999), part 1, pp. 17-106. See also Miroslav Volf, *Exclusion and Embrace: A Theological Exploration of Identity, Otherness, and Reconciliation* (Nashville: Abingdon Press, 1996).

conforms to the mind of Christ acting convictionally on the mind of the hermeneutist. Such a hermeneutical framework can incorporate with integrity higher critical concerns ("behind the text"), literary meanings and structures ("within the text") and theological concerns ("in front of the text") in a comprehensive interpretative movement that gets "inside" the four-dimensional conflict that gave rise to the classic or canonical texts themselves. Similarly, through this framework one gets "inside" congregational con-"texts" in order to help congregations interpret their life together and their symbolic world in four dimensions, so that congregations so engaged might become "canonical" expressions of life in the Spirit. Elements of a convictional hermeneutic are manifest in Loder's reading of Scripture (i.e., his programmatic interpretation of Luke 24, the road to Emmaus), but Loder never fully developed his hermeneutical approach.[46] Similar hermeneutical intuitions are visible in a curriculum project developed for Indian Christians by Beth Frykberg and Ajit Prasadam, two of Loder's students.[47] A full-blown convictional hermeneutic begs to be developed out of insights from his work.

P. Loder's model of transformation is beginning to be discovered by certain well-known secular organizational theorists and adult educators in the Unites States who recognize the potential in his thought for discerning the spiritual nature of leadership and of creativity in business settings or for reconceiving andragogy and curriculum theory.

Loder's understanding of transformation as a constitutive element of the nature of reality itself parallels the discovery of transformation in postmodern science — such as the emergence of new order out of chaos associated with chaos theory. Scholars in business schools and in teacher colleges are appropriating these understandings of the nature of reality as transformative for rethinking the nature of leadership and creativity in the business world and in secular adult educational theory. As business leadership and adult education theories move from models of mastery and control and transmission of information and authority to models of self-organization through transformation, Loder's thought may become an important resource in the secular academy as well as in congregations.[48]

46. New Testament scholar Paul Anderson developed an interpretation of John's Gospel using hermeneutical implications from Loder's work and that of James Fowler. See his *The Christology of the Fourth Gospel: Its Unity and Diversity in Light of John Six* (Harrisburg, PA: Trinity International Press, 1995), chaps. 3 and 4.

47. See the bibliography, the last citation.

48. See Robert Martin's essay in this volume, "Leadership and Serendipitous Discipleship: A Case Study of Congregational Transformation" for insight into the difference between

Conclusion

No doubt there are many other implications of the practical theological science of provident-contingent relations developed by James Loder to challenge practical theologians and Christian educators, but these will have to suffice. My hope is that, taken together, they provide the reader with an incentive to investigate his work as a generative resource for practical theologians, Christian or religious educators, and theorists of Christ-culture relations. The concern here is not to become Loderites, or to establish a Loderian "school" of practical theology, but to allow Loder's close contact with the "things of the Spirit" and with the spirit of science to compel practical theologians and Christian educators to live closer to the center of divine-human relations revealed in Jesus Christ, where alchemy in the Spirit becomes a real possibility.

Loder's practical theological science of provident-contingent relations was designed to take practical theologians, church leaders, Christian educators, and all disciples of Christ on a journey of intensification into the heart of the human condition, where the boundaries of human knowledge are confronted by the dread of non-being and then also by a Life so compelling and pure that they cannot but help see all things, including themselves and their disciplines, as if for the first time as a work of the Spirit, and as a work uniquely their own. Loder's practical theological science could be propaedeutic for learning to think and live "in the Spirit" in the twenty-first century compelled by the themes of "science" and "spirit" and by the gospel of Jesus Christ. Who knows, it might, as Basil Mitchell warned, even choose us by "its sheer impressiveness" or demand to be imitated by us in a way that "radically revises our previous notions about what is worth imitating."

---

leadership as "mastery" and as "self-organization." I have learned of Loder's influence on business school theory from Loder's (and my) former student Ajit Prasadam, who is involved in a study group looking into Loder's relevance to business and management concerns. Theorists like Jim Emrick (adjunct faculty, University of Pennsylvania) and Robert Quinn (University of Michigan) are avid readers of Loder's work, according to Prasadam. For Loder's use in secular theories of adult education, see Jack Mezirow, *Transformative Dimensions of Adult Learning* (San Francisco: Jossey-Bass, 1991) and *Learning as Transformation: Critical Perspectives on a Theory in Progress* (San Francisco: Jossey-Bass, 2000). Postmodern curriculum theory also resonates to Loder's vision, though I have not yet seen his work being appropriated there. See William Doll, *A Post-Modern Perspective on Curriculum* (New York: Teachers College Press, 1993).

Bibliography

PRIMARY SOURCES

Archives

Loder, James E., Jr. Papers. Catalogued papers and manuscripts, Luce Library, Princeton Theological Seminary, Princeton, N.J.

Dissertation

Loder, James E., Jr. (1962). The nature of religious consciousness in the writings of Sigmund Freud and Søren Kierkegaard: A theoretical study in the correlation of religious and psychiatric concepts (Doctoral dissertation, Harvard University).

Books

Loder, James E., Jr. (1965). *Religion in the public schools.* New York: Association Press.

———. (1966). *Religious pathology and Christian faith.* Philadelphia: Westminister Press.

———. (1979). *Transformation in Christian education.* Princeton Theological Seminary (from inaugural address delivered Dec. 12, 1979, includes response from James Lapsley).

———. (1981). *The transforming moment: Understanding convictional experiences.* San Francisco: Harper & Row.

———. (1990). *The transforming moment* (revised 2nd edition, including two additional chapters and a glossary). Colorado Springs: Helmers & Howard.

———. (1993). *The Holy Spirit and human transformation* (Korean translation of *The transforming moment*). Seoul: Yonsei University.

———. (1998). *The logic of the Spirit: Human development in theological perspective.* San Francisco: Jossey-Bass Publishers.

———. (unpublished). *Educational ministry in the logic of the Spirit.*

Loder, James E., Jr., and Jim Neidhardt. (1992). *The knight's move: The relational logic of the Spirit in theology and science.* Colorado Springs: Helmers & Howard.

Chapters in Edited Volumes

Loder, James E., Jr. (1966). Sociocultural foundations for Christian education. In M. Taylor, ed., *Introduction to Christian education* (pp. 71-84). Nashville: Abingdon Press.

———. (1972). The medium for the message. In J. Westerhoff III, ed., *A colloquy on Christian education* (pp. 71-79). Philadelphia: Pilgrim Press.

———. (1974). The fashioning of power: A Christian perspective on the life-style phenomenon. In A. McKelway and E. D. Willis, eds., *The context of contemporary theology* (*Festschrift* in honor of Paul Lehmann) (pp. 187-208). Atlanta: John Knox.

———. (1976). Developmental foundations for Christian education. In M. Taylor, ed., *Foundations for Christian education in an era of change* (pp. 54-67). Nashville: Abingdon Press.

———. (1979). Creativity in and beyond human development. In G. Durka and J. Smith, eds., *Aesthetic dimensions of religious education* (pp. 219-235). New York: Paulist Press.

———. (1980). Negation and transformation: A study in theology and human development. In Christiane Brusselmans, convener, *Toward moral and religious maturity* (pp. 166-190). Morristown, NJ: Silver Burdett Co.

———. (1994). Incisions from a two-edged sword: The Incarnation and the soul/spirit relationship. In B. Childs and D. Waanders, eds., *The treasure of earthen vessels: Explorations in theological anthropology* (*Festschrift* in honor of James N. Lapsley) (pp. 151-173). Louisville, KY: Westminster/John Knox Press.

———. (1996). Transformation in Christian education. In J. Astley, Leslie Francis, and C. Crowder, eds., *Theological perspectives on Christian formation: A reader on theology and Christian education* (pp. 270-284). Leominster, England/Grand Rapids, MI: Gracewing/Eerdmans (a reprint of Loder's inaugural address).

———. (1999). Normativity and context in practical theology: The "interdisciplinary issue." In F. Schweitzer and J. A. van der Ven, eds., *Practical theology: International perspectives*, pp. 359-381. Frankfurt am Main: Peter Lang.

Loder, James E., Jr., and Jim Neidhardt. (1996). Barth, Bohr and dialectic (including a reply by Christopher Kaiser). In W. Richardson and W. J. Wildman, eds., *Religion and science: History, method, dialogue* (pp. 271-298). New York: Routledge.

Brochures or Pamphlets

Loder, James E., Jr. (1969). *Adults in crisis.* John Sutherland Bonnell Lecture in Pastoral Psychology. New York: Fifth Ave. Presbyterian Church (delivered Sunday, Nov. 9, 1969).

Journal Articles

Loder, James E., Jr. (1964). Conflict resolution in Christian education. *The Princeton Seminary Bulletin* LVII, 3, old series, pp. 19-36.

———. (1965). The other mystique (reply to M. F. Pierson). In *Theology Today* 22 (July): 283-284.

———. (1966). Dimensions of real presence (sermon). *The Princeton Seminary Bulletin* LIX, 2, old series, pp. 29-35.

———. (1967). Acts and academia (chapel talk). *The Princeton Seminary Bulletin* LX, 2, old series, pp. 60-62.

———. (1970). Adults in crisis. *The Princeton Seminary Bulletin* LXIII, 1, old series, pp. 32-41.

———. (1976). The corrective: An educational mandate (chapel talk). *The Princeton Seminary Bulletin* LXVIII, 3, pp. 77-79.

———. (1980). Transformation in Christian education (inaugural address, Dec. 12, 1979). *The Princeton Seminary Bulletin* III, 1, new series, pp. 11-25.

———. (1981). Transformation in Christian education. *Religious Education* 76, 2, pp. 204-221 (reprint of inaugural address).

———. (1985). Transformation in liturgy and learning. *Liturgy* 4, 4, pp. 39-41.

———. (2000). The place of science in practical theology: The human factor. *International Journal of Practical Theology* 4, 1, pp. 22-44.

———. (2001). A meditation on evangelism in a scientific culture. *The Princeton Theological Review* VIII, 2/3, pp. 8-12.

———. (2001). The great sex charade and the loss of intimacy. In *Word & World* 11, 1, pp. 81-87.

Loder, James E., and Mark Laaser. (1973). Authenticating Christian experience: A research request. *The Princeton Seminary Bulletin* LXVI, 1, old series, pp. 120-124.

Loder, James E., and James W. Fowler. (1982). Conversations on Fowler's *Stages of Faith* and Loder's *The Transforming Moment. Religious Education* 77, 2, pp. 133-148.

Articles in Dictionaries or Encyclopedias

Loder, James E., Jr. (1984). Creativity. In John M. Sutcliffe, ed., *A dictionary of religious education.* London: SCM Press Ltd., in association with The Christian Education Movement, pp. 101-102.

———. (1990). Theology and psychology. In Rodney Hunter, gen. ed., *The dictionary of pastoral care and counseling.* Nashville: Abingdon, pp. 1267-1270.

———. (1990). Epistemology; Existentialism; Interdisciplinary studies. In K. Cully and I. Cully, eds., *Harper's encyclopedia of religious education.* San Francisco: Harper & Row.

———. (1998-2001). Affect; G. Allport; Anxiety and fear; Behaviorism; Karen Horney; Pragmatism vs. practical theology. In H. D. Betz, D. Browning, B. Janowski, and E. Jüngel, gen. eds., *Religion in Geschichte und Gegenwart: Handworterbuch für Theologie und Religionswissenschaft.* Tübingen: Mohr/Siebeck, six volumes.

———. (2003). Paradox; Self-reference. In J. W. van Huyssteen, ed., *Encyclopedia of science and religion.* New York: Macmillan Reference USA, vol. 2, pp. 648-649, 799.

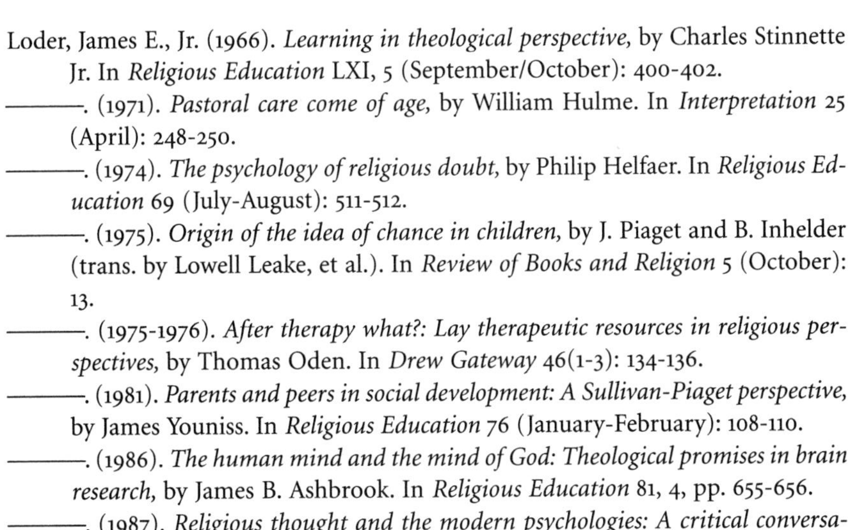

Book Reviews

Loder, James E., Jr. (1966). *Learning in theological perspective,* by Charles Stinnette Jr. In *Religious Education* LXI, 5 (September/October): 400-402.

———. (1971). *Pastoral care come of age,* by William Hulme. In *Interpretation* 25 (April): 248-250.

———. (1974). *The psychology of religious doubt,* by Philip Helfaer. In *Religious Education* 69 (July-August): 511-512.

———. (1975). *Origin of the idea of chance in children,* by J. Piaget and B. Inhelder (trans. by Lowell Leake, et al.). In *Review of Books and Religion* 5 (October): 13.

———. (1975-1976). *After therapy what?: Lay therapeutic resources in religious perspectives,* by Thomas Oden. In *Drew Gateway* 46(1-3): 134-136.

———. (1981). *Parents and peers in social development: A Sullivan-Piaget perspective,* by James Youniss. In *Religious Education* 76 (January-February): 108-110.

———. (1986). *The human mind and the mind of God: Theological promises in brain research,* by James B. Ashbrook. In *Religious Education* 81, 4, pp. 655-656.

———. (1987). *Religious thought and the modern psychologies: A critical conversa-*

tion in the theology of culture, by Don Browning. In *Princeton Seminary Bulletin* 8, 2, new series, pp. 76-79.

———. (1988). *Otherworld journeys: Accounts of near-death experiences in medieval and modern times,* by Carol Zaleski. In *Theology Today* 44 (January): 525, 528-529.

———. (1991). *Kierkegaard in golden age Denmark,* by Bruce H. Kimmerse. In *Theology Today,* 49 (January): 557-558.

———. (1991). *An introduction to systematic theology,* by Wolfhart Pannenberg. In *Theology Today* 49 (January): 557-558.

———. (1993). *A fundamental practical theology: Descriptions and strategic proposals,* by Don Browning. In *Princeton Seminary Bulletin* 14, 3, new series, pp. 327-330.

———. (1995). *Between Athens and Berlin: The theological education debate,* by David Kelsey. In *The Princeton Seminary Bulletin* 16, 3, new series, pp. 387-390.

———. (1995). *To understand God truly: What's theological about a theological school?,* by David Kelsey. In *The Princeton Seminary Bulletin* 16, 3, new series, pp. 387-390.

———. (1997). *Kierkegaard as humanist: discovering my self,* by Arnold B. Come. In *Theology Today* 54, pp. 130-134.

———. (1999). *Faith of our foremothers: women changing religious education,* ed. Barbara Anne Keely. In *Journal of Presbyterian History* 77, 2, pp. 135-136.

———. (2000). *Kierkegaard's vision of the incarnation: by faith transformed,* by Murray A. Rae. In *Theology Today* 56 (January): 638-641.

Audiotapes (Princeton Seminary)

Loder, James E., Jr. (06/06/63). Meaning in the middle years of life. *Current Issues in Ministry.*

———. (07/08/68). Sex identification and education. Presuppositions about education: Sex in theological context. *Institute of Theology.*

———. (07/09/68). Sex identification and education. The problem of authority: That which is inside a person. *Institute of Theology.*

———. (07/10/68). Sex identification and education. The issue of achievement orientation. *Institute of Theology.*

———. (07/11/68). Sex identification and education. Communicating with adolescents. *Institute of Theology.*

———. (07/06/70). Aggression and reconciliation: A psycho-social perspective. The aggression factor: Its nature and role in reconciliation. *Institute of Theology.*

———. (07/07/70). Aggression and reconciliation: A psycho-social perspective. Patterns of socializing aggression. *Institute of Theology.*

———. (07/08/70). Aggression and reconciliation: A psycho-social perspective. Ways to reverse self-destructive socialization patterns. *Institute of Theology.*
———. (07/09/70). Aggression and reconciliation: A psycho-social perspective. Teaching the transformation of aggression into creative patterns of behavior and interaction. *Institute of Theology.*
———. (07/07/75). Experiential theology: The structure of convictional experience. *Institute of Theology.*
———. (07/08/75). Experiential theology: The dynamics of convictional experience. *Institute of Theology.*
———. (07/09/75). Experiential theology: The nature of the enemy. *Institute of Theology.*
———. (07/10/75). Experiential theology: Our fear of grace. *Institute of Theology.*
———. (04/06/79). God and psychotherapy. *C. S. Lewis Society of Princeton.*
———. (11/28/79). Religious experience in theology. *Theological Forum.*
———. (12/12/79). Transformation in Christian education (Inaugural Address).
———. (07/01/80). Faith and human development, part I. *Institute of Theology.*
———. (07/02/80). Faith and human development, part II. *Institute of Theology.*
———. (07/03/80). Faith and human development, part III. *Institute of Theology.*
———. (07/04/80). Faith and human development, part IV. *Institute of Theology.*
———. (12/08/82). The holy spirit vs. the seminarian. *Theological Forum.*
———. (09/13/83). Sermon (untitled). *Small Church Symposium.*
———. (05/30/91). Lecture I (Alumni/ae reunion).
———. (05/30/91). Lecture II (Alumni/ae reunion).
———. (05/31/91). Lecture III (Alumni/ae reunion).
———. (5/5/97–5/7/97). Seminar given at University Presbyterian Church, Seattle, WA.
———. (5/5/97–5/7/97). Holy Spirit and human transformation: Lecture I, Dimensions: Damascus reality.
———. (5/5/97–5/7/97). Holy Spirit and human transformation: Lecture II, Dynamics: Emmaus vision.
———. (5/5/97–5/7/97). Holy Spirit and human transformation: Lecture III, Direction: The Golgotha mirror.
———. (5/5/97–5/7/97). Holy Spirit and human transformation: Lecture IV, Denouement: Betrayal betrayed.
———. (5/5/97–5/7/97). Holy Spirit and human transformation: Lecture V, Discernment: The eye of God.

Audiotapes (Academic Technology Center, Fuller Theological Seminary)

Loder, James E. (n.d.). Theology of faith and human development (CN531). Tape one, #2844ab.

———. (n.d.). Theology of faith and human development (CN531). Tape two, #2845ab.

———, and David Augsburger. (7/19/2000). Interdisciplinary reflections on Kierkegaard. Tape #2943.

Audiotapes (miscellaneous)

Loder, James E. (1988). The creator spirit and faith formation. 5-part course given through Continuing Education. Seattle, WA (tapes held by Dana Wright).

———. (June/July 1997). The Holy Spirit and human transformation (5 parts). India Sunday School Union, Bangalore, Coonoor, Bombay, Calcutta, and New Delhi.

Lecture 1, The dimensions of transformation
Lecture 2, The dynamics of transformation
Lecture 3, The direction of transformation
Lecture 4, The denouement: Betrayal betrayed
Lecture 5, The discernment: The eye of God

Videotapes

Loder, James E. Jr. (2001). James E. Loder on prayer (7-part series). Taped for *Mountain Views,* a television program of Drew Seminary, Madison, NJ, Oct. 23/30 (approx. 1 hour), with Angela Pak Sun. Held in Reigner Reading Room, Princeton Theological Seminary (n.n.).

1. The prayer of thanksgiving (shown 11/17/01)
2. The prayer of confession (shown 11/24/01)
3. The prayer of covenant (shown 12/01/01)
4. The prayer of petition (shown 12/08/01)
5. The prayer of intercession (shown 12/15/01)
6. The prayer of adoration (shown 12/22/01)
7. The prayer of healing (shown 12/29/01)

Bibliographies

Loder, James E. (n.d.) Annotated bibliography of the education disciplines. Unpublished.

Loder, James E., Jr., and F. LeRon Shults. (1999). Annotated bibliography for practical theology and interdisciplinary method. Unpublished.

Interviews (audio or video)

Audiotape. (2001). Interview of Dr. James E. Loder by Dana Wright (approximately 8 hours). Held by Dana Wright (transcribed).

Videotape. (1985). The transforming moment. Interview of Dr. James E. Loder on his book *The transforming moment,* by Laura Lewis (Austin Theological Seminary) at The Presbyterian School of Christian Education (approximately ½ hour). Held in Reigner Reading Room, Princeton Theological Seminary.

Unpublished manuscripts

Loder, James E., Jr. (1993). *Educational ministry in the logic of the spirit* (bound edition).

———. (n.d.). *Transformational dynamics in Christian education: A study in practical theology* (Note: only parts of this manuscript have been found as of spring 2004--D.W.).

Unpublished addresses, sermons, lectures, etc.

———. (1983). The Christian education of our times (paper delivered at the Wyckoff colloquium, May 5, 1983, Princeton Theological Seminary).

———. (1990). The journey of intensification and Christian education. Paper delivered on April 27, 1990 (paper delivered at unspecified location).

———. (1992). Research in theology and human development, two volumes (transcription of doctoral seminar PY902 by Dana Wright).

———. (1992). Case study model from PY902.

———. (1992). Theology and the human sciences (transcribed discussion from a doctoral seminar of that title, by Dana Wright).

———. (1992). The holy spirit and human transformation (four-part lecture delivered at Yongsei University, Seoul, Korea: (1) The dimensions of transformation: The Damascus reality; (2) The dynamics of transformation: The Emmaeus vision; (3) The direction of transformation: The Golgotha mirror; (4) Discernment and transformation: The eye of God).

———. (1993). The crux of Christian education (faculty seminar paper delivered at Princeton Theological Seminary).

———. (1993). Philosophy of education (lectures from ED 218 transcribed by Dana Wright).

———. (1993). Pressing issues facing practical theology in the 21st century (unpublished lecture given on Oct. 21, 1993, in the Reigner Reading Room).

———. (1993/2000). The educational ministry (unbound ED105 lecture notes, several editions).

———. (1994). Theology of faith and human development (summer course at Fuller Theological Seminary).
———. (1995). Christian education in the spirit of Christ (paper delivered at the annual conference of the National Association of Professors of Christian Education [NAPCE], Chicago).
———. (1996). Casebook for ED215 (a folder of verbatims).
———. (1999). Theology and human development (ED216 lectures transcribed by Dana Wright).
———. (1999). The relevance of Kierkegaard: Attack on Christendom (1854-55) (unpublished paper delivered in ED583 "Training in Christianity").
———. (n.d.). Christian spirituality in Christian education (unspecified setting).
———. (n.d.). From organism to universe: Nature and the constructive capacities of the human spirit in Jean Piaget: (A) Piaget, (B) Polanyi (chapter 5 of the unpublished *Transformational dynamics in Christian education: A study in practical theology*).
———. (n.d.). Revelation as a way of knowing (unspecified setting).
———. (n.d.). Teaching as the act of creation (paper on reserve file for Ed15 course, "Educational Psychology").
———. (n.d.). Transformed dialectical hermeneutic (an outline of a method of interpreting experience in relation to Christ's presence).

SECONDARY SOURCES

Ph.D. or D.Min. Dissertations on James E. Loder's Work (in whole or in part)

Bateson, C. Daniel. (1971). Creativity and religious development: Toward a structural/functional psychology of religion (Th.D. dissertation, Princeton Theological Seminary).
Nichols, John Randall. (1971). Conflict and creativity: The dynamics of the communication process in theological perspective (Doctoral dissertation, Princeton Theological Seminary).
Conrad, Robert Leroy. (1975). Christian education and creative conflict: Relations between creative intra-psychic conflict as understood in Luther's experience and theology and as understood in social psychological theories with conclusions for Christian education principles and practice (Ph.D. dissertation, Princeton Theological Seminary).
Dykstra, Craig. (1978). Christian education and the moral life: An evaluation of and alternative to Kohlberg/Piaget? (Ph.D. dissertation, Princeton Theological Seminary).
Schipani, Daniel S. (1981). Conscientization and creativity: A reinterpretation of

Paulo Freire, focused on his epistemological and theological foundations with implications for Christian education (Ph.D. dissertation, Princeton Theological Seminary).

Goldstein, Robert Morris. (1982). On Christian rhetoric: The significance of Søren Kierkegaard's "Dialectic of Ethical and Ethical-Religious Communication" for philosophical and theological pedagogy (Ph.D. dissertation, Princeton Theological Seminary).

Tiller, Darryl J. (1983). Pastoral counseling: A means through which God brings salvation to the lives of the people (Doctoral dissertation, Louisville Presbyterian Theological Seminary, advisor David Steere).

Johnson, Susanne. (1984). Religious experience as creative, revelatory and transforming event: The implications of intense Christian experience for the Christian educational process (Doctoral dissertation, Princeton Theological Seminary).

Moyer, David Lloyd. (1984). Making Christ our head: The transformation of a parish environment (D.Min. thesis, Princeton Theological Seminary).

Krych, Margaret Anne. (1985). Communicating "justification" to elementary-age children: A study in Tillich's correlational method and transformational narrative for Christian education (Doctoral dissertation, Princeton Theological Seminary).

Harkey, Martin Luther, III. (1985). A theology for the ministry of volunteers: With reference to Calvin's doctrine of vocation, and with particular focus on developing leadership for Christian education in the congregation (Moltmann, Laity, Calling) (Doctoral dissertation, Princeton Theological Seminary).

Frykberg, Elizabeth Anne. (1990). Spiritual transformation and the creation of humankind in the image of God, male and female: A study of Karl Barth's understanding of the *"analogia relationis"* correlated with psychosexual and psychosocial developmental theory (Doctoral dissertation, Princeton Theological Seminary).

Hess, Carol Lakey. (1990). Educating in the Spirit (Doctoral dissertation, Princeton Theological Seminary).

Hess, Ernest P. (1991). Christian identity and openness: A theologically informed hermeneutical approach to Christian education (Doctoral dissertation, Princeton Theological Seminary).

Rogers, Frank, Jr. (1991). Karl Barth's faith epistemology of the spirit as a critical constructive framework for Christian education (Doctoral dissertation, Princeton Theological Seminary).

Wigger, James Bradley. (1992). Texture and Trembling: A theological inquiry into perception and learning (Doctoral dissertation, Princeton Theological Seminary).

Cook, Carol Jean. (1994). Singing a new song: Relationality as a context for identity development, growth in faith, and Christian education (Doctoral dissertation, Princeton Theological Seminary).

Martin, Robert Keith. (1995). The incarnate ground of Christian education: The integration of epistemology and ontology in the thought of Michael Polanyi and Thomas F. Torrance (Doctoral dissertation, Princeton Theological Seminary).

Reese, Daniel Brian. (1995). The feast of wisdom: Thomas Merton's vision and practice of a sapiential education (Doctoral dissertation, Princeton Theological Seminary).

Lee, Kyoo-Min. (1996). Koinonia: A critical study of Lewis Sherrill's concept of koinonia and Jürgen Moltmann's social understanding of the Trinity as an attempt to provide a corrective to the problems of the Korean church and its educational ministry (Doctoral dissertation, Princeton Theological Seminary).

Pooler, Alfred D. (1996). Images that move us: The power of metaphor in spiritual transformation (Doctoral dissertation, Catholic Theological Union, Robert Schreiter, advisor).

Spencer, Gary Allen. (1996). A study of the founders at Suntree United Methodist Church (Congregation, Florida) (D.Min. thesis, Princeton Theological Seminary).

Turner, David. (1996). Story and vision: Shared praxis in service to an institutional mission (Roman Catholic, Rule of St. Benedict, values) (D.Min. thesis, Princeton Theological Seminary).

Brown, Sanford Webster. (1997). Creating and testing a church curriculum resource for the study of men's spirituality based on the Jacob to Israel story (D.Min. thesis, Princeton Theological Seminary).

Kuentzel, John Douglas. (1999). The ethic of care and Christian education: Implications for the theory and practice of Christian education (Doctoral dissertation, Princeton Theological Seminary).

Wright, Dana Rogan. (1999). Ecclesial theatrics. Toward a reconstruction of evangelical Christian education theory as critical dogmatic practical theology: The relevance of a second "Barthian reckoning" for reconceiving the evangelical Protestant educational imagination at the metatheoretical level (Doctoral dissertation, Princeton Theological Seminary [chapter four]).

Fredrickson, Johnna Lee. (2000). Iconic Christian education: Pointing to and participating in the reality of God (Doctoral dissertation, Princeton Theological Seminary).

Fairless, John Patrick. (2001). The meaning of the meal (D.Min. thesis, Princeton Theological Seminary).

Forster-Smith, Lucy Ann. (2001). A grammar of transformation: Language used by non-religiously affiliated college students in describing life-changing experiences (D.Min. thesis, Princeton Theological Seminary).

Hess, Lisa Maguire. (2001). Practices in a new key: Human knowing in musical and practical theological perspective (Edwin Gordon, Howard Gardner, Hildegard of Bingen) (Doctoral dissertation, Princeton Theological Seminary).

Frawley, Matthew J. (2001). Søren Kierkegaard's Christian anthropology and the relation between his pseudonymous and religious writings (Doctoral dissertation, Princeton Theological Seminary).

Buckles, Susan M. (2001). The perichoretic ministry of the Holy Spirit in formation and transformation of persons in the thought of James E. Loder and Thomas F. Torrance (Doctoral dissertation, Fuller Theological Seminary).

Kovacs, Kenneth. (2003). The relational phenomenological pneumatology of James E. Loder: Providing new frameworks for the Christian life. (Doctoral dissertation, St. Andrews University).

Hastings, Thomas J. (2003). Practical Theology and the one body of Christ: Toward a missional-ecumenical model (Doctoral dissertation, Princeton Theological Seminary.

Boyd-MacMillan, Eolene. (2004). Christian transformation: An engagement with James E. Loder, mystical spirituality, and James Hillman (Doctoral dissertation, Cambridge University).

Discussions of Loder's Work in Books, Chapters, Journals

Anderson, Paul. (1995). *The christology of the fourth gospel: Its unity and disunity in light of John six.* Harrisburg, PA: Trinity International Press, chapters 3 and 4, esp. pp. 148-151 and 185-186.

Barker, Patrick. (1995). The relevance of James Loder's grammar of transformation for pastoral care and counseling. *Journal of Pastoral Care* 49 (Summer): 158-166.

Batson, C. Daniel, J. Christiaan Beker, and Clark W. Malcom. (1973). *Commitment without ideology: The experience of Christian growth.* Philadelphia: Pilgrim Press. Though Loder's work is not explicitly used in this book, the authors admit, "The seeds for many of our ideas lie in the work of James E. Loder" (from the acknowledgments, p. 9).

Batson, C. Daniel, and Larry Ventis. (1982). *The religious experience: A social-psychological study.* New York: Oxford University Press.

Batson, C. D., L. Ventis, and P. Schoenrade. (1993). *Religion and the individual: A social-psychological perspective.* New York: Oxford University Press, esp. chapter 4. A reprint of *The religious experience.*

Berryman, Jerome, Richard Davies, and Henry Simmons. (1981). Comments on the articles by Eugene J. Mischey. In *Character Potential: A Record of Research* 9 (1981): 175-191. Reprinted in J. Astley and L. Francis, (1992), *Christian perspective on faith development.* Leominster, England/Grand Rapids, MI: Gracewing/Eerdmans, pp. 192-200.

Bube, Richard. (1993). The "strange loop" of complementarity (review essay on *The knight's move*). *Perspectives on Science and Christian Faith* 45 (December): 270-271.

Dean, Kenda C. (2004). *Practicing passion: Youth and the quest for a passionate church.* Grand Rapids: Eerdmans.

Dykstra, Craig. (1981). *Vision and character: A Christian educator's alternative to Kohlberg.* New York: Paulist Press, chapter 3.

———. (1982). Transformation in faith and morals (review article, *The transforming moment). Theology Today* 39 (April): 56-64.

———. (1999). *Growing in the faith: Education and Christian practices.* Louisville: Geneva Press, chapter 3.

Dykstra, Craig, and Sharon Parks. (1986). *Faith development and Fowler.* Birmingham, AL: Religious Education Press, pp. 41, 42, 63, 151-154.

Erdman, Daniel. (1983). Liberation and identity: Indo-Hispano youth. *Religious Education* 78, 1, pp. 76-89 (see in particular p. 86).

Faber, Heije. (1982). Zicht op de structuur van de godsdienstige ervaring: twee boeken (J. E. Loder, J. Scharfenberg, and H. Kampfer). *Nederlands Theologisch Tijdschrift* 36 (October): 311-331.

Frawley, Matthew. (2000). Loder on Kierkegaard. *Princeton Theological Review,* Spring/Summer, pp. 8-16.

Frykberg, Elizabeth. (1993). Karl Barth's theological anthropology: An analogical critique regarding gender relations. *Studies in Reformed Theology and History* 1, 3, pp. 1-54.

Gaventa, William C. (1986). Singing the Lord's song in a foreign land: A theoretical foundation for growth and education in the CPE process. *Journal of Supervision and Training in Ministry* 8, pp. 21-32.

Grannell, Andrew. (1985). The paradox of formation and transformation. *Religious Education* 80 (Summer): 384-398.

Groome, Thomas. (1983). Old task: Urgent challenge. Response to William Kennedy, Pursuing peace and justice. A challenge to religious educators. *Religious Education* 78, 4, pp. 477ff.

Heywood, David. (1986). Piaget and faith development. *British Journal of Religious Education* 8, 2, pp. 72-78, reprinted in J. Astley and L. Francis, (1992), *Christian perspectives on faith development.* Leominster, England/Grand Rapids, MI: Gracewing/Eerdmans, pp. 153-162.

Hess, Carol Lakey. (1991). Educating in the Spirit. *Religious Education* 86, 3, pp. 383-398.

———. (1996). Educating in the Spirit. In *Christian Education in Theological Perspective.* J. Astley and Jeffrey Crowder, eds. Leominster, England/Grand Rapids, MI: Gracewing/Eerdmans.

Johnson, Susanne. (1985). *Christian spiritual formation in the church and classroom.* Nashville: Abingdon, chapter 7.

Kaiser, Christopher. (1996). Quantum complementarity and christological dialectic (pp. 291-298). In W. M. Richardson and W. J. Wildman, *Religion and science: History method, dialogue.* New York: Rutledge.

Koenig, Matthew. (2000). Essays in honor of James E. Loder (introduction). *Princeton Theological Review,* p. 3.

Krych, Margaret. (1987). *Teaching the gospel today: A guide for education in the congregation.* Minneapolis: Augsburg, esp. chapters 4 and 5.

Lumsden, Scott. (2000). Theology that matters! James Loder's significance for pastoral ministry. *Princeton Theological Review,* pp. 4-7.

Mezirow, Jack. (1991). *Transformative dimensions of adult learning.* San Francisco: Jossey-Bass.

———. (2000). *Learning as transformation: Critical perspectives on a theory in progress.* San Francisco: Jossey-Bass, pp. 26-27, 163-164.

Morton, Nelle. (1967). Review article: James Loder: *Religious pathology and the Christian faith. Princeton Seminary Bulletin* LX, 2, old series, pp. 74-83.

Nelson, C. Ellis. (1989). *How faith matures.* Louisville: Westminster/John Knox, p. 94.

Osmer, Richard R. (1990). James W. Fowler and the Reformed tradition: An exercise in theological reflection in religious education. *Religious Education* 85, 1, pp. 51-68.

———. (1997). Rationality in practical theology. A map of the emerging discussion. *International Journal of Practical Theology* 1, 1, pp. 11-40.

———. (2003). The role of practical theology in Protestant religious education theory. *International Journal of Practical Theology.*

Parks, Sharon. (1986). *The critical years: Young adults and the search for meaning, faith and commitment.* San Francisco: Harper & Row, pp. 116-132.

———. (1986). Imagination and spirit in faith development: A way past the structure-content dichotomy. In C. Dykstra and Sharon Parks, eds., *Faith development and Fowler.* Birningham, AL: Religious Education Press, pp. 137-156, esp. pp. 151-152.

———. (2000). *Big questions, worthy dreams: Mentoring young adults in their search for meaning, purpose, and faith.* San Francisco: Jossey-Bass, chapter 7, pp. 104-126.

Pazmino, Robert. (2001). *God our teacher: Theological basics in Christian education.* Grand Rapids: Baker, pp. 47, 60, 88, 101, 109.

Rhodes, J. Steve. (1986). Conversion as crisis and process: A comparison of two models. *Journal of Psychology and Christianity* 5, 3, pp. 20-27.

Schipani, Daniel. (1984). *Conscientization and creativity: Paulo Freire and Christian education.* Lanham, MD: University Press of America.

———. (1988). *Religious education encounters liberation theology.* Birmingham, AL: Religious Education Press, esp. chapter 1 and pp. 109, 114, 152, 208, 247, and 260.

———. (2003). *The way of wisdom in pastoral counseling.* Elkhart, IN: IMS.

Shults, F. LeRon. (1997). Structures of rationality in science and theology: Overcoming the postmodern dilemma. *Perspectives on Science and Christian Faith* 49, 4, pp. 228-236.

———. (1997). "Holding on" to the theology-psychology relationship: The underlying fiduciary structures of interdisciplinary method. *Journal of Psychology and Theology* 25, 3, pp. 329-340.

———. (1999). *The postfoundationalist task of theology: Wolfhart Pannenberg and the new theological rationality.* Grand Rapids: Eerdmans, esp. chapter 4.

———. (1999). Pedagogy of the repressed: What keeps seminarians from transformational learning? *Theological Education* 36, 1, pp. 157-169.

———. (2000). One spirit with the Lord. *Princeton Seminary Review* 7, 2, pp. 17-26.

———. (2003). *Reforming theological anthropology: After the philosophical turn to relationality.* Grand Rapids: Eerdmans, esp. chapters 3 and 4.

———, with Steven Sandage. (2003). *The faces of forgiveness: Searching for wholeness and salvation.* Grand Rapids: Baker Academic, pp. 45-51, 121-122.

Thomas, Harold R. (1999). Conversion process: James E. Loder in missiological perspective. In C. van Engen, N. Thomas, and R. Gallagher, eds., *Footprints of God: A narrative theology of mission.* Monrovia, CA: MARC World Vision, pp. 5-18.

Webster, Derek. (1984). James Fowler's theory of faith development. *British Journal of Religious Education* 8, 2, pp. 79-83, reprinted in J. Astley and L. Francis, (1992), *Christian perspectives on faith development.* Leominster, England/ Grand Rapids, MI: Gracewing/Eerdmans, pp. 77-84.

Welton, Michael. (1993). Seeing the light: Christian conversion and conscientization. In Peter Jarvis and Nicholas Walters, eds., *Adult education and theological interpretations.* Malabar, FL: Krieger Publishing Co., pp. 105-123.

Wigger, J. Bradley. (1998). *The texture of mystery: An interdisciplinary inquiry into perception and learning.* Lewisburg: Bucknell University Press (Cranbury, NJ: Associated University Presses).

Wright, Dana R. (2002). The contemporary renaissance in practical theology in the United States: The past, present and future of a discipline in creative ferment. *International Journal of Practical Theology* 6, 3, pp. 289-320.

Research Entries (CD Rom)

Wright, Dana R. (2002). James E. Loder Jr. (1931-2001). In Kevin Lawson, gen. ed., Christian educators of the 20th century. Database website research entry. Includes biographical essay, exhaustive bibliography, annotated bibliography, essay on the contribution of Loder to Christian education, photographs, reading guide See www.talbot.edu/ceacademic.

Reviews of Loder's Books

Stendahl, Krister. (1963). Summaries of doctoral dissertations. In *Harvard Theological Review* 57, p. 89.

Green, John R. (1966). *Religious pathology and the Christian faith.* In *The Princeton Seminary Bulletin* LIX, 2, old series, pp. 66-67.

Rosen, S. (1966). *Religion in the public schools.* In *Journal of Church and State* 8 (Spring): 299-300.

Morton, Nelle. (1967). *Religious pathology and the Christian faith.* In *The Princeton Seminary Bulletin* LX, 2, old series, pp. 74-83.

Deconchy, Jean-Pierre. (1968). *Religious pathology and the Christian faith.* In *Archives de Sociologie des Religions* 13 (January-June): 211-212.

Outler, Albert. (1968). *Religious pathology and the Christian faith.* In *Theology Today.*

Gay, Volney. (1981). *The transforming moment.* In *Living Light* 18, pp. 276, 77.

Smith, J. (1981). *The transforming moment: Understanding convictional experiences.* In *Religious Education* 76 (November/December): 676-677.

Brownell, T. (1982). *The transforming moment: Understanding convictional experiences.* In *Epiphany* 3, 1, pp. 90-93.

Dykstra, Craig. (1982). *The transforming moment: Understanding convictional experiences.* In *The Princeton Seminary Bulletin* 3, 3, new series, pp. 339-341.

Hunt, R. A. (1982). *The transforming moment: Understanding convictional experiences.* In *Pastoral Psychology* 30 (Summer): 194-196.

Philibert, P. J. (1982). *The transforming moment: Understanding convictional experiences.* In *Horizons* 9 (Fall): 390-391.

Russell, J. F. (1982). *The transforming moment: Understanding convictional experiences.* In *Theological Studies* 43 (March): 185.

Faber, H. (1982). *The Transforming Moment: Understanding Convictional Experiences.* In *Nederlands Theologisch Tijdschrift* 36, pp. 311-331.

Dorrien, G. J. (1983). *The transforming moment: Understanding convictional experiences.* In *Sojourners* 12 (Fall): 36-38.

Dunlap, P. C. (1983). *The transforming moment: Understanding convictional experiences.* In *Journal of Supervision and Training in Ministry* 6, pp. 234-235.

Fuller, R. C. (1983). *The transforming moment: Understanding convictional experiences.* In *Zygon* 18 (December): 463-464.

McClendon, J. W. (1983). *The transforming moment: Understanding convictional experiences.* In *Journal of the American Academy of Religion* 51 (March): 127.

Fiet, Thom. (1990). *The transforming moment* (2nd ed.). In *Reformed Review* 44 (Winter): 170.

McKenna, John. (1991). *The transforming moment* (2nd ed.). In *Perspectives on Science and Christian Faith* 43 (Summer): 199-201.

Rogers, Frank. (1991). *The transforming moment* (2nd ed.). In *Religious Education* 86 (Spring): 323-325.

Wright, Dana R. (1992). *The knight's move: The relational logic of the Spirit in theology and science.* In *Koinonia* 4 (Fall): 273-276.

Bube, Richard H. (1993). *The knight's move: The relational logic of the Spirit in theology and science.* In *Perspectives on Science and Christian Faith* 45, pp. 270-271.

Buis, Harry. (1993). *The knight's move: The relational logic of the Spirit in theology and science.* In *Reformed Review* 47 (Autumn): 64.

Carlson, Richard. (1996). *The knight's move: Relational logic of the Spirit in theology and science.* In *Zygon* 31, pp. 731-735.

Durbin, William. (1993). *The knight's move: The relational logic of the Spirit in theology and science.* In *Journal of Interdisciplinary Studies* 5, 1 and 2, pp. 193-195.

Reich, K. Helmut. (1993). *The knight's move: The relational logic of the Spirit in theology and science.* In *CTNS Bulletin* 13 (Spring): 20-23.

Alsford, Mike. (1994). *The knight's move: The relational logic of the Spirit in theology and science.* In *Science and Christian Belief* 6 (October): 133-134.

Palmer, Michael (1994). *The knight's move: The relational logic of the Spirit in theology and science.* In *Paraclete* 28 (Spring): 30-32.

Haught, John F. (1995). *The knight's move: The relational logic of the Spirit in theology and science.* In *Journal of the American Academy of Religion* 63 (Spring): 168-169.

Richardson, W. Mark. (1995). *The knight's move: The relational logic of the Spirit in theology and science.* In *The Princeton Seminary Bulletin* 16, 3, new series, pp. 345-347.

Torrance, Thomas F. (1995). *The knight's move: The relational logic of the Spirit in theology and science.* In *The Scottish Journal of Theology* 48, 1, pp. 139-140.

Ivy, Steven S. (1999). *The logic of the spirit: Human development in theological perspective.* In *Journal of Pastoral Care* 53 (Winter): 495-496.

Torrance, Thomas F. (1999). *The logic of the spirit: Human development in theological perspective.* In *Princeton Seminary Bulletin* 20, 3, pp. 316-317.

Flett, Eric G. (2000). *The logic of the spirit: Human development in theological perspective.* In *Christian Scholar's Review* 29, 3, pp. 622-623.

Frohlich, Mary. (2000). *The logic of the spirit: Human development in theological perspective.* In *Horizons* 27, 1, pp. 213-215.

Bregman, Lucy. (2000). *The logic of the spirit: Human development in theological perspective.* In *Journal of Religion* 80, 4, pp. 689-691.

Tributes or Memorial Addresses

Alumni News. (1981). Synnott chair (announcement of Loder's appointment to the Mary Synnott Chair).

———. (1981). Transformation (announcement of the publication of *The transforming moment*), p. 4.

Chaapel, Barbara. (2002). A transforming life: James Edwin Loder, December 5, 1931–November 9, 2001. *Inspire* 6, 3, p. 18.

Englemann, Kim (Loder). (2002). Remembering Dr. James Loder as father: Reflections on the moments we shared. *Princeton Seminary Bulletin* XXIII, 1, new series, pp. 67-70.

Gaskill, William. (2002). A work of love in the presence of an absence. *Princeton Seminary Bulletin* XXIII, 1, new series, pp. 65-66.

Gillespie, Thomas. (2002). Words of welcome. *Princeton Seminary Bulletin* XXIII, 1, new series, p. 64.

Gardner, Freda. (2002). Memorial minute. *Princeton Seminary Bulletin* XXIII, 2, new series, pp. 188-194 (based on the tribute to James E. Loder given at the faculty meeting, February 13, 2002).

Hess, Lisa. (2002). A transforming life: Apostle of the living light. *Inspire* 6, 3, p. 19.

Tiss, Tamara (Loder). (2002). James Loder: Our Christlike father and gracious friend. *Princeton Seminary Bulletin* XXIII, 1, new series, pp. 71-74.

Wright, Dana. (2002). Prophetic practical theology as testimony: A Loder legacy? *Inspire* 6, 3, pp. 20-21.

———. (2002). Ruination unto redemption in the spirit: A short biography of a reformed "wise guy." *Princeton Seminary Bulletin* XXIII, 1, new series, pp. 75-85.

———. (2002). What have Athens and Jerusalem to do with Golgotha? A tribute to James E. Loder. Templeton Foundation/Princeton Seminary workshop on Spirituality and the Adolescent (unpublished).

Dissertations Supervised by James E. Loder

Roberts, William Lloyd. (1970). The supervisory alternative to the custodial contract in the educational ministry (Ph.D. dissertation, Princeton Theological Seminary).

Batson, C. Daniel. (1971). Creativity and religious development: Toward a structural/functional psychology of religion (Th.D. dissertation, Princeton Theological Seminary).

Nichols, Randall. (1971). Conflict and creativity: The dynamics of the communication process in theological perspective (Ph.D. dissertation, Princeton Theological Seminary).

Conrad, Robert Leroy. (1975). Christian education and creative conflict: Relations between creative intra-psychic conflict as understood in Luther's experience and theology and as understood in social psychological theories with conclusions for Christian education principles and practice (Ph.D. dissertation, Princeton Theological Seminary).

Dykstra, Craig. (1978). Christian education and the moral life: An evaluation of and alternative to Kohlberg/Piaget? (Ph.D. dissertation, Princeton Theological Seminary).

Schipani, Daniel S. (1981). Conscientization and creativity: A reinterpretation of Paulo Freire, focused on his epistemological and theological foundations with implications for Christian education (Ph.D. dissertation, Princeton Theological Seminary).

Goldstein, Robert Morris. (1982). On Christian rhetoric: The significance of Søren Kierkegaard's "Dialectic of Ethical and Ethical-Religious Communication" for philosophical and theological pedagogy (Ph.D. dissertation, Princeton Theological Seminary).

Johnson, Susanne. (1983). Religious experience as creative, revelatory and transforming event: The implications of intense Christian experience for the Christian education process (Ph.D. dissertation, Princeton Theological Seminary).

Cram, Ronald Hugh. (1984). Cultural pluralism and Christian education: Laura Thompson's design for anthropology and its use in Christian education for ethnic groups. (Doctoral dissertation, Princeton Theological Seminary).

McClure, John. (1984). Preaching and the pragmatics of human/divine communication in the liturgy of the word in the western church: A semiotic and practical theological study (Doctoral dissertation, Princeton Theological Seminary).

Ford-Grabowsky, Mary E. (1985). The concept of Christian faith in the light of Hildegard of Bingen and C. G. Jung: Critical alternatives to Fowler (Ph.D. dissertation, Princeton Theological Seminary).

Krych, Margaret. (1985). Communicating "justification" to elementary-age children: A study in Tillich's correlational method and transformational narrative for Christian education (Doctoral dissertation, Princeton Theological Seminary).

Ruiz, Lester Edwin Jainga. (1985). Toward a transformative politics: A quest for authentic political personhood (Ph.D. dissertation, Princeton Theological Seminary).

Croteau-Chonka, Clarisse C. (1987). Intuition: A paradigm of the wholeness necessary for holiness and its relationship to Christian education (Ph.D. dissertation, Princeton Theological Seminary).

Shoberg, Georgia Helen. (1987). Salvation, sanctification, and individuation: A study of the relationship between Jungian individuation and New Testament views of salvation and sanctification (Ph.D. dissertation, Princeton Theological Seminary).

Frykberg, Elizabeth A. (1989). Spiritual transformation and the creation of humankind in the image of God, male and female: A study of Karl Barth's understanding of the "analogia relationis" correlated with psychosexual and psychosocial development theory (Ph.D. dissertation, Princeton Theological Seminary).

Hess, Carol L. (1990). Educating in the Spirit (Ph.D. dissertation, Princeton Theological Seminary).

Proffitt, Anabel C. (1990). The technological mindset in twentieth-century American religious education curriculum (Ph.D. dissertation, Princeton Theological Seminary).

Hess, Ernest P. (1991). Christian identity and openness: A theologically informed hermeneutical approach to Christian education (Ph.D. dissertation, Princeton Theological Seminary).

Rogers, Frank. (1991). Karl Barth's faith epistemology of the spirit as a critical and constructive framework for Christian education (Ph.D. dissertation, Princeton Theological Seminary).

Reese, Daniel Bryan. (1995). The feast of wisdom: Thomas Merton's vision and practice of a sapiential education (Ph.D. dissertation, Princeton Theological Seminary).

Martin, Robert K. (1995). The incarnate ground of Christian education: The integration of epistemology and ontology in the thought of Michael Polanyi and Thomas F. Torrance (Ph.D. dissertation, Princeton Theological Seminary).

Lee, Kyoo Min. (1996). Koinonia: A critical study of Lewis Sherrill's concept of koinonia and Jürgen Moltmann's social understanding of the Trinity as an attempt to provide a corrective to the problems of the Korean church and its educational ministry (Ph.D. dissertation, Princeton Theological Seminary).

Kuentzel, John D. (1999). The ethic of care and Christian education: Implications for the theory and practice of Christian education (Ph.D. dissertation, Princeton Theological Seminary).

Wright, Dana. (1999). Ecclesial theatrics: Toward a reconstruction of evangelical Christian education theory as critical dogmatic practical theology (Ph.D. dissertation, Princeton Theological Seminary).

Fredrickson, Johnna Lee. (2000). Iconic Christian education: Pointing to and participating in the reality of God (Ph.D. dissertation, Princeton Theological Seminary).

Frawley, Matthew J. (2001). Søren Kierkegaard's Christian anthropology and the relation between his pseudonymous and religious writings (Ph.D. dissertation, Princeton Theological Seminary). (By special arrangement, Loder supervised this dissertation even though Dr. D. Allen was technically the advisor.)

Hess, Lisa M. (2002). Practices in a new key: Human knowing in musical and practical theological perspective (Edwin Gordon, Howard Gardner, Hildegard of Bingen) (Ph.D. dissertation, Princeton Theological Seminary).

Haitch, Russell. (2002). Baptizing and teaching: Three theological positions and their educational significance (Ph.D. dissertation, Princeton Theological Seminary). (Haitch finished his dissertation under the advisorship of R. Osmer.)

Curriculums Based upon Loder's Transformational Paradigm

India Sunday School Union. (1997-2000). Elizabeth Frykberg, chief ed., and Ajit Prasadam, assoc. ed., *Windows to encounter. Workbooks and teacher's guides for grades K-10.*

Contributors

Marilyn McCord Adams was Horace Tracy Pitkin Professor of Historical Theology, The Divinity School, Yale University, and became Regis Professor of Divinity at Oxford in January, 2004. She is the author of *Horrendous Evil and the Goodness of God* (1999); *What Sort of Human Nature? Medieval Philosophy and the Systematics of Christology* (1999); and *William of Ockham* (1987) among other publications.

Eolene Boyd-MacMillan is completing her doctorate in the Faculty of Divinity, Cambridge University. She has studied at UCLA, Fuller Seminary, and the University of Hong Kong, and has served several parishes, parachurch organizations, and in government. At Cambridge she organized a year-long seminar on interdisciplinary studies. Her dissertation is entitled "Transformation and Ego-Relativization in Contemporary Mystical Theology and in James E. Loder and James Hillman."

Kenda Creasy Dean is Assistant Professor of Youth, Church and Culture, Princeton Theological Seminary. She is the author of *Practicing Passion: Youth and the Quest for a Passionate Church* (2004); *The God-Bearing Life: The Art of Soul Tending for Youth Ministry* (1998); *Youth Ministry as the Transformation of Passion* (1997), as well as numerous articles on youth ministry.

Russell Haitch is Assistant Professor of Christian Education, Bethany Theological Seminary. He served in the pastorate and taught Christian education at the Pacific School of Religion. Among his published articles is "How Tillich and Kohut Both Find Courage in Faith" in *Pastoral Pyschology* (1995).

Thomas John Hastings is Professor of Christian Education, Tokyo Union

Theological Seminary. He is the author of numerous articles in English and Japanese, including "A Tale of Two Selves in Japan and the United States" (*International Journal of Practical Theology*). He is also translator of the Presbyterian Church (USA)'s First Catechism and Study Catechism into Japanese. He completed his Ph.D. dissertation, entitled "Practical Theology and the One Body of Christ: Toward a Missional-Ecumenical Model," in 2003 at Princeton Theological Seminary under Richard Osmer.

Susanne Johnson is Associate Professor of Christian Education, Perkins School of Theology, Southern Methodist University. She is the author of *Christian Spiritual Formation in the Church and Classroom* (1989), and other publications.

Margaret A. Krych is Charles F. Norton Professor of Christian Education and Theology, and Associate Dean of Graduate Education, Lutheran Theological Seminary at Philadelphia. She has authored several books, including *Teaching the Gospel Today: A Guide for Education in the Congregation* (1987), as well as numerous articles in books and journal essays.

John D. Kuentzel is Lecturer in Religion and Education, The Teachers College, Columbia University. *Redemptive Transformation in Practical Theology* is his first book.

Robert K. Martin is Assistant Professor of Congregational Leadership, St. Paul's School of Theology. He has written *The Incarnate Ground of Christian Faith: Towards a Christian Theological Epistemology for the Educational Ministry of the Church* (1998), and various essays and articles, including "Theological Education in Epistemological Perspective" (*Teaching Theology and Religion*, 1998).

John S. McClure is Charles G. Finney Professor of Homiletics, The Divinity School, Vanderbilt University, Nashville, TN. He is the author of *Other-wise Preaching: A Postmodern Ethic for Homiletics* (2001); *The Roundtable Pulpit: Where Leadership and Preaching Meet* (1995); *The Four Codes of Preaching: Rhetorical Strategies* (1991), and many other publications on preaching.

Daniel S. Schipani is Professor of Christian Education and Personality, and Chair of the Church and Ministry Department, Associated Mennonite Biblical Seminary. He has authored *The Way of Wisdom in Pastoral Counseling* (2003); *Educación, Libertad y Creatividad: Encuentro y Diálogo con Paulo Freire* (1998); *Religious Education Encounters Liberation Theology* (1988); *Conscientization and*

Creativity: Paulo Freire and Christian Education (1984), and other publications in Spanish and English.

F. LeRon Shults is Professor of Theology, Bethel Seminary. He is the author of *Reforming Theological Anthropology: After the Philosophical Turn to Relationality* (2003); *The Faces of Forgiveness: Searching for Wholeness and Salvation*, with Steven Sandage (2003); *The Postfoundational Task of Theology: Wolfhart Pannenberg and the New Theological Rationality* (1999), and many articles and essays.

Dana R. Wright is Adjunct Professor of Christian Education, Fuller Theological Seminary Northwest (Seattle). He is the author of several articles, including "The Contemporary Renaissance in Practical Theology in the United States: The Past, Present and Future of a Discipline in Creative Ferment" (*International Journal of Practical Theology*, 2002). *Redemptive Transformation in Practical Theology* is his first book.